International Directory of
COMPANY
HISTORIES

International Directory of

COMPANY HISTORIES

VOLUME 164

Editor

Tina Grant

ST. JAMES PRESS
A part of Gale, Cengage Learning

GALE
CENGAGE Learning·

Farmington Hills, Mich • San Francisco • New York • Waterville, Maine
Meriden, Conn • Mason, Ohio • Chicago

GALE
CENGAGE Learning®

International Directory of Company Histories, Volume 164

Tina Grant, Editor

Project Editor: Paul Schummer II

Editorial: Virgil Burton, Donna Craft, Miranda H. Ferrara, Peggy Geeseman, Hillary Hentschel, Matthew Miskelly, Holly Selden

Production Technology Specialist: Mike Weaver

Composition and Electronic Prepress: Gary Leach, Evi Seoud

Manufacturing: Rhonda Dover

Cover Photograph: Chicago's Cloud Gate (Big Bean) in Millennium Park. © Tammyleung/Dreamstime.com/Chicago Bean photo. 2014.

For product information and technology assistance, contact us at **Gale Customer Support, 1-800-877-4253.**
For permission to use material from this text or product, submit all requests online at **www.cengage.com/permissions.**
Further permissions questions can be emailed to **permissionrequest@cengage.com**

Gale
27500 Drake Rd.
Farmington Hills, MI, 48331-3535

LIBRARY OF CONGRESS CATALOG NUMBER 89-190943

ISBN-13: 978-1-55862-924-0

This title is also available as an e-book
ISBN-13: 978-1-55862-908-0
Contact your Gale, Cengage Learning, sales representative for ordering information.

BRITISH LIBRARY CATALOGUING IN PUBLICATION DATA
International directory of company histories, Vol. 164
TIna Grant
33.87409

Printed in Mexico
1 2 3 4 5 6 7 19 18 17 16 15

Contents

Preface

The St. James Press series *The International Directory of Company Histories (IDCH)* is intended for reference use by students, business people, librarians, historians, economists, investors, job candidates, and others who seek to learn more about the historical development of the world's most important companies. To date, *IDCH* has profiled more than 14,100 companies in 163 volumes.

Inclusion Criteria

Most companies chosen for inclusion in *IDCH* have achieved a minimum of US$25 million in annual sales and are leading influences in their industries or geographical locations. Companies may be publicly held, private, or nonprofit. State-owned companies that are important in their industries and that may operate much like public or private companies also are included. Wholly owned subsidiaries and divisions are profiled if they meet the requirements for inclusion. Entries on companies that have had major changes since they were last profiled may be selected for updating.

The *IDCH* series highlights 25 percent private and nonprofit companies, and features updated entries on approximately 40 companies per volume.

Entry Format

Each entry begins with the company's legal name; the address of its headquarters; its telephone, toll-free, and fax numbers; and its web site. A statement of public, private, state, or parent ownership follows. A company with a legal name in both English and the language of its headquarters country is listed by the English name, with the native-language name in parentheses.

The company's founding or earliest incorporation date, the number of employees, and the most recent available sales figures follow. Sales figures are given in local currencies with equivalents in U.S. dollars. For some private companies, sales figures are estimates and indicated by the abbreviation *est*. The entry lists the exchanges on which the company's stock is traded and its ticker symbol, as well as the company's NAICS codes.

Entries generally contain a *Company Perspectives* box which provides a short summary of the company's mission, goals, and ideals; a *Key Dates* box highlighting milestones in the company's history; lists of *Principal Subsidiaries*, *Principal Divisions*, *Principal Operating Units*, *Principal Competitors*; and articles for *Further Reading*.

American spelling is used throughout *IDCH*, and the word "billion" is used in its U.S. sense of one thousand million.

Sources

Entries have been compiled from publicly accessible sources both in print and on the Internet such as general and academic periodicals, books, and annual reports, as well as material supplied by the companies themselves.

Cumulative Indexes

IDCH contains three indexes: the **Cumulative Index to Companies**, which provides an alphabetical index to companies profiled in the *IDCH* series, the **Index to Industries**, which allows researchers to locate companies by their principal industry, and the **Geographic Index**, which lists companies alphabetically by the country of their headquarters. The indexes are cumulative and specific instructions for using them are found immediately preceding each index.

Special to this Volume

This volume of *IDCH* profiles RCHC-Raketa ZAO, a watchmaker housed in Russia's oldest factory, built by Peter the Great, as well as Haw Par Corporation Ltd., the Singapore-based maker of the world-renowned Tiger Balm ointment.

Suggestions Welcome

Comments and suggestions from users of *IDCH* on any aspect of the product as well as suggestions for companies to be included or updated are cordially invited. Please write:

> The Editor
> *International Directory of Company Histories*
> St. James Press
> Gale, Cengage Learning
> 27500 Drake Rd.
> Farmington Hills, Michigan 48331-3535

St. James Press and Gale, Cengage Learning, do not endorse any of the companies or products mentioned in this series. Companies appearing in the *International Directory of Company Histories* were selected without reference to their wishes and have in no way endorsed their entries.

Notes on Contributors

Gerald E. Brennan
Writer and musician based in Germany.

M. L. Cohen
Novelist, business writer, and researcher living in Paris.

Ed Dinger
Writer and editor based in Bronx, New York.

Paul R. Greenland
Illinois-based writer and researcher; author of three books and former senior editor of a national business magazine; contributor to *The Encyclopedia of Chicago History*, *The Encyclopedia of Religion*, and the *Encyclopedia of American Industries*.

Evelyn Hauser
Researcher, writer, and marketing specialist based in Germany.

Chris Herzog
Researcher and writer based in Evansville, Indiana.

Christina M. Stansell
Writer and part-time lecturer based in South Lyon, Michigan.

Frank Uhle
Ann Arbor-based writer, movie projectionist, disc jockey, and staff member of *Psychotronic Video* magazine.

List of Abbreviations

€ European euro
¥ Japanese yen
£ United Kingdom pound
$ United States dollar

A

AB Aktiebolag (Finland, Sweden)
AB Oy Aktiebolag Osakeyhtiot (Finland)
A.E. Anonimos Eteria (Greece)
AED Emirati dirham
AG Aktiengesellschaft (Austria, Germany, Switzerland, Liechtenstein)
aG auf Gegenseitigkeit (Austria, Germany)
A.m.b.a. Andelsselskab med begraenset ansvar (Denmark)
A.O. Anonim Ortaklari/Ortakligi (Turkey)
ApS Amparteselskab (Denmark)
ARS Argentine peso
A.S. Anonim Sirketi (Turkey)
A/S Aksjeselskap (Norway)
A/S Aktieselskab (Denmark, Sweden)
Ay Avoinyhtio (Finland)
ATS Austrian shilling
AUD Australian dollar
Ay Avoinyhtio (Finland)
AZN Azerbaijan manat

B

B.A. Buttengewone Aansprakeiijkheid (Netherlands)
BDT Bangladeshi taka
BEF Belgian franc
BHD Bahraini dinar
Bhd. Berhad (Malaysia, Brunei)
BND Brunei dollar
BRL Brazilian real
B.V. Besloten Vennootschap (Belgium, Netherlands)
BWP Botswana pula

C

C. de R.L. Compania de Responsabilidad Limitada (Spain)
C. por A. Compania por Acciones (Dominican Republic)
C.A. Compania Anonima (Ecuador, Venezuela)
C.V. Commanditaire Vennootschap (Netherlands, Belgium)
CAD Canadian dollar
CEO Chief Executive Officer
CFO Chief Financial Officer
CHF Swiss franc
Cia. Compagnia (Italy)
Cia. Companhia (Brazil, Portugal)
Cia. Compania (Latin America [except Brazil], Spain)
Cie. Compagnie (Belgium, France, Luxembourg, Netherlands)
CIO Chief Information Officer
CLP Chilean peso
CNY Chinese yuan

Co. Company
COO Chief Operating Officer
Coop. Cooperative
COP Colombian peso
Corp. Corporation
CPT Cuideachta Phoibi Theoranta (Republic of Ireland)
CRL Companhia a Responsabilidao Limitida (Portugal, Spain)
CUC Cuban convertible peso
CUP Cuban peso
CZK Czech koruna

D

D&B Dunn & Bradstreet
d.d. Deiniška družba (public limited company/joint-stock company) (Slovenia, Croatia)
d.o.o. Družba z omejeno odgovornostjo (limited liability company/private limited company) (Slovenia, Croatia)
DEM German deutsche mark (W. Germany to 1990; unified Germany to 2002)
Div. Division (United States)
DKK Danish krone
DZD Algerian dinar

E

E.P.E. Etema Pemorismenis Evthynis (Greece)
EBITDA Earnings before interest,

taxes, depreciation, and amortization

EC Exempt Company (Arab countries)

Edms. Bpk. Eiendoms Beperk (South Africa)

EEK Estonian Kroon

eG eingetragene Genossenschaft (Germany)

EGMBH Eingetragene Genossenschaft mit beschraenkter Haftung (Austria, Germany)

EGP Egyptian pound

Ek For Ekonomisk Forening (Sweden)

EP Empresa Portuguesa (Portugal)

ESOP Employee Stock Options and Ownership

ESP Spanish peseta

Et(s). Etablissement(s) (Belgium, France, Luxembourg)

eV eingetragener Verein (Germany)

EUR European euro

F

FIM Finnish markka

FRF French franc

G

G.I.E. Groupement d'Interet Economique (France)

gGmbH gemeinnutzige Gesellschaft mit beschraenkter Haftung (Austria, Germany, Switzerland)

GmbH Gesellschaft mit beschraenkter Haftung (Austria, Germany, Switzerland)

GRD Greek drachma

GWA Gewerbte Amt (Austria, Germany)

GYD Guyanese dollar

H

HB Handelsbolag (Sweden)

HF Hlutafelag (Iceland)

HKD Hong Kong dollar

HNL Honduran lempira

HTC Haitian gourde

HUF Hungarian forint

I

IDR Indonesian rupiah

IEP Irish pound

ILS Israeli shekel (new)

Inc. Incorporated (United States, Canada)

INR Indian rupee

IPO Initial Public Offering

I/S Interesentselskap (Norway)

I/S Interessentselskab (Denmark)

ISK Icelandic krona

ITL Italian lira

J

JMD Jamaican dollar

JOD Jordanian dinar

K

KB Kommanditbolag (Sweden)

KES Kenyan schilling

Kft Korlatolt Felelossegu Tarsasag (Hungary)

KG Kommanditgesellschaft (Austria, Germany, Switzerland)

KGaA Kommanditgesellschaft auf Aktien (Austria, Germany, Switzerland)

KK Kabushiki Kaisha (Japan)

KPW North Korean won

KRW South Korean won

K/S Kommanditselskab (Denmark)

K/S Kommandittselskap (Norway)

KWD Kuwaiti dinar

Ky Kommandiitiyhtio (Finland)

L

L.L.C. Limited Liability Company (Arab countries, Egypt, Greece, United States)

L.L.P. Limited Liability Partnership (United States)

L.P. Limited Partnership (Canada, South Africa, United Kingdom, United States)

LBO Leveraged Buyout

Lda. Limitada (Spain)

LSL Lesotho loti

Ltd. Limited

Ltda. Limitada (Brazil, Portugal)

Ltee. Limitee (Canada, France)

LUF Luxembourg franc

LYD Libyan dinar

M

MAD Moroccan dirham

mbH mit beschraenkter Haftung (Austria, Germany)

Mij. Maatschappij (Netherlands)

MUR Mauritian rupee

MXN Mexican peso

MYR Malaysian ringgit

N

N.A. National Association (United States)

N.V. Naamloze Vennootschap (Belgium, Netherlands)

NAD Namibia Dollar

NGN Nigerian naira

NLG Netherlands guilder

NIO Nicaraguan Cordoba

NOK Norwegian krone

NZD New Zealand dollar

O

OAO Otkrytoe Aktsionernoe Obshchestve (Russia)

OHG Offene Handelsgesellschaft (Austria, Germany, Switzerland)

OMR Omani rial

OOO Obschestvo s Ogranichennoi Otvetstvennostiu (Russia)

OOUR Osnova Organizacija Udruzenog Rada (Yugoslavia)

Oy Osakeyhtiö (Finland)

P

P.C. Private Corp. (United States)

P.L.L.C. Professional Limited Liability Corporation (United States)

P.T. Perusahaan/Perseroan Terbatas (Indonesia)

PEN Peruvian Nuevo Sol

PHP Philippine peso

PKR Pakistani rupee

P/L Part Lag (Norway)

PLC Public Limited Co. (United Kingdom, Ireland)

PLN Polish zloty

PTE Portuguese escudo

Pte. Private (Singapore)

Pty. Proprietary (Australia, South Africa, United Kingdom)

Pvt. Private (India, Zimbabwe)

PVBA Personen Vennootschap met Beperkte Aansprakelijkheid (Belgium)

PYG Paraguay guarani

Q

QAR Qatar riyal

R

REIT Real Estate Investment Trust

RMB Chinese renminbi

Rt Reszvenytarsasag (Hungary)

RUB Russian ruble

S

S.A. Sociedad Anónima (Latin America [except Brazil], Spain, Mexico)

S.A. Sociedades Anônimas (Brazil, Portugal)

S.A. Société Anonyme (Arab countries, Belgium, France, Jordan, Luxembourg, Switzerland)

S.A. de C.V. Sociedad Anonima de Capital Variable (Mexico)

S.A.B. de C.V. Sociedad Anónima Bursátil de Capital Variable (Mexico)

S.A.C. Sociedad Anonima Comercial (Latin America [except Brazil])

S.A.C.I. Sociedad Anonima Comercial e Industrial (Latin America [except Brazil])

S.A.C.I.y.F. Sociedad Anonima Comercial e Industrial y Financiera (Latin America [except Brazil])

S.A.R.L. Sociedade Anonima de Responsabilidade Limitada (Brazil, Portugal)

S.A.R.L. Société à Responsabilité Limitée (France, Belgium, Luxembourg)

S.A.S. Societe Anonyme Syrienne (Arab countries)

S.A.S. Societá in Accomandita Semplice (Italy)

S.C. Societe en Commandite (Belgium, France, Luxembourg)

S.C.A. Societe Cooperativa Agricole (France, Italy, Luxembourg)

S.C.I. Sociedad Cooperativa Ilimitada (Spain)

S.C.L. Sociedad Cooperativa Limitada (Spain)

S.C.R.L. Societe Cooperative a Responsabilite Limitee (Belgium)

S.E. Societas Europaea (European Union Member states)

S.L. Sociedad Limitada (Latin America [except Brazil], Portugal, Spain)

S.N.C. Société en Nom Collectif (France)

S.p.A. Società per Azioni (Italy)

S.R.L. Sociedad de Responsabilidad Limitada (Spain, Mexico, Latin America [except Brazil])

S.R.L. Società a Responsabilità Limitata (Italy)

S.R.O. Spolecnost s Rucenim Omezenym (Czechoslovakia)

S.S.K. Sherkate Sahami Khass (Iran)

S.V. Samemwerkende Vennootschap (Belgium)

S.Z.R.L. Societe Zairoise a Responsabilite Limitee (Zaire)

SAA Societe Anonyme Arabienne (Arab countries)

SAK Societe Anonyme Kuweitienne (Arab countries)

SAL Societe Anonyme Libanaise (Arab countries)

SAO Societe Anonyme Omanienne (Arab countries)

SAQ Societe Anonyme Qatarienne (Arab countries)

SAR Saudi riyal

Sdn. Bhd. Sendirian Berhad (Malaysia)

SEK Swedish krona

SGD Singapore dollar

SIT Slovenian tolar

S/L Salgslag (Norway)

Soc. Sociedad (Latin America [except Brazil], Spain)

Soc. Sociedade (Brazil, Portugal)

Soc. Societa (Italy)

Sp. z.o.o. Spólka z ograniczona odpowiedzialnoscia (Poland)

Ste. Societe (France, Belgium, Luxembourg, Switzerland)

Ste. Cve. Societe Cooperative (Belgium)

SRG Surinamese guilder

T

THB Thai baht

TND Tunisian dinar

TRL Turkish lira

TRY New Turkish lira

TTD Trinidad and Tobago dollar

TWD Taiwan dollar (new)

TZS Tanzanian shilling

U

U.A. Uitgesloten Aansporakeiijkheid (Netherlands)

u.p.a. utan personligt ansvar (Sweden)

UGX Ugandan shilling

V

V.O.f. Vennootschap onder firma (Netherlands)

VAG Verein der Arbeitgeber (Austria, Germany)

VEB Venezuelan bolivar

VERTR Vertriebs (Austria, Germany)

VND Vietnamese dong

VVAG Versicherungsverein auf Gegenscitigkeit (Austria, Germany)

W–Z

WA Wettelika Aansprakalikhaed (Netherlands)

WLL With Limited Liability (Bahrain, Kuwait, Qatar, Saudi Arabia)

XOF Central African franc

YK Yugen Kaisha (Japan)

ZAO Zakrytoe Aktsionernoe Obshchestve (Russia)

ZAR South African rand

ZMK Zambian kwacha

ZWD Zimbabwean dollar

Ackerman McQueen, Inc.

1601 Northwest Expressway, Suite 1100
Oklahoma City, Oklahoma 73118
U.S.A.
Telephone: (405) 843-7777
Fax: (405) 848-8034
Web site: http://www.am.com

Private Company
Founded: 1939 as George Knox Agency
Employees: 175
Sales: $208 million (2013 est.)
NAICS: 541810 Advertising Agencies

■ ■ ■

Ackerman McQueen, Inc., is an Oklahoma City–based advertising agency best known for its work with the National Rifle Association. It is the largest and oldest continuously operating ad agency in the state of Oklahoma. Additional offices are maintained in Tulsa, Oklahoma; Dallas, Texas; Colorado Springs, Colorado; and Washington, D.C. Subsidiaries include public relations firm Mercury Group; Ackmac Production Svc, a video production services company; AMID (Ackerman McQueen Interactive + Digital), an integrated digital solutions provider; and Videodigm, a managed online streaming video delivery platform.

AGENCY FOUNDED: 1939

Ackerman McQueen was founded in Oklahoma City on January 1, 1939, as the George Knox Agency by George

Washington Knox Jr. He had worked as the advertising manager for Hales-Mullally, an Oklahoma City–based appliance distributor. He started his advertising agency with Hales-Mullally serving as his first account. His second client was the Hank Moran Insurance Agency, for which Knox crafted the deceptively effective tagline "Hank Moran the Insurance Man." Thereafter, whenever Moran was introduced in the Oklahoma City area, a new acquaintance would typically reply, "Oh, you're the insurance man."

During World War II, Knox went to work for the nearby Tinker Air Force Base but kept his agency operating on a part-time basis. Following the war, he returned all of his focus to advertising and took on two partners to grow the agency. By the end of the 1940s, the Knox Agency was billing more than $1 million in a year. To his dismay, Knox realized that he was making less money than when he was the sole owner. As a result, he terminated the partnership. By the time he hired Raymond Basil "Ray" Ackerman in 1952, annual billings had dropped to $250,000.

Ackerman was born in a suburb of Pittsburgh, Pennsylvania, in 1922. During World War II he served as a fighter pilot in the U.S. Navy. While stationed on Saipan, he began to toy with the idea of pursing a career in advertising after the war. His sister, who was an advance publicist for the Ice Capades, introduced him to advertising people she knew in Los Angeles, and they recommended that he launch his career in a medium-size city working for a newspaper. He repeated the advice while visiting his uncle in Oklahoma City. His uncle suggested that Oklahoma City was an ideal choice, and he used his connection with George Knox to land Ackerman an interview with the advertising director of the *Daily Oklahoma* and *Oklahoma City Times*. Ackerman was hired in 1947 and spent the next five years selling newspaper ads, as well as providing marketing ideas and writing and laying out ads. Because much of Knox's business was placing newspaper ads for retailers across the state of Oklahoma, Knox eventually decided to hire Ackerman for his agency.

ACKERMAN ACQUIRED AGENCY: 1954

When Ackerman joined the Knox Agency, there were just three other staff members. Most of the creative work was contracted out to freelancers. Ackerman quickly became a cornerstone of the agency, especially after Knox began spending a growing amount of time in Colorado running a luxury soap company. At the start of 1953, the agency was renamed Knox-Ackerman, but Knox retained all of the equity. With Knox spending more time in Colorado than in Oklahoma, Ackerman offered to buy the agency. Knox agreed, and in 1954 Ackerman acquired the agency.

Ackerman expanded his staff. To reward his best people, he began to share ownership of the agency, which led to a name change in 1956. Knox-Ackerman now became Ackerman Associates, Inc. It was just one of about a dozen ad agencies based in Oklahoma City but gradually grew to become the largest. In 1963 Ackerman was approached by two friends who ran an engineering firm and wanted to own their office space rather than continue to pay rent. The three men agreed to construct a new building, which was completed a year later. Because Ackerman Associates was the largest tenant, it became known as the Ackerman Building.

Ray Ackerman set a goal of becoming a true statewide agency. He added to his business in 1964 with the acquisition of another Oklahoma City ad agency, the owner of which wanted to move to Florida. Three years later Ackerman Associates opened an office in Tulsa, Oklahoma, where it always had difficulty winning accounts from local agencies. Ray Ackerman had initially attempted to acquire an existing agency, but had been turned down. A few months after opening the Tulsa office, however, the owner of one of Tulsa's largest

ad agencies, John Whitney, offered to sell his business in order to pursue his first love, teaching.

MARVIN MCQUEEN JOINS AGENCY: 1972

Much of the Whitney Agency's $1.5 million in business left, however, with the departure of John Whitney. By the end of the decade Ackerman Associates was billing just under $5 million a year, but growth appeared to have stalled. In 1969 a large New York agency, Lennen & Newell (L&N), offered to acquire Ackerman Associates, and Ray Ackerman agreed. It proved to be a difficult relationship, as L&N began experiencing financial problems. There was one silver lining. Through L&N Ackerman met his future partner, Marvin McQueen, who worked for D'Arcy Advertising in New York, which was considering an acquisition of L&N. McQueen was able to review L&N's books and took note of the profitable subsidiary in Oklahoma City. McQueen was approaching retirement age and had decided he had wanted to spend the remaining years of his career at a local ad agency in the middle of the country. He met with Ray Ackerman and signed a deal to join Ackerman Associates on January 1, 1972. In the meantime, Ackerman also reached an agreement to buy back the agency from L&N.

McQueen initially worked out of the Tulsa office and soon took charge. He then moved to Oklahoma City to become the agency's president. Not pleased with the creative work, McQueen recommended the agency hire a new creative director. He recommended another D'Arcy employee, his son Angus McQueen, who joined Ackerman Associates in 1973. The younger McQueen brought considerable experience, having previous served as a television director in St. Louis and Houston and worked on national advertising campaigns for the likes of Gerber Baby Foods, General Tire, Lufthansa Airlines, and Royal Crown Cola. Upon his arrival, Angus McQueen joined his father and Ray Ackerman as the triumvirate that led Ackerman Associates. Later the two older men readily admitted that Angus McQueen began running the shop as soon as he arrived. His gift for creativity elevated the agency above the local shops and led to national recognition.

ACKERMAN MCQUEEN NAME ADOPTED: 1979

The value of father and son McQueen was such that on January 1, 1979, Ackerman Associates was renamed Ackerman McQueen, Inc. Angus McQueen now became president of the agency, while his father and Ackerman served as cochairmen. At the start of the 1980s

Ackerman McQueen was billing $10 million a year. By the end of the decade that amount increased to $84 million.

In 1981 the agency landed its highest profile national account, the National Rifle Association (NRA), which was disenchanted with New York ad men who, according to a biography of Ackerman, "didn't know which end of the gun the bullet came out of." Ackerman McQueen crafted the "I'm the NRA" print campaign that featured celebrities as well as everyday people holding guns and smiling. It was designed to show that NRA members came from all walks of life and to combat the negative image of firearms in some segments of the population. Because of the NRA's lobbying efforts, Ackerman McQueen opened a Washington, D.C., office and established the Mercury Group to handle the NRA's public relations' needs.

The agency also expanded its regional footprint in the 1980s with the opening of an office in Dallas. The decade was a period of transition as well for Ackerman McQueen. In 1984 Marvin McQueen was involved in an automobile accident and died from the injuries he suffered. In that same year, the agency moved to a new location in Oklahoma City, having outgrown its space in the Ackerman Building. In early 1987 the Tulsa business expanded through the acquisition of Hood, Hope and Associates, a transaction Marvin McQueen had discussed with Chuck Hood shortly before his death. The addition of Hood increased Ackerman McQueen's billings to $70 million, making it one of the largest ad agencies in the Southwest.

RAY ACKERMAN RETIRES: 1992

When Ray Ackerman retired in 1992 at the age of 70, the agency was generating $92 million in annual sales. He became chairman emeritus, but had no day-to-day responsibilities, devoting most of his time to his many civic projects, as well as to family and traveling. The agency was left in good hands with Angus McQueen, who continued to grow the agency. An office was added in Colorado Springs to service the Colorado Springs Convention & Visitors Center account, and a fiber-optic network was installed to allow the five Ackerman McQueen locations to work smoothly together. In addition to the NRA, other major accounts included Premier Parks, Inc., owner of Six Flags theme parks, and Brunswick Indoor Recreation Group. Business increased significantly in the latter half of the 1990s, and by the end of the decade, annual billings topped $200 million. New clients included King's Step golf shoes, software supplier Solarc, and Cherokee Casinos.

In the late 1990s and into the next decade, Ackerman McQueen considered moving its headquarters to Dallas, but ultimately decided to maintain its headquarters in Oklahoma City. After winning the consolidated global advertising account for Six Flags, Ackerman McQueen launched an international division in 2001, which led to the opening of an office in Brussels the following year and a second European outpost in London in 2003. After the agency lost the Six Flags account later in the year, however, the international division was shut down.

Ackerman McQueen expanded on other fronts in the new century. The agency added the AMID digital division, providing clients with internet and mobile marketing services. Ackerman McQueen also introduced the Videodigm division, an online streaming video platform for organizations involved in advocacy, tourism and travel, law, health care, and the arts. The NRA, for example, used the Videodigm platform to disseminate its message direct to the public.

In October 2012 Ray Ackerman died at the age of 90, severing the last tie to the agency's origins. By this time Ackerman McQueen had annual billings of more than $200 million, an amount that ranked it in the top 2 percent of ad agencies in the country. Angus McQueen remained in charge, but by now he was 70 years old. The agency had long operated out of the spotlight in Oklahoma City, but as gun violence in the United States became an increasingly controversial subject in the wake of several mass killings and the NRA's efforts to defeat any attempts to restrict the sale or use of firearms, attention began to be paid to the ad agency that for the past three decades had so adroitly crafted NRA's advertising and handled its public relations. How Ackerman McQueen would adapt to life without Angus McQueen and whether the agency might suffer a backlash because of its close ties to the NRA were questions yet to be answered.

Ed Dinger

Ackerman McQueen, Inc.

PRINCIPAL DIVISIONS

Ackmac Productions; AMID; Mercury Group; Videodigm.

PRINCIPAL COMPETITORS

GSD&M Advertising; Insight Creative Group; The Richards Group.

FURTHER READING

"Advertising Agencies to Negotiate Merger." *Daily Oklahoman*, September 25, 1986.

Brus, Brian. "Advertising Pioneer, Oklahoma City Leader Ray Ackerman Dies at 90." *Oklahoma City Journal Record*, October 17, 2012.

Bunyan, Clytie. "Ackerman McQueen Agency Wired for Future Growth." *Daily Oklahoman*, September 27, 1998.

Burke, Bob, and Joan Gilmore. *Old Man River: The Life of Ray Ackerman*. Oklahoma City: Oklahoma Heritage Association, 2002, 311p.

Finn, Peter, and Sari Horwitz. "Ackerman McQueen PR Firm Has Been behind NRA's Provocative Ads for Decades." *Washington Post*, February 13, 2013.

Monies, Paul. "Ackerman McQueen Examines Options." *Daily Oklahoman*, August 21, 2004.

Altavia S.A.

1 rue Rembrandt
Paris, 75008
France
Telephone: (+33 1) 49 48 00 00
Fax: (+33 1) 49 48 01 01
Web site: http://www.altavia-paris.com

Private Company
Founded: 1983 as PBE
Employees: 1,250
Sales: EUR 581 million ($755 million) (2013)
NAICS: 541810 Advertising Agencies; 541512 Computer Systems Design Services; 541611 Administrative Management and General Management Consulting Services

■■■

Altavia S.A. is one of Europe's leading advertising companies, focused on providing marketing services and print and media support to the retail distribution sector. Altavia operates across two main divisions, Marketing Services Agency, providing communication, brand content, trade marketing, and related support services; and Publishing Services, including print and cross-media content management. Altavia also has a number of specialized businesses, such as Shoppermind, focused on consumer research; MyStudioFactory, providing support for web, mobile, tablet, and other media platforms; Capital Innovation, which assists companies in developing new products and services; and CPO, a design agency. Based in Paris, Altavia has built a network of of-fices and subsidiaries across Europe, reaching more than 23 markets. The company also has an expanding presence in the mainland Chinese market. International revenues accounted for 46 percent of the group's total of EUR 581 million ($755 million) in 2013. Altavia is led by founder and Chairman Raphaël Palti.

ADMAN IN 1983

Raphaël Palti was born in Saint Nazaire, France, in 1958 into a family of entrepreneurs; among Palti's distant relatives was the founder of the Orangina soft drink company. As a youth, Palti dreamed of moving to Paris, where he hoped to become a film director. Palti's parents agreed to send him to Paris but on the condition that he continue his education. Palti enrolled in the private business school, ESLSCA (École Supérieure Libre des Sciences Commerciales Appliquées) in the late 1970s. There, Palti discovered a new vocation, advertising, which combined his interest in film and his background in entrepreneurship. He also gained experience working for two major French advertising groups, Publicis and Eurocom, part of the Havas media empire.

By 1983, while still a student, Palti decided to create his own advertising agency. For this, Palti was inspired by Bernard Brochand, a noted figure in the French advertising industry, who promoted the idea of developing new methods for advertising to the youth market. Palti set up shop in an office in Saint-Ouen en Seine-Saint-Denis, outside of Paris. The office was located in a building that functioned as a sort of incubator for young businesses. In exchange for a small stake, Palti's business, called PBE, was given free rent and other support services.

PBE grew swiftly through its first five years. The company built a strong portfolio of clients almost entirely through word of mouth. This success, however, helped mask a number of fundamental problems with the company's organization. As Palti himself later declared in a televised interview: "In fact, I had created nothing. [PBE] was merely an adventure with a bunch of friends."

In 1988 PBE hit its first major road bump, when in a single week it lost its three largest clients. The sudden loss of business exposed the weakness of the company's organization, and its lack of a long-term strategy. Nonetheless, the crisis proved an important turning point for Palti and the company.

RETAILER FOCUS IN THE NINETIES

Palti recognized the need to put into place a true business structure and organization. At the same time, he redeveloped the company's business strategy, now focusing its operations more specifically on providing marketing and media support services for the retail sector. The company's primary objective became to assist retailers in attracting customers to their stores, help them ensure customer purchases, and encourage customer loyalty. This objective remained a cornerstone of the future Altavia empire as well.

With its strengthened business structure, PBE set out to rebuild its client base, now targeting many of France's leading retailing groups. Into the 1990s PBE also expanded its range of operations, setting up a number of dedicated businesses. These included CFA, a specialist in outsourced print and media management, opened in 1988, and others, such as the Argile, focused on design; Palti-Malinkowski, a graphics agency; events specialist Aïda; and a consulting and direct marketing business, Coda, added in 1998.

By then too PBE had already taken its first steps outside of France, starting with the opening of an office in Madrid, Spain, in 1995. This was followed by an office in Barcelona as well. PBE's international strategy continued to focus on the southern European market through the end of the decade. The group entered Italy in 1997, with an office in Milan. The company's Spanish subsidiary also extended its operations into Portugal, adding an office in Lisbon.

ALTAVIA IN 1999

By the end of the 1990s Palti stood at the head of a diversified marketing services company generating operating profits of FRF 160 million (approximately $25 million) per year. The company had also succeeded in building an impressive list of clients, including French retailing juggernaut Carrefour, as well as French automotive leader Renault, clothing group Etam, and the Lustucru pasta brand.

Instead of resting on this success, Palti once again redeveloped the company's strategy. This effort began in 1999, when the company adopted a new name, Altavia, meant to evoke both "the high road" and "alternative route." Then, at the beginning of 2000, the company carried out a reorganization of its operations. These were now regrouped into three main business areas, Consulting, including its events, design, and direct marketing businesses; Altavia Junium, for the group's youth market-oriented marketing services; and Altavia Prodity, for its publishing services division. The latter division was further expanded by the acquisition of La Publicité Française, the former editorial subsidiary of the PSA automotive group.

The reorganization set the stage for an impressive growth spurt, as Altavia's sales swelled past EUR 400 million into the turn of the century. The company also continued its international expansion, continuing farther south into Greece and Turkey, before beginning its assault on the northern European market, starting with the creation of Altavia Belgium in 2001. By then, the group already achieved half of its sales outside of France.

As the world slipped into recession following the September 11, 2001, terrorist attacks on the United States that year, Altavia too found itself struggling. The company's consulting division lost two of its largest clients, Marks and Spencer and Carrefour, contributing to a drop of more than 16 percent the group's profits. The company also found itself confronted with a suddenly morose advertising sector.

REFOCUSED IN 2002

Palti once again seized on the group's difficulties to revise the company's strategy. Altavia now redefined

KEY DATES

1983: Raphaël Palti founds advertising agency PBE.

1988: Company loses three major clients and reorganizes to focus on the retail distribution sector.

1995: First international expansion, into Spain, is made.

1999: Altavia brand name is adopted.

2002: Altavia restructures to focus on the publishing services sector.

2005: Company opens its first office in China.

2010: Altavia enters Russia and Romania.

2014: Company acquires point-of-sale specialist IMS.

itself as a specialist in publishing services. To this end, the company began selling its noncore businesses, including Mideos, the newest name for the group's consulting business, acquired by Publicis in October 2002. Other operations sold during this period included Novatrice, a web-based advertising business, and the group's events division, sold to Lever de Rideau. The company shut down other operations, such as a web magazine called Urban Pass. The company nonetheless retained its retail marketing services operations, and notably subsidiary Altavia Junium.

Altavia's streamlining provided the company with the treasury it needed to achieve its aim of building itself into a European leader. The company now set its sights on conquering the northern and eastern European markets. By the end of 2002, the company had taken its first step into the latter market, opening offices in Prague, Czech Republic, and Warsaw, Poland. The company added subsidiaries in Düsseldorf, Germany, in 2003, and in London in 2004.

Altavia's ambitions had by then taken a significant step forward. In 2003 the company acquired majority control of Groupe Victor, a publishing services specialist based in Nantes, with offices in Paris and Lille. Founded in 1984, Victor brought Altavia new strength in local communication strategies, with experience working in a wide variety of areas, including the industrial, financial, business-to-business, mail-order, and entertainment sectors. Importantly, Victor had also developed its own expertise in the retail sector, bringing a client list including such French retail leaders as Décathlon, Système U, Leclerc, and Castorama. Following the acquisition, Altavia reorganized again, creating a new geographic-based structure. As such, the company's French operations were regrouped under a new subsidiary, Altavia France.

ADDING CHINA IN 2005

The Victor acquisition became the first of a series of purchases as Altavia claimed not only the leadership in the French publishing services market but across Europe as well. Among the company's acquisitions were Saint-Étienne–based Connexion, in 2005, and three other French companies, CPO, RVB, and Le Parti du Client, in 2006. Altavia also made its first international acquisition that year, buying the United Kingdom's HTT. This company was then merged with the group's London office, becoming Altavia HTT.

The company's acquisition of RVB, a specialist in the use of digital media, played a role in another successful extension by the company. Carrefour, once again one of the company's clients, had begun building its operations in mainland China at the turn of the century. At Carrefour's request, Altavia entered China as well, setting up its first office there in 2005. Altavia was able to leverage the expertise gained through RVB to take advantage of the ubiquity of digital communication media supports and outlets in China. By the end of the decade, Altavia had built up a network of four Chinese offices, in Beijing, Shanghai, Guanzhou, and Chengdu. With more than 150 employees, the group's Chinese operations became one of its largest outside of France. Alongside Carrefour, the company secured a number of major contracts, including for the Chinese operations of Germany's Media Mart, the do-it-yourself chain B&Q, and Watson, the Hong Kong–based retail cosmetics leader.

In 2006 Palti took the decision to step down from day-to-day direction of the group, retaining his position as chairman of the company. Instead, Altavia brought in Jimmy Anidjar, former head of Oracle's operations in Europe, the Middle East, and Africa, to take over as the company's CEO.

EUROPEAN LEADER IN 2014

Altavia had by then cemented its reputation as one of Europe's leading communications services groups. This reputation was further reinforced in 2007 when the company was named the European Communication Group of the Year in the Prix de l'Ambition awards held by Banque Palatine and La Tribune. Altavia was particularly singled out for the strong growth of its international operations. These continued to expand, notably into Switzerland in 2008 and into Romania and Russia in 2010. The following year it entered Hungary for the first time.

The company continued to develop its communications and publishing services tool kit into the new decade. In 2009 the company introduced its print-to-web Actipaper concept, providing clients with linked print and digital capabilities. The company also began developing environmentally friendly and sustainable operations, and in 2010 became the first communications company in Europe to achieve both FSC and PEFC certification. The company followed this up in 2012 with the introduction of its Ecopublishing service, bringing together various advancements in environmentally responsible inks, paper production and paper, and transport under a single banner. The company quickly converted some 10 percent of its clientele, including such heavyweights as the Picard frozen foods retail group and tire giant Michelin, to the new formula.

Altavia added to its range of operations again in 2011, with the creation of subsidiary, ShopperMind, dedicated to consumer research. The following year, the company added several new markets, including Ukraine, Sweden, Finland, and Hungary, where it created a dedicated subsidiary located in Budapest. The following year, the group expanded its Asian operations, opening offices in Japan and South Korea.

Into the middle of the decade, Altavia completed two new acquisitions. The first of these came in 2013, with the purchase of Agence Cosmic, a small Paris-based agency with complementary operations to Altavia's own. This was followed by the acquisition of point-of-sale specialist IMS, based in Lille, in July 2014. IMS brought its own strong client portfolio, which included Orangina Schweppes, Leroy Merlin, Go Sport, Carrefour, and Nocibé. With sales of EUR 581 million ($755 million) in 2013, Altavia had consolidated its position as one of Europe's leading communications and marketing specialists.

M. L. Cohen

PRINCIPAL SUBSIDIARIES

Altavia Benelux NV (Netherlands); Altavia Ceska (Czech Republic); Altavia China Ltd.; Altavia Deutschland (Germany); Altavia France; Altavia HTT Ltd. (UK); Altavia Hungaria; Altavia Iberica (Spain); Altavia Italia (Italy); Altavia Polska (Poland); Altavia Romania; Altavia Rus (Russia); Altavia Swiss (Switzerland); Altavia Turkiye (Turkey); Altavia Ukraine; Capital Innovation SARL; CPO SARL; Shoppermind SARL.

PRINCIPAL DIVISIONS

Marketing Services Agency; Publishing Services.

PRINCIPAL OPERATING UNITS

Altavia; CPO; Agence Cosmic; Capital Innovation; Shoppermind; Mystudiofactory.

PRINCIPAL COMPETITORS

Adrexo; Clear Channel Inc.; Hi-Media S.A.; JCDecaux SA; Leo Burnett; McCann-Erickson Inc.; Oakley Europe; Publicis Groupe S.A.

FURTHER READING

"Altavia Achète Cosmic et se Renforce en France." *FrenchWeb.fr*, October 18, 2003.

"Altavia Table sur les Imprimés Verts." *Environnement Magazine*, April 12, 2012.

Brusset, Olivier. "Altavia Rachète le Groupe Victor." *eMarketing.fr*, October 1, 2003.

Chalmet, Eric. "Altavia, un Stratège Commercial au Coeur du Boom Chinois." *La Tribune*, January 16, 2011.

Dussausaye, Daniel. "Entretien avec Raphaël Palti, Président du Groupe Altavia." *Presse Edition*, June 26, 2008.

"Eric Borreil Prend la Tête d'Altavia." *Stratégies Magazine*, January 9, 2014.

Laugier, Edouard, and Raphaël Palti. "Altavia: Le Client-Roi Devient une Réalité." *Le Nouvel Economiste*, January 16, 2014.

"Raphaël Palti se Retire de la Direction Opérationnelle d'Altavia." *GraphiLine*, December 11, 2006.

Anytime Fitness LLC

12181 Margo Avenue South
Hastings, Minnesota 55033
U.S.A.
Telephone: (651) 438-5000
Fax: (651) 438-5099
Web site: http://www.anytimefitness.com

Private Company
Founded: 2002
Employees: 166
Sales: $634 million (2013)
NAICS: 713940 Fitness and Recreational Sports
Centers; 533110 Lessors of Nonfinancial Intangible
Assets (except Copyrighted Works)

■ ■ ■

Anytime Fitness LLC operates and franchises a chain of more than 2,400 health and fitness clubs in 19 countries. The clubs are open 24 hours a day, every day of the year. The company's 2 million member clients are issued a key card embedded with a microchip that allows them access to the facilities when no staff is present. The company also operates the Anytime Health Web site, which allows members to track their progress, obtain fitness tips, and connect with other clients.

EARLY YEARS

The three founders of Anytime Fitness, Jeff Klinger, Chuck Runyon, and Dave Mortensen, came together in the 1980s, when they all worked in various positions as-

sociated with the Minneapolis–St. Paul–area fitness club scene. Runyon and Mortensen, both college dropouts, shared an interest in business and physical fitness. They formed a friendship with Klinger while employed in the marketing department of Medalist, an arca gym chain.

In 1989 the trio left to create the Health & Fitness Group, a consulting company designed to serve fitness chains in need of a sales boost. The endeavor was financially successful enough to enable the trio to purchase their own gym, the Southview Athletic Club, an established facility that had fallen on hard times. Southview would provide the laboratory the three partners needed in their quest to improve the health club business model.

Runyon, Klinger, and Mortensen would own Southview for seven years while continuing their work with the Health & Fitness Group. During that time, membership at the gym climbed from around 500 to more than 4,000. By this point, the three partners had learned quite a bit from their experiences running the facility. The gym was a typical "big box" workout club with amenities such as a swimming pool, courts for racquetball and basketball, and spacious locker rooms.

During the course of business, the partners observed that much of Southview's floor space went unused by its members, who tended to gravitate toward specific workout and weight machines. In an effort to both cut costs and provide data for their consultancy business, the partners began to poll clients about their favorite fitness machines, desired workout schedule, and general likes and dislikes about fitness clubs.

```
COMPANY PERSPECTIVES
```

Over 2 million members choose Anytime Fitness. Why? Because it's convenient, affordable, and fun. And with 24/7 access to thousands of our clubs around the globe, you can work out on your terms. Fitness has never been so easy.

DEVELOPING A NEW CONCEPT

Using their members' preferences and usage patterns as a template, the partners began to put together a business plan for a line of small facilities that concentrated on only the most popular fitness offerings and eliminated much of the wasted space and accompanying high overhead of big-box clubs. In 2001 the partnership sold the bustling Southview and used the $1.1 million in proceeds to start a new company. Anytime Fitness LLC established a brand of small, basic workout facilities that would be open 24 hours a day, 365 days a year, and offer the workout equipment that customers used the most and little else.

The gyms were designed for busy customers who wanted a quick and easy workout any time of the day or night. Operating with an emphasis on low overhead costs, Anytime Fitness locations would be staffed only during peak hours. Some stores would have an attendant on duty as few as five hours per day. Rather than paying to build multiple clubs, the partners opted for a franchise operation through which they licensed the Anytime Fitness brand name, business model, and corporate support system to independent operators.

These franchisees assumed most of the financial responsibility for their stores and paid various fees to the company. The first Anytime franchisee was Eric Keller, who had worked for the partners at Southview. Working closely with Klinger, Mortensen, and Runyon, Keller opened the first Anytime Fitness gym in Cambridge, Minnesota, later in 2002. He remained closely associated with Anytime Fitness, eventually becoming its vice president of international franchising.

FRANCHISE EXPANDS

With the first Anytime Fitness franchise established, the partners offered franchise opportunities to other former Southview employees, opening locations in Duluth and Albert Lea, Minnesota. Anytime Fitness continued selling franchises through 2003, concentrating primarily on areas of their native Minnesota that were underserved by health clubs.

By the end of their first full year in business, the company had earned just $52,000 in corporate revenue and had eight franchise stores in operation around Minnesota. The partners supplemented their revenues from the nascent business with income from their continuing work for Health & Fitness Group, which was bringing in several million dollars a year. In addition to a stripped-down focus on featuring only the most popular fitness machines in a 2,000 to 4,000-square-foot space, the Anytime Fitness stores all followed the same, no frills, self-serve business model.

Customers paid $30 to $55 per month, depending on the package, and had 24-hours-per-day, 365-days-a-year access to club facilities. Often unstaffed during slower hours, the clubs offered access and security via computerized ID tags provided to each customer. Clubs were monitored with video surveillance at all times.

Eventually, security systems were introduced to ensure that customers could not bring nonmember friends in with them. During the company's start-up period, costs to franchisees were kept deliberately modest in order to attract business. Franchise owners paid a $9,000 licensing fee and $399 per month in royalties. While some fees rose as the brand became more lucrative, Anytime Fitness's management always strove to keep them affordable.

FRANCHISES EXPAND

The $399 monthly royalty remained unchanged for years to come. At all stages of the start-up process, franchisees received support and assistance from the corporate offices. The strategy seemed to work. By the end of 2004 more than 50 Anytime Fitness franchises dotted the upper Midwest. The same year, the partners finally took the plunge themselves, opening Anytime Fitness's first corporate-owned location.

Highlighting the company's emphasis on franchising over corporate ownership, Runyon told the *Twin Cities Business Magazine*, "We sold 29 franchises before we opened our first [corporate-owned] club in Bemidji, Minnesota. We had a wealth of industry experience, but we did not open up our own Anytime Fitness center until store No. 30." The company went on to open 15 more corporate stores across the country, although typically the local manager would hold a minority ownership stake as well.

In early 2005 the company opened its first international franchise in Halifax, Nova Scotia. That year, the Anytime Fitness store count nearly tripled from the previous year, reaching 148. The following year saw the franchise continue to expand rapidly with more than 300 locations operating in 46 states by the end of 2006.

KEY DATES

2002: Company is founded.
2005: Company opens first location outside the United States.
2009: Cofounder and CEO Jeff Klinger leaves the company.
2012: Company purchases Waxing the City chain.
2014: Roark Capital Group becomes minority owner of the company.

Corporate revenues had also risen, reaching $3 million in 2005 and tripling to around $10 million in 2006. Systemwide, Anytime Fitness was bringing an estimated $70 million a year in membership fees. In 2007 systemwide revenues hit $98 million.

INTERNATIONAL EXPANSION

In 2008 Anytime Fitness opened its 1,000th location while corporate revenues topped $20 million, derived from $135 million in revenues across the chain. The company continued to expand its international presence that year, signing agreements that could bring up to 350 clubs to New Zealand and Australia. Within the next few years, Anytime Fitness clubs opened in the United Kingdom, Japan, Poland, and Qatar, among other countries. Usually, the partners signed a master franchise agreement with a firm in each country, which would then sell and service individual franchise contracts in the territory.

Anytime Fitness simply received royalties and left management issues to the local master franchisor. In a few countries, including Spain and Canada, Anytime Fitness worked directly with local franchisees. Among all the gains of this period came one loss. At the end of 2009 CEO and cofounder Klinger sold his stake in the company and moved on to other interests.

Runyon assumed his duties as CEO. "The growth of Anytime Fitness has been exciting and gratifying," Klinger stated in a press release, "But I am an entrepreneur at heart, and I love to take a new idea and get it started. Dave Mortensen, Chuck Runyon and I have been working alongside each other and building things together since 1989. It has been a tremendous pleasure for me to work with these guys—they are like family—but I felt the time was right for me to move on."

Throughout the transition, company revenues continued to climb, with $221 million in system-wide grosses earning $28.9 million for the corporation. As 2010 began, Anytime Fitness had some 1,300 locations operating across 49 states and in four other countries. With around 1,000 more franchise agreements signed and in various stages of development, the company's momentum seemed unstoppable.

DIVERSIFYING WITH NEW PARTNERS

Along with the number of store locations, revenues across the system had risen appreciably. The year 2010 saw corporate revenues of $33.7 million, based on $284.4 million in systemwide grosses. The next year saw Runyon and Mortensen's partnership earn $40.3 million against the chain's overall take of $364.7 million. By this point, the partners had formed a holding company, Self Esteem Brands, an umbrella under which they ran Anytime Fitness and several other associated businesses.

Along with the partners' ongoing consultant work, they also operated Provision Security, which oversaw the clubs' security systems, and Healthy Contributions, which provided services for health benefits providers. Anytime Fitness joined the social media revolution in 2010, when it implemented the Anytime Health online platform. While the company had always maintained a Web site, the new platform served as an interactive tool for Anytime members. Customers were able to track their progress, design workout programs, and engage with the company and other members in a social media–structured environment.

The platform was designed to increase brand loyalty, making Anytime Fitness a key part of its clients' lives, even when they were at home or using their smartphones. In late 2012 Runyon and Mortensen added another company to their portfolio when they purchased the Waxing the City chain, which provided cosmetic body-waxing services. The small network of stores was immediately overhauled in preparation for a franchised expansion, following the same basic model Anytime Fitness used.

DIVERSIFICATION AND EXPANSION

At the time of the purchase, Waxing the City had one store in Dallas, Texas, and four locations in Denver, Colorado. True to form, the partners opened their first franchise location in Woodbury, Minnesota. Forty more franchises were sold over the next year. The year 2012 also saw the beginning of a notable trend that garnered the company some media attention. Runyon had noted a fad among some faithful Anytime Fitness employees and customers for getting tattoos of the company's stylized "running man" logo.

At the height of the fad, the company hired celebrity tattoo artist Jimmy Hayden, famous for inking prominent NBA players, to provide free tattoos at Anytime's annual conference in 2013. Around 200 employees opted for the tattoo over the weekend. Runyon then announced that the company would reimburse anyone in the world for the costs of getting the tattoo, as long as they submitted a photo and a personal story. The company eventually estimated that more than 1,000 people got the tattoo.

The company continued to focus on international expansion in October 2013, when it launched a Singapore location that had more than 200 members signed up before the doors even opened. Soon, the company announced that it was working to open more than 100 new locations in Singapore and Hong Kong. Plans were also underway for a franchise in Malaysia. With 10 clubs already in operation in Japan, the company saw the Asian market as a promising new frontier.

HEADQUARTERS MOVED: 2014

The early months of 2014 saw two announcements with long-range implications. As the year began, the company announced that it would soon move its corporate headquarters from Hastings, Minnesota, to a new, significantly larger facility in Woodbury. In March, the company announced that the Atlanta-based public equity firm Roark Capital Group had made a significant investment in Anytime Fitness, acquiring a minority ownership stake.

Two of Roark's directors, Steve Romaniello and Erick Morris, joined the Anytime Fitness LLC board of directors in the wake of the news. Runyon and Mortensen continued to run the company and maintain controlling ownership. At this point, Anytime Fitness LLC was operating more than 2,400 fitness clubs worldwide.

The company had brought in $634 million in system-wide revenue the previous year and had more than 2 million member clients. It was ranked first on *Entrepreneur* magazine's list of the top 500 franchises. The average Anytime Fitness location had more than 800 members. Roark's decision to invest seemed another vote of confidence in the prospects of the growing company.

Chris Herzog

PRINCIPAL COMPETITORS

Fitness Together Holdings Inc.; PFIP LLC; Snap Fitness.

FURTHER READING

"Achieving Goals with Anytime Fitness." National Center for the Middle Market. Accessed October 13, 2014. http://www.middlemarketcenter.org/company-of-month/anytime-fitness.

"Entrepreneur 2014 Franchise 500; No. 1: Anytime Fitness." *Entrepreneur*, January 2014.

Howard, Fran. "Anytime Fitness: The Fastest Growing Club." *Twin Cities Business Magazine*, September 2012.

Johnson, Cheryl. "Chuck Runyon; Dave Mortensen; Fitness Guys Make a Smooth Move." *Minneapolis Star-Tribune*, November 4, 2012.

Runyon, Chuck. "Level Brand Loyalty." *Fast Company*. Accessed October 13, 2014. http://www.fastcompany.com/1837855/anytime-fitness-ceo-chuck-runyons-4-rules-tattoo-level-brand-loyalty.

Vomhof, John, Jr. "Anytime Fitness Lands Private Equity Investment." *Minneapolis/St. Paul Business Journal*, March 3, 2014.

Youngblood, Dick. "A Lesson in Bulking Up Bottom Line; Anytime Fitness Clubs Offer Affordability, Convenience and a First-Class Array of Exercise Equipment." *Minneapolis Star-Tribune*, December 20, 2006.

Arvind Ltd.

———————————■———————————

Naroda Road
Ahmedabad, 380 025
India
Telephone: (+91 79) 3013 8000
Fax: (+91 79) 3013 8668
Web site: http://www.arvindmills.com

Public Company
Founded: 1931
Employees: 3,900
Sales: INR 47.75 trillion ($908.7million) (2013)
Stock Exchanges: Bombay
Ticker Symbol: 500101
NAICS: 313210 Broadwoven Fabric Mills; 424330
Women's, Children's, and Infants' Clothing and
Accessories Merchant Wholesalers; 315220 Men's
and Boys' Cut and Sew Apparel Manufacturing

■ ■ ■

Arvind Ltd. is one of India's leading textiles and cloth-ing manufacturers and retailers, and one of the world's largest producers of denim. Based in Ahmedabad, Gujarat, Arvind is focused around several primary divisions, including Denim, Woven Fabrics, Knit Fabric, Garment Exports, Advanced Materials, Retail, Engineering, and Real Estate. The company's has an installed denim production capacity of 110 million meters per year, which is complemented by its annual woven fabrics production capacity of 84 million meters and knit fabric capacity of 5,000 tons per year. The company's Garment Export division oversees global sales of company-produced bottoms, formal and casual tops, and knit tops, shipping nearly 17 million pieces per year for such brands as Gap, Patagonia, Tommy Hilfiger, Quicksilver, Brooks Brothers, Calvin Klein, FCUK, Pull & Bear, Esprit, Mexx, and Benetton. The company also holds the domestic distribution rights to a number of these brands, as well as others, including Arrow, Wrangler, Izod, Cherokee, and Mossimo, which it sells through a network of 273 branded stand-alone stores and 975 in-store counters.

Arvind also operates two retail chains of its own, The Arvind Store, focused on bespoke tailoring featur-ing the company's fabrics, as well as the Megamart department store chain. This chain has more than 200 locations, as well as six larger-scale stores operated under the Big Megamart name. Arvind has also pursued diversification beyond the textiles industry. The company's Anup Engineering subsidiary produces a variety of metal-based components, such as heat exchangers, pressure vessels, columns and towers, and expansion bellows. Arvind has also been pursuing expansion into the real estate development sector, focus-ing principally on the city of Ahmedabad. A public company with a listing on the Bombay Stock Exchange, Arvind continues to be led by the founding Lalbhai family. The company reported revenues of INR 47.75 trillion ($908.7 million) in 2013.

COTTON MILL IN 1896

The Lalbhai family had long held a place of prominence on Ahmedabad, tracing its roots in the city as far back as the 16th century. Through the 19th century, the family became important gem traders and jewelers. By the 1870s under the leadership of Dalpatbhai Bhagubhai, the family had also branched out into cotton trading. This activity led Dalpatbhai's son, Lalbhai Dalpatbhai, born in 1863, to build a cotton mill in Saraspur in 1896. The following year a new family business, Saraspur Manufacturing Company, began producing cotton yarn. The family added a second textile mill, called Raipur Mills in 1905.

Soon after, Dalpatbhai Bhagubhai divided up the family's businesses among his children. As part of the division, Lalbhai Dalpatbhai and his sons were given the Raipur Mills and other related textile businesses. Lalbhai Dalpatbhai died at the age of 49 in 1912, however, leaving the mill under the direction of his second-born son, Kasturbhai Lalbhai, then 17 years old.

Kasturbhai Lalbhai joined the company while the Raipur mill was still under construction. Although serving as chairman of the company, Lalbhai also took an active role in its operations, initially serving as the mill's timekeeper. Lalbhai quickly switched positions, however, and began working as the company's cotton buyer. Traveling and negotiating with suppliers not only provided Lalbhai with a strong overview of the market, it also allowed him to spot the potential for extending the company's operations into the production of textiles themselves.

This move was accomplished in 1920, when the company opened its Asoka Mill. The new mill became the largest in the Ahmedabad area, requiring an investment more than double the cost of its largest rivals. Lalbhai's business continued to grow through the decade, enabling him to gather in the family's other textiles businesses as well. These included three mills owned by his sisters, the first of which, Aruna Mills, became part of Lalbhai's growing empire in 1928. The company added a second mill, Nutan Mills, from another sister in 1931, and Ahmedabad New Cotton Mills from a third sister in 1938.

FOUNDING ARVIND IN 1931

This expansion came amid the growing strength of the Swadeshi movement, which sought to push forward India's independence from British control through the use of economic pressure. The textiles industry played a central part of the *swadeshi* (or "self-reliance") strategy. In 1931 Kasturbhai Lalbhai, a committed nationalist, regrouped the family's textiles holdings into a new company, called Arvind Ltd., and set out to build an Indian textiles leader. He was also joined in the business by other family members, including younger brother Narrotam.

Through the end of the 1930s, Arvind expanded to a total of seven mills, which, backed by strong investments, were refitted to become among the most modern in India. Arvind also seized on the Swadeshi movement boycott of foreign-made clothing to expand into the production of clothing fabrics, setting up a new state-of-the-art mill, called Arvind Mill, in 1939. By the outbreak of World War II, Arvind had already grown into one of India's leading textile firms, responsible for more than 10 percent of the country's total spun fabrics production. The company also became the largest producer of woven fabrics in Ahmedabad.

Arvind showed an early interest in vertical integration-oriented diversification as well. The company took its first step beyond textile production in 1939, with the founding of Anil Starch Ltd. In the years following World War II, the company added the production of textile dyes and chemicals through Atul Products Ltd., founded in 1952. The company later teamed up with such Western companies as Ciba-Geigy, American Cyanamid, and the United Kingdom's ICI.

NEW GENERATIONS IN THE SIXTIES AND SEVENTIES

Kasturbhai and Narrotam Lalbhai began transitioning the company to the family's next generation during the 1960s. Arvindbhai took over the leadership of the company, joined by brother Niranjanbhai and four of their cousins. During the decade, the company took over one of its struggling rivals, Ahmedabad Laxmi Cotton Mills Co., which was then merged into Arvind and renamed as Ankur Textiles. Through the 1970s Arvind also invested in more diversified areas of operation, adding an engineering business, Anup Engineering Ltd., which specialized in producing heat exchangers and

KEY DATES

1896: Lalbhai Dalpatbhai founds a cotton mill in Saraspur.
1905: Family builds a textile mill in Raipur.
1931: Kasturbhai Lalbhai and his brothers found Arvind Ltd.
1952: Company founds Atul Products Ltd. to produce textile dyes and other chemicals.
1980: Arvind begins denim production.
2003: Arvind creates Arvind Brands Ltd. as part of its branded clothing strategy.
2008: Company opens its first retail stores under the Megamart brand.
2014: Arvind acquires 49 percent of the Calvin Klein brand in India.

other industrial equipment. Other diversified businesses added during this time included a joint venture for the production of filters and perlite products in partnership with U.S.-based General Refractories.

The fourth generation of the family, led by Sanjay Lalbhai and including 13 brothers and sisters, took over amid the disastrous market conditions of the late 1970s. Born in 1954, Sanjay Lalbhai had earned a management degree from Jamnalal Bajaj Institute in Bombay (now Mumbai), before returning to the Arvind empire in 1977. Sanjay first started working for the group's Anil Forging subsidiary, before transferring to Arvind Mill itself as the group's purchasing manager. Sanjay also displayed an entrepreneurial bent of his own, starting several companies, including an advertising agency.

The advent of new industrial production technologies in India and elsewhere had led to a surplus of cheaply produced textiles and fabrics. At the same time, the Indian textiles industry faced additional pressures due to the depressed economic conditions arising from the oil shocks of the 1970s. Arvind itself suffered from this situation, and by 1979 the company found itself unable to pay dividends to its shareholders for the first time since its founding.

DENIM TO THE RESCUE IN 1980

Amid Arvind's struggles, Sanjay Lalbhai ultimately sold his stakes in these other companies and instead took over the lead at Arvind Mill. Under his leadership, the company introduced a new business strategy, dubbed "Renovision," which the company described as "looking

at the same situation from different perspectives." As a result, while many of the company's rivals were engaged in shutting down their looms in order to reduce the glut on the market, Arvind decided to invest in building a new business focus for the company.

Sanjay Lalbhai spotted opportunity in the rising demand for denim, as the designer jeans fad swept the Western world. Lalbhai became determined to introduce denim and denim clothing into India as well. The company established its first denim manufacturing facility in 1980. Through most of the decade, the company focused on supplying rising demand for denim from the domestic market. The group's early success in this effort encouraged it to expand its production for the export market as well. In 1987 the company launched an extensive expansion effort, enabling it to triple its denim production capacity by 1988. The company set up a dedicated export division, called Arvind Exports, in 1988. The company also modernized its other operations, allowing it to offer new lines of double-yarn and other fabrics. By 1991 Arvind's annual denim production had topped 100 million meters.

In the beginning of the 1990s Arvind invested more than INR 1 trillion to carry out its expansion. The group added a woolen mill in Rajasthan and in 1992 an expanded denim factory in Khatraj with a daily capacity of 23,000 metric tons. These investments helped Arvind grow into the world's fifth-largest denim producer by 1995, with a total capacity of 77 million yards per year. In India, the company commanded 80 percent of the domestic denim market, and more than one-fourth of the country's total production of shirting fabrics. The company also boosted its export operations, particularly into the United States, where it opened an office in New York in 1993.

Arvind had also begun a new diversification, this time entering the telecommunications market with the production of switching and networking equipment in a factory in Pune in 1989. The company also began developing specialty textiles capacity, acquiring Nagri Mills in 1990. This business was renamed as Arvind Intex Ltd. At the same time, the group retooled its Saraspur Mills plant, which became known as Arvind Poly Coat.

GARMENTS IN 1995

Arvind began preparations for its next step toward vertical integration in 1994, when it restructured its operations under three divisions, Textiles, Telecom, and Garments. The latter division represented a major milestone for the company as it began producing its first clothing lines in 1995. The group's first garment product, under the Ruf & Tuf brand name, was sold as a do-it-yourself kit, including denim, rivets, and zippers. If the Ruf & Tuf concept proved slow to take off, the group had better success with its entry into full-fledged garment production soon after. The company added new brands, including Newport, Flying Machine, and Ruggers. In 1997 the company added a franchise network for the Ruf & Tuf brand, setting the stage for the brand's growth.

Arvind continued to invest heavily in expanding its denim production through the decade as well, building up its total production to 150 million yards per year by 1998. Among the company's most ambitious projects was the construction of a massive INR 10 trillion shirting factory on 450 acres of land in Santej.

Much of the new capacity was earmarked toward the export market. The economic crisis that swept through much of the Asian region, and the company's own miscalculation of the market, caught Arvind short, however. By the end of 1997 the company faced a debt mountain of INR 28 trillion. The company found itself faced with shutting down its operations.

Instead, Sanjay Lalbhai once again led an about-face in Arvind's strategy. Over the next four years, the company set to work renegotiating its debts with its banks and other creditors, including swapping debt for equity. Arvind also restructured its business processes, bringing in an SAP-based enterprise resource planning platform, starting in 1998.

ESTABLISHMENT OF LIFESTYLE APPARELS UNIT IN 2000

Arvind also began developing its brand strategy into the turn of the century. In addition to its growing stable of company-owned brands, Arvind began acquiring its first brand licenses, starting with the rights to produce and distribute the Lee jeans and clothing brand for the Indian and Middle Eastern markets. As part of its effort to build this operation, the company established a new Lifestyle Apparels unit as part of its Garments Exports Division in 2000.

The growth of Arvind's branded clothing operations led the company to establish a dedicated subsidiary, Arvind Brands Ltd., in 2003, in partnership with ICICI Ventures. The company acquired full control of Arvind Brands in 2005. Arvind also stepped up its design component, notably by setting up a dedicated denim showroom in New York's SOHO neighborhood. Called Arvind Design Lab, the new showroom permitted the company to work directly with designers.

Arvind's brand strategy brought the company into the retail sector into the second half of that decade. The

company's first retail offering opened in 2008 under the Megamart name. This store format positioned itself as a value-oriented department store. The Megamart chain grew quickly, topping 200 locations into the next decade, and also inspired the creation of an expanded large-scale store format, called Big Megamart.

This success encouraged Arvind to seek expansion into the higher-end clothing market as well. In 2010 the company introduced its Arvind Store format, which featured the company's top-line fabrics as well as bespoke tailoring services. At the same time, Arvind had been building up its portfolio of international brands, acquiring the rights to distribute such well-known labels as Tommy Hilfiger and Geoffrey Beene in 2011, Billabong in 2012, Hanes and Wonderbra in 2013, and a 49 percent stake in Calvin Klein's India business. By 2014 the company's portfolio included such brands as Arrow, Wrangler, Gap, Patagonia, Izod, Mossimo, Quicksilver, Brooks Brothers, FCUK, Pull & Bear, Esprit, Mexx, and Benetton.

NEW DIVERSIFICATION INTO 2014

Arvind supported these brand extensions with the development of a third retail network, including more than 275 stand-alone stores and nearly 1,000 in-store corner boutiques. The company made a number of acquisitions, including the Indian operations of the Debenhams, Next, and Nautica retail chains. By 2014 the company had expanded into the production of formal suits, forming a joint venture with Japan's Goodhill Corporation.

Arvind's growing branded clothing and retail businesses helped reduce its reliance on denim production, which dropped from 60 percent of sales in 2006 to just 35 percent in 2012. At the same time, Arvind had begun a new diversification program designed to lower its total textiles operations from 72 percent of its business to just half into the middle of the decade. Arvind also hoped to double its total sales, to as high as INR 80 trillion by 2015. The company's sales already neared INR 50 trillion ($910 million) by the end of 2013.

As part of this effort, Arvind extended its textiles expertise by forming a new Advanced Materials division. The company's investments in this area included the creation of a glass fabrics joint venture with Germany's PD Fiber Glass Group in 2011. This joint venture set up a factory for the production of textiles for automotive, aerospace, and energy applications. The company also invested in developing production capacity for bulletproof and fireproof fabrics and clothing. Sanjay Lalbhai's son Punit became head of the new division.

Lalbhai's younger son, Kulin, also joined the company, serving as executive director of Arvind Ltd. and also spearheading the group's push into the e-commerce market with the creation of Arvind Internet Ltd. That subsidiary set out to revolutionize Internet clothing sales in India with the introduction of its custom clothing brand, Creyate. The new brand allowed online shoppers to personalize their clothing purchases.

In the meantime, Sanjay Lalbhai continued to lead the group's diversification drive. A centerpiece of this effort was the group's decision to enter the real estate development market, creating Arvind Infrastructure Ltd. The company began its first development, in Ahmedabad, in 2010. By the end of 2014 the group already had 11 major building projects in the works, with a total of 5.3 million square feet across 360 acres of land, primarily in Ahmedabad but also in Bangalore. Arvind also laid plans to enter the Pune, Mysore, and other tier-2 and tier-3 cities in India. The Lalbhai family hoped to replicate its long-standing success as one of India's textile leaders in India's fast-growing real estate sector in the new century.

M. L. Cohen

PRINCIPAL SUBSIDIARIES

Arvind Accel Ltd.; Arvind Brands and Retail Ltd.; Arvind Envisol Private Ltd.; Arvind Infrastructure Ltd.; Arvind Internet Ltd.; Arvind Lifestyle Brands Ltd.; Arvind PD Composite Private Ltd.; Arvind Textile Mills Ltd. (Bangladesh); Arvind Worldwide (M) Inc.; Arvind Worldwide Inc. (USA); Asman Investments Ltd.; Syntel Telecom Ltd.; The Anup Engineering Ltd.

PRINCIPAL DIVISIONS

Denim; Woven Fabrics; Knits Fabric; Garment Exports; Advanced Materials; Engineering; Real Estate; Agri Business; Internet.

PRINCIPAL OPERATING UNITS

The Arvind Store; Mega Mart Retail; ANUP Engineering; Arya Omnitalk.

PRINCIPAL COMPETITORS

Cotton Corporation of India Ltd.; National Textile Corporation Ltd.

FURTHER READING

"Arvind Acquires Hanes Brands' India Operations." *Indian Textile Journal*, March 23, 2013.

"Arvind Eyes 100% Growth in Four Years." *Franchise Plus*, May 23, 2011.

"Arvind Mills: From Near Bankruptcy to Reinvention." *Economic Times*, December 14, 2012.

"Arvind Opens Flagship Store in Bangalore." *Point-of-Purchase*, July 15, 2014.

"Arvind to Be Rs 2000 cr Mega Brand in 5 Years." *IPR*, June 8, 2013.

"Arvind's e-Commerce Foray." *Media Nama*, August 22, 2014.

Gupta, Bhawna. "Arvind to Demerge Real Estate Business, to List on Stock Exchange." *VC Circle*, July 31, 2014.

Loewe, Erin M. "New Traditions." *Design:Retail*, August 2014.

Tiwari, Ashish K. "Brands, Retail, Technical Textiles and Real Estate Are New Growth Avenues for Us." *DNA (Daily News & Analysis)*, August 25, 2014.

Umarji, Vinay. "Now, Textile Major Arvind Aims to Be Real Estate Brand Too." *Business Standard*, September 4, 2014.

Audix Corporation

No. 8, Lane 120
Section 1, Nei-Hu Road
Taipei,
Taiwan
Telephone: (+886 2) 8797 6688
Fax: (+886 2) 2659 7115
Web site: http://www.audix.com

Public Company
Incorporated: 1990
Employees: 3,690
Sales: TWD 13.47 billion ($447.6 million) (2013)
Stock Exchanges: Taipei
Ticker Symbol: 2459
NAICS: 334419 Other Electronic Component Manufacturing; 334515 Instrument Manufacturing for Measuring and Testing Electricity and Electrical Signals

■ ■ ■

Audix Corporation is a Taiwan-based producer and distributor of electronic components. The company's Manufacturing Business Group operates primarily through its subsidiaries in Xiamen, Miaoli, and Wujiang in the People's Republic of China. These factories manufacture an array of electronic components, including backlight modules, optical disk drives, relays, transformers, electroplating, and precision molded- and plastic injection-molded components, as well as automated production machinery. The company also operates a joint venture in China with Japan's Hitachi

Corporation. This company, Hitachi Electronic Device (Wujiang) Co., Ltd., produces large-scale cold cathode fluorescent lamps (CCFL) for monitors and televisions. Audix's Marketing Channel Business Group is a major distributor of electronic components for such brands as Alps, Fujitsu, Harvatech, Hitachi, KMOT, Lontium, NDK, NEC-Tokin, PTE, Renasas, and Transtouch Technology. The company operates sales and distribution subsidiaries in Taiwan and Hong Kong and in Shenzhen and Shanghai in mainland China. Audix's third division is its Technical Services Business Group, based in Taipei, as well as in Shenzhen, Shanghai, and Wujiang. This division provides a range of testing and certification services, including safety standards testing, EMC certification, and IECEE CB certification. Audix Corporation is listed on the Taiwan Stock Exchange and is led by Chairman Cheng-Huang Chung. The company reported sales of TWD 13.47 billion ($447.6 million) in 2013.

DISTRIBUTION BEGINNINGS IN 1980

Audix Corporation was founded amid the Taiwanese government's efforts to transform the island state from a producer of low-cost consumer goods into a global high-technology center. This effort began when Dr. T. Y. Cheng developed the technology to produce Taiwan's first semiconductor in 1965. Soon after, the Taiwanese government began promoting the development of Taiwan's semiconductor and electronics industries by attracting foreign investment. In September 1965 the General Instrument Company agreed to set up a factory producing germanium alloy transistors, the first 100

KEY DATES

1980: Audix Inc. is founded as a distributor of electronics components in Taiwan.

1982: Company adds its first services business.

1988: Audix forms Taiwan Tokin Electronics Co. and enters the testing and certification market.

1991: Company opens a factory in Jimei, Xiamen, Fujian Province, in mainland China.

2001: Audix Corporation lists its shares on the Taiwan Stock Exchange.

2002: Company forms a production joint venture in Wujiang, China, with Hitachi.

2007: Audix acquires Lily Medical Products Co.

2014: Company adds IECEE CB certification.

percent foreign-owned facility on the island. This became the first of many foreign technology transfer agreements that defined Taiwan's early electronics industry.

By the middle of the 1970s Taiwan's bustling electronics industry featured both homegrown enterprises, such as Fine Product Corporation, which began producing transistors and integrated circuit (IC) assemblies from 1972, and foreign companies, such as Tokyo Sanyo, which opened a transistor and diode assembly plant in 1976. By the end of the decade Taiwan had moved into more sophisticated electronics technologies, importing, for example, ICs and metal oxide semiconductors from RCA in the United States. Another company, Taiwan Litton, began producing light-emitting-diode (LED) assemblies, using technology developed by Texas Instruments. At the same time Tatung Corporation brought in silicon crystal production technologies from Germany's Siemens.

The increasing sophistication and complexity of Taiwan's electronics manufacturing output opened up new opportunities within the sector at the beginning of the 1980s. The rapid growth of the industry, and the appearance of dozens, and then hundreds, of electronics manufacturers introduced the need for intermediate companies focused on the marketing and distribution of electronic components and finished products. Audix Inc. was founded in 1980 in order to meet this demand. With a capital of TWD 1 million, the company initially focused entirely on the distribution of electronic components.

SERVICES DIVISION IN THE EIGHTIES

The marketing and distribution of electronics components remained one of Audix's core business areas through the turn of the century. Audix developed an impressive list of products, supplying parts and components from many of the largest names in the semiconductor and electronics manufacturing industry. In addition to supplying products from the fast-growing Taiwanese electronics industry, the company also built up a portfolio of Japanese brands.

Audix's distribution business also expanded beyond Taiwan. The company entered Singapore in 1989, setting up subsidiary Singapore Audix Co. Ltd. This was followed by a move into Hong Kong, where it established the distribution company Toyo Kuni Electronics Co. Ltd. in 1991. The move into Hong Kong also provided the company with a crucial entry into mainland China, as the electronics manufacturing industry began to shift its center to that market into the turn of the century.

Audix had in the meantime already begun to develop two more business areas. The first of these was its services division, starting in 1982 with the creation of a Technology Department. The company initially focused on providing ASIC design services as well as developing applications for the microcomputer market. In the second half of the 1980s, however, Audix's services division turned to a fast-growing area, that of testing and certification.

Audix's first entry into this sector came in 1988, when the company formed a joint venture with Tokin Corporation, called Taiwan Tokin Electronics Co. Ltd. This company initially focused on electromagnetic interference (EMI) testing. Audix further expanded its services division in 1991 with the opening of a new test laboratory. The new facility added testing capability for the ergonomics ZH/618 specification and ISO 9241-3 graphics specification. In 1993 the company set up a new subsidiary, Taiwan Dong Jin Technology, focused on EMI testing for the European Union's CE standard.

Audix's range of testing and certification capacity expanded to include both Federal Communications Commission and VCCI Japan certification in 1990; Swedish MPR safety standards certification in 1992; Germany's TUV testing certification in 1993; and full CE certification in 1994. In 1997 the company added testing for Canadian Standards Association certification, while adding certification for other markets, including Australia and New Zealand, as well. The company also expanded its testing operations into China, setting up its first subsidiary in Shenzhen in 1992.

MANUFACTURING IN THE NINETIES

In the meantime, Audix had also been putting into place its third business pole. The company's first move into manufacturing came in 1988, when the company teamed up with Japan's Takamisawa Corporation to produce relays. For this the companies formed the joint venture Kaohua Electrics Co. Ltd. Audix took full control of the joint venture in 1990 and created a new Mechatronic department. The company then extended its production to include the original equipment manufacturer production of precision molded- and plastic injection-molded products. Through the Taiwan Tokin joint venture, the company also expanded its operations into magnet core and coil processing.

By the early 1990s Taiwan had succeeded in establishing itself as a major center for the global electronics and semiconductor markets. By then, too, Taiwan's electronic industry had successfully positioned itself as a developer and producer of highly sophisticated, higher value-added technologies. This push had come in part as a response to the emergence of mainland China as the world's low-cost manufacturing center, particularly for relatively less-sophisticated commodity components.

Audix responded to this trend as well, opening its first factory on the Chinese mainland, in Jimei, Xiamen, Fujian Province, in 1991. The company founded a new subsidiary, Audix M&E (Xiamen Co. Ltd.), and by 1992 had begun production of relays. That year Audix created a new subsidiary, Audix Technology (Xiamen) Co., focused on the production of transformers, as well as components for the Chinese automotive industry, such as electronic starter components.

The company soon expanded its production capacity, building a new factory in Jimei, Xiamen, in 1995. This enabled the company to develop new product lines, including the manufacturing of precision machinery, as well as a range of finished plastic products. In 1997 Audix merged its two Xiamen subsidiaries into a single company, Audix Technology (Xiamen) Co.

PUBLIC COMPANY IN 2001

Audix Technology continued to expand through the turn of the century, adding the production of automation equipment in 2001. By the end of the year, the company had added its third factory, located like its first two factories in the Jimei, Xiamen. The new facility permitted the company to develop a new manufacturing area, that of the production of thin-film-technology assemblies and components, starting in 2003.

During this time Audix also strengthened its services division. In 2001 the company succeeded in earning certification in seven major electronics testing categories, including ergonomics and safety standards testing, from China's National Laboratory Accreditation. The following year, Audix took full control of the Taiwan Tokin Electronics joint venture, which was then merged into the group's services business group. Through the middle of the decade, the growing demand for testing and certification services in Taiwan led Audix to found a dedicated subsidiary there, also called Audix Technology, in 2006.

Audix also began raising its profile into the beginning of the new century. In 1999 the company received approval from Taiwan's Securities & Futures Institute to convert to public company status. In anticipation of this, Audix carried out a series of capital increases, raising its total paid-in capital to TWD 410 million. Audix went public in October 1999, at first listing its shares on the over-the-counter market. The company formally listed on the Taiwan Stock Exchange in September 2001.

Audix soon attracted a new manufacturing partner. In 2002 the company teamed up with Japan's Hitachi to found Hitachi Electronic Device (Wujiang) Co., Ltd. The two companies invested $25 million in building a state-of-the-art automated production facility, including a cold cathode fluorescent lamps (CCFL) clean room and three CCFL production lines. This factory began production of CCFLs in January 2004. Following the initial success of the venture, the company added new capacity, with the addition of a clean room for the production of LED backlight panels as well. The success of the company's partnership with Hitachi helped drive up Audix's revenues to TWD 7.66 billion for the year.

LILY MEDICAL

Wujiang emerged as a new center of Audix's growing operations into the middle of the decade. In 2002 the company established a second operation there, through Audix Technology, and invested $50 million in building a 160,000-square-meter factory. The new fully automated and air-conditioned facility permitted Audix to expand its range of products to include components for digital cameras, as well as the production of precision pressing molds and mold cavities and related components. The site, which began production in 2005, also featured such amenities as a dormitory, cafeteria, laundry, grocery, and other shops, as well as sports facilities, a library, and a cinema.

In the second half of the decade, Audix had also begun looking beyond its core electronics components industry for other expansion opportunities. In 2007 the company added a new business line, that of medical supplies and equipment, with the acquisition of 51 percent of Lily Medical Supplies Co. This company had been founded in the early 1980s and, after completing construction of its factory in 1985, had become a major supplier of medical tubes and bags to the Taiwanese, U.S., and other markets. Audix's investment in the sector came amid the changing demographics of the Taiwanese population. Like Japan and other Asian counterparts, the proportion of elderly in the total population was expected to expand sharply into the new century, stimulating a heavy demand for medical products. Under Audix, Lily Medical Supplies expanded its product range to include syringe sets, suction catheters, urodynamic bags, and other medical care products. In 2007 Audix bought out a number of Lily Medical's minority shareholders, raising its own stake to 81.97 percent.

NEW CERTIFICATIONS IN 2014

Audix's three-prong approach to the electronics industry helped the company resist the growing pressure toward consolidation of Taiwan's highly fragmented IC and electronics distribution sector. Instead, Audix focused on building up its portfolio of brands through the decade. These included the LED product line of Wang Qi Technology and the memory products of Elpida in 2000. In 2002 the company began distributing products from Hitachi Metals and Konica Minolta. The following year, the group picked up distribution contracts from Japan's Renesas, as well as the touch-screen product line of Transtouch.

Audix also invested in expanding its distribution operation in mainland China, setting up a dedicated electronics logistics center in Wujiang. This facility was followed by a new warehouse in Shenzhen in 2004 and a logistics facility in Beijing in 2006. Through the end of the decade, the company gained the distribution rights for sales of SensorDynamics products throughout the Greater China, starting in 2009. The company also added products from NIDEC and PTC in 2010 and the semiconductor line of Long Xun in 2012.

The company's Product Verification Business Group made its own advances through this period. The company added a new dedicated toxicity testing subsidiary, Shenzhen Xinhua Detection Technology Co., Ltd., which opened its own testing center in 2009. The

group's range of services also expanded to include Taiwan BSMI and CNS small appliance certification in 2009 as well as Japan's JQA S-Mark and PSE Mark in 2011. In 2014 the company added IECEE CB certification from the IEC System of Conformity Assessment Schemes for Electrotechnical Equipment and Components. By then, Audix Corporation had grown from revenues of TWD 13.47 billion ($447.6 million) in 2013.

M. L. Cohen

PRINCIPAL SUBSIDIARIES

Audix Hi-Tech Investment Ltd. (Hong Kong); Audix Technology (Wujiang) Co., Ltd. (China); Audix Technology (Xiamen) Co., Ltd. (China); Hitachi Electronic Device (Wujiang) Co., Ltd. (China; 50%); Lily Medical Supplies Co., Ltd.; Toyo Kuni Electronics Ltd. (Hong Kong); Yuka Precision (Wujiang) Co., Ltd. (China).

PRINCIPAL DIVISIONS

Electronic Components; Optoelectronic Components; Automotive Electronic Components; Precision Molds and Injection Molding; Internet Communications Components; Automation Equipment.

PRINCIPAL OPERATING UNITS

Manufacturing Business Group; Marketing Channel Business Group; Product Verification Business Group.

PRINCIPAL COMPETITORS

Au Optronics Corp.; China Electronics Corp.; Flextronics International Ltd.; LG Display Company Ltd.; Soulbrain ENG Company Ltd.; Taiwan Hitachi Asia Pacific Company Ltd.; Wuxi Sharp Electronic Components Company Ltd.

FURTHER READING

"Audix Expects NTDlr602 Mil Pretax Profit in 2004." *Telecompaper*, July 15, 2004.

"Audix to Post Revenue of NT$500 Million for First Time in July." *Asia Africa Intelligence Wire*, July 1, 2003.

"Taiwan Province of China Renesas May Integrate Distribution Networks." *TendersInfo*, April 8, 2010.

Axiata Group Bhd

—■—

Axiata Centre
9 Jalan Stesen Sentral 5
Kuala Lumpur, 50470
Malaysia
Telephone: (+60 3) 2263 8888
Fax: (+60 3) 2263 8822
Web site: http://www.axiata.com

Public Company
Incorporated: 1984 TM International Bhd
Employees: 23,000
Sales: MYR 18.4 billion ($5.8 billion) (2013)
Stock Exchanges: Bursa Malaysia
Ticker Symbol: 6888
NAICS: 517210 Wireless Telecommunications Carriers

■ ■ ■

Axiata Group Bhd operates as one of the largest Asian telecommunications groups in Asia with over 240 million mobile subscribers. The group's mobile subsidiaries operate under the brand name Celcom in Malaysia, XL in Indonesia, Dialog in Sri Lanka, Robi in Bangladesh, Smart in Cambodia, Idea in India, and M1 in Singapore. The company's nonmobile telecommunications operations are based in Thailand and Pakistan. Axiata also oversees edotco Group Sdn Bhd, a communications infrastructure solutions and services company. The group is one of largest corporations traded on the Bursa Malaysia and had a market capitalization of over $18 billion at the end of 2013. The company was created in 2008 when Telekom

Malaysia Bhd (TM) went through a demerger, leaving TM International Bhd (TMI) to focus on its mobile operations. TMI adopted the Axiata Group name in 2009.

ORIGINS AS STATE TELECOM AGENCY

Malaysia's first telephone line was installed in 1874, linking the British colonial government's Resident's Office in Perak with one of its administrative offices. The colonies, then known as Malaya, remained unconnected. Over the next decade underwater cable was laid, linking Perak with the island of Panang. The country's first telephone exchange, however, was not installed until 1891, in Kuala Lumpur.

In 1964 Malaysia became a country independent of British rule. The years immediately following were turbulent as Indonesia sought control of the area and Singapore seceded from the new country. Once the government was stable, however, it took control of the country's telephone network, already organized as Jabatan Telekom Malaysia (JTM). Telephone penetration had remained extremely low in the country, and by 1960 had not yet reached 50,000 lines, for a total market penetration of less than 1 per 100.

GOVERNMENT INTERCEDES

As a government agency, JTM took a first step toward developing a corporate culture when it received authorization in 1971 to begin operating as an independent, profit-driven enterprise. In 1982 the

COMPANY PERSPECTIVES

At Axiata, there are two core values that we embrace across the Group: Uncompromising Integrity and Exceptional Performance. These two values define who we are and how we operate.

Malaysian government announced its intention to privatize JTM during the decade and to deregulate the Malaysian telecommunications market. JTM braced itself for the change, restructuring its operations.

In the meantime, JTM had continued to build up the country's network, topping one million access lines and raising the penetration rate to nearly seven per 100 by the mid-1980s. The company had also installed a national network of pay telephones, counting more than 60,000 by the end of the decade. In the meantime, JTM launched Malaysia's first cellular telephone service in 1985.

That service, called ATUR 450, was based on the NMT analog standard technology. By the end of the decade the company had developed a new generation of cellular telephone service, based on the ART 900 standard. An important step forward for the country's national telephone backbone came with the installation of a 1,500-kilometer underwater fiber-optic cable linking the Malaysian Peninsula with the Sabah and Sarawak regions.

DEREGULATION BEGINS IN 1987

The deregulation process of the Malaysian telecommunications market was formally launched in 1987, when JTM was split into two entities. The first, and smaller, retained JTM's industry regulation arm, and remained a government-run department. The second, which took over JTM's fixed-line and mobile telecommunications operations, became Telekom Malaysia (TM).

TM's privatization was slated for 1990. As part of the preparation for that process, the company sold its ART 900 cellular business in order to create a competitor for the soon-to-be-privatized telephone monopoly. As part of the government's efforts to promote the commercial interests of the ethnic Malay community, which while politically powerful had long played a secondary role to the economic clout of the country's ethnic Chinese community, the cellular company was sold to Tajudin Ramli for just MYR 250,000 (less than $110,000).

Included in the sale was a guarantee of a five-year monopoly for cellular services in Malaysia. Ramli launched the cellular services as a company called Celcom in 1989. As a result, TM was locked out of the cellular market and became one of the few incumbent telecommunications monopolies not to control the fast-growing mobile market in the late 1990s.

INTERNATIONAL INTERESTS

The Malaysian government moved forward with TM's privatization in 1990, placing 25 percent of the company on the Kuala Lumpur Stock Exchange. As such, TM became one of the first in the region to emerge from under government protection. The government continued to reduce its stake through the decade, selling another 5 percent of the company to private shareholders, and placing a further 5 percent among TM's employees by mid-decade.

In 1992 TM created TM International Bhd (TMI) to seek out international mergers, acquisitions, and joint ventures. The public offering enabled TM to launch a massive investment program in the early 1990s. The company's expansion effort came as part of the Malaysian government's ambitious "Vision 2020," a long-term plan meant to raise the country to developed nation status by 2020.

The role of the telecommunications sector in general placed TM at the center of the government's plans, and as such the company received the backing for its own MYR 17 billion ($5.6 billion) investment program, launched in 1994. By the end of the 1990s TM had boosted its total number of access lines to four million and its penetration rate to 19 per 100 population.

The company had also expanded its exchange capacity, launching a fully digital network with a capacity of nearly six million lines. The end of Celcom's five-year monopoly allowed TM to enter the cellular market in the mid-1990s, when the company received one of the country's eight new mobile telephone licenses.

TM TOUCH LAUNCHES

TM launched its own network, called TM Touch. At the same time, the government issued new licenses allowing entry into the country's fixed-line and international telephone markets. However, the high cost of entry, especially into the fixed-line local market, meant that TM maintained a de facto monopoly on this market into the 21st century. While building its network at home, TM also turned its attention to the regional telecommunications player.

KEY DATES

1946: State-run telecommunications agency, Jabatan Telekom Malaysia (JTM), is established.

1971: JTM begins operating as a for-profit corporation.

1985: JTM launches a cellular phone service.

1987: Privatization and deregulation begin as JTM is split into two bodies, and Telekom Malaysia (TM) is created as telecommunications provider.

1989: Cellular service is sold to Tajudin Ramli, who establishes Celcom.

1992: Company creates TM International Bhd (TMI).

1994: TM acquires control of cellular service in Sri Lanka (later Dialog Telekom) and launches its own cellular service, TM Touch.

2002: Company acquires an initial stake in Celcom and gains control the following year.

2008: Demerger separates TM and TMI.

2009: TMI is renamed Axiata Group Bhd.

2014: Axiata's subscriber base reaches 240 million people.

The company's first international effort came in Sri Lanka, where it backed the launch of that country's MTN (later Dialog) Telekom in 1993. By mid-decade TM had also added a joint venture in India, where it began operating GSM-based cellular phone services in the Calcutta market, as well as paging services in six other cities. The company also expanded into Malawi, formed a 60-40 joint venture with Malawi Telecommunications Ltd. to launch the TNM GSM-based cellular service in 1995.

Also that year, the company acquired 60 percent of Sotelgui SA, the former government-controlled, fixed-line and mobile service provider in Guinea. Bangladesh became another target market for the company, and in 1995 TM formed a joint venture with AK Khan & Co. to launch the Aktel GSM cellular service. In Malaysia, TM responded to the growing interest in Internet access with the launch of its own Internet service provider, TMNet.

That operation became the country's second, and soon largest ISP. TM's control of the nation's fixed lines also enabled it to capture the broadband market into the next decade. The company entered Cambodia acquiring a 19.4 percent stake in Samart in 1997, then acquiring a

51 percent stake, compared to Samart's 49 percent, in mobile telephone provider Casacom in 1998.

MOBILE LEADER IN THE NEW CENTURY

TM expanded its Malaysian cellular business in 1998, taking control of Mobikom, founded in 1993. Mobikom had built a network based on the AMPS protocol, covering all of the Malaysian peninsula, as well as Sabah and Sarawak. TM's TM Touch network operated on the GSM 1800 standard. In order to overcome incompatibilities between the two companies' networks, TM announced its intention to roll out a dual-band handset. Nonetheless, TM's cellular phone operation at this time remained a small, money-losing operation, lagging far behind leaders Celcom, Maxis, and GiGi.

Incompatibility was only one of the problems dogging the Malaysian mobile telephone market. The presence of eight cellular providers had proved to be too many for the Malaysian market. Into the early 21st century, therefore, the Malaysian government began encouraging a consolidation of the market. TM played its part in that effort, acquiring a stake in Celcom's parent company, Technology Resources Industry (TRI), in 2002.

By 2003 the company had acquired full control of TRI, and of the country's leading cellular service provider. TM then received one of only two licenses for the new third-generation (3G) high-speed cellular phone services. By 2004 the company had launched its first 3G service. Because of low initial demand for the service, however, the 3G the company offered remained on a limited scale, serving only a few hundred subscribers in the country's so-called Multimedia Super Corridor.

Elsewhere, TM's regional ambitions hit a setback when it failed to win its 2001 bid for a stake in Indonesian Satellite, thwarting TM's attempt to enter the Indonesian cell phone market. The company had also run into trouble with an attempt to enter Ghana's telecommunications market, where its investment reached some $150 million.

ACQUIRES MOBILEONE

TM bounced back toward mid-decade. In July 2005 the company brought its Sri Lankan operations to the Colombo Stock Exchange, selling a 9.6 percent stake in what became that country's largest-ever initial public offering (IPO). Soon after the company joined with Malaysian state investment agency Khazanah Nasional Bhd to acquire a 17.7 percent stake in Singapore's MobileOne, becoming the cellular service provider's largest shareholder.

Meanwhile, TM had found its entry into the Indonesian market, buying a 27.3 percent stake in Excelcomindo (XL), owner of that country's third-largest mobile phone provider. In order to consolidate its growing international profile, Telekom Malaysia announced in 2005 that it was adopting TM as its new brand identity. By this point, the company had reorganized into four main business units including Malaysia Business, Celcom, TMI, and TM Ventures.

DEMERGER CREATES AXIATA GROUP

The group's next big move came in 2007. At this time TM decided to separate its businesses in order to take advantage of opportunities in the mobile industry in emerging markets. As such, the company went through a demerger, leaving TM to focus on its fixed-line and various other telecommunications businesses while TMI, once responsible for TM's international ventures, focused on the regional mobile telecommunications operations. Khazanah remained a majority shareholder in TMI.

The transaction was finalized in April 2008, and TMI took over 100 percent control of Celcom. It also acquired stakes in XL and Sunshare from Khazanah. TMI, now listed on Bursa Malaysia, continued to strengthen its business in its first year of operation. In order to expand its footprint in India, the company acquired stakes in India's Idea Cellular Ltd. and Spice Communications Ltd. and then merged the two companies.

The combined firm stood as India's fifth-largest mobile provider at that time. TM International (Bangladesh) Ltd. also partnered with Japan's largest cellular operator NTT DoCoMo, Inc. During 2009 TMI officially changed its name to Axiata Group Bhd. Jamaludin Ibrahim, named CEO at the end of 2008, set forth a strategy at this time to position the company as one of Asia's leading telecommunications firms by 2015.

ONGOING DIVESTITURE PLAN

By the end of 2009 Axiata's total subscriber base had grown to 120 million, increasing by nearly 35 percent from the previous year. The company remained on solid financial ground despite intense competition in the mobile market in 2010. That year the company sold noncore assets and sold shares of XL on the Indonesian stock market. The company's divestiture program continued over the next several years and included the 2014 sale of Samart I-Mobile Public Co. Ltd.

Suntel Ltd., the second-largest wireless fixed-line operator in Sri Lanka, was acquired in 2011. During 2012 Axiata acquired Latelz Company Ltd. Those operations were then merged with Hello Axiata Company Ltd. to create Smart, the second-largest mobile telecommunications provider in Cambodia. During 2013 the company created Axiata Digital Services to oversee operations in digital-related entertainment, commerce, and advertising services. It also launched edotco Group Sdn Bhd as a communications infrastructure solutions and services firm.

By this point, Axiata had secured a position as a leading Asian telecommunications firm. Indeed, from 2007 through early 2014, Axiata's subscriber base had grown from 40 million to over 240 million people, group revenue had increased by nearly 85 percent, and its market capitalization had increased more than four times to MYR 58.9 billion, making it one of the largest firms to trade on the Bursa Malaysia.

In addition, Axiata had been awarded the Frost & Sullivan Asia Pacific ICT Award for Best Telecom Group for five consecutive years by 2013. Although the mobile market remained highly competitive, the Axiata Group appeared well-positioned to maintain a leadership position in the years to come.

M. L. Cohen
Updated, Christina M. Stansell

PRINCIPAL SUBSIDIARIES

Celcom Axiata Berhad; PT XL Axiata Tbk; edotco Group Sdn Bhd; Robi Axiata Ltd.; Dialog Axiata PLC; Smart Axiata Co., Ltd.; Idea Cellular Ltd.; M1 Ltd.; Multinet Pakistan (Private) Ltd.

PRINCIPAL COMPETITORS

Deutsche Telekom AG; Maxis Communications Berhad; Teliasonera AB.

FURTHER READING

Arnold, Wayne. "Telekom Malaysia Pushes for the Fast Lane." *New York Times*, February 21, 2003.

"Axiata Group Berhad Unveils New Brand Identity." *Daily News* (Sri Lanka), April 10, 2009.

Chew, Elffie. "Axiata Draws Strength from Overseas Strategy." *Wall Street Journal*, August 10, 2010.

Colquhoun, Lachlan. "Testing the Waters in KL." *Wireless Asia*, January–February 2004.

Lloyd-Smith, Jake. "Khazanah, Telekom Malaysia in M1Deal." *Financial Times*, August 18, 2005.

"Straight-Talking Axiata CEO." *Business Times*, May 2, 2014.

Tanner, John C. "3G Results Play the Wild Card in Malaysia's Cellco Shuffle." *Wireless Asia*, August 2002.

"Telekom Malaysia: A Leader in Telecommunications." *Institutional Investor International Edition*, June 2004.

"Telekom Malaysia Is Seeking a Controlling Share in Excelcomindo." *Wireless Asia*, January–February 2005.

Yeap, Cindy. "Axiata Marks TMI's New Lease of Life." *Edge Malaysia Weekly*, March 2, 2009.

Balsam Brands LLC

50 Woodside Plaza, Suite 111
Redwood City, California 94061
U.S.A.
Telephone: (650) 348-3655
Web site: http://www.balsambrands.com

Private Company
Founded: 2006
Employees: 49
Sales: $51.7 million (2013)
NAICS: 454111 Electronic Shopping

■ ■ ■

Redwood City, California–based Balsam Brands LLC is primarily an online retailer, operating several e-commerce web sites. The flagship subsidiary is Balsam Hill Christmas Tree Company, which markets artificial Christmas trees, wreaths, and garlands. The products are handcrafted and realistic, imitating most of the popular tree varieties, including the Balsam Fir, Fraser Fir, Noble Fir, White Spruce, and Norway Spruce. The trees come apart in sections and have hinged branches for compact storage. Balsam Hill also offers pre-lit trees and ornaments. In addition to its web site, Balsam Hill maintains a showroom and outlet store in Burlington, California. Balsam Brands' other subsidiaries help to balance out the seasonal nature of the Christmas tree business.

Concepts include Backyard Ocean, an online retailer of above-ground swimming pools, equipment, and accessories; Hinkley Lighting Gallery, an online retailer of lighting products, including ceiling lights, wall lights, outdoor lights, and specialty lights and accessories; and Kichler Superstores, which offers similar lighting products as Hinkley as well as lamps and ceiling fans. Balsam Brands is owned by its founder and CEO Thomas M. Harman.

FOUNDER'S ENTREPRENEURIAL BACKGROUND

Harman was born in Cleveland, Ohio, where his father, Thomas L. Harman, owned and served as president of Progress Wire Products, a steel wire manufacturing company that made industrial parts and merchandise displays. The younger Harman later claimed that he launched his first business venture at the age of three when he hawked used tennis balls to his neighbors. A year later he began growing and decorating gourds for sale. As a five-year-old he ran a lemonade and popcorn stand, before becoming dissatisfied with customer traffic, when he began using a wagon to sell his merchandise door to door.

After receiving an undergraduate degree from Williams College in Massachusetts, Harman went to work as a consultant for McKinsey & Co. His father was diagnosed with lung cancer in the summer of 1999 and died a year later. At the time, the founder of Progress Wire Products, William M. Folberth Jr., was still the CEO, but he was 80 years old. Although just 24 years old, Harman stepped in to replace his father while continuing to work for McKinsey. He developed an Internet marketing strategy for the struggling company and attracted new customers to stabilize the business. Progress Wire was eventually sold in 2007.

After his stint at Progress Wire, Harman entered Stanford Graduate School of Business and earned a master's of business administration in 2005. He then went to work in marketing at Clorox Company, but it was not long before he was inspired to start a side business. While visiting his in-laws for Christmas he was taken back by their artificial Christmas tree, which the family had been using for many years because one of the children had an allergic reaction to the mold spores that emanated from real trees. The sight of the tree stayed with Harman, who eventually decided that with new technology it had to be possible to create a more realistic artificial Christmas tree.

BALSAM CHRISTMAS TREE COMPANY STARTED: 2006

In 2006 Harman founded Balsam Christmas Tree Company to develop and market a next-generation artificial Christmas tree. Harman had some familiarity with trees, having minored in environmental studies as an undergraduate and taken a tree identification course. Using real tree samples, photographs from Christmas tree farms, and U.S. Forest Service research data, he designed trees modeled after real species. Although he was careful to imitate needle shape, color, and texture, he made sure his artificial trees conformed overall to the traditional Christmas tree shape though that was not necessarily found in the wild.

In just four months Harman succeeded in setting up a manufacturing, supply chain, and retail business, just in time for the 2006 Christmas seasons. Balsam trees, some of which included pre-strung lights, ranged in height from four feet to 12 feet and prices from $72 to $2,299. Matching wreaths and garlands ranged in price from $39 to $279. To generate interest and serve as a showroom, Harman opened a temporary storefront in the Stanford Shopping Center in San Jose, California, but most of his sales came from the Balsam Hill web site.

During the 2006 holiday season, Balsam Hill generated $3 million and turned a profit. At the time Balsam

Hill was a part-time job for Harman, who had no full-time employees. He ran the business out of his apartment but now decided to build a true company. His first step was to open an office. He used mass transit in considering potential locations, walking from the BART (Bay Area Rapid Transit) station to the building in order to determine if an area was safe and offered an inviting environment. Having worked as a McKinsey consultant and run a family business, Harman was aware of the value of culture in a company's success, and he kept that in mind as he laid the foundation for Balsam Hills. He ultimately settled on a second floor office in a retail building in Redwood City, California. He consciously avoided an office park setting, preferring a retail area where customer interaction was commonplace and could help establish the tone for a customer-oriented company such as Balsam Hills.

BACKYARD OCEAN LAUNCHED: 2008

Because the sale of Christmas trees was a seasonal business, Harman looked for a summertime product to sell, not only to balance out revenues over the course of the year, but to also keep full-time employees busy. Moreover, Balsam Hill's artificial Christmas trees were designed to last 20 years. As a result, there was little opportunity to develop repeat business. Harman settled on the online sale of above-ground swimming pools as an appropriate opposite cycle business, and in the summer of 2008 he launched Backyard Ocean. The web site sold frame pools, ring pools, kiddie pools, pool toys, and accessories. Harman designed the pools himself and had them manufactured in China. With a second business in operation, Harman formed Balsam Brands to serve as the holding company for his online retail ventures.

The company culture Harman put in place was immediately challenged. A financial crisis in 2008 led to a recession by the start of the holiday season. Most retailers suffered and purveyors of artificial Christmas trees were hardly exempt. After a difficult holiday season, Harman gathered his employees in early 2009 and guaranteed that their jobs were secure for the next year. He also bolstered the company's infrastructure and increased the marketing budget. It would be a turning point for the young company, which would enjoy low employee turnover and high morale that led to an excellent holiday season in 2009. Moreover, other artificial Christmas tree companies struggled, many of which went out of business, opening the field to even greater growth for Balsam Hill, which already had the infrastructure in place when consumer spending improved.

KEY DATES

2006: Thomas Harman starts Balsam Hill Christmas Tree Company.
2008: Backyard Oceans is launched.
2010: Balsam Brands adds Hinkley Lighting Gallery and Kichler Super Store brands.
2011: Idaho call center opens.
2013: Permanent Balsam Hill store opens.

Also important to the success of Balsam Hill in 2009 was the introduction of new tree varieties. Harman was always looking at conifers, often while skiing, searching for a type to imitate. In 2009 Balsam Hill introduced two new white Christmas trees, the Mount Washington White Christmas Tree and the Pikes Peak White Christmas Tree, along with matching wreaths and garlands. The company also added three new tree styles to its lower-priced Classics Collections: the Timberline Fir, Douglas Fir, and Black Spruce. In addition, the company offered two new Christmas ornament collections for 2009, the Silver Falls and Copper Valley ornaments sets that were handpicked by Balsam Hill designers.

NEW BRANDS ADDED: 2010

Balsam Hill enjoyed another year of increasing sales in 2010. Balsam Brands added to its stable of brands with the introduction of Hinkley Lighting Gallery and Kichler Super Store, both of which sold residential brand name lighting products. Kichler was also able to expand into other home decor categories. Harman believed that both web sites would be well positioned for success when the housing market eventually recovered.

The new online ventures helped Balsam Brands to accelerate revenue growth. Annual sales improved to $12.1 million in 2010. The following year they jumped to $22 million. Playing an important role in the growth of Balsam Brands was a sister company Harman started called ProService that provided customer service support for the Balsam Brand companies as well as some outside clients. In the summer of 2011, ProService opened a new call center in the Central Valley Corporate Park in Meridian, Idaho. In February 2012 ProService closed down its previous location in San Mateo, California. The Boise operation maintained a full-time staff and hired many others for large portions of the year. With growth in the home decor businesses, Balsam Brands hoped to minimize the length of employee layoffs.

Revenues for Balsam Brands increased to $34.7 million in 2012. During the year the company tested direct-response television (DRTV), but did not enjoy much success, due in large part to the decision to repurpose existing video that was not intended for a DRTV campaign. In 2013 Balsam Brands hired New York–based THOR Associates to create a true DRTV campaign with multiple spot lengths, which began to air in time for the 2013 holiday season.

PERMANENT STORE OPENS: 2013

Balsam Brands expanded on other fronts as well in 2013. It printed the first Balsam Hill print catalog, the success of which would determine if subsequent catalogs would be produced. In August 2013 Balsam Hill opened its first permanent brick-and-mortar store. The 2,000-square-foot site was located in Burlington, California, near San Francisco International Airport. It was open only Thursday through Sunday from 10 a.m. to 7 p.m., but as the holiday season approached, the hours were extended. The plan was to at least maintain weekend hours during the spring and summer months. The store served several purposes. It helped to promote the Balsam Hill brand, provided some warehouse space, and acted as a factory outlet store where returned merchandise and the previous year's tree model could be sold at a discount.

When 2013 came to an end, Balsam Brands reported sales of $51.7 million. Over the previous three years, the company had enjoyed a 327 percent growth rate. It was a performance that earned Balsam Brands a place on the 2014 Inc. 5000 list of the United States' fastest-growing private companies.

Each year, Balsam Brands tested a new marketing approach. Whether the print catalog or direct response TV campaigns would prove successful enough to continue remained to be seen. At the very least, the efforts helped to build brand awareness. What was not in question, however, was Harman's willingness to try new tactics. He had demonstrated it as a youngster when he decided to sell his popcorn and lemonade door to door rather than wait for customers to happen by. It would likely remain the hallmark of his business ventures in the years to come.

Ed Dinger

PRINCIPAL SUBSIDIARIES

Backyard Ocean; Balsam Hill Christmas Tree Company; Hinkley Lighting Gallery.

PRINCIPAL COMPETITORS

Amazon.com Inc.; National Tree Company; Vickerman Company.

FURTHER READING

Boatman, Kim. "Faux Firs, Pines Look Genuine, Attracting Lots of Customers." *San Jose Mercury News*, December 6, 2006.

Duxbury, Sarah. "Balsam Brands CEO Looks to Branch Out." *San Francisco Business Times*, December 16, 2011.

Esqueda, Hannah. "Thomas Harman, Founder and CEO of Balsam Brands." *San Francisco Business Times*, July 27, 2012.

Haire, Thomas. "O, Christmas Tree. ..." *Response*, December 2013.

Scott, Sam. "O Tannenbaum." *Stanford Magazine*, November/December 2012.

"Silicon Valley 40 under 40: Thomas Harman, Balsam Brands." *Silicon Valley Business Journal*, December 3, 2013.

Somerville, Heather. "When Clicks Aren't Enough, Online Retailers Become Old-Fashioned Stores." *San Jose Mercury News*, September 4, 2013.

Bayerische Staatsbrauerei Weihenstephan

———■———

Alte Akademie 2
Freising, D-85354
Germany
Telephone: (+49 8161) 536-199
Fax: (+49 8161) 536-200
Web site: http://www.weihenstephaner.de

State-Owned Company
Incorporated: 1923
Employees: 85
Sales: EUR 25 million ($32 million) (2013)
NAICS: 312120 Breweries

■ ■ ■

Located on the grounds of a historical monastery in Freising, Bavaria, Bayerische Staatsbrauerei Weihenstephan brews a full line of beers for the retail market and the restaurant and tavern trade. Weihenstephan produces 14 kinds of beer, the most popular being Weihenstephan *Hefeweissbier* (yeast white beer) made from wheat. The firm brews a variety of other wheat-based beers too, including crystal wheat beer, as well as light, dark, and alcohol-free versions. In all, wheat beers constitute approximately 75 percent of Weihenstephan's total sales. In addition, the brewery produces a pilsner, light and dark lager beers, an extra-strong bock beer, an annual beer brewed for Freising's yearly beer festival, and a *Radler*, a 50-50 mixture of pilsner and soda pop similar to Sprite. In addition to its beer brewing, Weihenstephan provides university-level education in brewing science through the Weihenstephan Science

Center for Nutrition, Agriculture and the Environment at Munich's Technical University. The Weihenstephan Research Center for Brewing and Food Quality is the science center's commercial arm. It conducts research in brewing technology and provides information to brewers, especially in Bavaria, on all technical aspects of the beer-making industry. Weihenstephan exports approximately half of its yearly output to about 50 different countries on every continent but Africa.

ORIGINALLY ESTABLISHED BY A SAINT

Weihenstephan Brewery traces its founding to the eighth century when the later-canonized St. Corbinian, on orders of Pope Gregory II, established the church of St. Stephen in Freising with the intention of converting the peoples of Bavaria to Christianity. About 100 years later, a monastery was also founded on the site. Its location atop a hill made it an ideal site for brewing, as cellars could be dug for the storage of beer while it aged. Documentary evidence shows that hops were being grown at the monastery in 768, and historians speculate that beer was probably already being brewed there then. In 1040, however, the city of Freising granted the monastery's monks a license to brew and to sell beer to the public, so the present-day brewery cites this year as its founding date.

The brewery took as its emblem a bear carrying two kegs of beer on its back. Legend has it that the monastery's founder, Corbinian, was making his way from Bavaria to Rome to see the pope when he was set upon by a bear. When Corbinian's horse was killed in the struggle, he subdued the bear and forced it to carry his belongings—including beer he had made for the pope—to Rome. Weihenstephan would continue to feature this image on the grounds of its brewery into the 21st century.

COMPETITIVE ADVANTAGE

The Benedictine brewers of Weihenstephaner beer in the Middle Ages enjoyed certain advantages over their secular competition. They had access to cheap or, if they raised it on their own grounds, free raw materials. Their monks provided free labor. The monastery paid no taxes. In addition, monasteries were not subject to the brewing bans regularly handed down by Bavarian rulers, such as when crop failures meant that grain had to be reserved for the making of bread.

A signal event in German brewing history took place a short distance from Weihenstephan in Ingolstadt, Germany, in 1516, when the first *Reinheitsgebot* (Beer Purity Law) was declared. Until then there was no restriction on the ingredients that could be used when making beer for retail sale, and these typically included herbs, fruit, and even the bark of trees. Under the new law, however, brewers were allowed to use only barley, hops, and water. The official reason for the act was to conserve wheat and rye crops exclusively for the baking of bread. Yeast was added to this list later, and to this day in Germany only those four ingredients (barley, hops, yeast, and water) can be used in the brewing and selling of anything called beer.

ROYAL WHEAT BEER IS LICENSED

While the lion's share of Weihenstephan's beers would one day be *Weissbier*, brewed with wheat rather than barley, production of wheat beer at the time was licensed to one man only, the baron of Dennenberg, who was granted permission by the German duke who had enacted the purity law. The royal monopoly on wheat beer was jealously guarded. Wheat beers were of higher quality than the so-called brown beers brewed at Weihenstephan and other breweries. They were extremely popular, so much so that they became the main source of income of their licensees.

As the Middle Ages drew to a close German brewing was undergoing massive changes. By the 1600s improved equipment and innovations in brewing techniques had transformed brewing from primarily a small local activity to a large preindustrial export business. Beer tasted better and beer consumption grew continually, in part because beer was safer to drink than water, which was often polluted and a carrier of diseases. The making of brown beer had developed to such an extent, in fact, that its popularity began to overtake that of the wheat beers. That trend continued for the next three centuries. By 1812 demand for wheat beers had declined to such an extent that nearly all the royal breweries that had been making it were sold or closed down. The right to brew *Weizenbier* was extended to all brewers. The right was an empty one for many years, though, because wheat beers had passed completely out of style.

The Revolutionary and Napoleonic Eras also contributed significantly to the trend democratizing the industry. The French Revolution, however, also brought an end to most brewing by German monasteries, including Weihenstephan in Freising. When the armies of antireligious, revolutionary France overran German lands, they seized monasteries and their lands, and dispossessed the clergy as had already been done in France. In 1803 they forced the closing of the Benedictine monastery in Freising. Its buildings and grounds passed into the secular ownership of the kingdom of Bavaria. Brewing operations there continued, however, under the administration of the Royal Holdings at Schliessheim.

EDUCATIONAL AND RESEARCH FACILITIES

In 1852 the Weihenstephan brewery established its first ties with an educational institution when the Central College of Agriculture moved to Freising. The school included a brewing program and Weihenstephan's brewing facilities began to be used to train apprentice brewers. The school was reorganized into an academy in 1895 and in 1919 became the University of Agriculture and Brewing. In 1930 it was merged into the Technical College of Munich.

KEY DATES

768: First beer is brewed at Weihenstephan Monastery.

1040: Weihenstephan Monastery is granted license to brew beer and sell it to the public.

1516: Declaration of the German Beer Purity Law.

1803: Weihenstephan Monastery is closed and properties pass into the ownership of the Bavarian king.

1852: First brewing educational activities in partnership with Central College of Agriculture begin.

1855: Experimental Station for Brewing Technology is established.

1923: Company is incorporated.

1928: First wheat beer is brewed.

2009: Company works with Boston Brewing Company to create Infinium beer.

2010: Contract is signed to brew Kirin beer in Bavaria.

In addition, in 1855 a Bavarian privy councilor established the Experimental Station for Brewing Technology, a private-sector attempt to promote innovation in brewing and to develop practical knowledge that could be used by small and middle-sized breweries in Bavaria. The facility, renamed the Testing and Experimental Station for Brewing Technology, was relocated to Weihenstephan in 1892. The Bavarian government took over control of the station in 1922 and placed it under the administration of Munich's Technical College as part of its Department of Brewing Technology. The station continues operations in the 21st century as the Weihenstephan Research Center for Brewing and Food Quality. As a result of its close association with these educational institutions, the Weihenstephan brewery has become one of the world's leading centers for research into the science of making beer.

WEISS BEER BREWED IN 1928

In 1923 the brewery and its training and research facilities were renamed Bayerische Staatsbrauerei Weihenstephan, or Bavarian State Brewery Weihenstephan. The company first began brewing its popular line of wheat beers in the same decade. Wheat beers had eventually returned to popular favor again in the late 19th century after the family of Georg Schneider purchased the old

Bavarian royal brewery and put it back into operation. Weihenstephan took note of weiss beer's new popularity after the end of World War I, but it was not until 1928 that it brought its first wheat beer onto the market, a *Kristallweizen* it called *Champagnerweizen*, or champagne wheat beer. Weihenstephan *Weizen* was slow to take off, sales grew but slowly. By the 1960s, however, the company had firmly established its reputation as the maker of Germany's finest weiss beers. By 1972 most of the beer Weihenstephan was brewing was wheat beer and it was being distributed to stores and taverns throughout Germany. The company's production was severely curtailed by the outbreak of World War II. German beer production as a whole fell from 31.3 million barrels in 1939, the first year of the war, to 8.6 million barrels in 1949, four years after the war's end. Production picked up again rapidly in the 1950s, so much so that demand overwhelmed Weihenstephan's facilities. As a consequence, a wide-ranging renovation program was launched. The brew house was modernized; new fermentation tanks were installed, and larger lagering cellars were built. The new facilities were state of the art and expected to carry Weihenstephan through the rest of the century.

In the late 1990s the Bavarian government announced the privatization of Weihenstephan Dairy, another state-owned company located near, but independent of, the brewery. That decision set off rumors that the brewery was to be sold as well. Although the rumors were quashed, in 1999 officials in the Bavarian department of finance made clear that Bavaria planned to encourage much closer cooperation between Weihenstephan and another state-owned brewery, *Staatliches Hofbräuhaus München*, the Munich Hofbräuhaus.

The synergies thus created, it was hoped, would enable both companies to better compete in Germany's tightening beer market, where the dominant trends for the previous two decades had been steadily lower beer consumption and constant downward pressure on beer prices. Nonetheless, Weihenstephan was able to turn a small profit on revenues of DEM 29 million, approximately $15.7 million in 1999. The Hofbräuhaus boosted its sales slightly that year as well, which seemed to bode well for the planned cooperation. Under the cooperation agreement, the two breweries would maintain the independence of their production and planning but share back office operations such as personnel and accounting.

FLOUTING THE TREND

By the early years of the first decade of the 21st century the dismal trend that had taken hold of the German beer market was impossible to ignore. In 2002 bottled water had passed beer as Germans' most popular cold drink. Per capita consumption was in decline, with younger Germans buying more nonalcoholic fruit beverages; when they did purchase alcohol, they were opting more for spirits than beer. At the same time, the cost of brewing, including energy, glass, and beer ingredients, was climbing steadily.

Weihenstephan managed consistently to buck this trend. In 2005 it boosted the amount of beer it sold from 216,000 hectoliters to 220,000 hectoliters, an increase of about 1,000 gallons. At the same time, its revenues climbed 3 percent to EUR 19 million (about $22 million). A prime reason for the company's success was that it was one of the first German brewers to make a concerted effort to market its beers abroad and some 36 percent of the company's total output was being sold outside Germany. Frequently, in its foreign markets, most significantly New York, Weihenstephan beer was sold as a high-priced, premium beer, in contrast to the German market trend to force the price of beer as low as possible. New foreign markets were constantly being opened in the first decade of the 21st century. In 2005 alone, it began selling its beers in Brazil, Kazakhstan, Monaco, Poland, Romania, and Russia. Revenues continued to climb, albeit slowly, and in 2007 they reached $27.2 million, with profits of about $160,000.

The firm launched an innovative partnership in 2009 when it invited the Boston Beer Company, the makers of Sam Adams beers, to collaborate in the production of a new beer similar to others that Sam Adams had pioneered. This new beer would be known as an "extreme beer" and would respect the extreme limitations imposed by the *Reinheitsgebot*. In order to achieve this, new brewing techniques had to be developed. The result was Infinium, a beer that Jim Koch, the founder of the Boston Beer Company, described in a 2010 interview with *Modern Brewing Age* as "a beer that sits in between a champagne, a good dessert wine, and a Sam Adams Noble Pils." Public reactions to the new brew were mixed.

2010 DEAL WITH KIRIN

Another collaboration was begun in 2010. Weihenstephan signed a deal to brew Kirin Ichiban beer in Bavaria. The beer was Japanese, but since it was being brewed in Germany, it too had to conform to the strictures of the *Reinheitsgebot*. Corn starch and rice, both essential ingredients of the Japanese recipe, could not be used and new ways had to be found to brew

European Kirin that tasted like the Kirin in Japan. The deal with Weihenstephan was intended to lower the costs of transport for Kirin and to improve its quality by getting the beer onto store shelves more quickly.

Weihenstephan continued to strengthen its export sales in the following years. Between 2003 and 2013 export destinations exploded from 11 countries to 42. The efforts were not always easy. Exporting a foodstuff, and an alcoholic beverage at that, to nearly 50 countries required adherence to many sets of laws concerning bottling and labeling. Moreover, ensuring delivery in a timely manner proved a challenge. In 2012 India was added to the roster, with distribution in seven major cities, Delhi, Mumbai, Pune, Kolkata, Goa, Bangalore, and Chennai.

Weihenstephan's most important export market during this time was the United States, in particular in New York City, where its beers were considered a gourmet delicacy. Other strong foreign markets for the company were Austria and Italy. With a shrinking and unprofitable domestic market, export growth was likely to remain an important priority at Weihenstephan in the coming years. The brewery would undoubtedly continue to pursue joint projects with foreign breweries as well, in the spirit of innovation that has been a signet of Weihenstephan for more than 1,000 years.

Gerald E. Brennan

PRINCIPAL COMPETITORS

Augustiner-Bräu Wagner KG; Hacker-Pschorr Bräu GmbH; Paulaner Brauerei GmbH & Co KG; Privatbrauerei Erdinger Weissbräu; Spaten-Franziskaner-Bräu GmbH; Weisses Bräuhaus G. Schneider & Sohn GmbH.

FURTHER READING

"Boston Beer to Roll Out Infinium." *Modern Brewery Age*, November 12, 2010.

"Glass Half Full for the German Beer Industry." *Irish Times*, April 19, 2014.

"1,000 Years Later, Germans Still Brewing." April 18, 2014. http://www.businessworld.com.

Risen, Clay. "When Bad Beers Happen to Good Breweries." *Atlantic*, January 19, 2011.

Wang Fangqing. "Kirin Holdings Signs Brewing Deal." *Just-Drinks*, August 10, 1020.

Wehring, Olly. "Weihenstephan Enters India through Cerana Tie-Up." *Just-Drinks*, June 11, 2012.

Blair & Associates Ltd.
(dba VCI Entertainment)

11333 East 60th Place
Tulsa, Oklahoma 74146-6828
U.S.A.
Telephone: (918) 254-6337
Fax: (918) 254-6117
Web site: http://www.vcientertainment.com

Private Company
Incorporated: 1961 as United Films Inc.
Employees: 20
Sales: $90 million (2013 est.)
NAICS: 512191 Teleproduction and Other Postproduction Services; 423990 Other Miscellaneous Durable Goods Merchant Wholesalers; 517110 Wired Telecommunications Carriers; 512120 Motion Picture and Video Distribution

∎ ∎ ∎

Blair & Associates Ltd., which does business as VCI Entertainment, produces and distributes home video products on Blu-ray and DVD and via electronic download. VCI is the oldest and largest independently owned home video company in the United States. Considered a pioneer in the home video industry, the company was one of the earliest to distribute movies on videocassette and was the very first to produce a movie specifically for home video release. The company is owned and operated by the family of its founder, Bill Blair.

A HOBBY BECOMES A BUSINESS

When Bill Blair graduated from high school in the late 1940s, he did not initially set out to become a pioneer in the field of home entertainment. Indeed, the young Eufaula, Oklahoma, native began his adult life with a degree from the Colorado School of Mines. Nevertheless, Blair had always been obsessed with watching movies. Not satisfied with the film selection at rural Oklahoma theaters, he had saved up money from his summer cotton picking job and purchased a film projector. Further savings were spent on acquiring battered, used film prints advertised in the backs of magazines. Soon the young man was enjoying a pleasure experienced by few during this era: movies at home.

The teenage Blair experimented with turning his hobby into a business. On pleasant nights he would set up a tent, run a film and charge 25 cents admission to his friends and neighbors. The profits from this venture proved modest at best, particularly when Blair began simply letting people in for free, valuing the pleasure of the shared viewing experience over the practical benefits of a full cashbox. When the time came to choose a career path, the region's bustling mining industry seemed distinctly more promising than the entertainment business.

After obtaining his degree, Blair moved with his wife, Edith, to the comparatively large city of Tulsa, Oklahoma, in 1952. While ostensibly seeking work in the mining business, he ended up with a succession of retail jobs culminating in a tenure at Hatfield Appliances, where he sold, installed, and repaired television sets for several years. During this period Blair's interest

---

COMPANY PERSPECTIVES

Classic movies never go out of style.

---

in movies, and watching them at home, continued unabated. He had accumulated a very respectable collection of film prints, and as he neared the end of his first decade in Tulsa, he began to reconsider the possibility of turning his hobby into a source of income.

THE UNITED YEARS BEGIN IN 1960

Blair understood that he did not have the finances or the industry connections to become a theatrical exhibitor. His initial plan was to keep his day job at Hatfield's while renting out his collection of film prints. Because the collection consisted primarily of older films, and most were printed on 16-millimeter stock rather than the 35-millimeter standard used for theatrical distribution, Blair's customer base would consist mostly of home hobbyists like himself, who had their own projectors. Like Blair, many of these film buffs were interested in watching some films only once or twice without the expense of purchasing a print. Because the size of this market was limited, the business at first yielded only a modest income. It did, however, provide the funding the young store clerk required to continue building his film collection.

After a few years serving the needs of private customers and learning how to operate what was essentially a two-way mail-order business, Blair had developed a strong aptitude for the film rental business and a respectable library of titles. At this point he began to expand his customer base and turned his side job into a legal corporation under the name United Films Inc. in 1961. Around the same time, Blair began renting films to institutions such as schools, churches, and airlines. In addition to his own collection, he began acquiring stock through licensing agreements with major film studios, who allowed him to rent 16-millimeter versions of their older titles in return for fees or royalties.

United Films continued to grow through the 1960s. It eventually became a primary nontheatrical distributor for the Warner Brothers, Columbia, and Universal film studios. Around the beginning of the 1970s, Blair began somewhat presciently designing contracts that guaranteed United all nontheatrical distribution rights to the client studios' catalog titles, regardless of format, for a number of years. Because of the company's solid

performance as a distributor over the years and the secondary priority afforded to nontheatrical rights, the studios agreed to the terms. These agreements would boost United's fortunes tremendously a few years later.

THE HOME VIDEO ERA BEGINS IN 1971

In 1971 the Sony Corporation introduced the first viable videocassette format intended for standard use. Although it was clear that the format was experimental, expensive, and would likely take years to catch on, the concept of playing video recordings at home was equally clearly the wave of the future, at least to Blair and his industry peers. The following year Blair created a side company, Video Communications International (VCI). Initially, VCI's mission was to provide videotape archiving and production services. Sony's new format, Broadcast Video U-Matic, or BVU, was intended for use mainly by broadcasters and other professional firms. The new company's revenues were modest at first but Blair and his staff acquired valuable experience with the videotape format.

A few years later Sony changed the game once again. In 1975 the Japanese electronics innovator introduced the Betamax system, which consisted of a compact videocassette format and player/recorders designed for use with home televisions. Although the technology was still priced beyond the reach of average consumers, the product's appeal and commercial potential were clear. Besides the home taping of television programs, the technology's most obvious application was the viewing of movies and other recorded entertainment in the privacy of the home. In 1976 VCI began releasing United's catalog of licensed titles on home videocassette.

As the home video market gathered steam through the late 1970s, Blair's company began focusing more and more on videotape sales and rental and less on film print distribution. By the end of the decade Blair had left the film rental business entirely. The United Films name was retired and he reorganized his company as Blair & Associates Ltd. Although Home Video would technically become a division of Blair & Associates, the company would do business almost exclusively under the VCI name for the next several decades.

VCI PRODUCES FILMS: 1980

As home video equipment became more affordable in the early 1980s, VCI's customer base expanded rapidly. The Victor Company of Japan (JVC) had introduced the VHS format, which would overtake the Betamax in

KEY DATES

1961: Bill Blair begins renting films, establishing United Films Inc.
1972: Video Communications Inc. (VCI) is formed.
1985: VCI produces and releases the first film produced exclusively for home video release.
2013: VCI adds two new distribution labels: Indie Go! Movies and Heartland Family Films.
2014: VCI begins offering films via digital download and streaming.

popularity, in 1976, though both formats would coexist into the 1980s. VCI still enjoyed the benefits of its licensing agreements with major studios, but Blair grew concerned that as the home video market became more lucrative, the studios would balk at accepting the same terms when it came time to renegotiate. One alternative to relying on the studios for future product, he mused, might be for VCI to produce its own content.

Up to this point it was understood that VCI and other home video companies simply provided the physical media and the distribution services needed to convey entertainment product to the public. Movies were produced by studios for theatrical exhibition and later distributed to the home video market. It had not occurred to anyone that a home video company might produce its own film and distribute it directly on videocassette, bypassing theaters and retaining all rights and revenues. Blair, lifelong film lover, was ready to try producing and distributing his own film.

While ever an admirer of great cinema, Blair went into the new venture as a businessman, determined to produce a saleable product at a low cost. For his first outing, he chose one of the more popular home video genres, a horror film. With a script cowritten by Blair, *Blood Cult* was shot on videotape in March 1985 using a budget of around $27,000 and a deal with Sony, which provided video cameras in exchange for promotional consideration. The film was shot in and around Tulsa using a cast and crew of local professionals.

Blood Cult, the first film ever produced exclusively for home video release, proved handsomely profitable for Blair and changed the home video industry forever. In addition to its production budget, Blair spent $100,000 promoting the film. Because the cassettes were marketed at $59.95 apiece, actually a modest price point for a mid-1980s video release, the film brought in

$400,000 on its first day of release in August 1985. Despite less than enthusiastic critical reviews, *Blood Cult* went on to gross more than $1 million and single-handedly proved the viability of the direct-to-video film market. Blair, as well as his competitors, scrambled to repeat the success.

TURMOIL AND TRANSITION

VCI would go on to produce several more films over the next decade, beginning with *The Ripper* in late 1985. Other titles included *The Killing Device*, *The Last Slumber Party*, and *Murder Rap*. Sticking mostly to the horror and action genres, the company's in-house productions remained profitable until the 1990s, when larger studios began producing direct-to-video releases with budgets and technical sophistication that VCI could not match. The market that Blair's company had created had now passed him by.

VCI faced other challenges during the 1990s. To this point, videotapes had mainly been marketed to rental stores at price points ranging from $40.00 to $100.00, not always affordable for individual consumers. When several major competitors began pricing their videos at $20 to $30 and marketing them to individuals, VCI had little choice but to lower prices and adapt the "sell-through" business model. By this time, Bill Blair's son Robert had become president of the company while Bill remained as CEO.

In the face of faltering profits, the Blairs actually made several attempts to sell the company, all of which fell through. When a Texas investment firm actually purchased VCI then defaulted on completing its payments, the resulting legal entanglement cut into company revenues and resulted in a two-year freeze on acquiring new films. The company had more than 2,000 titles in its catalog by this time but was having trouble capitalizing on them. By the end of the 1990s, however, VCI was poised to take advantage of a new technology and an accompanying surge in the popularity of home video.

DVD AND BEYOND: 2000

The late 1990s saw the emergence of the DVD as the dominant home video platform. For consumers, the technology provided a better picture and more storage capacity in a smaller, space saving package. For video companies such as VCI, it provided the opportunity to repackage and resell their catalog all over again, using a medium that was significantly less expensive to press and ship. The new format proved immensely popular with consumers during the early years of the new century and provided a much-needed revenue boost for VCI and the rest of the home video industry.

In 2001 VCI Home Video celebrated its 25th year in the home video business by changing its trade name to VCI Entertainment, a name designed to encompass DVD technology as well as any other delivery platform that might come along in the future. In 2006 Blair & Associates founder Bill Blair passed away at the age of 75. He left behind a bustling video company with more than 3,000 titles in its catalog. Robert Blair, along with siblings Rebecca, David, and Don and their spouses, continued to own and operate the company as a family business.

Over the next several years, VCI continued adding to its catalog, passing the 5,000-title mark in 2010. In 2013 the Blair family began marketing two new labels alongside its traditional VCI Entertainment brand releases. Heartland Family Films would release films considered family-friendly, while Indie Go! Films would feature quirkier fare from independent filmmakers. In 2014 the company began offering a selection of titles via digital download and Internet streaming.

Electronic delivery appeared to be the wave of the future at this point. With sales of DVDs, CDs, and other physical media declining, companies such as Netflix, which delivered video via the Internet had begun to dominate the home video market. Clearly VCI would have to change its business model once again in order to maintain its position in the industry. The Blair family had weathered technological transition and economic uncertainty before and seemed determined to do so again.

Chris Herzog

PRINCIPAL COMPETITORS

Lions Gate Entertainment Corporation; Sony Pictures Home Entertainment; Time Warner Inc.; 20th Century Fox Home Entertainment.

FURTHER READING

Elder, Bud. "VCI Brings Home the Entertainment." *Distinctly Oklahoma*, April 4, 2010.

Parker, Kit. "An Oklahoma Handshake." June 6, 2014. Accessed October 26, 2014. http://kitparkerfilms.wordpress.com/2014/06/06/an-oklahoma-handshake.

Wells, Rick. "Tulsa's VCI Entertainment Makes Movie Magic." September 10, 2009. http://www.tulsacw.com.

Wilharm, Sharon. "VCI Entertainment—With Executive Vice President Don Blair." June 18, 2013. http://faithflixfilms.wordpress.com.

Wooley, John. *Shot in Oklahoma: A Century of Sooner State Cinema*. Norman: University of Oklahoma Press, 2011.

Bonduelle S.A.

Rue Nicolas Appert, BP 30173
Villeneuve d'Ascq, 59653 Cedex
France
Telephone: (+33 3) 20 43 60 60
Fax: (+33 3) 20 43 60 00
Web site: http://www.bonduelle.com

Public Company
Incorporated: 1853
Employees: 9,758
Sales: EUR 1.92 billion ($2.62 billion) (2013)
Stock Exchanges: Euronext Paris
Ticker Symbol: BON
NAICS: 311421 Fruit and Vegetable Canning; 311411
    Frozen Fruit, Juice, and Vegetable Manufacturing

■ ■ ■

Based near Lille, France, Bonduelle S.A. is one of Europe's leading producers of prepared vegetables. The company operates in four primary markets: canned vegetables, frozen vegetables, processed fresh vegetables, and prepared vegetables. Its products, ranging from canned corn and peas to frozen beans, prepared salads, and fresh cut vegetables, are marketed under the Bonduelle, Cassegrain, ArticGardens, and Globus brands. Bonduelle's canned vegetables business, with roots dating back to the 1920s, accounted for 52 percent of its revenues in the 2013 fiscal year. The company's frozen vegetables segment represented 28 percent of the company sales, while its fresh vegetables business accounted for 20 percent of the company's sales in the same period. Nearly 70 percent of the company's sales, which topped EUR 1.92 billion at the end of its 2014 fiscal year, came from outside of France. While Europe represents the company's primary market, Bonduelle has been present in North and South America since the late 1990s. Its products are found in over 100 countries and it has contracts with over 3,700 farmers across the globe. Bonduelle is listed on the Euronext Paris Stock Exchange but remains majority owned by the founding Bonduelle family.

EARLY HISTORY

Bonduelle began as an offshoot of the Bonduelle family grain and food oil farm in northern France. In 1853 two members of the Bonduelle family, Louis Bonduelle and Louis Lesaffre joined together to open a grain alcohol distillery in Marquette-sur-Lille. The business prospered, and the family added a second distillery nearby in Renescure. By the end of the century the family's business included seven distilleries. At that time, the family decided to divide up the assets among its three main branches.

The Bonduelle branch continued to run a family farm. In the 1920s the family spotted a new opportunity in the development of new canning equipment. The Bonduelles purchased sterilizing and other equipment and planted their first crop for canning in 1926. The original crop was based on a 20-hectare plot, yielding some 120 tons of canned peas.

Demand for canned vegetables soared throughout the 1930s. In 1936 the Bonduelle company increased

COMPANY PERSPECTIVES

Backed by its unique agro-industrial expertise, Bonduelle offers consumers in more than 100 countries a range of ready-to-use vegetables in all formats. A family-run company, Bonduelle has maintained the founding values that have shaped the course of its 160-year history. This entrepreneurial vision, combining a long-term view, innovation, international expansion and the diversification of businesses and technologies, aims to position the Bonduelle Group as "the world reference in 'well living' through vegetable products."

planting to 230 hectares. Bonduelle expanded its canning facilities as well, although the company restricted itself to producing and canning, turning over marketing and distribution to another company.

The German invasion of France in 1940 put an end to the company's activity. Production did not begin again until the end of the war. Soon after, instead of turning to its former distributor, Bonduelle decided to place its own name on its products, launching the Bonduelle brand in 1947. Bonduelle quickly became a widely recognized brand name for canned peas. The growth of the Bonduelle brand soon outpaced the company's own farm production, and Bonduelle began putting into place a network of farmer suppliers in the northern region.

POSTWAR GROWTH

The mid-1950s saw the company's breakthrough. In 1957 Bonduelle introduced a new product, canned peas and carrots, which established the Bonduelle brand as one of the leading names in the French canned vegetables market. Bonduelle continued to build on its success, putting into place quality standards that contributed to boosting the brand's reputation.

Bonduelle continued to expand during the 1960s, adding a new production facility in Estrées-en-Chaussée, in the Picardie region, in 1963. The company then moved into other prime agricultural areas in France. At the end of that decade Bonduelle expanded its operations, adding frozen vegetables to its product line. This new area proved a success on the French market,

confirming Bonduelle's reputation as a vegetable specialist.

INTERNATIONAL EXPANSION: 1969

Bonduelle also expanded beyond France, opening its first foreign subsidiary in Germany in 1969. That was followed in 1972 by the opening of a subsidiary in Italy, then in the United Kingdom in 1973. The export market quickly became a crucial one for Bonduelle. By the mid-1970s half of the company's sales came from outside of France. Bonduelle's expansion had brought it into contact with a number of new crops, including corn and mushrooms, both added at the end of the 1970s.

While mushrooms remained a more limited category for the company, the growth in sales of canned corn sales led the company to establish a dedicated facility for that product in Labenne, in the French southwest, in 1978. Bonduelle's international expansion continued into the next decade. In 1980 the company turned to Belgium, acquiring Marie Thumas, a major supplier of canned vegetables in that country. A move into the Netherlands followed in 1982. The company next turned to Spain, acquiring Malagro as the basis of a new subsidiary for that country in 1986.

By this time, Bruno Bonduelle had taken over Bonduelle's leadership. The new generation of the Bonduelle family proved highly ambitious, launching the company toward a new goal of becoming the European leader by the early 1990s. For this, Bonduelle stepped up its acquisition drive, acquiring a new corn canning facility in southwest France and launching a new subsidiary and factory, Primeurop, in 1987. The following year the company purchased Talpe, based in Belgium, adding that company's factory in Kortemark. Bonduelle also moved into Portugal, building a new production plant there.

By the end of the 1980s Bonduelle had already captured the lead in several individual European markets, including Germany, the Netherlands, and Belgium. It had also gained the position of Europe's leading canned and frozen vegetable producer. In 1989 the company cemented that lead through the acquisition of Cassegrain, a producer of high-end canned vegetable products. The acquisition gave Bonduelle the lead position in the French market as well. Meanwhile, Bonduelle had stepped up its marketing campaign, launching the successful slogan, "Quand c'est bon, c'est Bonduelle" (When it's good, it's Bonduelle).

KEY DATES

1853: Louis Bonduelle and Louis Lesaffre-Roussel found a grain and juniper distillery near Lille, France.

1926: Bonduelle family begins a pea canning operation.

1968: The Bonduelles begin producing frozen vegetables.

1969: Company establishes its first foreign subsidiary, in Germany.

1980: Marie Thumas of Belgium is acquired and Bonduelle becomes the leading canned vegetable company in that country.

1989: Bonduelle acquires Cassegrain to become the leading producer of canned vegetables in France.

1998: Company begins production of chilled vegetables and makes a public offering on the Euronext Paris Stock Exchange's secondary market.

2000: Company restructures into five autonomous subsidiaries; Cielo e Campo of Italy is acquired.

2007: Canada's Aliments Carrière is acquired.

2010: France Champignon is purchased.

GLOBAL EXPANSION EFFORTS CONTINUE

By the beginning of the 1990s Bonduelle's sales had topped FRF 4.3 billion (EUR 655 million). Bonduelle had also expanded into a number of new markets, including Denmark in 1989. The company was quick to seize on the opportunity presented by the end of the Cold War, entering the former East Germany in 1990, then launching new subsidiaries in the Czech Republic, Poland, and Hungary in 1991 and 1992. These were followed by entries in Russia and Slovenia in 1994.

At this time Bonduelle was led by Christophe Bonduelle and Daniel Bracquart, who was the first nonfamily member to head the company. The company turned to South America, launching a joint venture with Iansa in Chile in 1992. A subsidiary opened in Brazil in 1994. In 1996 the company added an Argentine subsidiary. By the mid-1990s Bonduelle's sales neared FRF 5 billion. However, the company's core product markets, canned and frozen vegetables, had matured, and the company's growth slowed. In response, Bon-

duelle sought entry into the new and promising market of prepared fresh vegetables.

ACQUIRES SALADE MINUTE: 1997

Bonduelle found its entry point in 1997 with the acquisition of French fresh vegetables specialist Salade Minute. The purchase, which gave Bonduelle four new factories and business of more than FRF 400 million, enabled the company to launch a new brand, Bonduelle en Frais. Targeting at first the restaurant sector, the new brand was rolled out to the consumer market in 1998.

The move into the fresh vegetables sector completed Bonduelle's prepared vegetables offering. The company, which, in addition to its European lead in canned vegetables, held the second-place spot in the frozen vegetables segment, and sought to build a leadership position in fresh vegetables as well.

In order to fund this effort and the company's further expansion, Bonduelle went public in 1998, listing on the Paris Stock Exchange's secondary market. The Bonduelle family nonetheless maintained majority control of the company. Following the stock listing, Bonduelle opened new subsidiaries, entering the United States for the first time, as well as launching its first subsidiary in Africa in Zimbabwe.

In 1999 the company returned to external growth with the acquisition of Avril, also based in the north of France, with operations in Italy as well. That acquisition strengthened the company's position as a private-label producer for supermarket groups. The company then reorganized its operating structure, separating its activities into five independently operating divisions.

ENTERING THE NEW MILLENNIUM

After launching the Bonduelle en Frais brand in Italy in 1999 and in Germany in 2000, the company made a new acquisition, of Italy's Cielo e Campo, the number-two Italian producer of fresh prepared vegetable products. The company also deepened its position in Spain, acquiring former Unilever subsidiary Frudesa, a specialist in frozen vegetables, at the end of 2000. Then, at the beginning of 2001, Bonduelle acquired Ortobell, the Italian leader of the fresh vegetable segment, giving Bonduelle not only the lead in Italy but also a leading position in that category across Europe.

The company then merged its Italy holdings into a single subsidiary. Bonduelle continued to target new expansion opportunities in 2002. In June of that year the company agreed to acquire Inter Champ, a Polish subsidiary of struggling France Champignon. The acquisition added mushrooms, long a weak link in Bonduelle's chain of more than 240 vegetables.

The acquisition agreement also called for an eventual Bonduelle takeover of all canned and frozen production for France Champignon in Europe. During 2003 the company established a prepared food subsidiary after its takeover of the French food and catering company Michel Caugant. It also began construction of a new plant in Russia and inaugurated a new cut-and-washed salad facility in Germany that year.

GROWTH CONTINUES

In 2005 Bonduelle partnered with Groupe Euralis, Maïsadour, and Vivadour to establish a joint venture under the name Soléal. The venture was created to strengthen and sustain the vegetable market in the southwest region of France. In 2006 the company gained a stronger foothold in Spain's market with the purchase of Unilever's Spanish frozen food brands.

The company's focus on growth in international markets continued over the next several years. During 2007 the company acquired Canada's Aliments Carrière. Shortly thereafter, Bonduelle North America was created. During 2010 the company finally acquired France Champignon, the European leader in button mushrooms. Bonduelle increased its footprint in the United States in 2011, when it acquired the frozen foods business of Allens Inc.

That same year Bonduelle opened a new plant in San Paolo d'Argon, Italy. According to the company, this facility was the largest plant in Europe dedicated to the production of fresh-cut salad as well as the largest completely automated fresh-cut operation in the world. Bonduelle also took over various canning operations of Kelet-Food in Hungary and the Russian operations of the Centrale Coopérative Agricole Bretonne (CECAB) French cooperative.

PARTNERS WITH CROWN FOOD

Despite political unrest in the Russia during this time, company management remained dedicated to growth in this region. In early 2014 Bonduelle partnered with Crown Food Europe to install a new production line in

Bonduelle's Novotarovskaia plant in southern Russia. While Bonduelle experienced revenue and profit growth in its fiscal years of 2011 to 2012 and 2013 to 2014, investors remained cautious due to growing unrest between Russia and Ukraine in the summer of 2014.

Meanwhile, Bonduelle celebrated its 160th anniversary in 2013. The company aimed to accomplish this goal through new product development as well as continued growth into new markets. Some new products launched at this time included a new canned mix of sweet corn and gherkin in Germany, Vapeur steamed products in Spain, sweet corn cups available in schools in Slovakia, and vacuumed-packed canned vegetables in Europe. In 2013 the company launched VegeGo!, a new project that was designed to place Bonduelle as the world leader in healthy living through vegetables by 2025.

M. L. Cohen
Updated, Christina M. Stansell

PRINCIPAL OPERATING UNITS

Bonduelle Europe Long Life; Bonduelle Fresh Europe; Bonduelle Americas; Bonduelle Development.

PRINCIPAL COMPETITORS

Dole Food Company, Inc.; Pinguin N.V.; SOLECO S.A.S.

FURTHER READING

Best, Dean. "Bonduelle Sales Up but Shares Down amid Russia Fears." *Just-Food*, August 7, 2014.

"Bonduelle Acquires Unilever's Frozen Vegetables Activities in Spain." *European Report*, December 6, 2000.

"Bonduelle and Crown Partner in Russia." *Food Trade Review*, February 1, 2014.

"Bonduelle Group Sees Profit, Sales Rise." *Mena Report*, October 7, 2013.

"Bonduelle to Acquire Italian Fresh Vegetables Group." *European Report*, February 21, 2001.

"Bonduelle to Buy France Champignon Subsidiary." *Eurofood*, June 20, 2002.

"Strong Growth at Bonduelle." *Eurofood*, February 14, 2002.

Bossini International Holdings Ltd.

Level 1, The Long Beach
8 Hoi Fai Road
Tai Kok Tsui
Kowloon
Hong Kong
Telephone: (852) 2371-1688
Fax: (852) 2786-0869
Web site: http://www.bossini.com

Public Company
Founded: 1975 as Laws Fashion Knitters
Employees: 4,400
Sales: HKD 2.51 billion ($324.77 million) (2013)
Stock Exchanges: Hong Kong
Ticker Symbol: 00592
NAICS: 448110 Men's Clothing Stores; 424320 Men's
and Boys' Clothing and Furnishings Merchant
Wholesalers; 424330 Women's, Children's, and
Infants' Clothing and Accessories Merchant
Wholesalers; 448120 Women's Clothing Stores;
315220 Men's and Boys' Cut and Sew Apparel
Manufacturing

∎∎∎

Bossini International Holdings Ltd. is a Hong Kong–
based clothing retailer with operations in more than 40
countries. At the beginning of its 2014 fiscal year, the
company oversaw a network of more than 1,000 directly
managed and franchised stores. Hong Kong, where the
company operates 41 directly managed stores, remains
the group's primary market, accounting for 65 percent

of group revenues of HKD 2.51 billion ($ 324.77 mil-
lion) in 2013. Bossini has also expanded strongly into
mainland China, where it operates 144 directly managed
stores and 156 franchised locations. These operations
combined to generate 15 percent of group sales in 2013.
Other major markets for the company include Taiwan
and Singapore, where it operates 85 and 30 directly
managed stores, respectively, and which each
contributed 10 percent to group sales. Other markets
include Brunei, Cambodia, the Czech Republic, the
Dominican Republic, Egypt, India, Indonesia, Libya,
Malaysia, most of the Middle East, Myanmar, Romania,
Thailand, Vietnam, and Venezuela. Bossini positions its
clothing designs as everyday casual wear; the company is
a family-oriented retailer, with clothing lines for the
women's, men's, youth and children's segments. In addition to its flagship bossini brand, Bossini has
developed a number of cross-branding and co-branding
marketing relationships, such as with Angry Birds, Walt
Disney's *Cars*, and Winnie the Pooh. The company is
listed on the Hong Kong Stock Exchange and is led by
CEO Mak Tak Cheong (Edmund) and Chairwoman
Tsin Man Kuen (Bess). The founding Law family, led by
Law Ka Sing, remains the major shareholder in Bossini.

GARMENT-MAKING ORIGINS IN THE SIXTIES

Bossini International Holdings had its origins in a small
textiles business founded by Law Ting Pong in Hong
Kong in the early 1970s. In 1975 Law, then 65 years
old, decided to branch out into garment manufacturing.
Law set up a workshop in a small Hong Kong apartment, where he and other members of the family sewed

garments for delivery to local wholesalers. This business formed the basis for what later grew into one of Hong Kong's largest family fortunes.

Laws Fashion Knitters, as this initial business became known, started out with a single U.S.-based customer. From there, however, the company expanded quickly, in part by becoming one of the first to take advantage of the newly announced economic reform policy on the Chinese mainland. The company entered the mainland in 1978, establishing the first of several manufacturing facilities. Laws soon added operations in other nearby markets, including factories in Taiwan and Macau, and a sweater factory in Sri Lanka.

At the same time, Laws Fashion Knitters became a leading player in Hong Kong's own clothing and textiles boom into the early 1980s. By 1984 the company already operated four factories in Hong Kong, with a total of 120,000 square feet of production space, and employing more than 2,000 workers. This included the company's newest factory, a 40,000-square-foot plant located in Taipo, in the fast-growing New Territories area. By 1985 the company's total production included 500,000 dozen sweaters per year, as well as 400,000 dozen knit T-shirts, and 150,000 dozen knit blouses. The company's total sales that year neared $51 million.

RESPONDING TO IMPORT QUOTAS IN 1985

The United States represented the company's primary market during these early years. The company supplied a number of the country's large department store groups. Into the middle of the 1980s, however, the United States began tightening restrictions on clothing imports, in part by adopting new country-of-origin rules. Laws Fashion Knitters responded to the changing market in a number of ways. For one, the company, like many of its competitors, began investing in automated production technologies. Laws, for example, invested nearly $6 million in automated knitting machinery from Japan in 1985. The company could then outfit new factories in markets unaffected by the import quotas. These factories could be operated more or less by remote control from the company's Hong Kong base.

Laws also set out to expand its own quota levels, which reached 750,000 dozen units in 1985. The company began seeking acquisitions of other companies, adding their quota levels to its own. These included a local T-shirt producer in 1985, adding some 200,000 dozen quota units.

Laws Fashion Knitters sought out other means to maintain its growth. This led the company to begin developing its first interest both in retailing and in the production of its own branded clothing line. At the beginning of 1985 the company made its first venture into retail with the purchase of a 5 percent stake in Millies, a Hong Kong–based footwear chain. This was followed by a move into apparel retail, as the company acquired majority control of Hong Kong's upcoming men's and women's retail clothing chain Sparkle.

With this acquisition, the Laws family also set out to develop its own men's and women's clothing lines. For this, the company began working with European and Japanese designers, in order to develop fashions for the United States and other overseas market. Laws planned to sell its designs both to the private-label circuit and also under its own Sparkle brand name. The company also intended to sell any excess production through its existing Sparkle chain stores in Hong Kong.

The Laws family also explored other expansion opportunities during this period. The company recognized the opportunity for setting up new retail concepts in mainland China, as that country's economic reforms slowly took hold into the second half of the decade. They began drafting plans to develop a retail chain introducing well-known U.S. and international brands into the Chinese market.

BOSSINI IN 1987

While this idea ultimately proved somewhat ahead of its time, the Laws family continued to pursue its diversification, even as it expanded its core clothing manufacturing business. The company invested in new production facilities, including a $2.6 million factory in Manila, Philippines, in 1987. The new facility, set up to produce some 200,000 dozen clothing items each year, helped expand the group's ability to supply its main U.S. markets, as well European markets. The success of this venture quickly led the company to establish a second factory in the Philippines that same year. In order to provide further fuel for the group's expansion, the company went public as Laws Fashion Knitters Ltd. in 1987, listing its shares on the Hong Kong Stock Exchange.

That year also saw the debut of a new successful venture. Backed by its experience developing the Sparkle

KEY DATES

1975: Law Ting Pong establishes Laws Fashion Knitters in Hong Kong.
1985: Laws acquires majority control of Hong Kong retail chain Sparkle.
1987: Laws launches its casual wear retail brand Bossini.
1988: Bossini introduces its franchise concept.
1993: Bossini International Holdings goes public on the Hong Kong Stock Exchange and opens its first stores in mainland China.
2006: Bossini expand its mainland store network to more than 600 locations.
2009: Company introduces its "be happy" slogan.
2013: Bossini opens its first franchise in Kenya.

retail chain, which grew to 30 locations in Hong Kong by the end of the decade, Laws set out to develop a new low-priced, casual wear brand concept, called Bossini. The brand hoped to benefit from the strong reputation for Italian clothing designs and quality among Hong Kong consumers. Laws backed the launch of the Bossini retail chain with the creation of its own lines of men's and women's fashions.

The Bossini brand became an instant success. The chain expanded quickly, reaching 30 locations in Hong Kong by 1989. Bossini also enabled the group to enter the broader international market. The company opened its first store in Singapore, which became one of the chain's core markets, starting in 1987. By the end of the decade, the company had already opened nine stores in that market. Another early international market for the company was Taiwan. By 1989 the company had already opened 16 stores there. The company also opened two stores in Macau during this period and eyed the introduction of the Bossini brand into the United States as well.

MAINLAND ENTRY IN 1993

Laws, which relocated its domicile to Bermuda and changed its name to Laws International Holdings in 1989, had also put into place another element in the growing success of the Bossini brand. The company's earliest stores were also owned and directly managed by the Bossini division itself. These operations were supplemented in 1988 by the introduction of a franchising operation. In this way, the company was able to

work with local partners in order to penetrate other foreign markets.

Laws International continued to expand its own clothing manufacturing business into the 1990s, while the Laws family also invested their growing fortune into the real estate and development market. This latter business ultimately led the family into hotel ownership, and department stores operations, with a growing portfolio of prime properties in Hong Kong, Singapore, China, and elsewhere.

These increasingly diversified interests led to a restructuring of the family's holdings, starting with the spinoff of the property business as a separate publicly listed company in 1991. Bossini's turn came two years later, when the company listed its shares on the Hong Kong Stock Exchange, changing its name to Bossini International Holdings.

The public listing paved the way for a new expansion phase for the Bossini brand. The company entered the mainland Chinese market, setting up its first stores there in 1993. In 1995 the company extended its franchise formula to the mainland as well, helping the group gain scale, and building the brand's reputation, amid the stirrings of China's soon-to-boom middle class.

Bossini also began working with partners in the Middle East during this time, setting up its first franchised stores in those markets in 1995. Through the next two decades, Bossini and its partners opened more than 270 locations in such countries as the United Arab Emirates, Bahrain, Kuwait, Iran, Iraq, Jordan, Lebanon, Qatar, Saudi Arabia, and Syria.

THE 7 HABITS IN 2002

Bossini's international expansion suffered a rare setback in the late 1990s. Amid the economic crisis sweeping much of Southeast Asia, the company's entry into Malaysia fell flat. By 1997 the group's operations in that country posted losses as high as HKD 13 million. The company was forced to pull the plug on this business the following year.

Bossini itself hit a bump into the turn of the century, amid the weakening of the global markets following the September 11, 2001, terrorist attacks against the United States. The company slipped into losses, starting in 2002, returning to profits only in 2004. Bossini responded to these difficulties by shutting down more than a dozen underperforming stores. The company also brought in a new board of directors in an effort to revitalize its flagging growth.

At the same time the company set to work developing a new vision of its corporate culture, which it dubbed "the bossini way," in 2002. The group developed a series of core values for its business, based around a list of so-called 7 Habits. These included such imperatives as: Be Proactive; Begin with the End in Mind; and Seek First to Understand, then to be Understood. In 2004 the company worked with consulting firm Right Management Hong Kong Ltd. to develop a training program for its employees based on the 7 Habits.

By then, Bossini's total store network had reached 678 stores, including 400 stores in mainland China, including a number of stores selling low-end clothing under the Sparkle brand. The company laid out new expansion plans, eyeing such developing markets as Eastern Europe, as well as further expansion in the broader Asian region. For this the company targeted the entry into markets including Indonesia, South Korea, and India, as well as a return to Malaysia, in 2005. The company added its first franchise in India the following year.

MAINLAND SLUMP IN 2008

Bossini also moved aggressively to take advantage of the surging retail clothing market in mainland China, adding more than 200 stores there by 2006. By 2008, however, Bossini's expansion appeared to have run out of steam. As then-CEO Kathy Chan So-kuen told *South China Morning Post*, "We were aiming too high and opened new stores too fast at the time and overlooked existing stores." The company also admitted its low-end Sparkle chain did not provide enough brand differentiation to allow it to rise above the fast-growing tide of competing chains.

While the company took steps to put its mainland business back in order, it continued to develop its core Hong Kong business, where it generated the majority of its sales (as much as 65 percent in 2013) and profits. The company added a new youth-oriented clothing range, called Yb by bsn, in 2007. Bossini also launched a major brand revamp that year, targeting its Hong Kong and other core markets.

Through the end of the decade, the revitalized Bossini brand completed a series of new international incursions. The group added its first franchise operations in Europe, notably in the Czech Republic, and in North Africa, including in Morocco and Egypt. The company also expanded into the Latin American markets starting in 2008, adding franchise stores in the Dominican Republic and Venezuela.

ADDING AFRICA IN 2013

The Bossini brand continued to build its international presence into the next decade as well. The group introduced its new "be happy" marketing strategy in 2009. This helped ease the group's entry into such new franchise markets as Armenia and Cambodia in 2010 and Brunei in 2011.

Bossini celebrated its 25th anniversary the following year with record sales and store numbers. By then, the company oversaw an international empire of more than 1,300 stores, generating revenues of HKD 2.74 billion. These figures appeared to be something of a high water mark for the company, however. By 2013 the sluggish global economy had caught up with mainland China, as well as other major markets for the company. As a result, the company shed nearly 300 stores over the next year. Most of these store closings came in the group's mainland China business and included 206 of the company's directly managed stores there.

Bossini's 41 Hong Kong stores were able to take up much of the slack, however, helping to stem the group's sales losses to just eight percent over the year. The company also continued to explore further expansion of its international franchise network, which picked up 18 stores through the year. These included the group's first entry into the broader African continent, with the opening of its first franchise stores in Kenya in 2013. Bossini hoped to fulfill its "be happy" values with further expansion into the second half of the decade.

M. L. Cohen

PRINCIPAL SUBSIDIARIES

Active Link Ltd.; Bossini Clothing Ltd.; Bossini Distribution Ltd.; Bossini Enterprises Ltd.; Bossini Garment Ltd.; Bossini Idea Ltd.; Burling Ltd. (BVI); J&R Bossini Fashion Pte Ltd. (Singapore); J&R Bossini Holdings Ltd.; Land Challenger Ltd.

PRINCIPAL DIVISIONS

Directly-Owned Stores; Franchise Network.

PRINCIPAL OPERATING UNITS

Hong Kong; Mainland China; Taiwan; Singapore and Malaysia.

PRINCIPAL COMPETITORS

Anson's Herrenhaus KG; Giordano International Ltd.; Tarchini FoxTown S.A.; Ted Baker PLC; Trinity Ltd.; Zara SA.

FURTHER READING

"Bossini Exalts the 'Bossini Be Happy' Brand Value." *China Weekly News*, July 7, 2009.

"Bossini Profits Fall after Expansion Moves." *just-style.com*, June 22, 2007.

"Bossini to Cut Stores in Taiwan & China Mainland." *Alestron*, April 12, 2007.

"A Bridge to Britain from China." *Forbes*, April 22, 2010.

Kusterbeck, Staci. "Bossini Brings Visibility to Its Enterprise." *Apparel*, November 2006.

Sim, Melissa. "Early Check-In for Allen Law." *Straits Times*, September 7, 2013.

Smith, Katie. "Bossini H1 Profit Slumps on Weak Sales." *just-style.com*, March 8, 2013.

Wang, Jasmine. "Bossini Suffers after Bold Expansion on Mainland." *South China Morning Post*, April 7, 2008.

Woodard, Richard. "Bossini Cautious Despite FY Profit Hike." *just-style.com*, September 22, 2011.

The Boy Scouts of America

<table>
<tr><td>

1325 West Walnut Hill Lane
Irving, Texas 75038
U.S.A.
Telephone: (972) 580-2000
Fax: (972) 580-2079
Web site: http://www.scouting.org

</td></tr>
</table>

Nonprofit Organization
Incorporated: 1910
Employees: 2,800
Sales: $248.2 million (2013)
NAICS: 813410 Civic and Social Organizations; 511120 Periodical Publishers; 511130 Book Publishers

■ ■ ■

The Boy Scouts of America (BSA) is one of the largest youth organizations in the United States, with nearly 2.6 million youth members and over one million adult volunteers. BSA is unique among the country's largest nonprofit groups in that volunteers at the local level are responsible for much of its planning. There are over 280 local councils throughout the United States that offer scouting activities focusing on education, leadership, and fitness. BSA's membership declined during the early 21st century. Its stance on gay membership as well as failure to disclose information regarding child and sexual abuse in past years led to public outcry and loss of corporate sponsorships. During 2013 BSA began allowing openly gay youth to become members while gay adults remained unable to participate in leadership roles.

Robert Gates, former secretary of defense and former director of the Central Intelligence Agency, was named president of BSA in 2014.

EDWARDIAN ORIGINS

Although many ideas were incorporated into the Boy Scouts of America, a chance encounter on a foggy London night in 1909 connected all the threads. Chicago publisher William D. Boyce was on his way to a safari in Africa. On a layover in London, he became lost and was rescued by a helpful Boy Scout who refused to take a tip for his good deed. This inspired Boyce to set up a meeting with the man who had started the movement in 1907, Major General Robert S. S. Baden-Powell.

Baden-Powell, a plucky Boer War hero, penned *Scouting for Boys* in 1908 after learning the popularity of his survival manual among schoolboys. Believing that modern males lacked the kinds of initiation rites found in primitive society, and disdaining the urban decadence and declining influence of the British military in Edwardian Britain, Baden-Powell developed his own program for building character among youths in a setting of outdoor recreation. Besides African tribes, he looked to the early British and Irish, the Japanese, the Spartans, and contemporary American youth movements for inspiration.

Although scouting was in its infancy when Boyce discovered it, the movement had already recruited more than 100,000 Boy Scouts across the British Empire. Baden-Powell was knighted for his work in 1910. Initially unable to obtain a federal charter, Boyce incorporated the Boys Scouts of America on February 8, 1910, in the District of Columbia. He then delegated some of the start-up work to Edgar M. Robinson, who was heading a scouting program for the YMCA (Young Men's Christian Association). On June 21, 1910, dozens of representatives from various boys' agencies met at BSA's temporary headquarters at a New York YMCA to elect a steering committee. By this time, newspaper magnate William Randolph Hearst had organized his own "American Boy Scouts."

ILLUSTRIOUS START

From the start, the Boy Scouts of America (BSA) was surrounded by men of influence and means. President William Howard Taft and former president Theodore Roosevelt were named honorary president and vice president. The group's president was Colin Livingstone, president of the American National Bank of Washington. Scottish émigré Ernest Thompson Seton, who had founded the Woodcraft Indians and would write the BSA handbook, was chosen first chief scout in 1910.

Another buckskin-wearing naturalist, Daniel Carter Beard, was first national scout commissioner. He designed the original uniform and merged his own boys' group, the Sons of Daniel Boone, with BSA. James E. West, the first chief scout executive, was an inspirational figure. Handicapped and an orphan, he had furthered himself along the lines of a Teddy Roosevelt. However, he antagonized the more athletic types, like Seton, who was forced out of the organization.

BSA established its National Council office at 200 Fifth Avenue in New York City on January 2, 1911. It had just seven staff members but membership reached 61,495 that year. President Taft spoke at the group's first annual meeting, held at the White House. *Boys' Life* magazine was launched that same year and scouting spread to all states by the next year.

In 1913 BSA commenced publication of *Scouting* magazine for scout volunteers. BSA finally received a federal charter in June 1916, which limited membership to U.S. citizens. Membership stood at 245,183 at year-end. Boy Scouts soon became known for their patriotic service, selling millions of dollars worth of war bonds during World War I.

FIRST WORLD JAMBOREE: 1920

In 1920 BSA sent 301 members to the first World Jamboree in England, attended by Boy Scouts from 32 of 52 scouting countries. The Boy Scouts adopted the left-handed handshake in 1923. By this time, more than two million people had participated in the program and active membership, including boys and volunteers, was nearly 600,000.

Boyce's Lone Scouts merged with BSA in 1924. The next year BSA sent a promotional delegation to South America. In 1927 the headquarters relocated to roomier accommodations at 2 Park Avenue, New York. The Cub Scouts program for younger boys was officially launched in 1930. Total membership exceeded one million by BSA's 25th anniversary in 1935. Unfortunately, an epidemic of infantile paralysis that year caused the national jamboree to be canceled.

In 1938 BSA received an enormous gift from Waite Phillips, who gave the agency 36,000 acres of land in the Rocky Mountains near Cimarron, New Mexico. Three years later Phillips added another 91,000 acres to the gift, which became the Philmont Scout Ranch, the world's largest. The Philtower Building in Tulsa, Oklahoma, accompanied the donation and provided income to run the camp.

DURING AND AFTER WORLD WAR II

Boy Scouts again assisted their country during World War II. The range of tasks undertaken included distributing war bonds and propaganda, salvaging critical materials such as rubber, and helping medical and fire brigades. After the war, BSA's World Friendship Fund gave money to help restore scouting in war-torn areas including the Philippines, which received $10,000. Conservation education featured highly in the scouts' program at home. Membership passed two million in 1946.

The U.S. Post Office issued the first stamp honoring the Boy Scouts in 1950. The next year, the scouts collected two million pounds of clothing for various relief efforts. Another "Good Turn" was hanging millions of "Get-Out-the-Vote" reminders on doorknobs. Civil defense education was also on the agenda.

KEY DATES

1907: Scouting begins in England as the brainchild of Robert Baden-Powell.

1909: American William D. Boyce is introduced to scouting through a chance occurrence.

1911: National Council offices are launched in the United States; first issue of *Boys' Life* is published.

1912: Scouting spreads to all 50 states.

1920: First Boy Scout World Jamboree is held in England.

1930: Cub Scouts, a program for younger boys, is launched.

1982: The millionth Eagle Scout is registered; the Tiger Cubs program for first graders is launched.

2000: The Boy Scouts of America celebrates its 90th birthday.

2013: BSA allows openly gay youth to become scouts; gay adults are barred from leadership roles.

The National Council relocated to New Brunswick, New Jersey, in October 1954. BSA started a foreign exchange program with the gift of transportation on U.S. military planes. The International Geophysical Year, 1958, saw an Explorer Scout, or adult volunteer, accompany an arctic expedition sponsored by the National Academy of Sciences. Total membership reached five million the next year.

BOYPOWER '76

As part of its golden jubilee, BSA opened the Johnston Historical Museum in New Brunswick in June 1960. By 1965, 40 million boys had been part of the BSA program, 500,000 of them becoming Eagle Scouts. The National Council launched the Boypower '76 eight-year plan in 1968, aiming to boost membership and to raise $65 million.

In the 1970s the scouts launched Save Our American Resources (SOAR). An antidrug campaign, Operation Reach, was also launched. In conjunction with the Bicentennial, Boy Scouts displayed a massive exhibition of scouting skills on the Mall in Washington, D.C. Twelve scouts gave the Report to the Nation to President Gerald Ford, himself a former Eagle Scout.

Under pressure to keep membership numbers up in order to maintain donations from the United Way, some

troop leaders were found to have exaggerated their enrollment statistics in 1974. At any rate, the Boypower campaign ultimately proved unsuccessful. BSA had but 4.6 million members in 1976, down 1.1 million from 1969. Membership continued to wane. BSA had even introduced an action figure, Steve Scout, which also failed.

In 1978, updating its image, BSA unofficially dubbed itself "Scouting USA." It launched a new "Campaign for Character" to raise $49 million. National Council headquarters relocated again in 1979, to Irving, Texas, while the 15th World Jamboree was postponed due to events in the host country of Iran.

RISING MEMBERSHIP

Membership figures started to rise again in 1980. Perhaps the new uniforms designed by Oscar de la Renta helped. Scouts nationwide urged participation in the census. They formed new relationships with other government agencies, such as the Department of the Interior and the Department of Energy. Cub Scouting turned 50 and signed up its 30 millionth Cub Scout.

BSA counted its one millionth Eagle Scout in 1982. At the same time, the organization had launched its "Shaping Tomorrow" program. New categories of scouting including Tiger Cubs for 7-year-old boys and athletics-oriented Varsity Scouting for 14- to 17-year-olds emerged. In 1985 the year of BSA's 75th anniversary, scouts lit campfires outside each state capital and carried the ashes in a three-month procession across the country. Membership continued to climb, exceeding five million by the end of 1986.

That year, Boy Scouts promoted the cause of organ donation. Societal issues ("unacceptables") tackled by BSA in the late 1980s included drug abuse, child abuse, illiteracy, youth unemployment, and hunger. Backed by corporate supporters such as Quaker Oats and the United Way, scouts collected 60 million containers of food in 1988 alone. BSA recognized the potential for child abuse in its own organization and structured activities to eliminate one-on-one encounters between scouts and adult volunteers.

NEW FRONTIERS

The collapse of the Soviet Empire opened new frontiers for the Boy Scouts. Czechoslovakia and Hungary soon began their own programs. In 1990 a BSA delegation sought opportunities in Moscow, then continued to the Vatican City to present Pope John Paul II with a commendation. At home, the Hispanic Emphasis and Urban Emphasis targeted underrepresented segments of the population.

A sophisticated TV ad campaign aimed to swell the ranks of the Boy Scouts in the United States, who numbered only one million in 1990. Cub Scouting, aimed at younger boys, was much more popular as teenagers found traditional Boy Scout activities such as knot tying decidedly unhip. In-school scouting brought many new members in urban areas, although purists protested the perceived dilution of the curriculum.

In 1992 BSA's policy barring gay members and volunteers prompted Levi Strauss, Bank of America, and Wells Fargo to cancel their support for the organization, which together amounted to about $100,000 a year. Conservative groups boycotted the three San Francisco–based firms in response, and Bank of America soon resumed its contributions. BSA also banned atheists, as one of its three founding principles was a belief in God. An appellate court ruled that the Boy Scouts was a private group not subject to civil rights laws. Although it won a 1987 lawsuit from a woman scorned, BSA subsequently allowed women into scoutmaster positions.

A restructuring in 1992 reduced the number of councils from 408 to 340 and the number of regions from six to four. BSA also sold underutilized real estate, switched from mainframe computers to personal computers, and began benchmarking practices from the world of business. It also began to reduce its staffing levels. Jere Ratcliffe was picked to lead the National Council in 1993, taking over from Norm Augustine, CEO of Lockheed Martin.

BSA started systematically searching for more endowment money. Operating revenues were $411 million in 1995, a fifth of it provided by the United Way, which was cutting back its contribution. While it had 3,300 professional employees, more than a million volunteers did most of the work. Operation First Class sought adults from diverse backgrounds to fill the ranks.

MOVING INTO THE MILLENNIUM

Although a much-beloved organization among many Americans, Boy Scouts of America was not without its share of ongoing problems and controversies. For example, in 1999 the New Jersey Supreme Court ruled in favor of James Dale, a scoutmaster whom BSA had expelled for being gay. BSA appealed the case to the U.S. Supreme Court and won in 2000. The organization's stance on gay membership would prove to be a hotly contested topic throughout the early years of the new millennium.

While BSA welcomed its one millionth member in 2000 and its two millionth Eagle Scout in 2009, its overall membership waned during this time period. A

BSA communications director explained the numbers in a May 2014 *Christian Post* article. "The BSA has seen, in its past 10 years, some years with a decline of 2 to 4 percent in members each year with some years being flat. At the end of December, we had served nearly 2.5 million youth members and close to 960,000 adult members. This is a decrease of approximately 6 percent from the same time in 2012."

CHANGES IN POLICY

As BSA worked to develop new programs and attract new members, it remained surrounded by negative publicity. In 2012 over 1,200 internal BSA files that detailed accusations of sexual abuse within the organization from 1965 to 1985 were made public. Dubbed the "perversion files," these records brought to light inadequate BSA policies that often allowed cover-ups and repeat offenders to remain involved in the organization.

After the release of the files, BSA focused on developing new policies to protect its youth members, which included mandatory reporting to local authorities any suspicion of abuse. At the same time, the organization came under fire once again for its policy banning gay members and leaders. In 2012 Ryan Andresen, an openly gay scout, was denied the rank of Eagle Scout due to his sexual orientation. His story quickly spread through social media, news outlets, as well as through an appearance on the *Ellen DeGeneres Show*.

Public outcry and potential loss in corporate sponsorships forced BSA to review its policy. In 2013 it announced that it would allow openly gay youth to participate in its scouting programs. Gay adults, however, were banned from serving in leadership roles. Robert Gates, who had served as secretary of defense and director of the Central Intelligence Agency, and was strong advocate for the repeal of the "Don't Ask, Don't Tell" military policy, was elected BSA president in 2014. Although he applauded the change in policy and believed gay adults should be able to participate, he did not advocate for additional changes at this time.

AN EYE TO THE FUTURE

Gates explained his rationale in the aforementioned *Christian Post* article. "Given the strong feelings involved among our volunteers on both sides of this matter, I believe strongly that to reopen the membership issue or try to take last year's decision to the next step would irreparably fracture and perhaps even provoke a formal, permanent split in this movement with the high likelihood that neither side would survive on its own. That is just a fact of life."

Moving forward, BSA continued to focus on providing its members with educational, leadership, and fitness-oriented programming and activities. During 2013 the organization opened its Summit Bechtel Family National Scout Reserve near Beckley, West Virginia. It held its 2013 National Scout Jamboree at the new location. The Paul R. Christen National High Adventure Base debuted the following year at the reserve. While membership growth remained uncertain at this time, BSA remained dedicated to preparing its members to be responsible leaders of society.

Frederick C. Ingram
Updated, Christina M. Stansell

PRINCIPAL DIVISIONS

Cub Scouting; Boy Scouting; Varsity Scouting; Venturing and Sea Scouting; Learning for Life; Exploring.

PRINCIPAL COMPETITORS

Boys & Girls Clubs of America; Young Men's Christian Association (YMCA).

FURTHER READING

Barnhart, Melissa. "Boy Scouts of America Sees 6 Percent Decline in Membership; Stands Firm on Banning Openly Gay Leaders." *Christian Post*, May 30, 2014.

Cochran, William F. "Confessions of a Jamboree Scoutmaster." *Harper's*, February 1951.

Fowler, Geoffrey A., and Ana Campoy. "Boy Scouts Rethink Gay Ban; Proposed Change Comes after Petition Drives and Pressure by Corporate Backers." *Wall Street Journal*, January 29, 2013.

Schneider, Craig, Katie Leslie, and Ernie Suggs. "Abuse Scandal: Georgia Scout Leaders Accused: 97 Listed in Group's 'Perversion Files' Dating from 1947–2004." *Atlanta Journal-Constitution*, October 19, 2012.

Wagner, Carolyn Ditte. "The Boy Scouts of America: A Model and a Mirror of American Society." PhD diss., Johns Hopkins University, 1978.

Williams, Timothy. "Former Defense Secretary Gates Is Elected President of the Boy Scouts." *New York Times*, May 23, 2014.

Boyd Coffee Company

19730 Northeast Sandy Boulevard
Portland, Oregon 97230
U.S.A.
Telephone: (503) 666-4545
Toll Free: (800) 545-4077
Fax: (503) 669-2223
Web site: http://www.boyds.com

Private Company
Incorporated: 1900 as Boyd Importing Tea Company
Employees: 400
Sales: $120 million (2013 est.)
NAICS: 311920 Coffee and Tea Manufacturing; 333318 Coffee Makers and Urns, Commercial-Type, Manufacturing

■ ■ ■

Boyd Coffee Company is a leading distributor of coffee, tea, hot and cold beverages, and brewing equipment. Its products are found in over 2,500 convenience stores, more than 2,000 restaurants, nearly 550 hotels, approximately 1,000 business offices, and 75 casinos. Boyd Coffee was the first American coffee roaster to import Rainforest Alliance Certified coffee in 1999 and the first coffee roaster to be certified organic in North America. Jeffrey Newman became the first nonfamily CEO in 2010, while David and Dick Boyd remained owners and cochairmen. During 2013 the company produced nearly 12.5 million pounds of coffee, which accounted for just over half of company revenue.

PORTLAND ORIGINS

Percival Dewey "P. D." Boyd was born in New Zealand in 1879. The son of a Presbyterian missionary from Scotland, P. D. immigrated to the United States at the age of three. He worked at grocery and sales jobs until about 1900, when he started the Boyd Importing Tea Company in downtown Portland, Oregon. P. D. made door-to-door deliveries of tea and coffee with a horse and a red wagon he had bought for five dollars. Trucks replaced horses around 1910. By 1920 Boyd had stopped delivering to homes.

Among other measures P. D. Boyd initiated to keep his company in business was the practice of lending brewing equipment to foodservice customers. Rudy Boyd took over his father's business after World War II. In December 1946 the company became known as Boyd Coffee Company. A few years later a frost wiped out Brazil's coffee crop and nearly took Boyd Coffee with it.

Boyd introduced vacuum-packed coffee in cans in 1955. About this time, the company began manufacturing automatic coffee brewers for restaurants. The company also introduced paper coffee filters to restaurant users. A home version, the Flav-R-Flo Brewer, was rolled out a few years later. Boyd Coffee was also ahead of its time in hiring practices. Its longtime coffee buyer, Veda Younger, was one of the first females in her line of work.

Although Rudy Boyd never finished high school, his sons David and Dick went to the University of Oregon. Like their father, they both grew up working for the family business. David began stripping tape from

COMPANY PERSPECTIVES

Boyd's Coffee believes that everyone deserves a thoughtfully sourced, skillfully roasted and properly brewed cup of coffee. At Boyd's, we don't believe that coffee bestows status or makes a statement about the person who drinks it. We believe that people are capable of making their own statements. We hold that coffee is fuel, not fashion. It is what it has always been: a reward for good work, done well; and a kick in the pants to get back out there and do some more. That's the legacy of coffee in America and that's the Boyd's legacy, as well.

cartons at age 12. Dick began at age 16, counting coffee can lids. In 1975 David took over as CEO of Boyd Coffee upon Rudy Boyd's retirement. Rudy maintained a presence as chairman. In the late 1980s Boyd opened five of its own Red Wagon retail stores. It also opened espresso cafés in Portland and Seattle.

GOING GOURMET

Gourmet products would be the fastest-growing segment of the coffee market in the 1990s. In 1990 Boyd, which claimed to be the country's largest purveyor of gourmet coffee, had more than 50 gourmet varieties. Its coffee carts were supplying colleges, supermarkets, department stores, and hotels. With annual sales of $100 million and 400 employees, Boyd Coffee was profitable and growing in the early 1990s. Its plant was enlarged by 60 percent and going to double shifts.

In November 1991, however, Boyd's board replaced David with Richard for undisclosed reasons, reported *Fortune FSB* in a 2002 article on sustaining family businesses. The brothers eventually began sharing the position of president/CEO equally after bringing in a business/family therapist. Dick Boyd also brought in Los Angeles–based Flamhlotz Management Systems Consulting Corp. to facilitate some strategic planning.

In 1991 Boyd sued the coffee businesses of Denver's Boyer family over trademark infringement. Boyd claimed the Boyer name was similar enough to confuse consumers. The next year, Boyd acquired another Denver-based business, Ambassador Office Coffee Service. Boyd expanded its sales and service operations to Minnesota, Wisconsin, and the Upper Peninsula of Michigan in 1993. The company was part of the Dine-More consortium of regional roasters servicing national foodservice accounts such as ServiceMaster.

PREPARING FOR THE NEW MILLENNIUM

By the mid-1990s Boyd was packaging 75 different types of coffee. The company had installed electronically controlled roasters and was increasing production to 19,000 tons of beans a year. Boyd was rolling out espresso entertainment centers and coffee carts under the Italia D'Oro brand. The firm also imported espresso equipment. Company executives credited Starbucks with boosting awareness and sales in this segment.

Boyd began selling organically grown coffee around 1990, and it was certified organic by Quality Assurance International in 1997. The certification process, which documents the processing as well as the growing of the coffee, took three years. Boyd claimed to be the only national distributor of certified organic coffee. Boyd was the main supplier for Tuscany Premium Coffees, a small upscale chain that had eschewed its Seattle origins to focus on markets new to gourmet coffee, such as Cleveland, Pittsburgh, Philadelphia, Dallas, Houston, and Denver.

Tuscany Inc. went bankrupt in April 1997 after a failed initial public offering. Boyd was also heavily involved in the foodservice business, an outgrowth of its coffee packaging. It prepared packaged dry mixes for soups, sauces, beverages, desserts, and other products. To foster ties with the foodservice community, Boyd prepared an educational program for Johnson and Wales University, a leading culinary institute. The company also sponsored a culinary competition for high school students in Washington State.

By the late 1990s Boyd products were being distributed in Japan, Korea, and Taiwan. Boyd participated in a joint roasting venture in the Philippines. In early 2001 Boyd began a partnership with Vitality Foodservice Canada, Ltd., the largest Canadian foodservice beverage manufacturer and distributor.

EXPANSION IN 2001

By 2000 the expansion of Boyd Coffee's Sandy Boulevard plant had dragged on for several years. The company had scouted areas elsewhere in the country, including Utah, which was a surprising choice since traditional Mormon wisdom frowned upon caffeine in any form, including coffee. Ultimately, however, Boyd decided to stay in Portland.

A new plan called for adding 132,000 square feet to the facility, doubling its size. Boyd aimed to have all of its operations under one roof, and the space would house a new warehouse distribution facility. The

KEY DATES

1900: P. D. Boyd begins coffee and tea deliveries in Portland.
1946: Rudy Boyd takes over his father's business.
1972: Boyd relocates to a new factory and headquarters complex.
1975: David Boyd succeeds father Rudy as head of Boyd Coffee.
1991: Dick Boyd replaces brother at top spot.
2001: Boyd breaks ground on plant expansion.
2003: Company forms a partnership with the Rainforest Alliance.
2010: Jeffrey Newman is named CEO; launches restructuring effort.
2013: Company buys Harvested by Women certified coffee.
2014: Boyd launches single-cup coffee for use in K-Cup brewers.

company had been leasing 55,000 square feet of warehouse space near the airport. Boyd finally broke ground on the $8 million expansion in March 2001.

Oregon Business magazine named Boyd Coffee number 49 of Oregon's top 100 companies to work for in 2001. Dick and David Boyd attributed the company's success to integrity, respect for employees, and contribution to the local community. More good media coverage came from the Food Network. The cable network's *Unwrapped* series took a five-minute look behind the scenes at Boyd Coffee in a 2002 episode.

GROWTH CONTINUES

Boyd Coffee continued to move forward, looking for innovative ways to stay ahead of its competitors. During 2003 the company formed a partnership with the Rainforest Alliance. As part of the deal, Boyd Coffee supplied Rainforest Alliance–certified coffees to restaurants, hotels, and consumers in the United States.

A 2003 company press release explained meaning behind a Rainforest Alliance designation. "On Rainforest Alliance–certified farms, workers are treated fairly, soil and water quality are not compromised, waste is managed efficiently, chemical use is dramatically reduced and relations with surrounding communities are strong." The release further explained, "The Rainforest Alliance–certified seal of approval gives buyers the assurance that they are acquiring products from a farm that complies

with comprehensive social and environmental guidelines."

Along with introducing new coffees, Boyd Coffee also developed new brewing systems. The Coffee Profiler debuted in 2008 for restaurants across the United States. The programmable system included a push-button operation to brew hot coffee drinks, iced coffee, and hot and iced tea.

FOURTH GENERATION TAKES OVER

In early 2009 the fourth generation of the Boyd family joined the management ranks. Katy Boyd Dutt, David Boyd's daughter, took over as director of marketing while David's son, Michael Boyd, became director of risk management. Matthew Boyd, Dick Boyd's son, was named director of information technology. At the same time, the family began to search for its next CEO. Jeffrey Newman became the first nonfamily member to lead Boyd Coffee in 2010, while David and Dick remained cochairmen.

As president and CEO, Newman set out to restructure various operations in order to secure revenue and profit growth. Under his leadership, the company trimmed its employee count, shuttered unprofitable product lines, launched a rebranding campaign, and sold its Philippines-based subsidiary. The company closed its Portland retail locations, stopped selling spices and soup mixes, and discontinued its Coffee House Roasters brand, which had been sold mainly at truck stops.

Boyd Coffee also revamped its packaging and adopted a new logo. By 2013 revenues and profits were on the rise and the company had increased its production levels. That year the company became the first coffee roaster in the United States to purchase Harvested by Women certified coffee. The Harvested by Women designation ensured coffee was grown, harvested, and sold in a manner that provided a fair and sustainable lifestyle for the women involved in coffee production. The product, called ¡Café Libre!, was sold in grocery stores and on the company's Web site.

Boyd Coffee launched its single-cup coffee for brewers using the K-Cup systems in 2014. It also developed a new line of cold beverages that year including Boyd's Iced Tea, Boyd's Ice Cap, and Boyd's Iced Coffee. With a solid strategy in place, it appeared as though coffee lovers across the United States would enjoy the company's products for years to come.

Frederick C. Ingram
Updated, Christina M. Stansell

PRINCIPAL COMPETITORS

Farmer Bros. Co.; Keurig Green Mountain, Inc.; Starbucks Corporation.

FURTHER READING

"Boyd Coffee Company Forms Partnership with Rainforest Alliance to Provide Certified, Sustainable Coffees." *Business Wire*, February 10, 2003.

"Boyd Coffee Management Movement." *Tea & Coffee Trade Journal*, March 1, 2010.

Giegerich, Andy. "Boyd Coffee Jumps into the Singles Market." *Portland Business Journal*, April 22, 2014.

Goldfield, Robert. "Boyd Coffee Co. Looks Back to Its 113-Year-Old Roots." *Portland Business Journal*, May 24, 2013.

Junia, Catherine C. "Enterprisers: Over a Cup of Coffee." *Businessworld* (Manila), August 24, 2000.

Layton, Randy. "Boyd Coffee Company Serves a Fine Cup of Coffee." *Tea & Coffee Trade Journal*, August 1, 2009.

Strom, Shelly. "Boyd Coffee to Consolidate by Expanding Sandy Facilities." *Business Journal of Portland*, August 11, 2000.

———. "Boyd Seals Major Deal for Organic Coffee Line." *Business Journal of Portland*, December 15, 2000.

———. "Local Roaster to Be Showcased on Food Network." *Business Journal of Portland*, May 15, 2001.

Whitford, David. "Century-Old Companies Built to Last." *FSB: Fortune Small Business*, June 2002.

Cara Donna Provision Company Inc.

—■—

200 Commerce Drive
Braintree, Massachusetts 02184
U.S.A.
Telephone: (781) 794-3030
Toll Free: (800) 439-1565
Fax: (781) 794-1616
Web site: http://www.caradonnaprov.com

Private Company
Founded: 1930
Employees: 67
Sales: $87.8 million (2013)
NAICS: 424410 General Line Grocery Merchant
 Wholesalers; 424420 Packaged Frozen Food
 Merchant Wholesalers

■■■

Cara Donna Provision Company Inc. is a Braintree, Massachusetts–based full-service distributor of foods and food-related products, delivering to most of Massachusetts, all of Rhode Island, and portions of Connecticut, Maine, and New Hampshire. Cara Donna serves independent pizza shops, as well as restaurants and delis. The company also acts as a redistributor, serving smaller wholesalers. Products include meats, poultry, cheese and other dairy products, deli meats, produce, canned foods, appetizers and other prepared foods, frozen bread, frozen entrees, condiments, oils and other cooking supplies, foil and film wrap, pizza boxes, food trays and clam boxes, guest checks, and cleaning supplies and other janitorial products. In addition, Cara

Donna offers marketing solutions through a partner, Taradel LLC. Services include custom menu design and other printing services, direct mail, digital marketing, website development, and online and mobile phone pizza ordering services. Cara Donna is owned and managed by the third generation of the Donna family and is the largest family run and managed broad line foodservice distributor in the New England region.

COMPANY FOUNDED: 1930

Cara Donna Provision dates its history to 1930 when Joseph Cara Donna Sr. started the company as a one-man business in Boston. He was born in 1907 to Italian immigrant parents in Worchester, Massachusetts, one of 17 children. Initially, he was based in the Faneuil Hall district, which included Haymarket Square where traditionally fruits and vegetables had been sold in an open market. Cara Donna's focus was on fresh meats, delivering them to local Boston establishments. In 1945 he acted on a suggestion to begin offering authentic Italian deli meats to local markets, thus taking a major step in the direction of becoming a true foodservice wholesaler. He distributed Abromo Rae and Genoa Packing Italian deli meats, as well as cheeses and other Italian provisions.

Joe Cara Donna's business adopted the Cara Donna Provision Company name in 1945. It was a good time for the 38-year-old to expand his business. World War II came to an end that year, the country had finally escaped the Great Depression of the 1930s, and millions of servicemen were beginning to return home. Many would marry, sparking a population boom, and with a

---

COMPANY PERSPECTIVES

All the ingredients for your success.

---

economy that enjoyed extended growth following a brief postwar recession, there was ample opportunity for a wholesaler like Joe Cara Donna. People had more money to spend at delis and restaurants, and during the postwar years pizza became especially popular. Pizza had long been popular in Italian enclaves in the Northeast, but now pizza shops proliferated, ultimately providing Cara Donna with a core group of customers.

SECOND GENERATION JOINS COMPANY

Still a small supplier, Joe Cara Donna could handle only as much business as the one truck he drove allowed. With the arrival of his sons after they completed their military service, he was able to buy more trucks and expand further. The first son to join him was Leo Cara Donna in 1958. Joseph Cara Donna Jr. followed in 1960.

In addition to expanding the number of delivery trucks from one to three, the second generation of the Cara Donna family brought new energy to the business. Not only did the company add more customers and extend its delivery area, it expanded the products it carried to include fresh beef, pork, lamb, and veal. High quality was ensured by the Cara Donna brothers, who visited slaughterhouses in Somerville, Massachusetts, to personally select the company's own meats. They took further advantage of their relationship with suppliers to become a distributor to other wholesalers. To support this effort, Cara Donna Provision began renting a small warehouse space, just 1,000 square feet in size, in Newmarket Square in 1963. It shared a truck bay with another company.

Gradually the focus of Cara Donna Provision switched from supplying Boston-area neighborhood markets to meeting the needs of small distributors and truck jobbers as a redistributor. The company also expanded what it had to offer customers. While delis remained the primary end users for Cara Donna Provision, the pizza shop segment began to really come into its own in the 1960s. Because Cara Donna Provision carried tomato products, pepperoni, mozzarella cheese, and others products, it became a natural supplier to the pizza shop segment. As demand increased, Cara Donna Provision outgrew its warehouse. In 1969 the company moved into a 2,500-square-foot space in the New Boston Food Market, which had just been opened by the city of Boston as a home for food companies that had formerly made Faneuil Hall their home. The area was now becoming more oriented toward tourism rather than the foodservice business.

The new location provided Cara Donna Provision with a dedicated truck bay. By now, the second generation of the Cara Donna family was well in charge of the company, and in the 1970s the Cara Donna brothers continued to search out fresh opportunities. They recognized that the delis and neighborhood markets their father had long served were going through a period of transition. Specialty products that had appealed to Italian immigrants were not as popular with their Americanized offspring. On the other hand, there was a growing demand for prepared foods from the company's other foodservice customers.

PREPARED FOODS ADDED

Cara Donna Provision took advantage of its reputation as a wholesale food supplier to establish a prepared foods business. Joe Cara Donna Jr., who had initially made his mark with the family company as a salesman, spearheaded the new effort. He became knowledgeable about product formulation and manufacturing processes. As a result of his abilities, he was well suited to secure relationships with Eastern food production companies. Many of them had excess capacity and little if any business in the Boston area. Cara Donna Provision became an exclusive distributor with many of them. In this way, the company was able to expand the prepared foods it was able to offer. It was also able to arrange to have Cara Donna–labeled products made to its specifications by these food production partners.

As Cara Donna Provision continued to evolve into a full-service foodservice distributor, more space was required. In 1979 the company added three more truck bays and increased the total amount of warehouse space to 10,000 square feet. Another bay was added in 1987. In the meantime, the company computerized the operation.

While his brother made his contributions to the growth of Cara Donna Provision, Leo Cara Donna placed his own imprint on the business. He possessed strong administrative, personnel management, and customer services skills. In the late 1970s he also became interested in computers, which he saw as a potential answer to the challenges the rapidly growing company now faced. Cara Donna Provision had become buried in paperwork that resulted from the many small transactions it conducted each day. Not only was the

KEY DATES

1930: Joseph Cara Donna Sr. begins one-man distribution business.
1945: Cara Donna Provision is formed.
1958: Second generation of Cara Donna family joins company.
2000: Braintree distribution center opens.
2012: Cara Donna Provision offers marketing solutions through Taradel LLC.

paperwork burdensome, the sheer number of transactions magnified the potential for error. Technology assets included just three calculators until the fall of 1978 when the company paid $65,000 for an IBM System 34 mainframe computer.

The investment in a computer proved to be a wise choice. Not only was Cara Donna Provision able to handle its business better, permitting further growth, it opened up a new opportunity. In 1980, the company formed a joint venture, Prime Associates, a software development company that served the wholesale food distribution industry. Cara Donna Provision improved its information technology further in 1983 with an upgrade to an IBM System 36. It then invested $10,000 on a voice recognition system that allowed workers to read off weights as they walked through the warehouse to quickly take inventory.

THIRD GENERATION BECOMES INVOLVED

By the mid-1980s Cara Donna Provision was generating about $20 million in annual sales. Growth continued in the final decade of the century, and a third generation of the Cara Donna family began to play increasingly more significant roles in the business. Both Joseph Jr. and Lee Cara Donna had two sons, resulting in four new employees: Joseph Cara Donna III, Leo Cara Donna Jr., Joseph Anthony Cara Donna, and Chris Cara Donna. All of them had become familiar with the business at an early age. By the time they reached middle school, they began spending their school vacations working for Cara Donna Provision. They also worked for the company while attending college. Later as full-time employees they worked their way up through the organization, starting in the warehouse. They also drove trucks and delivered orders to become personally familiar with many of the customers they would eventually serve from an oversight position.

With the third generation of the family bolstering the operation and providing new leadership, Cara Donna Provision was poised to expand through organic and external means at the turn of the century. In January 2000 the company acquired Providence, Rhode Island–based Coastal Foodservice, adding $8 million in sales. Cara Donna Provision's annual revenue improved to about $50 million. To support further growth, the company opened a distribution center in Braintree in April 2000. The new 38,000-square-foot facility provided dry goods as well as cooler and freezer storage. In 2003 Cara Donna Provision completed two further acquisitions. First, it added Lowell Ice Cream, a small distributor based in Lowell, Massachusetts. Later in the year, Cara Donna Provision purchased the foodservice distribution unit of Worcester, Massachusetts–based Leroux Meats, a meat fabricator and distributor. The two deals helped to increased annual sales to about $57 million. "We are interested in smaller, well managed distributors with good quality employees within our geographic area," vice president Joseph Cara Donna III told the *Food Institute Report* in a September 8, 2003, article. He continued: "There's significant sales volume and a lot of untapped potential in many of the area's smaller distributors who are increasingly struggling against the forces of a concentrating marketplace."

COMPANY SETS $100 MILLION SALES TARGET

The company set a goal of increasing annual sales to the $100 million mark. Although a regional player, Cara Donna Provision remained a small company compared to the giants in the foodservice industry. In order to remain competitive and meet its goal, the company expanded the Braintree facility as well as its product offerings. Early in the first decade of the 21st century fresh produce was added. Just as important, Cara Donna Provision began offering other types of services to help its customers succeed. In 2006 an Internet Business Building program was introduced to design or redesign the websites of its customers as well as to provide rudimentary marketing services, such as e-mail coupon offers.

In 2012 Cara Donna Provision's website began offering Market Solutions to its customers, in particular pizza shops, that greatly expanded on the earlier Internet Business Building program. The company worked with Taradel LLC, a Virginia-based company established in 2003, to provide a host of new services. They included the design and printing of menus, flyers, mailers, and door hangers; a direct-mail program; an online pizza ordering system; and a tracking service to keep tabs on how customers rated an establishment. With a third generation of the founding family firmly entrenched and a commitment to remain relevant to its customers, Cara Donna Provision was well positioned to maintain its place in the New England foodservice market.

Ed Dinger

PRINCIPAL DIVISIONS

Operations; Purchasing; Sales; Transportation.

PRINCIPAL COMPETITORS

PFG Holdings, Inc.; Reinhart Foodservice L.L.C.; SYSCO Corporation.

FURTHER READING

"Acquisition Flurry in the Foodservice Sector." *Food Institute Report*, September 8, 2003.

"Cara Donna Provision Co., Inc." *Food Institute Report*, February 21, 2005.

"Cara Donna Provision Co., Inc." *ID: The Voice of Foodservice Distribution*, December 1999.

"Crown Equipment Corporation: Lift Trucks Provide Solutions for Food Distribution." *Material Handling Product News*, September 15, 2003.

"How Wholesaler Found Success by Talking to His Computer." *Quick Frozen Foods*, February 1985.

Cassano's, Inc.

———■———

1680 East Stroop Road
Kettering, Ohio 45429
U.S.A.
Telephone: (937) 298-8695
Toll Free: (888) 294-5464
Fax: (937) 294-8107
Web site: http://www.cassanos.com

Private Company
Founded: 1953
Employees: 400
Sales: $55 million (est.)
NAICS: 722513 Limited-Service Restaurants

■ ■ ■

Maintaining its headquarters in Kettering, Ohio, Cassano's, Inc., operates a chain of company-owned and franchise pizzerias in more than 30 locations in the Dayton, Ohio, area. In addition to full-size Cassano's Pizza King restaurants, the company operates the Cassano's Pizza Express format in convenience stores, gas stations, and hotels. The Cassano's menu includes a wide variety of pizzas, calzones, sub sandwiches, flat breads, pastas, salads, appetizers, and desserts. Two Cassano's locations offer the London Bobby's Fish and Chips menu. Cassano's also manufactures the dough for frozen pizza, sandwiches, and wraps, which it provides to its own restaurants as well as to outside customers in more than 20 states. In addition, the company offers frozen Cassano's The Pizza King pizzas, sold online to

the home market. The third generation of the Cassano family owns and manages Cassano's, Inc.

POSTWAR ORIGINS

Cassano's was one of many mom-and-pop pizzeria chains that emerged after World War II, when pizza first achieved widespread popularity in the United States. In 1953, five years before Frank and Dan Carney opened the first Pizza Hut in Wichita, Kansas, Victor J. Cassano Sr. opened a pizzeria in Kettering, Ohio. The son of Italian immigrants, he grew up under trying circumstance. He was only two years old when his father died. Unable yet to speak or read English, his mother was forced to place Cassano and his brothers in a Cincinnati orphanage, where they lived for several years before she earned enough money to take back her sons, one by one.

After serving in the military during World War II, Cassano began his career in the grocery business. A journalist friend who had visited New York and took note of the growing interest in pizza suggested that he bring the idea to the Dayton area. With the help of his mother-in-law, Caroline Donisi, Cassano opened the first Cassano's Pizza King in June 1953 in a 20-foot-by-15-foot space in the back of a combination party supplies store and deli.

The venture was an instant success. On the first evening, the company claimed the pizzeria sold 200 pizzas, although some sources say 400. Whether the tale is apocryphal or not, the business did well. Just two months later Cassano opened a second location in Dayton. By the time the first Pizza Hut opened it doors in Wichita, Vic Cassano was running a dozen Cassano Pizza King locations.

MOVE TO NEW FACILITY: 1968

Cassano continued to expand the business in the 1960s. In 1968 he moved into a new manufacturing facility where he also established his corporate headquarters. Pizza dough was produced for the chain at this location, and a test kitchen developed new products. Cassano did not limit himself to pizza. He also launched other restaurant concepts, including London Bobby's Fish and Chips, Sandy's Hamburgers, and Gabby's Restaurant.

The menu at the pizza stores also expanded and became eclectic, essentially offering whatever a particular market might buy. At its peak, the pizzeria chain was adding 50 stores a year in the early 1970s, eventually peaking at 125 stores, making it one of the country's top pizza chains. National players such as Pizza Hut and Domino's soon made inroads in the Midwest, forcing Cassano to close units.

By 1985 the chain was reduced to 75 stores, including 56 company-owned and 19 franchised units that generated about $18 million in annual combined sales. Cassano began to focus the menu. Not only did he remove fish and chips, he eliminated pastas and other dinner options and removed salad bars from the restaurants. He also attempted to open a smaller food-court format.

CASSANO'S SOLD: 1985

Cassano kept the details of his business affairs close to the vest, so much so that in 1985 he decided to retire. He sold the pizzeria chain without asking if his 40-year-old son and chief lieutenant, Victor Cassano Jr., might be interested in buying the business. In fact, his son very much wanted to own the chain. Instead, he accepted a token position from the new owners, Greyhound Food Management, a subsidiary of the Greyhound bus company. Cassano was essentially given a figurehead role because of his name.

After a two-year search for a fast-food company to acquire, Greyhound had settled on Cassano's, believing that it was a brand that could be taken nationally to compete against Domino's. With a focus on delivery and takeout, the plan was to open 100 to 150 stores a year. Greyhound faced no shortage of challenges with the Cassano's chain, which included a significant number of unprofitable stores. Despite recent changes, there was still no consistency to the menu or to the operation in general.

Some locations carried grocery items and were essentially convenience stores. The new owners developed a new prototype that focused on takeout and included a drive-thru. By the end of 1989 Greyhound hoped to have 375 Cassano's restaurants in operation, but the strategy was poorly executed. Due to inadequate sales, Greyhound began closing stores in 1988. Instead of laying a foundation for the future by the end of the decade, Greyhound was ready to exit its ill-fated venture.

FAMILY BUYS BACK BUSINESS

In 1989 Cassano Jr. teamed up with Greyhound executive Randy Leasher to buy the Cassano's chain. The partners began to retrench, closing select restaurants, some of which had only been open for two weeks. The hope was that once stabilized, the chain would be able to expand into the neighboring states of Indiana, Michigan, Pennsylvania, and West Virginia. Soon, sheer survival became the company's primary goal, as the decade saw a mass advertising blitz from national pizza chains that included Domino's, Pizza Hut, Papa John's, and the aspiring Donato's brand.

One bright spot for Cassano's was the launch of a wholesale frozen pizza dough business. Initially, the company was searching for a vendor to provide pizza dough to its restaurants as a way to save money. However, all of the available products were disappointing. Rather than cease manufacturing dough, Cassano and Leasher decided to expand their dough-making operation and become a supplier to outside customers. Thus, in 1994 the company teamed up with a food broker to become a wholesaler of frozen pizza dough.

Although the dough-making venture provided a much-needed new source of revenue, Cassano's financial health remained poor. In a decision Cassano Jr. would later regret, the company filed for Chapter 11 bankruptcy protection in February 1995. The company claimed assets of $7.2 million and liabilities of $4.9 million, mostly money owed to banks and suppliers. By the end of the year, Cassano's exited Chapter 11 with an agreement to pay back 87 cents on the dollar.

KEY DATES

1953: Victor Cassano Sr. opens first pizzeria.
1985: Cassano sells pizza chain to Greyhound Food Management.
1989: Victor Cassano Jr. and Randy Leasher acquire Cassano's.
2000: Leasher pleads guilty to embezzlement.
2014: Plans are made to open third co-branded unit with London Bobby's Fish and Chips.

TURNAROUND IN THE NINETIES

Cassano's began to turn around during the second half of the 1990s. In 1997 the chain returned to its old Cassano's Pizza King trade name after a decade of operating as Cassano's Pizza and Subs. The old mascot, a crowned waiter holding aloft a pizza pie, was also reintroduced. These steps were taken with an eye toward reestablishing the chain's roots in the Miami Valley in southwestern Ohio.

Cassano's relinquished its regional ambitions in favor of performing well in the area where it enjoyed the highest brand equity. The frozen dough business also enjoyed steady improvement. Annual sales increased to $3 million in 1998. Cassano's completed the decade by introducing the Cassano's Pizza Express format. With a smaller footprint than traditional Cassano's restaurants, it was designed for use in gas stations and convenience stores and such nontraditional locations as bowling centers and hotels.

CO-OWNER PLEADS GUILTY: 2000

In May 2000 Cassano's announced that co-owner Leasher had left the company but offered no explanation. The reason for his departure soon became known when Leasher was arrested for embezzling money from the company. Later in 2000, he pleaded guilty to embezzling more than $700,000 since 1994. He had written checks for travel expenses and country club dues and pocketed money that paid for imaginary store promotions. Leasher also pressured a Cassano's vendor to engage in a scheme in which Leasher paid for advertising that was not done, and the money kicked back to him was from the vendor's personal account.

In the end, Leasher was sentenced to three years in prison on two felony counts. Cassano Jr. became the sole owner of the Cassano's pizza chain. He was determined to avoid some of the mistakes his father had

made. After determining that his children, daughter Lora Cassano Hammons and sons Victor "Chip" Cassano III and Chris Cassano, were interested in eventually taking over the business, he began working with professional succession managers in 2000.

They developed a 10-year plan for his retirement and for turning over the reins to his children. In the meantime, his own father neared the end of his life; he passed away in 2002 at the age of 79. The third generation of the Cassano family played an important role in expanding the Cassano's chain in the first decade of the 21st century. All of the pizza ovens were upgraded. New menu items were added, including a Mexican pizza, pizza box nachos, and a flatbread called the Cassini Sandwich.

At the urging of Chris Cassano, the company expanded its dough manufacturing facility, and within two years frozen dough accounted for 15 percent of total revenues. Cassano's also improved its delivery and takeout business. A small call center was established to take food orders from four stores. In 2004 it was replaced by a $1 million, 35-desk call center that could serve the entire chain with a single phone number. The high-tech system also provided real-time tracking from the moment a pizza entered the oven until it reached the customer's door.

CASSANO JR. DIES: 2010

Cassano's was able to once again pursue new store openings. In the spring of 2005 the company unveiled a new flagship store and prototype. At 2,600 square feet, it offered seating for 80 and an outdoor patio, as well as such amenities as televisions and Wi-Fi Internet access. As the first decade of the new century came to an end, Cassano's replaced many stores with the new prototype and opened a few new locations.

Additionally, the company invested more than $1 million to increase frozen dough production. The succession plan developed by Cassano Jr. also played out. In May 2010, just one month before the transition to new leadership was to be completed, Cassano died unexpectedly from natural causes. The loss of Cassano was a shock to the family and employees. However, because of his commitment to a succession plan, there was little adverse impact on the company and plans that were already in place were executed.

Later in 2010 frozen Cassano's pizzas for home baking became available for sale over the Internet. A new co-branded restaurant opened in November 2010 that combined the Cassano's menu with another family-owned concept, London Bobby's Fish and Chips. A second Cassano's location added the London Bobby's menu in 2012. Two years later plans were made for a third London Bobby's.

Whether more co-branded units were to follow or the Cassano's chain might once again attempt to spread beyond Ohio's Miami Valley remained to be seen. With Chip Cassano serving as chief executive officer and his younger brother Chris acting as president, Cassano's appeared determined to at least maintain its place as a major pizza chain in its home market.

Ed Dinger

PRINCIPAL DIVISIONS

Cassano's Signature Dough.

PRINCIPAL COMPETITORS

Domino's Pizza Inc.; Marions Pizza, Inc.; Pizza Hut, Inc.

FURTHER READING

Irwin, Stephanie. "Cassano's Cooking Up a Comeback." *Dayton Daily News*, April 17, 2005.

Long, Delores. "GFM Takes Cassano's for Its Potential." *Restaurant Business*, September 20, 1986.

McCall, Ken. "Vic Cassano Jr. Dies at 65, Remembered for Saving Pizza Chain." *Dayton Daily News*, May 31, 2010.

Roberson, Jason. "Founder of Kettering, Ohio–Based Pizza Chain Dies at 79." *Dayton Daily News*, January 2, 2002.

Robinson, Amelia. "Iconic Dayton Restaurant Celebrates Being 'King' 60 Years." *Dayton Daily News*, June 19, 2014.

Stephens, Caleb. "A Taste of Tradition." *Dayton Business Journal*, August 26, 2002.

Thompson, Julie. "Former Cassano's Executive Guilty." *Dayton Business Journal*, November 1, 2000.

The Christian Science Publishing Society

———■———

1 Norway Street
Boston, Massachusetts 02115
U.S.A.
Telephone: (617) 450-2000
Fax: (617) 450-2031
Web site: http://www.csmonitor.com

Nonprofit Organization
Incorporated: 1897
Employees: 320
Sales: $18.2 million (2013)
NAICS: 511110 Newspaper Publishers; 519110 News Syndicates; 519130 Internet Publishing and Broadcasting and Web Search Portals

■ ■ ■

The Christian Science Publishing Society is the nonprofit, independently run media arm of the First Church of Christ, Scientist, better known as Christian Science, a Boston-based religious sect that stresses spiritual healing. The Publishing Society is best known for its flagship venture, the *Christian Science Monitor*, a well-respected international daily newspaper that since its inception in 1908 has won numerous journalism awards. With the decline of the print journalism industry, the daily print version of the newspaper ceased publication in 2009, converting to a digital daily news service and weekly magazine format. The society continues to publish the works of church founder Mary

Baker Eddy and several other news and church periodicals.

EARLY YEARS

The founder of the Publishing Society, Mary Baker Eddy, was born Mary Morse Baker in 1821 and raised on a New Hampshire farm. She took the last name Eddy in 1877 after marrying her third husband, Asa Gilbert Eddy. As a child she suffered from an unknown nervous disorder that caused hysterical seizures and prevented her from attending school on a regular basis. Instead, she was educated by her older brother, Albert, who taught her Hebrew, Greek, and Latin.

Eddy also took to writing poetry, and at a young age had her work appearing in periodicals. As a young adult she continued to endure tribulations with her father. At the age of 21 she married builder George Washington Glover and moved to Charleston, South Carolina. Shortly after she became pregnant, her husband died from an illness, forcing her to return to New Hampshire, impoverished, to give birth to a son, whom she would eventually have to give up.

Continuing to suffer from nervous disorders and bouts of depression, which led to an abiding interest in methods of healing, Mary married in 1853 a homeopath and dentist named Daniel Patterson. Nine years later, at the outbreak of the Civil War, she was once again visited by misfortune. Patterson, visiting the Bull Run battlefield, was captured by Confederate troops and sent to a prison camp. Once again, Eddy was destitute and forced to return home to live with her family as an invalid. Now 40 years old, she reached a turning point.

EDDY CURED BY HEALER

Eddy turned to a Portland, Maine, mental healer, Dr. Phineas Parkhurst Quimby, who within three weeks cured her, essentially relying on the power of suggestion. Raised in a Congregational church in New Hampshire, she viewed through a religious prism Quimby's system, which assumed that disease had a mental rather than physical cause. Her own beliefs were then crystallized in 1866, when bedridden from a fall, she reported experiencing a revelation after three days of intensely reading the Bible.

She was instantly cured by what she called "Christian Science" and became completely devoted to promoting the truths that had been revealed to her. Namely, that physical matter was illusory, and that to be well one had to come into harmony with the infinite Mind as revealed through Jesus Christ. Within a few years, Eddy had a group of followers and a number of practitioners who performed healing. Her beliefs were codified with the 1875 publication of *Science and Health*. The original title, *Science of Life*, was found to be already in use. Friends George Barry and Elizabeth Newhall financially backed the publication.

For the rest of her life Eddy continually revised and expanded the book. It took its place alongside the Bible as an essential study aide for the First Church of Christ, Scientist, which she headed and which she and her followers founded in Boston in 1879. The church's present form dates to 1892, when it was reorganized. By the time of her death in 1910, combined editions of *Science and Health*, which targeted an educated middle-class audience, sold approximately 400,000 copies. It also made Eddy wealthy and a celebrity.

CHURCH BEGINS PUBLISHING

In 1883 the Christian Scientist Association established the Christian Scientist Publishing Company, and under Eddy's influence it became involved in publishing magazines. Its first periodical was the *Journal of Christian Science*, which made its debut in April 1883 and was at first mostly written and edited by Eddy. In 1885 the publication assumed its present name, the *Christian Science Journal*.

Unlike *Science and Health*, the *Journal* was meant to appeal to lower-income, less-educated readers, presenting Christian Science tenets in digestible form through testimonials, anecdotes, and letters to and from the editor. In 1890 Eddy established another monthly magazine, *Christian Science Bible Lessons*, to provide weekly Bible lessons for church services and individual study. It was subsequently cut back to a quarterly publication basis and renamed *Christian Science Quarterly*.

It was also in 1890 that the church printed a four-page leaflet of hymns, published by an entity called the Christian Science Publishing Society. In 1897 the Publishing Society was incorporated and obtained a state charter. In January 1898 the corporation sold all of its assets to Eddy, the corporation was dissolved, and she subsequently set up the current Publishing Society as a deed of trust.

The deed also provided independence for the three trustees of the society, an arrangement that would become a matter of controversy in the years following Eddy's death. Later in 1898 the *Christian Science Weekly* (soon renamed the *Christian Science Sentinel*) was founded. *Der Herold der Christian Science* premiered in 1903, a monthly or quarterly magazine of articles and testimonies of healing originally published in German.

MONITOR TAKES SHAPE

The Christian Science Publishing Society's best-known product, its daily newspaper, the *Christian Science Monitor*, was established in 1908 at the behest of Eddy, who despite having retired from active involvement in the running of the church nearly 20 years earlier still held considerable sway in the church. She had entertained thoughts of starting a newspaper for some 25 years, disturbed by the tawdry yellow journalism practiced at the time.

In 1906, at the age of 86, she and the rapidly emerging Christian Science church became the victim of that excess when Joseph Pulitzer's *New York World* launched a scathing crusade against her and *McClure's Magazine* published a virulent profile of Eddy. Suggesting that the wealthy elderly woman was either senile and

```
┌─────────────────────────────────────────┐
│                                         │
│            KEY DATES                    │
│              ■                          │
│  ─────────────────────────────────────  │
│  1875:  Mary Baker Eddy publishes the first edition
│         of Science and Health.
│  1897:  The Christian Science Publishing Society is
│         incorporated.
│  1898:  The Publishing Society assets are sold to
│         Eddy, the corporation is dissolved, and a deed
│         of trust is established.
│  1908:  The Christian Science Monitor begins
│         publication.
│  1961:  Last year the Monitor is profitable.
│  1984:  Monitor Radio is established.
│  1988:  World Monitor begins publication.
│  1996:  Official Monitor Web site goes online.
│  1997:  Monitor Radio ceases operation.
│  2009:  Christian Science Monitor ceases publication as
│         a daily newspaper.
│  2014:  The Monitor announces a Web site overhaul
│         and new focus on a more interactive news
│         service.
└─────────────────────────────────────────┘
```

being used by others, or was simply dead and replaced by an impostor, the *World* was not merely satisfied with making lurid claims.

It managed to persuade her son to sue for control of her estate, which led to a sensational trial in 1907. Although an interview with court-appointed officials short-circuited the suit, Eddy was clearly upset by her treatment in the press. Another important factor in her decision to launch a newspaper was a letter she received from John L. Wright in March 1908. A journalist as well as Christian Scientist, he made the case that there was a deep need for a truly independent newspaper that would be "fair, frank and honest with the people on all subjects and under whatever pressure."

On July 28, 1908, she sent a letter to the directors of the church, followed by an August 8 note to the trustees of the Publishing Society, stating, "It is my request that you start a daily newspaper at once, and call it the *Christian Science Monitor*. Let there be no delay. The Cause demands that it be issued now." Despite the misgivings of the directors and trustees, Eddy's request was fulfilled in an astonishingly short time.

FIRST ISSUE PUBLISHED: 1908

On November 25, 1908, the first issue of the *Monitor* was published, reflecting considerable direct input from Eddy herself. She was consulted about the type to be used and instructed that a better-quality paper be used. She also chose the publication's motto, "First the blade, then the ear, then the full grain in the ear," and she decided where it would be placed. Eddy also defeated attempts to find a more commercial name for the newspaper.

On the editorial page of the first issue she offered an insight into the naming of all the Publishing Society's major periodicals, "The first was *The Christian Science Journal*, designed to put on record the divine Science of Truth; the second I entitled *Sentinel*, intended to hold guard over Truth, Life and Love; the third, *Der Herold der Christian Science*, to proclaim the universal activity and availability of Truth; the next I named *Monitor*, to spread undivided the Science that operates unspent. The object of *The Monitor* is to injure no man, but to bless all mankind."

Aside from the mention of Christian Science in its title, and one religious article that would run each day, the newspaper quickly gained a reputation for its independence and journalistic integrity and soon became a thriving enterprise. Eddy died in 1910 and without her presence the trustees of the Publishing Society and the directors of the church came into conflict. What became known as the Great Litigation lasted from 1917 to 1921, initiated after the trustees sued to stop the directors from interfering with their running of the Publishing Society.

At issue legally was whether Eddy's 1898 trust deed granted the trustees and the Publishing Society authority independent of the directors. Most Christian Scientists supported the directors, firmly believing the Publishing Society should unquestionably serve the needs of the church. In the end, however, the courts agreed with the trustees' position that Eddy clearly intended a double, balancing power structure between the two entities.

WORLD LANGUAGE PUBLICATIONS

With the litigation settled, the Publishing Society continued to publish the works of Eddy and the periodicals she was so instrumental in founding. The *Herald*, which began publishing a French edition in 1918, added other languages over the years, including the Scandinavian languages in 1930, Dutch in 1931, Spanish in 1946, Japanese and Indonesian in 1962, and Greek in 1964. *Christian Science Quarterly* also expanded to more than a dozen languages over the years. The *Sentinel* changed formats in the 1940s, eschewing its original broadsheet presentation for a digest size that became extremely popular.

The *Monitor*, in the meantime, became the Publishing Society's most visible face to the world. It grew into an award-winning newspaper, ironically receiving a number of Pulitzer Prizes, endowed by Eddy's former tormentor, Joseph Pulitzer. Rather than rely heavily on wire services for international coverage, the *Monitor* maintained correspondents around the world as well as throughout the United States.

From a financial point of view the *Monitor* peaked in the 1950s, after which the growth of television, rising production costs, and the expense of maintaining an international operation made it impossible for the newspaper to turn a profit. Starting in 1962 it began operating at a loss, subsidized by the Publishing Society. By the mid-1970s the *Monitor* deficit reached $8 million, resulting in cutbacks that led to the resignation of a number of senior writers.

INSTITUTING A NEW MEDIA STRATEGY

In 1982 John Hoagland joined the Publishing Society as manager and developed a strategy of extending the *Monitor* brand to radio and television, with financial support from the church. On the radio side, the Publishing Society established Monitor Radio in 1984, producing a one-hour weekend program distributed by National Public Radio. In October 1985 a daily show was introduced, with an early edition added in July 1989.

A short-wave radio program was initiated in March 1987 with facilities located in Maine, South Carolina, and Saipan. From 1983 to 1985 the Publishing Society produced pilots for what became a 30-minute television news program relying on the *Monitor*'s news-gathering network. The show finally premiered in September 1988. The Publishing Society purchased Boston television station WQTV in 1986 with the original intent of operating it on a commercial basis.

The strategy resulted in a larger audience share than anticipated and led to the investment of $14 million in syndicated programming. Management then decided to change course and converted WQTV into a noncommercial, public service station, essentially making it a laboratory for an even grander vision, the Monitor Channel, a cable television service.

Not only was most of the syndicated programming shelved at the cost of $10 million, the Publishing Society had to buy out the contract of a high-priced consultant who had been hired to advise the station on commercial operations. Moreover, the executives involved in the nascent television operations were spending in a manner that was quite lavish in comparison to the way the Publishing Society traditionally had operated.

WORLD MONITOR LAUNCHES: 1988

In 1988 the Publishing Society launched a news magazine, *World Monitor*, taking on such entrenched competition as *Time* and *Newsweek*. A nightly cable news program, *World Monitor*, also debuted in September of that year. As a result of its rapid accumulation of media operations, the Publishing Society and the church faced a severe financial crunch. Although the *Monitor* remained the flagship product, on whose brand all the other ventures were dependent, it was the newspaper that was forced to hike its subscription price and accept cuts, while at the same time money was poured into television.

According to Hoagland, the Publishing Society was committed to publishing the *Monitor* at a deficit, "But television will have to prove itself." Staff reductions as well as scaling back the size of the *Monitor* did not sit well with some of the newspaper's top editors, who in December 1988 resigned in protest. Several prominent staff writers soon joined them. Although the circulation of the *Monitor* fell following the changes, its losses also dropped. Nevertheless, this relative improvement did little to compensate for the mounting investments in the other media ventures.

Furthermore, the Publishing Society elevated its television aspirations, deciding to launch a 24-hour, satellite-based cable programming network. In essence the directors of the church and the trustees of the Publishing Society were gambling that television would turn profitable before they were pressured to back off. Because of Christian Scientists' beliefs, the service refused to accept pharmaceutical- or alcohol-related commercials, which handicapped its chances from the outset.

MONITOR BROADCASTING GOES DARK

By March 1992 the situation reached a tipping point, following press reports that the church had borrowed $41.5 million from an employee pension fund and another $5 million from its trustee endowment. This had been done in order to keep afloat its television operations, which were consuming $1 million a week and already had cost the church and Publishing Society a total of $250 million.

Despite protestations from officials that the Monitor Channel remained on track to become profitable by 1996, prominent church members pressured several leaders to resign, the syndicated news was canceled, and the cable service put up for sale. The *Monitor* and *World Monitor* were not affected, but WQTV was sold in 1993, while on the radio side the weekend program came to an end in June 1996 and, later, the daily shows were terminated as well. The short-wave radio facilities were eventually sold, leaving a limited slate of religious short-wave radio programming.

Several years passed before the Publishing Society and the church recovered from their move into television. It was not until July 1998 that the church was able to repay the pension funds. The *Monitor*'s circulation, which fell to a low of 75,000 in 1997 for a loss of 100,000 since 1988, rebounded to 90,000 in 1998.

To help the newspaper stage a comeback, the Publishing Society renovated its newsroom and invested $500,000 in a national ad campaign. The *Monitor* also underwent a redesign, an attempt to appeal to a wider audience, and even looked into the possibility of home delivery rather than rely on the postal service. The *Sentinel* also was redesigned in 1998.

CONVERSION TO DIGITAL

The early years of the new century were dominated for the *Monitor*, as they were for most other news agencies, by the dawning realization that consumption of traditional print journalism had begun to dwindle. Increasingly, the public was obtaining its news from the Internet for free. During this period, the *Monitor* saw a marked decrease in paid subscriptions, down to 70,000 by 2004. The society's other publications saw less dramatic drops, but had always been marketed primarily to church members, thus accounting for a much smaller portion of the company's income than the more mainstream *Monitor*.

While print circulation decreased, the *Monitor* Web site saw a steady increase in traffic with several million individual site visits per month. When Richard C. Bergenheim became the newspaper's editor-in-chief in May 2005, he immediately focused his efforts on cutting costs and finding ways to convert the *Monitor*'s growing online readership into a comparable revenue stream. Advertising sales on the site simply were not paying the bills.

Cutting costs involved, among other measures, cutting about a dozen positions from the paper's 102-person editorial staff. At the same time, Bergenheim reorganized the 26-person publishing staff, actually adding several positions. Bergenheim left his position in 2008 to become overall head of the First Church of Christ Scientist. His replacement, John Yemma, would

see the *Monitor* through perhaps the most significant transition in its history. Near the end of October 2008, in the midst of the paper's centennial year, the society announced that the *Christian Science Monitor* would cease publication as a daily print newspaper the following April.

Subscriptions had dropped to around 50,000. The paper was projected to bring in just $12.5 million in revenue for the fiscal year, against operating costs of $25.8 million. As it had for years, the church made up the shortfall with an endowment. The *Monitor* continued print publication as a weekly magazine digest, but the company's Web site would serve as its primary outlet. The move seemed risky.

BENEFITING FROM RECESSION

Although the paper saved significantly on printing and shipping costs, revenue from online advertising was still not sufficient to offset the lost subscription income. Subscriptions to the weekly magazine ran $89 per year in comparison to the $219 rate for the daily paper. The paper also offered a digital subscription version of the magazine for $5.75 per month. Ironically, the *Monitor* arguably benefited in some ways from the overall decline of print media and the global recession, which occurred around the same time.

As many U.S. news agencies reduced their overseas staffing and reportage to cut costs, the *Monitor* largely held steady in its international reporting. Some analysts felt this factor enabled the agency to attract a readership interested in quality coverage of world events. "We think that's an opening for the Monitor as the world contracts and becomes more interdependent," managing publisher Jonathan Wells told *Advertising Age* in November 2009, adding, "We've got a journalistic enterprise that someone couldn't create in their garage tomorrow."

The *Monitor*, and the Christian Science Publishing Society as a whole, now focused on four sources of revenue. The weekly *Monitor* and *Sentinel*, the monthly *Herald* and *Journal*, as well as the church's *Quarterly* publication all continued to generate subscription dollars and advertising income. The society also sold much of its published content to various news syndicates. Finally, there was the relatively new stream of Web advertising revenue. It was this last source that became the society's largest source of income. In 2012 the society launched a combined Web site that brought its other periodicals to the Web for the first time.

DIGITAL SUCCESS

By 2013 traffic at the *Monitor*'s Website had surged to around 50 million page views per month, a 10-fold increase in just four years. This increase, attributed to the *Monitor*'s new emphasis on digital journalism and its reputation for quality international reporting and analysis, had attracted more advertisers and higher ad rates. During this period, Web ad revenue increased an average of 24 percent per year for several years running.

Print circulation of the weekly *Monitor* had stabilized at around 50,000 with an additional 6,800 digital subscribers. In the summer of 2014 the *Monitor* announced a plan to overhaul the look and feel of its Web site in an effort to attract more readers and maintain their loyalty. One aspect of this plan was the Take Action initiative, in which the paper sought to augment coverage of long-running or complex news stories with Web site content designed to engage readers further.

Stories might contain links to deeper coverage or sites where readers could take action regarding a particular issue or organize activities with other readers interested in the same topic. At the same time it was adding content, the *Monitor* was determined to give its site a less cluttered, more welcoming feel. The move to digital publishing seemed to have come at the right time for the Christian Science Publishing Society.

Web advertising had finally begun to replace much of the lost print subscription revenue. The company still had work to do, however. Although revenues had reached $18 million by the end of 2013, operating costs in excess of $20 million meant that the society was still reliant on subsidies from its parent church to remain in business.

Ed Dinger
Updated, Chris Herzog

PRINCIPAL OPERATING UNITS

Christian Science Monitor; *Christian Science Quarterly*; *Christian Science Journal*; *Christian Science Sentinel*; *Herald of Christian Science*.

PRINCIPAL COMPETITORS

Graham Holdings Company; The New York Times Company; The Tribune Media Company.

FURTHER READING

Canham, Erwin D. *Commitment to Freedom: The Story of the Christian Science Monitor*. Boston: Houghton Mifflin Company, 1958.

Fuller, Linda K. *The Christian Science Monitor: An Evolving Experiment in Journalism*. Santa Barbara, CA: Praeger, 2011.

Gill, Gillian. *Mary Baker Eddy*. Reading, MA: Perseus Books, 1998.

Hiltzik, Michael A., and Tiffany Hsu. "Monitor to Discontinue Daily Print Edition." *Los Angeles Times*, October 29, 2008.

Hirschman, David. "So What Do You Do, John Yemma, Editor of *The Christian Science Monitor*?" *Mediabistro*, March 31, 2010.

Ives, Nat. "What Life Is Like for Titles after They Leave Print." *Advertising Age*, November 16, 2009.

Peel, Robert. *Mary Baker Eddy: The Years of Authority*. New York: Holt, Rinehart and Winston, 1977.

Skodzinski, Noelle. "Christian Science Monitor Launches Multiphase Strategy for Growth." *mediaShepherd*, June 18, 2014.

Thompson, Mike. "Digital First." *EContent*, April 2013.

Commercial Contracting
Group, Inc.

—————————■—————————

4260 North Atlantic Boulevard
Auburn Hills, Michigan 48326
U.S.A.
Telephone: (248) 209-0500
Fax: (248) 209-0501
Web site: http://www.cccnetwork.com

Private Company
Incorporated: 1946
Sales: $304 million (2012)
NAICS: 238290 Other Building Equipment Contractors

■ ■ ■

Commercial Contracting Group, Inc. (CCG) is an Auburn, Hills, Michigan–based company that through its subsidiaries provides a variety of services for North American manufacturers. The flagship operation is Commercial Contracting Corporation (CCC). The installation division of CCC installs production equipment for both new plants and retooling projects. CCC's construction division offers general contracting, design-build, concrete construction, engineering, and steel fabrication services, as well as facilities management services. Canadian Commercial Contracting (CCC-Canada) offers full-service equipment installation services in Canada, while Commercial Contracting de Mexico (CCM) is the largest equipment installation contractor in Mexico. CCG companies have long served the automotive industry. Other markets include chemical and petroleum, food processing, health care, pharmaceutical, airports, and post offices and parcel

sorting centers. CCG is also involved in a joint venture, Tooles Contracting Group, LLC, a Minority Business Enterprise company that offers a full range of general contracting and equipment installation services. CCG is owned by the Pettibone family. Brothers Michael L. Pettibone and William H. Pettibone Jr. serve as cochairmen.

WORLD WAR II–ERA ORIGINS

The Commercial Contracting Corporation grew out of a company called Commercial Carriers Corporation, a company established in 1940 to haul new vehicles from Detroit manufacturing plants to dealerships across the country. The United States would soon be caught up in World War II, which was already raging in Europe and the Pacific. CCC's automaker clients dropped new car production in order to support the war effort by building airplanes, tanks, jeeps, and other vehicles needed by the military. In 1942 Commercial Carriers Corporation created a new unit, Commercial Contracting Corporation. It was hired by General Motors (GM) to remove car manufacturing equipment from its plants, primarily the Buick plant in Flint, Michigan, in order to begin building war materials.

The CCC division was sold after the war to partners Andrew D. "Don" Beveridge and William H. Pettibone. In January 1946 the two incorporated the company, with Beveridge owning a 60 percent controlling interest and serving as president, while Pettibone held a 40 percent stake and the title of vice president. Beveridge also became well known as a top American polo player with the Detroit CCC team, which won numerous national championships in the 1950s.

The services of CCC were much in demand after the war, as Detroit automakers returned to car production and contracted CCC to reinstall the necessary production equipment. In addition, CCC was contracted by the government to store the weapon-making equipment in the event it would be needed in a future emergency. Thus, CCC established "mothballing" warehouses and maintained the equipment, so that if necessary it could be reinstalled and operational in a matter of weeks.

CCC gained wider recognition in 1961, when it won a $9 million equipment installation contract from Chrysler for the automaker's new stamping plant in Sterling Heights, Michigan. CCC's success with this high-cost, high-profile contract led to a succession of installation projects from other major automakers over the years, including BMW, Ford, GM, Honda, Mercedes-Benz, Nissan, Saturn, Toyota, and Volkswagen. CCC prospered as a union company, employing operating engineers, ironworkers, millwrights, and other skilled tradesmen, as well as laborers.

PETTIBONE BUYS OUT BEVERIDGE: 1961

Also in 1961 Pettibone bought out Beveridge to become the sole owner of CCC. His sons Michael and William joined the company as well and ultimately inherited control of the company and shared the chairmanship. With its work with automakers serving as a calling card, Bill Pettibone was able to expand CCC into other industrial sectors and take on jobs across the country. The company won equipment installation contracts in glass manufacturing, food processing, power, and steel.

CCC's ties to automakers took the company into Mexico to help set up new auto plants. In 1981 CCC installed the equipment for the GM Saltillo Engine Plant. Other jobs in the country would follow, and in 1997 CCC formed Commercial Contracting de Mexico (CCM). The subsidiary operated across the country and became Mexico's largest equipment installation contractor. CCM assembled an array of construction equipment and added in-house fabrication capabilities to become a full-service operation.

CCC also expanded to the north in 1981, forming Canadian Commercial Contracting (CCC-Canada). Although CCC-Canada maintained its headquarters in Auburn Hills, Michigan, it was fully registered and compliant with all Canadian regulations. The unit was an equipment installation contractor, offering a full range of project management and construction services. Like its sister companies, CCC-Canada primarily worked for automakers and truck manufacturers. It completed projects for DaimlerChrysler, Ford, Freightliner, GM, and Toyota. CCC-Canada would also win contracts with multinational manufacturers in other industries.

PULTE CONSTRUCTION ACQUIRED: 1999

CCG reached a watershed moment in its history in 1999. In April of that year, it acquired Troy, Michigan–based Pulte Construction Company. As a result, CCC was able to offer clients turnkey solutions. Not only could the company install equipment, it could now build concrete foundations and complete other related construction projects. Pulte laid the foundation for CCC's construction division and its expansion into other areas of large-scale construction and general contracting work. In June 2002 the Pulte Construction name was retired, and the operation officially became the Construction Division of CCC.

By the late 1990s CCC had outgrown its longtime headquarters in Troy and was scouting for a new location. The company finally settled on Auburn Hills and construction on a new facility began in 1999. Sweetening the move was a tax break provided to the company from the government of Auburn Hills. The CCG divisions moved into the $3 million, 77,000-square-foot headquarters in April 2000.

Business in Mexico also expanded during the 1990s. CCM's main office was located in Chihuahua, Mexico, but it was just a temporary location and the company looked for a permanent home. In 2001 the subsidiary moved into its new headquarters in Saltillo, Coahuila, Mexico. Much of CCM's focus early in the first decade of the 21st century was on an 18-month project preparing an engine plant for GM in Silao, Guanajuato, Mexico.

CC RESPONDS TO OKLAHOMA CITY TORNADO: 2003

At the turn of the new century, CCC continued to serve the needs of perennial automotive customers Ford, DaimlerChrysler, and GM. The company also picked up

KEY DATES

1940: Commercial Carriers Corporation is established.
1946: Commercial Contracting Group, Inc., is formed by Don Beveridge and William Pettibone.
1961: Pettibone buys out Beveridge.
1999: Company moves headquarters to Auburn Hills, Michigan.
2013: Company wins contracts from the University of Michigan.

new clients in a variety of industries. They included Awrey Bakery, Marathon Oil, National Steel, and Parkdale Pharmaceuticals. Although the company was mostly involved in long-term projects, CCC was ready to help in the summer of 2003 when a tornado devastated Oklahoma City and caused major damage to a GM plant. Each day the plant was out of operation cost GM millions of dollars. Quickly, CCC brought in 200 workers to reopen the plant. With the crisis averted, CCC was able to return its focus to regular projects, including a model changeover for a DaimlerChrysler assembly plant in Delaware, and installation contracts for GM plants in Kansas City and Lordstown, Ohio. GM not only demonstrated its appreciation for CCG's work by awarding more contracts, the automaker named CCG its 2006 Supplier of the Year Award for overall business performance.

CCG had long been known for its use of minority-owned companies as subcontractors. For several years, CCG worked closely with African American businessman Damon Tooles. The former stockbroker and commodities trader had drifted into the construction field through Detroit real estate developer Dwight Belyue. Eventually, CCG divisions began subcontracting with Tooles's Signature Industrial and Commercial Painting LLC. The Pettibone brothers and Tooles realized that they shared similar business philosophies, and they decided to form a joint venture. In 2006 they acquired BrixCom Construction LLS, which was renamed Tooles Contracting Group LLC. Because Tooles owned a 51 percent controlling share and CCG the remaining 49 percent, it was designated a Minority Business Enterprise.

Tooles Contracting served as an equipment installation, construction management, and general contractor. One of its first projects was to serve as the project

manager for the @water Lofts development project on the east riverfront in Detroit. Other clients included Ford, GM, DTE Energy Co., and Federal Express. The company also did preconstruction work on the Motor-City Casino that led to Tooles Contracting opening an office in Las Vegas in September. CCC already operated a satellite office in southern Nevada as a way to diversify its business, which was overly reliant on Michigan. CCC's home state was experiencing some economic difficulties, especially in the auto industry. Quickly, Tooles Contracting secured work with MGM Mirage's $8.4 billion CityCenter. The project's general contractor, Perini Building Co., was making a concerted effort to hire women-owned and minority-owned subcontracting companies.

AIRPORT BUSINESS ESTABLISHED: 2007

In addition to diversifying geographically by seeking work in southern Nevada, CCC looked to expand its client base. In 2007 the company won a contract at Hartsfield International Airport in Atlanta that provided entry into the baggage handling installation services sector. The long-term project commenced in 2009 and was completed in 2012. CCC won another airport contract in 2008, hired by the Bay County, Michigan, MBS Airport to build a new $48 million terminal building. CCC also entered the facility management services business in 2009 through its relationship with Chrysler.

The Mexico division won its share of projects as well during this period. CCM continued to do work in GM's Silao facility. In 2006 CCM was awarded a contract on the engine plant. Over the next 18 months, the company was responsible for the installation of all production machinery as well as support equipment. When that contract was completed in 2008, CCM won a yearlong transmission plant project to install all of the machining and assembly equipment needed to produce GM's six-speed rear-wheel-drive transmissions.

The effort at diversification paid off for CCG. The group was able to weather the downturn in the automotive industry in 2009 and then rebounded strongly in 2010. With all divisions performing well, CCG increased total revenues from $135 million in 2009 to more than $250 million just two years later. The trend continued in 2012 when CCG recorded revenues of $304 million.

The launch of an interiors division in 2011 helped to provide further diversification. The new business also opened the door to a wider group of clients. In May 2013, for example, CCC was awarded a contract from the University of Michigan to renovate the interior of the Union Grill in the school's historic Student Union. A second $1.21 million contract called for CCC to renovate the basement and first floor of the university's College of Pharmacy. It was perhaps the start of another long-term relationship for a company that already held deep ties with Detroit's automakers. With their repeat business as a foundation, the CCG companies looked forward to further revenue growth in the years ahead.

Ed Dinger

PRINCIPAL DIVISIONS

Commercial Contracting Corporation Installation Division; Commercial Contracting Corporation Construction Division; Canadian Commercial; Commercial Contracting de Mexico.

PRINCIPAL COMPETITORS

BECHTEL Group, Inc.; Marubeni Plant Contractor, Inc.; Turner Construction Company.

FURTHER READING

Ankeny, Robert. "Las Vegas Gamble Pays Off Big for Tooles Contracting." *Crain's Detroit Business*, December 8, 2008.

Davis, Cary. "Commercial Contracting Corporation: Champions of Adaptation and Reliability." *Frontiers*, Spring 2004.

John, Libby. "Auto Projects Drive CCC." *Construction Today*, May 2007.

Pinho, Kirk. "Upward Bound." *Crain's Detroit Business*, July 15, 2013.

Robison, Jennifer. "What's Cooking in Michigan?" *Las Vegas Review-Journal*, March 19, 2007.

Truby, Mark. "Troy OK's Firm's Move." *Detroit News*, August 17, 1999.

Cramer Cos.

153 West Warren Street
Gardner, Kansas 66030
U.S.A.
Telephone: (913) 856-7511
Toll Free: (800) 345-2231
Fax: (913) 884-5626
Web site: http://www.cramersportsmed.com

Wholly Owned Subsidiary of Performance Health Inc.
Founded: 1918
Employees: 50
Sales: $112.3 million (2009)
NAICS: 339920 Sporting and Athletic Goods Manufacturing

■ ■ ■

Doing business as Cramer Sports Medicine, Gardener, Kansas–based Cramer Cos. is a well-known provider of athletic training room supplies. Products include tapes, wraps, padding, braces and supports, analgesics, mouthpieces, and athletic trainer kits, as well as videos, books, and software. The company also develops sports-related and general medical products for the retail market. Divisions include Active Ankle Systems, a leader in ankle support products; Active Innovations, which acts as Cramer's medical division and serves the non-sports market; Stromgren Athletics, a sports medicine company that focuses on compression and protective performance apparel; and Cosom by Cramer, which offers products for physical education teachers and students. Cramer products are sold around the world through a network of distributors and dealers. Cramer Cos. is a subsidiary of Performance Health Inc., an Akron, Ohio–based physical therapy products company owned by the Connecticut private-equity firm of Gridiron Capital LLC.

FOUNDER: PHARMACIST AND ATHLETE

The man behind the Cramer name was Charles C. "Chuck" Cramer. He was born in 1892 in Gardner, Kansas, where his father ran a construction company. Unhappy with the hard labor involved in working for his father, Cramer found a job in high school with the local pharmacist and then decided to make a career of it. After graduating from high school in 1910, Cramer enrolled in a two-year pharmaceutical chemistry program at the University of Kansas.

Cramer also joined the track team as a pole vaulter. During practice in 1912, he tripped over a bench and injured his ankle. To help in the healing process, he and his roommate, fellow pharmacy student Bruce Killian, concocted their own liniment, mixing together chloroform, camphor, alcohol, and soap. Cramer did not win his next competition, as marketing material would later claim, but Cramer was still pleased with the effectiveness of his liniment.

After completing his degree, Cramer returned home, rejoined his old boss, and became a registered pharmacist. He was soon asked by a local sports coach for a liniment, prompting Cramer to continue the development of the liniment he had made at college.

The improved formula proved so popular that Cramer began formulating it at home for sale.

In 1917 he bought out the owner of the drugstore, but sales of his liniment were so strong that a year later he formed a separate company, Cramer Chemical Company, to make and sell the product to high schools and colleges. Although he continued to operate the drugstore for several more years, Cramer Chemical soon became his main interest.

COMPANY INCORPORATED: 1922

In 1922 Cramer Chemical was incorporated in the state of Kansas. In that same year, a trademark was granted to Cramer for the term *athletic*. It was a one-product company during the early years, offering only Athletic Liniment, which he cooked in his mother's kitchen and packaged in his parents' basement. Cramer personally delivered the product in a pickup truck. He received a major break in 1923, when Kansas City–based sporting goods distributor Lowe and Campbell agreed to carry Athletic Liniment.

Also that fall, the Kansas State University football coach provided Cramer with an introduction to Notre Dame football coach Knute Rockne, who purchase the "rub down" and in 1924 offered an endorsement in an advertisement for the company. With sales picking up, Cramer Chemical moved into its first permanent building in 1926. It was constructed by Cramer's father next to his parents' home. It was also designed to serve as a garage once Cramer Chemical folded, as Cramer's father blithely predicted.

Rather than fail, however, the company began to grow. Lowe and Campbell were eager to include a medicinal line in their catalog and persuaded Cramer to expand his product line. In 1929 Cramer Chemical added onto its building, and Cramer's older brother Frank joined the company as a salesman. In addition to Athletic Liniment, Frank Cramer would soon be representing foot power and rosin bags. Chuck Cramer

also began reaching out to athletic trainers and coaches to learn what kinds of products they would like. He then took the products to his old college for testing.

OLYMPIC ENDORSEMENT: 1932

In addition to liniments, balms, ointments, and antiseptic powder, the company produced its own shaving lotion for the consumer market. Also helping to raise the stature of Cramer Chemical, the U.S. Olympic track team named Chuck and Frank Cramer as its first athletic trainers in 1932. Given that the country was mired in the Great Depression, every marketing edge helped. It was only through sales to high schools that Cramer Chemical remained afloat during this period.

To reach the secondary school market, the company depended greatly on a free quarterly publication, the *First Aider*, which it began publishing in 1932. It started out as a newsletter but adopted a newspaper format by the end of the decade. In 1941 the *First Aider* began publishing installments of a book produced by Cramer Chemical, *A Training-Room Manual*, which became available as a paperback in 1945.

NEXT GENERATION GETS INVOLVED

Cramer Chemical was generating about $250,000 in annual sales by the early 1940s. After World War II, the next generation of the Cramer family became involved in the company. During the Great Depression everyone pitched in to help, including the youngest children. Chuck Cramer's son Bill joined the company in 1945. He had earned a degree in chemistry from the University of Kansas and spent a year as the athletic trainer at Kansas State Teachers College, which became known as Emporia State University.

A year later, Frank Cramer's son Jack began working at the family company as well. As a student at Kansas State University, he had served as the school's head athletic trainer. During the post–World War II era, Chuck and Frank Cramer played an important role in elevating the status of athletic trainers. In 1950 they helped to found the National Athletic Trainer's Association to teach proper treatment techniques. For the first four years, Chuck Cramer served as executive secretary.

In 1957 Cramer Chemical began offering student trainer workshops, laying a foundation for formal education in the training field. Cramer Chemical continued to evolve as athletic trainers played an increasingly important role in both amateur and professional athletics. Because many of the new products did not depend upon chemical formulations, the Cramer family

KEY DATES

1918: Chuck Cramer starts Cramer Chemical Company to sell athletic liniment.
1929: Cramer's brother Frank joins company.
1968: Company changes name to Cramer Products Inc.
2001: Company becomes employee-owned.
2013: Performance Health Inc. acquires Cramer.

decided in 1968 to change the company name to Cramer Products Inc.

Other changes were soon to follow, especially in the leadership ranks. Frank Cramer died at the age of 83 in 1971. Two years later Chuck Cramer, at 80 years old, turned over the presidency to his son Bill. By this point, annual sales had improved to about $2 million. Chuck Cramer died at the age of 91 in 1984.

EMPLOYEES ACQUIRE STAKE: 1985

Under the next generation of leadership, Cramer Products introduced a wide range of new products. In 1974 the company's Quickkick became one of sports medicine's first electrolyte replacement drinks. In 1980, as personal computers became more prevalent, Cramer Products introduced its first software product, serving both athletic trainers and coaches. By the early 1980s, however, the second generation of the Cramer family was ready to retire. The business was simply not large enough to support a third generation of family ownership, so several members on the board of directors advocated that Cramer Products be sold.

It was not a decision that was embraced by everyone in the family. The matter was finally resolved in 1985 when an employee stock ownership plan (ESOP) was established, providing a way for family members to sell 65 percent of the company's stock to the employees. By selling to an ESOP, they were able to defer the taxes on capital gains. Cramer Products was highly regarded among athletic trainers but little known to the general public. In order to increase sales, the company decided to pursue the retail market and seek out an endorsement from a prominent athlete.

Although management believed it was unlikely they could meet his price, Cramer Products contacted the representatives of Bo Jackson, who was both a star football and baseball player and had become a market-

ing juggernaut through his association with Nike. To their surprise, Cramer executives learned that Jackson was interested in becoming involved in a sports-related venture beyond a mere endorsement. The result was the Bo Med line of sports medicine products introduced in retail stores in 1990.

ROGGE BECOMES CEO: 1991

Shortly after the launch of Bo Med, Jackson suffered a severe hip injury. Following hip replacement surgery, he attempted to resume his baseball career and managed to play only 23 games in 1991 and 85 games the following year before finally retiring. Jackson's injury also proved devastating to Cramer Products. In the fall of 1991 a new president and chief executive officer, Thomas K. Rogge, was hired.

At the time, the company still held out hope for Bo Med, but it quickly became apparent that with Jackson injured the line had lost its luster and few products were ever sold. The condition of the company was such that its accounting firm in 1992 expressed doubts about its ability to remain in business.

Under Rogge's leadership, Cramer Products returned the focus to its core business. About one-quarter of the workforce was laid off to cut costs, and new products were added to generate additional income. The measures worked, and in 2001 Cramer Products was able to pay off the debt incurred with the launch of Bo Med. Moreover, the ESOP was able to purchase the remaining 35 percent interest in the company, also bringing an end to Cramer family involvement in the company.

GROWTH THROUGH ACQUISITIONS

Cramer was once again ready to make an attempt to expand into new markets. Rather than start new product lines, the company pursued an acquisition strategy. In 2004 it acquired Cosom Sporting Goods, a New Jersey–based manufacturer of physical education equipment. Cramer had actually been selling physical education equipment to elementary schools since the 1980s, but the addition of Cosom greatly expanded the business.

Cramer then acquired Active Ankle Inc. in 2008, adding a well-respected line of athletic ankle braces. Cramer also made a commitment to new product development, aided in large measure by an athletic trainers advisory council that suggested improvements to existing products as well as new product ideas. The company also kept an eye out for suitable companies to acquire.

In 2011 Cramer purchased Stromgren Athletics, a Hays, Kansas–based maker of sports medicine, compression, and protective performance apparel. In 2013 Cramer Products itself became an acquisition target. An agreement was reached to sell the business to Akron, Ohio–based Performance Health Inc. for an undisclosed amount. Cramer Products became Cramer Cos., but it remained an independent operation in Gardner, Kansas, under Rogge's direction.

Rogge had been considering retirement, but stayed on to help with the transition to new ownership. Finally, in August 2014, he decided the time was right to leave. It was the beginning of a new era for a company that was approaching its centennial. Still well-regarded in the athletic training field, and bolstered by a wider range of products and markets to serve, Cramer appeared well-positioned for the future.

Ed Dinger

PRINCIPAL DIVISIONS

Active Ankle Systems; Cosom by Cramer; Stromgren Athletics.

PRINCIPAL COMPETITORS

McDavid Inc.; Mueller Sports Medicine Inc.; 3M Company.

FURTHER READING

"Cramer Products Buys Stromgren Athletics." *Kansas City Business Journal*, June 17, 2011.

"Cramer Products Will Buy PE Equipment-Maker." *Kansas City Business Journal*, May 3, 2004.

Dornbrook, James. "Acquisition Braces Cramer Products for Run on Growth." *Kansas City Business Journal*, July 6, 2008.

———. "Cramer Products Gets Back on Top of Its Game after Long Rehab." *Kansas City Business Journal*, October 1, 2006.

———. "Cramer Products Sells to BioFreeze Producer." *Kansas City Business Journal*, August 8, 2013.

Webber, Matt. *Dropping the Bucket and Sponge: A History of Early Athletic Training*. Prescott, AZ: Athletic Training History Publishing, 2013.

Deutsche Presse-Agentur GmbH

Mittelweg 38
Hamburg, 20148
Germany
Telephone: (+49 40) 4113-0
Fax: (+49 40) 4113-32305
Web site: http://www.dpa.com

Private Company
Founded: 1949 as Deutsche Presse-Agentur GmbH
Employees: 1,200
Sales: EUR 82 million ($114 million) (2011)
NAICS: 519110 News Syndicates

■ ■ ■

Deutsche Presse-Agentur GmbH (DPA) is Germany's leading news agency, and one of the leading providers of newswire services in the world. DPA's basic German-language newswire service covers a broad range of subjects, including major events and politics, economic and business news, sports, culture, and lifestyle. German regional news services are produced by regional offices located in major cities. In addition to its German-language services, DPA offers international newswire services in English, Spanish, and Arabic, which are distributed to media outlets, digital content providers, and other organizations in about 100 countries.

DPA is also a leading provider of press photos, images, and illustrated charts. Its subsidiary dpa-AFX Wirtschaftsnachrichten provides real-time German financial and business news to the financial industry, companies, and the media. Headquartered in Hamburg,

DPA's central editorial team is based in Berlin. Major editorial offices abroad for the agency's foreign-language services are located in Spain, Cyprus, and Ireland. They are supplied with information by a worldwide network of more than 1,000 correspondents working from DPA offices in big cities around the globe. The agency is owned by roughly 190 German newspaper and magazine publishers, radio and TV broadcasters, and other media companies.

POSTWAR ORIGINS

The defeat of Adolf Hitler's Third Reich in Germany in May 1945 put an end to the National Socialist propaganda that had dominated the German media and public opinion for more than a decade. Immediately after the war the victorious Allied forces of France, the United Kingdom, and the United States established independent news services in each of the three occupied western German zones to provide the German media and public with information about what was happening in their country and the world.

The British occupation forces seized the communication facilities of the Naval High Command in Flensburg and moved the equipment and staff to Hamburg, where they established the German News Service. In 1947 they handed the agency over to German publishers who founded the German press service Deutscher Pressedienst (DPD). The U.S. military administration had established a news agency named Deutsche Allgemeine Nachrichten-Agentur in 1945, which started distributing news via a radio transmitter in a tent.

COMPANY PERSPECTIVES

Independent, reliable, up-to-the-minute. 24 hours a day, 365 days a year. The German Press Agency DPA is a trusted, accurate and independent provider of news with the digital and multimedia content to power the media at home and abroad. Our customers benefit from the extensive global network of correspondents and editors maintained by Germany's leading newswire. News gathering is completely free of outside influence which in turn guarantees that coverage lives up to the strict requirements of the DPA charter: This document lays down that reporting must be free of bias and unfettered by political, economic or governmental ideologies. Print media, radio stations, online and mobile communication providers in more than 100 countries rely on this journalistic excellence around-the-clock.

In October 1946 its successor, the news agency Deutsche Nachrichtenagentur (DENA), based in Bad Nauenheim near Frankfurt am Main, was licensed in the U.S.-occupied zone. German-language news services in the French-occupied zone were first provided by the Paris-based Rheina news agency. In 1947 the southwestern German news agency Südwestdeutsche Nachrichtenagentur (SÜDENA) was founded. It was taken over by an association of German newspaper publishers two years later.

FORMATION OF DPA: 1949

In August 1949, three months after the foundation of the Federal Republic of Germany, the shareholders of DENA, DPD, and SÜDENA decided to merge the three regional news agencies in West Germany to form the national newswire service Deutsche Presse-Agentur (DPA) GmbH. Set up as a private company, the agency was collectively financed by the newspaper publishers who owned it. According to DPA's charter, the share capital had to be evenly distributed between the shareholders to ensure its independence from political parties and private interests.

On September 1, 1949, the new German press agency issued its first news from company headquarters in Hamburg. Twenty days later the Allied forces declared the freedom of the German press. Within a few weeks, there were about 400 newspapers Germans could choose from.

FIRST STEPS IN POSTWAR GERMANY

Recruiting qualified staff was a big challenge because most experienced journalists had worked for the Nazi "propaganda machine." The agency hired mainly young people and trained them on the job. Office space and furniture, paper, and telephones were in short supply. By 1950, however, DPA was up and running, with a staff of 750. In addition to text-based information the agency provided image services for print publications. DPA also acquired a 33 percent stake in the German business news agency Vereinigte Wirtschaftsdienste (VWD).

DENA provided the necessary communication infrastructure for the distribution of DPA's newswire service. New technologies increased the speed at which DPA news was disseminated. Beginning in 1956 DPA's basic news service was transmitted via teletype machine. In the same year the agency launched its long-distance news-by-phone service. In 1964 the first permanent teletype line across the Atlantic Ocean went into service.

In the 1950s press photos were delivered as paper copies from the agency's photo service division in Frankfurt by railway express. Press photos of local interest were produced and distributed by DPA's regional offices. The speed of the delivery chain, from the photographer to the photo lab and from there to the local train station determined if a press photo was used by the media. Beginning in 1959 DPA distributed images of national interest via long-wave radio transmission, a step that strengthened the agency's market position.

EARLY INTERNATIONALIZATION

Initially, DPA provided its comprehensive news service mainly to German newspapers and public radio broadcasters. In 1956, however, the strategic decision was made to expand abroad by launching the agency's foreign-language services. In 1957 the agency started broadcasting its European News Service via long-wave transmitter. DPA's English-language news service was also broadcast overseas on five short-wave frequencies.

In 1960 the agency launched its newswire service for South America in Spanish and for African countries in French. Eight years later DPA started its newswire service for the Middle East in cooperation with the Egyptian news agency MENA. MENA translated DPA's English news content into Arabic and transmitted it from Cairo to the media in Middle Eastern countries. Although this cooperation became a success and was continued for a quarter century, the French-language news service was discontinued in 1975.

Parallel to its foreign-language services DPA established an extensive network of journalists abroad.

KEY DATES

1949: German news agency Deutsche Presse-Agentur is founded by newspaper publishers.
1957: European news service and the English-language news service are introduced.
1986: Global Media Services subsidiary is founded; DPA's audio and radio news services are introduced.
1988: DPA acquires image service provider Globus Kartendienst and launches its graphics service.
1999: Financial and business news subsidiary dpa-AFX Wirtschaftsnachrichten is founded.
2000: Agency's new office in Berlin is opened.
2013: DPA enters a strategic partnership with U.S. news agency Associated Press.

The agency's first correspondents outside of Germany in the 1950s reported from London, Paris, Amsterdam, Stockholm, Copenhagen, Rome, Madrid, Vienna, and Washington, D.C. In 1957 the agency also sent journalists to Moscow and Warsaw and to Beijing in 1964. At the same time DPA hired journalists from other nationalities with different professional and cultural backgrounds in their respective countries, particularly in developing countries.

EXPANSION OF FOREIGN NEWS SERVICES

By 1966 the agency's international network of correspondents covered 75 countries around the world. In the following years the agency further expanded its foreign-language news services. On the other hand, DPA cooperated with news agencies from other countries to complement its own service. Up until 1969 the British news agency Reuters was an important partner.

In 1967 DPA started cooperating with the press photo division of the U.S. news agency United Press International (UPI). Five years later UPI became DPA's new main partner for its international news service. From 1967 on DPA's basic news and photo services could be received 24 hours a day. Within two decades DPA's revenues had more than tripled, reaching about DEM 37 million by 1970.

NEW TECHNOLOGIES, IMPROVED SERVICES

The dawning age of electronic data processing radically changed the way news was produced and transmitted. It also opened up new opportunities for improving DPA's services. In 1973 the company introduced ERNA, its first electronically controlled information transmission and desktop editing system, which allowed editors to copyedit text messages displayed on a monitor at a computer terminal. The new system did not just increase the speed at which news messages could be produced.

Receiving, editing, and transmitting information was united in one process and controlled by DPA's editorial team. The new desktop system included several hundred terminals that were also installed at DPA's regional offices in the mid-1970s. The improved ERNA II system, launched in 1979, directly connected DPA's media customers with its computer network for the first time and gave the agency a competitive edge. Its new communication equipment allowed the faster transmission of more detailed information.

Text messages included full punctuation and special characters that enabled customers to retrieve and modify them on their own computer terminals. In 1979 DPA also introduced a standardized format for its news messages. From 1980 on the agency's European newswire service was available for customers around the clock. The press photos generated by the agency's regional offices were included in its nationally transmitted photo service.

In the early 1980s it took about seven minutes to transmit one image such as a press photo via the service. Beginning in 1983 images could be edited on a computer with the new "electronic picture desk." One year later DPA started setting up its electronic news database. In the mid-1980s DPA transmitted color images for the first time. A technological breakthrough followed in 1989, when images could be scanned directly from the developed film and fed into the electronic picture desk.

ADDITIONAL VENTURES AFTER 1980

The 1980s saw DPA introduce a range of new and improved services and launch new ventures. In 1981 the agency introduced a press review service and established its own economic and business news division, which continued to cooperate with German business news agency VWD. Together they launched a joint economic and business news service.

Three years later the agency introduced the dpa-Select service, which allowed customers to choose from different categories or subjects they were interested in to provide them with a customized news package. In 1986 DPA together with a number of news media publishers and agencies established Global Media Services (GMS), a provider of an extended range of editorial services.

The German newspaper service produced by GMS featured a survey of important articles and commentary from major German newspapers. The service also included sports columns, images, comic strips, and trivia. In 1987 a group of European national news agencies, including DPA, founded the European Pressphoto Agency B.V. (EPA), an international press photo service based in Frankfurt.

In 1988 DPA acquired the Hamburg-based Globus Kartendienst GmbH, a provider of info graphics and geographic maps, to German newspapers. Since 1972 DPA had distributed Globus content along with its own photo service.

LAUNCH OF DPA-AUDIO NEWS

As the demand for illustrated information increased, the renamed Globus Infografik GmbH produced charts that visualized statistical data in connection with recent events and developments, covering various political, economic, and social subjects, for the media as well as for educational institutions. With the number of commercial radio broadcasters on the rise in Germany, DPA launched dpa-Audio news service in 1986.

It contained a short message service and an hourly package of ready-to-use news reports covering recent events, politics, and sports. During the 1980s the agency gradually reduced its reliance on content from other major news agencies abroad. The cooperation between UPI and DPA ended in 1988. By 1989 DPA's international coverage was generated exclusively by its own worldwide network of correspondents. In 1994 DPA sold its stake in VWD.

In 1989 DPA, with other partner agencies, founded mecom Medien Communications-Gesellschaft mbH, a new subsidiary for satellite-based communication. DPA's technical services provider DENA consequently lost in importance and was finally shut down in 1998. By the end of the 1980s DPA's revenues had quadrupled compared to 1970, reaching DEM 142 million in 1990.

REUNIFICATION STIRS GROWTH

The sudden fall of the Berlin Wall on November 9, 1989, and the world-changing political, economic, and social developments that followed in its aftermath made the DPA news headlines for several years. Moreover, the opening of East Germany opened up a new market for DPA. In 1989 the agency concluded a distribution and technical cooperation agreement with the East German

state-controlled news agency Allgemeiner Deutscher Nachrichtendienst.

One year later DPA had acquired 41 eastern German newspapers as well as the formerly state-controlled East German TV and radio stations as new customers. In 1990, the year of the reunification of the two German states, a new editorial office in the eastern part of Berlin's city center and 14 regional news bureaus in eastern Germany were added to DPA's existing network in western Germany.

It included the head office in Hamburg, an office in Bonn, the West German capital, the image services branch office in Frankfurt, seven regional service branches, and 19 local editorial teams. DPA also acquired the newly founded eastern German press photo agency zb Zentralbild GmbH and hired eastern German journalists and technical support staff. During the 1990s DPA's revenues continued to climb, reaching more than DEM 220 million in 1998.

MOVES TO NEW OFFICES

As Berlin became the capital of the united Federal Republic of Germany in 1999, DPA moved into a larger office near the new government district. Its editorial team covered German politics and national news as well as regional news for Berlin and the surrounding state of Brandenburg. DPA's services for radio stations were also relocated to Berlin. By the late 1990s DPA was the leading news agency in Germany and an internationally respected provider of reliable information.

Newspaper publishers still made up the majority of its shareholders, owning a combined two-thirds stake in the company. Meanwhile, radio and TV broadcasters held almost one-fifth of DPA's total capital. The agency served more than 2,500 customers in about 100 countries, including 75 news agencies abroad. However, the ongoing globalization, diversification, and digitalization of the media industry and the rise of the Internet posed major challenges to the company.

GOING DIGITAL AND ONLINE

Changes in the dissemination of information on a global scale were brought about by two major factors at this time. One was the emergence of a more liberal political climate after the end of the Cold War and the dissolution of the Soviet Union in 1991. The other was the rise of the Internet in the second half of the 1990s as an easily accessible, world-spanning communication network and universal media platform. As the necessary communication infrastructure became available almost anywhere in the world at comparably low costs, more and more players entered the market for information products and services.

To keep up with the growing competitive pressure from other news agencies in Germany and abroad, DPA reorganized and strengthened its international division and extended its range of services. In the mid-1990s DPA established additional editorial teams for its world news service in Washington, D.C., and in Bangkok, Thailand, for news coverage from Asia. The agency's Spanish world news service branch was moved from Hamburg to Madrid, Spain, and Buenos Aires, Argentina.

An independent editorial team for the Arabic world news service was set up in Nikosia on Cyprus. In 2002 DPA's central international editorial office was moved to Cork in Ireland. DPA subsidiary GMS launched GMS Themendienst in 1995, which provided more in-depth coverage and background information on important events and issues.

ONLINE PORTAL LAUNCHES: 1997

The year 1997 saw the launch of DPA's Internet-based online portal, which was constantly improved in the following years. Meanwhile the agency's press photo and graphics service transitioned to fully digitalized production and data storage. In 1998 DPA acquired RUFA Rundfunk Nachrichtenagentur, a specialized news agency for radio broadcasters. The takeover strengthened the agency's audio service department, which by then delivered about 50 audio news messages per day. They were accompanied by ready-to-broadcast audio recordings of statements at press conferences and interviews.

In 1999 DPA added the news category "modern life," covering culture and lifestyle, celebrities and personalities to its basic news service. With AFX News and Austria Presse Agentur, the agency founded dpa-AFX-Wirtschaftsnachrichten GmbH, a financial and business newswire service the same year. The digital age also brought about the proliferation of images, which became ever-more important in the news business.

In 2002 DPA together with partner agencies established the dpa Picture Alliance, a subsidiary for the distribution of press photos and images. In that year, the agency's revenues generated by marketing photos and images to nonnews media exceeded the amount derived from its press news service for the first time, as reported by *General-Anzeiger* on June 27, 2003.

ADAPTING TO CHANGE

Of all news services providers competing for customers in Germany at the dawn of the 21st century, DPA's basic newswire service offered the most comprehensive coverage across subjects and geographic regions and was used by most of the country's daily newspapers. Early in the first decade of the 21st century, this service accounted for more than half of the agency's total turnover, according to *Stuttgarter Zeitung* on May 24, 2003.

Newspaper publishers whose dues to the agency were linked to their print run were DPA's main revenue source. However, as more media consumers used the Internet to get their daily news, fewer newspapers were sold and DPA's revenues declined. After several longtime customers unsubscribed from the service or threatened to do so early in the first decade of the 21st century, DPA completely reorganized its regional offices in Germany to cut costs.

In 2004 the agency introduced a new pricing scheme that substantially lowered subscription rates for bigger customers with large print runs. It also offered additional rebates to clients who signed long-term contracts with the agency. In 2007 DPA launched "dpa News for Kids," a news service designed for children with pictures, animated graphics, and podcasts. Two years later 55 German newspaper publishers subscribed to the service, according to *SDA* on November 9, 2009.

GEOCODING INTRODUCED

Another new DPA service called geocoding allowed users to find relevant news stories and images connected to a certain city or other location on a map online. In 2012 the agency introduced "dpa Insight EU," a new information service for political organizations, companies, associations, and institutions, featuring extensive coverage of European Union politics and regulations. At the frontlines of a global media landscape that was undergoing fundamental change in the second decade of the 21st century, DPA was facing the challenge to create innovative and affordable information services for its customers.

Ten years after the opening of DPA's Berlin office in 2000, all of the agency's central editorial teams started working closely together under one roof in a large open-space newsroom. Its editors produced news in exchange with journalists and editors in the media who gave them real-time feedback on what information they were interested in. In January 2013 DPA started a new strategic partnership with the U.S. news agency Associated Press.

Evelyn Hauser

PRINCIPAL SUBSIDIARIES

dpa Agencia Alemana de Prensa S.L. (Spain); dpa English Services GmbH; dpa-infocom GmbH; dpa-infografik GmbH; dpa mediatechnology GmbH; dpa news international Ltd. (Ireland); dpa Picture-Alliance GmbH; zb Fotoagentur Zentralbild GmbH; Global Media Services GmbH; dpa-AFX Wirtschaftsnachrichten GmbH (76%); AWP Finanznachrichten AG (50%); dpa-digital services GmbH (50%); news aktuell GmbH; news aktuell international GmbH; Zimpel Media-Daten GmbH; Rufa Rundfunk-Agenturdienste GmbH; mecum MedienCommunikations-Gesellschaft mbH (50%).

PRINCIPAL COMPETITORS

Agence France-Presse; Austria Presse Agentur eG; EFE; Evangelischer Pressedienst; Getty Images, Inc.; Katholische Nachrichten-Agentur; Schweizerische Depeschenagentur AG; Sport-Informations-Dienst (SID) GmbH & Co. KG; Thomson Reuters Corporation; United Press International.

FURTHER READING

"Deutsche Presse-Agentur mit weniger Umsatz und Gewinn." *General-Anzeiger*, June 27, 2003.

"Deutsche Presse-Agentur testet neuen Dienst in Lateinamerika." *SDA*, November 9, 2009.

"DPA kommt den Verlagen entgegen." *Horizont.net*, December 18, 2003.

"Dpa started Zusammenarbeit mit AP in Text und Bild." *SDA*, January 8, 2013.

"Dpa und APA uebernehmen Thomson Reuter-Anteile and dpa-AFX." *Original Text Service*, June 15, 2009.

"Goldene 90er fuer die dpa vorbei." *Horizont*, July 1, 1999.

Hardt, Matthias, ed. *DPA meldet … 50 Jahre Deutsche Presse-Agentur GmbH*. Hamburg, Germany: dpa Deutsche Presse-Agentur GmbH, 1999.

Langer, Bettina. "Was nicht über den Ticker läuft: die Sorgen der dpa." *Stuttgarter Zeitung*, May 24, 2003.

Stahr, Volker S. "Deutsche Presse Agentur; Den Erfolg nicht gepachtet." *Hamburger Abendblatt*, June 1, 2001.

DFC Global Corporation

1436 Lancaster Avenue, Suite 300
Berwyn, Pennsylvania 19312-1200
U.S.A.
Telephone: (610) 296-3400
Fax: (610) 296-7844
Web site: http://www.dfcglobalcorp.com

Private Company
Incorporated: 1979 as Monetary Management Corporation
Employees: 6,600
Sales: $1.12 billion (2013)
NAICS: 522291 Consumer Lending

■ ■ ■

DFC Global Corporation, formerly known as Dollar Financial Corporation, is a financial services company based in Berwyn, Pennsylvania, a Philadelphia suburb. DFC Global serves what it calls Asset Limited, Income Constrained, Employed (ALICE) and Asset Rich, Temporary Illiquid (ARTI) clients. The company operates a network of more than 1,500 stores in the United States and Canada as well as in the United Kingdom, Sweden, Finland, Poland, Spain, the Republic of Ireland, the Czech Republic, and Romania. DFC Global offers a variety of consumer financial products and services including unsecured short-term consumer loans, secured pawn loans, check cashing, and gold-buying services. Its retail network includes Money Mart, The Money Shop, Insta-Cheques, Suttons & Robertsons, The Check Cashing Store, Sefina, Helsingin PanttiSM, Optima, Money-Now!, Super Efectivo, and ExpressCredit. DFC Global adopted its current name in 2011.

ORIGINS

Dollar Financial Group was created in 1979 as Monetary Management Corporation by the United States Banknote Company (USBN), a printer of paper currency, as a private distributor of government benefits in the Philadelphia area. The company expanded to Ohio, California, and Michigan in the mid-1980s, and in addition to distributing benefits the USBN centers they offered check cashing services. The chain was incorporated as Dollar Financial Corp. in April 1990, and a month later USBN sold the business to a private investor group affiliated with the Wall Street investment firm Bear, Stearns & Co. Inc. Serving as DFG's chief executive officer and chairman was Jeffrey Weiss, a Bear, Stearns managing director who oversaw the firm's investment in small and midsized companies, for many of which he served as CEO and chairman. Also joining the board was another Bear, Stearns executive, Donald Gayhardt, who in 1993 left Bear, Stearns to become DFG's chief financial officer and executive vice president.

In June 1994 Weiss and Gayhardt bought the company, which by then was operating as Dollar Financial, from Bear, Stearns. A year earlier the company had acquired the PenNet system, an electronic benefits transfer system, which distributed food stamps and other public benefits via magnetic cards in Pennsylvania. The system was then incorporated into Dollar Financial's Philadelphia-area check cashing stores as well as grocery stores in other parts of the state. Dollar Financial received a monthly fee from the state to operate and support the PenNet system.

By 1995 Dollar Financial, under the Check Mart banner (and "Almost a Bank" in Virginia), operated the second largest chain of check cashing stores in the United States and was the largest distributor of government benefits. The chain had done especially well establishing kiosk outlets in convenience stores, many of which were open 24 hours a day. In addition to check cashing they offered utility and other bill paying, money orders, money transfer, postal services and mailbox rentals, and copy and fax services.

PAYDAY LENDING

Dollar Financial also offered consumer loans, becoming involved in the increasingly popular, and controversial, payday loan business, which many critics called loan sharking, a predatory lending practice that took advantage of low-income customers. Proponents called it a "deferred presentment" service. A customer with an active checking account and proof of employment could write a postdated check to the lender for an amount that covered the loan plus a fee, generally $15 to $20 per $100 received, rather than an interest charge. The agency deposited the check on the date written, generally the day of the customer's next paycheck. All too often, however, the cash-strapped borrower fell into a refinancing trap and a second loan was taken out to cover the first, a "rollover" loan that created a vicious cycle for some borrowers who continued to pay fees but were unable to reduce the principal of the loan.

Payday lending was hardly new in the United States. In the late 1800s the practice thrived with "five for six" lenders whose customers borrowed $5 on Monday and repaid $6 when they received their pay on Friday or Saturday. The interest rate seemed modest in the context of a week, but at 20 percent per week it amounted to more than 1,000 percent per annum. These salary lenders, mostly found in northeastern cities, became known as loan sharks. They targeted lower-middle-class people who held steady jobs but lacked the assets to obtain a bank loan if they suffered a financial setback. Because they had jobs and families they were not likely to flee town. Lenders could also play on their Victorian sense of guilt about going into debt.

Some lenders hired a "bawler-out," usually a vocal woman, to visit a workplace to denounce and humiliate the negligent borrower. The primary goal of the loan shark was to extract as many payments as possible without having the principal of the loan reduced, thus creating "chain debt." Such high-cost lending became a major problem in the late 19th century. Not only were laws eventually enacted to combat loan sharking, charitable lending institutions and mutual savings and loan organizations arose to meet the credit needs of the middle class. Loan sharking, conducted by organized crime, continued to prey on people in the shadows of society, however.

ALLIANCE WITH EAGLE NATIONAL BANK EXPANDS PAYDAY LENDING

The payday lending business was reinvented in the 1980s following deregulation of the banking industry that lifted interest rate caps and the demise of traditional small loan providers. It enjoyed explosive growth in the early 1990s. To many, payday lending was a return to the days of loan sharking, but others portrayed the practice as filling a need, providing a service to people who were neglected by traditional banks, which were focused on more highly profitable areas than short-term loans to less-affluent people.

By the end of the fiscal year ending June 30, 1996, Dollar Financial was operating about 425 outlets in 14 states, generating $91.7 million. A few months later, in November 1996, the company expanded into Canada by acquiring 36 company-owned Money Mart stores and 107 franchised locations. It was also around this time that Dollar Financial bolstered its domestic business through an alliance with Eagle National Bank of Upper Darby, Pennsylvania. With Eagle's imprimatur, Dollar Financial's check cashing units were able to make payday loans in states where they would not normally be allowed. As a small bank, Eagle found that the relationship with Dollar Financial provided it with the reach of a large bank that could maintain multiple branches. It was a mutually beneficial arrangement, but one that would last only six years.

By 2000 Eagle was making payday loans at 250 Dollar Financial outlets, but the partners were also receiving some unwanted attention. In January 1999 a San Diego, California, law firm filed a suit that charged Eagle with National Bank Act violations and Dollar Financial with racketeering law violations. The federal

KEY DATES

1979: Monetary Management Corporation is established to distribute government benefits.
1990: Chain is incorporated as Dollar Financial Corp. and sold to a private investor group.
1996: Company expands into Canada.
1999: Company makes its first U.K. acquisitions.
2002: Relationship with Eagle National Bank is severed.
2005: Company is taken public.
2009: Controlling interest in Polish consumer lending company is acquired.
2011: Company changes its name to DFC Global.
2014: Lone Star Funds LLC takes DFC Global private.

government also took notice of Dollar Financial's "Cash 'til Payday Loans," which had grown in volume from $3 million the first year to $400 million in 2001, offered in 40 states through Dollar Financial outlets. The Office of the Comptroller of the Currency investigated that arrangement and found that Eagle had provided inadequate monitoring or control over loan origination, quality assurance, compliance, or auditing of Dollar Financial outlets. In some cases, Dollar Financial began operating stores and offering payday loans without Eagle's knowledge, let alone approval. Thus, in 2002 Eagle was ordered to stop funding Dollar Financial's payday loan business.

GROWTH AND ACQUISITIONS AT HOME AND ABROAD

Dollar Financial continued to grow its outlets in the United States and abroad in the late 1990s. The first Loan Mart units opened in fiscal 1998, and in February 1999 the company made its first U.K. acquisitions, buying five stores. In July 1999 Dollar Financial added 44 stores in the United Kingdom by purchasing the outstanding shares of Cash A Cheque Holdings Great Britain Limited. The year ended with the acquisition of Cash Centres Corporation Limited, which operated five company-owned stores and 238 franchise units in the United Kingdom.

Also in December 1999 Dollar Financial bolstered its Canadian holdings through the purchase of Cheques R'Us, Inc., and Courtenay Money Mart Ltd., bringing into the fold another six stores, located in British Columbia. As a result of this activity, Dollar Financial's revenues increased from $121 million in fiscal 1999 to $165.8 million in fiscal 2000, of which nearly $100 million came from check cashing fees and another $35 million from consumer lending.

Further growth took place as the new decade arrived. In February 2000 the payday loan business of CheckStop, Inc., which operated in 150 independent document-transmitting outlets (mail stores and insurance offices) in 17 states, was acquired. The August 2000 purchase of West Coast Chequing Centres, Ltd., added another six stores in British Columbia. Later in the month, Dollar Financial acquired Fast 'n Friendly Check Cashing and its eight Maryland outlets. Also in August, Ram-Dur Enterprises, Inc., operator of five AAA Check Cashing Centers in Tucson, Arizona, was added. Dollar Financial closed calendar 2000 by acquiring Fastcash Ltd. and its 13 company-owned and 27 franchise stores in the United Kingdom.

GOING PUBLIC

Revenues increased to $195.5 million for the fiscal year ending June 30, 2001, and $202 million a year later. To pay down $200 million in debt taken on to grow the company, Dollar Financial issued $220 million in senior notes in late 2003. Little more than a year later, in January 2005, the company was taken public in a stock offering that raised $118 million. By this time, Dollar Financial operated a network of 1,122 locations, of which 650 were company owned.

The company also renewed its expansion efforts in 2005. Early in the year it acquired International Paper Converters, doing business as Cheque Changer Limited, as well as Alexandria Financial Services. In March 2005 Dollar Financial acquired We the People Forms and Service Centers USA, Inc., a legal-documentation preparation firm that operated through 170 franchise stores in 30 states and served the same low- and middle-income customers as Dollar Financial outlets. Two months later the five financial services stores in Arizona operated by Tenant Financial Enterprises, Inc., were added as well.

When fiscal 2005 came to a close on June 30, the company posted sales of $321 million. Consumer lending accounted for nearly half of the company's revenues, totaling $153 million compared to $128.7 million from check cashing fees. The disparity continued to grow over the next three years. Total revenues topped $572 million in fiscal 2008, but by this time consumer lending fees approached $300 million while check cashing fees approached the $200 million mark.

Along with greater rewards from payday lending came problems, however. A Canadian class-action suit filed in 2003 alleging violation of Canadian lending law was settled in early 2006, an agreement in which Dollar Financial admitted no wrongdoing. Also in 2006 the Federal Deposit Insurance Corporation pressured Wilmington, Delaware–based First Bank of Delaware into severing its payday lending partnership with Dollar Financial. A $515 million lawsuit in Canada received class-action status in early 2007. Begun in 2003, it alleged Dollar Financial and its payday loans charged fees and interest that exceeded Canadian law. Another settlement that allowed the company to avoid admitting guilt was reached in 2009.

Despite the stigma attached to payday lending, it remained a lucrative business, one of the few in the financial sector that was doing well in the early months of 2009. Unlike other companies that were scaling back, Dollar Financial looked to grow its operations, especially overseas. Four stores offering check cashing, payday loans, and pawnbroking services were acquired in Northern Ireland in the summer of 2009. In that same month a pair of 170-year-old pawnshops located in Edinburgh and Glasgow, Scotland, were added as well. Dollar Financial also extended its reach to the European continent by purchasing a controlling interest in a Polish consumer lender, Optima S.A.

CONTINUED GROWTH LEADS TO A NAME CHANGE

With ample growth opportunities in the United States and abroad, Dollar Financial continued to steadily expand over the next several years. The company added Sefina Finance AB, a Scandinavian pawn lending store operator, to its holdings in 2010. It also acquired Suttons & Robertsons Ltd., the fourth-largest pawnbroking network in the United Kingdom.

The company's coffers were bolstered again in 2011 with the purchase of Purpose U.K. Holdings Ltd., the parent company of Month End Money (MEM). MEM, which was established in 2003 and offered Internet-based loans, operated under the brand name PaydayUK. The company's European Internet business continued to grow with the purchase of Risicum Oyj, a leading provider of Internet-based loans in Finland and Sweden, later that year.

Dollar Financial's growth strategy proved successful revenues and profits were on the climb. During the 2011 fiscal year, the company issued $2.2 billion in payday loans. At this time Dollar Financial decided to change its name to DFC Global Corp. The new identity reflected its growth in international markets and range of product and services, which by now included secured pawn lending, consumer lending, small business ad-

vances, debit cards, gold purchasing, money transfer, check cashing, and foreign exchange.

Moving forward as DFC Global, the company continued to strengthen its international operations. During 2012 the company purchased Super Efectivo S.L., a Spain-based pawn lending store operator. DFC Global also began offering Internet-based loans in Poland that year.

The company entered the Romanian market in 2013 with the acquisition of Express Credit Amanet, which operated a chain of 32 stores that offered pawn lending on gold jewelry, electronics, and automobiles, as well as gold buying services. It also bought Monte Caja Oro, a Spanish pawn lending and gold buying stores operator. Revenues in 2013 reached $1.1 billion, an increase of 5.7 percent over the previous year.

DFC Global's financial performance was threatened in early 2014 as regulatory changes in the United Kingdom, a weak Canadian dollar, and lower gold prices began to eat into company profits. Nevertheless, DFC Global became an attractive investment opportunity for private-equity group Lone Star Funds LLC. Lone Star agreed to take the company private in a deal worth $1.3 billion.

DFC Global CEO Jeff Weiss's comments on the purchase were reported in an April 2014 *Philadelphia Business Journal* article: "Lone Star Funds is a sophisticated investor with broad-based financial and retail expertise, and we look forward to taking advantage of enhanced financial flexibility to find new ways to build our business while continuing to meet and exceed the needs of our global customer base." Lone Star completed the purchase in June of that year.

Ed Dinger
Updated, Christina M. Stansell

PRINCIPAL COMPETITORS

Ace Cash Express, Inc.; Cash America International, Inc.; Check into Cash, Inc.

FURTHER READING

Bergquist, Erick. "Dollar of Pa.'s IPO Raises $118 M." *American Banker*, January 31, 2005.

———. "Payday Lender Buys Document Prep Firm." *American Banker*, March 9, 2005.

Blumenthal, Jeff. "Payday Lender Agrees to Be Sold for $1.3 Billion." *Philadelphia Business Journal*, April 2, 2014.

Campbell, Colin. "Yes, It's a Good Time for Money Mart." *Maclean's*, February 16, 2009.

Dela Cruz, Katherine. "DFC Global Enters Romania with Pawn Loan Provider Acquisition." *SNL Specialty Finance M&A*, July 1, 2013.

"DFC Global Takes Over Spain's Monte Caja Oro." *M&A Navigator*, December 10, 2013.

Huckstep, Aaron. "Payday Lending: Do Outrageous Prices Necessarily Mean Outrageous Profits?" *Fordham Journal of Corporate & Financial Law*, 2007.

Mason, Todd. "Dollar Financial's Stock Falls." *Philadelphia Inquirer*, February 23, 2006.

Peterson, Christopher. *Taming the Sharks: Toward a Cure for the High-Cost Credit Market*. Akron, OH: University of Akron Press, 2004, 451 p.

Powell, Betsy, and Dale Anne Freed. "Payday Loan Victims Get $100 Million." *Toronto Star*, June 10, 2009.

Dorothy Lane Market, Inc.

———■———

2710 Far Hills Avenue
Dayton, Ohio 45419
U.S.A.
Telephone: (937) 299-3561
Fax: (937) 299-3568
Web site: http://www.dorothylane.com

Private Company
Founded: 1948
Employees: 700
Sales: $70 million (2013)
NAICS: 445110 Supermarkets and Other Grocery
(Except Convenience) Stores

■ ■ ■

Based in Dayton, Ohio, Dorothy Lane Market, Inc. (DLM) operates three nationally respected gourmet grocery stores, including two Dayton locations and a third in Springboro, Ohio. DLM is known for its high-quality produce, meat, cheese, bakery, wine, and deli and kitchen departments. DLM also sells many of its signature items through its Web site, provides catered boxed lunches and dessert trays, and provides an online shopping service. The DLM Culinary Center offers cooking lessons and hosts special "foodie nights." The second and third generation of the Mayne family owns and manages DLM.

FRUIT STAND ORIGINS: 1948

DLM began as downtown Dayton produce stand that Calvin D. Mayne opened in 1948, financed by $500

from his wife Vera. Her first husband had owned a wholesale produce company in Dayton that she ran after his death in the 1930s. Because of the location at the corner of Lebanon Pike and Dorothy Lane, Mayne named his stand Dorothy Lane Market. One of his regular customers was a Japanese American gardener, Frank Y. Sakada.

The two men regularly conversed and discovered they had similar interests, soon deciding to become business partners in the stand. They invested in a truck and began bringing in fresh produce, later adding other food items as well. During the post–World War II era, the United States experienced a housing boom as servicemen and servicewomen returned home, married, and began raising the baby boom generation. Dayton was no different, and the area around Dorothy Lane, once thinly populated, became the site of new housing developments around 1950.

NEW STORE OPENS: 1953

To take better advantage of the influx of potential new customers, Mayne and Sakada opened an 8,000-square-foot grocery store a few blocks north of the original produce stand in August 1953. The new store prospered, and by 1957 it was doing more than $100,000 in business a week. The store was expanded in 1958, the same year that Mayne bought out Sakada. It was also in the late 1950s that another Dayton-based company, the National Cash Register Company (NCR), took note of DLM's success.

NCR was eager to help retailers succeed as a way to stimulate cash register sales and approached Mayne about serving as a brand ambassador. The company wanted to send him around the world to share his story of success in the grocery business to NCR customers. Accompanied by his 13-year-old son Norman, Mayne traveled throughout Europe and the Far East.

Because of the trip, DLM gained an outsized international reputation for a small Dayton grocery store. In a December 1993 article in *Supermarket Business*, Norman Mayne said he was attending an industry event in Australia a year earlier "when an older fellow came up to me, looked at my badge, and said, 'Hmmm—Dorothy Lane Market. That's a very famous name!'"

HYPERMARKET EXPERIMENT

Calvin Mayne was a visionary as well as a competent grocery. In early 1963 he became convinced that in the future, supermarkets would be combined with discount stores, essentially anticipating the rise of Wal-Mart and other hypermarkets. In 1963 he acquired a pair of discount stores, which he converted into Dorothy Lane Supercenters, essentially adding leased departments with their own separate checkouts. A third supercenter soon opened as well.

In 1966 Mayne suffered a stroke, forcing his 21-year-old son to take over as DLM's chief executive. Norman Mayne had not been an especially good student, and instead of college he had gone to work for his father after high school as a truck driver. In addition to his inexperience, he had to contend with the poor performance of the supercenters.

In 1967 DLM was forced to file for Chapter 11 bankruptcy protection. The supercenters were closed, but Norman Mayne was able to keep the original Dorothy Lane Market open by promising to pay back 100 percent of the debt to creditors within 10 years. By focusing on the original store, Mayne was able to pay off his creditors in just eight years, and DLM emerged from bankruptcy protection in 1975.

SECOND DLM FAILS

Mayne began to consider expansion again in 1979, when an opportunity arose to open a second Dorothy Lane Market. Although his distributor advised against the move, Mayne opened the new store. It proved to be a poor decision, and the store was closed just six months later. Although popular with customers, DLM was very much a traditional grocery store as the 1980s began.

The store performed well until sales flattened out in the early 1980s and soon began to decline. With just 15,000 square feet of retail space and parking for only 105 vehicles, DLM was unable to match the prices of a new wave of supermarket chains and their large-footprint stores and massive advertising budgets. By 1984 DLM was in danger of being forced out of business.

Mayne was forced to take stock of DLM's position. A customer survey indicated that the store's best hope was to carve out an upscale position rather than attempt to compete on price. "We realized that upscale meant more than fancy mustards and Dutch chocolate," Mayne told *Supermarket News* in a December 19, 1988, profile. "We saw it meant the very best in perishables and ongoing promotions with a sense of theatre. [It meant] consumer education, sampling, cooking classes and demonstrations. We had to be really superior in everything we did."

TAKE-HOME PROGRAM STARTED

DLM made steady improvements, focusing first on bringing contemporary styling to the store. The deli and bakery departments were also doubled in size and more importantly, the quality of the prepared foods was improved. A box-lunch program and soup bar were created and proved popular, as did the Gourmet Dinners to Go program, which found favor with families increasingly pressed for time but wanting high-quality, take-home dinners.

All of the meals were prepared from scratch, and at five o'clock a tuxedoed chef stood at the newly stocked deli case to answer customer questions about the entrees and other items. In addition to generating sales, the program helped to improve the brand image of Dorothy Lane Market. DLM also began publishing an annual, 16-page, full-color catalog that featured some of the store's new signature items packaged as gift baskets for the holidays.

Top sellers were Killer Brownies and Heavenly Hams, which became signature DLM items. Also key to the new upscale image was consumer education. Recipes, news articles, and other information were made available throughout the stores. On the weekends, demonstrations were conducted and samples distributed throughout the store.

```
┌─────────────────────────────────────────┐
│                                          │
│             KEY DATES                    │
│                                          │
│  ─────────────────■─────────────────     │
│                                          │
│  1948:  Dorothy Lane Market opens as     │
│         roadside produce stand.          │
│  1953:  First grocery store opens under  │
│         Dorothy Lane name.               │
│  1967:  Company declares Chapter 11      │
│         bankruptcy.                      │
│  1991:  Second location opens.           │
│  2002:  Third location opens in          │
│         Springboro, Ohio.                │
│                                          │
└─────────────────────────────────────────┘
```

WASHINGTON TOWNSHIP STORE OPENS

DLM's upscale strategy worked and sales rebounded. Mayne believed in the concept so much that despite the saturation of the Dayton market with Kroger, Cub Foods, and Meijer supermarkets he decided to once again attempt to add a second DLM location. In 1991 a new 37,000-square-foot store opened less than four miles from the original Dorothy Lane Market in Greater Dayton's Washington Township. It featured a 40-seat, cafeteria-style restaurant as well as the Galeria self-service, walk-around island that offered a wide variety of prepared foods.

Mayne's attempt at expansion appeared to be ill-fated yet again. The new store opened just as DLM's three large competitors engaged in an all-out price war that included triple coupons and a multitude of loss leaders. For several months, Dayton consumers chased bargains. The new Washington Township store attempted to cut prices too, but lost money without gaining core higher-income customers.

CLUB DLM DEBUTS: 1995

The store came close to closing just when many customers finally grew tired of the indifferent customer service and the quality of perishables and prepared foods of the large stores. They began to shop at the new DLM. The store gained a foothold in the market, and Mayne finally had a successful second location. He also decided to never again attempt to compete with the larger supermarket chains on price.

Rather than become complacent, DLM continued to be an industry innovator. In 1995 it became one of the first grocery stores in the United States to offer a loyalty program, Club DLM, and pioneered the concept of rewarding its best customers with price reductions beyond newspaper ads.

DLM was also quicker than most to embrace the Internet, launching a Web site in 1995. Initially, the site served only a promotional purpose but would eventually add e-commerce capabilities and supplant the catalog as a way to sell DLM's food gift items.

THIRD LOCATION OPENS: 2002

In the late 1990s DLM expanded and renovated both of its locations. The Washington Township store, for example, almost tripled the size of its in-store bakery and added a new $60,000 French hearth oven to establish a from-scratch European bread program. Soon, DLM was making plans to add a third location, this time a few miles farther south in Springboro, Ohio.

The $4 million, 39,000-square-foot store opened in March 2002. Unlike previous expansion attempts, the Springboro store did not teeter on the verge of failure before finding its footing in the market. DLM continued to shape its upscale image in the new century. Organic produce was embraced ahead of the market. After years of throwing away products customers did not recognize or want, DLM was well prepared when customers began clamoring for these same organic goods.

The stores also used numerous in-store demonstrations to teach customers about brown organic eggs. Traditional white-egg Daytonians eventually began to make the switch. In addition to organic foods, DLM became a supporter of freshly picked, local produce. In 2008 DLM decided to no longer sell tobacco products, as it was clashing with the company's image as a promoter of health foods.

VERA MAYNE DIES: 2011

As DLM entered the second decade of the new century, it was a successful three-store operation that generated about $70 million in annual sales. It faced a period of transition, however. Three generations were involved in the company until March 2011, when Vera Mayne passed away at the age of 105.

For many years Mayne had been a majority shareholder of the company, and while her son served as CEO, she acted as president from 1972 to 2005. She was far from a silent partner. Even as she approached 100 years of age, she personally signed all of the paychecks, reviewed invoices, and signed hundreds of vendor checks each week.

With the first generation of the Mayne family departed, the third generation in the form of the founder's grandson, also named Calvin Mayne, was being groomed to succeed his father as DLM's CEO. Not only was 69-year-old Norman Mayne on the verge of retirement in 2014, so too were many members of his management team.

Even as Calvin Mayne and a new group of young executives were being prepared to take charge, DLM faced an immediate concern. Whole Foods Markets was scheduled to open a store in Dayton in 2015. The two companies occupied the same market niche, but Whole Foods enjoyed much greater scale and national brand recognition. How DLM would respond to this fresh challenge remained to be seen.

Ed Dinger

PRINCIPAL DIVISIONS

Oakwood; Springboro.

PRINCIPAL COMPETITORS

Kroger Co.; Meijer, Inc.; The Stop and Shop Supermarket Company, LLC; Trader Joe's Company.

FURTHER READING

Barrow, Olivia. "DLM's Norman Mayne: Father of the Modern Grocery Store." *Dayton Business Journal*, February 7, 2014.

Bohman, Jim. "Recipe for Success." *Dayton Daily News*, December 18, 1993.

"Dorothy Lane Gourmet Hits; Dinners to Go, Box Lunches." *Supermarket News*, December 19, 1988.

"Dorothy Lane Market: A Brief History of Ups and Downs." *Supermarket Business*, December 1993.

Fensholt, Carol. "Dorothy Lane Market." *Supermarket Business*, December 1992.

Fisher, Mark. "Dorothy Lane Makes a Splash in Springboro." *Dayton Daily News*, March 8, 2002.

Kaplan, Rachel. "Exotic Events at Small Upscale Unit Build Big Sales." *Supermarket News*, September 15, 1986.

Koehnen, Adele U. "Roadside Fruit Stand Grew into Dorothy Lane Market." *Dayton Daily News*, July 2, 1997.

Doumak, Inc.

1004 Fairway Drive
Bensenville, Illinois 60106-1317
U.S.A.
Telephone: (630) 594-5400
Web site: http://www.doumak.com

Private Company
Founded: 1921 as Doumakes Marshmallow Company
Employees: 170
Sales: $85 million (2009)
NAICS: 311340 Nonchocolate Confectionery Manufacturing

■ ■ ■

Doumak, Inc., is a private company based in Bensenville, Illinois, that is devoted to the production of marshmallows. The company owns Campfire, the oldest marshmallow brand. Under the Campfire label, Doumak offers regular marshmallows, mini white marshmallows, one-ounce Giant Roasters, bite-size Fruitswirlers, Tutti Frutti Marshmallows, and MallowBurst marshmallows available in Lemon Meringue and Key Lime flavors. Doumak also exports products under the Campfire and Rocky Mountain labels to more than 35 countries in Central and South America, Europe, Africa, and the Middle East. For customers on a halal diet, the company offers a fish gelatin marshmallow. Doumak maintains two production facilities, a 52,000-square-foot plant in Elk Grove Village, Illinois, and a 70,000-square-foot plant in nearby Bensenville, Illinois. Doumak uses its ample production capacity for private-label

work. It supplies the specialty market with small-size packages of marshmallows for gift baskets and baking kits. Doumak also makes dehydrated marshmallows for a variety of uses and supplies food service and industrial customers with marshmallows in bulk quantities for making crisped rice treats and use in Jell-O, salads, and other dishes.

MARSHMALLOW'S ANCIENT ORIGINS

The history of the marshmallow dates to ancient Egypt. The treat, intended only for royalty or the gods, was made from of the mallow plant native to northern Africa and eastern Europe. Because it was found in marshy areas close to the sea, such as the Nile Delta, the plant was known as the marsh mallow. The sap from its roots was used to bind nuts and honey, creating the earliest form of the marshmallow.

Later, Greek and Roman doctors used hardened marshmallows for medicinal purposes, to soothe sore throats as well as to treat ulcers. The modern marshmallow was created in the early to mid-1800s, when French candymakers began combining marsh mallow sap with eggs and sugar, which was beaten into a foam. The mix was then poured into cylindrical molds and hardened into their familiar shape. Like its Egyptian forebear, however, the cast-method marshmallows, *pate de Guimauve*, were expensive to make and their consumption was limited to the wealthy.

Later in the 1800s German candymakers developed a less costly way to make marshmallows using gelatin, which became the foundation for the modern marshmallow. The new marshmallows found favor with Americans who began roasting them over campfires in the early 1900s. The first marshmallow brand in the United States was introduced in 1917 by the Imperial Candy Company/Redel Candy Corporation under the Campfire name.

CANDYMAKERS BEGIN PRODUCTION

Also to take advantage of the popularity of roasting marshmallows, other candymakers around the country began to make the product. One of them was James Doumakes of Los Angeles. Born in Sparta, Greece, he immigrated to the United States in 1898, first settling in Fresno, California. After living in San Francisco for a time, he moved to Los Angeles in 1911.

James Doumakes began making cast-mold marshmallows in the basement of his house and selling them to his neighbors. In 1921 he opened a plant and launched Doumakes Marshmallow Company, selling his product under the Doumak's Snow-White Marshmallows and Wonderfood brands. He was soon joined by his three sons, John, Alex, and Robert. John became president, Alex vice president, and Robert secretary-treasurer.

NEW PRODUCTION METHOD DEVELOPED

Candymakers such as the Doumakes family continued to produce cast-mold marshmallows, but it was a time-consuming, and therefore expensive, process. It was Alex Doumakes who worked with his father to develop a new way of making the confection. In 1948 they developed a new marshmallow recipe and an extrusion process that created a continuous cylindrical stream of candy that could be automatically cut to size.

Not only was the method quicker, the new formula kept the product soft for a longer time, eliminating the hard edges that soon appeared on cast-mold marshmallows. The new marshmallows were also lighter and more tender, and the quality was more consistent. A patent on the new marshmallow was granted in 1954. Not only did the Doumakes family use the new process in the production of marshmallows for its own brands, it licensed the rights to the patent, including to the Kraft Company in 1958.

Five years earlier, Kraft had introduced the Jet-Puffed marshmallow brand. With the newly acquired ability to produce mass quantities of marshmallows, Kraft began a major marketing campaign that would have a dramatic impact on marshmallow sales in the United States. Annual marshmallow sales industry-wide increased from $10 million to about $45 million over the next dozen years.

FOUNDER DIES: 1956

In April 1956 James Doumakes died of a heart attack at the age of 77, bringing an end the first phase of the Doumakes family's interest in the marshmallow business. In 1961 the company, which had become Doumak, Inc., using an Anglicized version of the family name, opened a second plant in Elk Grove, Illinois. The new 25,000-square-foot manufacturing and distribution facility was better located to serve the growing market for both regular marshmallows and the new mini marshmallows that quickly grew popular with consumers because of their many uses.

The product were packaged in polyethylene bags, replacing boxes and tins. The new plant was capable of producing 20 million pounds of marshmallows a year. The three-acre site also provided ample room for future expansion and ultimately led to the closure of the Los Angeles operation. At this stage, Doumak was not involved in the private-label business, preferring instead to market its products through food brokers under the Doumak, Snowwhite, and Wonderfood labels.

Doumak, Inc., grew alongside the demand for marshmallows in the United States. The s'mores campfire treat, the recipe for which was first published by the Girl Scouts in 1927 in *Tramping and Trailing*, grew in popularity, as did Rice Krispies treats, introduced by the Campfire Girls in 1939 as part of a fund-raiser. Mini marshmallows were also used in sweet potatoes, Jell-O, and salads, which became popular in school cafeterias as well as at the family dinner table. Doumak focused its marketing on its new Fireside brand and enjoyed strong growth.

```
┌─────────────────────────────────────────────┐
│                                               │
│              KEY DATES                        │
│              ──────■──────                     │
│                                               │
│   1921:  James Doumakes starts marshmallow    │
│          company in Los Angeles.              │
│   1948:  James Doumakes and son Alex develop new │
│          extrusion production process.        │
│   1961:  Doumak, Inc., opens Chicago-area plant. │
│   2003:  Doumak acquires Campfire brand.      │
│   2013:  Campfire MellowBurst is introduced.  │
│                                               │
└─────────────────────────────────────────────┘
```

A DISTANT SECOND

To keep up with demand, the Elk Grove plant was soon doubled in size. By the early 1970s the company ranked as the second-largest marshmallow manufacturer in the country, but it was a distant second to Kraft, which dominated the category. Only two other companies continued to make marshmallows. Campfire Marshmallows remained popular, but ownership of the brand regularly changed hands.

Over the years, Campfire was owned by the Angelus Company, better known as the maker of Cracker Jack. Other owners were Borden, Inc., International Home Foods, and Con Agra. As the second-largest marshmallow maker in the United States, Doumak did not lack for business. According to a January 15, 1974, article in the *Chicago Daily Herald*, the company was unable to keep up with demand, despite producing as much as seven million pounds of marshmallows each day. By this point, the company had added a private-label business to supplement sales of Fireside marshmallows.

DIVERSIFICATION AND EXPANSION

Doumak supplied about 30 supermarket chains with marshmallows packaged under the customer's name. The company also packaged a kosher marshmallow but opted not to produce flavored marshmallows, which lacked the necessary consumer demand. America's love for marshmallows only continued to grow in the years ahead, with Kraft continuing to dominate the field. Soon, only Doumak's Fireside and the Campfire brand, as well as Doumak-made store brand, remained competition for Kraft.

During the 1980s Doumak also manufactured Campfire Marshmallows under contract for Borden. In order to remain competitive, Doumak continually upgraded its operations. In the early 1990s the Elk Grove plant replaced canvas belt conveyors with a new system of vibratory stainless steel conveyors.

The old canvas belts had a tendency to fray, which could result in a contaminated product. Moreover, canvas was far more difficult to clean than stainless steel. Not only was there greater quality control, the new system helped to improve yield. According to company studies, productivity improved 8 percent because of the new conveyor system.

CAMPFIRE BRAND ACQUIRED: 2003

The marshmallow sector consolidated further in 2003 when Doumak acquired the Campfire brand from Con Agra. Doumak also added a second plant, 70,000 square feet in size, about four miles away in Bensenville, Illinois. Because Campfire was an established national brand, Doumak discontinued the use of the Fireside brand, which did not enjoy the same level of distribution. In order to maximize the potential of the Campfire name, Doumak conducted consumer focus groups.

In addition to modernizing the look, Doumak considered switching to a stiffer polypropylene bag. It soon learned that consumers insisted on keeping the squeezable old bags, so they could smell the product. The focus groups also indicated that more product options were desirable. In 2005 Doumak began incorporating changes to the Campfire brand that grew out of the focus group work. The logo and Campy mascot were redesigned and a color-coded system introduced.

Regular-size marshmallows were assigned a burnt orange color, while blue was associated with minis, and purple with colored marshmallows. New products followed as well. The company introduced one-ounce minis in a 24-count tray that provided entry into the convenience store channel as well as warehouse stores. An 8-count tray of regular-sized marshmallows also proved popular in camp stores as well as service station markets.

The changes Doumak made to Campfire caught the attention of a company that supplied flavored marshmallows to Hispanic customers but was disappointed with the inconsistency of the product its supplier provided. As a result, Doumak develop a Tutti Frutti flavor for its new client. It also tapped into the Hispanic market by creating a Campfire sub-brand, Sabrosos. Not only did the pink-and-white marshmallows find favor with Hispanic customers, they proved to have crossover appeal.

ZEBRAS INTRODUCED: 2008

As the first decade of the new century continued, Doumak pursued other innovations. In 2008 the company introduced chocolate-drizzle marshmallows, dubbed Zebras. A year later, Doumak added Campfire Fruitswirlers in both five-ounce bags for regular size and 24-count minis. They were available in strawberry, orange, lemon, and lime flavors. The popular new products helped to drive Doumak's annual revenues to about $85 million in 2009.

Americans' love affair with marshmallows appeared unbounded, and Doumak continued to look for new ways to satisfy their customers. In 2013 the company introduced the country's first sour marshmallow. Called MellowBursts, the new minis were produced in Lemon Meringue and Key Lime flavors and sold in eight-ounce bags. Doumak did not neglect a staple of the marshmallow trade, s'mores.

Also in 2013 the company introduced the Campfire S'mores Kit, which included regular Campfire Marshmallows, traditional honey graham crackers, and premium chocolate. Each 16.3-ounce kit made one dozen s'mores. With control of the Campfire brand as well as a strong private-label and foodservice business, Doumak was well-positioned for the future. The United States remained the largest market for marshmallows in the world, but future growth might very well come from overseas, where the sector was still developing.

Ed Dinger

PRINCIPAL DIVISIONS

Campfire; Private Label; Export; Ingredient/food Service; Specialty.

PRINCIPAL COMPETITORS

Gud Fud; Kraft Foods Groups Inc.

FURTHER READING

"Dual Services Planned for James Doumakes." *Los Angles Times*, April 2, 1956.

"Firing Up the Category." *Candy Industry*, October 1, 2009.

"Fresh Marshmallow Secret Key to Doumak's Success." *Chicago Daily Herald*, August 1, 1963.

Gallas, Bob. "Marshmallows Galore!" *Chicago Daily Herald*, January 16, 1974.

Geering, Deborah. "Fluff Over Substance." *Atlanta Journal-Constitution*, March 14, 2002.

Locke, Michelle. "Food Processor Put Creative Twist on Marshmallows." *Winchester Star*, October 3, 2009.

Earl May Seed & Nursery L.P.

---

208 North Elm Street
Shenandoah, Iowa 51601
U.S.A.
Telephone: (712) 246-1020
Web site: http://www.earlmay.com

Private Company
Founded: 1919
Employees: 500
Sales: $211 million (2010 est.)
NAICS: 444220 Nursery, Garden Center, and Farm
   Supply Stores

∎∎∎

Earl May Seed & Nursery L.P. is a privately owned company based in Shenandoah, Iowa, that owns and operates more than 30 garden centers and landscaping design centers in Iowa, Kansas, Missouri, and Nebraska. The company also sells merchandise through its Web site. Products include plants and nursery stock, seeds, fertilizers, herbicides, lawn and garden supplies, as well as garden gifts, wild birds, pet supplies, and seasonal holiday merchandise. Using research from regional universities, the company offers Earl May–branded soil, mulches, fertilizer, and chemicals formulated specifically for midwest conditions. In addition, Earl May stores offer such services as landscape consulting and planting, landscape cleanup, lawn checks, weed and pest identification, and container planting and maintenance.

The company is led by the third generation of the May family.

FOUNDER, NEBRASKA BORN

The founder of Earl May Seed & Nursery was Earl E. May. He was born near Hayes Center, Nebraska, in 1888. Despite growing up on a farm, he exhibited more of a penchant for selling than for agriculture. By selling turkeys and trapping wolves, he raised enough money for college. After graduating from Normal College in Fremont, Nebraska, in 1910, he returned to Hayes Center to become principal of the public school. He then decided to pursue a legal career and entered law school at the University of Michigan, paying for his education by working for the D.M. Ferry Seed Company.

May peddled garden seed by horseback to farmers, working a swath from the Midwest to the mid-Atlantic states. When his father died, May decided to finish his law degree at the University of Nebraska, where he began courting the daughter of E. S. Welch, the owner of Mount Arbor Nurseries in Shenandoah, Iowa, located in the southwest corner of the state.

The small town had become a center for the seed and nursery industry. Beyond Welch's wholesale business, the town was home to Shenandoah Nurseries and Henry Field Seed Co., both of which were retail operations. Rather than complete his law degree, May married Gertrude Welch and went to work for her father-in-law in Shenandoah. He learned the nursery business with a mind toward starting a catalog and mail-order business.

COMPANY PERSPECTIVES

Earl May Garden Centers pride themselves on being the "local" lawn and garden experts.

COMPANY FOUNDED: 1919

Not only did Welch serve as a mentor, he provided the financial backing that May needed when he launched Earl E. May Seed & Nursery in 1919. The business was far from an overnight success, however. Shenandoah Nurseries and Henry Field Seed were already well-established, forcing May to carry whatever merchandise that might sell. In addition to seed and baby chickens, he sold clothing, tires, batteries, and radios.

Radio was just coming of age at the start of the 1920s, and May was quick to recognize that the new medium could help stimulate catalog requests. He began hosting a radio program that was carried by WOAW in Omaha, Nebraska. May was not the only seed dealer to try his hand at radio. In February 1924 Henry Field started his own station, KFNK, which operated out of his Shenandoah seed house. He doubled his sales in a single year.

Not to be outdone, May started his own radio station, KMA, in 1925. A flair for promotion, May dubbed KMA "The Cornbelt Station in the Heart of the Nation." The station's powerful transmitter, combined with its location on the open plains of the Midwest, allowed the signal to travel great distances. Under the proper conditions, KMA could be heard in the entire continental United States and as far away as Australia.

A RADIO PIONEER

May used radio to increase the distribution of his mail-order catalog, but along the way he also pioneered some of the elements of radio, including the early-morning broadcast. In October 1925 he began reading the news to farmers who were up early to do their chores. May became a popular and trusted radio personality, as did Henry Field. The two men and their country radio stations waged a fierce, yet cordial competition.

After the readers of *Radio Digest* voted Field the "World's Most Popular Radio Broadcaster" in 1925, he withdrew his nomination the following year. With his rival's support, May won the *Radio Digest* honor in 1926. In addition to farm news, KMA began airing the musical offerings of Earl May Seed employees. May and

Field also sponsored harvest jubilees that featured free food and entertainment and attracted large crowds to Shenandoah.

It was money well spent. In the year following the first jubilee, Earl May Seed increased sales 400 percent. After Field opened a broadcast theater in 1927, May followed suit by building the 1,000-seat Mayfair Theater with a soundproof stage. Professional musicians regularly visited Shenandoah to make appearances at the two radio stations. May hosted a variety show, *Country School*, in which he oversaw the musical acts and skits in the guise of a principal.

The radio show proved highly popular with midwestern audiences. At its peak, Earl May Seed mailed more than two million catalogs in a year. The company also maintained a store in Shenandoah that attracted customers from all over the Midwest, due in large measure to the entertainment provided by KMA. Nevertheless, the mail-order business accounted for 90 percent of annual revenues. After the stock market crash of 1929, however, the country entered the Great Depression. Customers were less inclined to travel to Shenandoah, although the annual jubilee remained popular. May countered by opening branch stores, starting in 1930 when he opened the Earl May Trading Post Number 2 in Lincoln, Nebraska.

EXPANSION AND DIVERSIFICATION

Over the next two years, branch stores opened in Omaha, as well as in St. Joseph, Missouri, and in Council Bluffs, Fort Dodge, and Des Moines, Iowa. Other branch stores, including some that were open only from February through May, were added later in the decade. By 1938 all of the branch stores operated year-round. Moreover, the stores expanded their product offerings to include fertilizers, insecticides, farm tools, and other hard goods.

The following year, KMA was split off from Earl May Seed and incorporated as May Broadcasting Company. The branch stores, along with financial back from Welch and Mount Arbor Nurseries, Earl May Seed was able to survive the lean years of the 1930s until military spending in support of World War II sparked the U.S. economy.

May was also credited with boosting morale at an especially difficult moment of the Depression. To stem the failure of banks, the new Roosevelt administration in Washington declared a "bank holiday" in 1933. May told his listeners to not lose heart and assured them he would accept checks from his customers for whatever they ordered by mail. During the time the banks were closed, he accepted nearly $50,000 in checks.

EARL MAY DIES: 1946

A year after the war ended, in December 1946, Earl May died at the age of 58 following a lengthy illness. At the time of his death, the company operated 30 stores. His son Edward and his daughter Frances assumed control of Earl May Seed and KMA. During the postwar year, Earl May Seed and May Broadcasting pursued different tracks. The latter launched an Omaha television station in 1949. Earl May Seed, in the meantime, adjusted to the times.

As the farm population decreased steadily, the company began to cater to the gardening needs of customers in towns and cities. As a result, nursery plants replaced field seed as the core product line, and the branch stores evolved into garden centers. The company continued to run its mail-order business, but its importance lessened over time. Important to Earl May Seed's success were the annual test gardens the company began planting in Shenandoah in 1940, which attracted thousands of visitors each summer.

To supplement its retail business, the company began offering landscaping services in the 1960s. To keep up with demand for its merchandise, Earl May Seed opened a new distribution center outside of Shenandoah in the fall of 1971. In 1977 Earl May Seed closed the test garden because the lease on the land became too expensive. In the mid-1980s the company purchased 77 acres of land for a Show Garden that attracted as many as 20,000 visitors during the annual open house. The practice came to an end following the 1994 season, however.

BECOMES LIMITED PARTNERSHIP

The land was used to support the retail business by housing a new growing operation and distribution center. Other changes were made in the final 15 years of the century. On January 1, 1987, the business was reorganized as a limited partnership and renamed Earl May Seed & Nursery L.P. It remained under the control of the May family, as did May Broadcasting, which formally became a separate company as part of the reorganization.

Frances E. May Rankin became president of May Seed, while Ed May Sr. remained in charge of May Broadcasting The third generation soon took charge of the businesses. Rankin's daughter, Betty Jane Shaw, became president of Earl May Seed, while her husband, Bill Shaw, served as chief executive officer. Ed May Jr., in the meantime, succeeded his father as the head of the broadcasting business.

CATALOG BUSINESS TERMINATED

Another significant change occurred in 1991, when the catalog business was discontinued, due to the high cost of postage. Earl May Seed was also reacting to a changing marketplace, as big-box home improvement chains such as Home Depot, Lowe's, and Menards changed consumer habits. People began preferring to visit garden centers rather than use a catalog. To keep up with the times, Earl May Seed opened more new garden centers.

In 1992 the company opened one of the largest garden centers in the Kansas City, Missouri, metropolitan area. It included a 9,500-square-foot building and a 20,000-square-foot outdoor sales area. In the late 1990s Earl May Seed launched a program to remodel and relocate some of its outdated stores. The company also chose to close two underperforming divisions, Earl May Direct, a wholesaler to midwestern garden centers, and Earl May Corporate, which sold trees to public- and private-sector clients.

As the new century dawned, Earl May Seed harbored no desire to become a large national chain. Rather, it focused on becoming one of the strongest retailing brands in its region. Despite its lack of geographic reach, Earl May Seed ranked among the top 10 garden retailers in the United States. In 2003 the company revisited an old concept, the seasonal store.

HOME EXPRESSIONS OPENS

Instead of operating during the spring planting season, however, it opened Home Expressions stores in shopping malls in the autumn to offer seasonal holiday and home décor merchandise. Earl May Seed remained an independent, family-owned business that was forced to be nimble because of its big-box competitors.

"That has forced us to redefine our customer base and the way we do business," Bill Shaw told the *Omaha World-Herald* in a February 11, 2006, article. "We strive for quality service and attention to our customers' needs. ... Whether it's looking for a type of grain seed or the right tree to plant, we provide service along with a product." In order to offer high-quality service, the company created a program to train employees in horticulture, plants, lawn care, diseases, and chemicals.

Early in the first decade of the 21st century, Earl May Seed closed a dozen garden centers because of declining rural populations. The chain continued to adjust its operations in the second decade of the new century. In late 2011 the company added a second Sioux City, Iowa, location by acquiring the Mosher's garden center, bringing the total number of retail centers to 32.

While the garden centers remained at the heart of Earl May Seed, the online business was growing and likely to increase its contribution to the company's balance sheet. With a new generation learning the business, Earl May Seed appeared to determined to remain independent for years to come.

Ed Dinger

PRINCIPAL DIVISIONS
Landscaping Design Centers; Retail Stores.

PRINCIPAL COMPETITORS
The Home Depot Inc.; Lowe's Companies, Inc.; Menard, Inc.

FURTHER READING

Alexander, Deborah. "Garden Center Firm Still Family Owned." *Omaha World-Herald*, February 11, 2006.

"Death Silences Radio Voice of Earl May, 58." *Carroll (IA) Daily Times Herald*, December 19, 1946.

Dreeszen, Dave. "Earl May to Take Over Mosher's Site." *Sioux City Journal*, November 28, 2011.

"Earl May: The Man behind the Company." *Cedar Rapids Gazette*, April 1994.

Hudson, David, Marvin Bergman, and Loren Horton. *The Biographical Dictionary of Iowa*. Iowa City: University of Iowa Press, 2008.

Offenburger, Chuck. "5 Largest Nurseries in U.S. Are S.W. Iowa's Top Industry." *Des Moines Register*, January 7, 1973.

Taylor, John. "May Plans Moves." *Omaha World-Herald*, July 27, 1997.

Ed. Züblin AG

Albstadtweg 3
Stuttgart, 70567
Germany
Telephone: (+49 711) 7883-0
Fax: (+49 711) 7883-390
Web site: http://www.zueblin.de

Private Company
Founded: 1898 as Ingenieur-Bureau für Cement-Eisenconstructionen
Incorporated: 1919 as Ed. Züblin AG
Employees: 13,000 (2013)
Operating Revenues: EUR 3.1 billion ($4 billion) (2012)
NAICS: 236210 Industrial Building Construction; 327332 Concrete Pipe Manufacturing; 237990 Other Heavy and Civil Engineering Construction; 238910 Site Preparation Contractors; 236220 Commercial and Institutional Building Construction; 236116 New Multifamily Housing Construction (Except For-Sale Builders); 237310 Highway, Street, and Bridge Construction

∎ ∎ ∎

Ed. Züblin AG is one of Germany's largest construction companies. The company offers the whole range of construction services, from construction planning and engineering, foundation excavation, the manufacturing of prefabricated reinforced concrete components, and the drilling of tunnels, to the turnkey construction of office and apartment buildings, shopping malls, bridges, railroads, harbors, dams, and subway and auto tunnels.

A specialty of Ed. Züblin AG is the manufacturing of large concrete pipes used in water pipelines, sewer installations, and hydroelectric power plants. The company also builds warehouses, hangars, and other industrial structures.

Headquartered in Stuttgart, Germany, Ed. Züblin is involved in major construction projects in many countries. These are carried out by the company's subsidiaries in Belgium, Denmark, Sweden, the Netherlands, Poland, Hungary, Portugal, Romania, China, Malaysia, Qatar, Dubai, Chile, and Canada.

PIONEERING CONSTRUCTION

When Eduard Züblin, the son of a Swiss textile entrepreneur in Naples, established an engineering and construction firm in Strasbourg, Alsace, in 1898, he had gathered many years of professional experience in machine tool manufacturing and engineering in Switzerland, France, England, and Italy. In the mid-1880s Züblin started working for a German architect in Naples who mainly designed factory buildings for the Italian textile industry.

Right from the start in 1898 the 48-year-old entrepreneur built his business on reinforced concrete. Patented by the French engineer François Hennebique, his new construction method used embedded iron bars in prefabricated, pre-shaped concrete components such as column, beam, wall, ceiling, and roof elements to form monolithic structures, including towers, bridges, production halls, and storage facilities. The material and building blocks resisted tensile strain, had a high load-bearing capacity, were durable and fire-resistant, and could be cast into any shape.

Züblin became a licensee for the Hennebique system and used the new technology to create unique shapes for buildings and other structures. In 1899 the city of Strasbourg, at the time part of the German Empire, assigned Züblin to build a large grain silo at the Rhine River. He used artfully designed precast wall elements that gave the building the appearance of a palace rather than a warehouse. In the same year Züblin received his first contract from abroad for the construction of a textile factory in Russia.

RAPID GROWTH IN NEW CENTURY

The early 1900s were years of rapid growth. Züblin developed and refined the technology that he applied to various construction projects, including arched concrete bridges, roof structures for industrial buildings, public pools, and train stations. One of Züblin's specialties was the use of reinforced concrete piles in the foundations of large structures. For the foundation of Hamburg's new central train station, built in 1902, the company drove 800 reinforced concrete piles, each of them 20 to 40 feet long, into the ground.

Züblin broke a world record in 1912, when the company completed the world's tallest and widest-spanning railway bridge made of reinforced concrete. It stretched over roughly 100 meters (328 feet). The Langwieser Viaduct, which was part of the Chur-Arosa railway line in the Swiss Alps, became a national landmark.

The company generated about DEM 18 million in revenues, then a large sum, with 150 employees working at the new Strasbourg headquarters. Eduard Züblin's most ambitious project was the underpinning of the rotten foundation of the famous Strasbourg Cathedral, one

of Europe's tallest buildings at the time, to save it from collapse. The project was successfully completed according to Züblin's plan two years after his death in 1916.

NEW START IN POSTWAR GERMANY

By 1914 Ed. Züblin had established subsidiaries and branch offices in Switzerland, Austria, Italy, France, Belgium, Germany, and Russia. In 1913 the company had also set up a production plant for large concrete pipes in Kehl, east of Strasbourg. However, the beginning of World War I in that year suddenly halted the company's international expansion. Züblin's subsidiaries in Italy and Switzerland were transformed into separate companies, which from then on operated independently.

When the Alsace region became part of France after World War I, Züblin's German employees at Strasbourg headquarters were expelled from the country. In 1919 they established Ed. Züblin AG, a corporation based in Stuttgart. As part of the reparations imposed on Germany by the Treaty of Versailles, a large contract for harbor repair work in Dunkirk, France, helped Ed. Züblin get through the difficult postwar years.

When the French occupants withdrew from Kehl in 1923, the company's factory remained on German territory and resumed the manufacturing of concrete pipes, which became an important pillar of Ed. Züblin's business activities. In 1925 the company opened a new subsidiary in Frankfurt am Main. By then Ed. Züblin AG's workforce had risen to 1,500. Additional subsidiaries were established in Duisburg, Karlsruhe, and Munich, where the company built a reinforced concrete penstock two meters in diameter for the Middle Isar Canal, a system of water power stations along the Isar River in Bavaria.

SURVIVING THE GREAT DEPRESSION

The onset of the Great Depression in Germany in the early 1930s caused a severe economic crisis and a sudden downturn in the construction industry. While the company's share capital was cut in half, members of Züblin's executive managers were partly paid in company stock. After Adolf Hitler's National Socialist Party came into power in 1933, the Nazi-led government launched a construction program for highways all across Germany.

As part of the German Autobahn project, Züblin built mainly bridges. The company was also involved in the construction of the Volkswagenwerk in Wolfsburg. A second plant in Kehl, built in 1938, expanded Züblin's

KEY DATES

1898: Eduard Züblin starts a construction consulting business in Strasbourg.

1913: A production plant for large concrete pipes is set up in Kehl.

1919: Ed. Züblin AG is established in Germany.

1988: German holding Walter Industrie-Beteiligungs GmbH buys a majority stake in Ed. Züblin AG.

2005: Austrian construction group Strabag SE becomes Züblin's majority shareholder.

2006: Ed. Züblin AG acquires the building construction and civil engineering division of STRABAG AG including DYWIDAG Bau GmbH.

production capacity for concrete pipes. As Hitler prepared Germany for a new war, Züblin was assigned to work on the construction of the Siegfried Line, or Westwall, a giant concrete defense system along the western border to France, Belgium, and the Netherlands.

During World War II the company was involved in the construction of harbor facilities in France along the Atlantic coastline, and in many other construction projects crucial to the war in Germany and at the front lines. In 1940 a second subsidiary for the production of concrete pipes was established in Schönebeck near Magdeburg in northeastern Germany. As the war returned to Germany in 1944, almost all production sites and office buildings of Ed. Züblin AG were destroyed or heavily damaged. More than 200 former Züblin employees died in the war and most of the company's equipment was either destroyed or confiscated.

GROWTH AFTER RECONSTRUCTION

After World War II ended in 1945 Züblin worked on rebuilding the company and helped with rebuilding a whole country. The construction of airport facilities and living quarters for the French and U.S. occupation forces were among Züblin's first postwar assignments. Later the company was involved in reconstruction work to rebuild destroyed bridges and other infrastructure. In 1948 Züblin's concrete pipe plant in Kehl resumed production and was spun off as a separate company seven years later.

During the 1950s, the postwar "economic miracle" years in Germany, the renamed Ed. Züblin Aktiengesellschaft built new factories and other industrial structures for manufacturers and heavy industry clients in the Stuttgart region, the Rhineland, and the Ruhr. Due to a growing number of projects in the areas of water supply and wastewater treatment as well as hydroelectric power generation worldwide, the demand for Züblin's concrete pipes increased rapidly.

In the first half of the 1960s the company built two new concrete pipe production plants in Germany, one of them in cooperation with Preussag AG and one in Kilstett, France. The maximum pipe size increased frequently, reaching 4 meters in diameter in 1970. A major driving force behind Züblin's rapid growth in the 1950s and 1960s was the large infrastructure projects the company got involved in around the globe.

WINS WADI THARTHAR PROJECT

In 1953 the company was awarded a contract for the Wadi Tharthar project, a giant barrage on the Tigris River near Samarra in Iraq. Worth roughly DEM 120 million, or six times Züblin's annual sales, it was a major milestone in the company's history. In the second half of the 1950s the company also built harbor facilities in Aqaba, Jordan, and Rangoon, Myanmar. In addition, Züblin was involved in the construction of large power plants, dams, and bridges in Egypt, Venezuela, Honduras, Sri Lanka, and the United Arab Emirates.

In the second half of the 1960s Züblin built the barrage wall for the Marala Headworks, a water flow-control project on the Chenab River in western Pakistan. Worth DEM 160 million, it was the single-largest project Züblin had carried out as the sole contractor. A second major project in Pakistan was the company's participation in the construction of the Tarbela Dam on the Indus River, the world's largest earth-filled dam, which began in 1968. Züblin also built a landing pier in the Butterworth Penang harbor in Malaysia, where the company used 140-foot-long, hollow, reinforced concrete piles in the footing.

MAJOR PROJECTS ABROAD

Ludwig Lenz died in 1969. He had worked side by side with Eduard Züblin since 1910 and headed Züblin's executive management as CEO and president of the advisory board for a quarter century. Two years later Züblin's revenues passed the DEM 500 million mark. However, as a result of the 1973 oil price crisis Germany slid into a severe economic downturn in the mid-1970s, with the construction industry taking the hardest hit.

The company reduced its workforce, restructured its administration, spun off its electronic data-processing division, and intensified efforts to procure more business abroad. By 1976 Züblin's turnover from projects abroad accounted for roughly 40 percent of the total. Large projects from several oil-producing countries in the Middle East became a major revenue source for Züblin in the 1970s.

The company built a tile production plant, a ceiling fan factory, a paper mill in Iraq, and new harbor facilities on the Persian Gulf in Iran. In 1974 the company constructed a power station and a water desalination plant in Qatar on the Persian Gulf. Four years later a fertilizer factory with a shipping pier was built in Akaba, Jordan. Also in the late 1970s Züblin set up four production plants in Riyadh in Saudi Arabia to produce 80,000 large, precast concrete components for the construction of the new King Saud University.

Another important market abroad was Austria, where Züblin was a major contractor in the construction of a dam for the Kölnbrein Talsperre in Kärnten. Züblin was also involved in the construction of a subway line in Vienna and of the Pfänder auto tunnel in the northern Austrian Alps. In addition the company helped build a 28-kilometer-long (17.4-mile-long) water supply tunnel in northern England. Major harbor construction projects were carried out in Cilegon, Indonesia; Bangkok, Thailand; and Limon, Costa Rica.

BUILDING NEW INFRASTRUCTURE

In the early 1980s Züblin received large orders from Iraq. The company was involved in the construction of a 100.6-meter-high (330-foot-high) wall for the Mosul Dam in the northern part of the country and helped install a new wastewater collection system in Baghdad. Züblin also built 10 trade schools for professional training in the areas of agriculture and crafts and three factories for terrazzo tiling on a turnkey basis. These projects alone were worth roughly DEM 1 billion.

While orders from Arab countries dropped significantly in the mid-1980s, Züblin realized large projects in other parts of the world, including tunnels, water supply systems, power stations, and harbor facilities in Chile, Sri Lanka, Taiwan, and China. The company constructed large dam walls in Honduras, New Zealand, and Mali. On the border between Paraguay and Argentina, Züblin helped built the Yacyretá Dam and hydroelectric power plant.

The dynamic development of the company's activities outside of Germany was reflected in its workforce. It peaked at about 10,400 in 1982 but declined rapidly when business abroad slowed down, standing at 6,800 in 1986. At the same time investment in new buildings and infrastructure projects in Germany picked up again, and Züblin got involved in a rising number of commercial and civil construction projects.

As part of German national railway's modernization program, Züblin built the first tunnel on the line connecting Hanover and Würzburg for Deutsche Bundesbahn in 1981. Tunnel construction evolved as one of Züblin's most sought-after specialties. When a heightened public awareness for environmental issues emerged in the 1980s, environmental engineering became another important new field of business activity for the company. In 1988 Züblin's domestic annual turnover passed the DEM 1 billion mark for the first time.

REBUILDING AFTER 1990

The reunification of Germany in 1990 resulted in a construction boom in the new eastern German states. Züblin acquired several construction companies there and set up branches in major cities. The company participated in the reconstruction of the rundown infrastructure in the former East Germany, building and rebuilding bridges, roads, sewage treatment plants, and pipelines as well as shopping malls and apartment complexes.

Major construction projects were carried out in Berlin's city center, where the company's specialized ground engineering division excavated very large, waterproof foundation pits for new building complexes. The company even made the headlines with the spectacular relocation of the historical Kaisersaal Salon inside Berlin's upscale Hotel Esplanade, a historical landmark that was moved about 250 feet across Potsdamer Platz square to its new location in 1996. While construction activity in Germany slowed significantly in the second half of the 1990s, Züblin realized big water management and tunnel projects abroad.

NEW SHAREHOLDERS, NEW VENTURES

For half a century Ed. Züblin AG was led by members of the Lenz family, who had acquired a 43 percent stake in the company. The Swiss AG für Bauunternehmungen owned roughly 31 percent, while the remaining 26 percent were held by nine families of former Züblin executives. In 1988 German construction holding Walter Industrie-Beteiligungs GmbH took over control by acquiring 52 percent in the company. Ed. Züblin AG continued to act independently in the market, but the Lenz family lost its seat on the company's advisory board.

Shortly after Züblin celebrated its 100th anniversary in 1998, a major downturn in the construction business put both companies under severe financial strain. According to *Börsen-Zeitung* on May 16, 2002, Walter generated a DEM 240 million loss in 2001. Züblin's business abroad was DEM 56 million in the red, partly due to delays on major projects in Pakistan and Lebanon, where the company was building a new campus for the Lebanese University in Beirut as a turnkey contractor.

Walter put its shares in Ed. Züblin AG up for sale but did not reach a deal with any of the interested parties. Züblin continued to produce losses abroad in the two-digit millions as reported by *Börsen-Zeitung*, on May 25, 2004, and on February 5, 2005, but managed the crisis, thanks to a number of large projects in Germany. After the Walter construction group filed for bankruptcy in 2005, its share in Ed. Züblin AG, then Germany's fifth-largest construction firm, was sold to Austrian construction conglomerate Strabag.

FACING LEGAL CHALLENGES

The Lenz family, with a 43 percent stake in Züblin and thus the company's second-biggest shareholder, filed a series of lawsuits against the integration of Strabag's German building construction and civil engineering divisions into Ed. Züblin AG as well as against other management decisions. While the restructuring case was finally decided in favor of Strabag in 2009 in a ruling by the Bundesgerichtshof, Germany's Federal Supreme Court, the Lenz family won back a seat on the company's advisory board.

In 2010 the company announced that all disagreements between the two main shareholders and the management of Ed. Züblin AG had been settled, as reported by *Börsen-Zeitung* on June 29, 2010. After more than a century of specializing in building reinforced concrete structures and pioneering technologies in the construction of bridges, tunnels, and railways, Züblin ventured into new fields of activity in the new millennium. The company entered the alternative energies field when it got involved in the development of thermal energy storage units made from special concrete.

Its clients for these items were solar power plants and compressed air-storage plants. A prototype developed in cooperation with the German Center for Aviation DLR was tested in 2008. In 2010 Züblin participated in research on the use of geothermal energy in manmade tunnels and the development of precast concrete tubing elements to extract underground heat as an energy source. Considering the company's strategic steps in the second decade of the 21st century, the next chapter in Züblin's history was not written in stone.

In 2011 the company took over NE Sander, a company that specialized in steel engineering. Between 2011 and 2013 Züblin acquired several timber construction companies, including the Metsä Wood Merk GmbH, a manufacturer of wooden construction components and systems in Aichach near Augsburg in Bavaria. Convinced that timber construction would become an important and integral element of modern buildings and other structures, Züblin was planning to strengthen its capabilities in this area in the near future.

Evelyn Hauser

PRINCIPAL SUBSIDIARIES

Züblin Spezialtiefbau GmbH; Züblin Gebäudetechnik GmbH; Züblin Stahlbau GmbH; Züblin Umwelttechnik GmbH; Züblin International GmbH; Züblin Chimney and Refractory GmbH; Züblin Nederland BV (Netherlands); Züblin Scandinavia AB (Sweden); Züblin International GmbH; Josef Riepl Unternehmen für Ingenieur- und Hochbau GmbH; Eberhard Pöhner Unternehmen für Hoch- und Tiefbau GmbH; Wolfer & Goebel Bau GmbH; NE Sander Eisenbau GmbH; Merk Timber GmbH; Stephan Holzbau GmbH.

PRINCIPAL DIVISIONS

Building Construction; Ground and Civil Engineering; Tunneling; Steel Engineering; Environmental Engineering; Real Estate Development.

PRINCIPAL COMPETITORS

Bilfinger SE; Hochtief AG; Skanska AB; Vinci SA; Wayss & Freytag Ingenieurbau AG.

FURTHER READING

"Dietrich Lenz." *Börsen-Zeitung*, June 22, 2004.

Everts-Grigat, Senta, and Karlheinz Fuchs. *Züblin. 100 Jahre Bautechnik 1898–1998*. Stuttgart, Germany: Ed. Züblin AG, 1998.

"Familie Lenz will jetzt Mehrheit an Ed. Züblin." *Börsen-Zeitung*, February 5, 2005.

"Finnish Metsaliitto Sells Wood Division in Germany." *SeeNews Nordic*, March 12, 2013.

"Lenz rennt bei Züblin offene Türen ein." *Börsen-Zeitung*, May 16, 2002.

Pecka, Michael. "Wärmespeicher aus Beton." *Energie & Management*, September 17, 2008.

"Züblin noch ohne neuen Eigentümer." *Börsen-Zeitung*, May 25, 2004.

"Züblin und Lenz einigen sich." *Börsen-Zeitung*, June 29, 2010.

Editions JC Lattès

—■—

17 Rue Jacob
Paris, 75006
France
Telephone: (+33 1) 44 41 74 00
Fax: (+33 1) 43 25 30 47
Web site: http://www.editions-jclattes.fr

Private Company
Incorporated: 1981 as Editions JC Lattès
Employees: 25
Sales: EUR 18 million ($25 million) (2013)
NAICS: 511130 Book Publishers

■ ■ ■

Editions JC Lattès is one of France's best-selling publishing houses, home to such successful authors as Dan Brown, E. L. James, Grégoire Delacourt, John Grisham, Delphine de Vigan, Dean Koontz, and Scott Turow. The company, controlled at 100 percent by the Hachette publishing empire, publishes approximately 140 new books each year. JC Lattès is most well-known as a publisher of commercial and generalist fiction, particularly thrillers. Other areas of focus for the company are historical fiction, including such authors as Jean-François Parot and Jean d'Aillon, and Nordic literature, including novels by Åke Edwardson and Karin Fossum. Beyond fiction, JC Lattès publishes biographies and autobiographies, such as the autobiographies of Nobel Prize–winner Muhammad Yunus and soccer player Zlatan Ibrahimović, and current events-oriented nonfiction. Editions JC Lattès also

controls imprint Les Éditions du Masque, a leading publisher of mystery and detective novels in France.

FAMILY HISTORY

Little about Jean-Claude Lattès's background suggested he would one day emerge as one of the most powerful figures in the notoriously closed circle of the French publishing industry. Born in Nice in 1941 Lattès's father, Alfred Lattès, owned a textile shop and was one of the leaders of that city's small Jewish community. The Lattès family was one of the oldest members of that community, having arrived there as part of the so-called population of *Juifs du pape* (or Papal Jews), which had enjoyed papal protection from the 14th century, but which had been chased out of the nearby Languedoc region in the 17th century.

The family prospered in Nice, but nonetheless clung to their origins. When the French government under Napoleon granted citizenship to the country's Jewish population, it also imposed the adoption of surnames. The Lattès family chose their ancestral village, Lattès, near Montpellier, as their last name. The family's entry into the textiles trade dated to at least 1840, with the opening of the Lattès Tissus shop. This shop was to remain under the family's control, finally closing its doors in 1999.

In the meantime, Jean-Claude Lattès's career had taken him into a far different direction. After completing his studies at the University of Nice in 1959, Lattès moved to Paris, where he attended the city's prestigious École Supérieure de Commerce. Instead of a career in business, however, Lattès chose journalism, taking a

---

COMPANY PERSPECTIVES

•

An open and ambitious publishing house.

---

position in the culture department of *Combat* magazine in 1961.

ENTERS PUBLISHING: 1965

Lattès soon began focusing on the publishing market, writing book reviews and other articles for the literature sections of such magazines as *L'Express*, *Candide*, *L'Observateur*, and *Les Nouvelles Littéraires*. In 1965 Lattès entered publishing directly, taking a position in the publicity department of Editions Robert Laffont, then in the process of revolutionizing France's publishing industry.

Originally from Marseille and member of a prominent shipping family, Robert Laffont had founded his publishing house in 1942. He proceeded to shake up the French publishing industry, in part by being one of the first to adopt modern marketing methods. Laffont became responsible for introducing French readers to a long list of prominent foreign writers, including Dino Buzzati, John le Carré, and Graham Greene, and was one of the first to publish collections of short stories.

FOUNDING A PUBLISHING SUCCESS

Laffont was also credited with introducing the concept of the best seller to France, after publishing the autobiography of the previously unknown Henri Charrière, nicknamed Papillon. This book became an enormous success for Laffont, not only in France, where it was the first French book to sell more than a million copies, but also internationally. In addition, the book inspired the successful Hollywood film *Papillon*, starring Steve McQueen. *Papillon* ultimately sold more than 13 million copies worldwide.

Jean-Claude Lattès had already left Laffont to found his own publishing house, initially called Edition Spéciale, in 1968. For this, Lattès teamed up with Jacques Lanzmann, brother of famed film director Claude Lanzmann, who was by then was a prominent novelist, journalist, and songwriter in his own right. Edition Spéciale began with a focus on publishing books treating current events. The company's first book, *Ce n'est qu'un début* by Philippe Labro, published in 1968, discussed the events of Paris student revolts, which had taken place just a few months earlier in May 1968.

In 1971 as Lanzmann went on to great success by developing the French version of the popular stage musical *Hair*, Lattès took full control of the company. The company then changed its name, becoming Editions Jean-Claude Lattès. The new structure soon broadened its range of titles, with a particular focus on commercial and generalist fiction.

BUILDING A SUCCESSFUL CATALOG

Lattès proved to have strong instincts for discovering and developing strong sellers, such as *Un Sac de Billes* by Joseph Joffo, *Léon l'Africain* by Amin Maalouf, and *Le Vent du Soir* by Jean d'Ormesson. Lattès was also credited with introducing a number of important foreign writers to France, such as future Nobel Prize–winner Naguib Mahfouz. During its first decade, Editions Jean-Claude Lattès succeeded in building a catalog of some 2,000 titles, including many of France's best-selling novels and other titles at the time.

This success, and the strong reputation of both Jean-Claude Lattès and his publishing house, brought the company to the attention of French publishing and media giant Hachette. In 1981 Lattès agreed to sell his company to Hachette. He then took up the position as CEO of Hachette Livre, the company's books division. Direction of Editions JC Lattès was then turned over to Lattès's wife, Nicole Lattès.

LAFFONT CONNECTION IN 1995

Under Jean-Claude Lattès, Hachette Livre grew into one of the world's leading book publishers. This growth took place especially after Lattès pushed through the acquisition of U.S.-based Grolier Books in 1989. While the acquisition later proved to become a core piece of Hachette's international empire, the initial difficulties of integrating the new operations into Hachette Livre led Lattès into conflict with Hachette. Lattès resigned from Hachette in 1991.

Editions JC Lattès, in the meantime, floundered into the early 1990s. By the middle of the decade the house, once one of France's most successful, was considered by many to be on its deathbed. In 1995, however, Hachette turned over direction of the house to a new management team led by Isabelle Laffont, the eldest of Robert Laffont's five children. Jean-Claude Lattès later went on to become a successful author in his own right.

The company's former editor-in-chief, Nicole Lattès, by then divorced from Lattès, took over as head of Editions Robert Laffont in 1999. The Laffont family

KEY DATES

1968: Jean-Claude Lattès founds publishing house Editions Speciales.

1971: Company is renamed Editions JC Lattès.

1981: Company is acquired by Hachette; Lattès becomes president of Hachette Livres.

2001: JC Lattès acquires Editions du Masque from Hachette.

2004: Company discovers Dan Brown's *The Da Vinci Code*, which sells more than two million copies.

2013: JC Lattès publishes the *Fifty Shades* series by E. L. James.

2014: Laurent Laffont becomes president of JC Lattès.

had long ago lost control of the Laffont publishing house. Isabelle Laffont was no stranger to publishing, having cut her teeth in the industry working from the ground up in her father's publishing company. Laffont had joined Editions Robert Laffont after completing her education at Paris's Sciences Po, one of France's elite universities. Laffont began her career working in the company's storeroom.

At one point, Laffont was even pressed into temporary service as her father's secretary for several months. Laffont's struggles to be taken seriously were further compounded by her marriage to Richard Ducousset, already one of the leading figures of the French publishing industry and future head of one of the country's top publishers, Albin Michel. As the "daughter of" and then the "wife of," Laffont found herself having to prove herself on her own merits.

MAKING A MARK IN THE NINETIES

Laffont nonetheless quickly made her mark at Editions Laffont, when she rescued a novel the company's editorial staff was about to reject. That novel, *Les Valseuses* by Bertrand Blier, became a new best seller for Editions Laffont and established Isabelle Laffont's editorial career. Laffont developed into one of the company's top editors, even after her father lost control of the company when Time Life International acquired it.

Isabelle Laffont developed a particular specialty in foreign literature. In this capacity, she established a new collection, called "Best-Sellers," including such international best-selling authors as Robert Ludlum and John le Carré. Laffont earned a reputation as having a nose for talent, signing a contract to bring then unknown John Grisham to France. After more than 20 years with Editions Robert Laffont, Isabelle Laffont had succeeded in becoming a well-respected name in French publishing in her own right.

In 1994, however, when her father appointed Bernard Fixot to take over as head of the company, Isabelle Laffont resigned. She was soon tapped to join Editions Grasset, becoming managing editor of one of France's largest publishing houses, which by then had also become part of the Hachette group. In 1995 Laffont was approached by Hachette with the request that she take over at Editions JC Lattès. Laffont described the company's situation at the time to the *Nouvel Observateur*, "When I arrived, in February, I had nothing to publish for June."

LAFFONT SEEKS TO REBUILD

Editions JC Lattès not only suffered from lack of successful authors, the company also struggled against an increasingly poor reputation among France's booksellers. Laffont set out to rebuild the company from scratch, setting out a new editorial line, while also bringing her own flair for discovering new talent. Over the next decade, Laffont established a strong stable of well-respected and successful authors, such as Marc Dugain, Delphine de Vigan, and Serge Bramly.

The company maintained both the Lattès and Laffont traditions of focusing on the generalist and commercial fiction segment. This focus on popular fiction tarnished the company's reputation with France's literary elite. Despite the success of many of its titles, Editions JC Lattès often found itself passed over for nominations for the country's many literary awards. The company nonetheless enjoyed the comfort of strong sales. By 2001 the house had become one of the fixtures of Hachette's French book publishing division.

EDITIONS DU MASQUE IN 2001

The group's strength in commercial fiction also gave it a new imprint, Editions du Masque, which had also been part of the Hachette group. That imprint stemmed from the publishing house Librairie des Champs-Élysées, originally founded as a bookstore by Albert Pigasse in 1925. Pigasse had started his career working for Grasset in 1919 before joining another renowned name in French publishing, Gallimard.

In 1925 Pigasse left Gallimard to open his bookstore. Two years later Pigasse decided to become a publisher himself, creating his own collection devoted to the mystery, detective, and thrillers genres. The new collection, called Le Masque, started off strongly, introducing France to the works of Agatha Christie, starting with her novel *The Murder of Roger Ackroyd*.

From the start, Le Masque became associated with Hachette, which agreed to handle the imprint's distribution. Hachette took control of the Librairie des Champs-Élysées, which remained the publishing house's official name into the 1990s, in 1971. As part of Editions JC Lattès, the imprint became known as Editions du Masque.

The imprint continued to build its catalog of detective, mystery, and suspense titles, which grew to nearly 4,000 titles by 2010. Under Lattès, Editions du Masque also developed a number of special collections, including pocket book imprint Masque Poche and Grands Formats, which published such authors as Philip Kerr, Ian Rankin, and Don Winslow. In 2008 suspense, adventure, and humorous fiction for the youth market were produced under the MsK imprint.

CRACKING THE *CODE* IN 2004

In the meantime, Isabelle Laffont's leadership had led Editions JC Lattès to the ranks of France's top-selling publishing houses. At the turn of the century, Laffont had been surprised by the success of a book written by her brother detailing the history of codes and ciphers. The more or less scholarly book nonetheless sold more than 20,000 copies and gave Laffont the idea that there could be a market for such esoterica in fiction as well.

Soon after, Laffont came across a novel by then-unknown author Dan Brown called *The Da Vinci Code*. Laffont read the novel over the course of a weekend and placed a bid for EUR 30,000. The planetary success of Brown's novel was echoed in France as well, where sales of its translation quickly sold more than two million copies, displacing *Papillon* as the country's largest-selling novel. Brown was to remain a prominent member of Editions JC Lattès's stable of authors and continued to drive the group's sales. In 2013 the company's release of Brown's *Inferno* generated sales of more than 800,000 copies.

FIFTY SHADES PUBLISHED: 2012

Editions JC Lattès already had a new best seller on its hand. In 2012 Isabelle Laffont won a bid to publish French-language versions of the hugely popular *Fifty Shades* trilogy of erotic novels by British author E. L. James. France's literary establishment scoffed at the possibility of the trilogy's success in France, which had its own tradition of erotic literature, with one publisher describing the series as "American-style Puritanism." Laffont, however, spotted the potential for the book beyond the country's traditional book-buying public.

As one novelist told the *New York Times*, the trilogy "has a special appeal to ordinary Frenchwomen who don't read much and long for a classic fantasy fairy tale." Laffont's intuition paid off, and the release of the first volume in the trilogy generated sales of nearly one million copies within the first three months of its release. The second volume in the novel quickly passed 500,000 copies after its release in January 2013.

By mid-2014, with the release of the trilogy's third volume, the *Fifty Shades* series had sold more than four million copies in France, in a market where sales of 50,000 copies of a book already established it as a major success. The success of the *Fifty Shades* series helped propel Editions JC Lattès's total sales to more than EUR 21 million in 2012 and to EUR 18 million ($25 million) in 2013, placing the publishing house among the best selling in the Hachette book division.

In 2014 Isabelle Laffont was appointed as chairperson of the company, turning over its direction to younger brother Laurent Laffont. Isabelle Laffont remained an active presence in the company, continuing to work as an editor for her own list of authors. Under her leadership, Editions JC Lattès had flourished to become one of France's best-selling publishing houses in the early 21st century.

M. L. Cohen

PRINCIPAL SHAREHOLDERS

Hachette Livre S.A. (100%).

PRINCIPAL SUBSIDIARIES

Les Editions du Masque.

PRINCIPAL DIVISIONS

Les Éditions JC Lattès; Les Editions du Masque.

PRINCIPAL COMPETITORS

Actes Sud S.A.; Editions Albin Michel S.A.; Editions Gallimard S.A.; La Martiniere Groupe S.A.; Les Editions Hatier S.N.C.

FURTHER READING

Bianchini, Roger Louis. "La Cinquième Génération de Juifs de Pape." *L'Express*, November 1, 2001.

Casassus, Barbara. "French Object to Livres Hebdo Sales Stats." *Bookseller*, February 9, 2007, 19.

Caviglioli, David, and Grégoire Leménager. "Isabelle Laffont, la Best-selleuse." *Le Nouvel Observateur*, February 26, 2013.

Frain, Irène. "Jean-Claude Lattès: l'Esprit des Lettres." *Paris Match*, July 10, 2012.

"France's Havas Buys Small, Too." *Publishers Weekly*, June 7, 1999, 19.

"Isabelle Laffont Nommée Présidente des Editions JC Lattès." *FranceTV Info*, June 26, 2014.

"Scarlett Johannson Awarded $6,800 in Defamation Suit." *UPI*, July 7, 2014.

"Scarlett Johannson Porte Plainte Contre les Editions JC Lattès." *AFP*, June 7, 2013.

Sciolino, Elaine. "A Defiant 'Oui' for *Fifty Shades*." *New York Times*, January 16, 2013.

EMS-Chemie Holding AG

Fuederholzstrasse 34
Herrliberg, 9704
Switzerland
Telephone: (+41 44) 915 70 00
Fax: (+41 44) 915 70 02
Web site: http://www.ems-group.com

Public Company
Incorporated: 1962 as Chemie Holding EMS AG; 1981
    as EMS-Chemie Holding AG
Employees: 2,670
Sales: CHF 1.89 billion ($1.71 billion) (2013)
Stock Exchanges: SIX Swiss
Ticker Symbol: EMS
NAICS: 325211 Plastics Material and Resin
    Manufacturing; 424690 Other Chemical and Allied
    Products Merchant Wholesalers; 325520 Adhesive
    and Sealant Manufacturing; 325180 Other Basic
    Inorganic Chemical Manufacturing

■■■

EMS-Chemie Holding AG is a world-leading producer of high-performance polymers and specialty chemicals. EMS is composed of two primary divisions. The High Performance Polymers division operates through two main subsidiaries, EMS-Grivory and EMS-EFTEC. The former specializes in the production of a wide range of polyamide materials, including high-performance resins marketed under the brand names Grilon, Grilamid, and Grivory, and used in the production of a wide range of extruded and injection-molded goods. EMS-Grivory is

also a globally operating company, with subsidiaries in Europe, North America, and Asia. EMS-EFTEC is global supplier of adhesives, sealants, coatings, and damping products, with a particular focus on the automotive industry. EMS-Chemie's Specialty Chemicals division is composed of EMS-Griltech and EMS-Patvag. The former produces fibers, adhesives, and adhesive yarns used in the production of tires, powder coatings, textile production, and other technical applications. EMS-Patvag focuses on the production of igniters for automotive air-bag gas generators.

EMSER WATER FROM 1936

EMS-Chemie was founded by Werner Oswald as a small Zurich-based company producing wood-based ethyl alcohol, or ethanol, for use as automotive fuel. Oswald's business, originally called Holzverzuckerungs AG (Hovag), was based on the Scholler process, developed by Alexandre Scholler at the dawn of the 20th century. This process used sulfuric acid to break down the fibers in wood, permitting the sugars to be fermented into alcohol.

Oswald's business came into its own with the outbreak of World War II. With no petroleum resources of its own, Switzerland faced an extreme shortage of fuel. Oswald took advantage of the situation, building a large-scale factory in the small village of Domat/Ems in 1942. Because of the high cost of the ethanol production process, the Swiss government agreed to subsidize sales of the fuel.

Before long, Hovag's production expanded to account for 30 percent of the total Swiss fuel supply. The

COMPANY PERSPECTIVES

EMS's company strategy is based on the following focus points: EMS concentrates on operational growth with speciality products. EMS defines Performance Polymers as core business. EMS returns financial resources not required for operational business to the shareholders.

product itself became popularly known as Emser Wasser (Emser Water). Hovag's payroll swelled to 200 workers, and the company became the largest enterprise in the canton of Grisons.

By the end of the war, however, Oswald recognized the need to diversify Hovag's business away from its reliance on Emser Wasser. Pressure to end the government's expensive subsidy on ethanol purchases had already begun to build by the end of the 1940s, although the subsidies were not eliminated by popular vote until 1956.

AUSCHWITZ CONNECTION IN 1947

Oswald steered the company into a new direction. Soon after World War II, Oswald had struck up a relationship with Johann Giesen, a former director of the Auschwitz concentration camp, under whose responsibility more than 30,000 forced laborers died while building the Buna factory for IG Farben. Despite his role during the war, Giesen was appointed to head of a former IG Farben's plant in Uerdingen, near Düsseldorf, by the Allied authorities.

Oswald, seeking a new direction for his company, first met Giesen in 1947 and became interested in Giesen's knowledge of IG Farben's emerging new plastics technologies, notably those being developed in one of its largest factories in Leuna. Soon after, Giesen began supplying Hovag with technology and personnel, including a number of specialists at the former Leuna factory. Giesen was ultimately relieved of his position at the IG Farben plant in 1949 after British authorities discovered he had supplied Hovag with a complete production unit, as well as two technicians to install the equipment.

Soon after, Giesen himself moved to Ems at Oswald's invitation, taking up residence at the company's Haldenstein castle. Giesen then oversaw the construction of Hovag's plastics production facility, which reportedly was built as an exact copy of the Leuna fac-

tory, complete with many of the same personnel. The former Auschwitz director not only oversaw production at the Hovag factory but also joined the company's board of directors in 1952.

As part of its transition to its new business focus, Hovag established a research and development subsidiary, Inventa, in 1947. Two years later the company also established a marketing subsidiary, Fibron AG. Backed by Giesen's chemical expertise, the company succeeded in developing a new method for the production of caprolactam, the raw ingredient and precursor to the production of a unique new plastic, based on polyamide fibers and most commonly known as nylon.

GRILON IN 1952

Hovag began industrial production of caprolactam in 1951. This business also led to the creation of a side business, manufacturing fertilizers using the ammonium sulfate produced as a by-product of the caprolactam production process. Inventa developed another lucrative side business based on the Leuna scientists' know-how, when it began licensing its caprolactam production process, starting with a Japanese company, in 1954.

The company ultimately supplied its technology for the construction of more than 300 caprolactam factories around the world. In the meantime, the tiny Ems company had surprised the world, including such global chemical giants as DuPont, the original developer of polyamide fibers, with the introduction of its own nylonlike product in 1952. Hovag dubbed its product Grilon, after its Grisons home. Early products using Grilon included hosiery and socks.

Hovag continued to benefit from its association with Giesen and the other former Leuna scientists. The company's association with the former Auschwitz director arguably enabled the company to survive the loss of the ethanol subsidies, which forced the company to shut down its production of Emser Wasser. Through the 1950s Hovag developed a growing line of products and technologies, including a range of Grilon-branded engineering plastics.

INTERNATIONAL EXPANSION

Grilon was to remain a mainstay in the company's brand stable into the 21st century. During the 1950s the company also took its first steps into the international markets, setting up its first overseas sales office in England in 1956. The company capped its transition as a fast-growing chemical fibers producer in 1960 with a name change to Emser Werke AG.

KEY DATES

1936: Werner Oswald establishes Holzverzuckerungs AG (Hovag), in order to produce ethanol.

1947: Company creates Inventa AG in order to develop and exploit a caprolactam production process.

1952: Company introduces its polyamide-based fiber, Grilon.

1960: Company changes its name to Chemie Holding EMS AG.

1983: Christoph Blocher gains majority control of EMS.

1997: EMS forms a joint venture with HB Fuller in the United States.

2009: Company opens new factories in China and India and acquires Nexis Fibers in Germany.

2014: Company is named General Motors' Supplier of the Year.

Two years later the company restructured under a holding company, Chemie Holding EMS AG, which listed its shares on the Zurich Stock Exchange, in December 1962. The Oswald family nonetheless retained majority control of EMS, while Giesen remained on the company's board of directors until his retirement in 1967.

REFOCUSED IN 1970

EMS maintained its expansion through the 1960s. During that time, it debuted a number of new product lines, including Grilonit Epoxy Resins in 1963, Grilene polyester fibers in 1964, and new polyamides including Grilamid, for the production of plastic pipes. In 1966 it released Grilon co-polyamide, for the production of packaging films.

The company had established up a new research and development facility dedicated to developing industrial applications for its thermoplastics and epoxy resins. This helped lead to the development of such products as the Griltex line of co-polyamide based fusible adhesives, used to produce textiles interlinings, introduced in 1967.

EMS's success in exporting its caprolactam production technology, notably to the emerging Asian markets, meant that its own caprolactam had become increasingly unprofitable. In 1970 the company took the decision to discontinue its production of caprolactam, as well as

fertilizers, refocusing instead on its polyamides production. During this time, a new figure emerged within the company, who would soon have a profound impact on EMS's future growth.

BLOCHER'S FAMILY ORIGIN

Christoph Blocher was born in Laufen in 1940, the seventh son in an impoverished family of 11 children. Blocher's father was a pastor. His grandfather, Eduard Blocher, had achieved some notoriety as a theologian and passionate defender of social Darwinism, Swiss neutrality, and anti-Semitic and anticommunistic ideologies. While two of Blocher's brothers became pastors themselves, Blocher initially hoped to become a farmer, studying at the Winterthur agricultural school, then going on to study agronomic engineering in Zurich.

Blocher soon abandoned his dream of farming, in large part because he possessed no land. Instead, he took up the study of law, ultimately earning his degree in 1971. In the meantime, Blocher had formed a relationship with Oswald, becoming a tutor for one of the EMS head's sons, and then becoming a part-time employee in EMS's legal department.

The relationship between Oswald and Blocher quickly deepened, with the latter becoming the former's protégé, ahead of Oswald's own children. After completing his law degree, Blocher went to work full time for the company, quickly rising to the position of its vice chairman and secretary-general. When Oswald died in the middle of a meeting in 1979, Blocher took over as the company's chairman and CEO.

THE BLOCHER ERA FROM 1983

EMS continued to build its operations through this period, despite the increasing volatility of the global economy in the 1970s. The company expanded its network of sales offices, opening a subsidiary in Japan in 1977 and in Germany and France in 1979. The company also restructured its operations again, merging all of its EMS subsidiaries under Chemie EMS Holding in 1978.

By 1981 the company had established EMS as the main brand for all of its subsidiaries. As the textiles industry shifted toward the east, Blocher led EMS into a new direction and began developing engineering plastics as its core business. As a result, the company began phasing out its textile fibers operations from 1980. Instead, the group developed new business lines, such as its Grilesta polyester resins, used for producing powder-based metal coatings, introduced that same year.

The company also entered the United States, setting up EMS-American Grilon Inc. in South Carolina in 1982. Blocher, who had been developing his political ambitions during this time as well, took control of EMS the following year. Accounts of how this occurred vary. According to the *Tages Anzeiger*, EMS's fortunes fell in the early years of the 1980s, as it faced growing competition in its core polyamide business. By 1983 Blocher announced to the Oswald family, who were still in control of the company, that EMS was nearing bankruptcy.

FINDS BUYER

Blocher proposed that the family sell their stakes in the company, and he offered to find a buyer for their shares. Soon after, Blocher announced he had found an unidentified buyer for the company, who was willing to pay the family CHF 20 million for their majority control of EMS. That buyer turned out to be Blocher himself, enabling him to gain control of the company that subsequently would be valued at between CHF 70 million and 125 million.

The deal was seen as one of the first examples of a new generation of Swiss businessmen importing so-called American-styled corporate raider tactics. EMS reported a different version of how Blocher came to control the company. Oswald's sudden death had come while EMS was already been struggling amid the economic recession of the late 1970s.

Changes in Swiss tax laws had also left the Oswald family facing higher property taxes, which they were hard-pressed to pay given the company's financial difficulties. Blocher stepped in to find a buyer for the company, leading negotiations with a number of its multinational rivals. These included General Electric, whose head, Jack Welch, offered to pay CHF 20 million for EMS.

Welch, however, planning to shed as many as half of EMS's workforce in its Ems home base. In order to save these jobs, Blocher agreed to meet General Electric's price. In either event, Blocher became EMS's majority shareholder in 1983. Over the next 20 years he built the company into a world leader in its field and one of the largest chemical companies in Switzerland. Blocher himself emerged as one of Switzerland's wealthiest people, and he was to use his wealth to become an increasingly vocal, and controversial, presence in Switzerland's growing far right-wing political sphere.

ACQUISITIONS IN THE EIGHTIES

Under Blocher's leadership, EMS took a two-pronged approach to its expansion. The company continued developing new successful products, such as its Griltex fusible adhesive power in 1986 and the weather-resistant Primid powder coatings line in 1990. In 1991 the company debuted its Grivory GV line of hardened polyamides, which opened a new era for the replacement of metal component with lighter and durable plastic alternatives.

The company's launch of transparent polyamide Grilamid TR in 1995, used for the production of the glasses frames and sunglasses lenses, helped the company become the global leader in these categories. EMS claimed leadership in another category at the end of that decade with the introduction of its Grilbond bonding agent, used in the production of automotive tires and other applications. At the same time, EMS made a series of acquisitions, starting with the TOGO Group, based in Romanshorn, Switzerland, in 1985.

Other acquisitions included SSF Dottikon AG in 1987 and Germany's Olling GmbH in 1989. The company's acquisitions continued into the next decade, to include Dinol Group, a production of corrosion protection products for the automotive industry, in 1991. The company ended that decade with the acquisition of Germany's Karl Fischer Industrieanlagen in 1999. EMS's annual revenues had soared past $650 million, and Blocher himself had become a billionaire.

ENTRY INTO TAIWAN: 1989

EMS expanded in other ways during this period as well. The company entered Taiwan in 1989, creating a performance polymers production subsidiary in Hsin Chu Hsein. The group entered Mexico three years later, forming an automotive supply joint venture with Placosa Corporation.

The company also added a production joint venture in Japan that year with UBE for the production of laurolactam, a key ingredient in the group's Grilamid line. The company expanded its U.S. presence with a joint venture with HB Fuller Automotive USA in 1997. It added the Czech Republic to its international network with the creation of a joint venture with D-Plast there in 2000.

NEW CEO IN 2003

In the meantime, Blocher had become the rising star of Switzerland's far-right political spectrum, in part through his anti-immigration idea, as well as his highly vocal stance against Swiss reparations for Jewish victims of the Holocaust. In 1999, for example, Blocher was convicted by a Zurich court for anti-Semitic libel. By the end of the 1990s Blocher had succeeded in taking the leadership of the ultraconservative SVP, helping it grow to become the nation's second-largest political party.

In the 2003 election, the SVP managed to outscore the country's Socialist Party, earning Blocher a seat on Switzerland's Federal Council, where he became head of the Federal Department of Justice and Police. The move into national politics prompted Blocher to resign from his position as chairman and CEO of EMS-Chemie. Blocher went a step further, turning over his entire stake in the company to his four children.

Blocher's eldest daughter, Magdalena Martullo-Blocher, who had joined the company two years earlier, then took over as EMS's vice president and CEO, starting on January 1, 2004. EMS continued its strong record of growth into the next decade. The company added new sales offices in Shanghai, China, in 2005 and in Mumbai, India, in 2006. The company restructured part of its operations, spinning off its fine chemicals business, EMS-Dottikon, as a separate, publicly listed company led by Markus Blocher, who then sold his share in EMS to his three sisters.

CELEBRATING ITS 75TH

EMS also invested in expanding its production, notably through the construction of a dedicated air-bag igniter production plant, as part of its EMS-Patvag business unit, in Brankovice, Czech Republic. That plan began production in 2008. The company also began shifting part of its production to China, where it established a specialty products factory for its EMS-Grivory business in Suzhou in 2008.

The company's EMF-EFTEC business added two factories of its own, in Wuhu, China, and Pune, India, in 2009. The company also completed the acquisition of Neumunster, Germany–based Nexis Fibers, a producer of polyamide-based specialty technical fibers, that year. EMS began gearing up for the celebration of its 75th anniversary in 2011, opening a public exhibition detailing its history at its Domat/Ems headquarters, as well as releasing a corporate biography, which quickly became a best seller in Switzerland.

The company also continued to position itself for further growth, adding a new assembly line in Markdorf, Germany, for its EMS-EFTEC business and opening a new state-of-the-art warehousing facility at its Domat/Ems base. EMS also celebrated its success in positioning itself as a major supplier to the global automotive industry, winning the award as General Motors Supplier of the Year in 2011 and 2012, and again in 2014.

EMS had grown into a globally operating company, with nearly 30 production facilities in 16 countries.

EMS had also posted significant sales growth in the early years of the new century as its revenues neared CHF 1.89 billion ($1.71 billion). The company had also become a global leader in each of its two core business areas, High Performance Polymers and Specialty Chemicals. EMS Chemie hoped to continue this strong record of growth as it moved deeper into the 21st century.

M. L. Cohen

PRINCIPAL SUBSIDIARIES

EFTEC (Czech Republic) a.s.; EFTEC (Elabuga) OOO (Russia); EFTEC (India) Pvt. Ltd.; EFTEC (Nizhniy Novgorod) OOO (Russia); EFTEC (Romania) S.R.L.; EFTEC (Shanghai) Engineering Co. Ltd.; EFTEC (Slovakia) s.r.o.; EFTEC (Thailand) Co. Ltd.; EFTEC (Ukraine) LLC; EFTEC AG; EFTEC Asia Pte. Ltd. (Singapore); EFTEC Automotive Materials Co., Ltd (China); EFTEC Brasil Ltda.; EFTEC Chemical Products Ltd. (China); EFTEC China Ltd. (Hong Kong); EFTEC Engineering GmbH (Germany); EFTEC Europe Holding AG; EFTEC Ltd. (UK); EFTEC NV (Belgium); EFTEC Sàrl (France); EFTEC SL d.o.o. (Slovenia); EFTEC Systems S. A. (Spain); EMS-Griltech; EMS-Chemie (China) Ltd.; EMS-Chemie (Deutschland) GmbH; EMS-Chemie (France) S.A.; EMS-Chemie (Italia) S.r.l.; EMS-Chemie (Japan) Ltd.; EMS-Chemie (Korea) Ltd.; EMS-Chemie (Luxembourg) Sarl; EMS-Chemie (Neumünster) Holding GmbH (Germany); EMS-Chemie (Neumünster) Verwaltungs GmbH (Germany); EMS-Chemie (North America) Inc. (USA); EMS-Chemie (Taiwan) Ltd.; EMS-Chemie (UK) Ltd.; EMS-Chemie AG; EMS-Grilon Holding Inc. (USA); EMS-Metering AG; EMS-Patvag s.r.o. (Czech Republic); EMS-UBE Ltd. (Japan).

PRINCIPAL DIVISIONS

High Performance Polymers; Specialty Chemicals.

PRINCIPAL OPERATING UNITS

EMS-Grivory; EMS-EFTEC; EMS-Griltech; EMS-Patvag.

PRINCIPAL COMPETITORS

Australian Vinyls Corporation Proprietary Ltd.; Dow Chemical Co.; E.I. du Pont de Nemours and Co.; LyondellBasell Netherlands Holdings B.V.; Saudi Basic Industries Corp.

FURTHER READING

"Christoph Blocher—der Profi." *Tages Anzeiger*, December 28, 2011.

"EMS Chemie Wins Norma Group's First Global Recognition Award." *Plastics News*, July 30, 2014.

Kreutzberg, Martin. "How to Build a Group." *WOZ*, June 14, 2012.

Pilarski, Laura. "EMS to Spin Off Fine Chemicals Unit." *Chemical Week*, February 23, 2005.

Wessel, Birgit. "EMS-Chemie Feiert 75-jähriges Jubiläum." *K-Zeitung*, February 29, 2012.

Ergodyne Corporation

1021 Bandana Boulevard East, Suite 220
St. Paul, Minnesota 55108
U.S.A.
Telephone: (651) 642-9889
Fax: (651) 642-1882
Web site: http://www.ergodyne.com

Private Company
Incorporated: 1983 as Comp Equipment Corp.
Employees: 250
Sales: $50 million (2010 est.)
NAICS: 339920 Sporting and Athletic Goods Manufacturing

■ ■ ■

Ergodyne Corporation is a St. Paul, Minnesota–based manufacturer and global distributor of workplace safety and productivity products. Protective gear includes gloves, knee pads, head protection, eye protection, high-visibility apparel, footwear, and back and wrist supports. Ergodyne also provides workers with protection from the elements, offering warm work wear, cooling materials, and work shelters. Productivity products include tool belts and pouches, storage bags, lanyards, and work-site organizers. In addition to its Minnesota operation, Ergodyne maintains a facility in Amsterdam to distribute products in Europe and other parts of the world. Ergodyne products are distributed through a network of more than 400 authorized dealers. Ergodyne is a subsidiary of Tenacious Holdings, Inc., controlled by the Votel family.

COMPANY FOUNDED: 1983

Ergodyne was founded in St. Paul, Minnesota, in 1983 by Dr. Thomas Votel, a physician who specialized in occupational medicine. Votel developed the company to make and market a flexible strap-on back support device he invented to help prevent industrial lifting injuries. He named the company Comp Equipment Corp., the name indicative of his marketing focus, workers' compensation insurance companies.

His belief was that in order to reduce claims on back injuries, insurers would urge their clients to use the back support product. To launch the company, Dr. Votel raised $360,000. The first full-time employee to be hired was his 28-year-old son, also named Thomas Votel. He had recently completed his undergraduate degree in business management at the University of St. Thomas in St. Paul, where he would also pursue an MBA degree.

He joined a company that experienced an inauspicious beginning. There was no doubt that there was a market for an occupational back support product. Back injuries in the American workplace were commonplace. Unfortunately, the ergonomic field was still new, and the Comp Equipment name added little in the way of branding. The company failed to win a single customer over its first two years.

Three presidents fled the company, leaving behind three junior employees. One of them was Tom Votel, who in 1986 became the new president. He had already developed the foundation of a marketing strategy for a business school term paper and persuaded his father to allow him to attempt to turn around the struggling company.

COST-CUTTING MEASURES

One of Votel's first steps was to drop the Comp Equipment name for something with greater branding potential. Because he was targeting the nascent field of ergonomics, he renamed the business Ergodyne. He also cut costs, exchanging the $1,100-a-month office in St. Paul's Energy Park complex in favor of a small house at less than half the price. He also used the expensive furniture purchased by the original management team to pay off a debt with a video production house.

Votel erased the debt with the company's advertising agency by persuading it to accept stock in the company. The attorney who handled the private placement of stock forgave his fee until Ergodyne was able to afford it. He was finally paid in full five years later. In order to help put Ergodyne on a firmer financial footing, Votel made a concerted effort to build a distribution network in the industrial safety market. It proved to be a particularly difficult challenge.

Votel received a major break in 1986 when he met Tom Barnard, a retired 3M manager who had worked in the Occupational Health and Safety Products division. Because of his position and longevity, Barnard was well familiar with all of the industrial safety equipment distributors. Votel hired Barnard as a consultant, and Ergodyne quickly assembled a distribution network. After the first fiscal year under Votel's leadership, Ergodyne posted a small profit on revenues of nearly $1 million.

EXPANSION AND DIVERSIFICATION

To maintain growth, Ergodyne expanded its product offerings. For the industrial market, the company introduced a new type of work glove made with a polymer that absorbed the shock of jackhammers and other power tools. Ergodyne also exploited the market for office ergonomics, a field that was beginning to take shape as the use of personal computers became widespread and the effects of poorly designed work spaces and repetitive tasks began to take their toll on office workers.

In the early 1990s the company developed adjustable keyboard wrist rests and mouse rests as well as strap-on wrist supports, adjustable foot rests, back rests, and lumbar rolls. In addition, Ergodyne developed a strap-on support for people suffering from tennis elbow. Beyond ergonomic products, the company in 1991 introduced a pair of WorkFlex warm-up and body mechanics videos. Later, Ergodyne added the WorkSmart Warm-Up and Stretch software program for personal computers, providing exercises to reduce the chance of injury from prolonged computer use.

FIRST SALES MANAGER HIRED

Sales grew rapidly as the new products gained traction. After sales doubled to $12 million in 1991, Votel hired its first sales manager to help maintain momentum. Annual sales grew to more than $40 million for the fiscal year ending on April 30, 1994.

By this point, Ergodyne was dividing its products between two flagship brands, ProFlex for industrial workers and WorkSmart for the office environment. Additionally, in 1994 Ergodyne struck a private-label deal with Steelcase Inc., a global office furniture manufacturer, to package ergonomic products, training programs, and other services under Steelcase's Detail brand.

Ergodyne suffered a setback in 1994, as did other manufacturers of back support belts, when a working group of the National Institute for Occupational Safety and Health (NIOSH) declared that the available scientific evidence did not support the claims of Ergodyne and others that back belts reduced the risk of back injury. The NIOSH group maintained that more research was necessary. Manufacturers agreed additional study was needed but were outraged with the implication that back belts were a mere nostrum.

ON3 DEVICE RELEASED: 1998

With its original product line under fire, Ergodyne increased the attention it paid to other product categories. The ProFlex hand protection product line was redesigned and expanded. Ergodyne developed ergonomic seating products, but they did not sell

---

KEY DATES

1983: Company is founded as Comp Equipment Corp.
1986: Ergodyne name is adopted.
1998: On3 Lateral Transfer Device is introduced.
2008: Tenacious Holdings, Inc., becomes Ergodyne's parent company.
2014: New CFO is hired.

---

especially well. More successful was the 1998 introduction of the On3 Lateral Transfer Device that opened up the hospital market for Ergodyne.

The product eliminated the need to lift patients manually during lateral transfers. A single person could easily move a patient from a bed to a cart in just 20 seconds. It was not a product normally carried by its distribution network, however. In 2000 Ergodyne assigned exclusive North American distribution rights for the On3 to Hill-Rom, a medical technology subsidiary of Hillenbrand Industries, Inc., that distributed hospital beds.

It was also during the late 1990s that Ergodyne introduced the Chill-Its brand of evaporative cooling bandanas. It was followed by the ThermalWear cooling vest. In 1999 the company added a new line of elastic wraps and neoprene sleeves. The Ergodyne 400 series of elastic wraps included three wrist supports and two ankle supports. They could be worn on either wrist, next to the skin or over clothing. The Ergodyne 600 series sleeves included compression sleeves designed specifically for knees, thighs, calves, and ankles.

FURTHER PRODUCT EXPANSION

At the start of the new century, Ergodyne continued to expand its product lineup and increase sales. A new industrial seating line included ergonomic workbenches, suited for repetitive task work such as assembly and sorting. Other designs included sit stands, providing support for standing workers, and a mobile stool called a Work Trolley. Ergodyne redesigned its work gloves as part of creating the Tenacious Work Gear branding concept.

In 2001 the company unveiled six specialized hand protection products, including full or three-quarters-fingered mechanics gloves, trade gloves, utility gloves, box-handler gloves, and new vibration-reduction gloves for use with power tools. Later in the year Ergodyne added computer mitts, which included built-in wrists pads for further comfort. Ergodyne, in the meantime, did not neglect its original product line.

BUDGET BACK BRACE RELEASED

In 2002 it introduced the ProFlex Model 1650 Economy All Elastic Back Support. With a suggested list price of less than $10, it proved popular and provided Ergodyne with a position at another price point in the back support sector. The product pipeline remained full mid-decade. In late 2005 Ergodyne added to its cold-weather products with the introduction of Trex Ice Traction Grippers. The product was fitted with steel studs that could be attached to boots or shoes by way of a stretchable rubber frame.

The following year Ergodyne entered a new product category, introducing a new line of tool belts, tool bags, and accessories. Also in 2006 Ergodyne extended its knee protection products with ProFlex kneeling pads. The pads were made with thick, closed-cell foam rubber and were resistant to petroleum products and other corrosive liquids. They were nonconductive as well.

Ergodyne added to its cooling products in 2006 with the GloWear Ranger Hat, Hi-Vis Orange Mesh Gloves, and Hi-Vis Stop-Go Gloves for construction, utility, department of transportation, and other outdoor work. Several months later, Ergodyne introduced four products to help protect workers against winter conditions. They included two new gloves that provided warmth without sacrificing dexterity, and two winter work hats, including a high-visibility model for night work.

HOLDING COMPANY FORMED: 2008

Ergodyne broadened its product range further in 2007 and 2008. New items included Trex Footbeds, footwear inserts that offered support and shock absorption, and new Chill-It products, including a headband, neck shade, do-rag, cooling towel, and improved cooling vest. Other products included the Core Performance Work Wear line of protective apparel, including a premium black leather tool rig as well as a line of canvas tool and equipment bags to fill out the company's emerging tool belt line.

Also in 2008 the Votel family formed Tenacious Holdings Inc. to serve as the parent company for Ergodyne and a new sourcing service division called Basic Issue. As the first decade of the new century came to a close Ergodyne continued to roll out new products. Several foul-weather jackets helped to fill out the

GloWear line of high-visibility apparel. A variety of knee pads, including a new gel series, were added.

HOT ROX RELEASED: 2009

In 2009 Ergodyne introduced the Insect Shield treatment to its apparel lines. Using a synthetic version of a natural repellant, the treatment helped to ward off insects to prevent Lyme disease, West Nile virus, and other insect-borne diseases. Also in 2009 the company introduced a new technology, Hot Rox, for use in extremely cold conditions. The product was a heat-exchanger mouthpiece that captured heat and vapor and returned it to the worker's body through inhalation.

Not only did the device keep workers warm, it slowed dehydration. To help workers in hot conditions, Ergodyne introduced a new line of portable work shelters. Innovation continued in 2014 with the addition of a magnetic tray organizer. In that same year the company added flame-resistant apparel to its Core Performance Work Wear line.

Changes were also made in the management ranks in August 2014 with the hiring of Sue Horvath as the company's new chief financial officer and vice president of finance. Tom Votel remained president and CEO of the company that he had brought from the verge of ruin. It had become a leading provider of worker safety products in the United States and was well-positioned for ongoing growth.

Ed Dinger

PRINCIPAL DIVISIONS

Elements; Protection, Productivity.

PRINCIPAL COMPETITORS

Blauer Manufacturing Co., Inc.; Lion Apparel, Inc.; Norcross Safety Products LLC.

FURTHER READING

D'Amico, Esther. "Ergonomic Endeavors." *Home Office Computing*, March 1994.

"Ergodyne User Support Devices Bow." *HFD–The Weekly Home Furnishings Newspaper*, January 4, 1993.

LeBar, Gregg. "NIOSH Challenges Back Belt Use." *Occupational Hazards*, September 1994.

"Minnesota's Best Entrepreneurs: 1992 Entrepreneurs of the Year." *Minnesota Ventures*, August 1992, 30.

"When's the Right Time to Hire a Sales Manager?" *Inc.*, September 1993.

Youngblood, Dick. "Founder's Son Gets Pat on the Back for Turning Around Ergonomics Firm." *Minneapolis Star Tribune*, March 17, 1993.

Esther Price Candies Corporation

194 Woodman Drive
Dayton, Ohio 45431
U.S.A.
Telephone: (937) 253-2121
Toll Free: (855) 337-8437
Fax: (937) 253-6034
Web site: http://www.estherprice.com

Private Company
Founded: 1926
Employees: 120
Sales: $45 million (2013 est.)
NAICS: 311352 Confectionery Manufacturing from
    Purchased Chocolate

■ ■ ■

Esther Price Candies Corporation is a privately owned confections company based in Dayton, Ohio. The company is best known as a maker of boxed chocolates, offering a wide variety of solid and filled chocolates available in sizes that range from one-half pound to four pounds. Customers can also customize their own boxes, selecting their favorite varieties. Other Esther Price products include sugar-free chocolates, chocolate bars, chocolate-covered pretzels and potato chips, hot chocolate mix, ice cream and dessert toppings, and premium nuts. Esther Price products are sold through a catalog and the company's web site, as well as seven Esther Price retail stores located in the Dayton and Cincinnati, Ohio, area. Many Kroger, Meijer, and Remke Biggs supermarkets also carry Esther Price

products in parts of Ohio, Indiana, and Illinois. In addition, Esther Price assembles gift baskets, towers, and trays and offers special flavors and package sizes for its corporate, fund-raising, and wedding businesses. Esther Price is owned by the family of Jim Day, who along with three partners purchased the business from the founder, Esther Price.

ESTHER PRICE, OHIO BORN

Esther Price was born Esther Rose Rohman in 1904 in Hamilton, Ohio. A month after her birth, her father took a job with the National Cash Register Company as a toolmaker, and the family moved to Dayton. Here she received a public school education and in seventh grade took a home-economics class. Shortly before Christmas the class learned how to make fudge, and Esther became enamored with the candy, making it at every opportunity at home.

Esther quit high school early and worked at Rike-Kumler Department Store in Dayton. She soon began making fudge as a treat for her fellow employees. After she married Ralph Price in 1924 and left her employment at the store when she gave birth to twins, her friends at her old job encouraged her make fudge to sell to the department store employees. A friend then put together an order for 23 pounds of fudge. When Esther attempted to deliver the candy, however, she was intercepted by the head floorman, who maintained that if employees wanted candy at work, they had to buy it at the store's candy counter. After one taste of the fudge, he reportedly decided that Rike would sell her fudge to the employees from the candy counter, but at twice the price.

Thus by chance Esther Price became a de facto candy supplier to a department store. At the end of business each day, she was told how much fudge to prepare that night. When she was ill and unable to fill that day's order, Rike quickly found someone else to replace her and meet the demand for fudge she had created. Soon she was making candy again but this time selling it out of her house. She also sold fudge door-to-door to offices in downtown Dayton.

PRICE BEGINS DIPPING

One of Price's regular customers requested that she cover his fudge with chocolate, which led to her experimenting with chocolate. Once she became comfortable with the process, she began buying 10-pound cakes of chocolate and started dipping fudge. The resulting pieces were about the size of a golf ball. At the request of a customer, she made smaller pieces, and both sizes became popular with customers.

To keep pace with demand for her candy, Price bought a large mixer that she had installed in her basement. After the board of health learned of her business, she had to partition off her basement, which now became a makeshift factory. A woman from church helped to dip chocolate and became her first employee.

Running a small candy company proved challenging for a woman during this time. When local banks refused to lend her money for the mixer, she had to borrow money from friends. Without a line of credit, just buying ingredients for the candy often proved difficult, and she was frequently obliged to ask people for loans. Often Price was unable to make more candy until the batch she had just finished was sold.

A UNIQUE CHALLENGE

Price also lived in fear of her husband being fired from his job at the National Biscuit Company (Nabisco). Nabisco prided itself on paying a wage that would allow a man to have his wife stay at home, and a manager there had already fired a man whose wife worked for the telephone company. He believed that an employed spouse made the company look bad. Fortunately, that manager was replaced by a man who tasted Price's candy and enjoyed it so much that he became a customer.

Gradually, Price expanded her product lines. She made cream eggs for Easter and then began adding new varieties to her chocolate boxes, including chocolate-covered cherries and peanut butter creams. She also produced peanut brittle. When World War II led to sugar rationing, however, Price could make candy only if her customers provided the sugar.

With the war over, Price resumed making candy on a larger scale. The growing number of customers, however, disrupted family life. She set up a self-serve business on her front porch, allowing people to buy candy and make their own change, but her neighbors were not pleased with the constant traffic and blocked driveways. At the behest of the city, she looked for a new home with wider streets that could accommodate her customers. She found a suitable property in 1952 and had it modeled to include a candy kitchen in the back and a retail shop in the front. Steadily, she acquired more tables and new equipment and hired additional workers to help meet the growing demand for her candy.

Relatives in Cincinnati promoted Esther Price candies, and soon people were driving to Dayton to make purchases. Recognizing an opportunity, Price opened a small store in Cincinnati across from a shopping center under the name Price's Candies. Because there was an existing company called Price Candies, she eventually changed the name to Esther Price Candies. The shop proved so popular that the parking proved inadequate, and a new Cincinnati location had to be found in 1965.

To serve her customers who worked at the Wright-Patterson Air Force Base east of Dayton, Price leased a store in a nearby shopping center. A customer also told her that he found it difficult to reach her Dayton store before it closed at 6 p.m. He suggested it would be more convenient if a local Kroger Supermarket carried her products. She had always refused to sell candy to retailers, preferring to maintain exclusivity, but the Kroger store had just opened a gourmet section and she arranged to have her candy sold there in a refrigerated case bearing her name. In time, other Kroger stores carried Esther Price candies as well, and a long-term relationship blossomed. A variety of other area retailers, including florists, card shops, and Music City Discount Records in Hamilton, Ohio, also carried Esther Price candies.

COMPANY SOLD: 1976

After 50 years of running a candy business, Price was ready to retire and sell her company in 1976. When she failed to receive an acceptable price from Kroger, she

```
┌─────────────────────────────────────────┐
│  ┌───────────────────────────────────┐  │
│  │            KEY DATES              │  │
│  ├───────────────●───────────────────┤  │
│  │                                   │  │
│  │  1926:  Esther Price begins selling homemade fudge │
│  │         in Dayton, Ohio.          │  │
│  │  1952:  Price buys Dayton home to build candy │
│  │         kitchen.                  │  │
│  │  1976:  Price sells her business. │  │
│  │  2006:  Jim Day becomes the sole owner. │
│  │  2013:  A third Cincinnati-area store opens. │
│  └───────────────────────────────────┘  │
└─────────────────────────────────────────┘
```

sold Esther Price Candies, including three stores and the wholesale business, to four Dayton men: Jim Day, Ralph Schmidt, Jim Bates, and Joe Haarmeyer. Day, a concrete contractor, and Schmidt, an electrician, were childhood friends and often worked together. Initially, Esther Price Candies was just an investment for them. The business was to be run by a hired manager, but they quickly grew dissatisfied and took charge themselves. Schmidt and Day also bought out their two partners before the end of the first year.

With the help of Price, who stayed on as a consultant, the contractor and the electrician learned the candy business. Rather than risk tampering with a successful formula, they followed her philosophy as well as her recipes. Because she overfilled her boxes of chocolates so that they held more than the listed weight, they did the same. She also left them with experienced workers, who knew how to make candy to her specifications, and they refrained from tampering with success.

Schmidt and Day made contributions in their own way, bringing to bear their experience managing businesses and understanding of the importance of good equipment. They bought a new extruder that placed small pieces of candy on the enrobing belt, a task previously accomplished by hand by 14 people. Not only did the machine create a more efficient operation, it improved product consistency. To speed up the operation, the new owners also installed several conveyors to further eliminate time-consuming manual labor. In short, the quality of the candy remained the same; there was just more of it to sell.

With more available product, Schmidt and Day were able to expand the company's wholesale business. Around 1990 Esther Price Candies also added a mail-order business. The company remained, however, very much a regional business. Other than some radio and television spots around Valentine's Day, Easter, and Christmas, the company did little in the way of advertising, relying mostly on reputation and word of mouth.

Nevertheless, business grew at an annual pace of 5 percent during the 1990s. The decade also saw the passing of Price, who died at the age of 89 in 1994.

NEW CENTURY, CONTINUED GROWTH

Esther Price Candies began the new century with annual sales of about $10 million and expansion on multiple fronts as the per capita consumption of chocolate steadily increased. Moreover, boxed chocolates were enjoying double-digit growth, due in no small measure to such larger competitors as Russell Stover promoting the idea of boxed chocolates as a year-round treat. The company's mail-order sales continued to improve and were supplemented by Internet sales early in the first decade of the 21st century. In addition, the company launched a corporate awards program, and several companies in its region allowed the company to set up holiday kiosks on their properties.

In 2006 Day became sole owner of Esther Price Candies; Schmidt died the following year. Day was now assisted in running the company by his wife, Elaine, their three daughters, as well as several sons-in-laws and granddaughters. As the decade unfolded, the company added to its retail business. In the fall of 2006 Esther Price Candies acquired a farmhouse in the village of North Clayton, Ohio, where a new candy store opened to accommodate customers north of Dayton. In 2010 the company added a second store in Cincinnati, this one on the west side of the city, which took over a former Hollywood Video outlet. A third store in Greater Cincinnati, and the seventh retail outlet overall, opened in 2013.

Closing in on its 100th anniversary, Esther Price Candies maintained its popularity in its market. In 2013 readers of *Ohio Magazine* named Esther Price the best Ohio-made candy. Although expansion beyond the region was uncertain, Esther Price Candies was well positioned to enjoy continued growth as a family-owned regional business.

Ed Dinger

PRINCIPAL DIVISIONS

Retail; Wholesale; Fundraising; Corporate.

PRINCIPAL COMPETITORS

Godiva Chocolatier Inc.; The Hershey Company; Russell Stover Candies, Inc.

FURTHER READING
Driehaus, Bob. "Sweet Tooth for Success." *Cincinnati Post*, April 22, 2000.

Hills, Wes. "Chocolatier Esther Price Dies at 89." *Dayton Daily News*, January 10, 1994.

Morawski, Lisa. "Sweet Success." *Dayton Business Journal*, February 1, 1999.

Price, Esther, and Linda Otto Lipsett. *Chocolate Covered Cherries: Esther Price's Memories.* Dayton, OH: Halstead & Meadows Publishing, 1991.

Schwartzberg, Eric. "Esther Price Owner Dedicated to Chocolate Business." *Dayton Daily News*, August 17, 2014.

Scully, Carla Zanetos. "Preserving a Candy Tradition—Priceless." *Candy Industry*, May 2005.

Zimmerman, Susan. "Esther Price Candies: The Next Generation." *Candy Industry*, August 1993.

Fahlgren Mortine Inc.

—■—

4030 Easton Station, Suite 300
Columbus, Ohio 43219
U.S.A.
Telephone: (614) 383-1500
Web site: http://www.fahlgrenmortine.com

Private Company
Founded: 1962 as Fahlgren Advertising Agency
Employees: 200
Sales: $150 million (2013 est.)
NAICS: 541810 Advertising Agencies

■ ■ ■

Based in Columbus, Ohio, Fahlgren Mortine Inc. is an independent midsized marketing communications agency. The company's wide range of services include advertising, media buying, identity design, brand building, social media, trade show coordination, public relations, public affairs, corporate communications, and corporate crisis management. Fahlgren serves clients in such sectors as automotive, business-to-business, consumer packaged goods, education, financial services, healthcare, retail, technology, and tourism and economic development. Additional offices are maintained in Cincinnati, Cleveland, and Dayton, Ohio; Charleston and Parkersburg, West Virginia; Denver, Colorado; Fort Lauderdale and Tallahassee, Florida; Greenville and Myrtle Beach, South Carolina; Lexington, Kentucky; and New York City. One of Fahlgren's most enduring accounts has been a McDonald's restaurant owners group for which the agency has handled co-op advertis-

ing since 1975. Neil Mortine serves as president and chief executive officer of Fahlgren Mortine.

FAHLGREN NAME ORIGINS

Providing Fahlgren Mortine with the first half of its name was H. Smoot Fahlgren. Born in Parkersburg, West Virginia, he returned to his hometown in 1962 at the age of 32 after finishing his college education at the University of Virginia and Marietta College in Ohio and completing his military service. Although he had only a single marketing course as training, he decided to start an advertising agency. He soon received a break when O. Ames Lawn and Garden Tools cut its advertising budget from $500,000 to just $50,000, making the account too small for its agency of record, New York's D'Arcy Advertising. For Fahlgren, however, it was a plum account, providing him with a much needed $7,500 in income.

Next, the fledgling Fahlgren Advertising Agency added the business of a local savings and loan as well as a bank. In need a creative director, Fahlgren hired a sign painter named Don Whitlatch for the job. Whitlatch did not lack for talent. He eventually launched his own corporate design firm, and later in life, following a heart attack, Whitlatch became an acclaimed wildlife painter.

Fahlgren added more employees as his agency took on more accounts. To help manage the business while he drummed up business and wrote ad copy, Fahlgren hired James W. Swearington, a trained pharmacist looking for a new line of work. He would become vice president and general manager of the agency. As the agency grew larger, it was able to lure away accounts

COMPANY PERSPECTIVES

We "think wider," offering social media, digital, advertising, PR, media, research, branding and design services to clients looking to build brands and enhance reputation.

from more established shops. For example, it won the business of the Chesapeake and Potomac Telephone Company, which had been held by Philadelphia's N.W. Ayer & Son, the country's oldest ad agency.

FERRIS MERGER: 1970

As it expanded, the Fahlgren Advertising Agency was renamed Fahlgren & Associates. The firm also grew through external means. In 1970 the shop merged with the David Ferris advertising agency of Cincinnati to become Fahlgren & Ferris. The new business helped the agency to reach $6 million in revenues in 1974. More rapid growth followed, both organically and through acquisition. By the early 1980s additional full-service offices were also located in Toledo, Ohio, and Charlotte, North Carolina, while service offices were maintained in Lexington, Kentucky, and Columbus, Ohio. In the meantime, offices in Pittsburgh and Washington, D.C., failed to take root and were closed.

A major turning point in the history of Fahlgren Mortine came in 1984 when Fahlgren & Ferris merged with Marion, Ohio–based Howard Swink Advertising. The origins of the Howard Swink agency reached back to the 1920s with the launch of the mail and printing business of The Folks on Gospel Hill, which formed the Jay H. Maish Agency to handle its advertising. One of the young account executives was Howard Swink, who struck out on his own in 1937, taking with him five clients for his one-man agency. The business enjoyed steady growth.

By early 1960s the agency had more than 30 accounts in all of Ohio's major cities and opened an office in Toronto, Canada, to service one of its clients. Howard Swink gained greater recognition in 1964 by launching a long-running advertising campaign in the midwest edition of the *Wall Street Journal* with ads that featured the tagline "What's an agency like Howard Swink doing in Marion, Ohio?" For 18 years, the ads ran in the *Journal*, promoting the agency as well as its clients. Howard Swink died in 1968.

Although touting its connection to Marion, Howard Swink added offices in Cleveland and

Columbus, Ohio, and Greensboro, North Carolina, through mergers, leading the agency to stop running the *Journal* ads in 1982. In that year, the agency had merged with Columbus-based Kight, Haunty to become known as SwinkKight Haunty in Columbus. In Cleveland, it operated as Swink and Schurdell, and in Marion and Greensboro, it was known as Howard Swink Advertising. Some continuity resulted in the merger with Fahlgren & Ferris, with the combined operations assuming the Fahlgren & Swink name.

HEADQUARTERS MOVES TO COLUMBUS: 1986

Smoot Fahlgren served as chief executive officer and chairman of the $85 million firm. Later in 1984, Fahlgren & Swink grew even larger through the acquisition of a two-year-old Atlanta, Georgia, advertising agency, Nucifora & Associates. Because of the greater scope of the agency and high concentration of Ohio offices, Fahlgren & Swink moved its head office from Parkersburg to Columbus in March 1986. To help promote the agency's new home, the old *Wall Street Journal* ad campaign was resurrected, but now the tagline read "What's an agency like Fahlgren & Swink doing in Columbus?"

Fahlgren & Swink remained independent until it was acquired in 1988 by Lintas New York, Inc., a subsidiary of the Interpublic Group of Companies. At the time Fahlgren & Swink generated $135 million in annual billings. With the deep pockets of its new owners, the agency attempted to grow even larger. In 1988 an agreement-in-principle was reached to acquire Tampa, Florida's Stokes, Epstein, Moore, Caborn & Moore, in order to add the Cellular One account in Florida, which was in review at the time. The deal was scuttled at the eleventh hour in the spring of 1989. In the fall of that year, however, Fahlgren & Swink succeeded in acquiring the largest advertising agency in the Tampa Bay area, Benito Advertising Inc. During the previous year Benito enjoyed billings of $43.5 million.

Despite its success in building its Florida business, Fahlgren & Swink faced challenges elsewhere. In 1989 the agency lost several clients, including the $10 million Banc One Corp. account and Central Benefits Mutual Insurance Co. As a result, Fahlgren & Swink trimmed its workforce in early 1990. Other changes soon followed. The Cleveland office was consolidated with another agency in which Interpublic held a significant interest. Smoot Fahlgren was replaced as chairman by David Martin, although he remained CEO. Martin was the founder of a Richmond, Virginia, advertising agency, Hawley & Martin, which was subsequently acquired by Fahlgren & Swink's corporate parent. The combined business took the name of Fahlgren Martin.

MANAGEMENT ACQUIRES FAHLGREN: 1994

The association with Hawley & Martin proved to be short-lived. The business was sold in 1993, and Fahlgren & Martin now became known as Fahlgren Inc. Smoot Fahlgren stepped down as CEO, succeeded by Steve Drongowski, but returned as the firm's chairman. A more important change followed. In 1994 Interpublic acquired Ammirati & Puris, an agency that did work for Burger King. Because Fahlgren performed McDonald's franchise-group work, accounting for one-third of its business, Interpublic faced a conflict of interest within its ranks. To solve the problem, Interpublic helped Fahlgren's management team buy back the company.

Although independent, Fahlgren was now a small regional advertising agency without a deep-pocketed New York parent. The agency attempted to gain further scale and geographic reach in 1998 through a merger with Dallas-based Moroch & Associates. The two regional firms appeared a good fit because both were major McDonald's agencies. They also performed local marketing business for several film companies, including 20th Century Fox, Miramax, and New Line Cinema. The deal was never finalized, however, and in 1999 Moroch & Associates sold a minority stake to Leo Burnett USA.

In 2001 Fahlgren made another attempt at a major merger to help establish a national footprint, negotiating a possible combination with another Columbus-based advertising agency, HMS Partners. HMS was especially attractive to Fahlgren because in recent years it had added public relations and interactive units, capabilities that Fahlgren lacked. With a broader range of services, Fahlgren hoped to attract more business. Because management of the two agencies was unable to agree on

the future direction of a combined firm, the talks were terminated in late February 2001.

LORD, SULLIVAN & YODER ACQUIRED: 2003

Finally, in the spring of 2003, Fahlgren expanded its service offerings with the acquisition of Columbus-based Lord, Sullivan & Yoder (LSY), a marketing communications and public relations firm. LSY and Fahlgren also shared a common heritage. LSY was started in 1962 by three Howard Swink employees. LSY's public relations and investor relations unit was established by Neil Mortine in 1986. While the Lord, Sullivan & Yoder name was eliminated, and Fahlgren Inc. remained the name of the enlarged firm, Mortine served as president of his own unit, known as Fahlgren Mortine. Fahlgren's president and CEO since 1993, Steve Drongowski, stayed on as the head for the parent company. He had also by now succeeded Smoot Fahlgren as chairman.

In August 2009 Drongowski announced that he was stepping down as chairman and CEO of Fahlgren Inc. at the end of the year, although he would remain as a consultant for another year. Mortine, whose unit had emerged as one of the country's Top 100 public relations firms according to *PR Week*, was named to succeed him in both posts. Mortine wasted little time in expanding Fahlgren, completing several acquisitions in 2010. They included the Cleveland-based public-relations firm Edward Howard & Co., the Dayton-area marketing and public relations firm Sabatino Day, and Columbus-based Web-design firm GRIP Technology. An office was also opened in Charleston, West Virginia, to service the West Virginia Lottery Commission account.

In 2011 Fahlgren Inc. changed its name for the first time in nearly 20 years. In light of the contribution of its chairman and CEO, the firm now became known as Fahlgren Mortine Inc. Its desire for further growth continued apace. In January 2014 the agency acquired Denver, Colorado–based Turner PR, to grow its presence in the tourism market. Turner clients included Albuquerque, New Mexico, and the state of Utah. Later in the year Fahlgren Mortine expanded its western footprint by opening an office in Boise, Idaho, primarily to service client J.R. Simplot Co., a food and agribusiness company. The Boise office would also handle California-based clients. Moving forward, Fahlgren Mortine was likely to open new offices and scout for further acquisitions as part of a strategic effort to grow beyond the limitations of a midsize marketing communications agency.

Ed Dinger

PRINCIPAL SUBSIDIARIES

Turner PR.

PRINCIPAL COMPETITORS

Campbell-Ewald Company; The Martin Agency, Inc.; W.B. Doner & Company.

FURTHER READING

Barmash, Isadore. "Interpublic Group Unit Adds Fahlgren & Swink." *New York Times*, October 12, 1988.

Dougherty, Philip H. "Hometown Agency Success." *New York Times*, May 20, 1982.

Franklin, Peter D. "Agency Changes Its Name." *Columbus Dispatch*, May 17, 1990.

Lilly, Stephen. "Fahlgren & Swink Hit by Client Losses." *Business First-Columbus*, January 8, 1990.

"Swink Agency Continues to Flaunt It." *Columbus Dispatch*, January 7, 1986.

"Swink Firm Takes Giant Strike Here." *Marion (OH) Star*, August 3, 1963.

Wolf, Barnet D. "Fahlgren Completes Acquisition." *Columbus Dispatch*, June 24, 2003.

Fifth Group Restaurants LLC

———— ■ ————

229 Peachtree Street NE
Peachtree Center
International Tower, Suite 600
Atlanta, Georgia 30303
U.S.A.
Telephone: (404) 815-4700
Fax: (678) 302-3222
Web site: http://www.fifthgroup.com

Private Company
Incorporated: 1992 as South City Management Group
Employees: 556
Sales: $29.9 million (2012)
NAICS: 722511 Full-Service Restaurants

■ ■ ■

Fifth Group Restaurants LLC is a privately held company that operates several restaurants in the Atlanta, Georgia, area. The flagship eatery is the South City Kitchen, which has been serving its own style of classic Southern cuisine in midtown Atlanta since 1993. A second South City Kitchen is located in the Atlanta suburb of Vinings. Other Fifth Group restaurants include Alma Cocina, a modern Mexican restaurant; Ecco, offering Italian and Mediterranean cuisine; Lure, a seafood house; La Tavola Trattoria, a highly regarded Italian restaurant located in Atlanta's Virginia-Highland neighborhood; and The Original El Taco, a neighborhood taqueria offering Tex-Mex dishes. Smaller footprint versions of Ecco and The Original El Taco are also located at Atlanta's Hartsfield-Jackson International Airport.

In addition, Fifth Group offers catering and event design services through its Bold American Events-Catering subsidiary. Event spaces include the King Plow Event Gallery and a smaller venue, Studio 887. Both are housed in the King Plow Arts Center, a century-old renovated factory space in Atlanta's Westside neighborhood. Bold American also hosts weddings and corporate events in other Atlanta locations, including the Atlanta Botanical Gardens.

SOUTH CITY KITCHEN OPENS: 1993

Fifth Group Restaurants was founded in 1992 as South City Management Group by Christopher Goss, Robert Kukler, and Steve Simon to develop the original South City Kitchen Restaurant. Goss served as the first president of the company. He was the former chef and general manager of the popular Magnolias restaurant in Charleston, South Carolina, and served as vice president of the corporate owner, Hospitality Management Group, Inc. Simon had also worked at Magnolias and at one time had served as general manager. He held a degree in hotel, restaurant and institutional management from Michigan State University. One of his classmates was Kukler, who had been the general manager of L&N Seafood Grill in Atlanta. Another Magnolias staff member, Kris Reinhard, helped to open South City Kitchen and served as kitchen manager. Later, Reinhard became a partner in Fifth Group Restaurants as well.

For their new grill and soul food restaurant, the South City partners acquired and renovated a 72-year-old bungalow in midtown Atlanta, a neighborhood that was less than desirable at the time. The 3,500-square-foot South City Kitchen with 100 indoor seats and a 30-seat patio opened in April 1993. Initially it operated during dinner hours only. The plan was to add a lunch business after two weeks, but the restaurant proved so popular so quickly that the idea was postponed for six months.

By the time the dining critic of the *Atlanta Journal*, Elliott Mackle, reviewed South City Kitchen in late July 1993, the restaurant had already established itself in the city. Although Mackle encouraged people to patronize South City Kitchen, he recommended that "the overambitious menu would be considerably improved if cut in half." Candidates for "immediate exclusion" included "terrible seafood sandwiches and the entire dessert list," as well as "drugstore-cowboy fantasies (we needed another salmon quesadilla) and maladapted items seemingly filched from the *Food Arts* magazine (grilled seafood sausage with caper-peach chutney comes to mind)."

COFFEE SHOP CONCEPT INTRODUCED: 1994

Mackle's mixed review notwithstanding, South City Kitchen established a strong platform for South City Management to pursue new ventures. In 1994 the company opened the Urban Coffee Bungalow, a coffee shop concept, on Piedmont Road in midtown Atlanta. A year later a second location opened in the Peachtree Hills neighborhood, and a third followed in 1996 in Atlanta's High Museum of Art.

In the meantime, South City became interested in Atlanta's emerging warehouse district. The partners settled on the King Plow building, a 90-year-old former farm equipment manufacturing plant. The 165,000-square-foot factory had closed in 1986. Four years later it was converted into a community center for the arts, including artist studios. galleries, and performing and event spaces. South City leased 18,000 square feet of the building and in 1996 launched The Bold American

Food Co. to provide off-site catering. Serving as the centerpiece was a 68-seat contemporary Southern restaurant, The Food Studio. The King Plow space was also large enough to accommodate a bakery and administrative space for South City Management.

As the Food Studio was opening in the King Plow Arts Center, the decision had been made to close the Urban Coffee Bungalow in the High Museum. The location lacked kitchen space, limiting what the restaurant could offer. South City then decided that the concept itself no longer fit, and in 1997 the two remaining Urban Coffee Bungalows were sold. A more significant change followed in 1998 when Goss decided to leave the company, and he sold his interest to his partners. Kukler and Simon had carved out their own roles by now. Kukler was in charge of operations, marketing, and human resources, while Simon focused on administrative, financial, sales, and legal responsibilities.

It was also during this period that South City worked with a management and organizational consultant to develop a corporate structure that could support further growth without overburdening the partners. Moreover, the management team of each restaurant and the catering unit wrote an individual business plan and were given more autonomy in executing it. South City's managing partners could now devote more time to the development of new restaurant concepts. They traveled to such cities as New York, Chicago, and San Francisco, eating at multiple restaurants in a short time in search of inspiration.

New South's next restaurant was La Tavola, which opened in a renovated restaurant location in Atlanta's Virginia-Highland neighborhood. It sat 60 in the dining room and another 40 in the back patio. La Tavola was positioned as a "hip trattoria." The menu feature classic Italian cuisine but with a contemporary twist.

FIFTH GROUP RESTAURANT GROUP NAME ADOPTED: 2001

South City entered the new century with three restaurants and the catering and events business, which combined to generate $11 million in fiscal 2000. The partners, who now included Reinhard, decided to rebrand the company, and in 2001 the Fifth Group Restaurant Group name was adopted. Concurrent with the switch was a five-year plan to double the number of units and increase revenues to $25 million. In keeping with this effort, the company earmarked $1.7 million to expand Bold American Food's catering business.

A new restaurant was also in development in the Virginia-Highland area. Fifth Group acquired an exist-

KEY DATES

1992: South City Management Group is formed.
1993: South City Kitchen opens in Midtown Atlanta.
2001: Fifth Group Restaurants name is adopted.
2006: Ecco restaurant opens.
2012: Lure restaurant opens.

ing Italian restaurant, Camille, whose founder had died in 1999, and converted it into a Mexican restaurant. Named Sala, the 100-seat restaurant opened in the fall of 2002. Fifth Group also planned to open a restaurant called No. 11 in a former Atlanta fire station in 2003, but that project was never fulfilled.

Fifth Group did not add any further restaurants until 2006. A second South City Kitchen location opened in Vinings, Georgia, located a few miles northwest of Atlanta. It offered essentially the same menu but was twice the size. The new eatery was not particularly well received by the *Atlanta Journal-Constitution*'s Meredith Ford, who found little to recommend on the menu. She also admitted missing the "gritty charm that makes the Midtown locale special" and lamented "I'm in a strip mall. It's a chi-chi, John Weiland Home–designed strip mall, but a strip mall nonetheless."

Fifth Group received a far more favorable response from Ford on its second new restaurant opening in 2006, Ecco. Housed in the former Atlanta Fencing Club building, the restaurant offered Mediterranean cuisine, but Ford insisted that "Italian-inspired" was a more accurate description. Regardless, she complimented Chef Micah Willix for keeping things simple. "Here is a restaurant with a charming sophisticated setting," she concluded. "A kitchen, while not perfect, that seems to value fresh products above all else. A wine list with deep options. A competent, informed staff."

REBRANDING AND REINVENTION

In 2007 Bold American Food Co. was rebranded as Bold American Events. The following year, the Food Studio was renamed Studio 887, and now served as a private event venue rather than a public restaurant. Fifth Group also decided in 2008 to reinvent Sala as The Original El Taco. The company recruited well-regarded local chef Shaun Doty to help develop what the principals called a "fresh, healthy, affordable-but-chef-driven Mexican concept." When the partnership was an-

nounced, Kukler told the *Atlanta Journal-Constitution* that "The Original El Taco will be lively, bright, open and—most of all—fun." He added, "we have known Shaun for years, and when we found out he had been thinking about doing Mexican, too, we knew it was a great partnership."

A poor economy hampered Fifth Group's expansion plans at the end of the first decade of the new century. The company resumed growth in 2011. It added to its Bold American Events business through the acquisition of Event Design Group. Fifth Group also decided to develop another Mexican concept. Rather than the family-friendly The Original El Taco, the company opted for a more sophisticated approach for its new chef-driven restaurant, the 195-seat Alma Cocina. It opened in 2011 in the One Ninety One Peachtree Tower in downtown Atlanta. Roughly translated as "soul kitchen," Alma Cocina offered modern Mexican fare with Latin influences from star chef Chad Clevenger. The menu, atmosphere, and wait staff were generally well received, providing Fifth Group with another successful concept.

In 2011 Fifth Group looked to take advantage of its concepts. It teamed up with concession giant HMSHost Corporation to win a contract to open four restaurants at Atlanta's Hartsfield-Jackson International Airport. The first to open was a smaller version of The Original El Taco in 2012. It was housed in the new international terminal. A second unit opened in Concourse C a year later. Also in 2013 a small-format Ecco restaurant opened in the international terminal. Completing the four-unit contract was a Satchel Bros. Deli & Pickle Bar, a new deli concept, which also opened in Concourse C in 2013. Just as important as creating a new revenue stream, the airport locations helped to promote awareness of Fifth Group's brands. Given that the airport was the gateway for many visitors to Atlanta, higher visibility for Ecco and The Original El Taco could translate into more business from out-of-towners for the full-scale locations.

SEAFOOD RESTAURANT OPENS: 2012

While Fifth Group was establishing its airport business, it was also developing a new seafood restaurant concept. Called Lure, the new restaurant opened in midtown Atlanta in 2012. The kitchen was overseen by Willix, who would continue to serve as executive chef at Ecco. Lure was located not far from the original South City Kitchen. The restaurant celebrated its 20th anniversary in 2013, and despite a limited number of seats it averaged about $4.5 million in annual sales. It remained the flagship property of Fifth Group, which expanded its offices in preparation for additional restaurant openings. There was a chance that a third South City Kitchen might be in the offing. In any event, Fifth Group was poised for further growth in the Atlanta metropolitan area.

Ed Dinger

PRINCIPAL DIVISIONS

Alma Cocina; South City Kitchen Midtown; South City Kitchen Vinings; Ecco; La Tavola Trattoria; The Original El Taco; Lure; Bold American Events-Catering; Bold American Events-Design.

PRINCIPAL COMPETITORS

Concentrics Restaurants & Hospitality; Here to Serve Restaurants; Metrotainment Cafes.

FURTHER READING

Crabb, Cheryl. "South City Creators Cooking at King Plow." *Atlanta Business Chronicle*, August 19, 1996.

Ford, Meredith. "E.A.T. Got Grit?" *Atlanta Journal-Constitution*, March 30, 2006.

———. "EAT Pretty. Simple." *Atlanta Journal-Constitution*, July 20, 2006.

Garrett, Montgomery. "How Top Restaurateurs Keep the Plates Spinning." *Atlanta Business Chronicle*, October 26, 1998.

Hayes, Jack. "Fifth Group Looks to Secure Spot at Atlanta Dining Table." *Nation's Restaurant News*, May 15, 2006.

Mackle, Elliott. "Passable South City, with Revisions, Could Shine." *Atlanta Journal*, July 31, 1993.

Wenk, Amy. "South City Kitchen Celebrates 20 Years." *Atlanta Business Chronicle*, April 5, 2013.

Finasucre S.A./NV

Avenue Herrmann-Debroux 40-42
Oudergem, 1160
Belgium
Telephone: (+32 2) 661 19 11
Fax: (+32 2) 672 02 22
Web site: http://www.finasucre.com

Private Company
Founded: 1929
Employees: 3,000
Sales: EUR 438 million ($590 million) (2013)
NAICS: 311313 Beet Sugar Manufacturing; 311314
   Cane Sugar Manufacturing; 221122 Electric Power
   Distribution

∎ ∎ ∎

Finasucre S.A./NV is a major Belgian sugar producer with a total annual production of 638,000 metric tons. The company produces both raw and refined cane sugar and white and refined beet sugar. Part of the group's sugarcane supply comes from its own plantations, which include an 11,700-hectare estate and processing facility in the Democratic Republic of the Congo, and through its ownership of Bundaberg, 14,700 hectares in Australia supplying two processing plants in Queensland. Through its 71 percent control of the Iscal Sugar BV partnership, the company also processes much of the supply of beets in Belgium, as well as from beet farmers in the Netherlands, backed by one production site in Belgium and another in the Netherlands. Finasucre has also developed a number of ancillary operations to its core sugar production. The company is part of the Galactic joint venture, in partnership with Compagnie du Bois Sauvage, which produces lactic acid, lactates, and other food and feed ingredients. Through Galactic, Finasucre is also part of the Futerro joint venture with Total, which has been developing technology to produce poly-lactic acid from cane, beet, and other vegetable waste. Other Finasucre products include ethanol, molasses, caramel, and other by-products of the sugar refining process. The company also uses its waste by-product in order to generate electricity and owns a majority stake in Naturex, a French manufacturer of natural food ingredients.

SUGAR MILL IN 1869

Finasucre's origins reached back to the founding of a sugar mill in Moerbeke-Waes, Belgium, in 1868. Moerbeke at the time had become something of the fiefdom of the Lippens family. The Lippens had long played a prominent role in the political and economic development of the region, and, following Belgium's independence from the Netherlands in 1830, one of the country's wealthiest families.

The appointment of August Lippens as mayor of Moerbeke in 1847, however, set the stage for the foundation of the family's financial empire. Prior to his appointment, August Lippens was already one of the largest landholders in the region, which had seen its economy collapse in the postindependence period. Lippens's appointment came as the region struggled to emerge from a series of failed grain harvests, resulting in pervasive famine.

LIPPENS LEADS INFRASTRUCTURE GROWTH

Lippens soon emerged a driving force behind the region's economy, focusing on the one hand on boosting its agricultural sector, and on the other, encouraging the development of agricultural-based industries. An early example of this was the creation of a municipal dairy. Lippens also traveled extensively in order to discover new agricultural technologies and methods and introduce them to farmers in the Moerbeke region. At the same time, Lippens led the development of the region's infrastructure, including improving its roadways and its transport canals.

Lippens was also behind the establishment of the region's first beet sugar refinery, established as Sucrerie Jules de Cock & Compagnie in 1868. The production of sugar from beets had been introduced into Belgium as early 1812, with the first true sugar refineries opening in the 1830s. Improvements in the refining process after the middle of the century led to a true boom in the market, which saw the number of refineries rise to more than 100, and then to more than 170 by 1872.

The creation of the sugar refinery provided farmers with an outlet for their beet crops. At the same time, the waste by-products from the refinery process could be returned to farmers as fertilizer for their fields and feed for their animals. The sugar industry quickly became the major motor for the region's economic growth, stimulating several industries including construction and industrial machinery.

MERGER IN 1929

Although the sugar refinery was founded by Jules de Cock, who arrived in Moerbeke from Gent with a certificate authorizing him to produce sugar, the Lippens family, including August Lippens and his brother Eugène, became major shareholders in the plant. The Lippens also benefited indirectly from the success of the sugar refinery through the expansion of their agricultural landholdings through the end of the century.

A crisis swept through the Belgian sugar industry in 1871, forcing many of the Moerbeke refinery's rivals to close. The Moerbeke refinery itself survived in large part due to capital injections from the Lippens family, which also allowed them to increase their control over the company. In 1893 the Moerbeke refinery adopted limited liability status, becoming NV Sucrerie de Moerbeke-Waes. In the years leading up to the outbreak of World War I, the company completed a number of acquisitions of rival refineries, and also began refining raw cane sugar for the first time.

These developments led to a name change, to NV Sucrerie et Raffinerie de Moerbeke-Waes, in 1914. The Lippens family gained majority control of the company at this time. The Lippens family's sugar interests began to expand beyond the Moerbeke during the 1920s. In Belgium, the company merged with two other Belgian refineries, Sucrerie Franz Wittouck in Zelzate and the Sucrerie d'Escanaffles.

ORIGINS OF FINASUCRE

Both acquisitions were completed in 1929, at which time the company changed its name again, to Suikerfabrieken van Vlaanderen (or, in French, Sucrerie des Flandres). This formed the beginning of the future Société Financière des Sucres (Finasucre). By this time, the Lippens family had been granted the status of nobility. One of the most prominent members of the family was Maurice August Lippens, who served as mayor of Moerbeke before being appointed as governor general of Belgian Congo in 1921.

During his term there, Lippens became convinced that the best way for Belgium to conserve colonial control over the region was to invest in its industrialization. Although Maurice Lippens returned to Belgium in 1934 and became president of the Belgian Senate, the family recognized the potential for developing its own sugarcane plantation and refinery operations in the country. In 1925 the family, through Suikerfabrieken van Vlaanderen, established its sugar operation in Kwilu-Ngongo, naming the plant Moerbeke after the family's original sugar business.

FINASUCRE IN 1989

The Kwilu-Ngongo plantation remained a key component of the Lippens family's sugar empire until

KEY DATES

1868: Sucrerie Jules de Cock & Compagnie is founded in Moerbeke-Waes, Belgium, with August and Eugène Lippens as major shareholders.

1914: Company begins refining raw cane sugar; becomes NV Sucrerie et Raffinerie de Moerbeke-Waes.

1929: Lippens family merges its sugar mills to form Suikerfabrieken van Vlaanderen.

1989: Company acquires Sucrerie Frasnes and becomes Société Financière des Sucres (Finasucre).

1994: Company forms a partnership, later called Galactic, to produce lactic acid.

2007: Galactic and Total Petrochemicals found Futerro to develop a poly-lactic acid production process.

2014: Finasucre acquires a stake in Lippens family real estate holding Compagnie Het Zoute.

the beginning of the now-independent Congo's nationalization policies in the early 1970s. This resulted in the company being nationalized in 1971. Two years later the Mobutu government partially reversed its nationalization policy, returning 60 percent of the Kwilu-Ngongo site to the Lippens family. The Compagnie Sucrière of Kwilu-Ngongo as the company became known was placed under the holding company Sogesucre, which was absorbed into the larger Finasucre group in 1986.

The Lippens family had also gained full control of the Moerbeke sugar mill as well, buying out the other shareholders in 1982. Into the end of the decade the family continued to lead the consolidation of the Belgian sugar industry, acquiring Sucrerie Frasnes, based in Frasnes-lez-Buissenal, in 1988. Following this purchase, the family reorganized its sugar holdings, merging Sogesucre with the Frasnes and Moerbeke mills to formally establish Finasucre in 1989.

Finasucre restructured its operations the following year, shutting down production at the Escanaffles mill. Instead, this site became dedicated to Finasucre's first diversification effort. In 1994 the company formed a partnership, initially called Bioprocess Technology, to develop and exploit processes for the production of lactic acid and lactates. Later known as Galactic, the partnership started out with a production capacity of

1,500 tons, which was then boosted to 15,000 tons in 1997.

EXPANSION AND DIVERSIFICATION

By 1998 Galactic had grown to become the second-largest lactic acid producer in the world, with exports reaching 40 countries and accounting for 80 percent of its production. Galactic continued to expand, doubling its production to 30,000 tons in 1999. In that year, Finasucre brought in a new partner in the lactic acid business, Compagnie du Bois Sauvage. Galactic began developing its own international operations into the turn of the century. The company formed a joint venture partnership called B&G with China's COFCO Biochemical in Bengbu in 2002.

B&G then built its own lactic acid facility with a production capacity of 50,000 tons. Galactic also moved into the United States, setting up shop in Milwaukee in 2005. This facility boosted its own capacity to 15,000 tons in 2011. In another technology extension, the company created a joint venture with Total Petrochemicals, founding Futerro in order to produce poly-lactic acid polymers, used in the production of biodegradable plastics.

ENTERING AUSTRALIA IN 2000

Finasucre in the meantime continued the internationalization of its sugar production. This effort took a major step forward with the purchase of Australia's Bundaberg Sugar in 2000. Founded in 1882 Bundaberg was one of Australia's oldest and largest sugar companies and the largest sugarcane grower and refiner in Queensland. The purchase of Bundaberg gave Finasucre seven mills in the region, as well as a strong molasses and feed business. Bundaberg also brought Finasucre control of 14,700 hectares of sugarcane plantation, as well as its sugar machinery and equipment production subsidiary, Bundaberg Foundry.

The acquisition became the prelude to more investment by Finasucre into the region, starting with the purchase of the South Johnstone Mill in 2001. In 2003 Bundaberg Foundry acquired Walkers, another leading producer of sugar machinery and equipment. The two businesses were merged in 2008, becoming Bundaberg Walkers. By then, the company had carried out its Bundaberg Regional Milling Project, which involved the closure of three of its mills through 2008.

ISCAL SUGAR CREATED: 2003

The company then spun off three other mills, South Johnstone, Tableland, and Babinda, into a joint venture with Maryborough Sugar. Finasucre sold its stake in the joint venture in 2011. Finasucre's restructuring of its Australian operations had been preceded by changes in its European operations. In 2003 the company created a new holding structure in partnership with Belgian beet farmers called Iscal Sugar.

Finasucre transferred ownership of its Moerbeke and Frasnes mills to Iscal, which also acquired sugar mills in Fontenoy and Veurne. Finasucre retained majority control of Iscal, which took its name from abbreviations for the Latin names of the Isera and Scaldis river basins, which formed the main source of its beet supply. Also in 2003 Finasucre acquired a production facility in the Netherlands.

The creation of Iscal soon led to a restructuring of its operations as well, starting with the shutdown of the Frasnes sugar mill in 2004. The company also surprised the market by closing its Moerbeke plant, despite the facility's unbroken record of nearly 170 years of profitable operation. Part of the impetus, however, came from Finasucre's progress in its diversification effort, with the start-up of production of its lactic acid plant in Bengbu, China, in 2005, and the creation of Futerro in 2007. The latter company launched pilot production of polylactic acid in 2010.

NEW INVESTMENTS FROM 2010

With the collapse of Fortis during the economic crash of 2008, Finasucre took on greater importance for the Lippens family fortune. Through Finasucre, the family developed a range of new investment interests. Through its control of Compagnie Het Zoute, the family had long been one of Belgium's leading real estate and development companies. Finasucre helped serve as the family's vehicle for entry into the African real estate market, starting with the creation of Socagrim, in Congo, in 2007.

That company then began developing its first real estate development project in Kinshasha. Construction of that project, an apartment building, got underway in 2014. In 2010 Finasucre expanded its real estate investments again, buying a 5.46 percent stake in Luxembourg-based real estate company Aedifica. Olivier Lippens already served as chairman of Aedifica. Also in 2010 Finasucre acquired a 25 percent stake in Société Civile Anonyme des Galeries Royales Saint-Hubert, operator of the iconic glass-covered shopping arcade in Brussels. Finasucre continued to raise its stake in that company, participating in its capital increase in 2014.

The company's real estate holdings expanded to include a building in Brisbane, Australia, acquired in 2013. The company took a stake in Compagnie Het

Zoute in 2014. Finasucre also invested in an area closer to its core sugar business. In 2011 the company acquired an initial stake in Holding SGD, which in turn owned nearly 21 percent of Naturex, a leading French producer of natural ingredients for the food, health and personal care, and nutrition industries.

At the same time, the company reached an agreement with Naturex CEO Jacques Dikansky to raise its position in SGD to 58 percent but only take 39 percent of voting rights. In this way, Dikansky retained control of Naturex's direction, while raising funds for its further growth. In the event, Finasucre soon took complete control of SGD, consolidating its stake as Naturex's primary financial partner in 2013. While maintaining its core business as a leading Belgian sugar producer, Finasucre's new investment strategy pointed the way toward the company's future evolution as it moved deeper into the 21st century.

M. L. Cohen

PRINCIPAL SUBSIDIARIES

B&G (consolidated with B&G Import-Export and B&G Japan) (China); Bundaberg Sugar Group Ltd (Australia); Bundaberg Sugar Ltd (Australia); Bundaberg Walkers Engineering Ltd; Devolder S.A.; Finasucre Investments (Australia) Pty Ltd; Finasucre S.A.; Futerro S.A.; Galactic Incorporated (USA); Galactic S.A.; Iscal Sugar B.V. (Netherlands); Iscal Sugar S.A./N.V.; Naturex S.A.; Northern Land Holdings Ltd (Australia); R&J Farm Pty Ltd (Australia); S.G.D. Sas (France).

PRINCIPAL DIVISIONS

Europe; Africa; North America; Asia; Australia.

PRINCIPAL OPERATING UNITS

Iscal Sugar; Galactic; Compagnie Sucrière; B&G; Bundaberg.

PRINCIPAL COMPETITORS

AGRANA Beteiligungs AG; Nippon Beet Sugar Manufacturing Company Ltd.; Nordic Sugar A/S; SUCDEN; Suedzucker AG.

FURTHER READING

"Belgium's Finasucre Shuts One Australian Sugar Cane Mill." *FWN Select*, February 3, 2005.

Brannelly, Louise. "Belgians Snap Up Bundaberg for $425m." *Mercury*, June 9, 2000.

Cranston, Matthew. "Finasucre Sweet on Cane Land." *Australian Financial Review*, July 4, 2011.

"Finasucre Anticipeert op Suikerliberalisering." *Trends*, June 19, 2014.

"Finasucre Sweet on Cane Land." *North Queensland Register*, July 4, 2011.

Le Bec, Christophe. "Les Belges au Congo: Prospères Dynasties d'Affaires." *Jeune Afrique*, August 12, 2013.

Lush, Deanna. "Foreign Buy-Up: Belgian-Based Finasucre." *Stock Journal*, July 7, 2011.

Munster, Jean-François. "La Compagnie Sucrière Résiste dans le Chaos." *Le Soir*, April 24, 2010.

"Naturex, le PDG Organise un Nouveau Tour de Table." *Les Echos*, August 2, 2011.

Fox-Wizel Ltd.

P.O. Box 76
Airport City, 7019900
Israel
Telephone: (972 3) 905 0100
Fax: (972 3) 905 0200
Web site: http://www.fox.co.il

Public Company
Incorporated: 1942 as Tricot Fox Ltd.
Employees: 2,497
Sales: ILS 1.05 billion ($250 million) (2013)
Stock Exchanges: Tel Aviv
Ticker Symbol: FOX.IT
NAICS: 424320 Men's and Boys' Clothing and Furnishings Merchant Wholesalers; 424330 Women's, Children's, and Infants' Clothing and Accessories Merchant Wholesalers; 315220 Men's and Boys' Cut and Sew Apparel Manufacturing; 315223 Men's and Boys' Cut and Sew Shirt (Except Work Shirt) Manufacturing; 315240 Women's, Girls', and Infants' Cut and Sew Apparel Manufacturing

∎ ∎ ∎

Fox-Wizel Ltd. is one of Israel's leading retail groups; the group's Fox brand is also the leading clothing brand in the country, a fast-growing international brand as well. Fox-Wizel operates 140 company-owned Fox stores featuring its Fox-branded line of women's, men's, children's and infant fashions. The company operates its own in-house design team, sourcing the garments themselves from overseas, primarily China. The company also operates 32 Fox Home stores and 14 Marcha Ballerina footwear shops in Israel. Through subsidiary Fox International, the company has developed operations into 15 countries, largely through franchise partners. In 2014 the company's Fox retail network included nearly 270 stores in Belgium, Cyprus, Georgia, Germany, Greece, Kazakhstan, Mongolia, Panama, the Philippines, Romania, Russia, Serbia, Singapore, and Thailand. The company also operates as a wholesaler in Georgia, Greece, India, Kazakhstan, Panama, and Russia. The company has also developed another international retail concept, Laline, featuring soaps, candles, fragrances and other personal care products and gifts. This chain included 82 mall-based boutique shops in Israel, and 20 stores in Switzerland, the United States, the Caribbean, Japan, Singapore, and Italy. Fox-Wizel has also been actively developing a portfolio of retail licenses for leading international brands, including Billabong, Sack's, American Eagle Outfitters, Disney, and The Children's Place. These chains add another 200 stores to the group's total Israeli portfolio. Fox-Wizel is listed on the Tel Aviv Stock Exchange and controlled by the founding Fox and Wizel (also spelled as Wiesel or Weisel) families. Harel Wizel, the company's founder and largest shareholder, serves as CEO. Fox expects sales to top $250 million in 2014.

UNDERWEAR MANUFACTURER IN 1942

Fox-Wizel got its start as a small workshop producing undergarments for the wholesale market, founded by the Fox (or Fuchs) family in 1942. Over the next decades Tricot Fox Ltd., as the company was known, expanded

COMPANY PERSPECTIVES

The Vision: To be a successful, leading company in each of its areas of activity, while emphasizing a unique style, a new kind of shopping experience, and a distinctive marketing approach; to cultivate a loyal client base, based on reliability, service, quality, and fair pricing; to be a profitable company that strives for excellence attain maximum value for its shareholders and to benefit its employees and customers; to continue to grow and expand in the international market; to instill a sense of pride and belonging in its employees, and to allow them to grow and develop professionally within the FOX Group; to work on behalf of the community.

its operations to include other clothing items. By the beginning of the 1990s, the Fox factory had come under the leadership of Avraham Fox, and focused especially on producing colored T-shirts for the Israeli market.

The Wizel family's association with Fox began when Harel Wizel's father became an independent wholesale agent for the company, starting in 1990. Within two years, Wizel had expanded his sales network to as many as 30 stores throughout Israel. In that year, however, the elder Wizel died of a heart attack.

Harel Wizel and brothers Iftach and Assaf soon discovered that a number of outstanding payments among their father's customers, and went to visit them with the intention of winding up their father's affairs. The customers surprised them, however, when they asked the brothers to continue serving as their sales agent for the Fox factory's clothing. At the time, Wizel, then 26 years old, had already began a successful career as sales manager for an Israeli textiles producer, supplying such noted Israeli retail fashion groups as Castro and Rosh Indiani.

In the meantime, Wizel's mother had asked her sons to help her set up a small shop selling Fox-produced clothing in Ramat Gan. The store was immediately successful, and the family soon developed a franchise relationship with Tricot Fox through which the Wizels began developing the Fox-brand retail clothing concept. By the end of 1992 Wizel Textile Ltd., as the new company was called, had already operated three Fox-branded clothing stores. Just two years later, the Wizel family's retail holdings had expanded to 10 stores. The Ramat Gan store was then expanded to serve as the group's wholesale base. Harel Wizel soon quit his sales manager's job to take over as head of the growing Wizel Textile Ltd.

MERGER IN 2000

Not content with Fox's existing clothing line, the Wizel brothers began actively developing their own design range. For this, the brothers traveled to various fashion shows in the United States, Europe, and Asia. The brothers also paid close attention to emerging design trends especially in New York and other fashion capitals, which generally reached Israel after a year or so. The company then worked with Tricot Fox to produce their designs, which were sold in the Wizel Textile's fast-growing network of Fox clothing stores. The company at first focused solely on women's fashions.

In 1996, however, Wizel Textile took the leap into developing its own designs, hiring its first full-time designer. The company soon expanded its team to include eight full-time designers by 2003. Both Harel and Iftach continued to participate actively in the company's design process, however, traveling to fashion shows and holding the final say on the clothing that appeared in the group's stores. The Fox brand quickly developed a national reputation for its attractively priced, brightly colored designs.

Wizel Textile reinforced this reputation by launching a series of national advertising campaigns, including a popular series of adds featuring Israeli model and actress Yael Bar-Zohar in the late 1990s. At the end of the decade, the company also expanded beyond the women's clothing segment to introduce a line of highly successful children's clothing. This success was soon followed into the turn of the century by the launch of a men's collection. By 2003 the company had also developed its Fox Baby line of infant wear as well.

By then the Wizel and Fox families had strengthened their relationship, merging Tricot Fox and Wizel Textile to form Fox-Wizel Ltd., a process completed in 2000. The move came in part as a cost-reduction effort, as the group began shifting its garment sourcing to overseas, particularly the Chinese market. By 2004 China had already become the source of 80 percent of the group's clothing.

OVERSEAS EXPANSION IN 2004

By the end of 2002 Fox-Wizel's sales had risen to ILS 362 million ($80 million), generating profits of more than ILS 30 million ($7 million). The company had also expanded its range to include a number of branded partnerships, including socks and underwear produced

KEY DATES

1942: Fox family founds Tricot Fox Ltd. to manufacture underwear.

1992: Wizel Textile Ltd. is founded to develop a Fox-branded retail franchise.

2000: Wizel and Fox merge to become Fox-Wizel Ltd.

2002: Company goes public on the Tel Aviv Stock Exchange.

2004: Fox-Wizel begins its international expansion with a franchise in Singapore.

2010: Fox-Wizel launches a retail home furnishings format, Fox Home.

2014: Fox-Wizel opens its first The Children's Place store in Israel.

by Delta, and watches and stationery in conjunction with Gallery, and even a mobile telephone in partnership with Cellcom. In the meantime, the group had become Israel's retail clothing leader, selling as many as one million items of clothing each month in a nation with a total population of only seven million.

The flip side of this success, however, was that Fox-Wizel would soon begin to run out of growth opportunities in the relatively tiny Israeli market. The company began developing plans to introduce the Fox retail brand to an international market, initially eyeing the Czech Republic and other emerging Eastern European markets. In preparation for this next growth phase, the company went public, listing its shares on the Tel Aviv Stock Exchange in 2002. Harel Wizel then became the company's CEO and largest shareholder.

Fox-Wizel made good on its international ambitions in 2004. In the event, Singapore became the company's first overseas market, with the opening of the first Fox flagship store there. As with the group's future overseas expansion, the move came through the establishment of a local franchise partnership. This enabled the company to get off to a strong start, opening five more stores in Singapore through the year, with plans to double that number by the beginning of 2005. The group also planned to open six stores in Australia. While this latter plan ultimately failed to prosper, the company became a popular retail brand in Singapore, opening 25 stores in the city-state by the early years of the next decade.

Encouraged by this success, the company began developing new franchise partnerships elsewhere in the world. The company moved into Panama in 2005,

establishing both a retail chain, which grew to 33 locations, and a wholesale supply business. Thailand became the group's largest foreign market, starting with the opening of its first store in 2006. By the middle of the next decade, the company's retail network there had grown to 116 locations. Other new markets during this time included Romania and Moldava in 2006; Canada and the Philippines in 2008; and Russia, Cyprus, and Kazakhstan in 2009. The group's entry into Russia was eased by the arrival of a new major shareholder, Russian-born billionaire Lev Leviev, who acquired a 20 percent stake in the company in 2005. Unlike Fox-Wizel's other overseas operations, the Russian business was directly controlled by the company, growing to 15 locations and establishing its own wholesale business.

RETAIL LICENSES FROM 2007

Meanwhile, Fox-Wizel had been exploring new means of stimulating its growth in its domestic market. While continuing to develop its own Fox store chain, notably with the addition of its first footwear line in 2005, the company also began building up a portfolio of licensed brands. The first of these came in late 2006, when the company acquired a 50 percent stake in Australian surf apparel brand Billabong's Israeli operations. The partnership between the two companies enabled Billabong to expand its presence in Israel to 40 locations.

In January 2007 the company acquired half ownership of the Laline chain of bath products boutiques. This chain operated 30 locations, including eight overseas shops in Norway, Romania, and the United Kingdom. Within five years, Fox-Wizel built the Laline brand into a network of more than 80 Israeli stores, and more than 20 stores in Switzerland, the United States, Japan, Singapore, Italy, and the Caribbean. Also in 2007 Fox-Wizel formed a partnership to introduce another popular international brand into Israel, Sack's. Fox-Wizel succeeded in expanding the designer boutique concept into a chain of 15 shops by 2013.

Fox-Wizel faced a bit of controversy in 2008, when it signed on Israeli supermodel Bar Rafaeli for its advertising campaign. Rafaeli had sparked criticism for having avoided her compulsory service in the Israeli army in order to pursue her modeling career. As the *Independent* reported, Rafaeli did not help matters when she replied to the controversy by stating: "I really wanted to serve in the IDF [Israel Defense Forces], but I don't regret not enlisting, because it paid off big time. That's just the way it is, celebrities have other needs. I hope my case has influenced the army." Fox-Wizel helped defuse the situation by suggesting Rafaeli help the IDF by serving as an unofficial "enlistment officer" in order to promote military service.

Fox-Wizel took a break from clothing in 2010, introducing instead its own retail home furnishings format, Fox Home. These were large-scale stores with a minimum selling space of 400 square meters, featuring an extensive line of tableware, kitchenware, bathroom accessories, linens, bedding and other items. The new format was an immediate success, enabling the company to expand the chain to 32 stores by the beginning of 2014.

NEW LICENSES IN 2014

By the end of 2010 the Fox retail brand had expanded to 15 countries, with a total of 400 stores in operation. Into the new decade, the company added a number of other markets, including Serbia, Mongolia, and Georgia in 2011; Belgium and Greece in 2012; and a wholesale business in India in 2013.

The company also continued courting other international brands seeking entry into the bustling Israeli retail clothing market. In 2010 the company acquired the franchise to introduce the American Eagle Outfitters brand to Israel. The company quickly expanded the chain, topping 25 stores by 2012.

The company added a new format soon after, signing a franchise agreement for The Children's Place retail brand in 2013. The Children's Place had become the leading children's clothing specialist in the North American market, with more than 1,100 stores in the region. That company had begun its own international expansion only in 2012, and by 2013 operated 20 stores in the Middle East, including in Saudi Arabia. Fox-Wizel debuted its first The Children's Place store in 2014 and expected to have 20 locations for the brand by the end of the year. By then, Fox-Wizel's revenues had topped ILS 1 billion ($250 million), representing an increase of more than 13 percent over the previous year.

At the same time Fox-Wizel eyed two other brand extensions. The company signed an agreement to acquire 50 percent of Yanga, a retail clothing chain, in July 2014. In August 2014 the company reported it was in advanced negotiations with Nike International to acquire and operate its Israeli operations, including 27 franchised locations and four Nike Factory Stores. The addition of these chains would only help consolidate Fox-Wizel's stature as Israel's retail clothing leader in the early 21st century.

M. L. Cohen

PRINCIPAL SUBSIDIARIES

Fox International Ltd.

PRINCIPAL DIVISIONS

Fox; Fox International; Fox Home; Laline; Billabong; Sack's; American Eagle Outfitters.

PRINCIPAL OPERATING UNITS

Fox Women; Fox Men; Fox Kids; Fox Baby; Fox Home.

PRINCIPAL COMPETITORS

The Gap, Inc.; Levi Strauss & Co.

FURTHER READING

"American Eagle Outfitters Ties Up with Fox-Wizel to Expand in Israel." *Franchise Plus*, July 7, 2010.

Blackburn, Nicky. "A 'Fox' of Fashion." *Israel21c*, November 16, 2003.

Dawber, Alistair. "Palestinian Groups Furious as Israeli Jeans Company Fox Sets Up Shop in Ramallah." *Independent* (London), July 23, 2013.

Hayut, Ilanit. "Fashion Chain Fox Expands European Operations." *Globes*, October 20, 2009.

————. "Fox in Talks for Nike Israel Store Franchise." *Globes*, August 11, 2014.

————. "Fox to Open 44 New Stores." *Globes*, November 11, 2013.

Kalaw, Ana G. "Fox News." *Philstar.com*, December 3, 2008.

Levy, Aviv. "Leviev Sells 8% More of Fox Fashion Chain." *Globes*, March 12, 2014.

Sharon-Rivlin, Vered. "Fox-Wizel Entering in Shoe Business." *Globes*, April 6, 2005.

Sheva, Arutz. "Next American Brand in Israel: Children's Place." *VoiceofJews.com*, March 3, 2014.

Genomic Health, Inc.

—————————■—————————

101 Galveston Drive
Redwood City, California 94063-4700
U.S.A.
Telephone: (650) 556-9300
Fax: (650) 556-1132
Web site: http://www.genomichealth.com

Public Company
Incorporated: 2000
Employees: 684
Sales: $261.5 million (2013)
Stock Exchanges: NASDAQ
Ticker Symbol: GHDX
NAICS: 541712 Research and Development in the
    Physical, Engineering, and Life Sciences (Except
    Biotechnology)

■ ■ ■

Headquartered in Redwood City, California, Genomic Health, Inc., is a leader in the field of diagnostic medical testing. Specifically, Genomic Health offers genomic-based clinical laboratory services that doctors and patients use to make informed decisions about cancer treatment options. (Genomics is the study of genes, their functionality, and how they interrelate.) Marketed under the Oncotype DX name, the company's tests for breast, colon, and prostate cancer use information gained from patients' tumors to make individualized predictions regarding response to therapy and recurrence.

ORIGINS

Genomic Health traces its roots back to August 2000, when the company incorporated in Delaware. However, the inspiration for its formation came in early 1999, when a friend of founder Randal W. "Randy" Scott, was diagnosed with cancer. Realizing that information about the human genome could be used to help cancer patients make individualized decisions about their treatment, based on the molecular makeup of their tumors, Scott decided to part ways with the company, Incyte, and establish Genomic Health to focus on the emerging field of "personalized medicine."

After developing a rough business plan, Scott received feedback and support from his mentor and PhD thesis adviser, Joffre B. Baker. Baker, who became one of the company's cofounders, connected Scott with Genentech's Dr. Steve Shak, who had worked on a clinical program for the breast cancer treatment, Herceptin. Shak eventually became the company's chief medical officer. Another significant development occurred when Scott hired Genomic Health's first employee, a health consultant named Gene Early, followed by a patient advocacy expert named Pat Terry.

Scott and Early collaborated to further develop Genomic Health's business plan and raise funds needed to begin operations. The founders initially raised $7.9 million in seed money from their friends and family. A second round of funding was received in early 2001, when $29 million was received from investors such as Baker-Tisch; Kleiner, Perkins, Caufield & Byers; and Versant. This was followed by another $5 million from Scott's former employer, Incyte, around the same time.

COMPANY PERSPECTIVES

As the world's leading provider of genomic cancer diagnostic tests, we are focused on using genomic information about a patient's individual tumor to personalize cancer treatment, and have built a world-class research, clinical and commercial organization to support this goal.

ESTABLISHES OPERATIONS

After securing incubator space at Alameda Naval Air Station in early 2001, Genomic Health ultimately based its operations in Redwood City, California. The company began conducting clinical studies, and gained access to blocks of tissue that it could study through an agreement with the National Surgical Adjuvant Breast and Bowel Project. In early 2002 Genomic Health named Kimberly Popovits as its new president and chief operating officer. Prior to joining the company, Popovits had served as Genentech's head of commercial operations for 15 years.

That year, Genomic Health decided to focus its efforts on the development of a diagnostic test for a specific type of breast cancer. As the company would later explain in its 2005 annual report, the test specifically was for patients with early-stage breast cancers. Furthermore, the company indicated that the test was "focused on patients with early stage, node negative, or –, estrogen receptor positive, or ER+, breast cancer who will be treated with tamoxifen, a frequently used hormonal therapy."

Progress continued in late 2002 when Genomic Health raised $9.3 million through a fourth round of funding. Early the following year, the company completed its initial studies in the area of gene expression analysis. This was significant in that the results revealed that it was possible to help predict patients' survival based on genes within their breast cancer tissue.

ESTABLISHES ONCOTYPE DX

Following successful completion of a Clinical Laboratory Improvement Amendments (CLIA) lab inspection in November 2003, a major breakthrough took place in January of the following year when the company received CLIA certification to perform its first breast cancer test, which was named Oncotype DX. At that time the company received its first commercial tumor sample, generated its first patient report, and began efforts to communicate information about Oncotype DX to physicians.

Genomic Health ended 2003 on a high note when the clinical validity of its Oncotype DX breast cancer test was confirmed in the results of a study presented by Kaiser Permanente at the San Antonio Breast Cancer Symposium. Other positive study results followed, and the company was flooded with inquiries and orders for Oncotype DX. Positive developments unfolded at a rapid pace in 2005, beginning with accreditation for Genomic Health's clinical laboratory from the College of American Pathologists during the early part of the year. Following this, the *American Journal of Managed Care* published a report demonstrating the cost-effectiveness of Oncotype DX.

Another major development took place in September 2005 when Genomic Health went public, offering approximately 5 million shares of its common stock. The initial public offering generated $60 million for Genomic Health. The company appeared positioned for success as it offered women detailed information about their specific prognosis. Its test went beyond telling a woman what her general risk level was, providing a specific numerical score that helped to gauge the likelihood of cancer recurrence.

DEVELOPS COLON CANCER TEST

Progress continued midway through 2006 when Genomic Health completed an additional study in partnership with the National Surgical Breast and Bowel Project. The study explored connections between the recurrence of colon cancer and gene expression. This led to additional research for an Oncotype DX colon cancer test, which began clinical development early the following year, with an evaluation effort involving roughly 3,000 patient samples.

Toward the end of 2006 Genomic Health established a national reimbursement contract with the insurance company, Aetna. This made the Oncotype DX breast cancer test part of insurance plans covering roughly 80 million people. A similar contract was established with UnitedHealthcare, one of the largest insurance companies in the United States, in 2007. Following this, the Oncotype DX breast cancer test became available to approximately 90 million people. Midway through the year, Genomic Health expanded its footprint beyond the United States, making Oncotype DX available in the United Kingdom via an agreement with the health care and diagnostics company, Medical Solutions plc.

Genomic Health ended 2006 with a net loss of $28.9 million, a slight decrease from a net loss of $31.4

KEY DATES

2000: Genomic Health is established.
2004: Company launches its breast cancer test, which is named Oncotype DX.
2005: Genomic Health goes public, generating $60 million.
2010: Company announces the availability of its Oncotype DX colon cancer test.
2013: Genomic Health launches its Oncotype DX prostate cancer test.

million in 2005. However, sales of Oncotype DX helped to increase the company's revenues from $5.2 million to $29.2 million during the same time frame. Midway through 2007 the company moved forward with plans to offer an additional 3 million shares of stock to the public, providing roughly $43 million for research and development, laboratory operations, and sales and marketing activities.

At this time Genomic Health continued under the leadership of Chairman and CEO Scott. In addition, Vice President Chu Chang helped oversee the company's business development initiatives, including international expansion efforts. In addition to the aforementioned distribution agreement in the United Kingdom, Genomic Health was marketing Oncotype DX in Japan via a partnership with SRL, and also in Israel through an arrangement with Teva Pharmaceutical Industries Ltd. By early 2008 more than 46,000 women had benefited from Oncotype DX.

POPOVITS NAMED CEO

Genomic Health received positive recognition in early 2008 when President and COO Popovits was named Woman of the Year by the Women Health Care Executives of Northern California, in honor of 25 years of contributions to the biopharmaceutical industry. Early the following year the company promoted Popovits to CEO. She was succeeded as COO by G. Bradley Cole, who also continued to function as COO. Additionally, Scott became chairman on a full-time basis, allowing him to concentrate on Genomic Health's long-term strategy.

At this time Genomic Health's senior leadership team continued to include cofounder Baker, who functioned as chief scientific officer. Additionally, Tricia Tomlinson served as vice president of human resources, along with Vice President of Corporate Communica-

tions Laura Leber and Senior Vice President of Worldwide Commercialization David Logan. Under the team's collective leadership, the company continued to advance research regarding Genomic Health's DX colon cancer test.

In this regard, the results of a landmark validation study were presented at the American Society of Clinical Oncology (ASCO) during the early part of the year. In addition, the first research results regarding the use of the Oncotype DX Breast Cancer test in male patients also were presented at ASCO. By this time the test had been used by roughly 100,000 breast cancer patients throughout the world, and its usefulness in predicting chemotherapy benefits were documented in research published by journals such as the *Lancet Oncology*.

LAUNCHES COLON CANCER TEST

Genomic Health reached an important milestone in early 2010 when the company announced that its Oncotype DX colon cancer test was available worldwide. This provided patients with a tool to help determine their individual cancer recurrence risk. Around the same time, distribution of the Oncotype DX test in the markets of Portugal and Spain was made possible through an agreement between Genomic Health and Palex Medical S.A.

Toward the end of the year Genomic Health used a social media campaign to promote Oncotype DX and the promises of personalized treatments for breast cancer awareness. Called "Pass It On ... Until Every Woman Knows," the campaign also included its own Web site, www.untileverywomanknows.com. Another important development occurred in early 2011 when the company accelerated the pace of clinical development for a new Oncotype DX prostate cancer test. As with its Oncotype DX tests for colon and breast cancer, development of the prostate cancer test would involve numerous clinical studies.

On the leadership front, Genomic Health named Dean Schorno as its new chief financial officer in early 2011. This allowed COO Cole to concentrate solely on growing the business. Later in the year, the company's national contractor for the Oncotype DX test, Palmetto GBA, secured coverage for all Medicare patients with stage II colon cancer. By this time roughly 10,000 physicians in more than 60 different countries had ordered 200,000 of the company's Oncotype DX cancer tests. In addition to its operations in the United States, Genomic Health had established European headquarters in Geneva, Switzerland.

NEW SUBSIDIARY

In early 2012 Genomic Health formed a new wholly owned subsidiary, in which it invested $20 million over the course of two years. The new business focused on integrating the human genome into medical practice, in order to help patients and families with both rare and common genetic conditions. It was headed by Scott, who stepped down as Genomic Health's chairman to concentrate on the new venture. Following this, Popovits assumed the additional role of chairman. The company also established a partnership with OncoMed Pharmaceuticals Inc., which focused on the use of next-generation sequencing to develop biomarkers for cancer therapeutics.

Midway through 2013 Genomic Health launched its Oncotype DX prostate cancer test, which was developed in collaboration with the Cleveland Clinic and the University of California, San Francisco. By this time approximately 19,000 physicians in more than 70 countries had ordered approximately 350,000 of the company's Oncotype DX cancer tests. Toward the end of the year Genomic Health established a licensing agreement with Almac Group Ltd., which focused on the development of an anthracycline chemotherapy benefit test for high-risk breast cancer patients.

By the end of 2013 Shak was serving as Genomic Health's executive vice president of research and development. Phil Febbo had been named chief medical officer by the middle of 2014, when the company announced that the results of a large study, published in the *Oncologist*, revealed that its Oncotype DX colon cancer test changed treatment recommendations for nearly half of patients with a stage II form of the disease. More positive news followed in September of that year when the journal *PharmacoEconomics* published research results showing that the company's colon cancer test resulted in significantly lower direct medical costs, as well as improved quality of life for patients.

By the end of 2014 Genomic Health had cornered more than 90 percent of the U.S. market for breast cancer testing. At this time, 29 percent of the company's revenues came from international markets. In only 10 years Genomic Health had made great strides in the development of tests that provided patients and their doctors with useful information for making personalized treatment recommendations. Moving forward, it appeared that Genomic Health was positioned for continued growth and success.

Paul R. Greenland

PRINCIPAL SUBSIDIARIES

Genomic Health International Holdings, LLC.

PRINCIPAL COMPETITORS

Celera Corporation; GE Healthcare Ltd.; Hologic, Inc.

FURTHER READING

Cook, Kevin. "Bear of the Day: Genomic Health." *Zacks*, October 3, 2013. Accessed October 13, 2014. http://www.zacks.com/commentary/29253/bear-of-the-day-genomic-health-ghdx.

"Genomic Health and Almac Group Ink Exclusive In-Licensing Pact to Develop and Commercialize Anthracycline Chemotherapy Benefit Test for High Risk Breast Cancer." *Health & Beauty Close-Up*, December 2, 2013.

"Genomic Health Announces Publication of Colon Cancer Cost-Effectiveness Study in PharmacoEconomics." *CNNMoney*, September 12, 2014.

"Genomic Health Launches Oncotype DX PCA Test." *Business Monitor Online*, May 9, 2013.

Higgins, Andrew. "Genomic Health's International Business Continues to Stand Out." *BioTech Insights*, September 16, 2014.

Globalstar Inc.

300 Holiday Square Boulevard
Covington, Louisiana 70433
U.S.A.
Telephone: (985) 335-1500
Web site: http://www.globalstar.com

Public Company
Incorporated: 1991 as Globalstar L.P.
Employees: 267
Sales: $82.71 million (2013)
Stock Exchanges: New York
Ticker Symbol: GSAT
NAICS: 517919 All Other Telecommunications

■ ■ ■

Headquartered in Covington, Louisiana, Globalstar Inc. is a leading provider of mobile satellite services, offering wireless voice and data communications in locations where those services are either unavailable or available on a limited basis. The company's Globalstar System comprises a network of ground stations or gateways, as well as in-orbit satellites. Globalstar's 583,000 subscribers come from a variety of different markets, including construction; transportation; utilities; natural resources, mining, and forestry; oil and gas; maritime and fishing; recreation and personal; public safety and disaster relief; and government. Globalstar's communications services include two-way voice communication and data transmissions (duplex) and one-way data transmissions (simplex).

ORIGINS

Globalstar Inc. traces its origins back to 1991, when the company was established as Globalstar L.P., a technology partnership between Loral Space and Communications and Qualcomm Incorporated. In 1999 Globalstar launched its original first-generation satellite network. At that time the company's operations included a network of approximately 48 satellites, in which Loral had invested $48 million. Early leadership was provided by President Tony Navarra.

That year, the company received approval from the Federal Communications Commission (FCC) to offer satellite-based telephone service through a network of approximately 500,000 fixed and handheld telephones. By early 2000 the satellite telephone service was producing weak sales, prompting Loral to consider selling its 45 percent interest in Globalstar. Other shareholders then included Qualcomm, China Telecom (HK), Alenia, DaimlerChrysler Aerospace, Elsacom, Hyundai, TE. SA.M, DACOM, and Vodafone AirTouch.

Nevertheless, geographic expansion continued with the introduction of service in remote parts of the world where residents had limited or no access to telecommunications services. In 2000 the company rolled out coverage in areas such as Denmark, Finland, Iceland, Morocco, Russia, Sweden, and Venezuela, resulting in the availability of service in approximately 34 different countries. To generate additional revenues, the company also established a long-term partnership with In-Flight Network to offer commercial airline travelers with high-speed broadband Internet service.

Globalstar began 2001 by completing a $180 million communication network in Latin America, after bringing a new communications gateway/hub online in Brazil that provided the country with coverage throughout all of its 8.5 million square kilometers. That year, the company's Globalstar USA service provider introduced a new satellite-based information service for sailors, in partnership with Ocean and Coastal Environmental Sensing, which provided them with weather data, a chart library, and other oceanic information. It also was in 2001 that a commercial data service was introduced, allowing Globalstar's satellite network to be used for purposes such as asset tracking, fleet management, and telemetry.

BANKRUPTCY

With revenues of just $6.4 million in 2001, Globalstar was struggling. Although the company had 66,000 subscribers, it was limited by an inability to provide service coverage throughout most of South Asia, the Indian subcontinent, and Africa. With the exception of the Northeast Pacific and North Atlantic corridor, Globalstar also was not able to provide coverage over major portions of the world's oceans, putting the company at a disadvantage with other industry players such as Inmarsat and Iridium. In addition, Globalstar was plagued by high operating costs associated with the satellite ground stations that were a critical part of its operation. In February 2002 the company filed for Chapter 11 bankruptcy protection.

Under the leadership of Chairman and CEO Olof Lundberg, Globalstar began restructuring. In order to expand its geographic coverage, the company acquired the satellite gateway formerly operated by its service provider, TE.SA.M, in Aussaguel, France. In a similar move, gateways in the United States and Caribbean were acquired from Vodafone Americas Inc. These deals also allowed the company to gain full ownership of its sales and marketing operations, hire more sales people, and roll out more aggressive sales promotions.

Globalstar continue to introduce new services, including secure encrypted data transmissions, via a partnership with Rainbow Mykotronx. Through a tie-up with the small satellite and technology products company, AeroAstro, Globalstar also introduced a low-cost simplex modem designed for tracking and remote sensing. Finally, Globalstar rolled out products that allowed workers and residents of harsh environments to use satellite phones inside buildings, vehicles, and boats through the use of special antennas.

Globalstar began 2003 by announcing that the company would be acquired by the investment firm, New Valley, for $55 million. Led by Bennett LeBow, New Valley agreed to infuse $20 million in cash into Globalstar while the company finalized its reorganization, followed by an additional $35 million once the restructuring process was complete. Ultimately, the deal failed to materialize when New Valley withdrew its offer.

Another suitor emerged when the London-based satellite communications firm, ICO Global Communications Holdings, which was led by entrepreneur Craig O. McCaw, agreed to acquire a 54 percent equity interest in the company for $55 million. Midway through 2003, the deal appeared to be on its way to completion after receiving approval from both the FCC and the U.S. Bankruptcy Court. Lundberg stepped down in June, making way for new post-bankruptcy leadership. Navarra remained with the company as president.

ACQUIRED BY THERMO CAPITAL

In the wake of Justice Department concerns about the ICO Global Communications deal, Globalstar unveiled a new reorganization plan in November 2003 that provided the company with $43 million in financing from Thermo Capital Partners LLC in exchange for an 81.25 percent ownership interest. The remaining 18.75 percent was distributed to Globalstar's creditors. Following its acquisition by Thermo Capital, Globalstar resumed operations with a workforce of 200 people and no debt.

After bankruptcy, Globalstar maintained its headquarters in San Jose, California. While under bankruptcy protection, the company's customer base had increased from 40,000 subscribers to 110,000 subscribers in 120 different countries. Globalstar proceeded to introduce new offerings, including StarFax, a service that allowed customers to send and receive faxes on the company's satellite network, in mid-2004. Thermo Capital offered Globalstar access to $250 million in funding, as the company considered opportunities in new markets, including oil and gas extraction, maritime, defense, and homeland security. In early 2005 the company's subsidiary, Globalstar de Venezuela C.A., acquired the Globalstar service satellite ground station

KEY DATES

1991: The company is established as Globalstar L.P., a technology partnership between Loral Space and Communications and Qualcomm Incorporated.

1999: Globalstar launches its original first-generation satellite network.

2003: After declaring bankruptcy the previous year, company is acquired by Thermo Capital Partners LLC and resumes operations as Globalstar LLC.

2012: Company begins launching its second-generation satellite network.

2014: Globalstar's stock begins trading on the New York Stock Exchange under the ticker symbol GSAT.

and related assets from service provider, TE.SA.M de Venezuela.

Growth continued in early 2006 when the company acquired the authorized Globalstar service providers, Globalstar Americas Holdings Ltd., Astral Technologies Investments Ltd., and Globalstar Americas Telecommunications Ltd. Collectively, the companies provided Globalstar service in Central America, in markets such as Nicaragua, Panama, Guatemala, Honduras, Costa Rica, and El Salvador. Product introductions included a new satellite modem for laptop computers, as well as a next-generation satellite telephone handset that functioned on six different continents and in 120 different countries.

SECOND-GENERATION PREPARATION

By this time Globalstar was proposing to implement a second-generation satellite constellation. Led by Chairman and CEO Jay Monroe, in early 2008 the company acquired its independent gateway operator in Brazil, in a deal with Loral Space & Communications Inc. Midway through the year Globalstar installed a satellite gateway in Singapore, gaining satellite coverage in Southeast Asia and its surrounding maritime region. Singapore Telecommunications Ltd. agreed to operate the new gateway.

By 2008 Globalstar ranked as the largest provider of mobile satellite voice and data services in the world, with approximately 300,000 subscribers in more than 120 countries. In August of that year manufacturer Thales Alenia Space and launch provider Arianespace began assembling, integrating, and testing the company's 48 second-generation satellites. These would meet the company's needs through 2025, providing customers with faster data speeds and next-generation services such as mobile video applications. It also was in 2008 that Globalstar named Thomas M. Colby as its chief operating officer.

In early 2009 Globalstar was honored with an Innovation Award from the Mobile Satellite Users Association, in recognition of the company's SPOT Satellite GPS Messenger product. Coverage expansion continued during the latter part of the year as the company established a new satellite gateway ground station in Nigeria, improving service in both western and central Africa, the Gulf of Guinea maritime region, and the Atlantic coast. The independent service provider, Globaltouch, was chosen to operate the gateway, in which Globalstar had a 30 percent ownership interest.

Globalstar began 2010 by establishing Globalstar Asia Pacific, a new South Korea–based joint venture with Arion Communications. Operations consisted of a satellite gateway facility southeast of Seoul, which the company acquired in a deal with LG Telecom. Approval for operations was received by the Korea Communications Commission midway through the year. Around the same time the company finalized upgrades to its Milpitas, California–based satellite operations and control center, as well as a backup control center in El Dorado Hills, California. The improvements were made in preparation for the company's second-generation satellite constellation launch.

A major development took place in July when Globalstar relocated its corporate headquarters from California to Covington, Louisiana. The relocation also included the company's international customer care operations, global business functions, call center, and product development center. By this time Monroe was serving as Globalstar's executive chairman, with Peter Dalton fulfilling the CEO role.

SECOND-GENERATION LAUNCH

After commencing construction of a satellite tracking station in Botswana, southern Africa, which was part of a satellite telemetry control unit, Globalstar began launching its second-generation satellite network. By October 2012 the company had launched the network's first six satellites. In the United States Globalstar began working with Open Range Communications to introduce wireless broadband Internet service in approximately 200 rural communities.

Globalstar soon began laying the groundwork to establish a national Wi-Fi network utilizing the Wi-Fi band, Channel 14, as well as a terrestrial low-power service. The company sought approval for the service, which would provide roughly 20,000 access points for facilities such as schools and hospitals, from the FCC in 2013. Later that year word surfaced that the Internet retailer Amazon was piloting a national satellite-based wireless network to support its Kindle device using Globalstar's infrastructure.

Globalstar ended 2013 by issuing 3.17 million shares of its common stock, valued at $4.3 million, to EchoStar Corporation subsidiary, Hughes Network Systems LLC. The following month Globalstar issued another 6.33 million shares, valued at $10.1 million, to Hughes. In early 2014 the company was awaiting the final certification from the FCC that was needed to roll out its new Sat-Fi service, which provided individuals with laptops, smartphones, and tablet computers to use voice and data service when cellular coverage was not available. The service utilized satellite hot spots that connected to mobile devices equipped with a related app.

GOING PUBLIC

It also was in early 2014 that Globalstar filed applications with the New York Stock Exchange and the NASDAQ Stock Market, as it explored options to list its stock on one of the two exchanges. Ultimately, Globalstar's stock began trading on the New York Stock Exchange in April under the ticker symbol GSAT. By this time the company's satellite network was being used for more than just communications. For example, satellite communications chipsets connected to the Globalstar network were used by gas, oil, and chemical companies to monitor hazardous materials being transported in tank containers and rail tank cars.

Midway through 2014 Globalstar's Victorville, California–based value-added reseller, VehSmart, was awarded a contract to install Globalstar's SmartOne hardware on approximately 4,000 small fishing boats in Ecuador, connecting the vessels to that country's National Emergency Response System. This was but one example of the wide-ranging applications that existed for Globalstar's technology. Moving forward, the company appeared to have excellent prospects for continued success.

Paul R. Greenland

PRINCIPAL SUBSIDIARIES

GSSI, LLC; ATSS Canada, Inc.; Globalstar Brazil Holdings, L.P.; Globalstar do Brasil Holdings Ltda. (Brazil); Globalstar do Brazil, S.A.; Globalstar Satellite Services Pte., Ltd. (Singapore); Globalstar Satellite Services Pty., Ltd. (South Africa); Globalstar C, LLC; Mobile Satellite Services B.V. (Netherlands); Globalstar Europe, S.A.R.L. (France); Globalstar Europe Satellite Services, Ltd. (Ireland); Globalstar Leasing LLC; Globalstar Licensee LLC; Globalstar Security Services, LLC; Globalstar USA, LLC; GUSA Licensee LLC; Globalstar Canada Satellite Co.; Globalstar de Venezuela, C.A.; Globalstar Colombia, Ltda.; Globalstar Caribbean Ltd. (Cayman Islands); GCL Licensee LLC; Globalstar Americas Acquisitions, Ltd. (British Virgin Islands); Globalstar Americas Holding Ltd. (British Virgin Islands); Globalstar Gateway Company S.A. (Nicaragua); Globalstar Americas Telecommunications Ltd. (British Virgin Islands); Globalstar Honduras S.A.; Globalstar Nicaragua S.A.; Globalstar de El Salvador, SA de CV; Globalstar Panama, Corp.; Globalstar Guatemala S.A.; Globalstar Belize Ltd.; Astral Technologies Investment Ltd. (British Virgin Islands); Astral Technologies Nicaragua S.A. (British Virgin Islands); SPOT LLC.

PRINCIPAL COMPETITORS

Inmarsat plc; Iridium Communications Inc.; ORBCOMM Inc.

FURTHER READING

"Globalstar and VehSmart to Outfit Ecuadorian Fishing Fleet with 4,000 Globalstar SmartOne Satellite Tracking Devices." *ENP Newswire*, May 26, 2014.

"Globalstar, Arion Form JV in Korea." *Digital Media Asia*, February 9, 2010.

"Globalstar Launches Satellites for Planned Broadband Service." *Techweb*, November 2, 2010.

Parker, Tammy. "Globalstar's Sat-Fi to Deliver Satellite Coverage to Wi-Fi Enabled Devices." *FierceWirelessTech*, January 29, 2014.

"Satellite Carrier May Open New Wi-Fi Channel." *PC World*, February 2013.

Grand Candy Company Ltd.

---

31 Masis Str
Yerevan, 0061
Armenia
Telephone: (374 10) 44 99 98
Fax: (374 10) 44 99 01
Web site: http://www.grandcandy.am

Wholly Owned Subsidiary of Grand Holding
Incorporated: 2000
Employees: 3,200
Sales: $1.32 billion (2011)
NAICS: 311351 Chocolate and Confectionery Manufacturing from Cacao Beans; 311352 Confectionery Manufacturing from Purchased Chocolate

■■■

Grand Candy Company Ltd. is the leading food company in Armenia and one of the country's largest private-sector corporations. Grand Candy produces a wide range of confectionery products, including hard and soft candies; chocolate and chocolate candies and bars; cookies and wafers; fruit jellies; and a variety of cakes and pastries. The latter include *ponchik*, a popular doughnut-like pastry. The company's other lines include nuts, including peanuts, almonds, pistachio and sunflower seeds, and coffee prepared in the company's own roasting facility. The company produces 73 flavors of ice cream, including bulk, and glazed and non-glazed ice cream products. The company also manufactures its own cones.

Grand Candy operates its own packaging facility, producing corrugated cardboard boxes both for its own and third-party businesses. Another offshoot of the company's main business is the sales of packaged flour, including for the wholesale and consumer markets. In addition to its confectionery and related production, Grand Candy is also a major retailer in Armenia, operating 18 stores throughout the country. Seven of these stores feature in-store bakeries and cafés, including Yerevan's iconic Ponchikanots café. Grand Candy is a private company employing more than 3,200 people, with revenues of more than $1.32 billion. The company is part of Grand Holding, controlled by the Vardanian family. Other companies in the Grand Holding group include Grand Tobacco, Armenia's largest cigarette and tobacco products company, and Grand Sun, a leading producer of lightbulbs and lamps.

SOVIET-ERA ORIGINS

Although Grand Candy was founded in 2000, the company's industrial origins reached back to the Soviet era. Tiny Armenia was annexed by the Soviet Union in 1920, along with neighbors Georgia and Azerbaijan. This brought a period of relative prosperity to the region, particularly following the turbulence amid the collapse of the Ottoman Empire. Armenia prospered under Soviet rule, gaining greater access to consumer goods, medicines and other products. The country also benefited strongly from the Soviet Union's industrialization policies.

The new availability of modern industrial production technologies played a prominent role in the growth

---

COMPANY PERSPECTIVES

Every day the Grand Candy staff and the company's owner himself go to work with one conviction: we produce for our children, for our families and for our nation.

---

of Armenia's food industry during this time. One of the earliest and largest Soviet-era investments came in 1933, with the construction of the Yerevan Pasta Factory (also translated as Yerevan Macaroni Factory). This complex became an important supplier of pasta, macaroni and other food products, not only in Armenia, but throughout the Soviet Union.

Similarly, a second factory built the following year, Yerevan Confectionery Factory, became a primary supplier of candy and other confectionery in the Soviet Union. The two Yerevan factories operated independently for most of their first two decades. In 1951, however, the factories were merged under the same management, forming a company known as Yerevan Confectionery and Pasta Factory. By then Yerevan was home to a number of other Soviet-era industrial operations, including a lightbulb factory and, especially, a large-scale tobacco and cigarette factory. While operated independently of the Pasta and Confectionery factory, this latter business played a prominent role in the creation of the Grand Candy company.

Through the next decades, the Yerevan Confectionery and Pasta Factory became one of the largest suppliers of both of these products in the Soviet Union. The factory benefited from the strong investments by the Soviet Union to boost the productivity of its industries, including the union's production of fast-moving consumer goods, during the Cold War era. In this way, Soviet authorities yielded somewhat to growing consumer pressure, as the Soviet population became increasingly aware of the array of goods available in Western markets. The Yerevan factory was expanded with new production equipment and production lines, adding the production of hard candies, cocoa and chocolate, and cookies and biscuits.

The Yerevan factory also held the distinction of becoming the first in the Soviet Union to produce chewing gum for the Soviet market in 1977. The recipe for this chewing gum, however, did not incorporate chicle, the gumlike substance that provided the base for early chewing gums. Instead, the product the Yerevan factory produced was composed of leftover materials from its pasta production. The resulting "gum" was too hard to be considered a true chewing gum and tended to fall apart once chewed.

PRIVATIZATION IN 1995

The Yerevan company's fortunes changed dramatically when Armenia declared its independence in 1991. By then Armenia was already struggling to recover from a major earthquake, which devastated a large part of the country in 1988. More than one-third of Armenia's industries were damaged. Fearful of another Chernobyl-like disaster, Armenians took to the street in protest, forcing the government to shut down the country's nuclear power plant. The loss of this energy supply was to have devastating consequences for the country through much of the next decade.

Armenia's economy was further affected by its conflict with Azerbaijan over the Nagorno-Karabakh region, a part of Azerbaijan with a large Armenian population. War between the two nations broke out in 1988. The imposition of an economic blockade by Turkey and Azerbaijan further isolated the tiny country, which also struggled with a failing infrastructure, an underdeveloped agricultural industry, and few natural resources. Russia joined in on the blockade, preventing crucial supplies and equipment from reaching mountainous Armenia.

In the meantime Armenia's first democratically elected government began introducing economic reforms. The transition to a market-oriented economy proved a bumpy one, however. Political unrest, the breakdown of its cease-fire with Azerbaijan, the continued blockade of such crucial imports as natural gas, and especially the widespread corruption in the country's business sector, contributed to the near-paralysis of the Armenian economy. In addition, the lack of natural gas strained the country's electricity resources, and through the middle of the 1990s, blackouts were common, with electricity available for less than two hours each day. The country's reliance on hydroelectric power during this period also put a significant strain on its water supply.

As a result, operations at the Yerevan Pasta and Confectionery Factory came to a virtual standstill for much of the decade. The factory's privatization, as Armconfection OJSC, in May 1995, did little to revitalize the company. Through the end of the decade, the company limped along, operating at as low as 3 percent of its total capacity.

GRAND SUCCESS FROM 1997

The factory might have shut down altogether, had it not been for Hrant Vardanian, who by then had already

KEY DATES

1933: Soviet authorities found Yerevan Pasta Factory in Yerevan, Armenia.
1934: Yerevan Confectionery Factory is founded.
1951: The two factories are merged as Yerevan Confectionery and Pasta Factory.
1995: Factory is privatized as Armconfection OJSC.
2000: Grand Candy is founded as a joint venture by Hrant Vardanian's Grand Holding and acquires Armconfection.
2006: Grand Candy adds a packaging facility.
2010: Company enters the Guinness Book of World Records for producing the world's largest chocolate bar.
2014: Vardanian's sons take over leadership of the company.

begun to emerge as one of the most dynamic of Armenia's new generation of businessmen. Born in 1948, Vardanian (also transliterated as Vardanyan) graduated from the Yerevan State Engineering University, then started his career as a mechanic at the Yerevan Cigarette Factory in 1970. Over the next two decades Vardanian had worked his way up the ladder, becoming one of the factory's directors.

Into the 1990s, however, Armenia had come to rely heavily on imported consumer goods, including cigarettes and tobacco products. Vardanian gambled on the idea that there would be a strong market for new cigarette brands not only produced in Armenia, but incorporating Armenian-grown tobacco as well. In 1996 Vardanian led the privatization of the Yerevan Tobacco Factory. For this he formed a joint venture with a group of Canadian investors, founding the Grand Tobacco company. Grand Tobacco promptly invested $415,000 on developing its own tobacco fermentation technology, while also working with Armenian farmers to develop the country's tobacco crop.

By 2001 Grand Tobacco had reached supply deals with some 300 farms. Much of the funding for this growth came from Grand Tobacco's Canadian investors, who contributed more than $4 million to the company's development into the turn of the century. Along the way, the company had developed more than 50 cigarette brands, including fruit-flavored cigarettes, small-sized cigarettes with built-in holders, and cigarettes wrapped in a variety of colored papers. The company easily captured more than two-thirds of the Armenian

cigarette more, selling more than 6 billion cigarettes per year. Grand Tobacco's production capacity ultimately reached more than 30 billion cigarettes per year.

Importantly, Grand Tobacco also developed a growing business supplying the large Armenian diaspora. An estimated 8 million ethnic Armenians lived outside of Armenia, which itself had a population of just 3.5 million at the dawn of the 21st century. Many Armenians had been forced to leave the country in search of work during the chaotic conditions immediately following independence. The exodus continued, dropping Armenia's total population to just over 2 million by 2010. Grand Tobacco began catering to the growing and generally prosperous Armenian expatriate communities in Russia, the United States, and elsewhere. The company developed specific brands for these markets, such as the popular Tough Guy cigarette brand marketed in the United States.

GRAND CANDY IN 2000

Grand Tobacco itself branched out beyond Armenia. The company opened a tobacco processing facility in Nizhny Novgorod, Russia, where it became manufacturing and marketing a discount brand, Strelka, for the Russian market. The move into Russia also brought Vardanian new business contacts, as he pursued his goal of contributing to the revitalization of Armenia's economy. Toward this end, Vardanian added two more companies. The first was a joint venture with a Greek partner, called Masis Tabak, which produced discount cigarettes using Armenian tobacco both for the domestic and export market. For the second, Vardanian acquired another abandoned Soviet-era factory in Yerevan, the Armenia Lamp Factory. Grand Holding, as Vardanian's growing business empire was called, reopened the factory, which began producing lightbulbs and lamps for the Armenian market as the Grand Sun Company. Into the next decade Vardanian invested in other areas as well, founding a television broadcaster, AR TV, and a solar power plant.

With these businesses underway, Vardanian's attention turned to another promising fast-moving consumer goods category: food, specifically candy and other confectionery. At the end of 1999 Vardanian bought out the shareholders in Armconfection and in 2000 brought in a new partner, the Russian company Brogus, to found a new joint venture called Grand Candy Company Ltd.

Grand Candy's new owners invested heavily in rebuilding the factory and installing new modern production equipment. The company began marketing its first products in April 2000. From the start, Grand

Candy focused on producing confectionery featuring only high-quality and all-natural ingredients. In this way Grand Candy quickly established a reputation for quality. In response to this success, the company rapidly expanded its product line. Before long, the company was already producing more than 400 products. These included ice cream, which the company began producing starting from 2001. Grand Candy brand soon became Armenia's confectionery leader.

Grand Candy had made impressive gains in its production capacity. By the end of 2001 the company already produced 250 tons per year of hard candy, and 150 tons per year of chocolates. The company's total production of wafers, biscuits and other cakes, and cookies reached 80 tons. In addition, Grand Candy at first continued to produce pasta for the home market, with production levels of 120 tons per year.

PACKAGING BUSINESS IN 2006

Grand Candy had also become an important part of the Armenian economy in its own right. By 2001 the company already employed more than 700 people. Within a decade, its payroll would swell to more than 3,000. Grand Candy employees also benefited from Grand Holding's payroll policies. Grand Candy employees, like their counterparts at the other Grand Holding companies, were typically paid between $100 and $200 per month. This was well above the national average wage at the time of just $35 per month.

Grand Candy's products not only found favor in Armenia, they also found a ready market overseas, notably in the United States, Canada, Georgia, Iran, Lebanon, Russia, and other markets with large expatriate Armenian populations. Back at home, Grand Candy raised its profile by developing its own retail network. This effort began with its purchase of Ponchikanots, once an iconic confectionery shop in Yerevan that had been shuttered after Armenia's independence and converted into office space. Vardanian purchased the property and reopened the café, which once again began featuring the popular doughnut-like *ponchik* pastry. Grand Candy expanded the site, opening the first of its candy and confectionery shops. Through the next decade, the company expanded its retail chain. By 2014 Grand Candy would operate from 18 locations throughout Armenia.

In an effort to ensure quality, Grand Candy also invested in its own packaging facility. The new site opened in 2006, producing corrugated boxes and other packaging, both for Grand Candy's operations, as well as for third parties. The following year the company extended its packaging capacity with the addition of a modern printing facility as well.

By 2010 Vardanian had become Armenia's wealthiest businessman. He was also one of the few truly admired of the new "oligarch" class in Armenia, which, as in Russia and other former Soviet states, remained rife with corruption and crony capitalism. Vardanian was not necessarily an exception in this respect. As messages released during the so-called WikiLeaks scandal in 2012 revealed, Vardanian most likely enjoyed a close relationship with Armenia's political elite. According to messages from the U.S. embassy at the time, Vardanian was said to enjoy the protection of the Armenian president.

NEW PRODUCTS FROM 2010

Vardanian nonetheless could point proudly to his contributions to the Armenian economy, pointing out that he had single-handedly become the fourth-largest source of tax revenues in the country. Through Grand Holding, Vardanian had also invested massively in rebuilding the country's damaged economic infrastructure. In the first decade of the 21st century Grand Candy's investments alone topped AMD 11.5 billion, and the company was on track to reach 4,000 employees by 2020. For his role in Armenia's transformation as one of the most dynamic economies among the former Soviet satellites, Vardanian was awarded the title of Merited Figure of the Armenian Economy in 2009.

Grand Candy continued to develop new product lines as well. The company began producing coffee, starting in 2008. In 2010 the company expanded its production with a line of pastries. Grand Candy then extended its product line up to include packaged flour, selling both large-sized bulk packages for the wholesale market and consumer-sized packages for the retail market, starting in 2012.

Grand Candy by then had started to raise its international profile. In September 2010 the company entered the *Guinness Book of World Records* with its production of the world's largest chocolate bar. As part of this stunt, coinciding with the company's 10th anniversary, the company's produced a bar weighing more than 4,400 kilograms (9,700 pounds) and measuring 5.5 meters (18.6 feet) long.

The company suffered a blow in April 2014, when Hrant Vardanian died of a heart attack at the age of 65. Vardanian's sons, Karen and Mikael, took over the leadership of Grand Holding, ensuring the continuity of Grand Candy and the other jewels in the Vardanian empire. Grand Candy soon promised new growth, announcing plans to invest another $5 million through the year on expanding its operations. In less than 15 years,

Grand Candy had established itself as Armenia's largest food company, and one of the country's leading corporations in the beginning of the 21st century.

M. L. Cohen

PRINCIPAL DIVISIONS

Confectionery Products; Nuts; Cocoa Products; Ice Cream; Coffee; Corrugated Cardboard; Flour; Stores.

PRINCIPAL OPERATING UNITS

Ponchikanots.

PRINCIPAL COMPETITORS

Artsweet Pastry Shop LLC; Kaghtsrik Confectionery Plant; Mancho Group LLC; Sonagro Confectionery Plant; Tamara Co. Ltd.

FURTHER READING

"Grand Candy Factory in Armenia Makes World's Largest Chocolate Bar." *Daily Telegraph*, September 14, 2010.

"Grand Holding Owner Hrant Vardanyan Dies at 65." *ArmeniaNow.com*, April 22, 2014.

"Investments of Armenia's Grand Candy Confectionery to Total $5 Million Later This Year," *Arka*, June, 6, 2014.

"Major Businessman 'Wealthiest Man in Armenia' Dies." *Epress. com*, April 21, 2014.

"10,000." *Science World*, January 3, 2011.

Great Eastern Shipping Company Ltd.

Ocean House
134/A, Dr. Annie Besant Road
Worli
Mumbai, 400 018
India
Telephone: (+91 22) 6661 3000
Fax: (+91 22) 2492 5900
Web site: http://greatship.com

Public Company
Incorporated: 1948
Employees: 672
Sales: INR 1.6 billion ($266.08 million) (2014)
Stock Exchanges: Mumbai Luxembourg
Ticker Symbol: GESHIP
NAICS: 483111 Deep Sea Freight Transportation

■ ■ ■

The Great Eastern Shipping Company Ltd. is the largest private shipping company in India. Its operations are organized into two main business units. The company's Offshore unit serves the oil industry via a subsidiary named Greatship (India) Ltd., providing business services to companies involved in offshore exploration and production. Additionally, Great Eastern Shipping's ISO 9001: 2000–certified Shipping unit is engaged in the transport of petroleum products and crude oil, as well as gas and dry-bulk commodities.

ORIGINS AND EARLY LEADERS

Great Eastern Shipping traces its origins back to 1948. That year the company was established by the Sheth and Bhiwandiwalla families, as a means of expanding their existing trading business. Operations began following the acquisition of a surplus Liberty ship named the SS *Fort Elice*, which was used for importing sugar.

Early leadership was provided by Vasant J. Sheth. Credited by the company as the "prime architect" for its formation, Vasant played an instrumental role in establishing the company as a provider tramp shipping throughout India. His father, Jagjivan Ujamshi Mulji, also was among the company's founders and had established a sugar-trading firm with the Bhiwandiwallas, after an initial stint in the textile industry. Early leadership also was provided by Ardeshir Hormusji Bhiwandiwalla, who helped the Sheth brothers build India's largest sugar-importing firm. He served as chairman of Great Eastern Shipping from 1948 to 1973. As a tribute to his legacy, the company embosses his initials on the funnel and house flag of every vessel. Great Eastern Shipping's founders also included Maneklal Ujamshi Mulji, known throughout India as the "Sugar King," who worked closely with his brother, Jagjivan Ujamshi Mulji, during the company's formative years.

EARLY DEVELOPMENTS

Great Eastern Shipping achieved steady growth throughout its first several decades. When India was impacted by famine during the 1960s, the company broadened the scope of its bulk fleet to transport grain. A pioneering development took place during the 1970s when Great Eastern Shipping became the first shipping enterprise in India to offer direct service to both the United States and the Canadian West Coast. Progress

COMPANY PERSPECTIVES

From providing sea-logistics support in its initial years to venturing in tramp shipping, to diversifying into offshore oil field services, much against the industry norms, the company has often swum against the tide and in the process, turned the tides in its favour, thereby laying a path for others to follow.

continued in 1982 when the International Finance Corporation invested in Great Eastern Shipping.

It also was during the 1980s that Great Eastern Shipping expanded its fleet via the sale of $10 million in convertible debentures. Another milestone was reached in 1986 when the company went public on the Bombay Stock Exchange. As part of a strategy to encourage foreign investment, Great Eastern Shipping also was the first shipping player in India to issue global depositary receipts in 1994. By 1996 the company had become the nation's largest private sector shipping company. It was generating annual sales of $222 million and had amassed assets of $537 million. Great Eastern Shipping's main competitor was the Shipping Corporation of India, the nation's second-largest shipping company.

By the mid-1990s Great Eastern Shipping's operations included a 57-vessel fleet. Collectively, these vessels had a capacity of more than 1.35 million deadweight tons. The company continued to seek outside investment, generating approximately $70 million from Asia, Singapore, and Europe through a floating rate note issued in October 1996.

By 1997 Great Eastern Shipping was pursuing a plan to expand its fleet by an additional 10 vessels. In keeping with this strategy the company ordered two Aframax tankers from South Korea–based Samsung Shipyard, at a cost of $40 million each. Additionally, the company also formed a joint venture named Coastal Lighterage with Thailand-based Precious Shipping Public Co., as a means of decreasing congestion at Indian shipping ports.

ACQUIRES MUMBAI OFFICE COMPLEX

Great Eastern Shipping made a significant real estate purchase in late 1997 when the company acquired a 44,000-square-foot office complex in Mumbai from Germany's Siemens. The company also had acquired one floor in the Hongkong Bank Building and two

floors in South Mumbai's World Trade Centre. The former Siemens facility was part of a move to consolidate the operations of several Great Eastern Shipping divisions, so that more employees were in one location.

At this time the Indian government was concerned about the decline of its domestic shipping fleet. Indian ships' share of domestic cargo totaled about 27 percent by the second half of 1998, down from almost 35 percent during the mid-1980s. Nevertheless, companies such as Great Eastern Shipping were not engaging in major fleet expansions. The absence of substantial incentives and funds were among the leading roadblocks to the expansion of India's domestic fleet.

Great Eastern Shipping ended the 1990s by spinning off its property division as a separate company. Although the division, formed during the early part of the decade, had been quite profitable, declining property prices had negatively affected the business by the middle of the decade. Following a demerger on April 1, 1999, the property division was named Gesco Corporation Pte Ltd. The business was headed by Managing Director Ghanshyam Sheth, who moved forward with a focus on property-related project management, as opposed to property development. Singapore-based Sembcorp, a subsidiary of the SembCorp Group, then entered into an agreement with Gesco to secure an ownership stake in the business.

INTERNATIONAL ATTENTION

In late 2001 one of Great Eastern Shipping's vessels, a 450-foot-long vessel named the MV *Nisha*, attracted international attention when the ship was suspected to be carrying explosives or anthrax, in connection with a potential attack against Britain by terrorist leader Osama bin Laden. On December 21 the vessel was intercepted in the English Channel by the Special Boat Service. Dozens of armed elite special forces troops boarded the vessel, armed with stun grenades and automatic weapons.

Ultimately, the ship, which was carrying sugar from Mauritius to an East London refinery, was cleared following a two-day search. The inspection of Great Eastern Shipping's MV *Nisha* took place after the vessel had visited Djibouti, East Africa, near Somalia, where bin Laden's terrorist group, al Qaeda, was suspected of being active. The search jeopardized the company's £9 million sugar shipment to customer Tate & Lyle, which voiced concerns regarding potential contamination of the sugar following the investigation.

By 2003 Great Eastern Shipping's interests also had grown to include an ownership stake in *Business*

```
┌─────────────────────────────────────────────┐
│                                               │
│              KEY DATES                        │
│                   ●                           │
├─────────────────────────────────────────────┤
│  1948:  Company is established by the Sheth and│
│         Bhiwandiwalla families.                │
│  1986:  Great Eastern Shipping goes public.    │
│  1997:  A 44,000-square-foot office complex in │
│         Mumbai is acquired from Germany's      │
│         Siemens.                               │
│  2001:  Great Eastern Shipping's vessel, the MV│
│         Nisha, is cleared of suspected involve-│
│         ment in a terrorist attack against     │
│         Britain following a two-day search.    │
│  2014:  New subsidiary named GGOS Labuan is    │
│         formed within the company's Greatship  │
│         Global Offshore Services business.     │
└─────────────────────────────────────────────┘
```

Standard, India's second-leading financial daily paper. During the middle of the decade the company's board of directors approved a plan to separate Great Eastern Shipping's offshore business and operated as a separate company. To be named Great Offshore Ltd., the new operation would encompass port services, marine logistics and construction, and drilling services. Announced in September 2005, the plan was withdrawn in August of the following year when the organization was unable to meet conditions established by the Mumbai high court.

FLEET EXPANSION

Great Eastern Shipping expanded its fleet with a variety of vessels during the middle of the decade. For example, in late 2004 the company received a new medium-range product carrier named the *Jag Pahel*. Early the following year Great Eastern Shipping added its first ice-class vessel, a Suezmax tanker named the *Jag Lok*. Increased exploration and production activities in India led the company to order its first new jack-up drilling rig from Singapore's Keppel Fels. Costing approximately $182 million, the rig could accommodate 112 workers and support drilling as deep as 30,000 feet.

In late 2006 Great Eastern Shipping expanded its fleet even further with a new Suezmax crude carrier, which it dubbed the *Jag Layak*. The company rounded out the year with a $60.4 million order for four anchor handling tug supply vessels from Labroy Marine. In addition, it also ordered a Panamax carrier that expanded the company's capabilities in the dry-bulk trade market.

As Great Eastern Shipping welcomed new vessels to its fleet, it also sold a number of vessels during the middle of the decade. These included the crude carrier *Jag Larjish*, in late 2004, and the dry-bulk carrier *Jag Ratna*, the following year. In 2006 the company sold its product carrier, the *Jag Prachi*, and a crude carrier named the *Jag Leena*. By late 2006 Great Eastern Shipping's fleet included 73 vessels. Among its more than 39 ships were dry-bulk carriers and tankers capable of transporting products, crude oil, and liquefied petroleum gas. Additionally, Great Eastern Shipping also operated 34 offshore units.

In 2007 Great Eastern Shipping divested its ownership stake in subsidiary Routes Travel Ltd. The company then sold its Suezmax crude carrier, *Jag Laadki*. Offshore capabilities expanded during the early part of the year when subsidiary Greatship acquired a new platform supply vessel, which it named *Greatship Diya*. In late 2008 the company found itself in the midst of another dramatic situation when pirates attempted to board one of its bulk carriers off the Somalian coast. The pirates also attempted to hijack a Saudi Arabian vessel but were thwarted by efforts of the Indian Navy.

DIFFICULT INDUSTRY CONDITIONS

By the latter part of the decade Great Eastern Shipping remained the largest privately owned shipping company in India. At that time the nation's market for shipping-related coastal trading was valued at approximately $225 million. Other leading Indian shipping companies at that time included the government-controlled Shipping Corp. of India Ltd., Pratibha Shipping Co. Ltd., and Mercator Lines Ltd. Low return rates in the dry-bulk sector led Great Eastern Shipping to significantly reduce its fleet by selling older vessels.

By 2011 the industry was contending with falling rates in both the liquid bulk and dry-bulk segments, prompting Great Eastern Shipping to continue reducing the size of its fleet. Early that year the company revealed that it would sell three very large crude carriers that were on order from South Korea–based Hyundai Heavy Industries. Instead of receiving the new ships, the vessels would be sold directly to another party. By February 2012 the company already had sold two of the three vessels, which it had ordered in April 2010. Around that time the company's Greatship subsidiary dissolved its Greatship DOF Subsea Projects Private Limited business.

Great Eastern Shipping continued to scale back its fleet in mid-2012, selling a very large gas carrier that had been constructed in 1990. Later that year the company's Greatship subsidiary sold a multipurpose platform supply and support vessel named *Greatship Mamta*. Although the company welcomed the *Jag Vidhi*, a new very large gas carrier, to its fleet in 2012, another divestment occurred in mid-2013 when it sold the *Jag Leela*, an Aframax crude carrier that had been constructed in 1999.

It also was in early 2013 that the company's Great Eastern Chartering LLC subsidiary established a new business named Great Eastern Chartering (Singapore) Pte. Ltd. By the middle of the year the shipping industry continued to struggle with low return rates, caused by an oversupply of available ships. Although this presented difficulties for all shipping companies, the impact on Great Eastern Shipping was partially offset by success within its offshore business.

FLEET EXPANSION RESUMES

Following the aforementioned divestments, Great Eastern Shipping began bolstering its fleet once again during the second half of 2013. After ordering a new very large gas carrier, the company added a medium-range product carrier named the *Jag Prabha* to its fleet. In addition, subsidiary Greatship Global Energy Services ordered a new rig that was equipped with advanced technology. Great Eastern Shipping then rounded out the year by placing an order with China-based Jiangsu Yangzijiang Shipbuilding Group for three new dry-bulk carriers.

By the middle of 2014 Great Eastern Shipping's offshore business continued to provide the company with a buffer from more difficult conditions within the shipping sector, which continued to experience overcapacity and weak freight rates. In fact, during the first quarter of the year more than half of the company's revenues came from its offshore operations. It was around this time that a new subsidiary named GGOS Labuan was formed within the company's Greatship Global Offshore Services arm.

During the middle of the year Great Eastern Shipping added a new very large gas carrier named the *Jag Vishnu* to its fleet. At this time the company operated 29 ships, including eight dry-bulk carriers and 21 tankers. The future looked bright when, in September 2014, Great Eastern Shipping announced that it would spend $380 million to bolster its fleet by early 2017. This amount included $180 million for six new vessels, as well as $200 million for another offshore rig. As India's largest private shipping company, Great Eastern Shipping appeared to be positioned for continued success as the company headed into 2015.

Paul R. Greenland

PRINCIPAL SUBSIDIARIES

The Great Eastern Shipping Co. London Ltd. (UK); The Greatship (Singapore) Pte. Ltd.; The Great Eastern Chartering LLC (FZC); Greatship (India) Ltd.

PRINCIPAL OPERATING UNITS

Shipping; Offshore.

PRINCIPAL COMPETITORS

Mercator Ltd.; M/s Pratibha Shipping Company Ltd.; Shipping Corporation of India Ltd.

FURTHER READING

Barrock, Jose. "Corporate: MISC's AET Ventures into India." *Edge Malaysia*, September 21, 2009.

"GE Shipping Takes Delivery of *Jag Vishnu*." *Dion Global Solutions Limited*, July 9, 2014.

"GE Shipping to Invest INR23bn to Boost Capacity." *Business Monitor Online*, September 2, 2014.

"Great Eastern Shipping Company Establish Subsidiary 'GGOS Labuan.'" *Pivotal Sources*, June 27, 2014.

"Offshore Business Buoys GE Shipping." *MINT*, May 7, 2014.

"Shipping Corp Continues to Battle Rough Seas." *MintAsia*, June 7, 2013.

Harry-Brot GmbH

———— ■ ————

Kiebitzweg 15–19
Schenefeld, 22869
Germany
Telephone: (+49 40) 830 35-0
Fax: (+49 40) 830 35-10353
Web site: http://www.harry-brot.de

Private Company
Founded: 1688
Employees: 4,000
Sales: EUR 910 million ($1.2 billion) (2013)
NAICS: 311812 Commercial Bakeries; 722515 Snack
and Nonalcoholic Beverage Bars

■ ■ ■

Harry-Brot GmbH is one of Germany's largest bread bakers. The company bakes a broad variety of prepackaged sliced breads marketed under the Harry brand or under private labels. Harry-Brot also produces a partially baked line, including bread rolls and specialty breads. Manufactured in nine large bakeries in Germany, the company's products are delivered by its distribution arm Brotland Backwarenvertriebs- Gesellschaft from one of over 30 distribution centers to more than 9,300 supermarkets and grocery stores. Harry breads are also exported to Austria, Switzerland, France, Denmark, and the Czech Republic.

In addition to its line of fresh breads Harry-Brot manufactures a broad range of prebaked frozen breads and rolls, which are distributed by Backshop Tiefkühl GmbH to about 6,600 in-store bakeries in super-markets. Another Harry subsidiary, Back-Factory, operates roughly 130 snack bar outlets in Germany. Headquartered in Schenefeld near Hamburg, Harry-Brot is owned and managed in its 10th generation by members of the Harry family, with a baking tradition reaching back to the 17th century.

ESTABLISHMENT OF TRADITION IN 1688

On May 9, 1688, Johan Hinrich Harry became a member of the baker's guild in Altona, a harbor town west of Hamburg. After receiving his concession, the 20-year-old son of a master baker started his own bakery. At the time, bread was still the main staple food in northern Europe. The guild put strict requirements on its members. Bread had to be sold the same day it was made, and it had to be presented for sale on clean linen cloths and protected from dust.

To protect Altona's bakers from cheaper competition, baker's guild membership was strictly limited and hawking baked goods from elsewhere was penalized. Harry baked mainly mixed rye-and-wheat bread, which increasingly replaced the region's traditional dark rye sourdough bread. Other popular baked goods of the time were rolls, pretzels, and braided breads or *zöpfe*. After two years in business Harry was able to buy the property where his bakery was located. His sons Hans, David, and Andreas followed in his footsteps and learned the baker's craft. It involved sometimes more than 14 hours of hard work a day, such as carrying heavy flour sacks, sifting the flour and kneading the dough by hand, standing in front of the hot baking

COMPANY PERSPECTIVES

Harry is the most well known bread brand in Germany. Why are we so popular? There are a few simple but important guidelines we follow. Quality, freshness, and service are our foremost rules—and at a great price. This is only possible with state-of-the-art commercial bakeries located close to the customers and a perfectly organized distribution network with short and quickly covered distances. *The desires of the customer.* For Harry the wishes of the consumer are at the center of all its activities. This also means always being open to innovations, reacting to trends early and transforming them into first-class product ideas. *Acting collectively.* Quick decision making processes, team work and continuous human resource development result in a high commitment to performance at all levels of the company. *Organic growth.* Company development is future-oriented and aimed at organic growth. Therefore, Harry consistently makes investments above the average in the market and in operations.

oven, and lifting baked goods in and out with a wooden shovel.

HANS TAKES OVER BAKERY: 1698

In 1698 Johan Hinrich's brother Hans took over their father's bakery in Altona. At the time, the city's population was growing rapidly. By 1709 the year when Johan Hinrich's father passed away, Altona was the third-largest city in the Kingdom of Denmark.

While the Danish king Frederik IV invested heavily in the infrastructure of northern Europe's first free harbor to compete with neighboring Hamburg for ocean shipping business, Johan Hinrich Harry invested heavily in expanding the family business. In 1719 he acquired an additional bakery in Altona's King's Street, and took over his father-in-law's bakery.

The latter was taken over by his son David in 1722, the former by his son-in-law four years later. Hans acquired his uncle's bakery, but died two years later at age 30. After Johan Hinrich's death in 1726, his youngest son Andreas carried on the business, but survived his father by only 10 years. Despite times of war and famine, various members of the Harry family carried on their baking businesses in Altona throughout the 18th century.

LESS BREAD, MORE CAKE AFTER 1800

Around the dawn of the 19th century wars between the major European powers resulted in major changes in eating habits and trade law, with major consequences for Altona's baker's trade. Potatoes, which the Prussian king Frederick II had ordered his farmers to grow during the Seven Years' War to feed his soldiers more inexpensively, became very popular, while bread consumption declined.

The Napoleonic Wars brought French "white" bread to northern Europe. In 1815, when Napoleon was finally defeated, four of the 40 baker's guild members in Altona were members of the Harry family. Johann Jürgen Harry, a great-grandson of David Harry, had traveled abroad for seven years and was the first in the family to learn the craft of a pastry chef. Sweet breads had become the little luxury even the poor wanted to be able to afford, while artfully decorated cakes came into fashion among the wealthy bourgeoisie.

In 1839 Johann Jürgen Harry took over a bakery in Altona's King's Street. It thrived in the following two decades and attracted a loyal base of well-to-do customers. His youngest brother, Johann Friederich, who had operated his own bakery in Altona since 1844, built a brand-new bake shop on a newly acquired property on the same street in 1854, which was successfully operated by Harry family members for almost a century.

INCREASING COMPETITION

In 1866 Johann Friederich's eight sons were registered as baker's journeymen in Altona. As the seventh Harry generation joined the family business, new challenges had to be mastered. After Denmark's defeat in the German-Danish War in 1864, Altona became part of the Prussian province of Schleswig-Holstein, which in 1871 became part of the newly formed German Empire.

The centuries-old baker's guild was dissolved in 1867, and Altona's protected market for baked goods was suddenly opened to competition from everywhere. The established Harry family bakeries in Altona were competing against Hamburg-based bakeries and their door-to-door salespeople. The early 1880s saw the rise of farmers' markets, where various baked goods were sold as well. Bread consumption, on the other hand, had dropped by 70 percent within a century.

Moreover, bakers were no longer required to sell bread the same day it was made. One of Johann Friederich Harry's sons, who successfully claimed his stake in Altona's changing bakery business, was Hugo Harry

KEY DATES

1688: Master baker Johan Hinrich Harry becomes a member of Altona's baker's guild.
1815: Harry family operates four bakeries in Altona.
1929: Franz Andreas Harry Jr. acquires a bread and cookie factory in Hannover.
1999: Harry-Brot's first factory for frozen prebaked products is built.
2002: Back-Factory is founded as a self-service baker's shop chain.

who received his master baker certificate in 1884. In the following years he expanded and modernized the bakery on King's Street.

MECHANIZATION BRINGS CHANGES

One of the city's first electrically powered bakeries was built there on a solid concrete floor that was able to accommodate the new heavy kneading machines as well as a bread elevator that carried 40 loaves at a time to the next floor. The flour sifting and dough cutting was also done by machines.

The new storefront featured an artfully decorated shopping window with art nouveau ornaments and artfully decorated cakes with colorful bordures and little figurines made from sugar and marzipan. In the last decade of the 1800s Hugo Harry employed 16 bakers and helpers.

While some Harry family members carried on their baking tradition in Altona into the new century, four of Johann Friederich Harry's sons joined the roughly three million German emigrants who left their home country between 1850 and 1890. By the end of the 19th century there were four Harry-operated bakeries in Altona.

PRE- AND POSTWAR INDUSTRIALIZATION

Hugo Harry's older brother Franz Andreas was the first in the Harry family to fully embrace the idea of industrial mass production. As early as in the mid-1800s a newly built bread factory had started manufacturing nonperishable bread in Hamburg, just outside the Altona city limit. After he had become a master baker in 1889, Franz Andreas Harry was planning to build a new

production facility in order to extend his market beyond Altona.

It was his wife Johanna who carried out these plans after his early death at age 41 in 1897. In the first decade of the 20th century Johanna Harry invested heavily in the expansion and modernization of production facilities. The company, renamed Franz Andreas Harry, started mass manufacturing Brillantkuchen, a northern German sweet bread with sugar crystals on the surface that sparkled like little diamonds.

Another important new product line was zwieback, a main staple food on ocean liners. Not only did Johanna Harry secure major contracts with large German ocean-shipping companies, she also meticulously controlled the manufacturing process to ensure high product quality. Harry's zwieback traveled as far as Africa on German ocean liners, and the company also produced bread rolls in large quantities for the local and regional markets.

DEVELOPMENT OF NONPERISHABLE BISCUITS

During World War I, which began in 1914, the company supplied the German navy with biscuits for the pilots. While the young men of the eighth Harry generation served in the German army during the war, Johanna Harry developed a new kind of nonperishable wheat bread for soldiers.

After World War I had ended with Germany's defeat in November 1918, Johanna Harry completed the transition of her business to industrial mass production. She acquired a complex of commercial buildings on Bahrenfelder Chaussee at the outskirts of Altona and successfully established a new zwieback and cookie factory. By 1925 all other production lines had been moved to the new site.

COFFEEHOUSE CULTURE AFTER 1925

Germans had spent years eating rationed, low-quality wartime bread and had suffered through a severe shortage of sugar during the war. Also, sweet pastries had become unaffordable for many during the postwar hyperinflation. As such, Germans were eager to indulge in cake. The early 1920s saw imports of coffee, tea, and cane sugar in increasing quantities from colonies overseas, while new types of grain mills produced finer flour suitable for pastry making. Public teahouses and coffeehouses expanded at a fast pace in big cities such as Hamburg.

Hugo Harry's son Max had learned the confectioner's craft in renowned *patisseries* bakeries in Paris,

Vienna, and Munich. He banked on this trend when he took over his father's bakery and pastry shop on Altona's King's Street in 1912. In the mid-1920s he remodeled the shop and opened a Vienna-style coffeehouse that became a great success. The enlarged pastry shop continued to thrive over the next two decades and employed roughly two dozen.

PREWAR EXPANSION

In 1929 Johanna Harry's son, Franz Andreas Harry Jr., was offered the opportunity to take over a large bread and cookie factory in Hannover, about 80 miles south of Altona. Despite the risk, he agreed and became the owner of Habag-Werke A.G. Hannoversche Brotfabrik. Within a few years, he and his wife Friedel transformed the financially struggling venture into a profitable business.

The technically savvy entrepreneur invested in the development of new baking technologies that significantly increased production efficiency as well as product quality. Packaged bread, zwieback, cookies, and waffles were delivered to numerous mom-and-pop grocery stores in and around Hannover with a growing fleet of horse-driven carriages and automobiles. Friedel Harry oversaw the opening and operation of 26 new baker's shops in Hannover. Attractively decorated cakes, small but affordable, were best sellers during the years of the Great Depression in the 1930s.

In April 1938 Altona became a part of Hamburg. A few months later the Nazi government forbade German bakers to sell fresh bread and introduced bread stamps. In 1939 Max Harry's pastry shop on Altona's King's Street celebrated its 100th anniversary. During World War II bread production and distribution was controlled by the Nazis. Large commercial bakeries were ordered to produce pan loafs for the German army while Germans in the homeland received a shrinking ration of lower-quality "war bread."

POSTWAR RECONSTRUCTION

In 1943 Max Harry's bakery and pastry shop as well as Franz Andreas Harry's old bakery in Altona were completely destroyed by bombs. Max Harry's son Werner was killed in combat in 1944. After the war had ended in spring 1945, his son Otto operated the bakery, kneading bread dough by hand again, due to frequent power outages. Max Harry died two years later.

In 1955 the building was torn down. By the end of the 1950s all Harry family bakeries in Altona were closed. Although most of the renamed Harry-Habag-Brotfabrik in Hannover had been destroyed during

bombing raids as well, two bombs landed in flour sacks, leaving the two floors with the baking ovens intact.

Franz Andreas Harry Jr., with help by the British occupation forces, collected flour from farmers and grain mills in the region, and started baking bread again. The scarce commodity was distributed by horse-driven carriages to the starving population. After Harry Jr.'s early death at age 54 in 1946, his wife Friedel successfully led the company through the difficult postwar reconstruction period.

EXPANSION AND EXPORTS

In the early 1960s the Harry family members who were still involved in the baking business made the strategic decision to focus solely on mass-scale bread manufacturing. After Friedel Harry's daughters Inge and Marlis, members of the ninth family generation in the baking business, inherited the factory in Altona from their grandmother Johanna in 1951, Inge dropped out of medical school and managed the company until her sister Marlis finished her training in the baking business. She, with her husband Hans Jürgen Blohm, led the company through four decades of massive growth.

The rapid spread of self-service supermarkets in Germany provided the basis for Harry-Brot's national expansion, starting in the 1960s. These supermarket chains increasingly relied on large suppliers who were able to restock the bread shelves of all outlets in a whole region or state. To considerably increase production capacity, productivity, and product quality, a new bread bakery was built in Schenefeld near Hamburg in 1963 that replaced the old factory in Altona.

Five years later Harry's most modern bread-baking factory at the time started operations in Hannover, making it the most modern bakery in Germany. With the 1973 takeover of the Duisburg-based bread manufacturer Knäpper-Brot, the Harrys expanded their production and distribution network to North Rhine Westphalia, one of the country's most populous states in western Germany. To satisfy the rising demand there, a second bakery was built in Ratingen near Düsseldorf in 1980.

BUSINESS AFTER REUNIFICATION

In 1988 Inge Harry-Holthausen's son Hans-Jochen Holthausen joined the company, which had been transformed into Harry-Brot GmbH six years earlier. By the end of the 1980s a fleet of about 300 vehicles delivered Harry bread to roughly 5,000 stores in West Germany. After the reunification of East and West Germany, Harry-Brot expanded into eastern Germany.

In 1990 the company acquired Backwarenkombinat Berlin, a formerly state-owned commercial bakery in the eastern part of Berlin, and invested heavily in its modernization and expansion. Three years later a new bread factory in eastern Germany was built in Wiedemar near Leipzig. In 1995 Harry-Brot took over a bakery in Schneverdingen south of Hamburg. By then, eight production plants supplied northern, western, and eastern Germany with the Harry product range.

The early 1990s also saw fresh Harry bread cross borders when the company expanded its reach to neighboring Austria, distributed there by Austrian baker Ölz. In the following years Harry-Brot further extended its exports to other European countries, including Switzerland, France, Denmark, and the Czech Republic.

INNOVATION DRIVES GROWTH

By the mid-1990s, thanks to consistent investment in brand building and promotion, Harry bread had become a nationally recognized brand name. To generate further growth and to reach new customers the company invested in a stream of new products such as multigrain specialty breads, potato bread, sandwich breads, and pita bread. Harry-Brot also introduced a range of parbaked bread rolls, French baguette, and Italian ciabatta bread.

At the end of the 1990s the Harry range included over 50 different products. In 1996 Harry-Brot introduced the Baker's Fresh line of unpackaged rustic bread loaves, which were delivered daily to supermarkets. One year later the company took the idea of providing freshly baked goods one step further and launched its in-store "micro-bakery" concept.

Harry manufactured the prebaked, deep-frozen bread loafs and rolls that were then distributed to supermarkets by newly founded subsidiary Backshop Tiefkühl GmbH. They were baked on-site by trained market staff in in-store micro-bakeries. After only two years in operation, the output capacity of the new factory for prebaked goods in Magdeburg more than doubled in 2001. Four years later a second factory was built in Troisdorf near Bonn to meet the rapidly rising demand.

BACK-FACTORY OPENS

In 2009 Harry-Brot supplied more than 5,000 in-store bakeries with frozen prebaked goods. In 2002 Harry-Brot set out to transfer the prebaked concept to smaller stores and launched a self-service baker's store chain. The new subsidiary Back-Factory opened the first outlets in Bielefeld and Hamburg. Within two years the number rose to 50 and then climbed to 114 outlets five years later, generating EUR 67 million in annual sales.

In 2009 the concept was adjusted and the stores were transformed into partly franchise-operated snack bars. Located in highly frequented places such as train stations and popular shopping malls, shoppers, travelers, and lunch goers were offered freshly made snacks such as sandwiches, pizza, granola, and salads, as well as hot and cold beverages.

In addition to Harry-Brot's range of branded products, the company's private-label production grew quickly in the first decade of the 21st century. As a result of Harry-Brot's innovations and new lines of business, driven mainly by the rapid growth of the new prebaked products segment, the company's revenues roughly doubled within seven years. Sales climbed by an additional 40 percent between 2008 and 2013.

325 YEARS AND BEYOND

In 2013, when Harry-Brot celebrated its 325th anniversary, annual sales passed the EUR 900 million mark. Despite the fact that bread had become one among many other food products, the century-old Harry family tradition of bread baking had a promising future. In the anniversary year the company successfully launched its new Vital+Fit line of multigrain malted bread for health-oriented consumers and expanded production capacity in Berlin to satisfy the continuously rising demand.

The first Back-Factory abroad opened in Wrocław, Poland, in 2013. In 2014 Harry-Brot built a large, cooled, high-rise warehouse for up to 12,000 pallets of prebaked frozen bread, rolls, and snacks in Magdeburg. Marlis Blohm-Harry's son Thomas Blohm held a 45 percent stake in Harry-Brot GmbH while Hans-Jochen Holthausen, who became CEO in the late 1990s after Marlis Blohm-Harry retired, owned 48 percent.

Convinced that the Harry brand was strong enough to stand its ground in a rapidly consolidating German bread market, Holthausen saw opportunities for product innovations in new bread and snack creations for health-oriented consumers, gourmets, and people on the go. Holthausen also expected continued growth of the prebaked and private-label market segments.

Evelyn Hauser

PRINCIPAL SUBSIDIARIES

Brotland Backwarenvertriebs- Gesellschaft mbH; Backshop Tiefkühl GmbH; Backfactory GmbH.

PRINCIPAL COMPETITORS

BackWerk Management GmbH; D. Entrup-Haselbach GmbH & Co. KG; Glocken Bäckerei GmbH & Co OHG; Kamps GmbH; Klemme AG; Kronenbrot KG Franz Mainz; Lieken Aktiengesellschaft; Mestemacher GmbH.

FURTHER READING

"Erste Brotmarke in TK-Truhen." *Lebensmittel Zeitung*, April 19, 1996.

"Harry setzt auf TK." *Lebensmittel Zeitung*, October 1, 1999.

"Harry-Brot sein Sortiment lebendig." *Lebensmittel Zeitung*, March 5, 2010.

Holst, Jens. "Überschaubar halten; Hans-Jochen Holthausen." *Lebensmittel Zeitung*, December 23, 2009.

"Innovationen beleben Umsatz." *Lebensmittel Zeitung*, June 7, 1996.

"Innovatives grosses Berliner Back-Werk." *Lebensmittel Zeitung*, December 22, 1995.

Schönfeldt, Sybil Gräfin. *Die Harry-Bäcker. 300 Jahre Brotgeschichte 1688 bis 1988*. Hamburg, Germany: Harry-Brot GmbH, 1988.

Stürmlinger, Daniela. "Hamburger Back-Factory will im Ausland wachsen." *Hamburger Abendblatt*, May 7, 2014.

Vongehr, Ulrike. "Frische und Service; Deutschlands größter Brotbäcker baute 2012 den Umsatz aus." *Lebensmittel Zeitung*, April 5, 2013.

Wesp, Roswitha. "Frisch wie Harry; Hans-Jochen Holthausen geht im Brotbacken auf." *Lebensmittel Zeitung*, October 29, 2010.

Haw Par Corporation Ltd.

401 Commonwealth Drive
Suite 03-03 Haw Par Technocentre 149598
Singapore
Telephone: (65) 6337-9102
Fax: (65) 6336-9232
Web site: http://www.hawpar.com

Public Company
Incorporated: 1932 as Haw Par Brothers (Pvt) Ltd.
Employees: 437
Sales: SGD 141.12 million ($111.83 million) (2013)
Stock Exchanges: Singapore
Ticker Symbol: H02
NAICS: 325411 Medicinal and Botanical Manufacturing; 713990 All Other Amusement and Recreation Industries; 423830 Industrial Machinery and Equipment Merchant Wholesalers; 451110 Sporting Goods Stores

■ ■ ■

Haw Par Corporation Ltd. is the producer of one of the world's most iconic brands, the Tiger Balm line of ointments, plasters, mosquito repellents, and other products, first marketed at the dawn of the 20th century. Haw Par also operates in the leisure sector and as a property and investment vehicle. The company's Healthcare division remains its largest, accounting for more than 73 percent of the group's revenues of SGD 141.12 million ($111.83 million) in 2013. Haw Par operates its own factories in Singapore, Malaysia, Thailand, and China, while additional production is carried out through a number of licensed manufacturers in the United States, India, Indonesia, and Taiwan. The company's Leisure division oversees two aquariums, Underwater World Singapore and Underwater World Pattaya, in Thailand. The Leisure division contributed 14.5 percent to group sales.

Haw Par's Property division owns a number of prime properties in Singapore including Haw Par Centre, Haw Par Glass Tower, Haw Par Tiger Balm Building, and Haw Par Technocentre, as well as the Menara Haw Par in Malaysia, the Westlands Centre in Hong Kong, and the Xiamen Tiger Medicals factory in Xiamen, China. The property division contributed more than 12 percent to group sales. In addition, Haw Par maintains an active portfolio of securities and properties investments. These account for more than 60 percent of the group's profits, which reached SGD 96.5 million ($76.6 million) in 2013. Haw Par is listed on the Singapore Stock Exchange and is led by Chairman Wee Cho Yaw and CEO Wee Ee Lim.

CURE-ALL IN THE LATE 19TH CENTURY

Haw Par's origins reached back to the second half of the 19th century, when Aw Chu Kin left his native China in 1863. Aw, an ethnic Hakka from Zhongchuan, Fujian Province, had learned traditional Chinese herbal medicine at his father's shop in Xiamen. In order to escape poverty, he moved to Singapore, staying at first in a communal residence with other Hakka. Aw later moved across the strait, where he reestablished his herbal medicine practice.

When he left China, Aw had brought with him a recipe for a traditional Chinese medicinal ointment, which had long been used in China's imperial court for the treatment of aches and pains. In 1870 Aw moved to Rangoon, in what was then known as Burma, to set up a new business in order to improve the ointment. Aw called his new practice Eng Aun Ton, or the "Hall of Everlasting Peace." Soon after, Aw married and had two sons, Boon Haw (Gentle Tiger) born in 1882, and Boon Par (Gentle Leopard) born in 1888. (An older son, Boon Leng, or "Gentle Dragon," had died while still young.)

Boon Haw proved to be hard to handle, and in 1892 he was sent to China to study traditional herbal medicine with his grandfather. The more docile Boon Par remained in Rangoon, where he was educated in the then-colony's British schools. Following Aw's death in 1908, Boon Par was originally meant to take over the Eng Aun Ton practice. Then just 20 years old, however, Boon Par felt overwhelmed by the prospect. Instead, he wrote to his brother, asking him to come back to Rangoon and operate the practice with him. Boon Par proposed to study Western medicine, while Boon Haw handled the traditional medicine practice.

With Boon Haw's return, the brothers also set to work perfecting their father's ointment, converting their mother's kitchen into a makeshift laboratory. They called the salve Ban Kim Ewe, or Ten Thousand Golden Oils, and took Boon Haw's name as their trademark, creating the Tiger Balm brand. A natural salesman, Boon Haw soon persuaded every Chinese store in Rangoon to stock the ointment.

MOVING TO SINGAPORE IN 1926

Success was swift, and orders soon poured in from outside of Rangoon as well. In response, the brothers set up their first branch office in Thailand in 1911. By the end of the decade they were already considered the wealthiest Chinese in Rangoon. Orders for the Tiger Balm ointment soon poured in, and before long its popularity had extended to other ethnic Chinese. Boon Haw took the lead in expanding the company into new markets, notably into Malaysia and Singapore. In 1924 the brothers opened a new and far larger Eng Aun Tong factory on Singapore's Neil road. The company also extended the Tiger brand to include a range of other herbal-based medicinal products.

Having a flair for sales, Boon Haw had a car custom painted with tiger's stripes and a large tiger's head on the hood. Instead of a traditional horn sound, the car's horn let out a roar like a tiger. Boon Haw personally plied the roads and towns in Malaysia, handing out free samples of Tiger Balm and the company's other products. In this way, the company soon succeeded in replicating its success.

Back in Rangoon, the brothers ran into difficulties with the British authorities, which accused them of several crimes, including counterfeiting and trafficking in opium. The brothers were placed under house arrest but were ultimately exonerated. The experience encouraged them to abandon Rangoon altogether, and in 1926 they moved their company to Singapore.

The company also sought other means to promote their growing business. In 1929 the company established the *Sin Chew Jit Poh* newspaper, in large part as an advertising vehicle for the Tiger Balm brand. The brothers also extended their business interests in other areas, including banking. In 1932 the brothers incorporated a new company, Haw Par Brothers (Pvt.) Ltd. in order to serve as the holding company for their various business interests and trademarks.

REBUILDING AFTER WORLD WAR II

Boon Haw moved to Hong Kong in 1932 in order to expand the group's operations there and into mainland China. By then the company had established a growing network of international factories and distributor partnerships for the Tiger Balm brand. The Aw brothers also extended their newspaper empire, adding the English-language *Tiger Standard* in Singapore, the *Sing Tao Daily* in Hong Kong in 1938, and *Sin Ping Jit Pow*, later known as *Guang Ming Daily*, in Malaysia in 1939.

The move to Hong Kong helped shield part of the brothers' business empire following the Japanese occupation of Singapore during World War II. Boon Par was forced to close the Singapore factory in 1942 and flee with his family to Rangoon. He did not, however, survive to see the end of the war; he died in 1944.

Boon Haw returned to Singapore to rebuild the company after the war. Both the factory and the group's newspapers were reopened soon after the country's liberation in 1945. Boon Haw also completely restored Tiger Balm Gardens, much of which had been destroyed during the Japanese occupation. By the end of that

KEY DATES

1863: Aw Chu Kin leaves Xiamen, China, and establishes a traditional herbal medicine business in Rangoon, Burma (Myanmar).

1908: Aw's sons take over the business and develop the Tiger Balm brand.

1926: Company moves its headquarters to Singapore.

1932: Company incorporates as Haw Par Brothers (Pvt) Ltd. and expands to Hong Kong.

1969: Company goes public as Haw Par Brothers International Ltd.

1971: Slater Walker acquires the company.

1981: United Overseas Bank becomes Haw Par's largest shareholder.

1992: Haw Par begins revitalizing the Tiger Balm Brand.

2010: Company spends $5 million to build a factory in Xiamen, China.

2013: Company returns to Myanmar.

decade the Haw Par company was able to resume the expansion of its range of business interests. The company founded a new bank, Chung Khiaw Bank, in 1950, which quickly grew into one of Singapore's largest banks before expanding into Malaysia and Hong Kong. The company also founded its fourth newspaper, the *Sin Siam Jit Poh*, targeting the large ethnic Chinese population in Bangkok in 1951.

GOING PUBLIC IN THE SEVENTIES

By then Boon Haw had already begun preparing his succession. Management of Chung Khiaw Bank was transferred to his son-in-law, Lee Chee Shan. Boon Haw turned over control of Haw Par Brothers itself to Boon Par's son, Aw Cheng Chye, in 1953, with the caveat that the business must always remain in the family. The following year while returning from Boston, where he had undergone a stomach operation, Aw Boon Haw died of a heart attack at the age of 72.

While operations of the company's businesses were turned over to six of Boon Haw's nine children and four nephews, Aw Cheng Chye emerged as the controlling force of the company. Into the 1960s several disputes broke out among the various family members, which ultimately resulted in Aw Cheng Chye gaining still further control of the company. In 1969 Aw Cheng

Chye surprised the other members of the family with the decision to take Haw Par Brothers public. Despite objections from the family, including from Chung Khiaw Bank leader Lee Chee Shan, Aw Cheng Chye went through with the public offering. The company joined the Singapore Stock Exchange in August 1969, becoming Haw Par Brothers International Ltd. In order to sweeten the offering, Aw Cheng Chye bundled nearly all of the family's businesses, including a major part of Chung Khiaw Bank, into the newly public company.

Aw Cheng Chye, however, had no interest in running the family business empire. By June 1971 he had extended Haw Par's control over the Chung Khiaw Bank to 51 percent. This enabled him to reach a deal, which he kept hidden from the rest of the family, to sell his majority stake in Haw Par International to Slater Walker, a British firm that had already made a reputation for itself as one of the earliest corporate raiders. At the same time Aw Cheng Chye had already negotiated a separate deal, this time selling control of Chung Khiaw Bank to far-smaller rival United Overseas Bank (UOB), led by founder Wee Kheng Chiang and his son, Wee Cho Yaw.

NEW OWNERSHIP

If Aw Cheng Chye had betrayed the family, and Boon Haw's wishes, he did not profit for long from the sale. A scandal broke out over irregularities in the sale of Haw Par to Slater Walker, and Aw Cheng Chye fled Singapore, only to be found dead in a hotel in Chile less than two months after selling the Aw family's business empire.

Haw Par International became the vehicle through which Slater Walker carried out a series of acquisitions and other corporate maneuvers through the middle of the 1970s. These included the spin-off of Haw Par's newspaper business as Sing Tao Holdings in 1972, and the sale of the remainder of its stake in Chung Khiaw Bank to UOB. The Wee family bank, soon to become one of the region's largest, also acquired a major stake in Haw Par International.

Slater Walker also sold out the Tiger Balm brand, creating two joint ventures with Jack Chia Holdings to create two companies, Haw Par Eng Aun Tong, in Singapore, and Haw Par Tiger Balm International, which gained the rights for the next 20 years to the Tiger Balm for the entire ASEAN and Middle East markets. Slater Walker collapsed amid fraud allegations, which resulted in its chairman being sent to prison, in the mid-1970s. The Singapore government stepped in to rescue Haw Par International, while UOB, Jack Chia Holdings, and a third company, Hong Leong Group, fought to take control of the company. UOB ultimately succeeded in the effort, raising its stake above 30 percent in 1981. Under UOB, Haw Par International was streamlined and refocused on its core Tiger Balm business.

The takeover battle, however, pitted Haw Par against its largest distributor, Jack Chia, which controlled the licenses for most of the company's primary markets. The Tiger Balm brand had been allowed to languish, with little effort made in expanding its markets. As a result, the Tiger Balm brand came to be viewed as an old-fashioned product, used only by an older generation. The brand's situation worsened after 1989, when Haw Par International informed Jack Chia that it would not be renewing its license after this expired at the end of 1991. In response, Jack Chia carried out a series of price increases of the Tiger Balm line, while also introducing its own ointment, called Golden Lion Shield Balm. Also during this period the Malaysian health authorities enacted new rules regarding camphor levels in topical products. Instead of reformulating the product, Jack Chia simply withdrew from Malaysia, one of the largest Tiger Balm markets.

REVITALIZATION EFFORTS

Haw Par International, with Wee Cho Yaw as its chairman, had already put into place a revitalization strategy for Tiger Balm by the time it regained control of the brand. As early as 1988 the company had already mapped out its strategy to its major distributors. The company began carrying out this strategy in 1992, setting up four new manufacturing and distribution joint ventures in Indonesia, the Philippines, Thailand, and Taiwan. Haw Par International developed a new marketing strategy, spending SGD 10 million to revitalize the brand's image in its core Asian markets, while enhancing the brand in promising markets in North America and Europe.

The company also invested in its research and development in order to expand the range of Tiger Balm products. This enabled the company to release a steady stream of new products, including Tiger Balm–branded bandages, and other topical products, including mosquito repellents, through the turn of the century. Other efforts to expand the brand included a joint-venture marketing agreement with France's Laboratoires Pierre Fabre.

The Tiger Balm brand remained the core business for Haw Par through the turn of the century. Nonetheless, the company developed two strategic side businesses. The first of these was a small leisure division, starting with the investment in an aquarium park, Underwater World Singapore, built in 1991. The company later added a second Underwater World, in Pattaya, Thailand.

At the same time Haw Par developed a range of investments, most notably in real estate. Through the next decades, the company built up a small portfolio of properties in Singapore, Malaysia, and Hong Kong. These included the Haw Par Center and Haw Par Glass Tower in Singapore, the Menara Haw Par in Kuala Lumpur, in Malaysia, and Hong Kong's Haw Par Technocentre. Other investments, particularly in securities, proved even more lucrative for the company and by 2013 had grown to represent more than 60 percent of the group's net profits.

2013 RETURN TO MYANMAR

By 2010 the Tiger Balm brand was once again flourishing, reclaiming its place among the world's best-known brands, with sales in more than 100 countries. Haw Par continued to invest in building the brand, spending $15 million to build a new factory in Xiamen, Fujian Province, not far from the apothecary where Aw Chu Kin had his start more than 150 years earlier. The first phase of the new factory started operations in 2011.

Haw Par had another homecoming of sorts in 2013, when the company began exports of its Tiger Balm line to Myanmar, the former Burma, as the military junta there loosened its grip on the country's commercial sector. As Haw Par's director of health care told the *Financial Times*: "The reason why we are very keen on Myanmar is, of course, it's our origin. Tiger Balm has gone out into the world, made a name for itself and now it's coming back." With sales of SGD 141.12 million ($111.83 million), and one of the world's most famous brands, Haw Par Corporation appeared to have found the right formula for growth in the 21st century.

M. L. Cohen

PRINCIPAL SUBSIDIARIES

Haw Par (India) Pte Ltd.; Haw Par Brothers International (H.K.) Ltd. (Hong Kong); Haw Par Capital Pte Ltd.; Haw Par Centre Pte Ltd.; Haw Par Equities Pte Ltd.; Haw Par Healthcare Ltd.; Haw Par Hong Kong Ltd.; Haw Par Investment Holdings Private Limited; Haw Par Land (Malaysia) Sdn. Bhd.; Haw Par Leisure Pte Ltd; Haw Par Pharmaceutical Holdings Pte Ltd.; Haw Par Properties (Singapore) Pte Ltd.; Haw Par Securities (Private) Ltd.; Haw Par Tiger Balm (Philippines), Inc.; Haw Par Tiger Balm (Thailand) Ltd.; Haw

Par Trading Pte Ltd.; Hua Han Bio-Pharmaceutical Holdings Ltd.; M & G Maritime Services Pte Ltd.; Pickwick Securities Pte Ltd.; PT. Haw Par Healthcare; Setron Ltd.; Straits Maritime Leasing Pte Ltd.; Tiger Balm (Hong Kong) Ltd.; Tiger Balm (Malaysia) Sdn. Bhd.; Tiger Medicals (Taiwan) Ltd.; UIC Technologies Pte Ltd.; Underwater World Pattaya Ltd.; Underwater World Singapore Pte Ltd.; Xiamen Tiger Medicals Company Ltd.

PRINCIPAL DIVISIONS

Healthcare; Leisure; Property; Investments; Associated Companies.

PRINCIPAL OPERATING UNITS

Tiger Balm Haw Par; Underwater World; Haw Par Centre; Haw Par Glass Tower; Haw Par Technocentre; Menara Haw Par.

PRINCIPAL COMPETITORS

Huons Company Ltd.; Natco Pharma Ltd.; Queisser Pharma GmbH and Company KG; Reyon Pharmaceutical Company Ltd.; Xinjiang International Industry Company Ltd.

FURTHER READING

Chamikutty, Preethi. "What It Takes to Survive over 100 Years in Business? Like Tiger Balm." January 10, 2014. http://www.yourstory.com.

"Elder Pharma's Shelcal. Tiger Balm Headed for Pak." *India Business Insight*, February 16, 2006.

Grant, Jeremy. "The Last Word: Tiger Balm Goes Back to Its Roots as Myanmar Opens Up." *Financial Times*, January 11, 2013.

"Haw Par Corp Ekes Out 5% Rise in First Quarter Profit to $7.7 Million." *TendersInfo News*, May 15, 2013.

"Singapore's Haw Par Corp. Invests $15 Mln in Xiamen Subsidiary." *China Business News*, April 12, 2010.

"Temporary Pain for Tiger Balm as Partnership Comes Unstuck." *India Business Insight*, July 9, 2011.

Henny Penny Corporation

■

1219 U.S. 35 West
Eaton, Ohio 45320
U.S.A.
Telephone: (937) 456-8400
Toll Free: (800) 417-8417
Fax: (937) 456-8402
Web site: http://www.hennypenny.com

Private Company
Incorporated: 1957
Employees: 600
Sales: $175 million (2012)
NAICS: 335210 Small Electrical Appliance Manufacturing

■ ■ ■

Privately held Henny Penny Corporation is an Eaton, Ohio–based manufacturer and distributor of foodservice equipment, best known for its flagship commercial deep fat pressure fryers. The company also offers open fryers, breading systems, rotisseries, high-volume combi-ovens, humidified holding equipment, and merchandising-holding equipment. Products are sold in 100 countries around the world through a network of 135 distributors. Henny Penny's notable customers include quick-serve restaurant chains KFC, Chick-fil-A, McDonald's, and Wendy's. In addition to its Eaton campus with a total of 450,000 square feet of space, the company maintains offices in Paris, France, and Moscow, Russia, and a manufacturing operation in

Suzhou, China. Henny Penny is owned and managed by the Cobb family.

RESTAURANT ORIGINS

Henny Penny was founded by Chester Wagner, who in 1947 opened the Whispering Oak Restaurant on U.S. 127 in Eaton, Ohio. It became well known for its fried chicken, which became so popular that Wagner was unable to keep up with the demand on Sunday evenings. To solve the problem, he invented the deep fat pressure cooker, which used pressure to increase the temperature of the oil and create steam from the chicken to reduce cooking times to about 10 minutes. He installed the fryer in the Whispering Oak kitchen and patented the device in 1954. The commercial potential of the fryer became apparent to Wagner, and in 1957 he started a company to manufacture it. For a company name, he chose the Henny Penny character in his son's favorite bedtime story, *Chicken Little*.

At the time Henny Penny began marketing the pressure fryer, Harland Sanders was popularizing restaurant fried chicken under the Kentucky Fried Chicken (KFC) banner. In the early 1950s he began franchising KFC restaurants, and according to Henny Penny lore he actually worked with Wagner in developing the pressure fryer. The fast-food industry was also beginning to take shape, and Sanders became one of Henny Penny's first customers, using the fryers as a part of a successful formula to compete against hamburger-oriented rivals such as McDonald's. Wagner also opened several Henny Penny fried chicken restaurants in southwestern Ohio during this period.

INTRODUCTION OF ADVANCED FRYER: 1960

Wagner continued to make improvements to his fryer. In 1960 he introduced the Model 500 Electric Pressure Fryer. It eliminated the problem of breading material falling into the fat. After repeated use of the fat, these particles were recooked, became over-brown, and stuck to the frying food. Not only was the appearance affected but also the taste. Rather than having to replace the oil, a time-consuming process, Wagner's improved fryer included a filtering system that eliminated the particles and greatly extended the life of the oil.

In 1961 Wagner added a second piece of equipment to manufacture, an automatic breading machine that allowed restaurants to produce large batches of fried chicken, fish, and meat. Helping to grow Henny Penny by now was Wagner's son, Michael, who had joined the company in 1958 after graduating from Vanderbilt University. In the 1960s he would become president of the company. One of his chief lieutenants was Jack L. Cobb, who was also involved with Henny Penny from the beginning. Cobb was named vice president of operations in 1969.

DEATH OF FOUNDER: 1970

In 1970 Chester Wagner died, leaving Henny Penny to his wife and son. By now the company was running out of space. In 1973 Michael Wagner acquired property in Eaton where he constructed a 25,000-square-foot manufacturing facility. The foundation was laid for what would become the current Henny Penny building complex. Also of importance in 1973, the company hired its first engineer to make further refinements to the fryer and help develop new product lines.

When the Wagner family decided to sell the business, Cobb teamed up with marketing manager Cecil Pruett to acquire Henny Penny in 1975. The new owners quickly made their mark. The company added a new product line in 1975 with the introduction of its first

warming equipment. To keep up with demand for its pressure fryers and new Counter Warmer, the company more than doubled its plant that year. Another 30,000 square feet of manufacturing space was added. The company now employed 45 workers.

Under Cobb's leadership as chief executive officer and Pruett's salesmanship, Henny Penny grew at an accelerated pace. A new holding cabinet, the HC-900, was introduced in 1980. To meet the needs of its growing product line, Henny Penny completed another plant expansion, adding 121,000 square feet of fabrication, assembly, and warehouse space. The additional space and increased workforce would also be necessary to support growing foreign sales. In 1986 Henny Penny opened its first international office in Paris to better serve European customers.

COBB BECOMES SOLE OWNER: 1988

In 1988 Cobb bought out Pruett to become the sole owner of Henny Penny. Playing an increasing role in the management of the company was Cobb's son, Steven. The younger Cobb earned a degree in business from Bowling Green University and a master's degree in business administration from the University of Dayton, but he did not join Henny Penny immediately after graduation. Rather, he first gained experience working for Banc One Corp. in Dayton and LexisNexis in New York before joining Henny Penny in 1988 as a distributor sales representative in the Philadelphia area. He then became a regional sales manager, divisional sales manager, and manufacturing manager.

The final decade of the century saw further growth for Henny Penny. In 1990 the company introduced its first rotisserie as well as a commercial bun warmer. Two years later Henny Penny added its first open fryers and in 1993 sold its first heated merchandiser units, which became especially important as supermarkets expanded their take-home dinner programs. The company also took steps to protect its brand and intellectual property. In 1990 Henny Penny sued a rival firm, Chicken Little Corp., accusing it of using the Henny Penny name in ads and telephone listings, as well as service stickers placed on equipment. Moreover, Chicken Little pressure fryers looked almost identical to Henny Penny fryers, which the company argued caused confusion in the marketplace.

Despite the recession of the early 1990s, Henny Penny continued to expand, increasing annual sales to $45 million by 1992 and employment to 325. Much of the growth was due to foreign sales, which now accounted for 30 percent of the business and became especially

KEY DATES

1954: Chester Wagner patents a pressure fryer.
1957: Wagner founds Henny Penny Corporation.
1975: Wagner family sells the business.
2003: China Manufacturing plant opens.
2013: Wood Stone Corporation is acquired.

important as sales to the fast-food market in the United States were flat during the economic downturn. Net revenues improved to $59 million in 1993, marking the fifth consecutive year of double-digit improvement for Henny Penny. Saturation in the U.S. market, however, brought an end to the trend the following year when revenues were flat.

To regain momentum, Henny Penny invested in further research and development, including new computer technology. In 1995 the company introduced a major new product that was actually produced by a German company. Henny Penny began distributing the Combi-Steamer. The professional cooking device combined a traditional oven with steaming capabilities to allow the preparation of large quantities of vegetables and other items.

CHANGE IN LEADERSHIP: 1997

At the start of 1997 Steven Cobb succeeded his father as Henny Penny's president and CEO. Jack Cobb remained chairman of the board. Henny Penny now made plans for the largest expansion in company history. In addition to 75,000 square feet of new manufacturing space, Henny Penny opened a 45,000-square-foot headquarters, training, and demonstration facility in the summer of 1998.

The company grew on other fronts as well at the turn of the new century. Island merchandisers and blast chiller-freezers were added to the Henny Penny product lineup. Following an Asian recession in the late 1990s, Henny Penny also looked to expand its business in the Far East. Steven Cobb said he became aware of the potential of the Chinese market after visiting a KFC in Beijing in 1998. "It was three stories tall and had 11 of our pressure fryers and 17 cash registers," he told *Dayton Daily News* in a December 13, 1998, article. Most KFC restaurants in the United States only used three pressure cookers. To serve the exploding fast-food industry in China and other Far East markets, Henny Penny opened a 30,000-square-foot manufacturing plant in Suzhou, China, in 2003. Early in the first decade of

the 21st century KFC alone was opening a store a day in China.

New Henny Penny products introduced early in the first decade of the new century included large-volume open fryers and a new line of express merchandisers. To accommodate the expanded product offerings, the company opened a new 120,000-square-foot building at its Eaton campus. While organic growth was at the core of Henny Penny's strategy, the company kept an eye out for acquisition opportunities. In 2006 it bought Refcon Inc., a 20-year-old New Jersey–based refrigerated food display case manufacturer. Hot foods, however, were clearly Henny Penny's focus, and Refcon's intellectual property was ultimately sold to RPI Industries, which focused on refrigerated display cases.

INTRODUCTION OF
NEXT-GENERATION FRYER: 2007

In 2007 Steven Cobb replaced his father as chairman and remained CEO but turned over day-to-day responsibilities to vice president of marketing Rob Connelly, who was appointed Henny Penny's new president. Cobb was now free to focus on strategic issues as Henny Penny took steps to become a global company. A key to achieving that goal was to remain on the cutting edge of food preparation technology. Henny Penny worked with McDonald's to develop a new low-oil-volume fryer to reduce both oil costs and consumer oil consumption. In 2008 Henny Penny became one of two companies contracted by McDonald's to supply its global network of stores with the next-generation low-oil-volume fryers.

Annual sales improved to $127 million in 2008, but the financial crisis of that year triggered a global recession, adversely affecting Henny Penny. Compared to its competitors, however, the company performed well simply by holding steady. In 2010 Henny Penny rebounded, increasing sales by about 15 percent. The company also benefited from the recession by making changes that substantially reduced operating costs without the need for cuts in the workforce. Moreover, the savings were invested in new products and personnel development to support continued growth.

In 2012 Henny Penny reorganized its management ranks, which included the creation of new posts, to further lay a foundation for the future. To broaden the solutions it could offer to the foodservice industry, Henny Penny completed another acquisition. In December 2013 it purchased Wood Stone Corporation. The Bellingham, Washington–based company made stone hearth cooking equipment. Some of Wood Stone's customers included California Pizza Kitchen, Carrabba's Italian Grill, and Wolfgang Puck. Wood Stone would continue to operate as a separate company, but it provided Henny Penny with a new revenue stream as well as cross-selling opportunities. Henny Penny was likely to broaden its range of products and extend its global footprint even further in the years ahead.

Ed Dinger

PRINCIPAL SUBSIDIARIES

Wood Stone Corporation.

PRINCIPAL COMPETITORS

Edlund Company LLC; Frymaster Corporation; Pitco Frialator, Inc.

FURTHER READING

Bohman, Jim. "Sky's the Limit for Henny Penny." *Dayton Daily News*, December 13, 1998.

———. "Thriving in Hard Times." *Dayton Daily News*, February 2, 1992.

Bollinger, Julie. "Henny Penny Plotting Second-Largest Expansion." *Dayton Business Journal*, August 11, 1997.

Cogliano, Joe. "Henny Penny Buys Cooking Equipment Company." *Dayton Business Journal*, December 16, 2013.

———. "Henny Penny Cooks Up Sales Growth." *Dayton Business Journal*, August 23, 2010.

Kershaw-Staley, Tracy. "Henny Penny Sizzles with Growth." *Dayton Business Journal*, September 24, 2007.

Navera, Tristan. "Henny Penny Grows through the Decades." *Dayton Business Journal*, August 30, 2013.

Hogan Lovells

UK Headquarters:
Atlantic House
Holborn Viaduct
London, EC1A 2FG
United Kingdom
Telephone: (+44 20) 7296 2000
Fax: (+44 20) 7296 2001

U.S. Headquarters:
555 Thirteenth Street NW
Washington, DC 20004
U.S.A.
Telephone: (202) 637-5600
Fax: (202) 637-5910
Web site: http://www.hoganlovells.com

Limited Liability Partnership
Founded: 1899; 1904
Employees: 3,407
Gross Billings: $1.72 billion (2013)
NAICS: 541110 Offices of Lawyers

■ ■ ■

With over 2,500 lawyers and both U.S. and U.K. headquarters, Hogan Lovells is one of the top 10 law firms in the world. Its practice spans the globe with over 40 offices in Africa, Asia, Europe, Latin America, the Middle East, and the United States. It provides expertise in virtually all areas of domestic and international law, from antitrust, taxation, and litigation to intellectual property, mergers and acquisitions, and project financing. Its clients include corporations, financial institutions, and governmental entities. The firm was created by the 2010 merger of Washington, D.C.–based Hogan and Hartson LLP and London-based Lovells LLP.

GETTING STARTED AND HOGAN'S EARLY LAW PRACTICE

Frank J. Hogan, the founder of Hogan & Hartson, was born in 1877 in Brooklyn. In 1902 he received his LLB from Georgetown University, was admitted to the District of Columbia Bar, and thus began his long career as a lawyer. One of Hogan's early clients was Theodore Roosevelt. In addition to his private law practice, Hogan lectured on wills, evidence, and partnerships at his alma mater, Georgetown University. He also wrote articles for legal journals and in 1912 began serving as the advisory editor of the *Georgetown Law Journal*.

For several years Hogan's partnership remained a small practice based in Washington, D.C., where it concentrated on serving clients in their dealings with the federal government that grew from new agencies and laws passed during the Progressive Era. For example, Congress gained the authority to tax incomes with ratification of the Sixteenth Amendment in 1913.

Nelson T. Hartson left as the Treasury Department's Internal Revenue solicitor in 1925 to lead the growing tax practice of the Hogan law firm. Unlike most other early partners who were from the East and had gained their legal education at Georgetown University, Hartson was born in Spokane, Washington, and earned his LLB at the University of Washington.

COMPANY PERSPECTIVES

Hogan Lovells is distinguished by a highly collaborative culture which values the contribution of our diverse team both within Hogan Lovells and in the wider community. Our style is open, service focused, and friendly. We believe that our commitment to client service, commerciality, and teamwork provides benefits to our clients and enhances effective business relationships.

In the 1932 *Martindale-Hubbell Law Directory*, Hogan, Donovan, Jones, Hartson & Guider, with the five name partners and one associate, described itself as having a "Practice before United States Courts, Bureau of Internal Revenue, Federal Radio Commission, and Government Departments." The 1932 directory stated that the Hogan firm was general counsel for Riggs National Bank and the District of Columbia Bankers Association and counsel for Capital Traction Company, Travelers Insurance Company, and the Evening Star Newspaper Company.

The 1940 directory listed Liberty Mutual Insurance Company, Columbia Broadcasting System (CBS), and Crosley Radio Corporation as other clients of Hogan & Hartson. The firm at that time consisted of 13 lawyers. Nevertheless, the nation's largest law firms were headquartered in New York City, the nation's financial and commercial capital. They usually did not have offices in Washington, D.C., until after World War II.

HOGAN & HARTSON'S POST–WORLD WAR II GROWTH

Hogan & Hartson described itself in the 1950 *Martindale-Hubbell Law Directory* as practicing "before United States Courts, Bureau of Internal Revenue, Federal Communications Commission, Federal Trade Commission and Government Departments," but by 1960 it said it had a general practice. It also increased from 24 lawyers in 1950 to 36 lawyers in 1960. In the 1960s and 1970s, law firms grew rapidly due to more federal government laws and regulatory bodies, including the 1964 Civil Rights Act and the Environmental Protection Agency. Joseph C. Goulden, in his 1972 book about large Washington, D.C., law firms, estimated that in the previous decade the number of lawyers had increased 25 percent. According to Goulden, the capital had "less than one-half percent of the United States population, and almost five percent of the

lawyers." As part of this trend, Hogan & Hartson more than doubled its number of lawyers to reach 76 in 1973.

Hogan & Hartson in the mid-1970s gained Senator J. William Fulbright as one of its partners after he lost his reelection bid. The Arkansas Democrat was well known for serving five terms in the U.S. Senate from 1945 to 1975, creating the Fulbright scholarships, and being one of the main opponents of the Vietnam War. Fulbright remained with Hogan & Hartson until his death in 1995.

In 1976 Hogan & Hartson was praised in *Verdicts on Lawyers* for having "identified full-time pro bono partners and associates to coordinate the firm's public interest work." Such an example was then and continued to be rather unusual in large corporate law firms. This program was started in 1970 as a way to provide legal services to clients unable to pay regular fees. Over the years thousands of organizations or individuals thus were served, and pro bono work became a significant aspect of Hogan & Hartson's culture. It led to the firm receiving the American Bar Association's top pro bono award in 1991. Hogan & Hartson's example also inspired some other large firms, such as Holland & Knight, Florida's largest law firm, to establish similar programs.

In the 1980s Hogan & Hartson added new offices near its Washington, D.C., headquarters. Its McLean, Virginia, office was established in 1985 to serve mainly high-tech companies in Fairfax County. Hogan & Hartson in 1988 became the first large out-of-town law firm to establish a branch office in Baltimore. The firm's international growth started in 1989 when its partners decided that expansion would be their major goal.

HOGAN & HARTSON'S GROWING PRACTICE: 1990–95

Hogan & Hartson was listed in the 1990 *Martindale-Hubbell Law Directory* as having a total of 278 lawyers at its Washington, D.C., headquarters and also three nearby branch offices in Baltimore and Bethesda, Maryland, and McLean, Virginia. In 1990 it added new offices in London and Prague, its first overseas branches. By 1991 other new offices had been established in Warsaw, Paris, and Brussels.

Hogan & Hartson and several other law firms grew in response to the collapse of communism. In 1989 Germans destroyed the Berlin Wall and soon reunited East and West Germany, and in 1991 the Soviet Union dissolved, ending the Cold War and marking the independence of Russia and several other newly independent states. Free market reforms that included

KEY DATES

1899: John Spencer Lovell sets up a practice in the United Kingdom.
1904: Frank Hogan founds a firm in Washington, D.C.
1925: Nelson Hartson joins the firm to head its growing tax practice.
1938: Partnership is renamed Hogan & Hartson.
1970: Hogan & Hartson begins its unique pro bono Community Services Department.
1988: Lovell White Durrant is formed through the merger of Lovell White & King and Durrant Piesse.
1990: Hogan & Hartson starts its first overseas offices in London and Prague.
2000: Hogan & Hartson opens a Tokyo office, its first in Asia; Lovell White Durrant joins with Germany's Boesebeck Droste to create Lovells.
2007: Lovells converts to a limited liability partnership.
2010: Hogan & Hartson merges with Lovells to create Hogan Lovells.

new laws and privatizing former state-owned businesses provided new opportunities for foreign corporations and their law firms.

In 1991 the U.S. Agency for International Development announced it had selected three teams of accountants and law firms to help eastern European nations develop agency-approved regulations and privatize their economies. Hogan & Hartson and KPMG Peat Marwick constituted one of the teams that would receive up to $15 million during a three-year contract.

Hogan & Hartson helped the Slovak Republic's Ministry of the Environment and the Czech Republic's Ministry of Agriculture to write new regulations. Some critics contended that such work was a conflict of interest because law firms' corporate clients could benefit from favorable laws and regulations. "Hogan & Hartson and the other law firms who represent major ministries have gotten into the business of writing regulations that suit themselves," said Stanley Glod, chair of the Foreign Claims Settlement Commission of the United States, in a 1991 *Washington Post* article.

Opened in 1994, the firm's Moscow office illustrated Hogan & Hartson's role in the globalized economy. It helped a U.S.-based communications

company gain a $190 million loan guaranty from a Russian agency. The Moscow office helped clients not only in Russia but also in Ukraine, Kazakhstan, the Czech Republic, and other nations in the region.

In 1996 Hogan & Hartson continued its growth in Eastern Europe by opening an office in Budapest that focused on industrial and energy privatizations. "I'm very excited," said Bob Glen Odle that year in *International Financial Law Review*, adding, "Budapest is [a] step in our European strategy of having an office in every major country our client base is interested in." Hogan & Hartson also helped develop Eastern Europe's new municipal bond market. Under communism, local governments avoided debt, but by 1996 some municipalities were beginning to see the advantages of long-term bonds to help pay for badly needed infrastructure such as roads, water systems, and airports. Meanwhile, Hogan & Hartson opened new offices in Colorado Springs and Denver in 1994 and Los Angeles in 1996. Its New York City office commenced operations in 1998.

IMPORTANT CLIENTS

Hogan & Hartson clients in the 1990s included the U.S. Olympic Committee; Genentech Inc., the nation's first biotechnology company; Amgen Inc.; the Biotechnology Industry Organization formed in 1993; and the American Academy of Pediatrics. Jean-Bertrand Aristide, ousted as Haiti's president in 1991, paid the firm $55,000 a month in 1994 to have partner Michael Barnes, a former Maryland congressman, try to get him restored to power. The firm, however, lost a significant client in 1995 when Boston Bancorp replaced it with Boston's Hale & Dorr. Hogan & Hartson had served Boston Bancorp from at least its 1983 debut as a public corporation.

In the 1990s Hogan & Hartson had close ties to the Clinton administration and the Democratic Party. For example, one of the firm's lawyers served as the Clinton-Gore campaign's general counsel in 1992. President Bill Clinton chose Hogan & Hartson lawyers in 1993 to be his deputy national security adviser and his secretary to the cabinet. At the same time, the firm increased its government relations practice by adding 10 new lobbying clients in the first months of the new administration.

In the mid-1990s a Hogan & Hartson employee delivered a $50,000 donation from Greek citizen George Psaltis's company Psaltis Corporation, a firm client, to the Democratic National Committee (DNC). The DNC later returned the money and said it had not realized Psaltis was not an American citizen and his company had no U.S. operations. Hogan & Hartson also represented DNC fund-raiser John Huang for alleged improper activities.

HOGAN & HARTSON MOVES INTO THE NEW MILLENNIUM

Hogan & Hartson continued to have one of the nation's top lobbying practices in the years ahead. For example, in 2000 the firm earned $15.5 million from lobbying, an amount exceeded by only three other law firms and one non-law firm. This was according to Influence, a service owned by American Lawyer Media Inc. Influence published a newsletter and operated www.influenceonline.net to inform the public about lobbying activities. The Hogan & Hartson Political Action Committee donated money to both Republican and Democratic candidates. From 1997 to 2000 it gave between 55 and 64 percent of its contributions to Republicans.

In the November 2000 presidential election, George W. Bush used lawyers from Hogan & Hartson and several other law firms to help him win the struggle over Florida's contested electoral votes. In May 1998 the U.S. Justice Department, 19 states, and the District of Columbia had filed an antitrust lawsuit against Microsoft Corporation. Hogan & Hartson, in this much-publicized case, represented the states, the District of Columbia, and also Netscape Communications Corporation, the governments' main witness against the Seattle software developer. Although attempts to split Microsoft were dropped, the legal battle continued in 2001.

Meanwhile, the firm served other clients in antitrust matters. For example, partner Janet L. McDavid represented Mobil Corporation when it merged with Exxon, American Electric Power when it merged with Central and South West Corporation, and also General Dynamics, PacifiCare, American Express, and BT plc in various transactions or investigations.

In July 2000 Russia's Uneximbank with help from Hogan & Hartson finally reached a settlement on the bank's $1.4 billion bankruptcy. About 75 of the firm's lawyers worked on the 1,600-page settlement document. The authors of an article in the *International Financial Law Review* in 2000 said, "Uneximbank is important because it was the first Russian credit institution to declare itself bankrupt and the first to then settle its bankruptcy with foreign creditors."

The firm's Prague office represented Radio Free Europe/Radio Liberty when it moved from Munich to Prague, ICF Kaiser International in its Czech steel minimill, the Czech and Slovak American Enterprise Fund

that aided various businesses, and U.S. West International in a Czech cable television and telephony project.

Hogan & Hartson also counseled Stredoceska Energeticka a.s. in its investment in a power plant near Prague. According to the firm's Web site, the $400 million plant was "the first independent power project in the Czech Republic and probably in Central and Eastern Europe as a whole to raise financing on a non-recourse basis and without the benefit of government guarantees."

In 2000 Hogan & Hartson began an office in Miami as a means to increase its Latin American practice. One of its clients was Petrobras, a company owned by the Brazilian government, as it built and financed a major gas pipeline with Bolivia. Also in 2000, the firm opened a small Tokyo office and worked to absorb 35 lawyers recruited laterally from New York's Davis, Weber & Edwards, the largest acquisition in its history to that time. Hogan & Hartson continued its rapid growth in the new millennium by opening a Berlin office in January 2001 under the name Hogan & Hartson Raue. The 30-lawyer office was the third largest law firm in Berlin, according to *Legal Times*.

In 2001 California businessman Dennis Tito became the first person to buy a flight into space. In addition to paying $20 million to Russia, Tito paid Hogan & Hartson and two other law firms that helped him negotiate with three Russian agencies before he blasted off to visit the International Space Station.

With literally hundreds of new lawyers added in the 1990s, the firm faced numerous challenges. As Hogan & Hartson's first full-time managing partner, Odle traveled to each overseas branch at least twice every year. That personal interaction helped strengthen the firm, which closed no offices during this rapid growth period.

Odle stepped down as the firm's chairman at the end of 2000. Since 1979, when Odle became chairman, Hogan & Hartson had grown from one to 18 offices worldwide and more than quadrupled its number of lawyers to over 800. The new chairman was J. Warren Gorrell Jr. Based on its 2000 reported gross revenues of $320 million, Hogan & Hartson was the nation's 35th-largest law firm, according to the annual ratings by *American Lawyer*. The firm's gross revenues increased 22.1 percent from 1999, when it was ranked number 40.

PREPARING FOR A MERGER

Growth continued over the next several years. Hogan & Hartson continued to strengthen its global operations and in 2002 opened office in Beijing. New offices were opened in Hong Kong and Caracas in 2005. That year a former Hogan & Hartson partner, John Roberts Jr., was named chief justice of the U.S. Supreme Court.

During 2008 the firm extended operations into Abu Dhabi, San Francisco, and Silicon Valley. The recession and economic downturn in the United States at this time however, threatened the bottom line of many law firms. A December 2009 *Washington Post* article reported that profits per partner at the largest U.S. law firms declined by 4.3 percent in 2008, which was the first drop since 1991.

In response to market conditions, Hogan & Hartson set plans in motion to join forces with Lovells LLP, a London-based firm with a far-reaching presence throughout Europe and Asia. While Hogan & Hartson had avoided large mergers throughout its history, the firm confirmed that joining with Lovells would more than double its international presence. "The marketplace is changing and there is a huge amount of demand for high-end, global capabilities," explained chairman Gorrell Jr. in the December 2009 *New York Law Journal*. He added, "You couldn't get there fast enough by simply picking up lawyers in small groups."

Lovells, on the other hand, was no stranger to mergers. The firm's roots dated back to 1899 when John Spencer Lovell set up a practice in the United Kingdom. Lovell partnered with Reginald White and then in 1924 with Charles King. The three formed Lovell, White & King.

In 1966 Lovell White & King merged with Haslewoods, a firm with long and rich London-based history. Lovell White Durrant was formed in 1988 through the merger of Lovell White & King, which by now oversaw a large international commercial practice, and Durrant Piesse, known for its expertise in the banking and financial services sectors.

In early 2000 Lovell White Durrant joined with Germany's Boesebeck Droste, a firm that got its start in 1884, to create the Lovells that would eventually merge with Hogan & Hartson. Lovells strengthened its operations by merging with Dutch firm Ekelmans den Hollander in December 2000. It merged with France's Siméon & Associés in November 2001. Lovells opened an office in Shanghai in 2003 and an office in Madrid the following year. During 2007 Lovells entered Dubai and converted to a limited liability partnership.

CREATING HOGAN LOVELLS: 2008–14

Merger talks began in 2008 and were made public the following year. The union, which needed approval from partners at both firms, would create one of the largest law firms in the world with nearly $1.9 billion in revenue, 2,500 lawyers, and over 40 offices across the globe. Partners gave the nod in December 2009. "We're really excited. It's not often that I get to drink Dom Pérignon at 7:30 in the morning, but this is a great day for us," Gorrell Jr. explained in the aforementioned *New York Law Journal* article. "There is a lot of work ahead of us to put it together and make it work, but everybody at both firms is up for it."

The merger of equals was finalized in May 2010, creating Hogan Lovells. The firm was headed by co-CEOs Gorrell Jr. and former Lovells Managing Partner David Harris. Hogan Lovells International LLP would maintain the London office while Hogan Lovells US LLP would oversee the Washington, D.C., practice. At this time, Hogan Lovells had nearly 20,000 clients including the likes of Ford Motor Co., Barclays PLC, Bank of America, Merrill Lynch, JPMorgan Chase & Co., and Iberdrola S.A. Its major practices included corporate, litigation, finance, intellectual property, and regulatory matters.

Moving forward, Hogan Lovells continued to focus on growth. During 2013 the firm gained a foothold in the South African market when it merged with Routledge Modise, a leading South African firm with 120 lawyers. The company strengthened its presence in Mexico the following year when it joined with Mexico's Barrera Siqueiros y Torres Landa (BSTL). Hogan Lovells BSTL was one of the largest firms in Mexico with 70 lawyers in offices in Mexico City and Monterrey. Steve Immelt was named CEO of Hogan Lovells in July 2014. Under his leadership, the firm appeared to be on a path to strengthen its leading presence in markets across the globe.

David M. Walden
Updated, Christina M. Stansell

PRINCIPAL SUBSIDIARIES

Hogan Lovells International LLP; Hogan Lovells US LLP.

PRINCIPAL COMPETITORS

Baker & McKenzie LLP; Jones Day Limited Partnership; Skadden, Arps, Slate, Meagher & Flom LLP.

FURTHER READING

Blum, Vanessa. "In with the Old." *Legal Times*, June 26, 2000.

"Forty-Three Lobbying Practices Earned $5M+ in 2000." *PR Newswire*, May 16, 2001.

Goulden, Joseph C. *The Super-Lawyers: The Small and Powerful World of the Great Washington Law Firms*. New York: Weybright and Talley, 1972.

Grimaldi, James V. "Hearsay: The Lawyer's Column; For David Boies, Working for Gore in Florida Caps a Year of High-Profile Cases." *Washington Post*, December 25, 2000.

Grimaldi, James V., and Carrie Johnson. "Once More before the Bench as *U.S. v. Microsoft* Resumes on Appeal—A Guide to the Proceedings." *Washington Post*, February 25, 2001.

"Hogan & Hartson Expands in East Europe." *International Financial Law Review*, June 1996.

"Hogan Lovells BSTL to Be Launched in August." *Legal Monitor Worldwide*, July 15, 2014.

Jeffrey, Jeff. "The Starting Line; Hogan Lovells Must Now Turn 2,500 Lawyers into One True Firm." *National Law Journal*, May 3, 2010.

Jeffrey, Jeff, and Carrie Levine. "Hogan and Lovells Partners Approve Merger to Create 2,500-Lawyer Firm." *New York Law Journal*, December 16, 2009.

Kaplan, Sheila. "The Superlawyers Roll East; Big U.S. Legal Firms Elbow for Business beyond the Elbe." *Washington Post*, July 21, 1991.

Maiden, Ben, Daniel Gogek, and Georgy Borisov. "Lawyers Learn to Live in Russia after the Gold Rush." *International Financial Law Review*, October 2000.

Polantz, Katelyn. "New Hogan Chief Sees Likely Growth in Latin America, Africa; Immelt Says Firm's Success Depends on Trust, Discipline, Vision—And Straight Talk." *National Law Journal*, July 7, 2014.

Stogner, Amy. "National Law Firm Landing Boulder High-Tech Clients." *Boulder County Business Report*, January 26, 2001.

Hooters of America, LLC

———■———

1815 The Exchange
Atlanta, Georgia 30339
U.S.A.
Telephone: (770) 951-2040
Fax: (770) 618-7031
Web site: http://www.hooters.com

Private Company
Incorporated: 1984
Employees: 8,000 (est.)
Sales: $836 million (2012)
NAICS: 533110 Lessors of Nonfinancial Tangible Assets
(Except Copyrighted Works); 541613 Marketing
Consulting Services; 722110 Full-Service
Restaurants

■ ■ ■

Hooters of America, LLC, operates and franchises a
chain of more than 400 casual restaurants that feature
waitresses known as Hooters Girls. The first Hooters
Restaurant opened in Clearwater, Florida, in 1983. The
concept was licensed in 1984 to Hooters of America.
The franchiser bought the trademark from Hooters Inc.
in 2001.

FORMATION OF PARTNERSHIP

The first Hooters restaurant was opened on April Fools'
Day in 1983 in Clearwater, Florida, by six friends, all
businessmen who had no experience in the restaurant
industry. Apocryphally, the six combed Clearwater

Beach searching for attractive young women who were
interested in becoming the first Hooters Girls.

In addition to Gil DiGiannantonio, a sales
representative for a liquor distributor, the other founding partners were L. D Stewart and Dennis Johnson,
also partners in a general contracting business. Another
was Kenneth Wimmer, who had worked for Stewart and
Johnson before starting his own paint business, and also
Ed Droste, owner and chief executive of a resort
development business. The sixth was William Ranieri, a
former service-station owner who had retired to Florida.
Stewart was the majority owner.

FREE PUBLICITY LAUNCHES
CONCEPT

The restaurant struggled for almost a year before receiving a fortuitous break in the form of free publicity. In
January 1984 Tampa hosted the NFL Super Bowl
between the Los Angeles Raiders and the Washington
Redskins. John Riggens, then a star running back for
the Redskins, ate lunch at Hooters the day before the
game.

After the Super Bowl, he returned with several
teammates for a midnight snack. With the resulting
media attention, Hooters quickly went from grossing
$2,000 a night to nearly $4,000. In 1984 the original
owners, who had formed Hooters of Clearwater, Inc.,
sold expansion and franchise rights to Neighborhood
Restaurants of America, a group of Atlanta investors,
who formed Hooters of America, Inc.

Hooters of Clearwater received 10 percent of Hooters of America and 3 percent royalties on all Hooters

sales. Hooters of Clearwater also retained the final say on restaurant design and menu and the right to build Hooters restaurants in Pinellas and Hillsborough Counties in Florida.

EARLY SUCCESS

Within two years Hooters had become a $16 million chain with nine restaurants in Florida and two in Atlanta. By 1991 there were some 50 Hooters restaurants, and Hooters of America had revenues of more than $100 million. The chain had reached 100 restaurants and $200 million in revenues by the end of 1993.

Hooters continued to thrive on free publicity. When the Soviet national boxing team was in Tampa to fight the Americans in the summer of 1986, the Soviets ate dinner at Hooters. The next day, the *Tampa Tribune* ran a full-color picture of a Russian boxer eating chicken wings. A Hooters Girl, wearing a tight-fitting Hooters T-shirt, was standing next to him.

In July 1986 Hooters Girl Lynne Austin was *Playboy* magazine's Playmate of the Month. The men's magazine also included a small article about Hooters, and some of the pictures showed Austin in a Hooters outfit. Probably the greatest marketing coup came in 1995 when Hooters of America hired a hairy male actor, called him Vince, and dressed him in a Hooters waitress outfit to poke fun at allegations that Hooters restaurants discriminated against men.

DEVELOPS WAITRESS CONCEPT

Hooters of America ran full-page advertisements showing "Vince" in *USA Today* and the *Washington Post*. More importantly, television camera crews showed up at many Hooters restaurants across the country the same day to do local stories. Hooters of America liked to boast that "Hooters is to chicken wings what McDonald's is to hamburgers." The Hooters Girls, not the

restaurants' food or drink, were always the essence of the Hooters concept.

Hooters restaurants hired young, attractive women as waitresses and dressed them in orange running shorts that were "sized to fit comfortably," according to corporate literature, and white tank tops or T-shirts. Hooters of America readily acknowledged that "the concept relies on natural female sex appeal" and the waitresses were encouraged to sit down and chat with the predominantly male clientele.

Hooters Girls also made celebrity appearances at sporting events and charity functions and were pictured on billboards, trading cards, and calendars. Hooters of America published a glossy *Hooters Magazine* that featured Hooters Girls in everything from swimsuits to evening wear. According to the corporate literature, Hooters Girls were expected to "always maintain a prom-like appearance with hair, make-up and nails done neatly. Hooters Girls should project a positive attitude with a bubbling personality and the prettiest smile in the world."

Although the founders of the original Hooters in Clearwater always insisted the name referred to an owl in the restaurant's logo, they did so tongue-in-cheek, and it was a claim that few people accepted. Critics of the name and concept dubbed Hooters the nation's first "breastaurant."

HOOTERS VS. EEOC

Women's groups expressed outrage at the skimpy Hooters Girls uniforms. Hooters restaurants were also forced with some regularity to defend themselves against allegations of sexual harassment. In the most high-profile case, three former waitresses at a Hooters franchise operated by Bloomington Hooters Inc. at the Mall of America in Minnesota filed suit in 1993, claiming they had been fondled and verbally abused by male employees at the restaurant.

Hooters of America denied that Hooters restaurants fostered a "hostile environment" for women and publicly stressed a strict corporate policy against any form of sexual harassment. The suit was eventually settled out of court. Hooters restaurants also attracted the attention of the Equal Employment Opportunity Commission (EEOC), which launched an investigation in 1991 into alleged discrimination because Hooters refused to hire male waiters.

The EEOC demanded that Hooters of America pay $22 million to men who could show they had been denied jobs because of their gender. The EEOC findings were generally ridiculed by the news media and a public

KEY DATES

1983: First Hooters restaurant opens.

1984: Franchise rights are sold to Atlanta investors, who form Hooters of America, Inc.

1991: Equal Employment Opportunity Commission launches investigation of chain.

1996: Chain generates more than $300 million in revenues.

1997: Class-action lawsuit settlement allows Hooters servers to remain exclusively female.

2001: Hooters of America buys trademark from Hooters Inc.

2003: Hooters Air is launched.

2006: Majority owner Robert Brooks dies.

2011: Company is purchased by a group of investors led by Chanticleer Holdings LLC.

2013: Company implements a system-wide brand facelift.

that had grown skeptical of government interference, especially since the EEOC had a backlog of seemingly more serious cases.

Hooters of America argued that Hooters Girls, in addition to foodservice, provided entertainment, which entitled the restaurants to an exemption from equal employment laws under the "Bona Fide Occupational Qualification" section of the Civil Rights Act. Forcing Hooters to hire men as waiters, the restaurant chain said, would be like forcing Radio City Music Hall to hire male Rockettes for its famed chorus line.

MARCH ON WASHINGTON

In a more serious vein, Michael McNeil, vice president of marketing, pointed out that Hooters employed men as cooks and in management positions. Hooters fought back with a $1 million publicity campaign, featuring "Vince," the hirsute waiter in a skimpy Hooter's outfit, designed to ridicule the EEOC. Hooters of America also coordinated a "March on Washington" with a rally at Freedom Park in Washington, D.C., where more than a hundred Hooters Girls carried placards with such slogans as "Men as Hooters Guys—What a Drag."

In addition to the newspaper ads, Hooters used Vince on billboards, other print materials, and even on its radio commercials. In a brief statement, the EEOC called the public relations campaign an effort "to intimidate a federal law enforcement agency, and, more importantly, individuals whose rights may have been violated."

Eventually, the EEOC dropped its demands and the investigation. In 1996 Gilbert F. Casellas, then chairman of the EEOC, sent a letter to the U.S. House subcommittee on employment in which he concluded "it is wiser for the EEOC to devote its scarce litigation resources to other cases."

CONTROVERSY CONTINUES

While the company was waging battle with outsiders, an internal struggle ensued in the Hooters system. Hooters of America CEO Robert H. Brooks had bristled against the constraints of the franchise agreements with Hooters Inc. from the outset. Hooters Inc. filed a lawsuit against Hooters of America in 1997 claiming franchise violations, including requiring franchisees to buy products from a Brooks-owned company.

Brooks's first experience with the food industry came on his family farm in South Carolina. He earned a dairy science degree in 1960, and then he had a seven-year stint with a food company. He founded Eastern Foods Inc. in the late 1960s, introducing the Naturally Fresh line in 1980. In 1984, while recovering from a stroke, he put up money for an associate's purchase of a Hooters franchise. Brooks took possession of the endeavor when his partner was unable to pay him back.

By 1997 the Hooters of America owned or franchised restaurants outnumbered Hooters Inc. 192 to 12. Brooks's Hooters restaurants were bringing in an average of $2 million in annual sales. Part of his profits went to buying out Hooters shareholders, purchasing a country club, and donating to charity.

Among his donations was an art center at Clemson University, honoring his son, Mark Brooks. Mark had been killed in a 1993 plane crash along with Hooters of America–sponsored NASCAR driver Alan Kulwicki. The company had entered into sports sponsorships to build loyalty among members of its target market.

CONTROVERSY ACROSS THE BORDER

Hooters Girls remained all female with the settlement of a class-action lawsuit in 1997. The $3 million-plus out-of-court agreement compensated men denied employment as waiters because of gender. Hooters would continue to hire only women as Hooters waitresses but would consider men on an equal basis for other more visible positions, such as manager or bar assistant.

The company's ability to garner controversy was not limited to the states. In Mexico, where Hooters had begun opening restaurants, they faced the challenge of translating its name and sexy image in another culture. North of the U.S. border, Miss Canada International lost her crown when she became a Hooters Girl.

Two years later, an Edmonton lawyer moved to keep Hooters Inc. from gaining a Canadian trademark. The Hooters management maintained its sense of humor and even facilitated a negative product placement in the 1999 box-office hit *The Spy Who Shagged Me*.

TRADEMARK CHANGES HANDS

Hooters of America purchased the Hooters trademark from Hooters Inc. in 2001. At this time, Hooters of America operated 80 company-owned restaurants and had agreements with 25 domestic and 12 international franchisees, operating, respectively, 170 restaurants in the United States and 20 restaurants in countries including Canada, Argentina, Austria, Mexico, Singapore, Switzerland, and the United Kingdom, and the islands of Aruba and Puerto Rico.

Hooters Inc. would continue to operate in Tampa Bay, Chicago, and New York and gain rights of development elsewhere. Hooters Air was launched in March 2003. An attempt by Brooks to buy the belly-up Vanguard line in 2002 failed, but he was able to purchase charter air carrier Pace. The company began with flights between Atlanta and Myrtle Beach, where its golf course was located.

The going price for tickets exceeded that of discount flights, but two Hooter Girls aboard each flight, in addition to the professional crew, were the promised perks. The Hooters Air brand expansion lasted just over three years ending with the airline's closure in April 2006. Never on firm financial ground, the service had been hit hard by fuel price increases in the wake of Hurricanes Katrina and Rita.

Analysts estimated the marketing experiment had cost the company around $40 million. Earlier that year, Hooters had embarked on another brand expansion when the 396-room, 35,000-square-foot Hooters Casino Hotel opened near the Las Vegas Strip. In this instance, Hooters of America had simply licensed its trademarks to hotelier 155 Tropicana LLC, limiting its financial risk.

OWNERSHIP CHANGES

A few months after the Hooter Air closure, the company suffered a much more significant loss when Robert Brooks passed away suddenly from a heart attack, on July 15, 2006. After spending the previous few years buying the company's ownership shares, Brooks had emerged as principal owner and had transformed Hooters of America into something of a family business.

Brooks's will left 30 percent of the company's ownership to his son Coby Brooks, who became controlling owner and CEO. The rest was distributed to other family members. When Brooks's widow successfully challenged the will, however, the future of Hooters of America as a family business began to unravel. After Coby Brooks reached a financial settlement with his stepmother in 2009, the terms of the deal effectively forced him to bring in outside investors to purchase shares in the company.

Initially, the high bidder appeared to be Wellspring Financial Management, but just as the sale seemed imminent, Chanticleer Holdings, a North Carolina–based investment group exercised a right-of-first-refusal clause included in a $5 million loan agreement it had signed with the company several years earlier. Forming a consortium with several other investment firms, including H.I.G. Capital and KarpReilly, Chanticleer ultimately acquired controlling ownership in the company for the group in 2011.

BUSINESS SLOWS

By 2013 business at Hooters of America had begun to stagnate, even as the company continued to expand, opening 17 new locations in that year alone. The chain's store count stood at over 400, with 69 of those outside the United States. Still, sales had declined steadily over the previous few years, with only a meager 1 percent rise in 2012 to break the trend.

Company executives blamed a number of factors including a tired, slightly dated image and failure to maximize the brand's appeal to female customers. Accordingly, a company-wide "facelift" initiative was undertaken to freshen the restaurant's image. While company spokespersons assured the public that the company's most famous assets, the Hooters Girls, the menu, and the sports bar atmosphere, would not change significantly, a number of tweaks were made.

Restaurants were redesigned with improved lighting and a more open layout. Menus were updated with more salads and dishes for health-conscious diners. Even changes to the Hooters Girl uniforms were considered. As part of the promotion of the new changes, some choices were put to a public vote through social media outlets.

CHANGES BRIGHTEN PROSPECTS

By 2014 most of the changes were well underway. A redesigned prototype of the new Hooters restaurant layout had opened for business in the New Orleans market and 19 existing stores had been subsequently remodeled. Plans were underway to continue remodeling existing stores. Hooters had also redoubled its efforts to open new franchised locations, particularly overseas.

In a February 2014 interview for *Business World*, Mark Whittle, senior vice president for global development noted, "We are big believers in the franchise model and we expect that more than 90 percent of our unit growth will be driven by franchisees." Whittle continued, "One of the great things about selling this concept is that you never have to overcome a brand-awareness hurdle. Whether here in the U.S. or abroad, everyone knows Hooters and most people have a genuine fondness for the brand."

Dean Boyer
Updated, Kathleen Peippo; Chris Herzog

PRINCIPAL COMPETITORS

Brinker International Inc.; Carlson Restaurants Worldwide; DineEquity, Inc.

FURTHER READING

Baker, Ryan. "Hooters No Stranger to Controversy." *Ottawa Citizen*, June 8, 2000.

Covert, James. "Hooter's Assets Seeking Support as Family Feud Drives Sales Plans." *New York Post*, February 11, 2010.

Dostal, Erin. "Hooter's CMO Talks Marketing Strategy." *Nation's Restaurant News*, June 25, 2013.

"Hooters of America, Inc. Acquires Hooters Trademark." *PR Newswire*, March 23, 2001.

"Hooter's of America: On a Mission to Expand Franchise Business." *Business World*, February 2014.

Horovitz, Bruce. "Showing Serious Wrinkles at Age 30, Hooters Is Looking to Reinvent Itself with More than a Nip and Tuck." *USA Today*, April 27, 2013.

"Hostess with the Mostest." *Economist*, June 28, 2003.

Huettel, Steve. "Hooters Wings, Aisle 2, Servers Not Included." *St. Petersburg Times*, October 14, 2003.

McKay, Rich. "Hooters Celebrates 20 Years." *Orlando Sentinel*, May 25, 2003.

O'Daniel, Adam. "Why Hooters Thinks It Can Overcome 'Veto Vote'—Even from Your Mom." *Charlotte Business Journal*, October 4, 2013.

Stanford, Duane, and Leslie Patton. "Hooters: Fun for the Whole Family." *Bloomberg Businessweek*, September 13, 2012.

Watson, Bruce. "Hardship at Hooters: Family Feud Drives CEO to Seek Investment Partners." *DailyFinance*, February 11, 2010. Accessed October 26, 2014. http://www.daily nance.com/2010/02/11/hardship-at-hooters-family-feud drives-ceo-to-seek-investment-p.

Houghton Mifflin Harcourt Company

222 Berkeley Street
Boston, Massachusetts 02116
U.S.A.
Telephone: (617) 351-5000
Fax: (617) 351-1114
Web site: http://www.hmhco.com

Public Company
Incorporated: 1908
Employees: 3,300
Sales: $1.38 billion (2013)
Stock Exchanges: NASDAQ
Ticker Symbol: HMHC
NAICS: 511130 Book Publishers; 511210 Software
  Publishers

■ ■ ■

Houghton Mifflin Harcourt Company is an established leader in educational publishing, providing indispensable materials for the elementary and secondary education markets. The company also produces testing materials, reference books, children's literature, and a line of award-winning trade books of interest to the general public. Formed in the 1800s as a printing house, the company grew and diversified, playing an important role in the intellectual development of generations of Americans. In time Houghton's focus shifted to scholastic publications, and the company has become a major presence in the educational market, both in traditional materials as well interactive and electronic products.

FROM PRINTER TO PUBLISHER: 1820

Henry Oscar Houghton was born into poverty in Vermont in 1823. At age 13, he was apprenticed to a printer in Burlington. In 1842 he entered the University of Vermont, earning his way through college by working in various printers' offices. In an effort to pay off the debts he had amassed while in school, Houghton moved to Boston after his college graduation in 1846, where he held a series of jobs in journalism and printing. Houghton paid off his debts within two years and bought out one of the partners in one of Boston's premier printing businesses for $3,100 (paid in installments); thus Bolles & Houghton was formed. The business had changed its name by 1851 to Houghton & Haywood, when Houghton exchanged his former partner for one of his cousins. The company moved the following year to an expanded printing plant on the banks of the Charles River and began to call itself the Riverside Press. In 1852 the business changed hands again and took the name H.O. Houghton & Company.

Five years later, in 1857, Houghton was shaken by a widespread economic panic, the lingering effects of which wore on for the next four years. As banks and other businesses closed and paper money lost its value, Houghton found itself in possession of the stereotype plates, used to print off new copies, for a number of books. These assets were given to the printer in lieu of payment by insolvent publishers. Soon after, Houghton purchased the stereotype plates for a 39-volume book on English law from the Boston publisher Little, Brown & Company. With these moves, Houghton took the first step in the process of changing from a printer into a

COMPANY PERSPECTIVES

Curiosity is essential to lifelong learning. At Houghton Mifflin Harcourt, we aim to spark a lifelong love of learning in every individual we touch.

publisher. In order to exploit the value of the stereotype printing plates he owned, it was necessary for Henry Houghton to print the books, which then needed to be distributed.

By 1863 Houghton had amassed enough plates to flesh out a basic publisher's list: law books, general classics, and a lucrative arithmetic textbook. When one of his primary clients, Little, Brown & Company, terminated their contract, Houghton was forced to diversify to ensure his company's continued financial health. Accordingly, in 1864 Houghton entered into a partnership with Melancthon M. Hurd, a wealthy New Yorker with whose firm Houghton had previously produced a series of books by Charles Dickens. Houghton planned to handle the printing, advertising, and distribution aspects of the business, leaving authors, manuscripts, and editors in the hands of his partner, Hurd. The new New York–based company was called Hurd & Houghton, and a shield with two interlocked Hs became its colophon.

The first catalog of books published by the new firm included the texts for which Houghton owned the stereotype printing plates, works by Englishmen, and several books written by Americans. In January 1865 the company purchased an additional 20 titles, including works by James Fenimore Cooper. Later the same year, the fledgling enterprise found itself the object of a lawsuit by Hurd's former partners over the rights to publish the Dickens books. Eventually, this was resolved to Houghton's satisfaction.

In 1866 Hurd & Houghton was reorganized when one of Houghton's brothers contributed additional capital. With this money, the company moved to newer, more stylish offices in New York and expanded its Cambridge, Massachusetts, printing facilities. After purchasing the Riverside Press site, the company added a new four-story building and 10 new presses. These new facilities, inaugurated at the end of 1867, allowed the press to keep up with demand for its most popular product, the *Merriam Webster Unabridged Dictionary*, as well as to print newspapers, periodicals, and the books of the Hurd & Houghton line (which included law books, school books, Bibles, prayer books, theological

works, and children's literature). Although Houghton's Massachusetts-based printing operations were turning a profit, its New York publishing arm languished. Hurd & Houghton's periodicals, such as the *Riverside Magazine for Young People*, suffered from stiff competition and were expensive to produce. Nonetheless, by the end of the firm's second year in operation it remained profitable overall.

BECOMING HOUGHTON MIFFLIN

In 1872 Hurd & Houghton took on several additional business partners, among them Horace Elisha Scudder, who worked on the children's magazine, and George Harrison Mifflin, a rich young man who had joined the firm in 1868. In the 1870s Houghton & Hurd expanded steadily, acquiring publications in a number of fields, including the *Atlantic Monthly*, and garnered a number of lucrative government contracts. Gradually, it was becoming the predominant Boston publishing house.

Boston suffered a devastating fire in 1872, worsened by the fact that all of the fire department's horses had an equine illness. Many paper manufacturers and printing businesses were destroyed in the catastrophe, which ushered in a prolonged economic slump. The events had forced one of New England's oldest and most illustrious publishing houses, Ticknor & Fields (at the time known as James R. Osgood & Company), into dire economic straits. The 50-year-old publisher had published such leading intellectuals as Ralph Waldo Emerson, Henry David Thoreau, Nathaniel Hawthorne, Mark Twain, Henry Wadsworth Longfellow, Harriet Beecher Stowe, and John Greenleaf Whittier. In 1878 Houghton bought out the older firm and formed Houghton, Osgood & Company, moving the company more firmly into the realm of literary publishing, away from the lucrative printing and textbook publishing with which it had begun.

By the start of the 1880s Houghton, Osgood was operating under the burden of heavy debts assumed under the Osgood takeover. To ameliorate this dangerous situation, the company was reorganized in 1880, to become Houghton, Mifflin & Company. The company spent the next decade reducing its debt, helped by the publications of books by authors such as Henry James and Kate Douglas Wiggin (*Rebecca of Sunnybrook Farm*). During this time Houghton also established an educational department, which worked to update the company's academic offerings. Chief among the company's schoolbooks was the Riverside Literature Series, also inaugurated in 1882, composed of unabridged American classics annotated with study

KEY DATES

1864: Hurd & Houghton is formed.
1878: Company purchases Ticknor & Fields and renames itself Houghton, Osgood & Company.
1908: Partnership becomes a corporation and is renamed Houghton Mifflin Company.
1967: Company sells stock to the public for the first time.
1994: Company acquires McDougal, Littell for $138 million.
2001: Company is acquired by Vivendi Universal.
2002: Group of private investors buys company.
2006: Company is acquired by Riverdeep plc.
2007: Company acquires Harcourt education and other divisions, becomes Houghton Mifflin Harcourt.
2012: Company files for Chapter 11 bankruptcy.
2013: Company begins publicly trading its stock again.

guides, available to schools as cheaply as possible. One version of the project was printed on opaque paper, with inexpensive paper covers, and sold for 15 cents a volume.

In 1895 company founder Henry Oscar Houghton died and control of the firm passed to his younger partner, George Harrison Mifflin. Houghton left the firm in strong, if not invincible, economic shape, as it faced slowing profits in response to another general economic depression. In the late 1890s, in addition to the firm's standard list of children's works and educational tomes, Houghton added a number of novels designed to attract public attention. Several of these books sold well, moving significantly more than 10,000 copies. In addition to its fiction, Houghton also offered newly updated schoolbooks and the popular *Atlantic Monthly*.

A NEW ERA IN THE 20TH CENTURY

In 1901 Houghton Mifflin opened a book shop in downtown Boston. In the windows, the company mounted displays promoting its best-selling novels, and inside, samples of the fine printing and binding of the Riverside Press were available. Seven years later, in 1908, after a series of deaths among the firm's original partners, Houghton, Mifflin & Company restructured

itself, changing from a partnership into a corporation, under the name Houghton Mifflin Company. At this time, the firm sold its journal, the *Atlantic Monthly*, to a group of investors who planned to install new editors while maintaining some ties with Houghton.

By 1914 George Mifflin's desire to publish novels that would win widespread popularity had brought about a decline in the overall literary quality of the company's offerings. One of the publisher's most prominent poets, Amy Lowell, quit the house for another charging that the company had suffered a decline in prestige through its practice of publishing second-rate fiction. Houghton lost further literary currency when World War I broke out in Europe in 1914. Under the leadership of its Anglophilic editor-in-chief, the company avidly supported the Allied war effort, working with Wellington House, the propaganda division of the British Foreign Office, a policy that later earned Houghton the suspicion of many scholars.

Between 1914 and 1918 Houghton published more than 100 books related to the war effort. Many of Houghton's books concerning the war proved profitable. An additional, unexpected side effect of World War I was an increase in the size of the reading public, and consequently, the market for books. Programs to put inexpensive books in the hands of servicemen during the war had introduced the habit of reading to a vast number of men. In the years following the war American letters underwent a renaissance, as new authors introduced fresh literary movements. Despite its heritage of having published many of the leading literary lights of the 19th century, Houghton was, in large part, left out of the contemporary movements.

The company had a strong reputation for conservatism, a product of the archaic tastes of several of its key editors, who sought uplifting works with pleasant themes and found the new stark realism unpalatable. In addition, Houghton's editors perceived themselves to be handicapped in the publication of radical material by their location in Boston, where local authorities frequently banned books found objectionable or dangerous. The company feared the Boston police could seize the entire print run of an offending work as it came off the presses in Cambridge, preventing a book from even entering circulation.

Although the literary tumult of the 1920s passed by Houghton, the company did show more success with its nonfiction offerings, and its educational books division thrived. It had begun publishing intelligence quota, or "IQ" tests back in 1916, and continued to update these best sellers for decades.

POSTWAR REBOUND OF EDUCATIONAL PUBLISHING

Houghton relied on its perennial sellers and its solid educational lists throughout the economic depression of the 1930s. A key part of this approach was the development of the market for standardized tests. Working with educators at the University of Iowa, the company developed the Iowa Tests of Basic Skills. Also during this time, Houghton Mifflin added Adolf Hitler's *Mein Kampf* to its nonfiction list. All royalties from this work were paid to the Office of Foreign Litigation of the U.S. government. After publishing Hitler, the company went on to publish the works of his adversaries in the wake of World War II. In the late 1940s, Houghton paid its largest advance ever for Winston Churchill's six-volume account of World War II, for which he was later awarded the Nobel Prize in Literature. In addition, the company published the works of General George Patton and Field Marshal Bernard Montgomery.

Following World War II, the U.S. government passed the GI Bill, promising a free college education to all who had served in the military during the war. This move dramatically increased the market for college textbooks, and Houghton's operations in this area expanded greatly. In 1949 the company also introduced the McKee readers, which taught young children how to read, and were purchased by school systems expanding to accommodate the baby boom of the 1950s. Houghton also increased its participation in the standardized testing field.

The company grew in size throughout the 1950s and 1960s, adding such works as Rachel Carson's controversial *Silent Spring* to its nonfiction list. In 1967 Houghton sold stock to the public for the first time, listing its shares on the New York Stock Exchange. Two years later, Houghton introduced the best-selling *American Heritage Dictionary*, one of the first such works to be created using a computerized word base.

MODERNIZATION OF HOUGHTON

The company moved further into the field of computer publishing in 1971 when it began working with a small New Hampshire–based firm called Time-Sharing Information to develop computer programs for use in schools. Four years later, in 1975, Houghton purchased the company, to better integrate its operations with its textbook division. This year also was noteworthy because the company was sued by three women and charged by the Massachusetts attorney general with discrimination against women in hiring and promotions. Two years later, Houghton agreed to pay $750,000 to its

female employees and increase its affirmative action program. In a separate later settlement, Houghton paid an additional $325,000.

By the late 1970s as the number of school-age children dwindled, Houghton began to shift its emphasis in educational publishing. The company started to move away from primary and secondary school texts toward college texts, particularly business course and professional offerings. In 1977 it purchased the Pinecliff Publishing Company, a California-based medical publisher, and its textbook sales gained steadily. These gains attracted the attention of Western Pacific Industries, a railroad conglomerate, which had acquired 6.7 percent of the company's stock by March 1978. Concerned about a possible corporate takeover, Houghton authors such as John Kenneth Galbraith and Arthur Schlesinger organized an Author's Guild inquiry into the matter, wrote letters of protest to the buyer, and announced that they might quit the publisher if it was not able to remain independent. The campaign worked, and Houghton bought back its shares.

Houghton established a Chicago subsidiary in 1979, calling it the Riverside Publishing Company, to produce reading textbooks with a new approach. To sell this line, the subsidiary was given its own separate sales force. Further, in its trade books division, Houghton reintroduced the Ticknor & Fields imprint belonging to the venerated Boston publisher the company had purchased long ago. The division was set up to publish a small list of distinguished authors on politics, biography, and historical fiction. Another imprint, J.P. Tarcher, Inc., was added for science books, and all of Houghton's trade activities were consolidated into one division, in the hope of increasing profits.

In 1980 Houghton moved to secure its dominance of the textbook market by purchasing the educational publishing operations of Rand McNally & Company for $11.6 million, though these activities remained separate from Houghton's other businesses. Throughout the 1980s, textbooks reigned supreme in Houghton's publishing empire, growing at a rate of more than 10 percent annually.

NEW LEADERSHIP, NEW DIRECTIONS

In the early 1990s Houghton was revamped under the leadership of a new chief executive officer, Nader F. Darehshori. Darehshori, who had joined the company as a sales representative in 1966, trimmed Houghton's workforce and gave more autonomy to its publishing divisions. He was also keenly aware of the technological changes in publishing and sought not only to keep up but to lead the industry. Such titles as 1992's *International Electronic Thesaurus* and the latest edition of the *American Heritage Electronic Dictionary* were major sellers. To bolster the educational divisions, Darehshori spearheaded efforts to buy a 17.5 percent stake in Cassell for $4.4 million, spent $17 million for the testing assets of DLM, and acquired the publishing arm of College Survival Inc. for $10 million. The company also reorganized its foreign publishing operation by shedding a few units.

A major acquisition came in January 1994 when Houghton bought textbook publisher McDougal, Littell & Company for $138 million in an effort to enhance its secondary school market product line. At the same time, the company announced that it would fold its prestigious Ticknor & Fields imprint and merge its 20 or so trade books into the company's general line, in an effort to stem losses. In further restructuring, Houghton spun off its computer software division into a separate company, InfoSoft Corporation (later renamed Inso Corporation), of which it retained a 40 percent stake. Sales for the year had climbed to $483 million, but Houghton was soon on the move, announcing its acquisition of D.C. Heath and Company. To cover some of the debt incurred in the Heath purchase, Houghton sold a portion of its Inso shares in 1995. Darehshori believed the D.C. Heath purchase would play a significant role in the company's future and would help Houghton reach sales of $1 billion by 2000.

In general, Houghton, the country's ninth-largest publisher, weathered the cyclical nature of educational publishing well. Most educational publishers experienced losses in the first and fourth quarters annually, because the lion's share of textbook sales always fell in the second and third quarters; in addition, however, the adoption of new textbooks and programs occurred only every five to seven years, with sometimes even longer periods. Expenses incurred in developing new elementary and secondary programs were absorbed until the texts were sold and tested in schools. Fortunately for Houghton, several new curriculum projects were well received in 1996 and, along with further sales by D.C. Heath, revenues were up by 91 percent in the second quarter. Houghton Mifflin Interactive (later renamed Sunburst Technology Corporation), meanwhile, was also steadily gaining in both products and sales. Houghton finished the year strong, with net sales of $717.9 million, up 36 percent from the previous year's $529 million.

Houghton stockholders had reason to cheer in July 1997 when a two-for-one stock split was announced. Each of Houghton's seven divisions, even the traditionally stolid Trade & Reference unit, had strong showings for the first two quarters that followed through to the end of the year. Net sales for 1997 reached $797.3 million, an increase of 11 percent and on track to reach Darehshori's projections for the new century. The following year Houghton was back on the acquisition trail; one bid failed (for a unit of Simon & Schuster) while another succeeded (the purchase of Computer Adaptive Technologies, Inc. [CAT], a firm that designed and developed computerized testing services and products). Year-end results were still on an upswing, topping $861 million, though the 8.1 percent boost was not as sharp as in previous years (1997's increase of 11 percent or the 36 percent net sales leap in 1996).

In 1999 Houghton continued to buy companies with technologically based product lines, including the assets of the Little Planet Literacy Series, a literary program for preschool- to third-grade students, followed by the purchase of Sunburst Communications, Inc., an instructional software and video developer. To help finance its new acquisitions, Houghton sold the remainder of its equity in Inso Corporation and continued to climb closer to its 2000 goal: net sales hit $920.1 million and net income rose to $76.3 million.

CHANGES IN OWNERSHIP

As the new millennium began Houghton Mifflin's fortunes started to falter. Significant net losses posted in the first two quarters of 2001, in addition to a half-billion dollars in accrued debt, had made many stockholders nervous. When European media giant Vivendi Universal SA made a generous bid to buy the company outright, the offer was accepted relatively quickly. Vivendi purchased Houghton Mifflin for $60 per share, paying stockholders 10 percent more than the stock's last registered value. Adding in the $500 million in assumed debt, Vivendi had spent around $2.2 billion to acquire the company and take it private.

Despite Vivendi's apparent eagerness to acquire the publisher, Houghton Mifflin's tenure as a Vivendi subsidiary was brief. The European conglomerate had developed debt problems of its own, and less than a year after the purchase, it announced a plan to sell more than $16 billion in assets over several years. One of the first properties to go was Houghton Mifflin's recently acquired Sunburst Communications subsidiary. Shortly thereafter, Vivendi was in talks with a consortium of investment companies, including Thomas H. Lee Partners, Blackstone Group, and Bain Capital, which had offered to take Houghton Mifflin off its hands.

Eventually, the two sides agreed on terms. The consortium would pay Vivendi $1.28 billion in cash and assume $380 million of the publisher's debt. The sale became final on January 31, 2002. During this period, Houghton Mifflin maintained its position in the market as one of the top three educational publishers. However, it was a time of transition in the industry, as more tests and curricula were disseminated via the Internet, rather than in traditional paper form. Along with its competitors, Houghton Mifflin struggled to profitably balance traditional publishing with the demands of the new online frontier. Over the next several years, the company's debt load rose to more than $1 billion.

Investment consortiums, in the end, are dedicated to buying and selling for profit, and in 2006 Houghton Mifflin's ownership was offered a deal it could not pass up. A group of investors affiliated with Irish-owned educational software company Riverdeep Holdings formed HM Rivergroup plc with the specific intent of acquiring both Riverdeep and Houghton Mifflin. The plan was to combine a successful traditional publisher with a proven software company and cover both sides of the educational publishing market. HM Rivergroup eventually purchased Houghton Mifflin for $1.75 billion in cash and $1.61 billion in assumed debt. After completing its purchase of Riverdeep, the new parent company was renamed Houghton Mifflin Riverdeep Group plc.

TURBULENT TIMES

The new Irish publishing group, led by chairman and CEO Anthony Lucki, was not finished growing. In July 2007 Lucki announced that his group would also acquire the Harcourt Education and Harcourt Trade publishing operations. A venerable New York publishing house dating back to 1919, the Harcourt Brace Company had been owned by the English-Dutch publishing and information conglomerate Reed Elsevier since 2001. For a reported $3.7 billion in cash and $300 million in common stock, the Harcourt groups, as well as their subsidiary Greenwood-Heinemann operation, became part of the new conglomerate. Upon completion of the sale at the end of the year, the company changed its name to Houghton Mifflin Harcourt Publishing Company. To accommodate the merger, the structure of the Houghton Mifflin Riverdeep Group holding company was reorganized and reincorporated as Educational Media and Publishing Group (EMPG).

Although this period was in many ways one of expansion, one key move served to streamline the company's mission significantly. At the same time it was finalizing the Harcourt acquisition, the company announced plans to sell its college division to Stamford, Connecticut–based Cengage Learning for a reported $750 million in cash. Houghton Mifflin Harcourt's would now focus primarily on publishing K–12 educational materials, while still maintaining a respectable trade publication operation. While the flurry of expansion and reorganization suggested an air of optimism at the new publishing giant, the combination of recession and debt would bring a sobering reality by the end of the next year.

During 2008 Houghton Mifflin Harcourt underwent a series of staff layoffs and announced a temporary freeze on acquiring new manuscripts for its trade, or noneducational, divisions. The company was publicly frank about the reasons behind the moves. Jeremy Dickens, president of the EMPG division, told the *New York Times* that EMPG was $7 billion in debt after the acquisitions of the previous few years and paid $500 million annually in interest alone. More bad news arrived in early 2009 when both Moody's and Standard & Poor's reduced EMPG's credit rating and suggested that it was likely to default on its debts. In April of that year, Lucki retired as CEO and was replaced by EMPG founder Barry O'Callaghan.

BANKRUPTCY AND BEYOND

EMPG spent the next few years attempting to restructure its debts, with less than satisfactory results. In 2012 Houghton Mifflin Harcourt filed for Chapter 11 bankruptcy protection. Although the company reported $1.29 billion in sales for the previous year and $2.68 billion in assets, it remained $3.53 billion in debt. When it emerged from bankruptcy later the same year, it had retired around $3 billion of that debt by converting it into ownership equity in the company.

At this point, Houghton Mifflin Harcourt seemed poised to continue with business as usual, including acquisitions. New CEO Linda Zecher announced that the company's plan for a return to profitability included shifting investments from print to online publishing, expanding internationally and increasing sales directly to consumers. The implementation of these strategies included a partnership with Hachette Book Group to market Houghton Mifflin Harcourt publications internationally and a number of key acquisitions. Among these were the *Webster's New World Dictionary* and CliffsNotes brands.

During 2013 several of Houghton Mifflin Harcourt's largest shareholders, who had acquired their ownership shares through the debt-to-equity conversion, decided to convert some of their equity back to cash by taking the company public. In November of that year 18.3 million shares in the company were sold in an initial public offering at $12 per share. The company was now listed on the NASDAQ as HMHC.

The following year Houghton Mifflin Harcourt continued to acquire key companies and brands in its quest to refocus on electronic publication. In May 2014 the company purchased the Curiosityville early childhood education website. In July it acquired School-Chapters Inc., a Connecticut-based developer of online educational solutions platforms. As the educational publishing industry continued its transition to electronic media, Houghton Mifflin Harcourt seemed determined to maintain its position in the market.

Elizabeth Rourke
Updated, Nelson Rhodes; Chris Herzog

PRINCIPAL DIVISIONS

Channel One News; Great Source Education Group; Heinemann; Holt McDougal; Riverside Assessment; SchoolChapters; The Leadership and Learning Center.

PRINCIPAL COMPETITORS

McGraw-Hill Publishers; Pearson plc.

FURTHER READING

Ballou, Ellen B. *The Building of the House: Houghton Mifflin's Formative Years*. Boston: Houghton Mifflin, 1970.

Chesto, Jon. "Houghton Mifflin Harcourt Shares Rise 32% on First Day of Public Trading." *Boston Business Journal*, November 14, 2013.

Davis, Michelle R. "Digital Shift." *Education Week*, February 6, 2013.

"Global Publishing Leaders 2013: Houghton Mifflin Harcourt." *Publishers Weekly*, July 19, 2013.

Milliot, Jim. "HMH Continues to Evolve." *Publishers Weekly*, March 25, 2013.

Mirabella, Lorraine. "Houghton Mifflin Harcourt Acquires Cockeysville-Based Children's Website." *Baltimore Sun*, May 24, 2014.

Moore, Mary. "Houghton Mifflin Pushing Deeper into Digital Space." *Boston Business Journal*, December 16, 2011.

Rich, Motoko. "Publishing Displays Its Split Personality." *New York Times*, November 25, 2008.

Strahler, Steven. "Textbook Case of a Dying Biz; Publishing Industry Collapses as School Purchases Shift, Sink." *Crain's Chicago Business*, March 5, 2012.

Tivnan, Tom. "HMH Exits Bankruptcy, but Questions Linger." *Bookseller*, June 29, 2012.

Trachtenberg, Jeffrey A. "Houghton Mifflin Files Plan for $274 Million IPO." *Wall Street Journal*, November 1, 2013.

Williamson, Eugenia. "Houghton Mifflin Harcourt's New Chapter." *Boston Magazine*, January 2014.

Hoval AG

Austrasse 70
Vaduz, 9490
Liechtenstein
Telephone: (423) 399 2400
Fax: (423) 399 2411
Web site: http://www.hoval.li

Private Company
Founded: 1932
Employees: 1,300
Sales: CHF 336 million ($360 million) (2012)
NAICS: 333413 Industrial and Commercial Fan and Blower and Air Purification Equipment Manufacturing; 221330 Steam and Air-Conditioning Supply; 333415 Air-Conditioning and Warm Air Heating Equipment and Commercial and Industrial Refrigeration Equipment Manufacturing; 333414 Heating Equipment (Except Warm Air Furnaces) Manufacturing

■ ■ ■

Hoval AG is a leading developer of innovative heating, air-conditioning, and ventilation (HVAC) systems. Based in Vaduz, Liechtenstein, Hoval operates through two primary divisions, Heating Technology and Climate Technology. Hoval has also invested strongly in developing environmentally friendly systems, including solar thermal power and other technologies. The company has built an international network of sales and production subsidiaries, with locations in Austria, Croatia, the Czech Republic, France, Germany, Italy, Poland,

Romania, Slovakia, Spain, and the United Kingdom, as well as in Shanghai, China, and exports its products to more than 50 countries worldwide. The company has supplied equipment for such high-profile installations as Buckingham Palace and Windsor Castle in England, Vaduz Castle in Liechtenstein, the National Theater in Prague, the Palazzo Apostolico at the Vatican, Beijing's Hotel Pangu, and the Burj Dubai. Hoval remains a private company owned by the founding Ospelt family. The company is led by Peter Gerner (CEO of the Heating Technology division), Fabian Frick (CEO of the Climate Technology division), and Richard Senti (CFO). Former CEO Peter Frick serves as group chairman. Hoval last reported sales of CHF 336 million ($360 million) in 2012.

BOILER INNOVATION IN THE THIRTIES

Hoval founder Gustav Ospelt came from a family of locksmiths, starting with his grandfather, Christoph Ospelt, opened a shop in Vaduz, the capital of the tiny principality of Liechtenstein, in 1868. Ospelt's father, Gustav Ospelt Sr., took over the shop in 1897 and expanded it as a metalworking shop. Gustav Ospelt Jr. soon joined his father in the business, before taking it over in 1932.

The younger Ospelt's interests reached beyond the family's traditional locksmith and metalworking trades. In the same year he took over the family business, Ospelt received permission to extend the metal shop's operations to include the fabrication of heating systems. Over the next decade Ospelt experimented with various designs, before hitting on the innovation that was to mark the true start of the future Hoval company. Ospelt's idea was to convert the traditional kitchen stove into a more versatile unit that could also be connected into a home's central heating system. Ospelt succeeded not only in patenting the design in 1942, but also in winning certification from the Swiss Federal Laboratory for Material Science and Technology, or EMPA.

By 1945 Ospelt had perfected his design, introducing the Model H stove, which served as both a cooking stove and central heating unit, which each functioned controlled separately. That year Ospelt registered the trademark Hoval, which stood for Heizapparatebau Ospelt Vaduz Liechtenstein. The company soon began receiving orders for its heating systems from beyond Liechtenstein. This prompted the company to set up its first international subsidiaries, in Switzerland and Austria, in 1946.

The company's move into Switzerland proved particularly fruitful for the company. Soon after Ospelt began marketing the first Hoval central heating cooker, he was approached by Gusty Herzog, a native of Basel who had studied heating engineering in Cologne, Germany. Herzog at first worked as a heating engineer, but ultimately found his calling in sales, working for Strebelwerk, and then Sanitar-Kuhn Company. Ospelt and Herzog decided to form a partnership, founding the Ing. G. Herzog & Co. Company in Feldmeilen, Switzerland, in order to develop Hoval sales in that country.

Herzog's business expanded quickly through the 1950s, opening branch offices in several Swiss cities. By the middle of the 1960s, the Swiss company, now known as Hoval Herzog AG, had established a network of customer service centers throughout Switzerland, as well as in Liechtenstein. The Herzog family remained closely associated with Hoval through the next decades, with Herzog's sons, Peter and Walter, becoming long-serving members of the company's board of directors.

PARTNERING WITH KRUPP IN 1955

In the meantime, Hoval had begun its own evolution into a modern production company. The company began its shift toward industrial production in 1953, when the company became the first to market a heating system with an integrated hot-water tank. The new system was marketed as the Hovaltherm system, but soon earned the nickname as "the Rocket." This also became the first of the company's products to be produced in series.

Demand for the Rocket and other Hoval products, particularly from West Germany, quickly outstripped the company's production capacity. This prompted the company to seek out production partners. In 1955 the company signed a licensing agreement with German steel giant Friedrich Krupp to produce steel boilers under the Hoval brand. In this way, the company was able to expand its brand into Germany, quickly growing to dominate the market. Licensing agreements permitted the company to extend its brand into other major European markets during this time as well.

At the same time Hoval invested in developing its own production capacity. This led to the inauguration of the group's Neugut factory, located in the Vaduz industrial zone, in 1957. The factory not only gave Hoval modern production facilities, but it also became the site of company's permanent headquarters. The company also made its first acquisitions during this time, acquiring a factory in Italy. The company also entered the U.K. market, setting up a sales subsidiary there in 1958. In 1961 Hoval added its own production facilities there, buying up the Farrar boiler works in Newark. Founded in 1887, the Farrar works had long supplied boilers and heating systems throughout the British Empire. The acquisition of the company not only raised Hoval's production capacity, it also provided a major boost in its engineering expertise as well. The company's association with the Herzog family also strengthened during this time, as Walter Herzog joined Hoval to become manager of its new British operations.

The increased production capacity enabled the company to respond to the soaring demand for its heating systems. By 1967 Hoval had already built more than 100,000 boilers. Along with those built by the company's licensing partners, more than 350,000 Hoval boilers had been installed across Europe by then.

INNOVATIONS IN THE SIXTIES

At the same time, Hoval's expanding engineering base allowed it to roll out new and improved heating systems and designs. In 1960, for example, the company

KEY DATES

1868: Christoph Ospelt opens a locksmith shop in Vaduz, Liechtenstein.

1897: Gustav Ospelt Sr. takes over the business and expands it as a metalworking shop.

1932: Gustav Ospelt Jr. takes over the shop and receives authorization to develop home heating systems.

1942: Ospelt patents a home heating and cooking system.

1945: Ospelt begins selling his system under the Hoval brand.

1958: Hoval acquires Farrar in the United Kingdom.

1970: Company begins producing industrial ventilation systems.

1987: Company develops a wood gasification boiler.

2005: Hoval opens a sales office in Shanghai, China.

2014: Company markets the Ultrasol solar collector in partnership with goinnovate.

revolutionized the heating industry again with the debut of its first combination boiler. The new design incorporated a positive pressure system which permitted the use of different fuel types, whether solid, liquid or gaseous. The new design set new standards for efficiency of use.

Hoval scored a number of other successes during the decade. The company introduced its high-performance water heater, called the Modul-plus, in 1967, which became one of the company's best-selling products. Hoval's design and engineering efforts also began to pay off during the decade. In 1968 the company logged the first in a long series of product patents, with its *Fischgratrohr* (literally "fishbone tube") heat transfer surface. The result was impressive advances in heating efficiency.

During the next decade, Hoval set out to expand beyond its core heating technologies segment. The company became a full-scale HVAC company in 1970, with the introduction of its first industrial ventilation and heat exchange systems. Climate control systems quickly emerged as the group's second major business. The company also continued to make gains in heating efficiency. In 1976, for example, the company combined its new ventilation expertise with heat recovery equipment to produce a new fuel-efficient industrial heating

system. This system was capable of cutting fuel costs by as much as 60 percent.

Other innovations followed through the end of the decade. Hoval scored a new patent for its self-cleaning thermolytic heating surface in 1979. The company quickly incorporated the new technology into its small- and medium-sized boilers, released that year.

ROYAL CUSTOMERS IN THE EIGHTIES

Hoval's U.K. presence provided the company with a new boost to its reputation at the beginning of the 1980s. The company was tapped to supply equipment for the heating systems for the British royal family, and specifically for Buckingham Palace, Windsor Castle, and the Palace of Holyroodhouse in Scotland. The company was further honored to be named as official suppliers to the royal family. Other high-profile projects were to follow, including outfitting Vaduz Castle, in Liechtenstein, and the papal residence, the Palazzo Apostolico, in the Vatican.

Industrial systems, however, became an increasingly prominent part of Hoval's operations through the 1980s. The company set up a partnership with Ruhrgas Deutschland in 1982 in order to develop a new generation of gas premix burners. Introduced under the name Ultraclean in 1986, the new burners represented a breakthrough in reducing the levels of pollutants thrown off during the combustion process.

Other important Hoval innovations including its Air-Injector system, introduced in 1984, which utilized an air vortex distributor to improve heating and ventilation efficiency in large-scale industrial systems. In 1987 Hoval joined the growing interest in biomass technologies, introducing its wood gasification boiler, which soon emerged as an industry standard. Also during the 1980s Hoval's sales network expanded farther abroad, adding a number of new markets, including the People's Republic of China.

Hoval continued to innovate in traditional fuel technologies as well. The company patented a new aluminum-based heat exchanger in 1993, which it then integrated into its gas condensation systems starting the following year. The company began marketing another patented technology in 1994, a recirculation cooling unit designed to improve HVAC systems in high spaces. Another major product for the company was its MultiJet oil condensing boiler, introduced in 1999. The new technology enabled Hoval to achieve higher efficiency with lower noise levels, and in smaller form factors.

ALTERNATIVE ENERGIES IN THE 21ST CENTURY

Hoval took steps to position itself within the growing Eastern European markets into the turn of the century. The company established subsidiaries in the Czech Republic, Slovakia, and Poland, starting in 2001. In 2005 the company solidified its growing sales in China, opening a sales office in Shanghai in 2005. This allowed the company to score several high-profile projects, including the HVAC systems for the seven-star Hotel Pangu, which opened in time for the Beijing Olympic Games. Through the second half of the decade, the company also added operations in Romania and Croatia, while expanding its Western European presence with sales offices in Spain and France as well. Hoval also expanded its production capacity during this time, opening a factory in Slovakia in 2005.

A new management team took over leadership of the company at the turn of the century. In 2003, longtime CEO Peter Frick retired to the position of chairman. In his place, the company appointed joint management team consisting of Peter Gerner, Fabian Frick, and Richard Senti. In addition to providing joint leadership of the company, Gerner became CEO of the group's Heating Technology division, while Frick became CEO of the company's Climate Technology division. Senti became the group's CFO, heading its Finance & Service division.

Under the new management team, Hoval invested heavily in developing new environmentally responsible and renewable energy technologies. This process had already begun in 2001, with the introduction of a new horizontal tube burner design, used in the installation of wood pellet–based heating systems. The company later expanded this technology to include the BioLyt range of wood-pellet systems, introduced in 2005. The company also developed a strong business converting former fossil-fuel installations to use wood-pellet and other biomass fuel sources.

HEAT PUMPS IN 2008

Hoval continued shifting its business away from its former reliance on fossil fuel technologies. By the beginning of the next decade, more than half of the group's revenues came from alternative energy resources. As part of this effort, the company expanded its range of technologies. In 2008, for example, the company teamed up with Austria's Warmepumpen GmbH to develop and produce a new generation of heat pumps. In that year, the company added another high-profile project, when it was tapped to supply HVAC equipment for the Burj Dubai, set to become the world's tallest building.

Hoval also sought new ways to increase efficiency and lower the environmental impact of other aspects of its technologies. In 2007 the company debuted a new refrigerant-free recirculation method for its cooling systems. In 2010 the company also targeted expansion into the growing market for heat transfer systems and combined heat and power generation systems, establishing a dedicated business unit for these operations.

At the same time, Hoval also invested in building up expertise in solar-power and solar thermal heating technologies. The company developed a range of solar collectors and hot water storage tanks, as well as solar power–based heating and cooling systems, both for the residential and industrial markets. The company also developed combination systems, permitting HVAC systems to use both renewable and fossil-fuel energy supplies.

Hoval found a new partner for its renewable energy commitment in 2010, when it began working with go-innovate to develop a new type of solar collector developed by goinnovate. By 2014 the two companies had developed a commercial product, manufactured by Hoval, and marketed by Hoval as Ultrasol. Hoval also supplied the collectors to goinnovate, which began marketing them under its own Radius brand in markets not covered by Hoval's own network of subsidiaries and sales offices. After more than 80 years in business, Hoval remained a leader in HVAC technology in the 21st century.

M. L. Cohen

PRINCIPAL SUBSIDIARIES

Hoval a/s (Denmark); Hoval Aktiengesellschaft (Singapore); Hoval d.o.o. (Croatia); Hoval Gesellschaft m.b.H. (Austria); Hoval GmbH (Germany); Hoval Ltd. (UK); Hoval Ltd. (China); Hoval SAS (France); Hoval SK spol. S.r.o. (Slovakia); Hoval Sp. Z.o.o. (Poland); Hoval spol. S.r.o. (Czech Republic); Hoval Srl (Italy); Hoval Srl (Romania).

PRINCIPAL DIVISIONS

Heating Technology; Climate Technology.

PRINCIPAL COMPETITORS

Bosch Thermotechnik GmbH; Daikin Industries Ltd.; Danfoss A/S; National Tank Co.; Qingdao Haier Company Ltd.; Shanghai Boiler Works Ltd.; Trane Inc.; Viessmann Werke GmbH and Co.

FURTHER READING

Beck, Gebhard. "Die Erfolgsgeschichte des Roten Heizkessels." *Liechtenstein Innovation*, December 7, 2012.

Epp, Baerbel. "New and Innovative Collector Model." *Global Solar Thermal Energy Council*, July 24, 2014.

"Hoval: Grossauftrag aus Österreich." *Liechtenstein Innovation*, October 8, 2012.

"Hovalwerk Aktiengesellschaft Receives Approval for Trademark HOVAL." *ABClive*, July 27, 2011.

"Innergytech Inc. Has Formed an Alliance with the Hoval Company from Liechtenstein." *Engineered Systems*, October 2006.

"Peter Gerner Über Die Marke Hoval: Der Endkunde Wird Für Uns Immer Wichtiger." *Brand Trust Insights*, July 21, 2014.

"Turning Up the Heat." *Venture*, October–November 2007.

"Unternehmerische Initiativen Kommen An." *Volksblatt*, October 9, 2013.

Hrazdan Energy Company

1 Gortsaranani Street
Razdan, 2302
Armenia
Telephone: (+374 223) 607 12
Fax: (+374 223) 607 14
Web site: http://www.raztes.am

Wholly Owned Subsidiary of Inter RAO
Founded: 1963
Incorporated: 2004
Employees: 912
Sales: RUB 10.33 billion ($3 billion) (2013)
Stock Exchanges: Armenia
Ticker Symbol: HRPC
NAICS: 221122 Electric Power Distribution

■ ■ ■

Hrazdan Energy Company is the largest power generation and distribution company in Armenia. Hrazdan Energy operates thermal, hydroelectric, and nuclear power plants. The company oversees Armenia's sole nuclear power plant in Metsamor, with a generating capacity of 405 megawatts (MW). The nuclear power plant is considered the base supplier of energy to Armenia, responsible for 40 percent of the country's power supply. The company is also overseeing preparations for the construction of a modern nuclear power plant to replace the aging Metsamor plant, although this facility is not expected to be operational before 2020. Through JSC RazTEZ, which trades on the NASDAQ, the company operates Hrazdan Thermal Power Plant,

with a total generation capacity of 1,110 MW, including 440 MW generated by its youngest power plant, Block 5, commissioned in December 2013. A smaller thermal power plant (TPP), the Yerevan TPP, has a capacity of 50 MW and provides power chiefly for the Nairit Chemical Plant. Hrazdan Energy also operates Armenia's two large-scale hydroelectric plants, the Sevan-Hrazdan Cascade, with an installed capacity of 550 MW, and the Vorotan Cascade, with a capacity of 404 MW. Hrazdan Energy also maintains Armenia's high-voltage power transmission grid, consisting of 119 substations and a total length of 3,170 kilometers. In 2013 the company began building a 230-kilometer, 220-kilovolt power line linking the Hrazdan TPP with Iran, slated for completion by the end of 2014. Hrazdan Energy is controlled by Russian energy giant Inter RAO, which reported total Armenian revenues of RUB 10.33 billion ($3 billion) in 2014.

HYDROELECTRIC POWER IN THE TWENTIES

Armenia remained something of a backwater throughout much of its history as part of the Ottoman Empire. The tiny, mountainous country had few natural fuel resources. With no large, easily exploitable rivers, the country proved relatively inhospitable to the development of a hydroelectric power generation industry. Nonetheless, the country's first hydroelectric plant was constructed in 1903. This small facility primarily provided electricity for the operation of a copper mine in Syunik.

After a brief period of independence following World War I, Armenia was annexed by the Soviet

KEY DATES

1936: Construction begins on the first phase of the Sevan-Hrazdan Cascade hydroelectric power plants.

1963: Constructions begins on the first phase of the Hrazdan Thermal Power Plant.

1969: Construction begins on the Metsamor Nuclear Power Plant.

1995: Armenergo is broken up amid the privatization of the Armenian energy industry.

2003: Inter RAO acquires financial management of the Metsamor Nuclear Power Plant.

2013: Company commissions the fifth unit of the Hrazdan Thermal Power Plant.

2014: Company announces plans to invest AMD 21.5 billion upgrading the Sevan-Hrazdan Cascade.

Union, along with its Caucasus region neighbors, Georgia and Azerbaijan. Armenia soon began to benefit from the Soviet Union's industrialization policies, as well as its vast resources. Through the 1920s and 1930s Armenia became the site of a number of Soviet industrial projects, spanning a range of industries, including food, tobacco, and other goods.

In order to fuel this development, the Soviet authorities also began investing in developing a power generation and electricity distribution infrastructure in Armenia. A new body, later known as Armenergo, was established, which reported directly to the Soviet Ministry of Power and Electrification. Under Armenergo's auspices, work began on the development of the country's most ambitious hydroelectric power plant (HPP), tapping the major cascade from Lake Sevan, Armenia's largest lake.

The Sevan-Hrazdan Cascade HPPs were conceived as a series of six HPPs located downstream from the lake along the Hrazdan River. Construction of the first of these, the Yerevan HPP, situated at the lowest point on the cascade, began in 1936. At the top was the Sevan HPP. Construction of the full project spanned nearly 30 years, with the final phase of the project not commissioned until 1961. The full installed capacity of the Sevan-Hrazdan HPP was 550 MW. A seventh power plant, added later, would ultimately raise the cascade's total power output to 565 MW.

THERMAL POWER IN THE SIXTIES

The exploitation of the Soviet Union's vast oil and natural gas resources opened new possibilities for power generation in Armenia. This was particularly true as the Soviet Union began constructing a pipeline network, including into Armenia, greatly easing the transport of fuel across the country's vast distances. Given Armenia's limited waterways, the new availability of thermal fuels represented the country's best hope for expanding its power generation capacity.

Into the early 1960s, Armenergo laid out a new and still larger-scale power generation project, that of the Hrazdan TPP. This plant was designed to incorporate four, and later five power units, for a total operating capacity of 1,110 MW. Construction of the first of the power units began in 1963, and was placed in operation in 1966. Work continued on the project, and by the end of the 1980s, four of the five units of the plant had been completed. The fifth unit would not be commissioned until 2013.

In parallel to the Hrazdan TPP, Armenergo oversaw the construction of a second TPP, this time in Yerevan. This project also incorporated multiple units, with an initial design capacity of 550 MW. Parts of this plant remained in operation for more than 40 years, far exceeding the typical life span of 30 years for TPPs. Nonetheless, into the turn of the century, the plant was reduced to just a single power generation unit, outputting just 50 MW.

NUCLEAR POWER IN THE SEVENTIES

During the 1970s, construction began on a second major hydroelectric power project, known as the Vorotan Cascade HPPs. This project encompassed three power plants along the Vorotan River, with the highest unit, the Spandaryan HPP, located at an altitude of 1,694 meters. The first of the three power plants was commissioned in 1970, with the last not completed until 1989, bringing the project's total capacity to 404 MW.

Armenia also benefited from the Soviet Union's race to develop its nuclear power industry. Starting in the mid-1950s, the Soviet Union had been developing two types of nuclear power plants (NPPs). The first used a solid graphite-based system to regulate the fission process. The most notorious example of this type of plant was the Chernobyl NPP. The second type of nuclear power utilized a pressurized or heavy water design. This design, known as the VVER 440, emulated Western NPP designs, in that it used water to both regulate and cool the nuclear fuel. In Russian, VVER stood for "water-water power reactor."

Armenia was chosen to become one of the first sites for the new power plant design. Construction of the VVER 440 facility began in 1969, in Metsamor, in the shadow of Mount Ararat. This place the nuclear power facility within 20 miles of Yerevan, Armenia's largest city and home to approximately half of the Armenian population. The first of the two Metsamor units, containing two generators, began operations in 1980, supplying 400 MW. The second unit, containing two more generators, raised the plant's total capacity to 800 MW soon after.

The completion of the Metsamor facility represented a major milestone in Armenia's power generation history. In addition to ensuring a plentiful supply of electricity to Armenia and its industries, the added power generation capacity also enabled Armenia to become an electrical power exporter. Through the 1980s, Armenergo extended the country's high-voltage transmission grid beyond Armenia, supplying power not only to other member states of the Soviet Union, but also neighboring Turkey to the west.

POWER SHORTAGES IN THE NINETIES

Armenia's power generation industry lay at the heart of the country's economic collapse into the early 1990s. In 1988 an earthquake registering 6.8 on the Richter Scale devastated much of the country. More than 25,000 people died as a result of the quake, with more than 500,000 left homeless, and over one-third of the country's industries left in ruins. The Metsamor NPP was located just 60 miles from the epicenter of the quake, which occurred along a major fault stretching from Turkey to the Arabian Sea.

The Metsamor plant emerged from the earthquake undamaged; nonetheless, the potential for catastrophe (an anxiety fueled by the Chernobyl disaster just two years earlier) brought Armenians to the streets, demanding the plant be shut down. The Soviet authorities complied, taking the Metsamor facility offline in 1989.

By then, however, Armenia headed toward a new, tumultuous chapter in its history. With the weakening of the Soviet Union at the end of the 1980s, long-suppressed tensions between Armenia and neighboring Azerbaijan once again began to rise. By 1988 the two countries had emerged into an open dispute over the region known as Nagorno-Karabakh, home to a large Armenian population.

Armenia declared its independence from the Soviet Union, becoming the first in the region to do so. Shrug-

ging off Soviet domination, however, eliminated the moderating force that had helped restrain the growing hostility between Armenia and Azerbaijan. War broke out between the two countries over Nagorno-Karabakh in 1992. Turkey, which had its own long history of hostility with Armenia, took up the Azeri cause. With the outbreak of hostilities, both Azerbaijan and Turkey imposed a blockade on imports into Armenia, and most especially, gas and oil imports to the country.

With the Metsamor plant shut down, and its TPPs starved of fuel, Armenergo was left with only its aging HPPs to provide electrical power to the entire country. The reliance on these plants, and particularly on the Sevan-Hrazdan Cascade, placed too much pressure on Lake Sevan, causing a severe shortage in the country's water supply as well. The embargo also blocked Armenergo from receiving shipments of replacement parts for its aging power generation facilities. In order to carry out repairs, the company was forced to take several of its power generation units offline in order to harvest them for parts to fix its other units.

As a result, Armenia experienced a dramatic loss of electrical power. At the worst of the crisis, power was limited to just one to two hours per day; it was not uncommon for power to cut off for a week at a time. The country's industrial output plummeted, while its economy collapsed.

NUCLEAR RESTART IN 1995

Amid this crisis, the newly democratic Armenian government began carrying out its economic reform policies. The power generation and distribution sector became an important and early target of these reforms. Starting in 1993 the government began dismantling Armenergo, setting up a number of independent operating companies. These included the Armenian Nuclear Regulatory Authority, which became the owner and operator of the Metsamor NPP in 1993. In 1994 the government also established new power distribution businesses to take over these operations from Armenegro.

In 1995 the government began the privatization of the country's power generation and distribution sector. These operations were hived off from Armenergo starting from March 1995, leaving the body with oversight of only the country's transmission grid. This process continued in December 1995, when the unbundling of Hrazdan NPP and the Sevan-Hrazdan Cascade were set in motion. Both facilities were formally separated from Armenegro in 1996.

By then, Armenia's fortunes had begun to improve. In 1993 construction of a pipeline crossing Georgia succeeded in linking the Russian oil and gas supply to Armenia. While the pipeline became the frequent target of sabotage during the conflict between Russia and Georgia, these attacks ended by 1995. As a result, Armenia had once again been able to generate power at its thermal NPPs, relieving pressure on the struggling hydroelectric system.

Also in 1995 the Armenian government airlifted in more than 500 tons of new parts and equipment, largely from Russia, in order to restart the Metsamor facility. The government also initiated a long series of upgrades and improvements to the site, one of the last NPPs in the world to have no containment system. Over the next 15 years, more than 1,400 safety improvements were carried out at the site, including the introduction of seismic-resistant storage batteries and the reinforcement of the reactor's housing. The Armenian government benefited from aid from the United States as well, which contributed a new seismic-resistant coiling system. The choice was also made to recommission only one of the facility's two power plants, limiting capacity to 400 MW.

Nonetheless, the restoration of nuclear power marked the end of Armenia's power supply crisis. The country soon initiated its industrial redevelopment. By the dawn of the 21st century, Armenia had already become one of the most vibrant of the former Soviet economies. The country continued carrying out reforms of the energy industry. In 2002 the government tackled the inefficiency of the original privatization of the utility sector. Originally, power distribution had been placed under the control of 64 separate companies. These were streamlined into 11 companies, then into four regional operators. In 2002, however, the four regional operators were united under a single entity, Electric Networks of Armenia CJSC.

RUSSIAN TAKEOVER FROM 2003

Into the turn of the century, the Armenian government's privatization of the country's energy sector took a new turn. In order to pay off its debts, in particular to Russia, the government began transferring a number of assets, including part of its power generation sector, to Russia. These assets were placed under the control of a new and fast-growing force in the region's power industry, Inter RAO. That company had been founded in 1997 as part of RAO United Energy Systems of Russia, and initially focused on importing and exporting electricity.

Into the turn of the century, Inter RAO began developing its own portfolio of power generation assets, both in Russia and abroad. The company's first step

into Armenia came in 2003, when Inter RAO took over the financial management of the Metsamor NPP. In 2006 Inter RAO gained control of Armenia's power distribution market, when it acquired Electric Networks of Armenia. Also that year Inter RAO took over much of the country's power transmission grid.

By the end of the decade the Armenian government had ceded 100 percent control of the Hrazdan TPP as well. That company was subsequently placed into a joint stock company, JSC RazTES, or Hrazdan Power Company, which listed its shares on the NASDAQ OMX market in 2011. Through subsidiary International Energy Corporation, Inter RAO also gained control of the Sevan-Hrazdan Cascade, as well as the Vorotan Cascade. These companies were all placed under an entity known as Hrazdan Energy Company.

With the backing of Inter RAO, which had grown into one of the leading energy groups in the region, Hrazdan Energy could begin plans to upgrade and update its aging power generation infrastructure. Most of the group's power generation plants were by then operating beyond their normal life spans. Among the company's investments was the completion of the fifth unit of the Hrazdan TPP in December 2013. This raised the site's total power capacity by another 440 MW. Importantly, the new modern unit represented a significant advance in the plant's operating efficiency.

Into 2014 the company also pledged an investment of AMD 21.5 billion to upgrade the Sevan-Hrazdan Cascade, starting with the Yerevan HPP. At the same time, the Armenian government began plans to replace the aging Metsamor nuclear facility, with a new and modern NPP expected to cost $4 billion. The government hoped to have the new plant online by 2020. In this way, Hrazdan Energy Company expected to enhance its status as Armenia's major power provider in the 21st century.

M. L. Cohen

PRINCIPAL SUBSIDIARIES

JSC Elektricheskiye seti Armenii, JSC RazTEZ; Armenian Nuclear Power Plant; Sevan-Hrazdan Cascade Hydroelectic Power Plants; Vorotan Cascade Hydroelectric Power Plant.

PRINCIPAL DIVISIONS

Power Transmission; Hydroelectric Power Plants; Nuclear Power Plants; Thermal Power Plants.

PRINCIPAL OPERATING UNITS

Sevan-Hrazdan Cascade of Hydro Power Plants; Vorotan Cascade of HPPs; Armenian NPP; Yerevan TPP; Hrazdan TPP.

FURTHER READING

"Armenia to Launch New Power Line from Hrazdan Plant toward Iran by 2015." *Russia & CIS Business and Financial Newswire*, June 20, 2013.

Gharabegian, Areg. "Electricity Production in Armenia." *Armenian Weekly*, July 25, 2013.

"In Q1 2014 Sevan-Hrazdan Hydro Cascade Reduces Electric Power Output by Almost 50%." *ArmInfo Business Bulletin*, April 22, 2014.

"Is Armenia's Nuclear Plant the World's Most Dangerous?" *National Geographic*, April 11, 2011.

"New Power Line to Link Armenia and Georgia." *ArmInfo–Business Bulletin*, April 20, 2014.

Indorama Ventures Public Company Ltd.

—————■—————

75/102 Ocean Tower 2, 37th Floor
Sukhumvit Soi 19
Bangkok, 10110
Thailand
Telephone: (+66 2) 661-6661
Fax: (+66 2) 661-6664
Web site: http://www.indoramaventures.com

Public Company
Incorporated: 1994 as Indorama Holdings
Employees: 10,000
Sales: THB 229.12 billion ($7.46 billion) (2013)
Stock Exchanges: Thailand
Ticker Symbol: IVL
NAICS: 325211 Plastics Material and Resin
Manufacturing; 424610 Plastics Materials and Basic
Forms and Shapes Merchant Wholesalers; 313110
Fiber, Yarn, and Thread Mills; 325220 Artificial
and Synthetic Fibers and Filaments Manufacturing

■ ■ ■

Indorama Ventures Public Company Ltd. (IVL) is the
world's largest and most-vertically integrated producer
of polyethylene terephthalate (PET), and a world-
leading producer of polyester and wool yarns. IVL's
largest division is its PET Business, which operates on a
global basis with factories in Thailand, China,
Indonesia, the United States, the Netherlands, the
United Kingdom, Italy, Lithuania, Poland, and Nigeria.
The company had a total annual installed production
capacity of 3.8 million tons of PET resin at the beginning of 2014. In addition to PET resin, the PET Business has moved downstream into the production of
PET-based bottles, closures, preforms, and other packaging, with packaging plants in Nigeria and Northern
Ireland, and through its Petform joint venture with
Serm Suk Pcl. The PET Business generated more than
$4.75 billion in sales in 2013 (including sales to other
IVL divisions). IVL's Fibers and Yarns Business
encompasses the company's polyester fibers and yarns, as
well as its world-leading production of worsted wool
yarn. This division had total revenues of more than $1.5
billion in 2013. IVL vertical integration strategy has also
led the company upstream, through its Feedstock Business, which produces such PET and polyester
components as purified terephthalic acid (PTA), mono-
ethylene glycol (MEG), and ethylene oxide derivatives
and by-products. This division generated revenues of
$2.29 billion (including sales to other IVL operations).
Altogether, IVL reported total revenues of THB 229.11
billion ($7.6 billion) in 2013. The company is listed on
the Thai Stock Exchange and is led by founder and
CEO Aloke Lohia, and his brother Sri Prakash Lohia,
chairman and founder of Indonesia-based Indorama
Corporation.

INDIA-INDONESIA CONNECTION IN 1976

Although originally from India, the Lohia family had a
long history of establishing businesses throughout the
Asian region. The family, led by M. L. Lohia, originated
as Calcutta-based textile traders, a business that they
extended to Burma at the beginning of the 1940s. In
1952 M. L. Lohia began manufacturing textiles, at first

COMPANY PERSPECTIVES

Indorama Ventures will be one of the leading global producers in the polyester space with our key focus on people and processes, thus making us one of the most admired companies in the world.

in Thailand, and then in Nepal as well, while developing export markets as far away as France. M. L. Lohia also developed a business importing synthetic yarns from Japan.

M. L. Lohia was joined in his business by his son, M. P. Lohia, born in Rajasthan in 1931. M. P. Lohia at first worked in Burma, where he set up a business manufacturing lace. In 1964, however, he transferred his company to Thailand, founding Thonburi Lace Corporation. In the 1970s M. P. Lohia expanded the family's textile manufacturing empire to include a new company, Ashok Textile Corporation, set up in Nepal in 1972.

The Lohia family had by then decided to take advantages of new opportunities arising in Indonesia. In 1972 M. P. Lohia moved to Jakarta with his three sons, Om Prakash, born in 1949, Sri Prakash, born in 1952, and Anil (later Aloke) Prakash, born in 1958. This marked the start of Indorama Corporation, which grew to become one of Indonesia's leading textiles producers. In 1976 the family branched out into the production of synthetic spun yarns, when S. P. Lohia founded Indorama Synthetics.

In the meantime, Aloke Lohia had been sent to study commerce at the University of Delhi. Following graduation, Lohia rejoined the family's successful and growing business empire. Lohia at first worked as a trainee under his father, before becoming financial controller of Indorama Synthetics in 1979.

Aloke Lohia remained in this position through most of the 1980s. Toward the end of the decade, however, as Mohan P. Lohia neared retirement, he also began preparing the company's succession. Rather than turn over Indorama to all three of his sons, Lohia instead instructed them to seek out new business opportunities, for which Lohia would provide starting capital. O. M. Lohia chose to return to India, where he established the family's Indian operations as Indorama Synthetics (India) Ltd. in 1989. That business eventually became India's second-largest polyester producer. S. P. Lohia stayed on in Indonesia to lead Indorama Synthetics, and later took over as Indorama Corporation itself.

THE MOVE TO THAILAND IN 1988

Aloke Lohia decided to try his luck elsewhere. His opportunity came in 1988 when a family friend approached Mohan Lal Lohia with the idea of founding a factory in Thailand to produce furfural and furfuryl alcohol, derived from cereal bran, corn cobs and other agricultural by-products. Furfural served as a solvent for agricultural preparations, and was particularly prized for its ability to increase delivery of chemicals such as herbicides into plant leaves.

Aloke Lohia agreed to go to Thailand to examine the feasibility of the project. Despite a lack of experience in the chemicals industry, Lohia recognized the opportunities of operating in Thailand, with its low labor costs and abundant agricultural and petrochemical resources. Mohan Lal Lohia supplied his son with $5 million in start-up funding, which Aloke Lohia used to construct his first chemical complex in Saraburi, Thailand, calling the company Indorama Chemicals Ltd. Production at the new factory began in 1989. Through the next decades, Indorama Chemicals, later known as Aurus Speciality Company Ltd., became one of the world's leading producers of furfural.

While operating their companies separately, the three Lohia brothers remained in close contact, often sharing expertise and technologies. This permitted Aloke Lohia to extend his own business interests into the production of wool. For this, Lohia began importing wool from Australia, becoming the first to produce high-quality worsted wool in Thailand. Founded in 1994, the new business was called Indoworth Thailand (later Indorama Holdings) and formed the basis for the future Indorama Ventures. Indorama Holdings soon grew into one of the world's leading producers of premium worsted wool. The company also established a small business producing wool sweaters as well.

PET IN 1995

The Lohia family had by then spotted a new business opportunity in the production of PET. This relatively new plastic had come into increasing demand in the early 1990s, especially for the use in the production of plastic bottles and other packaging. PET offered a number of advantages, allowing for the production of lightweight but highly resistant bottles. The Lohia family's investment in this area started with the construction of a small PET factory in Java, under S. P. Lohia's leadership. The family soon decided to focus its PET operations on Thailand, to take advantage of proximity to the country's abundant petrochemicals resources. In 1995 Aloke Lohia established his first PET

KEY DATES

1976: Lohia family makes its first investment in synthetic spun yarns, founding Indorama Synthetics.

1988: Aloke Lohia opens the family's first operations in Thailand, founding a furfural factory in Saraburi.

1994: Lohia founds Indoworth Thailand to produce worsted wool.

1995: Lohia founds Indo Pet (Thailand) to produce polyethylene terephthalate (PET) resin.

2003: Company acquires StarPET in the United States.

2010: Lohia brothers restructure their PET and polyester holdings, founding Indorama Ventures Ltd. (IVL).

2012: IVL acquires the ethylene oxide and ethylene glycol operations of Old World Industries in the United States.

resin factory, under the name Indo Pet (Thailand) Ltd. This company later became known as Indorama Polymers.

By 1996 Indorama Polymers had already developed its first downstream business. In that year, the company teamed up with Serm Suk Pcl., the bottler for PepsiCo in Thailand, to found a PET bottle joint venture, called Petform. Indorama held a 60 percent stake in the joint venture.

The Lohia family continued to seek out new extensions for its growing, if still separate business empires. The move into polyester production appeared a natural extension on the one hand of the company's extensive textiles manufacturing experience, and on the other of its growing expertise in plastics and synthetic fibers. The move into polyester production was carried out by Indorama Corporation itself, with the acquisition of Thailand's Siam Polyester Ltd. in 1997. This company was promptly renamed as Indo Poly (Thailand) Ltd. This company soon grew into a leading Thai polyester producer.

GOING GLOBAL IN 2003

In the meantime, Aloke Lohia continued to build up the PET resin business. Lohia at first focused on producing for the Thai market. By the turn of the century had succeeded in expanding the company to become Thailand's leading PET producer.

With this success, Lohia set his sights on more ambitious horizons. In 2002 he drafted his so-called Dream Plan, in which he set out a goal of transforming Indorama into one of the world's top five PET producers within the next 10 years. Lohia was able to take advantage of the downturn in global PET demand, amid the recession at the beginning of the century. In 2003 the company picked up struggling U.S. PET producer, StarPet, for just $35 million. The acquisition provided Indorama with a crucial platform for its broader entry into the US market, then the world's single-largest PET market.

Proximity to markets played a crucial role in PET production, allowing to the company to avoid high transport costs from shipping the relatively heavy PET resin over long distances. This consideration was a central part of the group's decision to build its own factory in Europe, the world's other major PET market, the following year. The company turned to Lithuania, where offered lower operating costs, while providing strong access to the European markets. Lithuania was also slated to become among the first of the new entrants into the enlarged European Union, providing the company with duty-free access as well. The company's factory opened in 2007.

While Lohia was guiding the company's rapidly expanding PET business, brother S. P. was leading Indorama's diversification into the petrochemicals markets. The brothers soon brought these two interests together, forming a joint venture to produce purified terephthalic acid (PTA), a primary feedstock for both PET and polyester. This venture, which included partners IRH Rotterdam and TPT Petrochemicals, opened its production facility in Rotterdam in 2008.

INDORAMA VENTURES IN 2010

By then, Indorama Synthetics, the Indonesian company led by S. P. Lohia, already appeared to serve as the holding company for the Lohia brothers' increasingly global operations. Indorama Synthetics invested in many similar areas, starting with its acquisition of Tiepet Inc., a PET resins producer based in Asheboro, North Carolina, in 2003. In 2004 the company also began construction of a $240 million PTA factory in Map Ta Phut, with a production capacity of 600,000 metric tons per year in 2004. This facility began production in early 2006, providing Indorama with crucial expertise ahead of the Rotterdam PTA joint venture. Indorama had also added PET in Lithuania as well, acquiring UAB Orion Global Pet in 2006. This led to the creation of UAB Indorama Polymers Europe in 2007.

In 2010 Sri Prakash and Aloke Lohia decided to restructure the family's PET and polyester and related businesses. The brothers set up a new company, called Indorama Ventures Ltd. (IVL), which then took over the family's PET businesses, the various polyester fibers and yarn operations, the worsted wool business, and the PTA and other feedstock businesses. Following that deal, S. P. Lohia emerged as chairman of the group, and majority shareholder, with a 51 percent stake. Aloke Lohia became IVL's CEO, while his 49 percent stake also included 76 percent of the group's voting rights. Soon after, IVL went public, listing on the Thai Stock Exchange.

IVL had in the meantime continued to build up its range of operations. These included two European PET resin factories acquired from Eastman Chemical Company in 2008 and AlphaPet, based in Alabama, in 2009. In 2010 the company also acquired a PET resins business in Italy.

IVL soon made a move into the mainland Chinese market, as PET production there began to soar in the new century. For this, the company acquired a factory in Kaiping City, Guangdong Province, in 2011. By then, the company had completed its largest acquisition to date, paying $420 million for much of the PET production business, including factories in South Carolina and Mexico, of Invista. These acquisitions added more than one million metric tons per year to IVL's total production capacity.

GLOBAL PET LEADER IN 2011

IVL continued scouting for new acquisition candidates. This led the company to pick up two businesses from South Korea's SK Chemicals, including SK Eurochem, in Poland, and SK Keris and SK Fibre, in Indonesia in 2011. The former added 140,000 metric tons per year of PET chip production capacity, while the Indonesian operations boosted the company's PET chip and polyester yarns businesses, with nearly 200,000 metric tons per year. Also that year the company formed a joint venture with Italy's Sinterama SpA in order to acquire Trevira, a polyester producer based in Germany.

These purchases helped solidify IVL's new position as the world's largest producer of PET and PET resins. The company nonetheless continued building up its range of operations, carrying out a major expansion of its Rotterdam PTA factory and acquiring 50 percent of Indonesian PTA producer Polyprima Karyesreska. IVL also acquired the European PET recycling and fiber manufacturing operations of Wellman International, in order to meet the growing demand for recycled plastics. IVL made its first approach to integrating the family's Indian business with its own entry into that country. In 2012 the company announced plans to set up an integrated factory producing PTA, PET, and polyester fibers, at a projected cost of $700 million.

INTEGRATION IN THE EARLY 21ST CENTURY

Full-scale integration became the new spearhead of the company's growth strategy into the middle of the decade. The company took a major step in this direction in 2012, when it reached an agreement to pay nearly $800 million to acquire the chemical assets of Illinois-based Old World Industries. This gave IVL control of the largest ethylene oxide (EO)-ethylene glycol (EG) production complex in the United States. EG, particularly in the form of monoethylene glycol (MEG), was the key component in the production of PTA. As a result, IVL became the first globally operating PET and polyester to develop integrated operations not only in the production of PTA but in MEG as well.

The company continued to develop its core PET business as well. In 2012 the group consolidated its leading position in Indonesia, picking up the PTA and PET assets of PT Polypet Karyapersada, based in Cilegon. The company also announced plans to set up a new PET resin factory in the United States, with a projected capacity of 1.2 billion pounds per year. The company expected the new facility to be operational by 2015.

IVL also laid plans to deepen its vertical integration. In April 2013 the company announced plans to set up a plant to produce paraxylene, another major PTA component. For this, the company formed a partnership Abu Dhabi National Chemicals company, joining in on the development of that group's Tacaamol Aromatics Plant. This facility was expected to begin production by the end of 2014. IVL also entered into Africa during this time, acquiring a PET-based packaging business in Nigeria in 2013.

IVL sought out other downstream opportunities as well. In 2014, for example, the company formed an 80-20 joint venture with Japan's Toyobo Co. to acquire Germany-based PHP Fibers GmbH, a maker of polyester-based air bags. Soon after, the company expanded its international network again, buying 51 percent of Turkey's SASA, the country's leading producer of PET and polyester fibers. By June 2014 IVL had added a second business in Turkey, this time acquiring full control of Artenius TurkPET A.S., based in Adana, Turkey.

By then, IVL had swelled to a globally operating company with nearly $7.5 billion in total revenues. IVL had also established itself as one of the world's most fully integrated PET and polyester companies, controlling not only the production of its basic feedstock but also present in an expanding array of downstream markets as well. From its home base in Thailand, IVL looked forward to new expansion as the world's global PET leader in the 21st century.

M. L. Cohen

PRINCIPAL SUBSIDIARIES

Asia Pet (Thailand) Ltd.; Athens Holdings, Inc. (USA); Auriga Polymers Inc. (USA); Aurus Packaging Ltd. (Nigeria); Beacon Trading (UK) Ltd. ; Beverage Plastics (Holdings) Ltd. (UK, Northern Ireland); Covington Holdings, Inc (USA); ES FiberVisions, Inc (USA); FiberVisions L.P. (USA); FiberVisions Manufacturing Company (USA); FiberVisions Products, Inc (USA); FV Holdings, Inc. (USA); Guangdong IVL PET Polymer Co. Ltd. (China); Indorama Holdings Rotterdam B.V. (Netherlands); Indorama PET (Nigeria) Ltd.; Indorama Polymers Rotterdam B.V. (Netherlands); Indorama Polymers Workington Ltd. (UK); Indorama Trading (UK) Ltd. ; Indorama Trading AG (Switzerland); Indorama Ventures USA Inc.; IVL Singapore PTE Ltd. (Singapore); Petform (Thailand) Ltd.; StarPet Inc. (USA); UAB Indorama Polymers Europe (Lithuania); UAB Orion Global PET (Lithuania).

PRINCIPAL DIVISIONS

PTA, PET, Ethylene Oxide/Glycols, Polyester Fibers and Yarns; Wool.

PRINCIPAL OPERATING UNITS

Indorama Polymers; Asia Pet; Petform; Indorama Polypet; Auriga Polymers; StarPet; Beverage Plastics; Indorama Ventures Packaging; Indorama Polyester Industries; FiberVisions.

PRINCIPAL COMPETITORS

BASF SE; The Dow Chemical Company; E.I. du Pont de Nemours and Company.

FURTHER READING

Chang, Joseph. "Indorama in the Fray." *ICIS Chemical Business*, March 12, 2012.

———. "Indorama Targets Next Growth Phase." *ICIS Chemical Business*, June 30, 2014.

Esposito, Frank, and Gurdip Singh. "Indorama Plans PET Site." *Plastics News*, November 19, 2012.

"Indorama Launches Inviya I-300 Fibre." *Apparel Online*, May 8, 2014.

"Indorama to Double Spandex Fibre Production." *India Business Insight*, May 21, 2013.

"Indorama Ventures PCL." *Nonwovens Industry*, May 2014.

"Indorama Ventures Plans PX Plant in Middle East." *Apparel Online*, April 30, 2013.

"IVL to Buy 80 Per Cent of PHP Fibres." *Indian Textile Journal*, May 6, 2014.

Jagger, Anna, "Global Ambitions for Indorama." *ICIS Chemical Business*, July 4, 2011.

Lohia, Aloke, and Amit Lohia. "The Global PET Power." *Packaging Strategies*, December 15, 2010.

Lopez, Jonathan. "Thailand's Indorama to Buy Turkey PET Assets." *ICIS Chemical Business*, February 24, 2014.

Nan, Suzanne. "Building a Polyester Giant." *Forbes*, June 11, 2009.

Ramesh, Deepti, and Robert Westervelt. "Indorama Acquires Old World's Chemical Assets for $795 Million." *Chemical Week*, February 6, 2012.

Smith, Katie. "Charge Hits Indorama Ventures Q1 Profit." *just-style.com*, May 13, 2014.

Jazzercise, Inc.

—■—

2460 Impala Drive
Carlsbad, California 92010
U.S.A.
Telephone: (760) 476-1750
Fax: (760) 602-7180
Web site: http://www.jazzercise.com

Private Company
Incorporated: 1979
Employees: 260
Sales: $96 million (2012)
NAICS: 533110 Lessors of Nonfinancial Intangible Assets (Except Copyrighted Works)

■ ■ ■

Jazzercise, Inc., is a leading global franchiser of dance and fitness classes. The company pioneered its own brand of dance-based exercise routines. These are taught by certified Jazzercise instructors in 32 different countries worldwide. The company has more than 8,000 franchises and teaches an estimated 32,000 classes every week. Franchisees pay a nominal start-up fee to the company and then 20 percent of gross revenues monthly. Founder Judi Sheppard Missett choreographs new routines approximately every 10 weeks. The company also produces videos, music recordings, and other educational materials. In addition to the Jazzercise Apparel division, the company operates a video production division named JM DigitalWorks.

FUN DANCE CLASS

Jazzercise, Inc., was founded by Judi Sheppard Missett, a professional jazz dancer. Missett was born in Iowa in 1944. As a toddler, she was pigeon-toed and had to wear leg braces. Her doctor recommended the little girl take dance classes as therapy, and she took her first class at the age of three. Apparently, her talent was evident from the beginning. Her mother especially encouraged young Judi, although it was difficult to find qualified dance teachers in the small town of Red Oak where the family lived.

Ultimately, her mother recruited dance teachers to settle in towns within driving distance of Red Oak, promising the recruits a place to teach, students, and offering her own bookkeeping and costume-sewing services. By the time Missett was 10 years old, she was teaching dance herself. After she graduated from high school, she moved to Chicago and enrolled in the theater and dance program at Northwestern University.

She began focusing on jazz dance, studying with the choreographer Gus Giordano. She traveled widely with touring shows and ultimately began teaching jazz dance classes for her mentor Giordano. In 1966 she married a television news reporter, Jack Missett, and had a daughter, Shanna, in 1968. Judi Missett's professional career had taken her all over the world. She continued to perform, but she also began to focus more on teaching.

APPEALING TO MOMS

Missett was troubled, however, because so many of her students dropped out of her classes. These students were typically young mothers like herself or married housewives. They wanted to take a class for the fun of it as well as to keep fit, but they did not have the ambition to become professional dancers. Their choices were either to take a high-powered class such as Missett taught, or to take a calisthenics class.

If the dance class was too demanding, they dropped out after a few weeks. Their other alternative, the calisthenics class, typically had only soft background music, and Missett imagined it was dreary. Around 1969 she began developing jazz-based exercise routines that she thought fit somewhere between the two extremes. Her classes were meant to be enjoyable, musical, and good exercise. She did not critique form, as in a professional dance class, and she used a room without mirrors, to reduce inhibitions.

RELOCATES TO CALIFORNIA

In 1972 the Missetts moved near San Diego, California. It was primarily a career move for Jack Missett, who also had family in the area. Judi Missett thought Southern California might prove an excellent place to develop her new dance classes. The area was far ahead of the rest of the country in worshipping health and fitness. Missett began looking for community centers and gymnasiums where she could teach her class, which she advertised as a new technique developed in faraway Chicago.

She promoted herself and her classes, getting coverage in the local newspaper, and soon she had flocks of students. She stopped performing around this time and devoted herself to teaching. In 1974 Missett began using the name Jazzercise for her program. Jazzercise grew more and more popular. By 1977 Missett was teaching 20 classes a week, with a total of almost a thousand students. This was all she could handle, and she had to turn people away. Jazzercise had found a niche, but it was difficult for Missett to fill it single-handedly.

Missett was at first unwilling to let others teach her Jazzercise routines, but there seemed no other way to provide enough classes for the community. She began by

training five students who had been with Jazzercise since Missett's arrival in California. These new teachers set up in rented spaces and began teaching Jazzercise classes. They were almost immediately successful, and Missett trained five more teachers over the course of the year.

COMPANY INCORPORATES: 1979

At this point Jazzercise did not have a formal franchise arrangement. The new instructors paid a start-up fee to Missett and then promised her 30 percent of their gross revenues. They got to use the Jazzercise name and continued to train with Missett. By 1978 this arrangement included instructors outside the San Diego area.

In 1979 Jazzercise formally incorporated. Missett also began using videotapes of her routines to teach certified instructors new material. This method allowed her to keep instructors up to date, even if they were teaching far from Jazzercise's new corporate headquarters in Carlsbad, California. By the end of the year, Jazzercise had gone international, with instructors in Europe, Japan, and Brazil.

NATIONAL PROMINENCE

After Jazzercise, Inc., incorporated in 1979, Missett began promoting the company's fitness routines across the country. She performed on national television for the first time in 1980, where Missett's svelte physique advertised the benefits of her program. Her television exposure led to the development of the Jazzercise apparel division. When Missett appeared on a broadcast of the *Dinah Shore Show*, she wore a leotard with the Jazzercise logo emblazoned on it.

She wore this because she was afraid viewers would otherwise miss the connection between her and her company. It spawned inquiries from Jazzercise students, who wanted to know where they could get Jazzercise gear. The company began to sell Jazzercise logo togs through a mail-order catalog. By 1980 Missett had trained over 1,000 instructors. The franchises brought $1.9 million to Jazzercise, Inc., that year.

The boom was just beginning. Missett broadened the company's exposure by publishing a book in 1981 called *Jazzercise: A Fun Way to Fitness*. It was a best seller, going into four reprints and selling close to 400,000 copies. Translated editions also appeared in France and the Netherlands. Missett also put out the first of the Jazzercise videos for public consumption. The next year Jazzercise put out a record, which went gold, selling over 25,000 copies. The company followed the success of the *Jazzercise* album with *Jazzercise Looking Good!* later in 1982. In 1983 Jazzercise, Inc., formalized its franchise relationship with its certified instructors.

DIFFERENT FRANCHISEE FORMULA

The company broke with the norm in the franchise industry by charging a low start-up fee and a high royalty rate. Most franchises around the country went for upward of $25,000, but a Jazzercise instructor could buy a Jazzercise franchise for only $500. The typical royalty rate for a franchise in the United States was from 3 to 10 percent, but Jazzercise instructors sent 30 percent of gross receipts back to Jazzercise, Inc.

This cockeyed formula nevertheless worked well for both the company and the franchisees. Perhaps because the new instructors were able to make money quickly and did not have to worry about recouping a high start-up fee, Jazzercise retained a high percentage of its franchisees. A successful Jazzercise franchise could bring the owner $75,000 a year. This looked very good compared to other aerobics programs where instructors were paid an hourly wage. So despite the high royalty rate, Jazzercise instructors remained committed.

CONTINUED GROWTH

The company grew enormously in the early 1980s. By 1983 Jazzercise franchises had spread to all 50 states. The company put out a third album, and founder Missett gained more exposure by appearing frequently on Disney Channel's *Epcot Magazine* show. Jazzercise

instructors performed in the opening ceremony for the 1984 Los Angeles Olympics, and Missett herself ran in the relay to bring the Olympic torch to the city. When the entertainment company MCA put out a Jazzercise workout video in 1984, it went gold, like the record in 1982, selling over 25,000 copies.

Fitness had become something of a national craze. Aerobics classes of all kinds were popular, and actress Jane Fonda also had a huge following for her fitness videos. Gross receipts from franchises were $40 million in 1983, an astonishing rise from under $2 million at the start of the decade. Regardless, sales remained relatively flat for 1984 and 1985, held in check by competition from other exercise programs. Even so, the company was named one of the fastest-growing franchises in the country in 1985.

With sales holding steady, Missett redoubled her efforts to promote Jazzercise. In addition to her frequent television appearances, she began writing a syndicated newspaper column on fitness to get maximum media exposure. She also worked at a more grassroots level, making appearances, giving speeches, and distributing coupons for local Jazzercise classes.

INNOVATIVE MARKETING TACTICS

Jazzercise also advertised in innovative ways, promoting itself on packages of products deemed healthy. Jazzercise had space on the back of boxes of Nabisco Wheat Thins crackers, for example. Jazzercise entered a licensing agreement with an apparel manufacturer to produce a complete line of Jazzercise exercise clothes in 1987, which would be sold in retail stores. Previously, the company had sold its clothing only through its catalog. The Jazzercise clothes came with a certificate for two free Jazzercise classes.

The company also changed its focus somewhat in the late 1980s. Missett realized that she had begun her career teaching mostly young married women who did not work outside the home. They were happy to take classes in a church basement or school gym. By the late 1980s, however, the typical Jazzercise student was working outside the home and did not mind spending money on pampering herself. The company built its first permanent gyms in the late 1980s, the upscale Fit Is It facilities. The modern buildings housed juice bars and clothing stores as well as attractive workout rooms.

Missett also began offering more varied routines, to fit a variety of lifestyles. The Fast and Fit class offered more active aerobic exercise, while the Lighter Side class was slower and easier. The company debuted Junior Jazzercise for kids, and Jazzergym for mothers and their small children, at the new Fit Is It centers. In 1988 the company reduced the royalty rate it charged franchisees to 20 percent. Despite the cutback, gross revenue inched up. The company had earned national name recognition and had close to 4,000 franchises.

Jazzercise classes were found in over 30 countries abroad. In 1989 Jazzercise became more widely available in Japan when that country's largest operator of health clubs agreed to offer all its members Jazzercise classes. Moreover, even though the franchise business was not growing as quickly as it had early in the decade, Jazzercise had a substantial revenue stream from its videotape and apparel sales. By 1989 one-third of the company's sales came from tapes and clothing.

STILL FIT IN THE NINETIES

Missett continued her vigorous promotion of the company in the 1990s. She went to the Soviet Union in 1990 with other health and fitness experts as part of a People to People ambassador program, and in 1991 she helped present the Great American Workout at the White House. The company also launched a free fitness program for children called Kids Get Fit in 1991, which eventually reached more than a million children worldwide.

The company entered a marketing arrangement with the athletic shoe company Nike, Inc., in 1992. In this cross-promotional effort, both Judi Missett and her daughter Shanna gained the title Nike Fitness Athlete. The company also produced more videos in the 1990s. The year 1995 saw a series of videos, including *Sports Stretch*, *Healthy Backs*, and *Body Power!* The company listed about 5,000 franchises by the mid-1990s. Sales were around $15 million.

Judi Missett passed the age of 50 and showed no signs of slowing down. She continued to teach almost every day in California and to choreograph new Jazzercise routines. In order to keep things fresh, she put out as many as 30 new routines every 10 or 11 weeks, and sent them via videotape to certified instructors worldwide. Missett's daughter Shanna Missett Nelson also taught regularly. She had become a Jazzercise corporate executive, in charge of Jazzercise's international operations.

ALLIES WITH GENERAL MILLS

The company kept up various promotional efforts tied to healthful products. It allied with General Mills in 1996, naming that company's Total cereal as the Jazzercise official cereal and giving away Jazzercise class coupons on the back of nine million Total boxes. The

next year the company ran a similar promotion on boxes of Ore-Ida baked potatoes, and Jazzercise also promoted a new energy drink called Boost, made by Mead Johnson.

The company allied with another athletic footwear manufacturer, Ryka, Inc., in 1997, and formed other publicity links the next year with Smuckers jam and cereal-maker Quaker Oats. A new development in the late 1990s was the Jazzercise CyberStretch program. Introduced in 1998 this was a computer program that appeared as a screen saver. CyberStretch gave step-by-step instructions for stretches and relaxation exercises, geared toward desk-bound office workers.

Computer workers were subject to repetitive motion injuries such as carpal tunnel syndrome, and the program was designed to prevent or alleviate this kind of ailment. The insurance company Barney & Barney began offering Jazzercise's CyberStretch program to client companies, hoping to reduce worker's compensation claims for repetitive motion injuries. Jazzercise also marketed CyberStretch through an international network of insurance brokers.

30TH ANNIVERSARY CELEBRATION

Jazzercise celebrated its 30th anniversary in 1999. By 2000 sales were $17.9 million. About half of this came from franchise fees. Jazzercise franchises worldwide generated over $56 million. Jazzercise, Inc., brought in another third of its revenue from sales of apparel and other merchandise. Some 16 percent came from royalties and other miscellaneous sources, and the company's video production arm, JM DigitalWorks, accounted for 6 percent of gross revenues.

By this time the company had changed its franchise arrangement only slightly. In 2001 the cost of the initial franchise fee had gone up to $650, and instructors still paid the company 20 percent of gross revenues monthly. To stay current, Minneapolis advertising agency Colle + McVoy was hired to develop a results-oriented advertising campaign for franchisees.

KEEPING UP WITH THE TIMES

As creative director John Jarvis said in the December 17, 2001, issue of *Adweek*, "Jazzercise is still seen as legwarmers and 'poofy' hair. But in reality it's changed with the times as much as anything." In early 2002 Missett was inducted into the National Association for Sports and Physical Education's Hall of Fame. That year, the company withstood negative public relations after refusing to hire a five-foot-eight, 240-pound woman as an exercise instructor, due to concerns that students would perceive her as being unfit.

The woman, who had engaged in high-impact aerobics six days per week for 15 years, filed a complaint with San Francisco's Human Rights Commission. Acknowledging that body shape was not necessarily a reflection of fitness, Jazzercise changed its standards for hiring instructors. During the early part of the decade Missett continued to provide instructors with fresh material every 10 weeks, developing anywhere from 75 to 90 new routines each time.

From weight training to step aerobics, routines were incorporated into 10 different class formats. Jazzercise ended 2002 with record revenues of $62 million. By 2003 the company's classes included choices such as Circuit Training, Step by Jazzercise, and Body Sculpting. A program named Jr. Jazzercise also was developed to provide something for a growing number of younger participants.

CONTINUATION OF STRONG GROWTH

During the middle of the decade Missett received industry recognition once again when *Fitness Business Pro* magazine honored her with a Lifetime Achievement Award. At the age of 62, she had built Jazzercise into a business with 52 full-time employees, 6,000 franchised instructors in 30 countries, and revenues of $71 million in 2005.

As Jazzercise celebrated its 40th anniversary in 2009, the company's corporate staff had grown to include 228 employees. The company ended the decade with sales of $96 million. In 2010 Jazzercise extended a partnership with two-time *Dancing with the Stars* champion Cheryl Burke, who agreed to remain the company's spokesperson through 2011. That year, Jazzercise added Egypt as a new international location, and Shanna Missett Nelson was promoted to president.

In addition, the company climbed 24 positions on *Entrepreneur* magazine's franchise 500 ranking to number 20. In 2011 Jazzercise's District Manager Support department relocated from California to a new satellite office in Kansas City, Missouri. Jazzercise's connection with Burke was strengthened in 2011 when her self-branded apparel line was introduced in the company's fall catalog.

RELEASE OF NEW PRODUCTS

In early 2013 Jazzercise sponsored *Be the Boss*, a real-life competition series on A&E Network. This resulted in

instructor Kim McCulloch being named as the company's ambassador, a corporate position that functioned as a liaison between Jazzercise and its franchisees. In addition, instructor Sophia Hubbard also became part of the company's corporate team and was provided with her own Jazzercise Fitness Center. Jazzercise continued to stay relevant by introducing new products such as an intensity interval training *Dance HiiT by Jazzercise* DVD in 2013.

The following year the company sponsored Kids Get Fit dance parties in conjunction with National Physical Fitness and Sports Month. The parties featured easy dance moves and interactive fitness games and were offered throughout Jazzercise's franchise network, which had grown to include 7,800 locations. Jazzercise celebrated its 45th anniversary in 2014. Throughout its history, the company had demonstrated its ability to evolve with the times and achieve remarkable growth. Moving forward, it appeared that Jazzercise would continue on this path for the foreseeable future.

A. Woodward
Updated, Paul R. Greenland

PRINCIPAL DIVISIONS

Jazzercise Apparel; JM DigitalWorks.

PRINCIPAL COMPETITORS

Bally Total Fitness Holding Corporation; Curves International, Incorporated; 24 Hour Fitness Worldwide, Inc.

FURTHER READING

Baar, Aaron. "No Leotards, Leg Warmers: Colle + McVoy Attempts to Firm Up Exercise System's Image." *Adweek Midwest*, December 17, 2001.

Graham, Katy. "Fitness Exec Has a Whirlwind Romance with Dance: Jazzercise Founder Shares Her Love for Universal Language." *San Diego Business Journal*, August 7, 2006.

"Jazzercise Hosting Fitness Getaway." *Entertainment Close-Up*, June 4, 2014.

"Jazzercise Introduces New Dance HiiT." *Wireless News*, September 17, 2013.

"A Lifetime of Dance and Fitness." *Fitness Business Pro*, October 1, 2005.

Maio, Pat. "Jazzercise Restructures Business, Adds New Support Center in Kansas City." *North County Times* (Escondido, CA), August 26, 2011.

Kaltura Inc.

---

250 Park Avenue South, 10th Floor
New York, New York 10003
U.S.A.
Telephone: (646) 290-5445
Fax: (646) 349-5999
Web site: http://www.corp.kaltura.com

Private Company
Founded: 2006
Employees: 250 (2013 est.)
Sales: $100 million (2013 est.)
NAICS: 511210 Software Publishers

■ ■ ■

Kaltura Inc. designs and distributes software that allows content owners and publishers to create and post video content on the Internet. Kaltura's video platform comes with a number of desirable features, including various ways to charge for video content and analyze video consumption. The company offers its software in both an open-source format, which allows users to access its programming code and create their own applications, and a commercial format administered and managed by the Kaltura team. Kaltura video software is used on approximately 300,000 Web sites.

ORIGINS OF THE KALTURA TEAM

The four entrepreneurs who founded Kaltura Inc. were no strangers to the world of tech start-ups. All were young Israelis in their mid-30s who had already found success in various sectors of their country's information technology industry, which was experiencing something of a boom during the early years of the 21st century. Besides a high level of industry savvy, the company's founders brought solid academic credentials and practical experience in the Israeli military to the table when they decided to combine forces in early 2006. The mix of experience and drive would bring Kaltura to the forefront of the Internet video market within just a few years.

Ron Yekutiel, who would become the company's CEO, was a former military helicopter pilot. He and Dr. Shay David, Kaltura's financial chief, had previously worked together to found Destinator Technologies, a GPS software company. After selling the company to Canadian tech company Intrynsic, David and Yekutiel decided to enter the entrepreneurial arena once again with another start-up. To create a viable company that would eventually have resale potential, they would have to find a market niche that was either underserved or ripe with potential for reinvention.

The other portion of the Kaltura team consisted of its president, Dr. Michal Tsur, who had founded the Internet security firm Cyota in collaboration with a former Israeli minister of the economy in 1999, and chief technical officer Eran Etam, who had helped create ICQ, the first instant messaging system, in 1996. All four founders had seen firsthand the revenue potential of developing a company from scratch and then selling to the highest bidder when it attained a strong presence in the marketplace.

EXAMINING MARKET TRENDS

Destinator had sold for around $16 million while Cyota brought its owners around $145 million when it sold to Massachusetts-based RSA Security just six years after its founding. Etam had seen Mirabilis, the company that owned ICQ, purchased by AOL for some $400 million just two years after its founding. With these successes still fresh in their minds, Yekutiel, David, Etam, and Tsur came together in 2006 to brainstorm and attempt to identify emerging tech trends with the greatest market potential.

The sessions generated a wide variety of ideas centered on both hardware and software. One early idea involved an Internet-connected helmet for drivers. This was quickly put aside for a number of reasons, foremost of which was the partners' desire to create something with a wide range of applications, rather than a single product. Also, the partners wanted their company to embody a general philosophy that they, and a large portion of the Internet community, saw as the wave of the future and a path to innovation and discovery.

CONCEPT CREATED: 2006

"We knew what we wanted to be," Yekutiel told *Globes* news service in 2014. "The subject that interested all of us was pluralism. The Internet trend of empowering the user was just beginning. The best example is Wikipedia and joint writing. At the same time, video was beginning to pick up."

The four entrepreneurs had become fascinated by the open-source philosophy that had swept through the tech field during the preceding years. Web applications that allowed users to add or modify content as a collaborative effort with other users had been tagged with the term *wiki*, from the Hawaiian word for "quick." The Wikipedia Web site, and others like it, allowed users to write, update, and edit reference articles on a seemingly infinite variety of topics. The result was an exhaustive source of information created and fine-tuned by many, many hands.

OPEN-SOURCE EXPLORED

Open-source software reflected the same general principles. Under the open-source model, programming code for a particular application is made available to the general public, which is encouraged to improve and expand it. In this way, the software has the talents and imaginations of millions of potential programmers available to help it reach its potential, rather than just a finite group of employees. The Kaltura team decided that an open-source paradigm could give their new project an almost limitless potential to spread through the marketplace.

The other tech trend the Kaltura team had noticed was the increasing prevalence of video on the Web. Over the previous decade, dial-up services had given way to nearly ubiquitous high-speed Internet and video processors in home computing hardware, which had become faster and more sophisticated. The result was an increase in the popularity of video content on the World Wide Web. Internet users were increasingly using their computers like televisions. The team sensed that the near future would bring a demand for more sophisticated and user-friendly video technology.

The founders initially crafted their product as a combination of Wikipedia and the video-upload site, YouTube. Users could upload video clips, which would become more or less communal property for collaborative projects. A user could propose a video collage of the best hiking trails around San Francisco, for example. Other users could then upload their own clips and edit a presentation collaboratively, like a Wikipedia article. A family of tourists could create a video album souvenir of their trip from their individual cell phones or camcorder videos.

DEBUT AND REFINEMENT: 2007

Under their new company name Kaltura, a variation on the word *culture*, designed to evoke the team's pluralistic philosophy, the partners debuted the new platform at TechCrunch40, an invitational showcase and competition for tech start-ups, held in San Francisco in September 2007. By this point, the company had set up shop in Brooklyn, New York, in order to be closer to the U.S. media and tech markets. Kaltura began with about 20 employees and initial funding of a little over $2 million in investment capital from a combination of small investors and California venture capital firm Avalon Ventures.

KEY DATES

2006: Company is founded.
2009: Kaltura begins distributing platform in Japan.
2010: Company releases commercialized version of platform.
2012: European operations are expanded.
2014: Company acquires television services provider Tvinci.

Although the TechCrunch event promised a high-profile opportunity to show off Kaltura's flagship product, the debut did not go as planned. After arriving late for the sign-up portion of the event, the Kaltura team found that all the available presentation slots had been filled. The only way to enter the competition was a write-in process. Thinking fast, Yekutiel hired an off-duty bartender on the spot to make the rounds at the convention, lobbying attendees to vote Kaltura into the competition.

It worked. Kaltura left the conference with the People's Choice Award, based on the votes they had generated from other participants. Once Kaltura had introduced its platform to the marketplace, the next step was to put together a business plan that would generate profit. Yekutiel and his team first focused on advertising. Kaltura could feature its own advertising on sites or apps it directly controlled, like its home Web site and its Facebook application. It could also license the video software to other Web site developers and app engineers and take a share of their advertising revenues as part of the licensing fee.

WIKIPEDIA PARTNERSHIP: 2008

In January 2008 Kaltura moved to the forefront of the Web video revolution when it announced a partnership with one of its primary inspirations, the Wikipedia Web site. Wikipedia, which had built one of the world's largest bodies of information by allowing users to collaborate on text-based articles, would soon allow users to construct video content as well, using the Kaltura platform.

It was at this point that Kaltura officially made its source code open to the public. This partnership, along with several smaller deals, attracted another round of venture funding for Kaltura, primarily from the Boston-based .406 Ventures firm, in June 2008. Near the end of 2008 Kaltura struck another high-profile deal when it

partnered with New York's WNET, one of the country's most prestigious public television stations.

WNET was to provide the software for Talk to Us, a feature on the station's Web site that allowed viewers to upload video commentary and criticism of programming. Less than a month later, the company partnered with the popular blogging site Wordpress to add a video uploading and editing plug-in to the platform. In little over a year, Kaltura had gone from an intriguing concept with growing industry buzz to a high-profile media presence.

GLOBAL EXPANSION

During 2009 Kaltura focused on expanding its Web presence and refining its business model. While advertising continued to bring in money, the company began to focus on generating revenue through support and maintenance services on its commercial accounts. While the basic Kaltura software remained free and open-sourced, commercial Web sites that hosted the platform were usually willing to pay Kaltura to maintain the software and provide support services.

Kaltura engineers helped integrate their software into the site's existing framework and business model and monitor its performance over time. For these services, the company collected a monthly maintenance fee, as well as service charges for special requests and projects. As 2009 ended and 2010 began, the company started to expand its operations globally. First came a partnership with Japan's Digital Advertising Consortium that began integrating Kaltura software into Japanese Web sites. Soon after, Kaltura entered the European market, signing a deal with German Internet service provider Nacamar.

In May 2010 the company released a commercial version of its software that allowed Web sites to create their own video materials and control content and access. Customers could even create video content for sale. Besides its geographical expansion and its foray into the commercial video market, Kaltura had also begun establishing its presence in the educational world, designing video applications for use by colleges and other institutions. By the end of 2010 the Massachusetts Institute of Technology's TechTV online video service was running Kaltura software. Harvard and Yale Universities soon signed up as customers.

NEXUS VENTURE CAPITAL

The latest round of growth also brought another round of funding. In February 2011, $20 million in venture capital came in from new investor Nexus Venture partners, as well as old partners .406 Ventures and Avalon Ventures. In April 2011 Kaltura inked a deal with Fox Digital Media to provide online video services for nearly all of the broadcasting giant's Web sites.

July of the same year brought a major coup in another market sector as the company partnered with Blackboard Inc. to create video software for the widely used educational tool, Blackboard Learning System. Near the end of the year, Kaltura brought in another $25 million in investment funding, this time led by Japanese firm Mitsui & Co. Global Investment Ltd. The company was serving some 150,000 commercial customers, bringing in around $65 million annually. *Forbes* magazine named Kaltura one of the six fastest-growing tech companies in the nation.

LOOKING AHEAD

Kaltura continued to grow over the next several years. By this point, the company had left its Spartan start-up headquarters in Brooklyn for an upscale suite of offices on Park Avenue South, near Manhattan's Union Square. Having made significant inroads into the media and educational market sectors, Kaltura turned to providing in-house video platforms for businesses, colleges, and other organizations. Clients such as Bank of America and New York University used the company's MediaSpace software to communicate and share content with employees in a controlled manner.

With its three-pronged market approach, providing services for media, educational, and in-house, or "enterprise," use, Kaltura's client list quickly passed the 200,000 mark. The company had around 200 employees, split between the New York headquarters, engineers working in Israel, and its European headquarters in London. In 2012 the company began an accelerated European expansion, naming former vice president of strategy Leah Belsky as its European general manager.

Kaltura's European division serviced the same mix of clientele, including such commercial entities as Nestlé and AstraZeneca, as well as educational institutions Danish State University and Durham University. After turning a profit for the first time in 2013, Kaltura began 2014 with one more round of financing. A group of

investors led by SAP Ventures, Nokia, and Intel added another $47 million to the company's coffers. Kaltura's latest offering was MediaGo, a self-contained Video-on-Demand platform that could be used to stream ad-supported video content on any mobile device.

TVINCI ACQUISITION: 2014

As if to emphasize the company's commitment to MediaGo, Kaltura made its first major corporate acquisition in May 2014. The company purchased Israeli video services provider Tvinci, and it immediately began integrating its software with the MediaGo platform. By the middle of 2014 Kaltura's founders had begun openly speculating about the possibility of taking the company public. Tsur told *Globes* in April 2014 that an initial public offering would happen within 18 to 24 months.

More cautious, Yekutiel would only call it "a definite possibility." The company definitely seemed ripe for profitable sale, with a customer list topping 300,000 clients, revenues growing by 50 percent annually and approaching $100 million, and a clear commitment to staying ahead of the curve in both technology and business philosophy.

Chris Herzog

PRINCIPAL COMPETITORS

Brightcove Inc.; Ooyala Inc.; thePlatform for Media Inc.

FURTHER READING

Goldenberg, Roy. "Kaltura Aims to Be World's Biggest Technology Co." *Globes: Israel's Business News*, April 22, 2014.

Lagorio-Chafkin, Christine. "How Kaltura Went from Free-Spirited Collaboration Tool to the Future of Online Video." http://www.inc.com/christine-lagorio/kaltura-openness-and-growth.html.

Orpaz, Inbal, and Orr Hirschauge. "Israeli Start-Up Kaltura Raises $47 Million in Funding." *Haaretz*, February 11, 2014.

Pozin, Ilya. "How to Avoid Being a Startup Failure." *Forbes*, February 11, 2014.

Shamah, David. "Kaltura Raises Major Funds, Poised for 'Something Big.'" *Times of Israel*, February 16, 2014.

Keria SA

■

4 rue Tropiques
Echirolles, 38130
France
Telephone: (+33 4) 76 22 93 93
Fax: (+33 4) 76 23 12 00
Web site: http://www.keria.fr

Private Company
Founded: 1982
Employees: 550
Sales: EUR 250 million ($325 million) (2010)
NAICS: 442299 All Other Home Furnishings Stores

■ ■ ■

Keria SA is a family-owned operator of retail concepts focused on the lighting, furniture, and home furnishings sectors. The Grenoble-based company is the French leader in the lighting category, with more than 90 Keria Luminaires stores and 50 Laurie Lumière stores. In addition to offering a full range of home and office lamps and light fixtures, the company is also a leading supplier of lighting solutions to the hotel, restaurant, and other sectors. With the purchase of Newco in 2011, Keria has branched out into retail furniture franchising concepts.

The company's L'Inventaire is France's leading discount furniture specialist, selling remaindered and end-of-stock furniture, as well as specially selected furniture imported from Asia. In 2014 there were more than 50 Inventaire franchises. Another franchise network, Tousalon, focuses on sofas and other seating for the home, with more than 30 franchise stores

operating throughout France. The company's youngest franchise is Place de la Literie, a bedding specialist, with more than 20 franchise stores. The company also operates the small home decoration and furnishings chain Maison & Reflet. Altogether, Keria operates more than 250 stores, including shops in Switzerland and Spain. The company expects to expand to more than 400 stores by 2016.

GROCERY ORIGINS IN THE SIXTIES

Marcel Barbe founded Keria SA in 1982. He had already built up a strong career in France's growing chain retail industry. France's retail industry was by then undergoing a major evolution. Retailing in the country had traditionally been the province of small, independent shops, supplied by a network of wholesalers, or directly by largely local manufacturers.

The appearance of modern supermarkets in the 1950s, and then large-scale, department-style hypermarkets in the late 1960s, represented the first step toward the development of large-scale regional and national retail groups. Barbe started his own career in the supermarket sector, at first developing a chain of groceries.

Competition in that sector became especially fierce into the beginning of the 1970s, however, as a number of leaders, including Carrefour, E. LeClerc, Auchan, and Casino, rose to dominate the industry. In the meantime, the so-called big-box specialty retailing format, first developed in the United States, had begun to reach France and elsewhere in Europe.

KEY DATES

1982: Marcel Barbe founds Keria Luminaires as a specialist retail of lamps and lighting fixtures.

1989: Barbe's sons Frédéric and Christian join the company.

1997: Keria opens its first store in Paris.

2002: Company acquires Paris-based Cailleau and opens a store in Switzerland.

2008: Company acquires main French rival Laurie Lumière.

2011: Keria acquires Newco and its franchise brands Inventaire, Tousalon, Place de la Literie, and Maison & Reflet.

2013: Company stops development of the Maison & Reflet chain.

"CATEGORY KILLERS" DEBUT

This new style of store, also became known as "category killers" for their focus on a single product category, were able to emulate the high-volume purchasing approach of the large-scale supermarket groups, which enabled these companies to prosper despite often razor-thin margins. The new style of retailing also offered the potential for building national retail networks through another recently imported retailing concept, franchising.

Faced with competition in the grocery industry, Barbe sold his original business, and instead decided to invest in developing his own high-volume retailing format. For this, Barbe chose the furniture sector, then undergoing its own transformation in parallel with other branches of the French retailing industry. One of the major innovations in the sector was the growth of the flat-pack market, that is, furniture manufactured to be assembled by the customer, a market made most notorious by the rise of Swedish furniture juggernaut Ikea.

FROM FURNITURE TO CLOTHING

This new method of selling furniture, which permitted furniture to be more easily transported and warehoused than traditional furniture, became responsible for introducing new segments in France's furniture industry. Furniture in France had previously been highly traditional, both in design and fabrication. The flat-pack market, which also made use of new materials and production methods, became especially associated with a more youthful, design-oriented but lower-cost furniture market.

Traditional furniture retailers focused on fully built, solid wood furniture, with a reliance on classic and old-fashioned designs. At the same time, a new breed of fashion-forward, design-oriented retailers developed, focusing largely on the high-end sector. The early 1970s saw the growth of the first retail furniture chains as well.

Among these was Mobilier Européen, a company originally founded as a window and fittings manufacturer in Alsace in the 1920s by Joseph Rapp. In the 1950s Rapp moved into furniture distribution and began building the their first retail furniture format in 1964. In 1969 the family opened a logistics platform, as they began developing a new generation of retail furniture and home furnishings stores. The company introduced its first retail format, Atlas, in 1973.

BARBE AIDS ATLAS GROWTH

Barbe played an early role in the growth of the Atlas chain. Barbe had opened his own chain of stores, under the name "Barbe" in Grenoble. He soon teamed up with Mobilier Européen, changing the names of his stores to the Atlas signage. Barbe also became one of the pioneers of Mobilier Européen's most successful format, Fly, which grew into one of France's leading youth-market retail furniture retail chains. In 1975, however, Barbe sold his furniture stores to the Rapp family.

His interest turned to another bustling French retailing market, textiles. Clothing retailing was in the process of undergoing its own revolution, with the rise of designer clothing labels on the one hand, and the rapid expansion of low-priced and youth-oriented clothing on the other. Barbe spotted the opportunity for adapting the large-scale supermarket format for the retail sector and developed two retail clothing formats through the end of the 1970s.

LIGHTING ON A NICHE IN 1982

By the early 1980s, however, Barbe had become disenchanted with the retail clothing sector, as competition among the fast-growing numbers of retail clothing brands became particularly intense. Barbe began searching for his next retailing adventure. One day, while reading the newspaper, Barbe came across the mention of lighting as an underserved retailing sector.

Barbe researched the market and recognized the opportunity for building a specialist chain of stores focused on the sale of light fixtures, lamps, and related furnishings and equipment. Barbe opened the first Keria Luminaire store in 1982. Barbe's intuition had been correct, and with little competition, the company developed rapidly through the decade. By the beginning of the

1990s Keria had already captured the leading in France's retail lighting segment.

Barbe had been joined by his sons Frédéric and Christian. Both came to the company with their own strong background in retailing, having previously struck out on their own to build a national chain of 45 furniture stores. The furniture sector, which had developed strongly through the 1980s, had begun to run out of steam by then. The collapse of the building market at the end of the 1980s meant fewer new homes to decorate.

IKEA BRINGS COMPETITION

At the same time, the relatively long replacement rate for home furniture, and especially living room furniture at as long as 15 years, predicted a period of slow growth for the industry. At the same time, smaller furniture chains were under increasing pressure from the arrival of Ikea in France, as well as strong growth of the Fly chain, and the rapid expansion of such discount furniture and home furnishings groups as But and Castorama.

The Barbe brothers joined their father therefore in building the Keria business. This chain too had come under pressure, as a number of new rivals appeared into the 1990s. In order to differentiate itself, the company set out to revamp its image in 1990.

Recognizing that its core clientele, as well as 85 percent of its sales force, were women, the company brought in a female designer to restyle the stores to provide a more feminine atmosphere. The company's marketing campaigns also developed a more feminine touch, employing such celebrities as Spanish actress Victoria Abril to promote the Keria brand.

ADAPTING TO THE NEW CENTURY

Keria found itself confronted by a new type of competitor, as the country's do-it-yourself centers, including such national champions as Castorama and Leroy Merlin, began to expand beyond their original hardware focus to become full-fledged home decoration centers. As part of this evolution, the stores developed their own lighting departments. By the second half of the decade these two chains had captured the lead of the French lighting sector.

Other rivals also began to appear, notably a number of self-standing lighting shops operated by E. Leclerc and other hypermarket chains. Keria responded by engaging a more aggressive expansion strategy through the decade. By 1997 the company had expanded its network to 40 stores, including its first store in Paris,

opened in 1997. The company also began expanding its range of references to as many as 8,000 per store.

This permitted the group to featuring a wider price spread, positioning its products from the low- to mid-end of the lighting market. Into the next decade the company's product offerings swelled even higher, reaching as many as 15,000 items. Keria continued its expansion through the turn of the century, building up a network of more than 80 stores.

RECESSION BRINGS CHALLENGES

With claims to a 20 percent share of the French lighting market, the company had also strengthened its position as the leading independent lighting specialist. The company was nonetheless forced to confront the new realities of the market. Like most of the retail sector, Keria was hit by the sharp recession at the beginning of the decade. The introduction of the euro, and the perception of rising prices, helped further cool French consumer behavior.

In response to these pressures, the Barbe family brought in investors for the first time, selling 20 percent of the group to investment group Siparex for EUR 3 million. With Frédéric Barbe taking the leadership of the company, Keria began adapting to the market. The company streamlined its product offerings, trimming its catalog from 15,000 to just 10,000 items.

Keria also sought to reduce its reliance on the lighting category by expanding its product offerings to include a wider variety of home furnishing and home decoration products. Into the middle of the decade, these products represented as much as one-third of the company's total product offerings.

This effort was led by Barbe's younger sister Aurélie Hours, who joined the company with husband Sébastien Hours in 2004. Brother Christian Barbe died in 2003. Aurélie Hours also led a new revamp of the Keria store format. Among other features, the group's stores were rearranged into several "universes," each reproducing the ambiance of a particular theme or part of a home.

SWISS ENTRY IN 2002

Keria's expansion efforts sought out new horizons during the decade as well. The company made its first acquisition, of Paris-based Cailleau, in 2002. This company operated franchises under the Tousalon and Inventaire furniture formats, as well as its own chain of lighting stores, adding a total of 15 stores to Keria's network. At first, Keria sought to develop both the Keria and Cailleau chains, with each serving a different market segment.

This plan ran aground amid the growing morosity of the French lighting sector, in which the average annual lighting cost barely reached EUR 20 per person per year. The two chains also had a number of overlapping locations. Keria soon abandoned its dual-format approach, shutting down the nine Cailleau shops. This left the company with the six franchised stores, including four Inventaire and two Tousalon stores.

Tousalon, which specialized in sofas and seating, was one of France's earliest franchised furniture chains, having been founded in 1976. Keria's difficulties with the Cailleau acquisition also put the brakes on another expansion effort. Hoping to leverage the success of its stores in Granges-Paccot and elsewhere along the Swiss border, the company decided to enter that market at the beginning of the decade.

The Swiss market also held promise, in that the Swiss perceived lighting fixtures as an integral part of home decoration, which tended to generate higher annual spending rates, both in Switzerland and in France. The Swiss annual lighting expenditure represented more than five times that of the French market. The Etoy, Switzerland, store failed at first to live up to its promise, not turning a profit until 2005. With the company's attention further taken up by its troubled Cailleau acquisition, however, Keria put its further expansion into Switzerland on hold. The company did not open its second store there, in Geneva, until 2007.

NEWCO ACQUISITION IN 2011

Keria had not given up on its expansion, however. Through the end of the decade the company continued to open new stores, raising its total to 90, including its first stores in Belgium and Spain, by 2011. In the meantime, the company had completed two new acquisitions. The first of these came in 2008 with the purchase of Keria's largest rival in the French independent lighting sector, Laurie Lumière.

That acquisition gave the company its second national chain of lighting stores. The Laurie network, which counted 57 stores, was also complementary to Keria's own network. In 2010 the company bought out Siparex, restoring 100 percent control of the company to the Barbe family. By then, Keria's annual sales had topped EUR 110 million ($135 million).

In the meantime, Keria's small Inventaire and Tousalon franchise operations brought the company into contact with the operator of those formats, Newco. Newco had been founded in 1997 by Philippe Malbran, who had served as the CEO of Tousalon since 1995.

Newco operated purely as a developer of franchise concepts, providing purchasing, marketing, and logistics support to retailers in its franchise network. The company introduced its own format, Maison & Reflet, combining home decoration and furniture, with an emphasis on imports of Asian and other exotic furniture. In 1999 Newco purchased the up-and-coming Inventaire group, with 10 stores focused on sales of end-of-stock and remaindered furniture.

INTRODUCES EMBARCADÈRE: 2005

The company then introduced a second home decoration and furniture concept, this time specializing in exotic furniture, called Embarcadère. By 2005 Newco operations neared 125 franchised stores. Newco folded the Embarcadère format into its larger Inventaire stores in 2007. The company then filled the gap in its portfolio with the creation of a new brand specializing in beds and bedding called Place de la Litérie.

Keria's relationship with Newco, and its own furniture franchise operation, inspired the company to set out a new strategy into the beginning of the decade. Keria sought to redefine itself as a full-range supplier of home furnishings. To this end, the company reached an agreement with Malbran to buy Newco and its various franchise formats.

TARGETING 400 STORES BY 2016

Keria set to work revitalizing Newco's formats, most of which had run out of steam amid the global economic crisis at the end of the decade. The company focused its attention particularly on the Tousalon brand. At its height in the 1980s that brand had operated 100 stores throughout France. By the time of its acquisition by Keria, the Tousalon network had shrunk back to just 32 stores. Keria announced plans to invest in new growth for the network, with a target of 60 stores by the middle of the decade.

The group also announced a major refurbishment of the Inventaire chain, which by then represented 50 locations. While maintaining Inventaire's identity as a discount furniture supplier, the company set out to revitalize its offering with more contemporary furniture designs. To this end, Keria began developing a network of manufacturers in Asia, in order to supply its wholesale warehouse.

Franchisees could then buy directly from the company, placing orders as small as a single item of furniture. Keria also sought to revitalize the flagging Maison & Reflet chain, which barely topped 10 stores after more than a decade. The company redeveloped the chain's home decorations and home furnishing offerings.

This effort proved unsuccessful, however, and in November 2013 Keria announced it would no longer be developing the format. Despite this failure, Keria itself remained optimistic, as its sales jumped to EUR 250 million. The company also appeared on track to reach its goal of expanding its retail empire to 400 stores by 2016. This would place Keria among France's retail leaders in the early 21st century.

M. L. Cohen

PRINCIPAL SUBSIDIARIES

L'Inventaire SA; Tousalon SA.

PRINCIPAL DIVISIONS

Lamps; Furniture; Home Furnishings.

PRINCIPAL OPERATING UNITS

Keria Luminaires; L'Inventaire du Mobilier; Maison & Reflet; Place de la Literie; Tousalon.

PRINCIPAL COMPETITORS

Bois et Chiffons International S.A.; But International S.A.S.; Castorama France SASU; Conforama Holding S.A.; EuroCave S.A.; FinEuroCave S.A.; GiFi S.A.; Habitat France SASU; Meubles Ikea France S.N.C.; Neuftex S.A.S.; Sodice Expansion S.A.

FURTHER READING

Bray, Florence. "Le Groupe Keria Parie sur une Politique Multienseigne." *LSA*, April 29, 2011.

Guertchakoff, Serge. "Luminaires: La Tension Monte." *PME Magazine*, November 30, 2007.

"Keria Nouveau Logo, Nouveau Concept." *Logo News*, November 20, 2012.

Leroux, Olivia. "Maison et Reflet Stoppe Son Développement." *Franchise Magazine*, November 5, 2013.

———. "Tousalon Entame Sa Reconquête du Territoire." *Franchise Magazine*, July 11, 2011.

———. "Un Nouveau Concept pour Place de la Litérie." *Franchise Magazine*, February 8, 2012.

Leroy, Florence. "Une Famille aux Multiples Talents." *Dynamique Commercial*, January 2011.

"Newco Décline ses Concepts avec Succès." *Dynamique Commercial*, May 2005.

"Newco Équipe l'Ensemble de la Maison en se Mettant à la Literie. ..." *Dynamique Commercial*, January–February 2007.

Serraz, Gabrielle. "Siparex Laisse la Famille Fondatrice Seule à la Barre de Keria." *Les Echos*, August 13, 2010.

KVH Industries Inc.

50 Enterprise Center
Middletown, Rhode Island 02842-5268
U.S.A.
Telephone: (401) 847-3327
Fax: (401) 849-0045
Web site: http://www.kvh.com

Public Company
Incorporated: 1982 as Sailcomp Industries
Employees: 471
Sales: $162.29 million (2013)
Stock Exchanges: NASDAQ
Ticker Symbol: KVHI
NAICS: 334220 Radio and Television Broadcasting and
Wireless Communications Equipment Manufacturing; 517919 All Other Telecommunications

■■■

Headquartered in Middletown, Rhode Island, KVH Industries Inc. is a leading company within the satellite industry. KVH's offerings, which include TracPhone satellite communications systems, TracVision satellite television systems, and the mini-VSAT broadband network, provide satellite-based voice, television, and high-speed Internet services. KVH's customers use the company's services on land, as well as in the air and at sea. Additionally, KVH also manufactures navigational sensors and integrated inertial systems used in applications such as defense and commercial guidance and stabilization. Beyond the company's Rhode Island headquarters, KVH operates subsidiaries in Illinois,

Belgium, Bermuda, Brazil, Cyprus, Denmark, Japan, the Netherlands, Norway, Singapore, and the United Kingdom.

EARLY YEARS

KVH Industries traces its roots back to 1982 when Arent, Robert, and Martin Kits van Heyningen established Sailcomp Industries and introduced the PC202, the first digital compass for racing sailboats. As the company's offerings expanded beyond sailboats, the owners changed Sailcomp's name to KVH Industries in 1985, and the company reincorporated in Delaware in August.

In 1987 KVH unveiled the first commercial digital fluxgate compass for use in powerboats, followed by the first self-contained digital compass and display system in 1988. It also was in 1988 that KVH Industries began supplying the U.S. Navy with military versions of the company's digital compass. KVH rounded out the 1980s by introducing a handheld compass/rangefinder named DataScope in 1989.

KVH began the 1990s by introducing tactical navigation systems that the U.S. military incorporated into land vehicles during the Persian Gulf War. Referred to as TACNAV, the systems were developed through the combination of auto calibration and sensor technologies. These provided on-board navigation for vehicles such as tanks and armored personnel carriers. After acquiring Danaplus A/S in 1992, KVH expanded its global footprint by forming a sales and marketing office near Copenhagen, Denmark.

TRACVISION SYSTEM INTRODUCED

Product offerings continued to grow when the company introduced its TracVision satellite television system in 1994, followed by the TACNAV magnetic compass the following year. KVH ended 1995 with revenues of $14.15 million, up from $8.57 million in 1994 and $7.15 million in 1993. By the middle of the decade the company's TracVision system allowed customers to receive DirecTV and USSB satellite television service at sea.

In addition, the company positioned itself to produce mobile satellite television systems for maritime use via an agreement with American Mobile Satellite Corp. KVH's customer base included the likes of Westinghouse Electric Corp., Mitsubishi Electric Corp., Raytheon Marine Corp., and General Motors. Additionally, KVH served the U.S. Department of Defense and armed forces in the Middle East and Europe. A major development occurred in 1996 when KVH made its initial public offering and began trading on the NASDAQ under the ticker symbol KVHI.

Early the following year the company made further inroads into the defense sector when it received a $3.3 million contract to supply the Canadian Army with TACNAV systems for armored personnel carriers. The company was awarded the new business after completing a $2.6 million contract to equip Canadian armed reconnaissance vehicles with TACNAV systems. By this time the Swedish government had purchased nearly $10 million of TACNAV systems for its army's armored vehicle fleet.

NEW MILLENNIUM SUCCESS

KVH continued to find success with its TACNAV system in 2000. That year, the company received an award to equip the United Kingdom's armored vehicles with the technology. This was followed by a $4.7 million, two-year contract for the systems from an unnamed Southeast Asian country. It also was in 2000 that

KVH partnered with Crossbow Technology to develop a next-generation measurement device that replaced mechanical gyro systems. This involved the combination of Crossbow's dynamic measurement unit technology with KVH's fiber-optic technology.

Another breakthrough occurred in 2000 when KVH partnered with the National Football League (NFL) and Sportsvision Inc. on the development of the computerized "1st and 10" system, which displayed a yellow first-down line on television screens during game broadcasts. This allowed viewers to determine if a player had crossed the first-down marker. KVH's role in the partnership involved its fiber-optic gyro, which offset routine stadium vibrations to stabilize the yellow line.

By 2001 KVH's research and development initiatives were concentrating on projects in areas such as mobile broadband and photonic fiber, which was a next-generation optical fiber. To generate funding, the company completed the placement of 1.54 million shares of its common stock with institutional investors during the early part of the year, generating $10 million.

New international markets emerged in mid-2001 when KVH received regulatory approval in Russia to market the company's Tracphone 25 and 50 mobile satellite phone systems for maritime use. This also set the stage for the company to do business in several other Baltic countries. KVH rounded out 2001 by naming S. Joseph Bookataub, formerly an executive with the San Jose, California–based optical networking company, Mayan Networks, as chief operating officer.

RANKED AS LEADER: 2002

By the middle part of 2002 the company ranked as the leading provider of in-motion satellite television service for the coach, recreational vehicle, and trucking markets. That year, the luxury bus conversion manufacturer, Featherlite Inc., announced that it would make KVH's TracVision L3 in-motion satellite TV system standard equipment on its 2003 model year coaches. Additionally, the company would offer KVH's Tracphone 252 satellite telephone and TracNet mobile high-speed Internet system as optional equipment.

Around the same time, the company benefited from a contract from L-3 Communications Corporation, worth approximately $1 million, for its digital signal processing fiber-optic systems. New product introductions continued in 2003 as KVH unveiled what it described as the world's very first satellite TV system for cars, capable of receiving programming from DirecTV. In 2004 the company benefited from a $730,000 Small Business Innovative Research grant, in connection with its work with ActiveFiber technology.

KEY DATES

1982: Arent, Robert, and Martin Kits van Heyningen establish Sailcomp Industries and introduce the first digital compass for racing sailboats.

1985: Sailcomp's name changes to KVH Industries and the company reincorporates in Delaware.

1996: KVH makes its initial public offering and begins trading on the NASDAQ under the ticker symbol KVHI.

2007: Company launches its mini-VSAT broadband satellite communications network.

2013: KVH spends $24 million to acquire the media and entertainment services company Headland Media Limited.

MILITARY SUCCESS

By the middle of the decade, KVH had benefited from the sale of its TACNAV systems to the U.S. military, which used the technology for operations in both Afghanistan and Iraq. In addition to the U.S. Army, the company also sold the systems to the U.S. Navy and Marine Corps. Beyond the United States, countries such as Germany, Australia, New Zealand, Italy, Taiwan, Malaysia, and Saudi Arabia also had purchased the systems for use in their nations' military vehicles.

In 2005 KVH introduced a marine satellite TV system called TracVision M3, which the company claimed to be the smallest of its kind. That year, the research firm Frost & Sullivan awarded KVH with a Market Leadership Award in connection with its TracVision A5 technology, which had pioneered automotive satellite television. The technology also had received other recognition, including being named a finalist for *Automotive News*'s PACE award.

It also was in 2005 that KVH provided fiber-optic gyros to robot designers from Carnegie Mellon University, which were used as part of the guidance system needed to compete in the Defense Advanced Research Project Agency's Grand Challenge. This involved navigating driverless Hummers over 175 miles in the Mojave Desert.

JOHN MADDEN HELPS PR

Early the following year the company partnered with technology leader Microsoft to provide in-motion, high-speed Internet access and MSN TV service on boats.

The company's Mobile Internet Receiver allowed passengers to access services such as MSN Mail, MSN Radio, and MSN Video, and also provided a Wi-Fi network for any Internet-ready device.

KVH benefited from some public relations exposure when NFL broadcaster John Madden partnered with the company to equip his motor coach, the Madden Cruiser, with the company's equipment. This gave Madden access to satellite TV, phone, and Internet on the road. Madden traveled more than 100,000 miles annually in the vehicle, and the company's technology gave his vehicle the ability to function as a mobile office, enabling Madden to prepare for upcoming games via access to high-definition DirecTV game broadcasts.

LAUNCHES MINI-VSAT NETWORK

The company made more inroads in the recreational vehicle sector in early 2007 when it established a relationship with the national dealership, Lazydays. After becoming an independent KVH dealer, Lazydays began providing customers with live satellite TV and high-definition TV through the company's TracVision antennas, as well as TracNet mobile Internet service. That year, the company also launched its mini–very small aperture terminal (VSAT) broadband satellite communications network, offering customers coverage throughout North America, Europe, and the Caribbean.

VSAT terminals used small satellite stations on Earth to send and receive data via satellite. More breakthroughs took place in 2008 when KVH introduced the TracVision M1, which it claimed was the smallest stabilized marine satellite television system in the world. In addition, a customer in the airline industry awarded KVH with a $20 million contract to design and produce a commercial aircraft antenna. Additionally, the company shipped its 150,000 mobile satellite antenna that year, followed by its 25,000th fiber-optic gyro in 2009. Growth within the company's defense business occurred in 2009 when $1.3 million in TACNAV orders were received from three undisclosed international defense contractors.

Additionally, two leading defense contractors also ordered $10.2 million worth of the company's fiber-optic gyros, which were needed to equip remote stabilized weapon stations. Internationally, the company established a distribution agreement with Japan Radio Co. Ltd., which began distributing its products for maritime use. In 2010 KVH acquired the Norway-based software company, Virtek Communications AS.

The $6.5 million deal gave KVH access to software technology that helped maritime vessel and commercial fleet owners manage data transmitted to and from vessels via different satellite communications services. That year, the company also received a $1.1 million contract from a leading defense contractor for the use of its fiber-optic gyros in the U.S. Army's Javelin Basic Skills Trainer, which taught soldiers how to use Javelin antitank missile systems.

CONTINUED MILITARY PROGRESS

KVH benefited from the largest TACNAV order in its history, worth $13 million, in 2010. This was followed by a 10-year, $42 million contract from the U.S. Coast Guard to equip as many as 216 cutters with the Trac-Phone V7 system and mini-VSAT broadband service. Another milestone was attained in 2011 when KVH manufactured its 50,000th fiber-optic gyro. More defense-related growth occurred in 2011 when an international customer ordered $3.7 million in TAC-NAV systems for upgrading its light armored vehicles.

In addition to KVH's Middletown, Rhode Island, headquarters, operations had grown to include facilities in Illinois, Singapore, Norway, and Denmark. KVH rounded out 2011 by establishing a new Asia-Pacific headquarters in Singapore. Operating under the name KVH Industries Pte Ltd., the facility provided both customers and industry partners with a state-of-the-art demonstration and training lab for exploring the potential integration of the company's mini-VSAT broadband satellite communications network with various shipboard applications.

In 2012 KVH continued to expand internationally when the company established a new office in Tokyo, Japan, named KVH Industries Japan Co. Ltd. That year, KVH received another record-breaking TACNAV contract, worth $35.6 million. In addition, independent ship manager V.Ships chose the company to serve as its preferred satellite communications provider. The deal involved equipping more than 1,000 vessels with KVH's mini-VSAT enhanced data applications.

NEW TESTING FACILITY

KVH also opened a new testing facility in Middletown in 2012. Located next to its main headquarters building, the testing complex featured a motion simulator that replicated a ship's movements during bad weather. This provided the company with a means of evaluating how well its antennas maintained satellite signal connections.

On the leadership front, CFO Patrick Spratt retired and was succeeded by Peter Rendall. The company rounded out the year by completing a significant upgrade to its mini-VSAT broadband network. This benefited customers in Europe, the Middle East, and the North Africa region by increasing satellite capacity by 60 percent. On the social media front, KVH saw membership on its Crewtoo site, created specifically for mariners, reach the 60,000 mark after only 12 months.

In 2013 KVH spent $24 million to acquire the media and entertainment services company, Headland Media Limited, which provided licensed sports, movies, news, and music content to 1,700 retailers, 1,700 hotels, and 9,600 maritime vessels. The deal gave KVH a platform for creating its own satellite delivery service to provide on-board content services. Headland generated annual revenues of $12.2 million, about 85 percent of which came from subscriptions.

In early 2014 KVH further improved the capacity of its mini-VSAT broadcast network, benefiting maritime customers in the shipping, fishing, and offshore oil-field sectors. The company had experienced significant growth since its formation as a provider of digital compass solutions for racing sailboats during the early 1980s. Moving forward, it appeared that KVH would maintain a position of leadership within its industry for many years to come.

Paul R. Greenland

PRINCIPAL SUBSIDIARIES

KVH Industries A/S (Denmark); KVH Industries Pte. Ltd. (Singapore); KVH Industries Brasil Comunicacao Por Satelite Ltda. (Brazil); KVH Industries Norway AS; KVH Industries Japan Co. Ltd.; KVH Industries U.K. Ltd. (UK); KVH Media Group Ltd. (UK); KVH Media Group Services Ltd. (UK); KVH Media Group Entertainment Ltd. (UK); KVH Media Group Communication Ltd. (UK); KVH Media Group International Ltd. (UK); KVH Media Group Ltd. (Cyprus); Good Morning News Sprl. (Belgium); KVH Media Group ApS (Denmark); KVH Media Group Communication, Inc.; KVH Media Group, Inc.; Rigstream B.V. (Netherlands); Bamboo Option Ltd. (Bermuda).

PRINCIPAL COMPETITORS

Globalstar, Inc.; Iridium Communications Inc.; Northrop Grumman Corporation.

FURTHER READING

"KVH Doubles C-Band Capacity of VSAT Network." *Satellite Today*, January 16, 2014.

"KVH Industries Acquires Headland Media in a $24 Million Deal." *Satellite Today*, May 13, 2013.

"KVH Industries Expands with Japan Office." *Internet Business News*, November 6, 2012.

"KVH Opens New Antenna-Testing Facility in Middletown."

Providence Journal, April 4, 2012.

"Middletown Company Opens Singapore Office." *Providence Journal*, November 1, 2011.

Laird plc

100 Pall Mall
London, SW1Y 5NQ
United Kingdom
Telephone: (+44 20) 7468 4040
Fax: (+44 20) 7839 2921
Web site: http://www.laird-plc.com

Public Company
Incorporated: 1970 as Laird Group
Employees: 10,957
Sales: £537 million ($890.03 million) (2013)
Stock Exchanges: London
Ticker Symbol: LRD
NAICS: 334416 Capacitor, Resistor, Coil, Transformer, and Other Inductor Manufacturing; 334417 Electronic Connector Manufacturing; 334419 Other Electronic Component Manufacturing; 334220 Radio and Television Broadcasting and Wireless Communications Equipment Manufacturing; 334290 Other Communications Equipment Manufacturing

∎∎∎

Laird plc is the world's leading producer of electromagnetic interference (EMI) shielding materials, as well as a leading developer of other performance materials for such applications as thermal management and signal integrity. The company is also a leading supplier of wireless components and systems, including infrastructure antennas, telematic and machine-to-machine systems, and wireless automation and control systems. The group's Performance Materials division is its largest.

BRITISH INDUSTRIAL REVOLUTION ROOTS

Laird Group's roots lay in the early years of the British Industrial Revolution—and at the beginnings of one of England's great shipbuilding empires. The Laird name itself stemmed from William Laird, a Scotsman who founded the Birkenhead Iron Works in partnership with Daniel Horton in order to produce steam boilers in 1824. Four years later, Laird and Horton dissolved their partnership, and Laird was instead joined in business by his son John, creating William Laird & Son.

The Birkenhead works continued making boilers, but under John Laird's leadership branched out into what would become its defining industry, shipbuilding. The younger Laird recognized that the same methods for producing steam boilers could be used in the production of a new type of vessel, the so-called iron ship, which replaced traditional wood hulls with hulls made of iron plate.

The company received its first order, for the production of a paddle-steamer to be used on Ireland's inland lakes and waterways, in 1828. The company delivered this first ship, named the *Wye*, in 1830. Laird & Son quickly proved itself an innovator in the shipbuilding trade, becoming the first to incorporate bulkheads in its designs, while also branching out into the design of more power engines.

BRANCHING OUT

By the mid-1830s Laird & Son had already built its first gunships, and it had also shipped the first iron ship to a U.S. client. Later in the decade the company also became known for another specialty, prefabricated riverboats, which were put into use by many famous British explorers of the day. These included Dr. David Livingstone, whose steamer *Ma-Robert* was built by the company.

John Laird took over the company completely after his father's death in 1842. Laird later brought his own sons, William and John, into the business, which became known as John Laird, Sons and Co. in 1860. The elder John Laird retired the following year. In 1862, after Henry Laird joined his brothers in the business, the company's name changed again, to Laird Brothers.

CAMMELL LAIRD IN 1903

Laird Brothers established itself as one of the United Kingdom's preeminent shipbuilders through the end of the 19th century. The company became an especially important supplier of vessels to the British merchant marine, as well as to the British and other navies. Between 1870 and 1900, the company completed more than 270 merchant ships. Among the company's notable vessels was the ironclad *Alabama*, delivered to the Confederate navy in 1862. Other notable vessels included its line of Cock tugs.

Laird's production at the dawn of the 20th century included armored battleships and torpedo boat destroyers, for the British Royal Navy as well as others, including the Russian, Portuguese, Argentine, and Chilean navies. During this time, the company struck up a partnership with Sheffield-based Charles Cammell and Co., which delivered the armor plating for Laird's vessels.

A Hull native, Charles Cammell had started his business in 1837, initially producing steel files. By the 1860s Cammell's business had greatly expanded, and the company had become a major manufacturer of rails and railway materials. The company's production of armor plating began in 1863. The following year the company incorporated as a limited liability company, and Cammell retired to the position as chairman. Cammell died in 1879.

The relationship between Laird and Cammell proved highly fruitful and led to the companies merging in 1903. The merger had been encouraged by the Royal Navy, which preferred to have its armored vessels built by a single company. Following the merger, the company transferred Cammell's operations in Sheffield to Birkenhead, which became the home of the new Cammell, Laird and Co. Soon after, the company carried out an extensive modernization program, while also significantly expanding its shipyard.

GROWTH THROUGH WORLD WAR I

Cammell, Laird's early years were difficult ones, as the country endured a steep drop in the shipping trade. As a result, the company's shipbuilding business posted losses through most of the rest of the decade. The company also underwent a number of management changes. Following the deaths of the original Laird brothers, their children, including J. Macgregor Laird, Roy M. Laird, and J. W. P Laird, took over as heads of the company. By 1912, however, all three had left the company as well, marking the end of the Laird family's involvement in Cammell, Laird.

Cammell, Laird had developed a new area of business, that of the construction of passenger/cargo liners, particularly for South American operators, and also for the Norwegian-Amerika line, among others. Cammell, Laird had also expanded Cammell's original steel business to include the production of an ever-increasing array of products, ranging from tires and axles, to springs, rails, ammunition, including missiles, as well as boilers, forgings, and castings.

Cammell, Laird contributed significantly to the British war effort during World War I. The company carried out a number of ship conversions, constructed its first seaplane carriers, built submarines, and repaired more than 500 ships. The company also found a ready customer in neutral Norway, for which it built a number of commercial liners and other vessels. Cammell, Laird turned its steelworks to the British cause as well, opening the National Projectile Factory in Nottingham in 1915 and converting another factory in Nottingham, the National Ordnance Factory, in 1917.

POSTWAR GROWTH

In the postwar period, Cammell, Laird received a steady number of orders from the Admiralty for a new class of and 5.5-inch shells, while its shipyards produced nearly 110 destroyers, battleships, submarines, and sloops, and carried out repairs on more than 2,000 ships.

KEY DATES

1824: William Laird founds the Birkenhead Iron Works as a partnership producing steam boilers.
1828: John Laird joins his father and William Laird & Son builds its first iron ship.
1837: Charles Cammell founds a business producing steel files in Sheffield.
1903: Cammell and Laird merge to form Cammell, Laird & Company, one of the British Empire's leading shipbuilders.
1965: Cammell, Laird begins to diversify, acquiring Scottish Aviation.
1970: Industrial Reorganisation Corporation takes over Cammell, Laird and splits it in half, creating the new Laird Group for its non-shipbuilding assets.
2004: Laird enters the wireless systems sector with the acquisition of Centurion Wireless Technologies.
2013: Laird expands its thermal management business with the acquisition of Nextreme Thermal Solutions.

NATIONALIZATION IN THE SEVENTIES

Cammell, Laird continued to produce a limited number of vessels for the British navy following the war. Most of the group's operations, however, focused on the construction of cargo ships and tankers. The company also developed a strong business building passenger ferries. Cammell, Laird also ventured into other markets, notably through its acquisition of Patent Shaft and Axletree Company in 1956. Patent Shaft grew into the United Kingdom's largest private-sector steel plate producer. The company also acquired greater control of Metro-Cammell during this time.

By the mid-1960s, however, the great era of British shipbuilding was clearly on the wane. As the profitability of its shipbuilding operations began to falter, Cammell, Laird began taking steps to diversify its business. The company focused especially on developing its engineering expertise, at first targeting other areas of transport engineering.

To this end, the company acquired Scottish Aviation in 1965, a supplier of both aircraft engines and airframes, as well as aircraft maintenance and other airport services. This purchase was followed by that of British Federal Welder, based in the Midlands, a producer of welding equipment, in 1968. Cammell, Laird also bought out Vickers' remaining share in Metro-Cammell, then in the process of shifting its own business focus from rolling stock to buses and containers.

ACQUIRES SOLAR INDUSTRIES

Another major acquisition completed during this time was Solar Industries, based in Glasgow, active in aerospace engineering, roadway equipment, conveyor systems, and the production of aluminum components, acquired in 1969. This diversification helped buttress Cammell, Laird's slumping shipbuilding business through the decade. By 1970, however, after the cancellation of a major new order, Cammell, Laird was on the ropes, posting a loss of £8.6 million.

The British government stepped in to rescue the company, which was placed under the auspices of the Industrial Reorganisation Corporation (IRC). The IRC promptly split Cammell, Laird into the two companies, the first for the group's struggling shipbuilding operations, and the second, called Laird Group Limited, for its diversified businesses. Laird Group continued to hold

battleships and destroyers. The group's commercial production also soared, and between 1920 and 1930 the company built 44 passenger/cargo liners, cargo ships, and banana boats. Also during the time, Cammell, Laird began producing railroad carriages and other rolling stock, having acquired The Midland Railway Carriage and Co. Ltd. in Birmingham. The company's railroad business expanded strongly, including an order to supply the London Underground.

In 1929 the company agreed to merge its rolling stock business with that of the Metropolitan Company, then owned by Vickers Ltd., creating Metro-Cammell, one of England's leading manufacturers in this market. Cammell, Laird suffered through the early years of the Great Depression and was ultimately forced to shut down its shipyards between 1931 and 1933. The decision by the British Admiralty to accelerate its new ship orders was credited with saving the company.

Through the rest of the decade, the company turned out a steady string of vessels, including a growing number of tankers serving the deepwater and coastal markets. The company once again turned its production in support of the British war effort, converting its Nottingham factory to the production of two-pounder guns a 50 percent stake in Cammell, Laird as well, until this stake was nationalized in 1977.

REBUILDING INTO THE EIGHTIES

The IRC appointed John Gardiner, then 34 years old, to lead the new Laird Group. Gardiner quickly set to work, pulling the group into record profits by 1974. The company struggled again amid the OPEC oil crisis that year, particularly from its ill-timed investment in building two new electric-arc furnaces for its Patent Shaft steel business.

By the end of the decade the company was forced to shut down this business. The company also sold Scottish Aviation to the British government. Laird was already seeing strong growth in its other operations, most notably its transport engineering business. This became the company's largest division into the 1980s, scoring such high-profile contracts as the supply of the trains for the Hong Kong mass-transit railway, as well as the contract to supply all of the London Underground's trains.

Other growing businesses for the group included a business developing long-distance conveyor systems, including one project stretching over 13 miles, and the development and production of high-tech resistance welding equipment. The company also made its first major international acquisition, spending £22 million to acquire U.S.-based New York Twist Drill Corporation in 1980.

Laird also entered the automotive sector, starting with the production of auto-body seals. Through the 1980s automotive components became one of the company's major business areas. Laird built up a number of operations in this area, including Draftex, a German producer of rubber profiles, hoses, and other components with operations in France, Germany, and Spain.

SELLS METRO-CAMMELL: 1989

The shift toward automotive components prompted the company to shed its transport engineering operations, including Metro-Cammell, which it sold in 1989. By the early 1990s Laird's automotive supply businesses were the largest part of its operations. The company's holdings included Vickers, Stanton Rubber, Draftex, and, since its acquisition in 1989, CPIO, formerly part of French automaker Renault. By the end of 1992 Laird's total revenues had grown to £600.7 million ($902 million), generating profits of £20.7 million.

The company continued to expand its automotive business through the decade, acquiring the car body sealing business of Germany's Happich in 1993, and forming a car body sealing joint venture in China, Beijing Wanyuan-Draftex Sealing Products Co. Ltd.

Laird invested heavily in expanding its European operations, notably through a joint venture with Optimit AS to produce extruded seals in Odry, Czech Republic. In 1996 Laird announced plans to enter the North American market, spending $31.5 million on the construction of an extrusions plant in support of a contract to supply components for the Ford Escort.

ELECTRONICS ENTRY IN THE NINETIES

This expansion, however, came even as Laird was preparing to take a new business direction. In 1994 Laird sets its sights on entering the fast-growing electronics engineering sector. For this, the company invested in developing its own electromagnetic interference (EMI) shielding technology. This investment quickly led the company to acquire APM, a company specializing in the production of coated textiles used in EMI shielding, in 1996.

This was to become the first of a string of acquisitions as Laird began building up a portfolio of business focusing on the one hand on EMI shielding and other performance materials, and on the other, on wireless systems technologies. These investments came amid changes in the global automotive supply market, in part driven by the increasing complexity, and modularization, of automobile components themselves. The increasing competitiveness of the automotive sector encouraged Laird to continue its development of its new EMI and other high-technology oriented business lines.

The company began its exit from the automotive sector in October 2000, selling Draftex to GenCorp Inc. for $188 million. The company sold another major part of its automotive division two months later to Trelleborg for $156 million. It then completed its exit soon after, selling its remaining body seals business. Instead, Laird stepped up its acquisition strategy, acquiring Instrument Specialties, a leading EMI shielding products producer, in 2000.

Next came R&F Products, a producer of EMI absorption materials in 2001, followed by BMI, which developed EMI shields for printed circuit boards, in 2002. The company continued to expand its performance materials division, pushing into the thermal management sector in 2003 with the purchase of Kansas City, Missouri–based Orcus and U.K.-based Warth Ltd. These were followed by the acquisition of Cleveland, Ohio–based Thermagon Inc., a producer of silicone pads and other thermal interface materials, in

2004. In 2005 the company added thermoelectric cooler producer Melcor Corp. as well, gaining that company's Chinese operation.

GOING WIRELESS IN 2004

Acquisitions remained the key component of Laird's expanding high-technology interests. In 2004 the company moved into the booming wireless technologies sector, buying wireless antenna manufacturer Centurion Wireless Technologies. This purchase was followed up by three new acquisitions, of Antenex Inc. and RecepTec LLC, both antenna developers, and Steward Inc., a producer of signal integrity products, in 2006.

Also that year the company invested in expanding its own production, setting up factories in Beijing, Shenzhen, and Tianjin, China, and Reynosa, Mexico. Throughout this buildup, the company shed other non-core business. A plastics business was sold in 2004 and its security division, originally founded in the 1980s, was divested in 2007.

This enabled the group to focus on its new dual-division organization of Performance Materials and Wireless Systems. The latter received a major boost in 2007, after the company completed the purchases of AeroComm, South Korea–based M2Sys, and antenna producer Cushcraft. The company had by then established itself as a provider of full-scale wireless systems.

EXPANSION INTO INDIA: 2008

Laird expanded into India in 2008, spending $15 million to set up a factory in Sriperumbudur. The company also continued to seek out new extensions to its technologies, leading to its acquisition of U.S.-based Cattron Group International Inc. in December 2010. This purchase gave the company access to Cattron's wireless control and automation technologies. It also helped it extend its operations into new areas, such as the mining and railroad industries. Laird also extended its thermal management business into the new decade, when it acquired Kluver Aggregatebau GmbH in April 2011.

This company specialized in developing cooling systems for medical equipment, another new market for Laird. In the meantime, Laird's handset antenna business had hit a bump. Its largest customer, which accounted for as much as 70 percent of Laird's own orders, ran into trouble in 2011. Laird decided to exit the handset antenna market and began selling its assets, starting with its stake in its Beijing-based handset antenna factory in February 2012.

NEW TECHNOLOGIES IN 2014

Laird turned toward higher-value-added sectors of the wireless and performance materials sectors. In 2012 the company made a new acquisition, of Microwave Materials Group, a leading developer of microwave-absorption and related materials. Laird itself had already established itself as the global leader in EMI shielding technologies. The company also solidified its presence in the growing market for wireless machine-to-machine communications, buying Summit Data Communications that year.

Laird remained on the lookout for new acquisition opportunities as it moved toward the middle of the decade. This led the group to U.S.-based Nextreme Thermal Solutions Inc., adding that company's expertise in thin-film thermoelectric and thermal management technologies in 2013.

In the meantime, Laird successfully integrated its ever-expanding range of technologies in a number of next-generation products. These included a new range of integrated Wi-Fi and Bluetooth modules for use in such devices as bar-code scanners, medical devices, and machine-to-machine communications in July 2014. Although the company's origins reached back to the early days of the British Empire's Industrial Revolution, Laird had established itself as a driving force in the high-technology industry of the 21st century.

M. L. Cohen

PRINCIPAL SUBSIDIARIES

AeroComm, Inc. (USA); Antenex, Inc. (USA); Cattron-Theimeg Africa (Pty) Ltd. (South Africa); Cattron-Theimeg Americas Ltda (Brazil); Cattron-Theimeg Europe GmbH (Germany); Cattron-Theimeg Inc. (USA); Centurion Electronics (Shanghai) Ltd. (China); Emerson & Cuming Microwave Products Inc (USA); Emerson & Cuming Microwave Products NV (Belgium); Kunshan Cateron Electronics Co., Ltd. (China); Laird Asia Ltd. (Hong Kong); Laird Durham, Inc. (USA); Laird Technologies (M) SDN BHD (Malaysia); Laird Technologies (SEA) PTE Ltd. (Singapore); Laird Technologies (Shanghai) Ltd. (China); Laird Technologies (Shenzhen) Ltd. (China); Laird Technologies GmbH (Germany); Laird Technologies GmbH (Germany); Laird Technologies Gothenburg AB (Sweden); Laird Technologies Inc. (USA); Laird Technologies Japan, Inc.; Laird Technologies Korea Y.H.; Laird Technologies S. de R. L. de C. V. (Mexico); Laird Technologies S.R.O. (Czech Republic); Laird Technologies Taiwan, Inc.; R&F Products, Inc. (USA); RecepTec Corp. (USA); Steward (Foshan) Magnetic Materials Co., Ltd. (China); Steward (Foshan) Magnet-ics Co. Ltd. (China); Steward Pte Ltd. (Singapore); Steward, Inc. (USA); Summit Data Communications Inc. (USA); Thermagon Inc.; Tianjin Laird Technologies Ltd. (China).

PRINCIPAL DIVISIONS

Performance Materials; Wireless Systems.

PRINCIPAL OPERATING UNITS

EMI Shielding; Thermal Management; Signal Integrity; Telematics/M2M; Wireless Automation and Control; Infrastructure Antennae.

PRINCIPAL COMPETITORS

Doncasters Group Ltd.

FURTHER READING

"Bluetooth and Wi-Fi Modules Foster Connectivity Integration." *Product News Network*, July 30, 2014.

"Cascade Microtech Elects Martin Rapp to Board of Directors." *Entertainment Close-Up*, June 10, 2014.

Curley, John. "Laird Technologies Acquires Two Companies." *Microwaves & RF*, March 2007, 22.

"Laird." *Investors Chronicle*, September 23, 2005.

"Laird Exits Handset Antennae Business." *Total Telecom Online*, June 17, 2011.

"Laird Sells Chinese Antenna Subsidiary." *Telecommunications Mergers and Acquisitions Newsletter*, February 2012, 8.

"Laird Tech Sets Up Its First Offshore Facility in Sriperumbudur." *India Weekly Telecom Newsletter*, May 2, 2008, 4.

"Laird Technologies Acquires Cattron." *Hoist*, December 2010, 6.

Ojo, Bolaji. "Laird Builds Lab in India." *Electronic Engineering Times*, July 16, 2007, 27.

Wembridge, Mark. "Exit from Handset Antennas Business Takes Toll on Laird." *Financial Times*, March 3, 2012, 19.

Lenzing AG

Werkstrasse 2
Lenzing, 4860
Austria
Telephone: (+43 7672) 701-2696
Fax: (+43 7672) 701-3880
Web site: http://www.lenzing.com

Public Company
Founded: 1938
Employees: 6,675
Sales: EUR 2.14 billion ($2.9 billion) (2013)
Stock Exchanges: Vienna
Ticker Symbol: LNZ
NAICS: 313110 Fiber, Yarn, and Thread Mills; 325220
 Artificial and Synthetic Fibers and Filaments
 Manufacturing

■ ■ ■

Lenzing AG is a world-leading producer of manmade, primarily cellulose-based fibers used in the production of textiles and other fabrics and materials. Lenzing is the world's only producer of wood-based lyocell fibers, which it markets under the Tencel brand name. The company is also a leading producer of viscose, used in the production or rayon, and in modal fibers. Lenzing operates on a global basis. The group's Lenzing, Austria, headquarters is also the site of the world's largest integrated pulp and fibers plant, as well as the site of its newest large-scale Tencel plant, completed in August 2014. The company operates a second Tencel plant in Heiligenkreuz, Austria. The company also operates

plants in the United Kingdom, the United States, Germany, the Czech Republic, China, and Indonesia. The company sold a total of 890,000 metric tons of fiber in 2013. The group's Textile Fibers division is the group's largest, representing 72 percent of the company's total consolidated sales of EUR 2.14 billion ($2.9 billion) in 2013. The Nonwoven division added the remaining 28 percent. The company also produces much of its own pulp, and generates energy using primarily its own production by-products as fuel. Asia represents Lenzing's largest market, at 62 percent of group sales, while Europe including Turkey represented 29 percent, and the Americas 7 percent of sales. Lenzing AG is listed on the Vienna Stock Exchange. Peter Untersperger is the group's CEO and chairman.

PAPER MILL IN THE LATE 19TH CENTURY

Surrounded by forests, the tiny village of Lenzing, Austria provided the perfect location for the founding of a paper mill by Austrian industrialist Emil Hamburger in 1892. Into the 20th century, however, the site came under the ownership of Bunzl & Biach, which established a fast-growing presence in the European pulp and paper industry in the years leading up to World War II. Bunzl & Biach had originally been founded as a haberdashery called Emanuel Biach's Eidam in Bratislava by Moritz Bundl in 1854. Bunzl's sons changed the company's name to Bunzl & Biach, and moved its headquarters to Vienna in 1883. The company soon after moved into paper production, acquiring its first mill in 1888. Over the next decades, Bunzl & Biach acquired several more mills in Austria, including the mill in Lenzing.

Bunzl & Biach's major breakthrough had come in the mid-1920s, when one of the company's employees invented a method for producing cigarette filters from crepe paper. The company began commercial production of filters in 1927, enabling it to expand strongly through the next decade. By the late 1930s Bunzl & Biach had added factories in England and Switzerland, as well as operating several facilities in Austria. In the middle of the decade, in an effort to skirt the growing restrictions against Jewish ownership of Austrian businesses, Bunzl & Biach reincorporated as a limited liability company. The company initially shifted its headquarters to Switzerland, but by the outbreak of the war, the family had settled in England, where they established a new company in 1940.

FIBER PRODUCTION IN 1938

In the meantime, following the so-called Anschluss of Austria by Germany, Lenzing had been taken over by the Nazi authorities. The site then took on a new vocation, that of the production of viscose. Viscose, the fiber used to produce rayon fabrics, played a central role in the Nazi government's effort to reduce their reliance on imports of foreign cotton.

The Lenzing mill was placed under a new company, called Zellwolle Lenzing AG, and led by an SS brigade commander. Zellwolle Lenzing itself became a subsidiary of Thüringischen Zellwolle, based in Scharza an der Saale. The Lenzing mill was quickly expanded, seeing its pulp production volumes doubled, while at the same time being converted to the processing of beechwood. Construction also began on the site's viscose processing facility, which became one of the largest in the German Reich. The Lenzing site had a further shadow cast over its early years, when it became the location for a "sub-camp" of the Mauthausen concentration camp, using primarily female prisoners as forced laborers in the final months of World War II.

The Lenzing plant's future proved highly uncertain following the war. A struggle for control of the site broke out soon after the war, after a German American businessman attempted to seize control of the mill in 1947. The ownership issues surrounding the mill were at last resolved when Bunzl & Biach, which had regained possession of most of its prewar Austrian holdings, renounced its claim on the Lenzing site. The mill was then taken over by a number of Austrian banks. At last, given the importance of the plant to the local economy, the American occupation authorities granted permission for the company to resume production, ensuring its continued existence.

NEW TECHNOLOGIES IN THE FIFTIES

Lenzing next set to work tackling another major issue facing the company. The introduction of new synthetic fibers and fabrics, most notably nylon, in the early 1950s presented a major new challenge to the viscose industry. Lenzing was further saddled with outdated technology, which limited its total production to just 25,000 metric tons per year.

The company set out to rebuild its business, starting with developing new production methods in order to improve the consistency of its fibers. The company developed an innovative spinning technology, which enabled the company to raise production volumes significantly. The starting successful trial of a pilot spinning facility using the new design led the company to invest heavily in expanding its production into the end of the 1950s. During this time, the company also initiated an effort to minimize the environmental impact of its production process, which required large amounts of chemicals to break down the cellulose pulp.

This effort achieved a major milestone in 1962, when the company eliminated the use of calcium bisulfite from its processing method. The company instead incorporated magnesium bisulphite, a chemical that proved more environmentally responsible in that it was capable of being recycled. Lenzing ultimately developed an almost entirely closed-loop production

KEY DATES

1892: Emil Hamburger founds a paper mill in Lenzing, Austria, which is later acquired by Bunzl & Biach.

1938: Lenzing mill is taken over by Nazi authorities and converted to the production of viscose.

1962: Company changes its name to Chemiefaser Lenzing AG.

1980: Lenzing is a founding partner of South Pacific Viscose in Indonesia.

1985: Company goes public on the Vienna Stock Exchange as Lenzing AG.

1997: Lenzing inaugurates its lyocell plant in Heiligenkreuz, Austria.

2004: Lenzing acquires lyocell rival Tencel brand.

2007: Company builds a viscose factory in Nanjing, China.

2014: Company inaugurates its new Tencel factory in Lenzing.

process, which enabled the company to develop recycling rates reaching 99.8 percent. Also in 1962 the company changed its name to Chemiefaser Lenzing AG.

Lenzing also put into place a dedicated research and development department in order to extend this company's more modern fibers. This effort was inspired in part by the strong growth of petroleum-based fibers, such as polyesters and others, during the time. Lenzing, however, remained committed to its cellulose-based fiber technology. Through the 1960s the company's research efforts paid off, with the development of new automated filtration methods, which introduced a significant cost-savings while also boosting both quality levels and production volumes. In this way, viscose fibers remained competitive against the growing clout of the artificial fibers.

NEW FIBERS IN 1965

In face of this competition, Lenzing also joined with others in the viscose fiber industry to work on developing new high-performance fibers, called modal fibers, to compete with the advanced strength of the artificial fibers. Lenzing became one of the first to market this new generation of cellulose-based fibers, introducing its Hochmodul 33 brand of high wet modulus modal fiber in 1965. As part of the move into modal fibers production, Lenzing also set out to redevelop itself as an integrated pulp and fibers company. To this end, the

company took over another Lenzing business, Lenzinger Zellstoof- und Papierfabrick, which operated a pump and paper mill, in 1969.

An important part of Lenzing's growth over the next decade came with its ability to respond to the needs of its existing and potential customers. In 1976, for example, the company introduced a new highly flame-resistant viscose fiber. This fiber, which the company marketed as Lenzing FR, helped inspire a new generation of protective and safety clothing, and also became a popular material for the production of home textiles, such as curtain fabrics. Similarly, Lenzing worked closely with lingerie makers to convince them of the advantages of incorporating its ultrafine modal fibers into their garments. This effort paid off, positioning modal fibers as a major lingerie material starting in the 1990s. Lenzing's production of these fibers soared as a result, growing to more than 100,000 tons per year, and giving the company a 75 percent share of the global market for modal fibers at the dawn of the 21st century.

Into the 1980s, Lenzing took its first steps overseas. The company became the minority shareholder in a viscose production joint venture in Indonesia, called South Pacific Viscose, in 1980. Production at the new factory began in 1983. The following year, Lenzing changed its name to Lenzing AG. In 1985 the company went public, listing its shares on the Vienna Stock Exchange.

In the meantime, Lenzing had also been preparing its entry into the nonwovens market. The company developed its own technologies, which allowed viscose fibers to be processed or pressed directly into nonwoven materials and products, such as personal hygiene products and wipes. This effort ultimately led to the development of a new nozzle design, allowing the company to produce star-shaped fibers specifically for the nonwovens industry. Because products made from Lenzing's fibers were almost entirely biodegradable, they were far more environmentally friendly than those produced using petroleum-based fibers. As part of its entry into nonwovens, Lenzing also entered the United States, setting up a subsidiary and production facility in Lowland, Tennessee, in 1992.

LYOCELL IN THE NINETIES

Lenzing also began exploring another promising new area for cellulose-based fibers. By the 1970s the search was on for alternative processing methods for the production of cellulose fibers. Akzo, later part of Akzo-Nobel, hit on what was to become the most promising new method, using an entirely different solvent, N-methylmorpholine oxide, to break down cellulose in order to produce a new and still finer fiber. Akzo gave the new fiber the generic name of lyocell. In 1987 Akzo granted licenses to Lenzing and its chief viscose fibers rival, Courtaulds, to develop commercial production methods for the new fiber.

In any event, Courtaulds beat Lenzing to the market, introducing its lyocell fiber under the Tencel brand name in 1992. Lenzing responded by spending ATS 1.8 billion (approximately $177 million) on building its first lyocell plant, starting in 1994. The complex, built in Heiligenkreuz, Burgenland, started production with an initial capacity of 12,000 tons per year in 1997. The company began marketing its own lyocell as "Lyocell by Lenzing."

While slow at first, demand for lyocell, considered far more environmentally friendly than viscose rayon, began to pick up into the end of the decade. Lenzing responded by announcing plans to double its lyocell production capacity in 1999. This investment caught the company short, however, amid a sudden drop in demand for the fiber. In the meantime, Lenzing's own future once again appeared uncertain, as it emerged from a management shakeup in the late 1990s. At the same time Lenzing's major shareholder, Bank Austria, which owned 50.1 percent of the company, sought to sell its stake.

In 2000 Bank Austria agreed to sell Lenzing to CVC Capital Partners, which had earlier purchased control of Acordis, the new name for Courtaulds. The move would have allowed the merger of Lenzing and Acordis, creating the world's largest producer of viscose fibers. In anticipation of the deal, Lenzing sold its non-fibers businesses, including Lenzing Plastics, in 2000. That deal, however, was scuttled by the European Commission amid anticompetition concerns in 2001.

LYOCELL MONOPOLY IN 2004

The decision came as Lenzing faced growing pressure from imports of cheaply produced synthetic fibers from the Far East. At the same time, the global textiles industry itself had shifted east, as China emerged as the global manufacturing center for low-priced textiles. These market changes led Lenzing to sell its U.S. operations, to a private equity–backed management buyout, starting from 2002.

Instead, Lenzing invested in developing its higher value-added businesses, and its lyocell operations in particular. In 2002 the company began construction of a second 20,000-metric-ton-per-year lyocell plant in Heiligenkreuz, Austria, doubling the facility's size. This expansion was followed by a new EUR 90 million investment in the group's core Lenzing site, starting in 2004.

That year also marked another milestone for the company. In May 2004 Lenzing reached an agreement to the entire Tencel fiber business, including the Tencel brand, which by then had become the property of another CVC holding, Corsadi, based in the Netherlands. The deal gave Lenzing control over Tencel's two factories, in Alabama and in Grimsby, England. Although the purchase also gave Lenzing a de facto monopoly over the global lyocell market, the deal was allowed to proceed, in part because lyocell remained only a small part of the overall textiles industry. Lenzing phased out its own lyocell brand in favor of the Tencel brand in 2005.

CHINA PRODUCTION FROM 2005

Following the purchase, Lenzing, which had largely operated as an Austrian-oriented company, adopted a new internationalization strategy. The company decided to follow the direction of the textiles industry, and in 2005 began construction of a 60,000-metric-ton-per-year viscose factory in Nanjing, China. The new plant started up production in April 2007. By then the company had formed a joint venture, with Modi Group, to build a viscose fiber plant in India as well. Lenzing also invested in expanding its Indonesian operations, building a new fiber processing line there in 2005. The company also raised its stake in South Pacific Viscose, to nearly 86 percent, in 2007.

Into the second half of the decade, Lenzing also began exploring other growth options. The company set out to develop its integration strategy, moving downstream with the purchase of Hahl Group, a producer of industrial synthetic brushes. In 2007 the company acquired Germany's Pedex as well, gaining control of that company's production of plastic filaments used in a variety of applications, including the production of cosmetics and hygiene products. These acquisitions were followed soon after by the purchase of cut plastic filaments producer Glassmaster, based in Lexington, South Carolina. In 2013 the company created a joint venture with China's Nox Bellcow (Zhongshan) Nonwoven Chemical to produce facial masks using Tencel fibers.

Lenzing also began expanding its range of fibers. The company looked beyond cellulose-based fibers for the first time in 2007, when it started up a joint venture, in partnership with carbon fiber producers SGL Carbon and Kelheim Fibres in Germany, to produce polyacrylonitrile, a key component of carbon fiber. In 2010 Lenzing expanded its fibers portfolio again, acquiring the rights to market Viloft fibers, developed by Kelheim Fibres. The new fiber, which featured a flat profile, boosted superior insulation qualities over conventional viscose fibers.

These additions came as Lenzing benefited from the growing demand for wood-based fibers. In order to meet the expected expansion of the market, Lenzing announced plans to invest EUR 285 million ($381 million) in order to raise its total capacity past one million metric tons per year by 2014. A centerpiece of this investment involved the construction of a new EUR 130 million Tencel plant at the company's Lenzing base, adding 60,000 metric tons per year of lyocell capacity. This plant was inaugurated in August 2014. Along with an expansion carried out at the group's Alabama factory, Lenzing's total Tencel production capacity topped 220,000 metric tons. Lenzing, which celebrated its 75th anniversary in 2013, had succeeded in establishing itself as the world's leading producer of cellulose-based fibers in the early 21st century.

M. L. Cohen

PRINCIPAL SUBSIDIARIES

ASIA Fiber Engineering GmbH; Beech Investment s.r.o. (Slovakia); Biocel Paskov a.s. (Czech Republic); BZL – Bildungszentrum Lenzing GmbH; Cellulose Consulting GmbH; Dolan GmbH (Germany); European Carbon Fiber GmbH (Germany); LENO Electronics GmbH; Lenzing (Nanjing) Fibers Co., Ltd. (China); Lenzing Beteiligungs GmbH,; Lenzing Engineering and Technical Services (Nanjing) Co., Ltd. (China); Lenzing Fibers (Hong Kong) Ltd.; Lenzing Fibers (Shanghai) Co., Ltd. (China); Lenzing Fibers GmbH; Lenzing Fibers Grimsby Ltd. (UK); Lenzing Fibers Holding GmbH; Lenzing Fibers Inc. (USA); Lenzing Fibers Ltd. (UK); Lenzing Global Finance GmbH (Germany); Lenzing Holding GmbH; Lenzing Modi Fibers India Private Ltd.; Lenzing Plastics GmbH; Lenzing Technik GmbH; LP Automotive GmbH; Lyocell Holding Ltd. (UK); Penique S.A. (Panama); PT. South Pacific Viscose (Indonesia); Pulp Trading GmbH; Tencel Holding Ltd. (UK).

PRINCIPAL DIVISIONS

Textile Fibers; Nonwoven Fibers; Pulp; Energy.

PRINCIPAL OPERATING UNITS

Tencel; Lenzing Viscose; Lenzing Modal; Lenzing FR.

PRINCIPAL COMPETITORS

INVISTA S.A.R.L.; Sarpsfoss Ltd.

FURTHER READING

Drier, Melissa. "The Hills Are Alive. ..." *Daily News Record*, July 11, 2005.

Friedman, Arthur. "Lenzing Group Opens 'Jumbo' Tencel Plant." *WWD*, August 5, 2014.

"Lenzing Acquires Share in Indonesian Firm." *Nonwovens Industry*, September 2009.

"Lenzing Celebrates 75 Years." *Nonwovens Industry*, July 2013.

"Lenzing Starts New 600,000-Ton Capacity Plant in China." *Indian Textile Journal*, October 31, 2011.

"Lenzing to Examine Cost-Saving Measures." *Nonwovens Industry*, July 2014.

Ramesh, Deepti. "Lenzing Becomes Majority Shareholder of Indonesian Firm." *Chemical Week*, June 27, 2007.

Smith, Katie. "Lenzing Cuts Full-Year Forecasts." *just-style.com*, November 15, 2013.

Young, Ian. "Lenzing Acquires Tencel, Creating a Lyocell Monopoly." *Chemical Week*, May 12, 2004.

Lovejoy, Inc.

———■———

2655 Wisconsin Avenue
Downers Grove, Illinois 60515
U.S.A.
Telephone: (630) 852-0500
Fax: (630) 852-2120
Web site: http://www.lovejoy-inc.com

Private Company
Founded: 1900 as Lovejoy Tool Works
Employees: 280
Sales: $60 million (2012 est.)
NAICS: 333613 Mechanical Power Transmission Equipment Manufacturing

■ ■ ■

Lovejoy, Inc., is a leading manufacturer of power transmission and hydraulic products, primarily used in the aggregates, food and beverage, mining, power generation, pulp and paper, and steel industries. Lovejoy's signature product is the flexible shaft coupling, available in a wide variety of styles. For more than half a century, Lovejoy has also produced universal joints in standard and specialized styles. Other products include variable speed drives, shaft locking devices, powder metal components, and the ROSTA brand of multipurpose rubber suspension modules, vibration dampers, oscillating elements, motorbases, and chain-belt tensioners. Lovejoy products are sold around the world through a network of distributors. The company maintains its world headquarters in Downers Grove, Illinois, and a second manufacturing plant in South

Haven, Michigan. The company is also part of a German joint venture, R+L Hydraulics, which manufactures and modifies couplings to meet European standards and provides technical and customer support to the region. The Lovejoy Canada subsidiary provides support to Canadian customers. Lovejoy is owned by the fourth generation of the Dangel-Hennessy family. Michael W. Hennessy serves as chief executive officer.

COMPANY FOUNDED: 1900

Although he was involved for only a brief time with the company that would bear his name, Thomas Lovejoy founded Lovejoy Inc. as Lovejoy Tool Works in downtown Chicago in 1900. It was originally a railroad equipment company but also manufactured tooling and machinery for the steel industry. In 1912 Lovejoy sold the business to William H. Dangel, who had been born in Elizabeth, New Jersey, in 1875. The company continued to produce railroad equipment, but the direction changed in 1927 when Dangel acquired the patent for the jaw coupling from its inventor Louis Ricefield. The timing of the deal proved fortunate.

Following the stock market crash in October 1929, the country was plunged into the Great Depression that encompassed the following decade. Lovejoy sold its railroad business, focused on the manufacture of jaw couplings, and changed its name to the Lovejoy Flexible Coupling Company. Because of poor business conditions, the company also lost it original building and had to move to another Chicago location in 1930. The workforce was also reduced to just four employees, which included William Dangel, his son Merlin W.

Dangel, and a pair of machinists. The younger Dangel had been born in Chicago in 1897 and joined the company after serving in the U.S. Army in France during World War I.

MERLIN DANGEL SUCCEEDS
FATHER: 1946

Lovejoy survived the Depression, which was not completely overcome until government spending for World War II in the first half of the 1940s lifted the economy. As Lovejoy entered the postwar economic boom years, Merlin Dangel succeeded his father as the president of Lovejoy in 1946, but the elder Dangel remained very much involved as chairman. Also in 1946 the company began manufacturing universal joints. The following year, Lovejoy made a major addition to its product lineup by acquiring a variable speed pulley line, sold under the Ideal brand name.

During the postwar years Lovejoy began manufacturing motor bases and belt transmissions as well. A second manufacturing plant was added in 1958 through the acquisition of the Hi-Lo Manufacturing Company, a Minneapolis-based maker of variable speed pulleys and other power transmission components. In addition, a third generation of the family became involved in the business and assumed a position of responsibility. Merlin Dangel's son-in-law, Charles Patrick Hennessy, who had married into the family in 1950, became executive vice president in charge of international sales.

MICHIGAN PLANT OPENS: 1960

In 1958 Merlin Dangel bought a summer home in South Haven, Michigan. A year later the company announced that it planned to build a $92,975 plant in the community. It would be dedicated to the manufacture of variable speed pulleys. The new facility opened in March 1960 with four employees. Within two years, the workforce grew to 29.

Lovejoy soon added other products lines. In 1962 the company began the manufacture of the Uniflex line of couplings, followed a year later by the SAGA line of couplings. During this time, three generations of the Dangel-Hennessy family were still actively involved in the management of Lovejoy Flexible Coupling Company. Even at the age of 88, William Dangel continued to serve as chairman. In January 1964, however, he died suddenly on a Monday morning in his home, bringing to an end his 52-years with the company. Merlin Dangel was by now 66 years of age, his health failed, and late in 1964 he too died following a lengthy illness. In February 1965 Charles Hennessy was elected president of the company and was also named a director.

Hennessy continued to expand the company, but because the Lovejoy Flexible Coupling name was no longer representative of all the company had to offer, it was shortened in 1967 to Lovejoy, Inc. The Chicago plant remained Lovejoy's principal manufacturing site, but soon it would also become outmoded. In 1970 the company moved to a new headquarters and manufacturing plant in Downers Grove, Illinois. With greater production capacity, Lovejoy in 1971 began manufacturing torsional couplings, which eliminated torsional vibration problems common in diesel engine-driven equipment and other industrial engine applications. Through a partnership with Switzerland's Rosta AG in 1978, Lovejoy also began manufacturing products that used Rosta's elastomeric elements, including tensioners, motor bases, and other products.

FOURTH-GENERATION
LEADERSHIP: 1984

In 1984 Charles Hennessy passed away, and his son, Michael W. Hennessy, became the fourth generation of the Dangel-Hennessy family to become Lovejoy's chief executive officer. Like his father, the younger Hennessy continued to grow Lovejoy's portfolio of couplings. A year after he took the helm, the company introduced the S-Flex and Delta Flex coupling lines. By now it had become apparent that in order to remain competitive, Lovejoy had to expand internationally. Customers were growing overseas, and the company had no choice but to follow suit to meet their needs.

Lovely's first international office was established not too far from home in Canada in 1990. Two years later Lovejoy Canada opened a 14,000-square-foot distribution facility in Mississauga, Ontario. A warehouse opened in the Netherlands in 1994. To accommodate European standards, Lovejoy introduced the curved jaw coupling in 1995. Other new products were introduced as well during this period, including a full line of Sier Bath couplings and motion control couplings. In 1996 Lovejoy introduced a line of all-metal, flexible grid

KEY DATES

1900: Thomas Lovejoy founds Lovejoy Tool Works.
1912: William H. Dangel acquires company.
1960: South Haven, Michigan, plant opens.
1990: Lovejoy Canada marks first international expansion.
2013: South Haven plant is expanded.

couplings. Two years later the Jaw In-Shear coupling was added to the product lineup and represented a significant design upgrade over the standard jaw coupling.

As industrial quality standards became more stringent in the 1990s, it became apparent that Lovejoy needed to become ISO certified. In 2000 the company completed the process and Lovejoy plants received ISO-9001 certification, providing assurance to customers that the company's products were of the highest quality and reliability. Also during this period, Lovejoy made a significant upgrade to its technology. For many years the company had relied on a mainframe computer and dumb terminals. A new generation computer system was installed in 2000.

LOVEJOY EUROPE ESTABLISHED: 2001

Lovejoy celebrated its 100th anniversary in 2000. The company began its second century with the introduction of a new line of disc couplings. International growth also continued. In 2001 the company established a subsidiary in Germany, Lovejoy Europe B.V., to modify couplings for the European power transmission market as well as other export markets. Two years later Lovejoy expanded its ability to serve the continent as well as Southeast Asia. The company established distribution partnerships with Germany's FlexonGmbH and Singapore-based RO-QUIP Asia Pacific Pte Ltd.

In order to become even more of a global company, Lovejoy in 2003 acquired a majority stake in Wedohl, Germany–based Rahmer & Jansen GmbH, a major supplier of hydraulic components and flexible shaft couplings sold under the Spidex and Dentex labels. It served as the foundation for a joint venture with Rahmer & Jansen's management team, CEO Bodo Jansen and his son Jens Jensen, who would continue to run the business under the Raja-Lovejoy GmbH name. In that same year Lovejoy unveiled the next generation of its Jaw In-Shear coupling. Not only could the joint venture

offer a greater range of products, it inherited Rahmer & Jansen's established sales and distribution networks. Additionally, Lovejoy Europe now moved its home base from the Netherlands to Germany and closer to the manufacturing operation. It would also be more centrally located for distribution and customer service.

In 2004 Lovejoy entered into a new manufacturing sector with the launch of a new unit in Downers Grove, Lovejoy Sintered Technologies. The company focused on the manufacture of sintered metal parts for original equipment manufacturer applications. The way the parts were made was similar to how couplings were produced, making the venture an attractive way for Lovejoy to diversify its product offerings.

Raja-Lovejoy GmbH enjoyed strong growth with hydraulics products, leading to a name change to R+L Hydraulics. The products had performed so well in Europe that Lovejoy decided to also offer them to the North American market. In 2009 the Lovejoy Hydraulics division was established to manufacture and market hydraulic couplings, bellhousings, water-oil coolers, reservoirs, and accessories.

Lovejoy reached another milestone in 2012 when it celebrated 100 years of Dangel-Hennessy family ownership. The company was, however, far from content to rest on its laurels. In August of that year the company opened a new sales office in Shanghai, China. In early 2013 Lovejoy completed a major expansion of its 35,000-square-foot South Haven operation through the purchase of the nearby 95,000-square-foot Clarion factory building. The cost of the property plus new equipment was $3 million. The extra production capacity was needed to support Lovejoy's drive to increase market share in the company's gear product line. Moreover, Lovejoy was aggressively pursuing international sales. Employment at South Haven was increased from 75 to 100. A main reason for expanding the Michigan operation was the difficulty Lovejoy encountered in attracting suitable employees in Illinois. The Michigan Works! Association played a key role by providing Lovejoy with labor market information and developing a training plan. The nonprofit member organization also worked with Lovejoy's human resources department to recruit and assess the job-related skills of applicants. Lovejoy hoped to add another 50 to 75 workers over the next five years.

Lovejoy looked to expand on multiple fronts in the years ahead through organic means, acquisitions, and partnerships. In the fall of 2013, for example, Lovejoy forged an alliance with VibraAlign Inc., a leading specialist in laser shaft alignment. The two companies agreed to share knowledge and expertise for their mutual benefit. They also teamed up for a "Realigning America

Tour," a seven-city seminar program to help maintenance professionals solve coupling and alignment problems. Like Lovejoy, VibraAlign was a family-owned business and shared similar values. There was every indication that Lovejoy planned to remain a family-owned-and-managed company well into the future.

Ed Dinger

PRINCIPAL DIVISIONS

Lovejoy Canada; Lovejoy Hydraulics; Lovejoy - Manufacturing; Lovejoy Powder Metal Group; R+L Hydraulics.

PRINCIPAL COMPETITORS

Eaton Corporation; Kanemitsu Corporation; Zero-Max, Inc.

FURTHER READING

"Lovejoy Changes Corp. Name." *Oak Park (IL) Oak Leaves*, April 27, 1967.

"Lovejoy Enjoys Growth Spurt." *St. Joseph (MI) Herald-Palladium*, December 19, 2012.

"Merlin Dangel, Coupling Company President, Dies." *Oak Park (IL) Oak Leaves*, December 3, 1964.

"Name Hennessy President Lovejoy Flexible Coupling Co." *Oak Park (IL) Oak Leaves*, February 11, 1965.

"New Business for Lovejoy." *Diesel Progress North American Edition*, April 2004.

"Will Build Plant at South Haven." *Benton Harbor News Palladium*, October 31, 1959.

"William Dangel, Community Leader, Dies at His Home." *Oak Park (IL) Oak Leaves*, January 9, 1964.

Manna Inc.

1903 Stanley Gault Parkway
Louisville, Kentucky 40223-4159
U.S.A.
Telephone: (502) 254-7130
Fax: (502) 254-7031

Private Company
Incorporated: 1999
Sales: $500 million (2013 est.)
NAICS: 722511 Full-Service Restaurants; 722513
    Limited-Service Restaurants

■ ■ ■

Louisville, Kentucky–based Manna Inc. is the privately held umbrella company for the business ventures of former National Basketball Association (NBA) player Ulysses L. "Junior" Bridgeman. Through Manna subsidiaries, Bridgeman owns about 200 Wendy's quick-serve restaurants, making him the second-largest franchise owner in the system. Manna also owns about 120 Chili's casual restaurants and 45 Fannie May Chocolate shops. Other ventures include the Napa River Grill restaurant in Louisville and a venture to open 30 Blaze Fast Fire'd Pizza locations in Florida, Kentucky, and Tennessee. Manna is one of the largest black-owned companies in the United States.

FOUNDER, A BASKETBALL STAR

Junior Bridgeman was born in 1953 in East Chicago, Indiana. The son and grandson of steel mill workers, he grew up determined to escape the mills. While focusing on his studies, Bridgeman also grew tall and demonstrated athletic ability. After leading his high school basketball team to an undefeated season and an Indiana state championship in 1971, Bridgeman received a scholarship to play for the University of Louisville. He again enjoyed success, helping his team to reach the Final Four in the 1975 National Collegiate Athletic Association championship during his senior year.

After completing his degree in psychology, he became the eighth selection in the first round of the NBA's 1975 first-year player draft. Taken by the Los Angeles Lakers, he was quickly traded to the Milwaukee Bucks in a deal that sent Kareem Abdul-Jabbar to the Lakers. Although Bridgeman rarely started, the guard-forward proved to be one of the game's top reserve players.

During his 12-year NBA career, mostly spent in Milwaukee, he played 711 games for the Bucks, the most in franchise history. He was so well-regarded by the Bucks that his jersey was retired by the team. Despite his success, Bridgeman played during a period when NBA players did not receive multimillion-dollar contracts and lucrative endorsement deals. His highest NBA salary was $350,000.

INVESTMENT IN WENDY'S FRANCHISE

During the off-season, Bridgeman worked the front desk at a Howard Johnson hotel and had a stint selling insurance. He also attended law school at the University of Wisconsin–Madison with an eye toward a legal

KEY DATES

1983: Junior Bridgeman becomes passive investor in Wendy's restaurant.
1988: Bridgeman Foods acquires five Wendy's restaurants.
1999: Manna Inc. is formed.
2005: ERJ Dining is formed to become Chili's franchisee.
2014: Bridgeman becomes franchisee of Blaze Fast Fire'd Pizza.

career. Bridgeman would eventually find a different field of interest. In 1983 he became a passive investor in an Illinois Wendy's franchise and became familiar with the restaurant business.

Bridgeman was so impressed with the Wendy's system that in 1986 he attempted to acquire the Illinois restaurant but was turned down. After retiring from the NBA in 1987, he invested in another Wendy's franchise in Brooklyn, New York, with a friend, NBA player Paul Silas, and Lawrence Fleisher, a lawyer who served as executive director of the National Basketball Players' Association.

Bridgeman had been a former president of the association. Fleisher and another former NBA player, John Havlicek, were already established Wendy's franchisees. Havlicek had been a neighbor of Wendy's founder, Dave Thomas, and became a franchisee with Fleisher in 1978.

OFFERED FIVE STORES: 1988

Bridgeman made it clear to Wendy's that he was interested in becoming more than a passive investor and in 1988 was given the opportunity to acquire five low-performing restaurants in the Milwaukee area with financing provided by Wendy's. Bridgeman sought Fleisher's advice, as he had done with other business decisions in the past. Not only did Fleisher approve of the deal, he expressed interest in becoming a partner in the venture, Bridgeman Foods Inc.

Only at the 11th hour did Bridgeman learn that his partner would be in fact Havlicek/Fleisher Enterprises, Inc. The deal with Wendy's was completed and Bridgeman became the controlling shareholder of Bridgeman Foods. Unlike his previous relationship with Wendy's, Bridgeman was very much a hands-on owner. He learned all roles in the business, from cooking hamburg-

ers to mopping the floors. He also used his experience as a professional athlete to his advantage.

Bridgeman took care to hire the most talented people he could find, encouraged teamwork, and empowered his people. As a result, his restaurants experienced far less turnover than the industry average, a fact that would be positively reflected on the balance sheet. Due to his hard work and willingness to make personal appearances at the restaurants, the five Wendy's showed marked improvement.

BRIDGEMAN FOODS FORMED: 1989

Bridgeman quickly became interested in expanding his restaurant portfolio. In October 1988 he met with a Wendy's executive to discuss new opportunities. Over the following months, Wendy's created a 16-store deal for additional Milwaukee-area stores, as well as an option to open five more units. Bridgeman discussed the offer with Fleisher, but Fleisher advised against it.

Fleisher subsequently died from a heart attack in May 1989 after playing squash. The following week Bridgeman formed a new entity, Bridgeman Foods Inc. II, to purchase the Wendy's stores. When executives at Havlicek/Fleisher Enterprises learned about the transaction, they were not pleased. In 1990 Havlicek/Fleisher sued Bridgeman, alleging that he had been required to inform all the shareholders of Fleisher/Havlicek of his intentions and receive their consent before buying the 16 restaurants.

FACING LEGAL CHALLENGES

Moreover, the suit claimed that Bridgeman used the personnel and other resources of Bridgeman Foods Inc. to run the 16 Wendy's stores that constituted Bridgeman Foods Inc. II, and then transferred the staff of the first Bridgeman Foods to the second without the necessary consent. The courts ultimately dismissed the case in September 1992.

In the meantime, Bridgeman briefly pursued a broadcasting career, serving as a radio analyst for the University of Louisville basketball games and the NBA's Los Angeles Clippers and Chicago Bulls. At the same time he managed Bridgeman Foods and attempted to move beyond hamburgers to chicken in 1990 with the acquisition of a Popeye's Famous Fried Chicken & Biscuits restaurant franchise in Milwaukee.

Late in the year Bridgeman entered the grocery field by acquiring a Milwaukee Pick 'n Save supermarket. He quickly changed his mind, however. Just six months later he sold the store. Although Bridgeman decided to focus on restaurants, poor economic conditions and high real estate prices prevented external growth. He sold his Popeye's franchise in May 1991 and concentrated on increasing same-store sales in his Wendy's units.

EXPANSION RESUMES

Bridgeman was again able to add to his Wendy's portfolio in 1993, acquiring three stores in Madison, Wisconsin. He added to his holdings in southeastern Wisconsin in 1997 by acquiring eight Hardee's restaurants. He then converted them to the Wendy's concept, bringing the total number of Wendy's restaurants he owned in the region to 42. As the economy roared in the second half of the 1990s Bridgeman expanded as well.

By the fall of 1999 Bridgeman owned 22 Wendy's restaurants in Louisville, as well as another 20 in Fort Myers, Florida, the latter the result of another opportunity Wendy's International offered to him. Bridgeman also added units in the Chicago area, close to where he was raised, and looked to Nashville, Tennessee, as a place for future growth. Located about two-and-a-half hours from Louisville, Nashville appeared to be a market on the cusp of strong growth.

In October 1999 Bridgeman acquired Southern Hospitality Corp., the owners of 39 Wendy's restaurants in the Nashville area. Bridgeman controlled 120 units at this time. The regional operations were divided among different corporate entities, and in 1999 Bridgeman formed Manna Inc. to serve as an umbrella company.

RECEIVES FOUNDER'S AWARD: 1997

Junior Bridgeman entered the new century as one of the largest Wendy's franchisees in the United States. He was also the recipient of the 1997 Founder's Award, the highest award offered by Wendy's International. He was far from content, however. By the end of 2002 he added about 20 more Wendy's restaurants in the Nashville market.

According to *Black Enterprise* magazine, Manna Inc. generated $159.3 million in revenues in 2002, making it one of the largest black-owned companies in the country. Manna Inc. continued to open new Wendy's units in 2003, bringing the total number of stores to more than 150.

In addition, Bridgeman opened a Baja Fresh Mexican Grill restaurant. To support further growth, the company secured a $27 million credit agreement with GE Commercial Finance's franchise finance unit. With the financing in place, Manna hoped to open 35 to 45 new Wendy's restaurants over the next five years.

ADDS CHILI'S RESTAURANTS: 2005

Bridgeman did not limit Manna to the quick-serve format. In 2005 subsidiary ERJ Dining acquired four Chili's Grill & Bar restaurants in Louisville and Lexington, Kentucky, and signed a franchising and development agreement with Brinker International, Inc., to open 18 additional units. In 2006 ERJ acquired 15 Chili's restaurants in Wisconsin and Missouri from Brinker.

Bridgeman made an even greater commitment to Chili's the following year by signing an agreement with Brinker in which ERJ acquired 76 existing units and received the right to develop 49 new restaurants in the Midwest. Manna restructured some of its operations in 2007. As part of that effort, the company sold 15 Wendy's restaurants in southeast Wisconsin for $11.3 million to GE Capital Solutions Franchise Finance.

While the Wendy's and Chili's concepts were his core businesses, Bridgeman continued to look for new franchise opportunities. In 2011 he joined a franchise group to open 45 Fannie May Fine Chocolate shops over the following three years, primarily in Minnesota and Wisconsin. Bridgeman remained committed to Wendy's, as well as to helping other professional athletes make the transition to a business career.

In 2013 he entered into a partnership with basketball player Chauncey Billups, who would soon announce his retirement from the NBA. The new venture acquired 30 restaurants in the St. Louis, Missouri, market from the Wendy's Company, as part of Wendy's plan to refranchise 425 corporate-owned stores.

NEW PIZZA VENTURE: 2014

Bridgeman continued to expand Manna in a number of directions. He entered the fine-dining sector by purchasing Louisville's 15-year-old Napa River Grill. He also remained interested in the quick-serve sector. In 2014 Bridgeman partnered with Jim Patterson, the founder of Long John Silver's and Rally's Hamburgers, to become a franchisee of Blaze Fast Fire'd Pizza stores, with plans to open 30 units in Florida, Kentucky, and Tennessee.

At Blaze Fast restaurants, customers built their own 11-inch pizzas from a selection of more than 40 sauces, meats, cheeses, and vegetables. The pizzas were then cooked and ready within three minutes. Although turning 61 years old in 2014, Junior Bridgeman appeared committed to the pursuit of growth for the various ventures controlled by Manna Inc.

A second generation of the Bridgeman family was also involved, including Bridgeman's sons Justin and Ryan and daughter Eden. All three learned the restaurant business from the ground up. In preparation for a role within the Manna group of companies, the brothers earned MBA degrees.

Justin then worked as a general manager at a Chicago's Chili's and Ryan served an internship with Taco Bell in the finance department to prove themselves before joining their father. Because of the poor economy, Eden joined Manna straight after college, taking a position as marketing manager for 49 Chili's. With an infusion of new blood, the Manna group of companies appeared well-positioned for the future.

Ed Dinger

PRINCIPAL SUBSIDIARIES

Bridgeman Hospitality LLC; ERJ Inc.

PRINCIPAL COMPETITORS

Boddie-Noell Enterprises, Inc.; Heartland Food Corp.; Quality Dining, Inc.

FURTHER READING

Foran, Chris. "Bridgeman Hopes Popeye Proves Stronger than Cajun Chef." *Business Journal-Milwaukee*, January 8, 1990.

Johnson-Elie, Tannette. "Bridgeman, Havlicek Square Off in Court." *Milwaukee Sentinel*, October 8, 1991.

King, Paul. "Former NBA Star Scores on Wendy's Team." *Nation's Restaurant News*, August 23, 2004.

Kirchen, Rich. "Milwaukee Bucks Suitor Junior Bridgeman Diversifying His Restaurant Biz." *Milwaukee Business Journal*, March 3, 2014.

Lawrence, Andrew. "Junior Bridgeman: A Different Kind of Franchise Player." *Fortune*, July 7, 2014.

Punzel, Dennis. "Bridgeman Loves His Burgers." *Madison (WI) Capital Times*, May 20, 1993.

Sanders, Denise. "Once More than a Player, Bridgeman's Now More than a Boss." *Business Journal–Milwaukee*, December 4, 1989.

MaxamCorp Holding S.L.

Avenida Partenon 16
Madrid, 28042
Spain
Telephone: (+34 917) 220 100
Fax: (+34 917) 220 101
Web site: http://www.maxam.net

Private Company
Founded: 1896
Employees: 6,500
Sales: EUR 1.1 billion ($1.43 billion) (2014)
NAICS: 325920 Explosives Manufacturing; 332992 Small Arms Ammunition Manufacturing; 332993 Ammunition (Except Small Arms) Manufacturing

■ ■ ■

MaxamCorp Holding S.L. is one of the world's oldest and largest explosives companies, tracing its origins to a company founded by dynamite inventor Alfred Nobel in 1872. Maxam is the largest producer of civil explosives in Europe, and the second-largest worldwide. The company is also the leading European producer of detonators, fuses, and other initiation systems, and the largest European producer of ammonium nitrate, nitrocellulose, and other chemicals used in the production of explosives and ammunition. The group is a leading producer of ammunition, both for the civil and defense markets. The group's Outdoors division, which produces cartridges, as well as powder and other ammunition products for hunters and shooting clubs, is the world leader in this category. In addition to the production of ammunition, weapons, and systems, the company's Defence division is also the leading provider of demilitarization services in Europe. Civil Explosives remains the company's largest division.

NOBEL BEGINNINGS IN 1872

Alfred Nobel invented dynamite in 1867 and quickly began developing a global network of production companies. Among the earliest of these companies was Sociedad Anónima Española de la Pólvora Dinamita, founded in 1872 in Bilbao in order to take advantage of that growing industrial port's proximity to the region's rich mineral deposits. Nobel was initially joined by a group of French and Belgian investors in the creation of Pólvora, which built a factory in Galdacano, near the French border.

The Pólvora company, which soon became simply Sociedad Española de la Dinamita (SED) started out with a major advantage, after then-king Amadeo I granted it with the exclusive right to manufacture dynamite in Spain for a five-year period. The end of that period brought SED into direct competition for the first time. Other European dynamite producers, including other members of the Nobel network of companies, rushed into Spain.

This sparked a long price war in Spain, emulating the intense rivalry elsewhere in the world. The need to stabilize prices led a number of Nobel companies in other countries to form a cartel, known as the European Nobel Trust. SED led similar efforts to stabilize the Spanish dynamite market. In 1896 the company joined with two other German-backed dynamite producers, as well as six smaller companies operating mining interests in Spain's northern region, to found the limited liability company Unión Española de Explosivos, S.A. (UEE).

SED, still controlled by the Nobel trust, became the majority shareholder in the company, forcing through the consolidation of its partners' industrial operations into the factory in Galdacano. The company's other operations were converted to sales subsidiaries. The Pólvora site, for example, changed its name to Sociedad Anónima Española de la Dinamita y de Productos Quimicos.

CHEMICALS IN THE TWENTIES

The Spanish government held a strong interest in seeing the creation of the UEE. At the time, Spain was in the midst of a costly war with the United States and found itself desperately in need of a stable and certain revenue source. The fast-growing dynamite industry, and its importance to the related mining industry, was one of the country's most promising industries at the dawn of the 20th century.

The Spanish government encouragement the creation of the UEE, with the objective of establishing a monopoly on the dynamite market. This monopoly was formally granted in 1897. In this way, the UEE was able to raise its prices, thereby raising revenues for the government. At the same time, the company's production also expanded to include production of ammunition and explosives for the Spanish war effort.

UEE at first made good on its promise, posting profit margins as high as 67 percent, while transferring significant sums to the Spanish treasury in terms of taxes. The UEE's monopoly was to last for more than 20 years. During this time, the company came increasingly under Spanish ownership, as the Nobel trust gradually reduced its interest. By the 1920s UEE had become a fully Spanish-owned company.

WORLD WAR I INCREASES DEMAND

UEE benefited strongly through this period from the demand for explosives during World War I. The company not only expanded its explosives production during this time, it also invested in diversifying its operations, starting with the production of gunpowder for the Spanish army in 1911. The company also added the production of dyes and nitrogen. This diversification enabled the company to easily absorb the loss of its dynamite monopoly in 1917.

Into the 1920s the group's diversification led it into other areas, including fertilizer manufacturing, creating a more vertically integrated business structure. The group's entry into fertilizer took off especially after 1927, when it acquired Cartagena-based Sociedad General de Industria y Comercio, founded in 1903. This acquisition also enabled the company to enter the mining industry, with the rights to mine potassium salt in Cardona. UEE started the mine in 1929.

ERT IN THE SEVENTIES

UEE's expansion continued, leading it to acquire other mining interests, including in Catalonia, as well as in Morocco, where it operated a phosphate mine, and in Huelva, where it mined pyrite. Growth for the company continued after the Spanish Civil War, as it expanded its fertilizer production into the markets for other agricultural chemicals, including the production of insecticides and fungicides.

By the early 1960s the company had also emerged as one of Spain's leading chemicals producers. The group operated 20 factories located across Spain, with a total payroll of 8,500 employees. The group's products at the time included sulfuric acid, nitric acid, hydrochloric acid, acetic acid, caustic soda, liquid chlorine, and calcium carbide. By then, too, UEE had claimed the national leadership in many of its categories, such as accounting for 55 percent of the total Spanish potash market.

BUILDS SEVILLE FACTORY: 1963

UEE continued adding to its industrial capacity into the middle of the decade. The company began construction of a new large-scale fertilizer factory in Seville in 1963. In that year, UEE also began construction of a petrochemicals factory in Tarragona, marking the group's first extension into this area.

In 1970 UEE's expansion moved to a new level. In that year, the company merged with Compañía Española de Minas de Río Tinto, one of Spain's leading

KEY DATES

1872: Nobel group founds an explosives producer, Sociedad Española de la Pólvora Dinamita, in Bilbao, Spain.
1896: Company leads the creation of Unión Española de Explosivos (UEE), which acquires a 20-year monopoly on the Spanish explosives market.
1927: UEE expands into chemicals production.
1970: UEE merges with Compañía Española de Minas de Río Tinto, forming Unión Explosivos Río Tinto, S.A.
2006: UEE caps its internationalization strategy by changing its name to Maxam.
2011: Advent International acquires 45 percent of Maxam, alongside management.

mining companies, founded in 1954. The new company became known as Unión Explosivos Río Tinto, S.A. (ERT) and quickly began a new expansion phase as it joined the ranks of Spain's largest companies. Through the 1970s ERT set out an ambitious diversification strategy.

In 1974 the company moved into the pharmaceuticals market, acquiring Compañía Española de Penicilina y Antibióticos, a leading Spanish producer of antibiotics founded in 1949. The company's Tarragona petrochemicals plant was completed in 1973, allowing the company to add the production of ethyl acetate to its lineup. At the same time, ERT formed the petrochemicals joint venture Industrias Químicas Asociadas, which teamed up with France's Total to produce low-density polyethylene during the mid-1970s.

STUMBLING IN THE EIGHTIES

ERT also expanded its horizons beyond Spain during this time. The company entered the U.S. market, setting up an explosives production factory in Salt Lake City, Utah, in 1979. The company had also entered the Middle Eastern market, forming a joint venture to build a civil explosives plant in Dubai in 1978. Also during the decade, ERT expanded its mining interests to include the operation of a joint-venture uranium mine in Segovia. By the beginning of the 1980s ERT had grown to become the large private industrial conglomerate in Spain.

ERT's diversification at first appeared to buffer it from the increasing volatility of the global market dur-

ing the 1970s, as well as the upheavals in Spain following the death of Spanish dictator Francisco Franco in 1975. The company also diversified into nonindustrial areas, such as the real estate market, building up a portfolio of properties in Madrid and in the Canary Islands.

ENDURES MARKET CHALLENGES

In 1979, however, the company sales growth suddenly slowed, while its profits dropped sharply over the previous year. This signaled the start of an extended rough patch for the company. The company's troubles worsened into the beginning of the next decade.

By 1982 the company was forced to inform its creditors that it was unable to pay the principal on its debts, which by then had risen to $1 billion, a huge sum for the time. ERT was seen as having become too diversified, leaving it unprepared for the recession that hit Spain particularly hard at the end of the 1970s and beginning of the 1980s. ERT's diversification had come at a heavy cost for the company as well, leaving it saddled with a large and mostly short-term debt.

The group's exposure to the real estate market, in which it held assets worth approximately ESP 20 billion, left it especially vulnerable during the downturn. ERT responded by carrying out a restructuring of its operations. The group merged its various pharmaceutical operations into a single company, which it later sold. The company also sold a number of its chemicals joint ventures, while the group also sought to sell some of its mining interests.

INDEPENDENT IN THE NINETIES

ERT's difficulties eventually led it into the arms of Cros SA, originally founded as a fertilizer producer in Barcelona in 1817. By the late 20th century Cros had expanded to become one of Spain's largest private chemicals companies in its own right. Cros also enjoyed the financial backing of the Kuwaiti Investment Office, which had acquired nearly 39 percent of the company in the 1980s. The merged company became known as Ercros.

In the lead-up to the merger, ERT spun off its explosives and related operations into a reborn Unión Española de Explosivos, in 1988. The company only achieved full independence in 1994, however, as Ercros, hard hit by the new recession, scrambled to avoid bankruptcy. Ercros began selling a number of its assets, including its fertilizer business, in order to reposition itself as a chemicals company. This provided the opportunity for UEE's management, backed by private-equity group Pallas Invest Iberian Fund, to buy out the company.

The buyout, for more than $60 million, gave UEE's management a 20 percent stake in the company. UEE itself carried out an extensive restructuring process as it positioned itself for the next phase of its development. Into the middle of the 1990s UEE put into place an ambitious international expansion plan that was to see it transform itself from a largely Spain-focused group into one of the world's leading explosives and ammunition companies.

Acquisitions formed a central part of this strategy, enabling the company to gain significant positions in a number of new markets. These included Angola, following UEE's acquisition of majority control of that country's Companhia de Pólvoras e Explosivos de Angola SA (CPEA) in 2002. The group also added operations in Brazil, Australia, Russia, and Asia, as well as in South Africa.

MAXAM IN 2006

By the middle of the decade UEE had expanded far beyond its Spanish roots. The group's new international profile led the company to change its name, and in 2006 the company became known as Maxam. Despite the change in name, the company maintained its successful acquisition strategy, and through the second half of the decade completed a string of acquisitions providing it with entry into the explosives and ammunitions markets in Italy, Denmark, Germany, and Eastern Europe.

The company also entered Mongolia during this time, setting up an office to supply explosives to that country's Oyu Tolgoi mining group in 2006. Maxam also invested in building up its existing operations, as it climbed its way to world leadership in a number of its core business areas. By the beginning of the next decade the company had already positioned itself as the European leader and global number-two producer of civil explosives.

The group had also become the world leader in the outdoor ammunition sector, supplying cartridges for hunters and gun enthusiasts. Other acquisitions enabled the group to build up its materials business, including purchases of ammonium nitrate interests in France and Uzbekistan. The company's investments helped it to achieve solid growth through the decade. By 2010 the company posted an average compound growth rate of over 25 percent over a six-year period. The company had by then expanded its operations into 40 markets worldwide.

MOVES INTO CHINA: 2012

In the new decade Maxam set its sights on expansion into one of the world's fastest-growing markets, China. To this end, the company brought in new investors Advent International, which bought out the group's previous investors and took a 45 percent share of the company. Maxam's management, led by CEO and chairman José Sánchez-Junco, had raised its stake in the company to 55 percent. Backed by fresh capital, Maxam made its move into China in 2012, setting up a EUR 70 million manufacturing joint venture in Shandong.

This plant would produce Maxam's line of explosives, detonators, and other initiation devices for the Chinese mining, quarrying, and public works industries. The move into China helped raise the group's Asian sales to 11.5 percent of its total revenues by 2014.

Maxam had achieved its goal of becoming a global explosives heavyweight. The group's internationalization strategy had successfully transformed Maxam from a Spain-focused company to an industry leader with sales of EUR 1.1 billion ($1.4 billion) and operations in 45 countries, reaching more than 100 countries worldwide. It appeared well-positioned for continued success.

M. L. Cohen

PRINCIPAL SUBSIDIARIES

Denex SA; Expace On Board Systems, SL; Expace SA; Maxam Australia; Maxam CPEA SA (Angola); Maxam North America, Inc. (USA).

PRINCIPAL DIVISIONS

Civil Explosives; Outdoors; Chem; Defence; Energy.

PRINCIPAL COMPETITORS

Asean Explotech Inc.; Dyno Nobel Moranbah Proprietary Ltd.; Famesa Explosivos S.A.C.; Hanwha Corp.; Initiating Explosives Systems Proprietary Ltd.; Nippo Kogyo Company Ltd.; Orica USA Inc.

FURTHER READING

"Advent-Backed Spanish Explosives Maker Maxam Inks €280m Loan." *AltAssets*, January 4, 2013.

"Commission Clears Acquisition of Joint Control of Maxam by Advent and a Group of Individuals." *Plus NEWS*, February 10, 2012.

Daynes, Will. "Blasting through Barriers." *Bemining*, April 24, 2013.

Healing, Janice. "Maxam Dantex." *Mining Weekly*, September

20, 2010.

"Maxam Debuts in the Chinese Market." *China Mining*, October 17, 2012.

Ouass, Louisa. "Business Is Booming for Maxam." *Worldfolio*, September 2012.

"Portobello and Vista Exit Maxam to Advent for €900m." *Southern Europe Unquote*, September 12, 2011.

Millennium: The Takeda Oncology Company

—■—

40 Landsdowne Street
Cambridge, Massachusetts 02139-4234
U.S.A.
Telephone: (617) 679-7000
Fax: (617) 374-7788
Web site: http://www.millenium.com

■ ■ ■

Wholly Owned Subsidiary of Takeda Pharmaceutical
Company Ltd.
Incorporated: 1993
Employees: 1,500
Sales: $692.7 million (2011)
NAICS: 325412 Pharmaceutical Preparation
  Manufacturing

■ ■ ■

Millennium: The Takeda Oncology Company is a wholly owned subsidiary of Takeda Pharmaceutical Company Ltd. Formerly known as Millennium Pharmacuticals, the company was originally dedicated to the discovery and development of new drugs through research into disease-related genetic factors, but in later years decreased its emphasis on genetic research and dedicated its resources to a wider approach to drug research and marketing. Since its foundation in 1993, Millennium has been highly successful in landing lucrative research and development contracts with major pharmaceutical firms. The company developed the cancer drug Velcade, which is marketed in more than 90 countries.

BUSINESS BACKGROUND OF MILLENNIUM'S FOUNDER: THE SEVENTIES TO EIGHTIES

The driving force behind the creation of Millennium was its chairman and chief executive officer, Mark J. Levin. He grew up in St. Louis, the son of a businessman who owned several small shoe stores. Levin was forced to take on a great deal of responsibility early in life, following the death of his mother from cancer when he was 16. While maintaining his studies he cared for his three younger sisters and sold shoes for his father, ultimately earning a master's degree in chemical and biomedical engineering from an area school, Washington University.

For a brief spell he stayed in St. Louis selling shoes, and then in 1976 he accepted an engineering position in Indianapolis with Eli Lilly and Co. He next took a job in North Carolina, where his wife attended college, overseeing the setup of a new brewery for Miller Brewing Company, which provided him with exposure to a large production facility. A brief, unsuccessful stint owning a doughnut shop taught him the pitfalls of running a business. Levin and his wife moved to Massachusetts, where he took a job with the Foxboro Co. selling computers to biotech companies. He called on his former boss at Lilly, William Young, who now worked at Genentech, one of the pioneering biotechs, but instead of selling a process control system he found himself being offered a job.

In 1981 Levin relocated with his wife to San Francisco, where he gained experience managing a number of complex drug projects with Genentech. He

COMPANY PERSPECTIVES

At Millennium, we want to exceed expectations in terms of progress against cancer, distinguishing ourselves within the research-based biotechnology community. We're prepared to deliver on this goal by exclusively focusing on oncology, targeting best-in-class drug candidates, and cultivating the brightest talent. This puts us on an exciting path toward global oncology leadership.

then took a position in 1987 with the Mayfield Fund, a San Francisco venture-capital firm, where he served as the codirector of its Life Science Group. His job was to identify new scientific ideas, then help form companies to exploit them. Rather than wait for someone to approach him with an idea, Levin kept up on research journals and made contacts with scientists. In this way he was instrumental in the creation of Cell Genesys, Inc., in 1987; Cyto Therapeutics, Inc., in 1988; Tularik, Inc., in 1990; and Focal, Inc., in 1991.

While starting these companies and spending time with scientists, Levin became aware of research on the human genome. He visited the major genome centers in both the United States and Europe, meeting many of the prominent people in the field. It became clear to him that they believed all human diseases had some connection to genetics and that within the next decade the human genome would be sequenced. Levin recognized that genomics offered a way to produce a myriad of new drugs to cure specific diseases, as well as a business opportunity with significant potential. He was not alone in this belief, with differing business models developing to exploit genomics. Levin described the situation in a 2001 *Technology Review* interview: "Some formed diagnostic companies by identifying mistakes or [diversity] in genes. Some built companies by compiling genomic information and selling the databases that arose from the information. Others realized that there were going to be important technologies to develop and you could sell these tools and form alliances around them. Millennium was focused from day one on building the biopharmaceutical company for the future by developing personalized therapeutic products."

FOUNDING OF MILLENNIUM: 1993

From 1991 to 1992 Levin laid the groundwork for Millennium, recruiting a team of top scientific advisers with commercial appeal who would found the company in 1993: Eric Lander, with the Massachusetts Institute of Technology (MIT); Jeffrey Friedman, of Rockefeller University; Raju Kucherlapati, of the Albert Einstein College of Medicine; and Daniel Cohen, chief scientist at Genset, a French biotech. From the outset the advisers knew that in the beginning they would have to team up with a large pharmaceutical to provide major funding and to develop drugs out of Millennium's research, then take them through trials and bring them to market.

The founders also recognized that they would produce a great deal of intellectual property. As a result of this thinking, Millennium was determined to form partnerships that were narrowly defined, retaining as many rights as possible to the intellectual property the company produced, as well as earning royalties on any drugs that made it to market. Teaming with a number of companies targeting different diseases also served to spread the risk. In addition, Millennium chose to portray itself as a technology company involved in drug research, rather than an aspiring drug company, a label that was likely to drive away many investors.

At first Levin turned to Mayfield for $8.5 million in seed money, then raised additional money from other venture capital funds. His wife, who was an executive search professional, spent months looking for a suitable chief executive for the company before concluding that her husband was the only candidate with enough vision to run the business. Although Levin intended to head Millennium on a temporary basis, as he had with earlier start-ups funded by Mayfield, he ultimately decided to stay on as the permanent CEO.

In December 1993 Millennium Pharmaceuticals was incorporated. Levin leased space close to MIT and within six months the company recruited a team of 30 scientists. It also began to establish its technology platform, in many ways a testament to Levin's engineering background. A number of technologies, including robotics and computers, were combined with microbiology to create a complex, but efficient, production process.

By March 1994 the first cash-rich pharmaceutical signed on with Millennium. Hoffmann-La Roche agreed to pay $70 million over a five-year term to develop drugs to treat type 2 diabetes and obesity, two target areas with the potential to generate large revenues. In July Levin named Steven H. Holtzman as chief business officer for the company. Holtzman would be instrumental in the structuring of future agreements with pharmaceuticals, reserving as many rights as possible. Millennium's next major alliance, and Holtzman's first deal, came in October 1995, a $50 million

KEY DATES

1993: Company is incorporated.
1994: First strategic alliance signed with Hoffmann-La Roche.
1996: Company goes public.
1997: Subsidiaries Millennium BioTherapeutics and Millennium Predictive are formed.
1998: Strategic alliance is signed with Bayer AG.
2001: Company acquires Cor Therapeutics.
2003: Millennium releases Velcade.
2005: Mark Levin steps down as CEO.
2008: Takeda Pharmaceuticals Inc. acquires the company.
2013: Takeda folds Millennium into its corporate structure.

joint venture with Eli Lilly focusing on atherosclerosis, the blocking of arteries by fatty deposits. Two months later Millennium signed a five-year, $60 million collaboration with Swedish pharmaceutical Astra AB, targeting inflammatory diseases such as asthma, hay fever, and bronchitis.

PUBLIC OFFERING IN 1996

Millennium went public in 1996, netting $58 million. During the year the company's research efforts produced the first tangible results. A gene-based assay was produced for Roche to screen for obesity drug candidates. Millennium also identified a gene involved in the development of type 2 diabetes, triggering a milestone payment from Hoffmann-La Roche. Furthermore, a gene-based test developed for Eli Lilly was used to identify atherosclerosis drug candidates.

Millennium was active on a number of fronts in 1997. In an $89 million stock transaction, it acquired Chemgenics Pharmaceuticals, which allowed Millennium to broaden its research into antibacterial drugs. The company also forged a new important alliance: a $218 million, five-year deal with Monsanto Inc. involving research into bioengineered crops. Unlike previous partnerships, the agreement with Monsanto was not as narrowly defined. Because it wanted to maintain its focus on drugs, Millennium essentially agreed to a technology transfer to a new Monsanto unit, Cereon Genomics, which was set up next door. Under this arrangement Millennium received a hefty payment from Monsanto yet was not saddled with the costs of adding personnel and equipment.

Also in 1997 Millennium formed a pair of subsidiaries to enhance the value of the corporation. Millennium BioTherapeutics was established to develop therapeutic proteins, gene therapy, and antisense products. Lilly immediately signed a $70 million, five-year deal to develop medicines from proteins, in the process gaining an 18 percent stake in the subsidiary. Millennium next formed Millennium Predictive Medicine to produce diagnostic tests using bioinformatics and proteomics.

After gaining valuable experience in genomics, Millennium researchers developed a way to narrow down the number of target genes. Rather than conduct lengthy validation studies on each new gene, they concentrated on genes that reacted to known medicines. These so-called druggable genes were then studied, saving a considerable amount of time and effort. Needing a partner to put this new technique into use, Millennium turned to Bayer AG, which because it was late to embrace biotechnology was willing to assume some risk in order to catch up with its rivals. Bayer had been looking to team with a genomics company since late 1997 and by September 1998 agreed to a $465 million, five-year deal with Millennium.

Under the terms of the agreement, Millennium was to deliver 225 genomics-based proteins targeting cardiovascular diseases, cancer, osteoporosis, pain, liver fibrosis, hematology, and viral infections. In addition, Bayer gained a 14 percent stake in Millennium. It would be allowed to cherry-pick the target proteins, but the rights of 90 percent of the proteins would revert to Millennium. Although it still had no products on the market, Millennium was able to post a $10.3 million profit for the year because of its pharmaceutical agreements.

More research deals would follow in 1999. Bristol-Myers Squibb agreed to a $32 million, five-year alliance with Millennium Predictive Medicine to develop diagnostic tests in oncology. The subsidiary also signed Becton Dickinson to a $70 million, five-year strategic alliance. The parent company, meanwhile, moved closer to its goal of becoming a drug company capable of selling its own proprietary products when it agreed to a $750 million stock acquisition of LeukoSite Inc., providing latter-stage drug development capabilities as well as several possible drugs in clinical and late-stage preclinical development.

In June 2000 Millennium landed another major deal with a pharmaceutical company, which in the process forwarded its long-term aspirations. France's Aventis SA, Europe's fourth largest pharmaceutical, agreed to pay $450 million in a complex five-year deal that called for the two parties to create, develop, and market a new line of anti-inflammatory drugs to treat such diseases as rheumatoid arthritis, asthma, and certain allergies. The two companies would share profits equally in any drugs sold in the United States and Canada, and Millennium was to receive a royalty in all other markets. It was a highly advantageous deal for Millennium, but it was also of strategic importance to Aventis, which had been formed in a $25 million merger in 1999. A new management team conducted a thorough review of its operations to identify shortcomings. Establishing a relationship with Millennium was a quick and economical way for Aventis to fill its needs. Millennium then bolstered its ability to fulfill the Aventis agreement by paying $53 million to acquire Cambridge Discovery Chemistry, a British subsidiary with a large number of scientists experienced in pharmaceutical chemistry. Moreover, the addition of Cambridge Discovery extended Millennium's presence overseas.

Millennium had its first drug on the market in 2001, Campath, used to treat chronic lymphocytic leukemia, which it picked up in the LeukoSite acquisition. Although Campath was expected to reach only revenues of no more than $150 million a year, and Millennium had to share profits with two other companies involved in its development, it was still a major step for the company. As other products made their way through clinical trials, Millennium continued to forge partnerships with pharmaceuticals that might one day become rivals. Hoffmann-La Roche reached a three-year agreement to develop diagnostic products for rheumatoid arthritis. Because of the expiration of an earlier deal with Hoffmann-La Roche, Millennium was able to strike a new partnership to develop drugs and diagnostic tests for diabetes and obesity, this time with Abbott Laboratories for $250 million over five years.

By the end of 2001 Millennium also completed the largest acquisition in its brief history, a stock swap valued at $2 billion for San Francisco–based Cor Therapeutics. The transaction was a clear statement that Millennium intended to one day become a major player in the pharmaceutical business. The Cor purchase brought with it marketing rights to Integrilin, a popular cardiovascular drug, a sales and marketing staff experienced in launching new products, and a team of researchers working in heart disease, the most lucrative therapeutic area. Although some observers were critical of the Cor acquisition, others thought that Millennium had put itself in a solid position to realize future growth.

MILESTONES AND MAJOR CHANGES IN THE NEW CENTURY

In 2003 Millennium introduced another important pharmaceutical to its line with the release of Velcade for Injection, a treatment for several forms of blood cancer. Velcade would go on to become the company's flagship product for the next several years, particularly after Millennium sold its rights to Integrilin to Schering-Plough Corporation in 2005. Also in 2005, Millennium experienced the first of several major changes when Levin stepped down after 12 years as CEO. Despite relatively high sales for Velcade and Integrilin, the company had lost $252 million the previous year. Its focus on genetic research had not resulted in any promising new products in quite some time and had proven costly. As part of a transition to a research and development model with a broader focus, Levin agreed to step aside and allow a new CEO, with more practical experience marketing pharmaceuticals, to take over.

Levin's replacement was Deborah Dunsire, a South African MD who had successfully run the cancer drug division for Novartis for several years. Under Dunsire, Millennium did return to profitability as Velcade became more popular and was approved for several more uses. By 2007 the drug's success had attracted the attention of Japan-based Takeda Pharmaceuticals. Although Takeda was clearly interested in acquiring the rights to market Velcade, it also expressed interest in the skills of Millennium's research teams who had at least 10 other cancer drugs in development at the time. After a short round of negotiations, Takeda purchased Millennium outright for $8.8 billion, with the sale becoming final in 2008. Although many firms endure staff cuts after an acquisition, Millennium actually increased its workforce by almost 50 percent, to about 1,500 employees, as Takeda added another 10 cancer drug projects of its own to the company's development roster.

Although Dunsire's first several years as CEO proved profitable, several factors combined to threaten Millennium's success by 2013. First, after a very successful run, Velcade was facing stiffer competition from several new cancer drugs. Even though it answered these challenges by introducing a new form of the drug that patients could inject themselves at home, Velcade's days as a top-tier sales performer seemed numbered. Furthermore, and beyond Millennium's control, Takeda was facing other economic pressures and was looking for ways to streamline its operations and cut costs. It had lost patent protection on Actos, a diabetic drug that generated a significant portion of its global sales. Takeda had seen its net revenues fall by 28 percent in 2013 and its stock price drop by nearly 10 percent.

As part of its company-wide streamlining, Takeda decided to fold the previously autonomous Millennium organization into its general corporate structure. This would make the CEO position and several other office titles redundant. Although Takeda offered Dunsire the option of remaining with the company in another role, she chose to depart. Her effective replacement, now with the title of president of Millennium Pharmaceuticals was Anna Protopapas, who had been with the company for 16 years, primarily engineering the acquisition of several smaller pharmaceutical firms. Protopapas would oversee Millennium's business and marketing operations while research and development would now fall under the auspices of Tachi Yamada, Takeda's medical and science chief. The company's new name, Millennium: The Takeda Oncology Company, emphasized Millennium's tighter relationship with its corporate parent and Takeda's concentration of most of its cancer research on Millennium's Cambridge, Massachusetts, campus.

By the end of 2013 Millennium had fully released another promising new drug, Adcetris, in partnership with the Seattle Genetics company. Even though Seattle Genetics would retain North American marketing rights for the lymphoma treatment, Millennium would retain the global sales rights. No longer a one-drug company, Millennium seemed poised to move into the future as a vital part of Takeda's corporate mission. In January 2014 Millennium announced plans to build a new six-story, 246,000-square-foot laboratory facility in Cambridge.

Ed Dinger
Updated, Chris Herzog

PRINCIPAL COMPETITORS

Bristol-Myers Squibb Company; Celgene Corporation; Genentech Inc.

FURTHER READING

Aoki, Naomi. "Changing the Odds." *Boston Globe*, June 17, 2001.

"Custom-Made Medications." *Technology Review*, December 2001.

Looney, William. "Anna Protopapas: Takeda's Oncology Taskmaster." *Pharmaceutical Executive Magazine*, February 3, 2014.

"A Pharma Star Is Born?" *Business Week*, September 25, 2000.

Pollack, Andrew. "Shift Seen atop Millennium Pharmaceuticals." *New York Times*, June 29, 2005.

Seiffert, Don. "Millennium Is Starting Work on a New Lab Building in Cambridge." *Boston Business Journal*, January 8, 2014.

Stipp, David. "Hatching a DNA Giant." *Fortune*, May 24, 1999.

Thiel, Karl A. "The Millennium Minuet." *Forbes*, May 31, 1999.

Timmerman, Luke. "Millennium CEO Dunsire Juggles Growing Pipeline, Works to Maintain Nimble Culture—As New Owner Takeda Makes the Company Its Center for Cancer Drug Development." *Xconomy*, September 10, 2008. Accessed October 26, 2014. http://www.xconomy.com/boston/2008/09/10/millennium-ceo-dunsire-juggles-growing-pipe line-works-to-maintain-nimble-culture-as-new-owner-takeda-makes-the-company-its-center-for-cancer-drug-development.

Weisman, Robert. "Millennium CEO Resigns amid Changes." *Boston Globe*, May 9, 2013.

———. "Millennium Chief Faces Questions, Uncertainties." *Boston Globe*, June 18, 2013.

New Glarus Brewing Co.

—■—

2400 State Highway 69
New Glarus, Wisconsin 53574
U.S.A.
Telephone: (608) 527-5850
Web site: http://www.newglarusbrewing.com

Private Company
Incorporated: 1993
Employees: 80
Sales: $35 million (2013 est.)
NAICS: 312120 Breweries

■ ■ ■

New Glarus Brewing Co. is one of the 25 largest brewers in the United States, even though its distribution is confined solely to Wisconsin, where its Spotted Cow is the top-selling craft beer. The firm also brews five other year-round varieties including Wisconsin Belgian Red and Moon Man, seven seasonal beers that include Fat Squirrel and Totally Naked, and an ever-changing lineup of experimental styles released under the Thumbprint label. The company's brewery is a popular tourist destination that brings upward of 100,000 people to the small village of New Glarus, and founders Deb and Dan Carey have received national and international recognition for their business and brewing talents.

EARLY YEARS

Deborah and Daniel Carey founded The New Glarus Brewing Company in 1993. Deb, who had grown up in

Wisconsin and later moved with her family to Helena, Montana, had studied design and marketing at Carroll College before dropping out when she could no longer afford tuition. She began working at a local brewery, where in 1983 she met Daniel Carey, who had grown up in San Francisco and studied food science at the University of California, Davis. The young couple, both 23, was soon married and began to raise a family.

The Careys moved a number of times while Dan continued his brewing studies, which included apprenticing at the Ayinger brewery in Germany and studying at the Siebel Institute in Chicago. In 1987 he received a master brewer diploma from the Institute of Brewing in London, one of only a handful of Americans to do so, and he subsequently began working for an Oregon-based brewing equipment company.

In 1990 the family settled in Fort Collins, Colorado, where Dan took a job with industry leader Anheuser-Busch and Deb focused on their two daughters and side businesses doing graphic design and selling antiques. Dan appeared set to ascend the corporate ladder. Soon, however, he became frustrated by the lack of creativity the position offered. In the early 1980s a craft-brewing movement had begun gaining momentum in the United States after legal obstacles dating to Prohibition were rescinded. Drinkers had grown bored with the similar-tasting lagers offered by American brewers, who then numbered fewer than 100.

The success of start-ups such as the Sierra Nevada Brewing Co. and the Boston Beer Company inspired a host of other entrepreneurs. By the early 1990s several hundred new breweries and food-serving brewpubs had

COMPANY PERSPECTIVES

Welcome to our quaint little brewery nestled on the outskirts of New Glarus, Wisconsin. The brewery is run by an enthusiastic couple, Daniel & Deb Carey, who have successfully combined business management and brewing professionalism. Our philosophy is based on individuality, cooperation and the employment of 100% natural ingredients to produce world-class, handcrafted beers for our friends in Wisconsin. Cheers!

been founded. Spurred by her husband's unhappiness and an awareness that brewmasters employed by small breweries typically worked long hours for little pay, Deb Carey began to consider starting a brewery of their own.

ESTABLISHES BREWERY

Following a series of encouraging conversations with craft brewers she knew, Deb Carey began doing research to find areas of the country that would be ripe for a new local brewery. After looking at options including Montana and the East Coast, the idea of returning to Wisconsin to raise their daughters in a small town struck a chord. When she happened upon a failed brewpub's equipment being auctioned in Appleton, she decided to seize the opportunity.

Although they had no savings, she convinced Dan they should sell their house and put the money into starting a brewery. Madison, the state capital and home to the University of Wisconsin, was a good market for craft beer. Deb told her husband to choose a small town within a 30-mile radius to set up shop. As he drove through the wintry countryside in February 1993, the towns began to blur together, until he stopped for gas in New Glarus.

The village of 2,000, which had been founded in 1845 by Swiss immigrants from Glarus, had long taken pride in maintaining its heritage and old-world character. After a quick look around he called Deb to tell her that he had found their new home. The couple soon found an unused 10,000-square-foot warehouse, which they leased by giving its owner a stake in the brewery.

PRODUCTION BEGINS: 1993

In June 1993 the New Glarus Brewing Co. was formally established. After much work, which included digging a

drainage system in the warehouse floor, the brewery began operating in October. While Dan concentrated on setting up the equipment, Deb wrote a business plan and took care of everything from designing labels to rounding up the $400,000 they needed for the initial launch.

At year's end New Glarus brought out its first beers, which included Edel-Pils, a lager that used yeast imported from Germany, and darker brew Uff-da Bock. They would be sold on draft in bars and restaurants and in four-packs of bottles that retailed for about $4. The new firm's philosophy drew from the Careys' experiences in Germany, where nutrient-rich beer was viewed as a food and an integral part of the diet.

The company brewed 2,466, 31-gallon barrels in its first year, equivalent to about 34,000 cases in bottled form. With the Careys working most days from 5:00 in the morning until 10:00 at night and forgoing health insurance, they managed to break even financially.

New Glarus sought new customers via tastings and appearances at beer festivals. By mid-1995 distribution had grown to reach La Crosse to the northwest, Green Bay to the northeast, and Milwaukee to the east. Maximum brewing capacity had been boosted to 6,000 barrels through the acquisition of two 4,000-gallon lagering tanks, and the firm had also spent $65,000 to add bottling equipment.

WINS GOLD MEDAL: 1995

The Careys found success fairly quickly. In October 1995 New Glarus's Apple Jack Ale took the gold medal in the fruit beer category at the World Beer Championship, sponsored by Chicago's Beverage Testing Institute. Early the next year the firm also won a gold medal at the Brewing Industry International Awards in England for its Belgian Red, which used more than a pound of Door County, Wisconsin, cherries for each 750-milliliter bottle.

The sweet, fruity drink, which had made *Wine Enthusiast* magazine's list of top 10 beers for 1995, was a project Dan Carey had started some six years earlier. New Glarus was brewing Edel Pils and Uff-da Bock year-round. It was also offering Coffee Stout and Norski Honey Bock during the spring, Solstice Weiss and Apple Jack Ale in summer, Staghorn Oktoberfest in fall, and Belgian Red and Snowshoe Irish Ale in winter.

Company president Deb Carey had recently been named to head the 20-member Small Brewers Association of Wisconsin. In that post, she promoted interests of small brewers against the efforts of beer distributors and national brewers who wanted to sponsor legislation that protected their dominant positions.

```
┌─────────────────────────────────────────┐
│                                         │
│            KEY DATES                    │
│               ─■─                       │
│                                         │
│  1993:  New Glarus Brewing Co. is founded in │
│         central Wisconsin.              │
│  1997:  Firm introduces Spotted Cow beer. │
│  2007:  Second brewery begins operations in New │
│         Glarus.                         │
│  2014:  New $9 million expansion adds fruit beer │
│         aging cellar.                   │
│                                         │
└─────────────────────────────────────────┘
```

GERMAN BREWHOUSE PURCHASED: 1997

In 1996 New Glarus brewed 5,200 barrels of beer per year in its original 20-barrel brewhouse, which was nearing the limits of its equipment and small staff. Needing to expand, but unable to afford the $1 million a new brewhouse could cost, in 1997 the Careys began to look for used equipment in Germany, where the brewing industry was experiencing a wave of consolidation like the United States had endured decades earlier.

After looking at numerous rusty, worn-out examples, they came upon the recently shuttered Rauh and Ploss brewery in the small town of Selb, where the owners were about to scrap a 100-barrel Huppmann brewhouse that included two striking, 12-foot-tall, 14-foot-wide copper brew vessels. The price for the scrupulously maintained 35-year-old equipment was just $24,000, plus another $50,000 to get it to New Glarus. Dan Carey, who had installed dozens of brewhouses for JV Northwest, Inc., spent the month of April dismantling and packing the 50-ton shipment.

Relieved that it was going to a good home, the entire town turned out to watch it trucked away, with many pledging visits to Wisconsin to see it operating again. After a 5,000-mile journey by ship and truck, the equipment was lowered with cranes into the foundation of a new building adjacent to the firm's original facility, after which the walls and roof of the Bavarian-style building, designed by Deb Carey, were attached.

MORE MEDALS AWARDED: 1997

During the year the firm also added new offices and a 7,000-square-foot warehouse to store finished beer as part of its $650,000 expansion. In the fall of 1997 New Glarus's Wisconsin Belgian Red won a gold medal against 64 competitors in the fruit beer category at the Great American Beer Festival in Denver for the second year running, while its Apple Ale took bronze.

The tiny brewery's success, which had also included being ranked one of the 10 best breweries in the world by Chicago's Beverage Testing Institute, brought it to the attention of the Confederation Des Brasseries de Belgique, which threatened legal action if the word *Belgian* was not removed from the beer's name. When the press picked up the story, it provided much free publicity for New Glarus, and the Belgians quietly dropped the issue.

SPOTTED COW INTRODUCED: 1997

Dan Carey was continually making new brews in a variety of styles. In 1997 he developed a slightly sweet, easy-drinking, pre-Prohibition type of ale based on local ingredients. Believing it to be "the consummate Wisconsin beer," as she told the *Capital Times & Wisconsin State Journal* in 2007, Deb decided to call it Spotted Cow, a name she had already come up with when the Careys were in England accepting one of their beers' many awards. Noticing the large number of sheep that wandered the countryside, she realized that a visitor would have the same reaction to the many cows in Wisconsin, the "Dairy State," whose residents also took them for granted.

Carey designed a label that featured a cow jumping over a map of the state, and she believed the beer's name would resonate with Wisconsinites. Nevertheless, several distributors were reluctant to carry it, thinking the name might put off male drinkers. She persevered, and the refreshing flavor and quirky marketing that included "Spotted Cow Crossing" point-of-sale signs won drinkers over.

From the beginning the Careys had embraced a local focus, including sourcing as many ingredients from Wisconsin as possible. Residents of the state were proud of their many local traditions that ranged from cheese making to the Green Bay Packers, who sometimes played football games in subzero temperatures.

BEGINS CHICAGO DISTRIBUTION

Although its beer was available in many places around the state, Madison still remained New Glarus's primary focus. Even still, in 1998 the company began shipping its products to the huge Chicago market 150 miles southeast. Its beers were retailing for about $6 per six-pack and just under $7 for 750-milliliter bottles of Belgian Red. New Glarus's brewery began offering tours and tastings.

In 1998 production topped 6,500 barrels, and maximum potential capacity was increased by 50 percent the following year to 12,000 barrels with the addition of a pair of 200-barrel lagering tanks. Although the craft brewing industry was enduring a shakeout caused by too many start-ups and pushback from national brewers and importers, the firm continued to grow even as some craft brewers struggled or threw in the towel.

BEERS PULLED FROM ILLINOIS

In 2002 the firm completed a $500,000 expansion that added a new bottling line, four lagering tanks, and additional warehouse space. Still struggling to keep up with demand in Wisconsin, in November New Glarus withdrew distribution from Illinois, where it sold 7 percent of its output, as distribution regulations were notoriously unfriendly to small brewers. The Careys' decision to keep their loyal Wisconsin drinkers happy would prove a wise one.

New Glarus was producing six beers year-round and five seasonally, as well as occasional limited-edition brews. Spotted Cow had become its best-selling beer and was offered on tap in most bars in the state. The firm's beers continued to win medals, taking platinum honors at Chicago's 2002 World Beer Championships for both Belgian Red and Raspberry Tart, plus gold for Solstice Hefe Weiss, and silver for Copper Kettle Weiss.

The following year New Glarus was named Small Brewing Company of the Year at Denver's Great American Beer Festival. In 2003 production jumped nearly 40 percent to more than 19,000 barrels, which put New Glarus into the top 50 breweries in the United States for the first time. The company employed nearly 20, six of them part time, and sales increased to $4 million from $2.5 million. The following year the firm added a new automated kegging line, four additional lagering tanks, a new brewhouse for fruit beer, automation capabilities, and additional laboratory and refrigeration facilities. It took out a $2.2 million loan to fund the work.

SALES TOP $8 MILLION: 2005

As it strained to keep up with demand for popular beers such as Uff-da, Fat Squirrel, and Spotted Cow, which were accounting for three-quarters of sales, New Glarus put others such as Native Brown Ale and Edel Pils on hiatus, and cut to half the quarterly special-edition Unplugged line. While overall U.S. beer production had recently declined by 2 percent, craft brewers had an average 7 percent growth as the stronger companies that had survived the industry shakeout continued to grow.

For 2005 New Glarus brewed more than 39,000 barrels, a 52 percent increase, and had sales of $8.5

million. Having outgrown the 15,000-barrel production limit for the industry's small brewer category, in 2005 New Glarus was named best Mid-size Brewer of the year at the Great American Beer Festival over craft giants Sierra Nevada Brewing Co. and the Boston Beer Company, of Sam Adams fame. Dan Carey was also named Brewer of the Year. Both awards would be recaptured the following year as well.

Having considered a variety of ways to meet the ever-increasing demand for its beers, in May 2006 New Glarus Brewing broke ground on a second facility that would nearly triple its maximum capacity to 140,000 barrels annually. Largely financed by a $13.8 million loan that company president Deb Carey had secured from Wisconsin State Bank, it would be situated on a hill just south of New Glarus that offered views of the village and the surrounding countryside.

SEWAGE PLANT BUILT

Carey, who had once voiced opposition to brewing more than 30,000 barrels per year, designed the new complex, which would meld Bavarian and Wisconsin styles. A recent study done by Green County, where New Glarus was located, had found that the brewery was responsible for over $40 million in economic output per year. The expansion was widely supported by residents of the area, where it was one of the largest employers. The Village of New Glarus had pledged $2 million for a sewage pretreatment plant necessary to process the protein-, yeast-, and sugar-rich liquid waste generated by brewing.

Construction of the plant was held up for several months by negotiations over whether the village, which had agreed to annex the 30-acre site, would have rights to provide electrical service. After the firm threatened to move elsewhere, the village board agreed to let it use larger electricity provider Alliant Energy, which offered numerous incentives for the energy conservation measures the facility would use. New Glarus Brewing also agreed to accept the village's assessed value of $8 million for the property, which would determine its tax rate.

HILLTOP BREWERY OPENS: 2009

Although construction of the facility was still incomplete, the new Hilltop Brewery began production operations in late 2007. On June 13, 2009, a public grand opening was celebrated with live music, tours, and beer tastings. The 75,000-square-foot complex, whose final cost had grown to $21 million, incorporated a formal garden and gift shop. Its many energy-saving features included a system that recaptured heat from brewing and a wastewater treatment plant disguised as a barn, which pumped treated water back to the village of New Glarus and saved the firm $200,000 per year. Another barnlike building was solely devoted to Spotted Cow production.

The new facility boosted the firm's total workforce to 60, which now included the founders' daughter Nicole Carey, who served as company spokesperson. With the new brewery up and running, the firm's original location was devoted to Dan Carey's development of limited-edition Unplugged beers. Spotted Cow had become the most popular craft beer in Wisconsin and the second-best-selling beer in the state, behind SABMiller's Miller Lite.

The latter, the second-largest U.S. brewer, budgeted millions for advertising. New Glarus had spent little on marketing beyond creating a Web site and point-of-sale materials. The firm was ranked by *Inc.* magazine as one of the 100 fastest-growing food and beverage companies in the United States. New Glarus's reputation was so strong, and its distribution so limited, that beer lovers outside Wisconsin were constantly seeking ways to get its products.

PUSH TO STAY LOCAL

In November 2009, 50 cases of Spotted Cow were confiscated from the Mad River Bar & Grille in New York City after the New York State Liquor Authority discovered them on-site. The firm's decision to stay local proved a boon for some retailers close to the borders of Minnesota and Illinois, however, who sold large quantities of New Glarus beer to thirsty customers from out of state.

For 2010 New Glarus brewed just under 92,000 barrels of beer, up more than 16 percent from the year before, and had revenues of nearly $20 million. Spotted Cow accounted for half, with demand to the point that the firm was running two shifts per day. Craft brewers had grown to account for 5 percent of beer sold in the United States, up from 3 percent a decade earlier. The segment continued to expand even as overall beer consumption stagnated.

THUMBPRINT LINE ADDED: 2011

New Glarus had long produced Dan Carey's experimental beers in limited release under the Unplugged brand, but in recent years other brewers had begun to use similar names. In early 2011 the firm relaunched them under the name Thumbprint, which was subsequently trademarked. The beers were sold only

at the Hilltop Brewery in editions of 1,500 bottles each. Dan Carey's reputation was such that they usually sold out within hours, with some beer lovers driving hundreds of miles to obtain them.

Their only publicity was an announcement on the firm's Web site. Over the years more than two dozen different styles had been produced, while a similar number of year-round and seasonal varieties had come and gone. The brewery's lineup had changed as sales of each brew rose or fell, although Spotted Cow had always been offered since its introduction. New Glarus seasonals included Yokel, Totally Naked, and Dancing Man, while recent additions to the year-round brews included Moon Man India Pale Ale (IPA), named after a brewer's cat, and Two Women Ale, a collaboration with German woman-owned brewing products supplier Weyermann Malting.

GOVERNMENT RECOGNITION

In March 2011 the U.S. Small Business Administration named Deb Carey Wisconsin Small Business Person of the Year, and in May she was named national first runner-up. New Glarus was the 21st-largest craft brewer in the United States, and the 30th-largest brewer overall, according to craft beer trade group the Brewers Association. There were now more than 1,700 breweries and brewpubs around the country, including 60 in Wisconsin.

The firm's success had brought considerable attention from outside investors, and the Careys had reportedly turned down a number of offers to buy the company. These included two attempts by Dan Carey's former employer, industry leader Anheuser-Busch InBev. More than 100,000 tourists had visited the brewery in 2011. With this figure expected to rise by as much as 50 percent, in 2012 the firm invested $7 million to double the size of its visitors' center, and to add another 17,000 square feet of warehouse space.

The firm sponsored a trolley from downtown to the Hilltop Brewery that often carried 600 visitors on a weekend day, and offered self-guided brewery tours along with tastings costing $3.50 for three samples. A weekly Hard Hat Tour gave a more extensive view of the operation, with the $20 all-access visits often sold out months in advance. For 2012 the firm brewed 126,000 barrels of beer, up 10 percent over 2011, and had revenues of $31.4 million.

WHITE HOUSE INVITATION

In November 2012 Deb Carey, who had begun serving on the White House Business Council, was one of 15 members invited to Washington to meet with President Barack Obama and Vice President Joe Biden, who were seeking advice on spurring economic recovery and job growth. Obama, who had recently become the first president to brew beer in the White House, traded Carey three bottles of his Honey Ale and Honey Porter for two of New Glarus's new Serendipity apple-cherry-cranberry beer, which had been created after the previous year's Door County cherry crop was wiped out by drought.

The Careys and a group of military veterans who worked for the brewery later posted a video of their favorable review of his beers on YouTube. In February 2013 Michelle Obama invited Deb Carey to sit in her box at the State of the Union address, where she sat next to Apple CEO Tim Cook. As New Glarus's latest expansion neared completion in 2013, the firm announced another $9 million project that would nearly double maximum brewing capacity to 250,000 barrels per year.

It would include a 7,500-square-foot fermentation cellar for aging fruit beers for up to three years, and a large copper "coolship" for creating spontaneously fermented sour beers, which Carey had recently begun experimenting with. In spring 2013 New Glarus celebrated its 20th anniversary with the release of a special Belgian Dubbel-style ale. For 2013 the firm was ranked 18th-largest U.S. craft brewer and 25th-largest overall. The craft industry's vitality was attracting more competitors. During the year a group of investors led by former Capital Brewery brewmaster Carl Nolen opened an $11 million brewery in Verona, Wisconsin, near Madison.

SECOND WHITE HOUSE VISIT

Production of up to 250,000 barrels per year was forecast by 2015, and the Wisconsin Brewing Co. would include a tasting room facing a pond and an outdoor beer garden, with an anticipated 200,000 visitors annually. In January 2014 Deb and Dan Carey were invited to Washington to attend the nomination of Maria Contreras-Sweet as administrator of the Small Business Administration.

President Obama cited the Careys in his remarks as examples of the organization's success in helping small business owners. The Careys, who had both started with little and succeeded because of their own hard work, had from the beginning striven to treat their employees fairly and pay them a living wage.

In just over two decades, New Glarus Brewing Co. had grown from a two-person operation into one of the 25 largest breweries in the United States, as well as a major central Wisconsin tourist destination. In a state long famed for its brewing, the firm's Spotted Cow was the most popular craft beer, and the company posted strong annual growth even as distribution remained limited to Wisconsin. With Deb Carey's business acumen and Dan Carey's beer-making talent leading the way, New Glarus Brewing appeared set for continued growth.

Frank Uhle

PRINCIPAL COMPETITORS

Boston Beer Company, Inc.; Capital Brewery; Jacob Leinenkugel Brewing Co.; Lakefront Brewery, Inc.; New Belgium Brewing Co.; Sierra Nevada Brewing Co.; Stevens Point Brewery; Wisconsin Brewing Co.

FURTHER READING

Adams, Barry. "Co-founder to Sit with First Lady at Speech." *Capital Times & Wisconsin State Journal*, February 12, 2013.

———. "Spotted Cow Out of Place in Big City." *Capital Times & Wisconsin State Journal*, November 25, 2009.

"Brewery Taps into History." *Capital Times*, June 23, 1997.

Daykin, Tom. "Crafted with Success." *Milwaukee Journal Sentinel*, March 10, 2008.

———. "New Glarus, Wis., Brewery Cuts Back to Take Advantage of Success." *Milwaukee Journal Sentinel*, December 30, 2002.

Leaf, Nathan. "Chance Taken, Leading to Spotted Cow." *Capital Times & Wisconsin State Journal*, January 1, 2007.

McDade, Phil. "Brewing in New Glarus: Beer Wizard Sets Up Shop." *Wisconsin State Journal*, September 6, 1993.

Nelesen, Marcia. "New Glarus Brewing Bottles Love for Wisconsin." *Janesville Gazette*, July 22, 2012.

"New Glarus Makes Belgians See Red." *Capital Times*, April 18 2000.

Reid, Peter V. K. "Brewing the Good Life." *Modern Brewery Age*, May 10, 1999.

Simms, Patricia. "New Glarus Founder: 'I'm a Game Changer.'" *Capital Times & Wisconsin State Journal*, July 3, 2011.

Troller, Susan. "Roll Out the Barrels; New Glarus Brewing Co. to Celebrate Grand Opening of Hilltop Brewery this Weekend." *Capital Times & Wisconsin State Journal*, June 11, 2009.

Williams-Masson, Ellen. "Pour Another Round; New Glarus, Brewery Reach Agreement." *Capital Times & Wisconsin State Journal*, August 4, 2006.

OKI Electric Industry Company Ltd.

—■—

1-7-12, Toranomon
Minato-ku
Tokyo, 105-8460
Japan
Telephone: (+81 3) 3501 3111
Web site: http://www.oki.com

Public Company
Incorporated: 1881 as Meikosha Company
Employees: 21,090
Sales: ¥483.1 billion ($4.74 billion) (2013)
Stock Exchanges: Tokyo
Ticker Symbol: 67030
NAICS: 334118 Computer Terminal and Other
Computer Peripheral Equipment Manufacturing;
334210 Telephone Apparatus Manufacturing

■ ■ ■

OKI Electric Industry Company Ltd. manufactures a vast array of telecommunications equipment and high-end electronics. OKI's network of subsidiaries are located throughout Japan, Asia, the Americas, and Europe and offer banking systems used in financial institutions, ticket reservation systems, cloud computing services, call center and videoconferencing systems, flight control systems, and optical network systems. Its products range from printers to automated teller machines (ATMs) and check-in terminals. With a history dating back to 1881, OKI has the distinction of being Japan's first telecommunications equipment manufacturer.

EARLY HISTORY

OKI Electric Industry's roots are inextricably tangled up with an American invention. OKI's founder, Kibataro Oki, was an engineer working for Japan's Department of Industry when the first telephones to be imported into the country arrived from the United States in 1877. He participated in the planning and production of Japan's first domestically manufactured telephones, but the Japanese version of the Bell System proved to be a technical failure.

Oki's faith in the future of the telecommunications, however, was not shaken by the experience. Instead, he left government service and founded his own manufacturing company, called Meikosha Company, in 1881 in the Shin-Sakanamachi area of Tokyo. Meikosha started out producing and marketing telephones, electric wires, and bells, and soon added switching equipment, telegraphs, lightning rods, incandescent and arc lamps, and medical equipment to its repertoire. Most of its customers were large institutions including government agencies, private companies, and the Japanese military.

In 1890 telephone exchanges were set up in Tokyo and Yokohama, and Meikosha was among the Japanese companies that manufactured telephones for these systems. It also supplied the nation's first domestically produced magneto serial repeating switchboard for the Tokyo exchange in 1896. That same year, the company separated its marketing and manufacturing operations, with the former shifting its headquarters to the Kyobashi Ward of Tokyo and changing its name to Oki & Company. The manufacturing plant had changed its name to Oki Electric Plant two years earlier.

COMPANY PERSPECTIVES

The people of OKI, true to the company's enterprising spirit, are committed to creating superior network solutions and providing excellent information and communications services globally to meet the diversified needs of communities worldwide in the information age.

Kibataro Oki died in 1906 at the age of 59. The next year Oki & Company was reorganized as a limited partnership, with a capitalization of ¥600,000. The company underwent further reorganization in 1912, when the manufacturing and marketing operations were again separated from each other. Then in 1917 the two groups were recombined under the name OKI Electric Company Ltd.

During this time OKI also diversified its product lines. Besides venturing into electric clocks and measuring equipment, it also was a pioneer in the manufacture and sale of radio equipment in Japan. By 1917 it had expanded its facilities to four manufacturing plants, and the company employed nearly 4,000 people.

After the Great Kanto Earthquake of 1923 caused severe damage to Tokyo's infrastructure, Japan's telephone exchanges became automated. In 1926 OKI entered into a joint venture with the General Electric Company of the United Kingdom, to manufacture automatic switching equipment. Oki also began to produce electric clocks in 1929.

THE WAR YEARS

The political climate in Japan in the 1930s was marked by increasing militarism. In 1931 the Japanese army invaded Manchuria, and in 1937 Japan went to war against China, marking the start of eight years of full-fledged war for Japan. By then, OKI had become one of the nation's leading electrical manufacturers and had built up an overseas sales network that covered China and Southeast Asia. In response to the increasing demand for military hardware, it built two more plants in the late 1930s, one in Shibaura, Tokyo, to produce communications equipment for the army, and another in Shinagawa to build hydrometers for the navy, as well as maritime and aeronautical radios.

After the United States entered World War II in December 1941, the manufacture of civilian communications equipment came to a standstill as Japan devoted more and more of its resources to the war effort. For the remainder of the war, military orders provided the vast majority of OKI's business. The company underwent significant expansion in the early 1940s, increasing its production of military equipment, such as field telephones, aeronautical radios, and hydrophones. When World War II ended in August 1945, OKI had 20 plants and nearly 23,000 employees despite the fact that its Shibaura plant had been completely destroyed in an American bombing raid.

OKI radically scaled back its operations after Japan's surrender, trimming itself down to five plants and 4,000 employees. It stopped producing military equipment and restored its remaining manufacturing capacity to civilian uses. Its plant at Warabi had somehow escaped damage during the war, and OKI began turning out automatic telephone switching equipment there. The company produced telephones and radios and, responding to the demand for simple consumer goods in war-ravaged Japan, began making portable cooking stoves and irons as well. Amidst the difficulties of reconstruction, however, OKI also found the time and resources to begin developing the teleprinter, laying the foundation for a business that would become one of its most successful four decades later.

POSTWAR GROWTH

OKI's resurrection was almost cut off in 1948, however, when the American occupation authorities ordered the breakup of large industrial concerns. Similar actions were undertaken in occupied Germany, partly as retribution, but also in the hope that decentralizing the economy would make future remilitarization more difficult. OKI was one of the Japanese companies marked for breakup. Later that year, however, the order was rescinded, and in 1949 the company was incorporated under its current name, OKI Electric Industry Company Ltd.

In 1953 OKI's rebuilt Shibaura plant opened and began manufacturing telephones and radios. In 1954 the company entered into a joint venture with Raytheon, a leading American defense electronics contractor, to produce radar equipment. Also during the 1950s OKI began making semiconductors and entered Japan's fledgling data processing and computer industry. By 1960 it had become one of the Big Six that historically dominated that business in Japan, along with Nippon Electric Company (NEC), Hitachi, Fujitsu, Toshiba, and Mitsubishi.

KEY DATES

1881: Kibataro Oki establishes the Meikosha Company.

1890: Telephone exchanges are set up in Tokyo and Yokohama.

1907: Oki & Company is reorganized as a limited partnership.

1917: Marketing and manufacturing operations merge to form OKI Electric Company Ltd.

1926: OKI enters into a joint venture with the General Electric Company to manufacture automatic switching equipment.

1949: Company incorporates under the OKI Electric Industry Company Ltd. name.

1953: OKI's rebuilt Shibaura plant opens and begins manufacturing telephones and radios.

1984: Subsidiary OKI America, Inc., is created.

2008: OKI sells its semiconductor business.

2014: Company buys Itautec's ATM business.

EXPANSION AND NEW PRODUCT DEVELOPMENT CONTINUES: 1960–75

Beginning in 1962 with the encouragement of the Ministry of International Trade and Industry (MITI), OKI joined other Big Six computer firms in a series of joint research-and-development ventures. The first of these was called FONT AC, and was intended to develop an IBM-compatible mainframe computer to make Japan less vulnerable to mainframe imports from the United States. Fujitsu developed the central processing unit, NEC the electronic peripheral equipment, and OKI the mechanical peripherals, and it resulted in the introduction of Japanese IBM-compatible mainframes in the early 1960s. The remaining Big Six firms were brought into the project in 1966, when work began on the next generation of FONTAC computers. OKI's task was to develop a way to process Kanji, the Japanese alphabet.

In 1963 OKI entered into a joint venture with the American computer company Sperry Rand to manufacture mainframes under the name OKI Univac Kaisha, Ltd. The 1960s also saw a substantial increase in OKI's overseas business, especially in Latin America. It constructed a nationwide communications network in Honduras in 1962 and a regional network in the Bolivian capital of La Paz in 1966. In 1971 OKI developed a microwave radio network in Brazil.

OKI established a new division in 1970 to develop computer software. In 1977 it added a research laboratory to its electronics plant at Hachioji and devoted it to research and development of large-scale integration (LSI) microcircuits, which can pack a relatively substantial number of transistors into a small space. But in this area OKI was somewhat behind because in that year the government initiated a research-and-development program devoted to very-large-scale integration (VLSI). VLSI circuits crammed more than 250,000 transistors onto a silicon chip less than one micron wide and they were in common use by the late 1980s. OKI was the only Big Six manufacturer to be left out of the project by MITI, although the company soon began work on VLSI at its Hachioji lab.

OKI was also in a state of severe financial crisis in 1977 and 1978. Sales barely increased between 1975 and 1977, and profits plummeted resulting in a loss of ¥1.5 billion in 1977. Following an extensive restructuring in 1979, however, the company made a dramatic recovery.

GLOBAL FOCUS: 1980–95

In 1980 OKI built a VLSI plant in Miyazaki. In 1981 it began to produce personal computers, one of the last of the Big Six to do so. And in 1984, OKI responded to increased business opportunities in the United States by merging its five American subsidiaries into one large subsidiary, OKI America, Inc., anticipating that the cost of doing business in the United States would be lower if its American activities were coordinated in the United States instead of Japan. In 1985, OKI began manufacturing cellular mobile telephones in the United States, one of the largest markets for cellular phones at the time.

The strong yen also persuaded OKI to begin construction of a plant in the United Kingdom for the local production of its popular dot-matrix printers. In the United States, OKI built a major manufacturing facility outside Atlanta in 1988 and an additional factory opened in Oregon two years later.

After its financial crisis in the late 1970s, OKI's profits dropped drastically again in 1985 and it lost ¥8.4 billion in 1986, reflecting a profound slump in the semiconductor industry. But OKI, like the industry, bounced back, and it remained a leading electronics and computer peripherals manufacturer into the early 1990s.

During 1990 the company established subsidiary OKI (Thailand) Company Ltd. and acquired the data business division of U.K.-based Technitron Corp. The company partnered with Hewlett-Packard Company in 1992 to develop integrated circuits. It completed construction of a printer plant in Thailand the following year. As part of a restructuring effort the company transferred its printer and fax businesses to subsidiary Oki Datasystems Company Ltd. This subsidiary's name was then changed to OKI Data Corporation in 1994. OKI entered a joint venture with U.S.-based Sensar, Inc., to develop iris recognition products the following year.

ENTERING THE NEW MILLENNIUM

As OKI prepared to enter the 21st century, the company adopted a new corporate mission statement and launched its "Vision 2000" business strategy that focused on streamlining company operations while developing new products that met global demand. New products in 1996 included the OKITAC-2500 banking information system, the CTstage Computer Telephony Integration (CTI) system, and the Discovery 2000 multimedia integrated communications node. Changzhou OKI-GEG Telecoms, Ltd., a Chinese subsidiary, was created in 1997.

During 1998 Katsumasa Shinozuka was named president. OKI's financial performance was faltering at this time due to falling prices in the semiconductor market, which greatly affected profits in its dynamic random access memory chips business. Waning demand for communications equipment also ate into the company's bottom line. As such, Shinozuka began to revamp its semiconductor business in an attempt to shore up profits. During 1998 OKI partnered with U.S.-based Cadence Design Systems, Inc., to develop new chip designs. The company also began to shutter underperforming businesses including its cellular phone operations. It acquired Toshiba Corp.'s ATM business in 1999.

Profits began to rebound in 2001, just as the company celebrated its 120th anniversary. Moving forward, OKI remained focused on new product development, forming key partnerships, and global expansion. During 2002 the company formed OKI Software Technology Company Ltd. in China. It also launched a semiconductor sales company in China. During 2003 OKI joined with Silicon Application Corp. of Taiwan to create OSAC Solutions Company Ltd. That same year, the company partnered with NEC to develop products for the Internet protocol (IP) telephony market in Japan.

In 2004 the German Federal Ministry of the Interior began using OKI's Iris Recognition System in the Frankfurt am Main Airport. The following year the company acquired Texas Instruments Japan's driver chip

business used for large thin-film-transistor liquid-crystal display, which were used in televisions, monitors, and notebook computers. The company acquired TCB Technologies Corporation's Visual Nexus software-based videoconferencing system in 2007.

OKI recognized the importance of the China market at this time and continued to strengthen its footprint in the region. The company opened a sales office in Beijing in 2006 and then completed construction on a new plant in Shenzhen the following year. OKI Telecommunications Technology (Changzhou) Company Ltd. was established in Jiangsu, China, in 2008.

EXITING THE SEMICONDUCTOR MARKET IN 2008

During the early 21st century the semiconductor market remained highly competitive and new product development proved costly. Once a market leader, OKI's rank had fallen to 13th among Japan's semiconductor firms. As such, the company began exploring options to exit this market. During 2008 the company created OKI Semiconductor Company Ltd. and then sold 95 percent of its shares to Japan's Rohm Company Ltd.

At the same time, the company created OKI Networks Company Ltd. to oversee its telecommunications business, which by now included products and services related to next-generation networks, network integration technology, IP network technology, and voice and video over IP.

Hideichi Kawasaki took over as president in 2009. Under his leadership, the company continued to streamline operations while developing its printers business and high-end electronics manufacturing services. It also continued to eye new markets for expansion and opened a printer sales office in Russia in 2010. Offices were opened in Indonesia and Germany in 2012. During 2014 the company completed the acquisition of the ATM business of Itautec S.A., which was renamed OKI Brasil S.A. Looking to the future, OKI management planned to launch the OKI brand in new markets across the globe.

Updated, Christina M. Stansell

PRINCIPAL DIVISIONS

Solutions & Services; Telecom Systems; Social Infrastructure Systems; Mechatronic Systems; Printers; High-End Electronics Manufacturing Services (EMS).

PRINCIPAL COMPETITORS

Canon Inc.; Fujitsu Ltd.; Hitachi Ltd.

FURTHER READING

Davidson, William H. *The Amazing Race: Winning the Technorivalry with Japan.* New York: John Wiley & Sons, 1984.

"Oki Electric Prioritizing Early Resumption of Dividend Payments." *Japan Chemical Web,* October 27, 2010.

"Oki Electric to Change President for 1st Time in 11 Yrs." *Kyodo News,* March 12, 2009.

"OKI Starts Operations of Its New ATM Business Company in Brazil." *China Weekly News,* January 28, 2014.

"Oki to Sell Chip Business to Rival Rohm for 100 Bln Yen." *Nikkei Weekly,* June 2, 2008.

Okimoto, Daniel I., Takuo Sugano, and Franklin B. Weinstein, eds. *Competitive Edge: The Semiconductor Industry in the U.S. and Japan.* Stanford, CA: Stanford University Press, 1984.

Sobel, Robert. *IBM vs. Japan: The Struggle for the Future.* New York: Stein and Day, 1986.

Omax Corporation

21409 72nd Avenue South
Kent, Washington 98032
U.S.A.
Telephone: (253) 872-2300
Toll Free: (800) 838-0343
Fax: (253) 872-6190
Web site: http://www.omax.com

Private Company
Incorporated: 1993 as Auburn Machine Tool, Inc.
Employees: 240
Sales: $85 million (2012)
NAICS: 333515 Cutting Tool and Machine Tool Accessory Manufacturing

■ ■ ■

Omax Corporation is a leading designer and manufacturer of computer-controlled abrasive water-jet cutting machines, which use a high-velocity stream of water mixed with an abrasive material to precisely cut metals, composites, glass, ceramics, and other materials. They are used in the aerospace industry and by other manufacturers, as well as metal and architectural fabricators, research and development and prototyping companies, tooling companies, repair shops, branches of the military, government agencies, and others. Premium machines are sold under the Omax name, while standard machines rely on the Maxiem brand. New and preowned water-jet machining systems are sold by the company's sales force and a global network of distributors. In addition, the company offers financing.

More than 3,000 Omax systems have been installed in about 60 countries. Omax also offers a wide range of accessories and software and provides installation, training, maintenance, and repair services. The Kent, Washington–based company is privately owned.

WATER-JET ORIGINS

The roots of water-jet technology date to the 1930s, when the Paper Patents Company developed the first water-jet nozzle that created a low-pressure water stream and could be used to cut paper. Although the lack of durable nozzles kept water-jet cutting from becoming a viable option, development of the technology continued. With the introduction of ultrahigh-pressure nozzles, water jets were used to cut metals in the aerospace industry in the 1950s.

Systems that could cut plastic followed, and in the 1960s a water jet was developed by Union Carbide to cut both metal and stone. It was not until the 1970s, however, that commercial water-jet-cutting machines became available. It was also in the early 1970s that in Kent, Washington, former Boeing Company researchers and scientists started Flow Research Company to develop commercial water-jet systems.

The two cofounders of Omax, Dr. John Cheung and Dr. John Olsen, both worked for Flow. Olsen had studied fluid mechanics at the Massachusetts Institute of Technology and in 1966 completed his doctoral thesis on the subject. He started a research and development partnership in 1970 to work on water-jet technology, which became the cornerstone for the work of Flow Research.

Olsen developed the first high-pressure intensifier pump in the early 1970s and played an important role in the development of a more efficient crankshaft high-pressure water pump. Cheung had begun working with water-jet technology as a research scientist with the U.S. Bureau of Mines after earning his PhD in mechanics and materials in 1973.

BECOMES FLOW INDUSTRIES

Cheung then joined Flow as a research scientist and in 1982 was named president of the company. By this time, Flow Research had expanded and was known as Flow Industries. In 1983 Flow Systems was spun off to pursue water-jet-cutting systems for industrial automation. Two years later another company, AD-MAC, Inc., was spun off to focus on water-jet systems for construction, industrial cleaning, and the mining industries.

A third company, FlowMole, was also formed to become involved in tunnel boring for cable and pipe installation. The businesses struggled in the late 1980s and were united in 1989 as Flow International. The management ranks were less unified, however. In March 1990 Cheung resigned. A month later three key senior executives resigned as well.

FOUNDING OF OMAX

Cheung and Olsen teamed up with the goal of providing abrasive water-jet technology to the manufacturing sector. They initially named the company Auburn Machine Tool, Inc., but soon adopted the OMAX Corporation name. The foundation of the company was a software patent by Olsen on motion control that addressed a major drawback of abrasive water-jet technology.

A water jet is essentially a soft tool. When it cuts, it bends, always changing shape and direction, thus making it difficult to produce a consistent finish to the material being cut. The solution to the problem was to adjust the traverse speed or change the angle of the water jet to compensate for the taper. It was a manual adjustment, however, and posed too many variables for the machine operator to properly take into account.

COMPUTERIZATION OF PROCESS

Olsen's answer was to computerize the process. Instead of selecting a speed, the water-jet operator would input values that included the type of material, thickness, and other set-up parameters. The motion control software then created a model of the proposed process, which was subsequently executed. This approach became known as "compute first, move later."

With this motion control technology, abrasive water-jet machines not only became more precise, they were easier to use and could be used for more applications. Operators could also determine the level of quality they desired. If the piece was going to be machined later, a simple separation cut was requested. If not, a fine edge could be applied. Using Olsen's motion-control software solution, Omax introduced its first product in 1993, the JetMachining Center Model 2448. It was intended for general machine shop use.

The following year the company added the JetMachining Center Model 2652, which was also intended for machine shop use but was able to handle projects with smaller dimensions and requiring a high level of precision. It was an integrated system that included motion control, an ultrahigh pressure pump, abrasive jet delivery system, and a two-axis machining table.

SOFTWARE IMPROVED

Omax continued to make improvements to the software, as well as to pump technology and the machining table. In 1995 the company was awarded a patent for Machine Tool Apparatus and Linear Motion for the Machine Tool. The following year, a patent was received for Motion Control with Precomputation. Also, in 1996 Omax introduced the Maxjet3 Nozzle and the Omax JetMachining Center Model 2652A, an updated version of the previous Model 2652.

Further improvements were made in the second half of the 1990s. Windows-based software, new direct-drive pumps and the Maxjet4 nozzle were introduced, as was a new cutting machine. The Omax JetMachining Center Model 55100 became the company's largest cantilever-style machine, designed for machine shops using larger stock. Also in the late 1990s Omax began selling its products in the European market.

CONTINUATION OF RESEARCH AND DEVELOPMENT

Although Omax had greatly improved abrasive water-jet technology, there remained many improvements to be

KEY DATES

1993: Company is founded.
1994: JetMachining Center Model 2652 is introduced.
2007: Agreement is reached to sell Omax to Flow International.
2009: Sale of company to Flow International is terminated.
2014: Next-generation Maxiem machine opens up new markets.

made as the company entered the new century. Taper remained an issue, and motion-controlling equipment also needed to evolve in order to improve accuracy. To meet these challenges and better serve its customers, Omax continued to invest in research and development.

Early in the first decade of the 21st century, the company made steady improvements in direct-drive pump technology. To help improve precision, Omax introduced the Precisions Optical Locator accessory, which allowed users to accurately place premachined components on the machining table for secondary machining operations.

The new Intelli-Max Software Suite also provided tools to improve accuracy and compensate for taper, as well as making the machine centers easier to use and faster to set up. Omax also introduced a new JetMachining Center. The Model 80160 was a large bridge-style machine that was designed to handle larger stock, offering unobstructed loading capability and other advanced features.

10TH ANNIVERSARY: 2003

In 2003 Omax celebrated its 10th anniversary. To date, the company had installed more than 600 systems. In addition to machine shops, customers included manufacturing facilities, universities, and government agencies around the globe. The year was also marked by the introduction of new features, including the Maxjet 5 Water Only Nozzle, Manual/Adjustable Tilt Nozzle, the Tilt-A-Jet cutting head, and the Omax Drill head.

While Omax had firmly established itself in the water-jet market, it also developed a fierce rivalry across town with Flow International. In 2004 Omax filed a $108 million lawsuit against Flow, accusing it of infringing on two software patents. Omax also asked that a Flow patent be declared invalid. Flow insisted that the claims lacked merit, and the two companies took the matter to court.

With the litigation against Flow in the background, Omax remained on the forefront of abrasive water-jet technology. Further advances were made in direct drive pumps, and new products were unveiled. The Omax JetMachining Center Model 2626|xp was introduced to serve the tool-and-die and medical device markets.

In 2006 Omax added the Collision Sensing Terrain Follower, an accessory that helped with the cutting of uneven surfaces. In that same year, the company added the Omax Fabricator JetCutting Center, an abrasive water-jet machine designed specifically for the cutting of large stone slabs or metal plates. Two new JetMachining Centers were then introduced in 2007, Model 60120, a small bridge-style machine, and Model 5555, a small footprint cantilever-style machine.

BROWN BECOMES CEO

In 2007 Omax and Flow made an effort to settle their differences, mainly the result of Flow hiring a new CEO, Charley Brown, who came from the outside and had not been party to the animosity that had festered between the two Kent companies. He arranged to meet with Cheung at a restaurant, and the two men quickly developed a good rapport.

They soon decided that both companies would be better served by joining forces rather than by spending more money in court. By the end of 2007 they struck a deal that called for Flow to acquire Omax for $109 million in cash and stock. While the sale to Flow underwent due diligence, Omax introduced more new products in 2008, including the Omax 80X Series JetMachining Centers that were designed for large or multiple-part projects.

The rotary axis rotary head was also introduced, as well as the third generation of motion control software. Omax was enjoying strong growth, as sales improved from $25.3 million in 2004 to $62.7 million in 2007. The following year the global economy lapsed into recession as a result of a financial crisis. Not only did sales decline, the poor business climate jeopardized the sale to Flow.

SALE TO FLOW SCUTTLED: 2009

In March 2009 Omax and Flow settled their patent infringement suit, but two months later Flow decided that because of the recession it would have to terminate the acquisition of Omax. According to the terms of the 2007 agreement, Flow was required to pay Omax $35 million if the deal was scuttled. Omax remained an independent company but now had the litigation with Flow behind it and additional cash in the bank.

Another significant development in 2009 was the introduction of the less-expensive Maxiem Waterjet line. Omax possessed two brands at this time, Omax for premium systems and Maxiem for standard systems. In the years that followed the company developed both lines further and introduced new enhancements. It also rebuilt sales, which had fallen to about $40 million during the recession. Omax increased sales to $85 million in 2012.

A year later Omax celebrated its 20th year. In October of that year the company introduced the narrowest-stream water jet it had ever produced. The MicroMax was ideally suited for the medical and electronics fields. In 2014 Omax introduced its next-generation Maxiem machine. It was an attractive option for a wide range of customers, including architectural, sign, stone, and gasket shops, as well as trade schools.

By this stage, Omax had sold more than 3,000 machines around the world but had barely dented its potential market. With ample opportunity at both the higher and lower price points, and still room for improvements in software, pumps technology,

and machining tables, the future appeared bright for Omax.

Ed Dinger

PRINCIPAL OPERATING UNITS

Maxiem; Omax.

PRINCIPAL COMPETITORS

Flow International Corporation; Jet Edge, Inc.; KMT Waterjet Systems, Inc.

FURTHER READING

"Flow Cancels Its Omax Acquisition." *Puget Sound Business Journal*, May 12, 2009.

"Flow Settles Litigation with Omax." *Puget Sound Business Journal*, March 13, 2009.

"OMAX Corp. Celebrates 20 Years of Waterjet Innovations with Aug. 20 Event." *Kent Reporter*, July 29, 2013.

"Omax Sues Flow for $108M." *Puget Sound Business Journal*, November 29, 2004.

Wilhelm, Steve. "The Tiniest Cut: Kent Company Unveils Fine-Focus Waterjet." *Puget Sound Business Journal*, August 29, 2013.

———. "Two Competitors Find a Common Ground in Kent." *Puget Sound Business Journal*, December 30, 2007.

Orion HealthCorp, Inc.

1805 Old Alabama Road, Suite 350
Roswell, Georgia 30076
U.S.A.
Telephone: (678) 832-1800
Fax: (678) 832-1888
Web site: http://www.orionhealthcorp.com

Private Company
Incorporated: 2004
Employees: 423
Sales: $32.5 million (2013)
NAICS: 561499 All Other Business Support Services

■ ■ ■

Headquartered in Roswell, Georgia, Orion HealthCorp, Inc., is a leading player in the field of medical billing. The company's customers are physicians, for whom it provides a wide range of business-related services. These include billing, collections, and practice management, with a goal of minimizing costs and maximizing earnings via the use of systematic processes. Additionally, the company also provides customers with a means of minimizing vaccine costs through access to its Vaccine Group Purchasing Alliance.

EARLY YEARS

Although Orion HealthCorp Inc. was established in December 2004, through its predecessors the company traces its origins back to the mid-1980s. The company initially operated as a Delaware corporation named Technical Coatings Incorporated, which was established on February 24, 1984. Eventually becoming inactive, the company changed its name to SurgiCare Inc. on July 11, 1999, and moved forward with a new focus, namely the development, acquisition, and operation of so-called freestanding ambulatory surgery centers, which were not organizationally or physically connected to a particular hospital.

Early leadership at SurgiCare was provided by co-CEO and Chairman Dr. David Blumfield, co-CEO and COO Charles Cohen, and a committee that comprised physicians who provided the organization with guidance. Initially, the company was focused on growing via acquisitions, mergers, and management contracts. In keeping with this strategy, Bellaire Surgical Inc. was acquired in July 1999.

In the spring of 2000 SurgiCare went public, and its stock began trading over the counter. Early the following year the company filed for a listing on the NAS-DAQ Small Cap exchange, seeking greater exposure with investors. The listing, however, never materialized. Instead, SurgiCare's common stock was listed on the American Stock Exchange and began trading under the ticker symbol SRG on July 11, 2001.

GROWTH BY ACQUISITIONS

SurgiCare ended 2001 with revenues of $12.9 million. The company began 2002 with a deal to acquire Baytown, Texas–based San Jacinto Surgery Center L.P. for $11.7 million. This was followed by an agreement to acquire a 51 percent stake in the Dover, Ohio–based Tuscarawas Surgery Center, as well as a $6.8 million deal to purchase the Colorado-based health care management consulting firm Aspen Healthcare Inc.

Midway through 2002 SurgiCare revealed that it had acquired an interest in Tuscarawas Surgery Center ahead of schedule. At the same time, the *Houston Chronicle* gave the company an eighth-place ranking on its 100 Leading Companies list, in recognition of increasing revenues nearly 104 percent from 2000 to 2001. In June SurgiCare made the first two payments in connection with the Aspen Healthcare deal, and the company was in the process of integrating Aspen's operations into its own.

EARLY CHALLENGES

Although things seemed to be going well, the climate at SurgiCare changed significantly a few months later as the company encountered financial difficulties. In September Keith G. LeBlanc was named CEO, and a new chief financial officer named Phil Scott was hired. At that time the company announced that it had sold its 20 percent stake in the Bayside Surgery Center and was evaluating other nonstrategic or unprofitable assets.

The following month the company pulled out of its merger with Aspen Healthcare at a cost of approximately $1.7 million. Additionally, SurgiCare pulled the plug on development of a plastic surgery center named First Street SurgiCare. In addition to a new CEO, SurgiCare experienced another senior leadership change when Blumfield resigned in November. Even though it had withdrawn from certain deals, SurgiCare moved forward with other plans, including the development of a freestanding gastroenterology center in Houston named Physicians Endoscopy.

SEEKING CAPITAL PARTNER

The company rounded out the year by raising $1 million of equity from International Diversified Corporation Ltd. As SurgiCare began 2003 the company continued to revamp its management team by hiring experienced health care executives for key positions. In addition, the company focused on ways to reduce its debt, indicating that between $2.5 million and $3 million was needed to rectify loan defaults.

CEO LeBlanc revealed that the company had stabilized its operations and was in search of a long-term capital partner to fund its growth strategy. This included the development of medical imaging services via joint ventures with existing physician partners, as well as the formation of a practice management division to offer billing and collection services. As part of its revitalization efforts, SurgiCare retained an advertising agency to develop a new logo, Web site, and image campaign.

The company also developed a new mission and vision statement to complement its strategic plans. In early 2003 SurgiCare received an additional $1.2 million from Houston-area physicians who were existing shareholders in the business. Nevertheless, the company remained in a difficult financial position, with liabilities exceeding assets by approximately $8 million as of March 31, 2003.

As SurgiCare continued to restructure, it revealed that, in keeping with a strategy to establish so-called outpatient medical malls, it would open a new magnetic resonance imaging (MRI) center in Dover, complementing its surgery center there. By this time SurgiCare had sold its equity stake in Physicians Endoscopy Center. By the middle of 2003 the company had generated $4.22 million in revenue, down 40 percent from the previous year, and had recorded a $1.59 million net loss.

RESTRUCTURES AS ORION HEALTHCORP

A major development took place on October 11, 2004, when SurgiCare's shareholders agreed to restructure ownership of the company. Completed in December of that year, this was accomplished via the acquisition of three new businesses, Integrated Physicians Services Inc. (IPS), Dennis Cain Physician Solutions Inc., and Medical Billing Services Inc. (MBS).

In addition, the company also received approximately $13.3 million in equity financing from Brantley Partners IV LP and completed a one-for-ten reverse stock split. Following SurgiCare's restructuring, the company changed its name to Orion HealthCorp Inc. Along with the new name came a new ticker symbol, ONH, under which Orion HealthCorp began trading on the American Stock Exchange on December 15. The company also elected a new board of directors and secured a two-year, $4 million revolving credit line.

SurgiCare's former common stock was converted into Class A shares of common stock for the new Orion

HealthCorp. Additionally, Class B and Class C common stock also was created, as part of the aforementioned acquisitions and equity investments. By 2005 Terrence L. Bauer had been named as Orion HealthCorp's new CEO.

That year, the company sold its IntegriMED subsidiary, which provided physicians with integrated business and clinical software and technology solutions, in a deal with the electronic medical records and practice management systems company, eClinicalWorks LLC. Additionally, Orion HealthCorp sold its MRI center and ambulatory surgery center in Dover to a local hospital.

REDUCES ANNUAL EXPENSES

Although it no longer owned the facilities, the company continued to manage them under a long-term management agreement, and stood to benefit from higher management fees as the hospital began referring a larger number of patients to the facilities. Moving forward, Orion HealthCorp consisted of three different business units, namely SurgiCare, which provided services to freestanding surgery centers; Medical Billing Services Inc., which provided hospital-based physicians with practice management solutions and billing/collection services; and Integrated Physician Solutions Inc., which was a provider of business and management services for physician practices.

By selling its ownership of the facilities in Dover, as well as the consolidation of functions at company facilities in Atlanta and Houston, Orion HealthCorp achieved a $1.45 million reduction in annual expenses. During the latter part of 2006 Orion HealthCorp was able to successfully settle a lawsuit that had been filed against the company by investor American International Industries Inc. in mid-2005. The suit alleged that the company had engaged in stock fraud, common-law fraud, civil conspiracy, misrepresentation, and violations of the American Stock Exchange's rules, causing American International to lose money. Ultimately, the two companies settled the matter for $750,000.

ACQUISITIONS CONTINUE

With that challenge behind, Orion HealthCorp made progress in late 2006 when the company acquired the Simi Valley, California–based full-service medical billing agency, Rand Medical Billing Inc., which had formed in 1985 and specialized in serving clinical and anatomic pathology practices. Additionally, the company also acquired the Mobile, Alabama–based payment-processing services company, On Line Payroll Services Inc., as well as the related data outsourcing business, On Line Alternatives Inc., which provided patient refund processing, collection follow-up, insurance filing, payment posting, patient statements, and data entry services. On Line Alternatives' roots dated back to 1973.

In connection with the aforementioned acquisitions, Orion HealthCorp secured $8 million in private placements from Brantley Partners IV LP, which continued to be the company's largest shareholder, as well as Phoenix Life Insurance Company. In preparation for future growth, a new senior secured credit facility worth $16.5 million was obtained from Wells Fargo Foothill Inc. The facility included $10 million specifically for acquisition purposes. Orion HealthCorp ended 2006 with net operating revenues of $23.4 million, up slightly from $22.8 million in 2005.

Profits continued to be elusive, with a net loss of $4.1 million. This was, however, a marked improvement from 2005 when the company generated a net loss of $14.6 million. In September 2007 a major leadership change occurred when CFO Stephen H. Murdock resigned from Orion HealthCorp to pursue another business opportunity. At that time the company also hired Ronald D. Wentling as its new director of business development. Additionally, William J. Suffich III was named regional vice president.

GOING PRIVATE

In addition to the leadership changes, another major development took place at this time when Orion HealthCorp announced plans to become a private company. This was accomplished via a one-for-2,500 reverse split of the company's Class A common stock, followed by a 2,500-for-one forward stock split. Completed in December 2007, the split resulted in the number of Orion HealthCorp shareholders being reduced to less than 300 and the company's shares being delisted from the American Stock Exchange.

Orion HealthCorp continued to grow as a private company, making two additional acquisitions in 2008. These included Western Skies, a medical and physician billing provider in Denver, Colorado. In addition, the medical billing and physician practice management firm RMI also was acquired. That company, which specialized in billing and collections for the radiology field, had been formed in 1994.

In 2010 Orion HealthCorp introduced a new data management and analysis tool named Osmium, which allowed physician clients to understand and make decisions based on the large volume of data associated with their respective medical practices. Specifically, the tool offered assistance with functions such as benchmarking productivity against similar practices, forecasting and managing cash flow, viewing the status of charges, and managing reimbursements. That year CEO Bauer was named to *Business-to-Business Magazine*'s Top 25 Entrepreneur list, with a 12th-place ranking.

By this time Orion HealthCorp's headquarters were based in Roswell, Georgia. The company also maintained operations in Texas and Ohio, as well as Colorado, Illinois, Alabama, and California. Following a third-party audit, in late 2010 Orion HealthCorp received the American Institute of Certified Public Accountants' Statement on Auditing Standards No. 70 certification, which pertained to the company's processes for handling critical client data reliably and securely.

SATISFIED CUSTOMERS

By late 2011 Orion HealthCorp's customer base included imaging centers, laboratories, physician groups, and other types of health care providers nationwide. At that time the company released the results of a client satisfaction survey, indicating that 94 percent of its clients were highly satisfied with Orion HealthCorp's services. At this time the company was serving medical imaging customers via a subsidiary named Orion RMI, which was led by CEO Jack McBride.

Orion HealthCorp continued to add new customers in 2013, such as the Los Angeles–based Kerlan-Jobe Orthopaedic Clinic, a widely recognized leader in orthopedics and sports medicine treatment and research. That year, the company instituted new leadership when it appointed Western Skies Billing Service founder Dale N. Brinkman as its new CEO. In addition, the company also named Joseph A. Seal as president.

By 2014 Orion HealthCorp had grown to include approximately 700 employees. Although the company had experienced challenging times during its early years as an operator of surgery centers, the organization had successfully transformed itself into a leader in the field of medical business and financial management services. Moving forward, Orion HealthCorp appeared to be positioned for continued growth and development.

Paul R. Greenland

PRINCIPAL SUBSIDIARIES

Orion—IPS; Orion—MBS; Orion—Rand; Orion—RMI; Orion—Western Skies Billing.

PRINCIPAL COMPETITORS

CBIZ, Inc.; McKesson Corporation; Team Health Holdings, Inc.

FURTHER READING

"Imaging Economics Chooses Orion HealthCorp Client, West Houston Radiology, as Best of 2011 Radiology Facilities." *Health & Beauty Close-Up*, December 15, 2011.

"Orion HealthCorp Attains SAS 70 Type II Certification." *Daily the Pak Banker*, December 16, 2010.

"Orion HealthCorp Inc. Appoints New Leadership Team." *Reuters*, June 26, 2013.

"Orion HealthCorp Receives High Marks from Clients." *Wireless News*, November 4, 2011.

Orr Safety Corporation

———— ■ ————

11601 Interchange Drive
Louisville, Kentucky 40229
U.S.A.
Telephone: (502) 774-5791
Fax: (502) 515-8020
Web site: http://www.orrsafety.com

Wholly Owned Subsidiary of Orr Corporation
Incorporated: 1948
Employees: 200
Sales: $267 million (2009 est.)
NAICS: 423840 Industrial Supplies Merchant Wholesalers

■ ■ ■

Orr Safety Corporation is a Louisville, Kentucky–based distributor of industrial safety products, representing more than 600 manufacturers and primarily serving the railroad industry. Categories include clothing and work wear; high-visibility vests, clothing, and accessories; protection products for head, eyes and face, hearing, and feet and legs; anchorage and attachment and other fall protection products; welding protection; respiratory protection; orthopedic and ergonomic products, including back, wrist, and elbow supports; and specialty work gloves. Orr also distributes emergency eyewash and showers; first aid and emergency response products; facility maintenance products; fire protection products; heat stress prevention products; temperature indicators and other instrumentation; head lamps, flashlights, and other lighting products; ladders and other material handling products; and traffic control products. In addition to its Louisville home, Orr maintains distribution facilities in nine other cities across the United States. Orr also sells products online. Additional services include on-site stores, vending, and programs for prescription safety eyewear and safety shoes. Orr Safety is a subsidiary of Orr Corporations, Inc., which also serves as the holding company for Orr Protection Systems and InspectionLogic Corporation. All are privately owned and managed by the Orr family.

ORR SAFETY FOUNDED: 1948

Orr Safety was founded in Louisville by Clark Orr Sr. in 1948 to fill the safety protection needs of utility workers, including helmets and work gloves. He initially visited utilities in central Kentucky and Indiana, showing samples from the trunk of his car. He expanded his business to include utilities throughout the Midwest and began serving the safety needs of other industries. As government regulations grew stiffer, industrial safety needs increased, resulting in further growth.

In 1967 the second generation of the Orr family joined the business in the form of Clark "Bud" Orr Jr. He soon took Orr Safety into the fire protection sector. In 1971 he secured a distribution agreement with Fenwal Incorporated for its fire and explosion suppression systems. Established in 1935, Fenwal had pioneered these products in the aircraft industry and played an important role in military aviation during World War II. In the years that followed, Fenwal became an international provider of fire protection products for mission critical facilities. Orr Safety's early projects with

COMPANY PERSPECTIVES

Worker safety means business.

Fenwal involved the installation of fire suppression systems at the Brown & Williamson Company tobacco firm and Kentucky's Ashland Oil. The Orr family decided to form a new company in 1971, Orr Protection Systems, to focus exclusively on this sector. Not only did the subsidiary distribute fire protection products, it provided the necessary engineering services, including the design and installation of fire, explosion detection, and fire suppression systems.

BUD ORR SUCCEEDS FATHER: 1973

Bud Orr succeeded his father as the chief executive of both Orr Safety and Orr Protection Systems in 1973. He also found a new market to serve, environmental protection products. Although the original Clean Air Act was passed by the U.S. Congress in 1961, subsequent amendments put teeth in the measure. In 1970 federal enforcement was greatly increased and called for the creation of the Environmental Protection Agency. The act was amended further in 1977, creating increased demand for products to protect the environment and another market to serve for Orr Safety.

Industrial safety products remained Orr Safety's primary business. Playing a key role in the continued growth in sales was Richard P. Harper, who joined the company in 1980. The 36-year-old Harper had fled Cuba with his family in 1960 and earned a degree in business administration from the University of Florida. Involved in operations at Orr Safety and ultimately becoming vice president of operations, Harper was instrumental in Orr Safety adopting computer technology before many of its competitors. It was an edge that allowed Orr Safety to begin national expansion in the mid-1980s.

An important factor in Orr Safety's decision to expand nationally was the desire of its customers for more safety services. In the mid-1980s Orr Safety opened field offices in California, Illinois, Missouri, Ohio, Texas, and West Virginia. With a wider footprint, Orr Safety, as well as Orr Protection, was better able to serve major corporations as well as midsized companies. Some of Orr Safety's and Orr Protection's customers included B.F. Goodrich Co., BellSouth Corporation, Conrail Inc., CSX Transportation Inc., Dow Corning Corp., Eli Lilly, GTE Corp., Sprint Corp., Union Carbide Corp., and Union Pacific Railroad.

Orr Safety's customers did not just want a provider of protection products with a robust distribution network; they needed solutions to help them remain in compliance with Occupational Safety and Health Administration (OSHA) regulations. By the start of the 1990s, however, companies also began to realize that improved safety and industrial hygiene was simply good business and could have a significant impact on the balance sheet. Accidents and injuries on the job interrupted work, disrupted schedules, increased insurance rates, and in the end cost money in a variety of ways. According to a National Safety Council study conducted in the early 1990s, each injury that resulted in lost work time cost a company $27,000. As a result of these factors, companies began to budget an increasing amount of funds for training to not only cut down on work disruptions but to improve the lives of their employees.

TRAINING UNIT FORMED: 1991

In 1991 Orr Safety's marketing manager, Bernie Gibson, began urging the company to start a safety training department to take advantage of the growing demand for training. By becoming more of a full-service operation, Orr Safety would also be in line to increase the sale of its protection products. Once Orr Safety decided to take the step, it elected not to start from scratch. Rather, it acquired another Louisville firm already involved in safety training, CRU Inc. In this way, Off Safety received an experienced staff of nationally certified occupational health and safety professionals, as well as an established client base. CRU was renamed Training and Environmental Sciences Group (TES) and operated as an independent business. In addition to providing group training sessions, TES also offered compliance evaluation services to ensure a client met OSHA requirements.

It was not just large companies that recognized the cost-benefit of safety and hygiene. Small privately owned companies had been traditionally reluctant to spend much money on safety products. Their attitude changed as OSHA had a growing impact on their businesses. Perhaps of even greater importance was the rising price of workers' compensation insurance and the potential cost of workers' compensation lawsuits. Hence, demand for safety products, training, and compliance evaluation also increased among smaller companies, playing to the benefit of Orr Safety and its sister operations. By the end of the 1990s Orr Safety increased annual sales to $70 million.

Also in 1991 Orr Safety formed a division dedicated to the environmental protection market called

KEY DATES

1948: Clark Orr founds the company.
1967: Bud Orr joins his father at the company.
1973: Bud Orr succeeds his father as chief executive.
1991: CRU Inc. is acquired.
2013: Miller Safety and First Aid Products is acquired.

Environmental Compliance Systems Corporation. It offered custom engineering services and used its expertise to develop compliance software to help reduce harmful air emissions and create other state-of-the-art monitoring systems. The new business would become part of Orr Protection Systems before splitting off as a separate subsidiary of Orr Corporation. At the turn of the century, EC Systems launched the LDAR business unit to provide training, auditing, and consulting services. LDAR soon became the company's primary business unit and its fugitive emission LDAR software the flagship product. Subsequently, EC Systems was renamed InspectionLogic Corporation.

NEW CORPORATE HEADQUARTERS: 2000

Other changes were in store for Orr Safety and its sister companies at the beginning of the new millennium. During this period, the third generation of the Orr family, Bud Orr's son, Clark, became more involved in the management of the family businesses, which would also have a new home. The four businesses of Orr Corporation had over the years spread across five buildings in the Louisville area. To bring some continuity to the group companies, and allow them to better cross-sell to one another's customers, the Orr family decided to construct a new 100,000-square-foot facility in Louisville's Commerce Crossings Industrial Park. The idea of attempting to find an existing site that could be renovated was rejected. Construction of the new building and the relocation of the Orr companies was completed in the fall of 2000. As an economic incentive to build in the area, the local government made an unusual agreement with Orr Corporation. In exchange for 20 years of reduced taxes, Orr Safety would supply the county with an equivalent amount of safety equipment and provide the public schools with safety audits, safety training, and other professional services.

Expansion was not limited to Louisville. In 2000 the Charleston, West Virginia, branch of Orr Safety exchanged its 5,000-square-foot location for a new 20,000-square-foot facility. Orr Protection also expanded in 2002 by acquiring Reno, Nevada–based TPG Inc., which designed and installed fire suppression systems for telecommunications companies. Because of the terrorist attacks against the United States on September 11, 2001, many of its customers had turned their attention to security systems rather than fire suppression projects. With revenues reduced, TPG was forced to either merge or be acquired in order to survive. The operation was relocated to the new Louisville facility.

NEW PRESIDENT: 2003

Orr Safety hired a new president in 2003. Replacing Jerry Nichter, due to health problems, was Bryan B. Slade, who had joined Orr Corporation a year earlier as the head of the e-business division. Although Bud Orr remained chairman, Slade assumed day-to-day responsibilities for Orr Safety, which continued to expand the range of products it carried. A steady stream of new products were added from such key suppliers as Aearo, offering hearing protection products; American Allsafe Company, a provider of goggles; Ergodyne, a manufacturer of work gloves and other worker safety products; Industrial Scientific Corporation, a maker of gas detection products; Lakeland Industries, a provider of protective clothing; Pelican Products, a manufacturer of watertight equipment cases, flashlights, and work lights; and Protective Industrial Products, Inc., which offered G-Tek gloves and other industrial safety products.

As the first decade of the new century unfolded, Orr Safety became more active in marketing value-added services to its customers, many of which had cut costs and had to make do with fewer safety managers. Orr Safety offered to pick up the slack by providing technical training. Although the company charged a fee for some of the programs, much of the training was offered as part of the sale of equipment. In addition, Orr Safety conducted training seminars around the country for the benefit of current and potential customers.

Growth continued in the 2010s. To keep up with demand and free up underused warehouse space, Orr Safety upgraded its Louisville distribution facility. A new narrow-aisle format was adopted and new narrow-aisle equipment was acquired in order to create additional space without the need for construction. Orr Safety also grew through external means. In the summer of 2013 it acquired Miller Safety and First Aid Products, a Pittsburgh, Pennsylvania–area distributor of industrial safety and occupational health products. Orr Safety inherited a number of new customers in Ohio and

Pennsylvania, as well as a few national accounts. The addition of another distribution center also bolstered Orr Safety's ability to pursue future growth.

Ed Dinger

PRINCIPAL COMPETITORS

Global Equipment Company Inc.; Protective Industrial Products, Inc.; W.W. Grainer, Inc.

FURTHER READING

Adams, Brent. "Orr Protection Systems Acquires Nevada Firm." *Business First*, February 12, 2002.

"Injury Cost Drives Safety Market." *Industrial Distribution*, July 1995.

"Orr Safety Gets New President." *Business First*, April 18, 2003.

"Proving Safety Still Pays." *Industrial Distribution*, July 1995.

Ray, Rebecca. "Safety in Number." *Business First*, December 20, 1999.

Pantone LLC

590 Commerce Boulevard
Carlstadt, New Jersey 07072-3013
U.S.A.
Telephone: (201) 935-5500
Toll Free: (866) 726-8663
Fax: (201) 896-0242
Web site: http://www.pantone.com

Wholly Owned Subsidiary of X-Rite, Inc.
Incorporated: 1962
Employees: 140
Sales: $20.3 million (2013 est.)
NAICS: 511140 Directory and Mailing List Publishers;
511120 Periodical Publishers; 511210 Software
Publishers

■ ■ ■

A wholly owned subsidiary of X-Rite, Inc., Carlstadt,
New Jersey–based Pantone LLC is a global authority on
color and color systems. Using a palette that includes
thousands of colors, the company develops, standardizes,
and forecasts colors for a worldwide clientele. It provides
both color systems and the technology that enables
industries to not only select colors accurately, but also to
communicate choices from designers to manufacturers
to retailers, and ultimately to customers and other end
users. The company explores the impact of color on human emotions, physical reactions, and thought processes
through its Pantone Color Institute.

EARLY YEARS

Pantone's emergence as a major force in color management systems did not start until Lawrence Herbert
became part of the company. As a young man, he had
an early interest in printing, but that was not the focus
of his education. He graduated from Hofstra University
with a double major in biology and chemistry. His plan
was to go on to medical school, but in 1956 he began
working for Pantone on a part-time basis. He became so
intrigued with his work that he scrapped his idea of
pursuing his studies as a physician.

At that point, Pantone was just a small printing
company in Manoochie, New Jersey. There were no
industry-wide or uniform standards for color printing.
Pantone printers in the 1950s employed a basic stock of
about 60 different pigments and used them to mix ink
colors in an inefficient, trial-and-error method. Through
his knowledge of chemistry, Herbert was able to reduce
the stock of pigments to a basic palette of just 12, from
which a full range of colored inks could be mixed.

By 1962 Herbert was running the printing half of
the business while the company's original owners
focused on promoting commercial displays. Herbert's
division was profitable, theirs was not, and even though
they drained off funds from his division, they soon ran
up $50,000 in debt. Herbert then bought the printing
division from them for $50,000, enough to pay off their
debt. The funds for the buyout were provided by a
woman who not only put up the money but also did it
without demanding a financial stake in the company as
collateral. The identity of this benefactor has never been
disclosed.

COLOR SYSTEMS AUTHORITY

Under Herbert, Pantone began its development into an international authority on color and color systems. The company took the initial step in 1963, when it introduced its first Pantone Matching System Printers' Edition, the basis for Pantone's evolution into a company with global prestige and influence. Although Herbert had previously developed a uniform system based on a carefully coded mixing of 12 basic pigments, it was not until he owned Pantone that he began an aggressive campaign to gain wide acceptance of his system.

He had also reduced the number of pigments to just 10 basic inks, making the generation of a wide array of colors remarkably simple. Herbert wrote to 21 major ink producers, describing the Pantone Matching System and offering to license them as manufacturers of the system's 10 basic inks. It took less than two weeks for all but one of them to sign on and pay a basic royalty to Pantone. It was an unheralded achievement, but, albeit quietly, it had revolutionized the color printing trade.

The Pantone Matching System soon began providing solutions to some of industry's problems. For example, it helped Kodak solve one that had stemmed from the fact that Kodak used more than one company to print its film packaging. Confronted with film boxes with varying shades of yellow, customers tended to leave the darker-shaded ones on retail shelves, thinking the film in them was not as fresh as that in the brighter ones. With Pantone's systems, companies printing the boxes for Kodak all began producing them with the exact same color tone and thereby solved Kodak's niggling problem.

Through the rest of the 1960s Herbert started to adapt his basic matching system, not just to printing, but also to other industries. In 1964 he launched the Pantone Color Specifier for the design market, and in the next year introduced the first artist materials application of the Pantone Matching System. Pantone also developed new systems and guides in Herbert's first decade as owner, including Pantone's first Four-Color Process Guide and its Color Tint Selector for the design field in 1968.

ENTERING THE DIGITAL WORLD

It was more of the same during the 1970s, a decade that also saw Pantone sign up some important clients and negotiate at least one major agreement. In 1971, 3M signed on as a Pantone Color Key licensee. Also in that year, Pantone by Letraset Color Markers were introduced in the design field. The following year, Pantone and Letraset entered an agreement granting Letraset global rights to produce and market Pantone Graphic Arts Materials, all of which were coordinated to the Pantone Matching System.

At that time, Pantone also entered a licensing arrangement with Day-Glo Color Corporation for the application of its system to fluorescent base colors. In 1974 Pantone made its first foray into the digital world of computing. The milestone was achieved when the company produced its Color Data System for computerized ink color formulation and matching. It was a significant step in an area of application that, as computer use burgeoned in the 1980s and beyond, became increasingly important.

Herbert took Pantone private in 1977. In its last year as a public company, Pantone's sales were about $2 million. Thereafter, Herbert did not divulge what the company's sales volume was each year. By the mid-1980s Pantone's trademark appeared on about $500 million worth of art supplies, ink, and other art and printing products marketed in over 50 countries.

TECHNOLOGICAL ADVANCES AND PARTNERSHIPS

Through the 1980s Pantone made some significant technological advances and launched new products. Among other things, in 1981 the company introduced its Two-Color Selector and its Color Selector/Newsprint, and in 1982 it launched its Process Color Simulator. In addition, in 1984, Pantone formed a new division. The Electronic Color Systems Division was established to reproduce the company's color standards in a digital system. By 1985 Pantone had also signed on its first software licensee, Via Video.

In the next year it inked a licensing agreement with Networked Picture Systems, Inc., its first client to adapt Pantone's software designed for the IBM-PC and compatible computers. In 1987 the company licensed LaserWare, Inc., as its first customer to adopt a version of the software for use with the Apple-Macintosh platform. Meanwhile, by that same year, Pantone had expanded its Matching System to 747 colors. Between 1988 and 1990 the company entered into licensing agreements with most of the world's major graphic and design software manufacturers.

KEY DATES

1956: Lawrence Herbert starts working part time at a printing company.

1962: Herbert acquires the printing operations from the original owners.

1963: Company introduces its initial Pantone Matching System Printers' Edition.

1977: Herbert takes company private.

2001: Company launches its Pantone TheRight-Color division.

2006: Pantone unveils a new brand identity and forms Pantone Japan Co.

2007: Company is acquired by X-Rite Inc. for $180 million.

2010: Pantone improves its Pantone Matching System by introducing the Pantone Plus Series.

2013: A color-matching device is developed for the cosmetics retailer, Sephora, for use in more than 800 stores nationwide.

EXPANSION AND DIVERSIFICATION

These agreements pertained to programs for both Macintosh and IBM-PC compatible computers. In 1988 it also signed up QMS Inc. as its first printer licensee, and in the next year added NEC Technologies, Océé Graphics, and Tektronix Inc. to its list. It also was in 1989 that Pantone expanded its Textile Color System to 1,225 colors. In a cooperative venture with Intergraph Corporation, the company developed its color interface for high-end computer systems. In a venture with another company, Purup Electronics A-S, it created and introduced The Purup System for designing sophisticated packaging.

By the late 1980s Pantone had energetically entered a period of partnering with other companies to develop new products. In that respect it was very much in step with what many large companies were doing in a variety of industries, particularly those that could derive benefits in cost and efficiency from outsourcing some part of their operations.

The company's co-development of products would continue through the next decade, starting in 1990, when it developed its Professional Color Toolkit in conjunction with Radius Inc. The toolkit consisted of a software library designed to achieve the best Pantone color in Pantone-licensed printers. Meanwhile, several other companies signed on as Pantone software licensees.

TECHNOLOGICAL ADVANCES

Over the next few years, with the phenomenal development of the home computer industry, Pantone's role in digital art and design grew by leaps and bounds. In 1991 the company expanded its textile color system to 1,701 colors. It also entered into a new licensing agreement with NeXT Computer Inc., marking the first time that its colors were provided at the system level. That meant that developers for the NeXT platform did not have to build support for Pantone colors into either their software or hardware products.

The company also entered into new licensing agreements with Ventura Software, Hewlett-Packard, and others. Its colors also became available for the UNIX operating system for the first time. Although NeXT, in many ways ahead of its time, would be absorbed by Apple in 1996 and end production, UNIX and its desktop computer versions began to give Microsoft some growing microcomputer operating-system competition as the 1990s wore on.

By 1992 Adobe, Bitstream, Deneba, MultiAd Services, Quark, and Ventura had all announced support for the Pantone color system in their newest software releases. In that year, too, Pantone introduced its color printer test kit, allowing users of Pantone licensed printers to find the closest possible matches to Pantone colors. In that year, the Xerox 4700 color document printer became the first color laser printer to support the full range of Pantone colors, while the Tektronix Phaser USD was the first dye-sublimation printer to provide similar support for the company's color-matching system.

PRODUCT ENHANCEMENTS AND INTRODUCTIONS

Between 1993 and 1995 Pantone launched several new products and continued to enhance its technology. Among other things, in 1993 it introduced its Open Color Environment, the first color management system allowing true WYSIWYG (what-you-see-is-what-you-get) color matching. In that year it also introduced its Plastics Color System, a universal plastic color-reference system, and ColorUP, a software color-management tool for business professionals designed to help them enhance color quality in their reports and presentations.

The next year, 1994, Pantone introduced its Color Systems Cross-Reference Software as well as ColorDrive, a desktop color-management program free of specific applications. Next, in 1995 Pantone introduced its Textile Color Swatch Files, its Foil Stamping Color Guide, and its SuperChip. These all represented technical refinements for making color delineation as accurate as possible in different applications of the Pantone systems. Meanwhile, in the same three-year period, Pantone continued to develop new partnerships and licensing agreements.

In 1993 alone, six new companies (AGFA, Aldus, Corel, Gold Disk, Linotype-Hell, and Serif) included support for the Pantone Process Color System in their most recent software releases. From 1995 to 1998 Pantone continued to produce an array of new products in its partnering and licensing arrangements with other companies, both at home and abroad. Among other things, in 1995 the company launched Hexachrome for commercial use and secured new licensing agreements with Hewlett-Packard, Lexmark, and Xerox. Pantone also entered into a distribution pact with Ingram Micro.

The following year, the company received ISO 9002 certification and entered a global distribution agreement with VISU. Next, in 1997, it signed a distribution agreement with ALTO Imaging Group N.V. for the marketing of Pantone's products abroad, published *Color Trends 1998* for graphic and Web design, and released a new version of ColorDrive for Windows. In 1998 Pantone began shipping ColorWeb Pro, introduced its OfficeColor Assistant, an operating system add-in, and, with Apple, launched a worldwide color seminar series called Expand Your Color Universe.

A NEW MILLENNIUM

By the end of the decade Pantone had expanded its global presence to the point where its name had virtually become synonymous with color management, and almost monthly it strengthened its position through new partnerships and licensing arrangements. By 2001 Pantone had built its palette to 1,757 colors. The company's aim at that point was to have not just professionals but the general public speaking its color language.

To that end, Pantone started up TheRightColor division, the focal responsibility of which was to provide a universal, uniform, and precise color language along with technological solutions for industry retailers needing a color standard for enhancing consumer shopping and sharpening their competitive edge through all their marketing channels. TheRightColor solutions adapted the universally used Pantone Textile Color System to their needs.

Among other things, the solutions allowed retailers to cut down on the number of merchandise returns stemming from faulty color matches, update their inventory tracking and restocking techniques, and enhance their ability to monitor customer color tastes and thereby make stocking and shelving adjustments to increase sales. The company also formed a partnership with The National Retail Federation for the purpose of providing a better color-coding system for electronic marketing applications.

Midway through 2002 Pantone introduced a handheld, portable spectrocolorimeter that was preloaded with the company's Pantone Matching System. This allowed the user to scan any flat surface and identify the closest matching color for a variety of outputs, including Web design and four-color printing. Around the same time the company established a new division named Pantone Custom Color Services, which was devoted to providing art directors and corporate managers in a wide range of industries with custom color standards. By this time the company's palette had expanded to include 1,932 different colors.

INTRODUCES INK-JET LINE

New product introductions continued in 2003 when Pantone introduced its own line of ink-jet products named ColorVANTAGE. Early the following year the company established a licensing agreement with the China Textile Information Center to co-market and co-brand Pantone's color system as part of the China National Color System. This gave Chinese textile manufacturers better tools with which to do business internationally. The company also partnered with Xerox to develop a color-matching system specifically for digital printing presses.

Pantone mourned the loss of vice president Michael C. Garin in 2004. A company employee for almost 42 years, the longtime executive had played an integral role in developing the Pantone Matching System with Lawrence Herbert. By this time Lawrence's son, Richard Herbert, was serving as the company's president and chief operating officer. Richard's educational background included both business and computer engineering, helping Pantone to stay on the cutting edge in a digital age.

Taking advantage of its proprietary colors, Pantone continued to introduce new products during the middle of the decade. In 2005 the company unveiled its own line of stationery and office supplies under the name Pantone Universe. The following year Pantone partnered with Fine Paints of Europe to create Pantone Paints. Selling anywhere from $7 to $95 per can, the paint line provided new options for homeowners, architects, and interior designers. Additionally, international growth took place when the company established Pantone Japan Co.

A major development took place at the end of 2006 when Pantone unveiled a new brand identity. This involved the development of a new company logo that was an interpretation of its widely recognized Pantone Chip, along with the tagline, "The Color of Ideas." The company ended the year with revenues of approximately $42 million, on the strength of relationships with licensees in more than 100 different countries.

ACQUIRED BY X-RITE

In August 2007 the publicly traded color solutions provider, X-Rite Inc., agreed to acquire Pantone for $180 million. The deal was finalized in October, at which time Pantone became an X-Rite subsidiary. That year the company introduced the PANTONE Goe System, a new color-matching system supported by recognized printing and design industry players such as Xerox, Hewlett-Packard, and Quark. This was followed by the introduction of an online color network for design and pre-media professionals called myPantone.com, which encouraged color-related collaboration and provided access to Pantone's color forecasts.

In 2010 Pantone improved its Pantone Matching System by introducing the Pantone Plus Series, which provided customers with expanded color options. That year, the company also introduced a new handheld digital color-measuring device named Capsure. More than a colorimeter, the device included a digital camera and spectrophotometer and had the ability to not only capture color measurements, but also textures. In 2011 Pantone and X-Rite shared their knowledge with industry professionals through educational color-management seminars that explored technical topics such as color immersion, flexographic press control, and offset process control.

By 2013 Pantone's color-matching expertise was being applied to many different types of products and industries. That year, the company developed a device that cosmetics retailer Sephora began using at more than 800 stores throughout the United States to help customers identify the right cosmetic products based on skin images. Working with clothing designers, the company also released a fashion color report for the spring 2014 season. Moving forward, it appeared that Pantone would continue to be a widely recognized color-matching expert for the foreseeable future.

John W. Fiero
Updated, Paul R. Greenland

PRINCIPAL COMPETITORS

Adobe Systems Incorporated; The Sherwin-Williams Company.

FURTHER READING

Kim, Crystal, and Robin Goldwyn Blumenthal. "Shakeup in Makeup." *Barron's*, October 7, 2013.

"Pantone Announces Spring 2014 Fashion Color Portfolio." *Seybold Report*, September 9, 2013.

"Pantone Reveals New Global Brand Identity." *Printing News*, December 4, 2006.

"Pantone Rounds Off Busy Year by Launching Its Colour Network Site." *Print Week*, January 4, 2008.

"Pantone Unveils Latest Handheld Unit to Identify & Measure Colour." *Print Week*, December 3, 2010.

"X-Rite Acquires Pantone." *Print Week*, November 1, 2007.

Paramelt B.V.

Postbus 86
Heerhugowaard, 1700 AB
Netherlands
Telephone: (+31 72) 575 06 00
Fax: (+31 72) 575 06 99
Web site: http://www.paramelt.com

Private Company
Founded: 1898
Employees: 430
Sales: $250 million (2011)
NAICS: 325520 Adhesive and Sealant Manufacturing;
325998 All Other Miscellaneous Chemical Product
and Preparation Manufacturing

■■■

Paramelt B.V. is the leading producer of industrial and specialty waxes in Europe and a prominent operator in the market for industrial adhesives. The group's Industrial Wax business forms the oldest part of its operations, stemming from the opening of the Netherlands' first wax factory at the dawn of the 20th century. This division produces a wide range of specialty waxes for a variety of applications, including coatings for cheese and other food products; wax paper and other flexible packaging; cosmetics; and automotive tires. The company's Heerhugowaard headquarters is also one of Europe's largest industrial wax factories. The company also operates production facilities in a factory in Suzhou, China. That facility is shared by the company's younger and fastest-growing business, that of Industrial Adhesives.

Since the start of the 21st century, Paramelt has established itself as a leading European and global producer of industrial adhesives, with a focus on water-based adhesives, as well as polyurethane and other adhesives. Paramelt operates a dedicated production facility in Veendam, Netherlands, for its adhesives business. This site is also the location of the group's research and development department. Since 2010, Paramelt has also become a leading producer of casting wax, through its acquisitions of U.S.-based M. Argüeso & Co. and The Kindt Company. Paramelt is a privately held company shared between Euro Schümann Wax GmbH, an equity group specialized in the wax industry, and Ter Hell & Co. GmbH, a producer of chemicals, resins, ingredients, and plastics. Both companies are based in Germany. Paramelt last reported revenues of $250 million for 2011.

NETHERLANDS WAX PIONEER IN 1898

Paramelt traced its origins back to the founding of the Netherlands' first paraffin-based polish factory, appropriately named the Eerste Noord-Hollandse Olie-en-Smeerfabriek, by Dirk de Wit, in 1898. Paraffin wax had been discovered in the 1830s but had become an increasingly versatile and prominent component of waxes and polishes with the development of methods to refine paraffin from petroleum in the 1850s. A largely colorless and odorless product, paraffin offered numerous advantages over natural waxes, particularly in the

While cheese represented a major market for the company, the future Paramelt also developed a wide range of other products, such as waxes for the paper and packaging industry, and microwaxes, used in the production of chewing gum. The company also developed ranges of natural waxes and synthetic wax blends for use in the production of facial creams and cosmetics and other personal care products. The company had also developed a strong import-export business, building a strong trade in oils, fats, and semi-refined paraffin wax. The company also became a wholesaler for a wide variety of waxes, such as casting wax for dental applications; impregnating wax for textiles production; polishing and floor waxes; and mon-tan wax, for use in the production of carbon papers.

The company itself became part of a larger concern in 1961, when it was acquired by Germany's Ter Hell & Co. GmbH. That company had been founded in 1908 in Hamburg by Hermann Ter Hell but had been major-ity controlled by the Westphal family since 1938. The Westphals had been a prominent trading family, before developing industrial operations ranging from chemicals to waxes to plastics and other products.

Under Ter Hell, the original de Wit company's operations were divided into two businesses, known as Syntac and Paramelt. These companies were merged, forming Paramelt Syntac in 1977. Through the 1980s, Paramelt benefited from Ter Hell's own growing international presence, as the German parent added a subsidiary in the United States in 1980 and in Hong Kong in 1984. The latter business also gave both Ter Hell and Paramelt access to the mainland Chinese market, as the Chinese government's economic reform policies took hold through the dawn of the 21st century.

EXPANSION IN THE NINETIES

Into the 1990s Paramelt set out to establish itself among the global leaders in the wax industry. Toward this end, the company initiated a series of acquisitions that lasted through much of the decade. The first of these came in 1993, with the purchase of RMC Belix, based in Antilly, France. That company had originally been founded as Raffineries Meridionale de Ceresine, before becoming part of petroleum giant Mobil. In 1996 Paramelt, still known as Paramelt Syntac, merged its business with RMC Belix, changing its name to Paramelt BV. The company then integrated the former RMC Belix's production operations into its main Netherlands factory in Heerhugowaard.

Soon after, Paramelt completed two other important acquisitions. For this, the company turned to

---

COMPANY PERSPECTIVES

Where we are heading: Over recent decades we have been driving rapid growth and diversification of our business. We are constantly exploring new markets and engaging in new opportunities wherever they are in the world. We have a history of looking ahead. The result is that we now have a global sourcing, produc-tion and marketing structure in place. Growth, though, is not an end in itself. For us it is a means to ensure continuity, to offer customers even greater reli-ability of supply, to remain independent and to stay ahead of the competition. We have been here for a long time and we're here to stay. After all, we have a history of looking ahead.

---

manufacture of candles but also as a base for the production of polishes for leather and carriage work.

Paramelt itself was founded to produce polishes for the latter categories. Into the start of the 20th century, de Wit's interest turned to other uses of paraffin wax. By then, techniques for refining paraffin had succeeded in eliminating virtually all of the petroleum from paraffin. This meant that the substance could be used by an increasingly diverse range of industries, including the food, cosmetics and pharmaceuticals industry. In the early 1900s, de Wit expanded the company into a new category, that of the production of wax for covering cheeses.

De Wit was credited with creating the concept of wax-coated cheese, which became a hallmark of Dutch cheeses, and especially of the Gouda and Edam varieties. By the 1930s this industry had grown strongly, especially in the region around Purmurend. De Wit also helped develop the color-coding system, put in place to denote both the variety and age of cheeses. Gouda, for example, was traditionally wrapped in yellow wax, while Edam's wax wrapper was colored red.

Was de Wit, as the company's wax business became known, emerged as a leading force in wax technologies by the 1950s. The company achieved a major breakthrough in the early 1950s when it developed a new method for wax coating cheeses. The method, called cheese coating dispersion, permitted larger quanti-ties of cheeses to be processed. This helped open new export markets for Dutch cheeses. As a result, Edam and Gouda both joined the ranks of the world's best-known cheeses.

KEY DATES

1898: Dirk de Wit founds Eerste Noord-Hollandse Olie-en-Smeerfabriek in the Netherlands.

1950s The de Wit company develops the cheese coating dispersion method.

1961: Company becomes part of Ter Hell of Germany.

1977: Paramelt and Syntac, both former parts of the de Wit company, are merged to form Paramelt Syntac.

1993: Company begins the first of a string of acquisitions, acquiring RMC Belix in France.

2001: Expanding into adhesives, Paramelt acquires Scholten Adhesives in Veendam, Netherlands.

2005: Company acquires Honeywell's European and Chinese industrial wax business.

2010: Paramelt acquires M. Argueso & Co. in the United States.

2014: Company upgrades its Heerhugowaard factory.

Germany, where it acquired Schlickum Werke, as well as the wax production business of the Van Stockum company. These acquisitions provided a springboard into the Scandinavian market the following year, with the takeover of the wax division of the Chr. Hansen group in Denmark. In 1998 the company acquired a larger share of the German market, buying the European specialty wax division of the H.B. Fuller Company.

As with its other acquisitions, Paramelt transferred its new industrial operations to its main factory in the Netherlands. In their place, the company built up an international sales office network, with locations in France, Germany, Sweden, and, in 2004, Denmark. The company also expanded into Asia, adding a sales office in Singapore, before adding a presence in the mainland Chinese market. By 2001 the company's total sales had reached EUR 45 million.

ADHESIVES INTO THE 21ST CENTURY

Into the turn of the century, Paramelt took a new strategic direction, designed to reduce the company's reliance on the wax market. The company targeted an entry into the adhesives market, and specifically the aqueous, or water-based adhesives sector. To this end, the company expanded its manufacturing capacity, add-ing the production of hot-melt adhesives, and, in 2001 a new production line for pressure-sensitive adhesives.

Paramelt took a major step toward achieving its goals that year, when it reached an agreement to acquire Veendam, Netherlands–based Scholten Adhesives, formerly part of potato starch producer Avebe. The purchase, completed in the beginning of 2002, provided the company with a new factory in Veendam and added another EUR 15 million to its annual sales.

The Veendam plant also provided Paramelt with room to grow in other directions. In December 2002, for example, the company added a new production line for producing water-based cheese coatings, which it began marketing under the Paracoat trade name. The new coating, to be used in conjunction with the group's cheese waxes, provided enhanced moisture control and mold prevention.

Paramelt completed another major acquisition in 2005, buying Honeywell's industrial wax operations in Europe and China. The purchase brought the company a factory in Eupen, Belgium, originally established as Astor Chemical Company in 1969, and a modern production facility in Suzhou, near Shanghai, China, built in 2001. The acquisitions not only raised Paramelt's production capacity, it also gave the company entry into a number of complementary products, and most notably into the global tire and rubber markets. The acquisition also provided a strong boost to the group's annual sales, which topped EUR 110 million.

Paramelt added another small business in 2005, buying up the industrial wax operations of U.K.-based Hansen & Rosenthal ESP Ltd., which operated a small plant in Chorley, England. This business focused on producing blended waxes for the flexible packaging and adhesive markets. Following the acquisition, Paramelt transferred the plant's production to its Heerhugowaard factory. The Chorley site was then converted into Paramelt's U.K. sales office.

U.S. OPERATIONS IN 2010

Paramelt took a temporary break from new acquisitions through the middle of the decade. The company itself came under a new shareholding arrangement between Ter Hell and Euro Schümann Wax GmbH. The latter company stemmed from a partnership formed in 1995 between South Africa's Sasol and Germany's Hans Otto Schumann, a company founded in 1942 to produce petroleum jelly. Schumann entered the paraffin wax business in 1951, and grew to become one of the leading European producers of paraffin wax through the next decades. After transferring its industrial assets into the joint venture, Euro Schumann became an equity investment company, held at 51 percent by Sasol Wax International. In 2005 Sasol sold its 51 percent of the Euro Schumann, instead acquiring 31.5 percent of Paramelt directly. Two years later, in order to avoid competing against its own interests, Sasol sold its stake in Paramelt, leaving Ter Hell and Euro Schumann as the company's two shareholders.

In the meantime, Paramelt had been investing in expanding its operations, notably through the construction of a dedicated research and development facility in Veendam. The new center opened in September 2006. The investment allowed Paramelt to introduce a number of new products through the end of the decade. These included a new low-melt metallocene hot-melt adhesive, which it began marketing as Plastomelt Excelta LM1 in 2009. Destined as an adhesive for corrugated boxes, bag closings, and the like, the new adhesive permitted strong bonding at lower temperatures. This not only reduced the risk of burning but also provided significant energy and cost savings as well.

The company returned to its growth-through-acquisition strategy the following year. For this, the company turned to the United States, where it acquired that company's M. Argueso & Co. Founded in 1908, Argueso had started out a producer of natural waxes, such as candelilla. The company later grew to become one of the world's leading manufacturers of casting waxes, starting with the opening of a factory in Mamaroneck, New York, in 1939. The company later focused on the production of casting wax, moving its production to two factories in Muskegon, Michigan, and Rosemead, California. Into the turn of the century, Argueso made the move into the Far East, setting up a third factory in Kunshan, Jiangsu Province, China.

Completed in January 2010, the purchase of Argueso raised Paramelt's total revenues past $230 million. Argueso also provided Paramelt with a vehicle to expand its U.S. operations, with the purchase of The Kindt-Collins Company in December 2010. Kindt-Collins had been founded in Cleveland, Ohio, in 1914 and specialized in the production of casting waxes for the jewelry and precision instrument industries. Following the acquisition, Paramelt combined its U.S. operations into Paramelt Argueso Kindt, which set up headquarters in Muskegon. As a result, Paramelt completed the year with total revenues of $250 million.

NEW EXPANSION IN 2014

Paramelt remained on the lookout for new acquisition candidates into the decade. The company boosted its product line with the acquisition of Dilavest, the expansion wax business of Germany's Evonik Industries, in October 2011. This purchase followed on the acquisi-

tion of the chemical labeling adhesives operations of BENEO-Bio Based Chemicals, part of the BENEO food ingredients group. The BENEO-Bio range added a variety of synthetic, starch-based, casein, and hybrid adhesives, complementing Paramelt's hot melt and pressure sensitive adhesive lines.

Paramelt continued adding to its technologies on its own as well. In 2013, the company introduced its Aquaseal line of water-based polyethylene coatings, designed as an alternative to more commonly used extrusion coatings. The company also prepared for new growth, renovating and expanding its Heerhugowaard plant. The upgrade was expected to be completed in November 2014. After more than 115 years in operation, Paramelt remained one of Europe's leading producers of industrial waxes in the early 21st century.

M. L. Cohen

PRINCIPAL SUBSIDIARIES

M. Argüeso & Co., Inc. (USA); Paramelt Belgium B.V.; Paramelt Singapore Ltd.; Paramelt Veendam B.V.; The Kindt-Collins Company Inc. (USA).

PRINCIPAL DIVISIONS

Industrial Wax; Industrial Adhesives; Casting Wax.

PRINCIPAL OPERATING UNITS

Paramelt; Syntac; Paramelt Argüeso Kindt.

PRINCIPAL COMPETITORS

Heraeus Materials S.A.; Innovene Inc.; LG Group; Polypore International Inc.; Sasol Chemiese Nywerhede Ltd.; SNF S.A.S.

FURTHER READING

"Aqueous Lacquers: A Sustainable Alternative." *Packaging & Converging Intelligence*, November 11, 2013.

D'Amico, Esther. "International Group Buys Honeywell's U.S. Industrial Wax Business." *Chemical Week*, June 8, 2005.

"Paramelt Acquires Adhesives Activities of BENEO-Bio Based." *Datamonitor Financial Deals Tracker*, October 4, 2011.

"Paramelt Buys Belgian Firm." *Chemical Week*, October 17, 2011.

Whitfield, Mark. "German Chemical Company Evonik Industries Has Agreed to Sell Its Dilavest Expansion Wax Business to Netherlands-Based Industrial Wax Producer Paramelt." *Chemistry and Industry*, October 10, 2011.

Party City Holdco Inc.

80 Grasslands Road
Elmsford, New York 10523
U.S.A.
Telephone: (914) 345-2020
Toll Free: (800) 727-8924
Fax: (914) 345-3884
Web site: http://www.partycity.com

Public Company
Founded: 1986
Incorporated: 1990
Employees: 14,627
Sales: $1.34 billion (2013)
Stock Exchanges: New York
Ticker Symbol: PRTY
NAICS: 453220 Gift, Novelty, and Souvenir Stores;
454111 Electronic Shopping

■ ■ ■

Party City Holdco Inc. operates the top U.S. chain of superstores dedicated to a one-stop approach to retailing party goods. The Elmsford, New York–based company comprises over 850 stores, about two-thirds of which are company owned. The other third is operated by franchisees. A typical Party City store ranges in size from 10,000 to 12,000 square feet and carries some 30,000 items. Although Halloween accounts for as much as one-quarter of yearly sales, Party City is continually promoting seasonal holidays, from traditional occasions such as New Year's Eve and the Fourth of July to modern marketing-driven events such as Father's Day and Super Bowl Sunday. Moreover, outlets offer a wide array of merchandise dedicated to birthday parties, bar mitzvahs, wedding and bridal showers, and baby showers. Products include costumes, gift wrap, balloons, greeting cards, personalized invitations, tableware, catering supplies, candy, and party favors. In addition to its chain of stores, the company also distributes its wares wholesale, selling to more than 40,000 retail operators.

FIRST STORE OPENS

Party City was founded by Steve Mandell, the son of a retailer who grew up dreaming of opening his own store. He started his business career as a manufacturer's sales representative. From 1972 until 1986 he served as president of The Marketing Group, an independent sales representative firm that handled such items as school supplies, stationery, and party goods. Mandell recognized that party goods were highly fragmented, with a lot of small mom-and-pop operations, a large number of retailers carrying limited supplies, and no big players dominating the market. He decided to specialize in the business when he struck out on his own to realize his long-cherished goal of running his own retail operation.

In 1986 after scraping together $125,000, he opened a 4,000-square-foot store in East Hanover, New Jersey, naming it Party City. The operation was immediately successful, and within a year Mandell started planning for a second location. He also began to hear from people asking to franchise the Party City concept, and as a result Party City began its evolution into a

COMPANY PERSPECTIVES

We believe we are the premier party supplies retailer, providing a one-stop shopping experience with a broad and deep selection of products offered at a compelling value seamlessly through our retail stores and our e-commerce platform. We keep our assortment current by frequently introducing new products, and we organize our stores by events and themes to make it easy to shop while consistently presenting customers with additional product ideas that will enhance their events and our sales.

national chain. After his first year in business Mandell also decided to concentrate on Halloween, so that in 1987 a quarter of his store was turned into a "Halloween Costume Warehouse."

The move proved highly successful and led to the company's ongoing focus on the holiday, and the major impact that the month of October would have on the company's bottom line. Year-round, Party City stocked an inventory of Halloween costumes, if for no other reason than to make customers aware of the items for the next Halloween season. The first Party City franchise store opened in 1989, and by 1990 Mandell also owned four Party City stores. At this point he incorporated the business as a franchising operation, with his stores forming the core of the chain.

CONCEPT IS REFINED

By the end of 1990 Party City outlets numbered 11. Five more franchised stores were added in 1991, 16 in 1992, and another 26 in 1993, bringing the total to 58. The company's annual revenues in 1993 topped $2.4 million and net profits approached $235,000. During these first four years of operation, Mandell refined the Party City concept, including store design, product mix, choice of suppliers, and the implementation of systems.

With a successful store model in hand, Mandell in late 1993 decided to de-emphasize franchising in favor of opening company-owned stores, which would generate greater returns for the corporation than it could receive on fees and royalties from franchised outlets, as well as allow Mandell to better control the destiny of Party City.

While franchisees might maintain a tighter control on inventory, Mandell was insistent that company-owned units would be amply stocked with a wide range of merchandise. The first of these company-owned stores opened in Orlando, Florida, in January 1994, followed by six others later in the year.

To help support this change in strategy, Mandell brought in two equity investors. Party City also opened 42 franchise stores (with one closing) in 1994, bringing the total number of units in the Party City chain to 99. Also in 1994 Mandell hired David Lauber as chief financial officer. Lauber was a seasoned executive with Mother's Stores, a 170-store chain specializing in maternity and children's clothing.

PARTY CITY GOES PUBLIC

Party City was clearly trending up, with sales in 1994 improving to $8.85 million and net profits exceeding $540,000. Strong growth continued in 1995, as nine more company-owned stores and 35 new franchised operations were added to the chain, and revenues for the year totaled $23.1 million with net profits approaching 1.3 million. Mandell talked about a chain of 1,000 stores and made plans to fuel further expansion by taking the company public, a move welcomed by a number of investors who saw Party City as a possible "category killer," the huge store phenomenon spawned by Toys "R" Us and emulated by other retailers including Office Depot and Home Depot.

Like these other retailers, Party City had the potential to leverage its size to gain discounts from suppliers that would allow it to stock an even greater selection of goods at lower prices than those of its competitors. Moreover, party supplies in the United States had grown into a business worth more than $3 billion a year and was accelerating at a 10 percent annual pace. Children's birthday parties were a significant engine of growth for the category.

In addition, baby boomers were spurring growth in adult parties, especially Halloween, which to Party City had become comparable to the Christmas season for most retailers. In March 1996 Party City completed its initial public offering (IPO), selling 1.7 million shares at $10 each, netting $15.1 million. Additionally, Mandell and another top executive each sold 150,000 shares. By the end of 1996 the chain reached the 200 mark in units with the opening of 20 company-owned and 32 franchised stores. For the year, revenues were more than double the amount generated in 1995, growing to $48.5 million, and net profits almost tripled, reaching $3.76 million.

DIVERSIFICATION AND EXPANSION

Party City continued its high-flying ways in 1997, opening 57 company-owned stores, as well as purchasing 24

KEY DATES

1986: Steve Mandell opens first Party City store.
1994: First company-owned store opens.
1996: Company goes public.
1999: Mandell resigns as CEO and chairman.
2001: Company resumes trading on the NASDAQ following delisting in July 1999.
2005: Company is purchased by AAH Holdings.
2008: Advent International acquires 38 percent of company.
2009: Company launches major online sales outlet.
2012: Thomas H. Lee Partners acquires majority stake in company.
2014: Company begins another initial public offering.

---

outlets from franchisees or affiliates, including all of the stores owned by Mandell. Business was so strong that the company declared a 3-for-2 stock split at the end of the year. Annual revenues topped $141.7 million and net profits totaled $7.7 million. Investor confidence in the company peaked in March 1998 as the price of its stock reached $35.25 per share.

Concerns set in when the company failed to meet third-quarter projections. Within six months the share price dipped below $10 and analysts dropped coverage. Nevertheless, Mandell persevered. By the end of the year Party City had launched another 69 company-owned stores and acquired 22 units from franchisees, while another 15 franchise units were also opened. Mandell was indicating that Party City planned to open another 100 company-owned stores in 1999. He was also thinking in terms of building a 1,500-store chain in the near future, but behind the scenes Party City was having trouble handling its rapid growth.

MANDELL STEPS DOWN

A worsening situation came to a head in March 1999, when the company announced that it was unable to conduct a year-end inventory of its stores or complete its 1998 audit and was therefore unable to comply with Securities and Exchange Commission filing regulations. Management blamed the failure on turnover in the finance department, which prevented the company from installing a new inventory tracking system made necessary by its rapid growth.

Nevertheless, the delay placed Party City in technical default of covenants on loan agreements and caused an immediate drop in the price of its stock, which quickly lost almost half its value, a slide further exacerbated by talk of selling assets that emanated from inside Party City. The company also faced a number of class-action lawsuits from disgruntled shareholders who claimed the company had misrepresented or omitted information to artificially inflate the price of its stock. Some of the suits further charged that insiders unloaded shares before the March audit announcement. When the year-end audit was still not completed in May, the NAS-DAQ suspended trading of Party City stock, then delisted it in July.

A restructuring effort was quickly mounted, starting with changes in the ranks of top management. In late May CFO Lauber resigned. Less than three weeks later Mandell stepped down as chairman and CEO, although he retained a directorship and stayed on as a $50,000-per-month consultant. This arrangement lasted only until September 1999, when Mandell resigned as a director and gave up his consulting contract as well. He remained, however, Party City's largest shareholder with a stake of more than 20 percent in the company.

AVOIDING BANKRUPTCY

Replacing Mandell as CEO on an interim basis was board member Jack Futterman, a former pharmacist who once headed Whelan's Drug Stores before becoming the CEO at Pathmark Stores Inc., where he was a pioneer in the drugstore/supermarket combination. Futterman managed to steer Party City clear of bankruptcy primarily because investors still believed in the chain's basic business model and vendors were willing to accommodate the company because the potential of large bulk sales to Party City remained highly desirable.

In early July 1999 Party City had outstanding borrowings of $58.6 million against its $60 million line of credit and was in dire need of refinancing. One of its major shareholders, Sidney Craig (husband of diet guru Jenny Craig), whose sons were Party City franchisees, played a pivotal role in saving the company by involving Los Angeles–based investor Michael E. Tennenbaum, who was able to arrange a $37 million cash infusion in exchange for a sizable stake in the business.

Party City raised an additional $9.8 million by selling 18 stores to franchisees. At the end of these maneuvers, the chain had a market capitalization of just $100 million, 25 percent of what it was worth a year earlier, but at least it was in a position to stock up for the all-important upcoming Halloween season.

With its finances stabilized, Party City also launched a search for a new chief executive to replace 65-year-old Futterman. After three months the board

---

settled on James Shea, who had previously served as president of the Lechters housewares chain, as well as holding executive positions with Eddie Bauer, May Department Stores, and Target Stores.

SHEA TAKES OVER: 1999

Taking over in December 1999, Shea focused on establishing a technical infrastructure capable of supporting a major retail chain, investing heavily in point-of-sales and inventory systems. He also led an effort to redesign the stores, which according to research were too dark for customers. As a result, halogen lights replaced overhead fluorescent fixtures, and the merchandise was organized by categories rather than the previous supermarket-aisle approach.

In a new circular orientation, seasonal merchandise was moved to the center of the store, forcing customers to pass by everyday items, and children's and adults' party items were clearly separated. The changes gave rise to a new prototype for a Party City store, one with high-energy colors and vivid signage, and merchandise organized according to category zones such as Kid's Parties, Grown-Up Parties, Party Basics, Costumes, and Cards, as well as an inviting area where balloons were inflated.

In addition, the prototype featured a centrally located "power aisle" running the length of the store and offering holiday and seasonal fare. All of the other category zones were clearly visible from this center aisle. Party City's recovery culminated in its return to the NASDAQ in the summer of 2001. As the company again achieved profitability the price of its stock rose accordingly.

The company suffered a minor setback early in 2002 when a 28-store Canadian franchisee, Partyco Holdings, went out of business. Of more importance to the fortunes of the company was the acquisition of 13 rival Paper Warehouse stores in Seattle. Moreover, Party City was well-positioned to take advantage of the misfortunes of its nearest rivals. Paper Warehouse with its 140 stores was delisted by the NASDAQ in June 2002, and 170-store Factory Card Outlet emerged from Chapter 11 bankruptcy protection only months earlier. All told in 2002, Party City posted revenues of $423.5 million, with net profits of $17.2 million.

PARTY CITY GOES PRIVATE

Despite its reorganization and return to profitability, Party City's profit performance remained unimpressive for the next few years. While overall revenues had exceeded $500 million in the fiscal year, which ended in

July 2005, profits had sunk to $4.4 million, the lowest level in five years. At this point, the company's board of directors began to seriously consider a buyout offer that had been recently extended by a private-equity consortium led by Berkshire Partners LLC and Weston Presidio. The firms had recently formed a new group, AAH Holdings, and had purchased Amscan Holdings, one of Party City's largest wholesale suppliers.

By combining Party City with Amscan, the consortium hoped to become the largest party supply company in the country, selling both at its own store outlets and to other retailers. The Party City board and stockholders eventually accepted AAH's offer to buy up the outstanding Party City stock at $17.50 per share, in a deal that finally amounted to some $360 million for the 500-store chain. Party City was a private company once again. The following year, the company's chief merchandising officer Lisa Laube was promoted to the position of president.

ACQUIRES PARTY AMERICA: 2006

The new owners continued to add new party supply companies to their Amscan-centered conglomerate over the next few years, acquiring the Party America chain in 2006 and Factory Card & Party Outlet in 2007. Most of these stores were converted to Party City locations. Seeking capital to fund the company's rapid expansion, the AAH partnership agreed to sell a 38 percent ownership stake in Party City to the international investment group Advent International in 2008.

The following year the company began an effort to add a significant online sales presence to its brick-and-mortar stores. A revamp of its Web site and a broad expansion of the products it offered signaled Party City's intention to become a major "e-tailer," as well as a traditional retail chain. In 2011 the company expanded further when it acquired the Canadian Party Packagers chain of stores and began converting them to its own brand.

PARTY CITY GOES PUBLIC AGAIN

By 2012 Party City's new owners had reason to celebrate. The previous year's profits had spiked 55 percent, reaching $76.4 million against a 17 percent rise in overall revenue. The new e-commerce site had generated $76 million in sales that year as well. The time seemed ripe for the AAH and Advent partnership to try to cash in on their investment. They first announced that they would take the company public once more with an IPO of stock.

Behind the scenes, however, the company was also negotiating with a private party. Venerable equity firm Thomas H. Lee Partners had offered $2.69 billion in exchange for a 70 percent stake in the company. After some consideration, the planned $350 million IPO was canceled and Party City's ownership agreed to buyout terms. Precise details of the deal were not announced, but AAH Holdings and Advent would both retain minority ownership stakes.

Despite the sale, Party City's days as a private company were numbered. In early 2014 about 18 months after the purchase, a public offering of Party City stock was announced once again. In the period following the buyout, debt incurred to finance the sale had wiped out the company's profits and led to a loss of $52 million against $1.34 billion in revenue. Public documents showed the company was carrying a debt of $2.3 billion.

HELIUM SHORTAGE

Planning to trade on the New York Stock Exchange under the symbol PRTY, Party City hoped to raise as much as $500 million from the stock sale and use the funds to pay down debt. In addition to the IPO preparations and debt woes, 2014 also brought another headache when a global shortage of helium resulted in double-digit increases in the wholesale price of the gas.

For Party City, where helium-filled balloons accounted for 4 percent of sales at its more than 850 stores, the shortage provided yet another challenge to the company's profitability. Nevertheless, the company reiterated its plan to continue expanding and add up to 30 stores per year over the next decade.

Ed Dinger
Updated, Chris Herzog

PRINCIPAL DIVISIONS

Halloween City.

PRINCIPAL COMPETITORS

Celebrate Express Inc.; Oriental Trading Company Inc.; Wal-Mart Stores Inc.

FURTHER READING

Abrams, Rachel. "Party City to Try Again to Go Public." *New York Times*, January 22, 2014.

Benoit, David. "Party City Skips Public Party for Private Deal." *Wall Street Journal*, June 5, 2012.

Coleman-Lochner, Lauren. "Party City Celebrating Modest Resurgence." *Record*, November 15, 2001.

Elstein, Aaron. "In the Markets." *Crain's New York Business*, January 27, 2014.

Gallagher, Leigh. "Act 2, Scene 1." *Forbes*, November 25, 2002.

Gara, Antoine. "Party City IPO Tests Private Equity Industry Carousel." *thestreet.com*, February 4, 2014.

"Party City IPO: Is Party City Worth $500 Million?" *Christian Science Monitor*, January 21, 2014.

"$360 Million Deal to Buy Party City." *New York Times*, September 28, 2005.

Wilson, Marianne. "Party City Makes Shopping Fun." *Chain Store Age*, August 2002.

PartyLite Worldwide Inc.

—■—

59 Armstrong Road
Plymouth, Massachusetts 02360
U.S.A.
Telephone: (508) 830-3100
Toll Free: (888) 999-5706
Fax: (508) 732-5818
Web site: http://www.partylite.com

Wholly Owned Subsidiary of Blyth Inc.
Incorporated: 1973 as PartyLite Gifts, Inc.
Employees: 400
Sales: $425 million (2013)
NAICS: 339999 All Other Miscellaneous Manufacturing; 454390 Other Direct Selling Establishments

■ ■ ■

PartyLite Worldwide Inc. manufactures candles, related scented items, and home décor accessories, which are then sold primarily at home parties through a multilevel, direct sales program. PartyLite fields around 60,000 independent sales contractors in more than 20 countries. The company offers around 600 different products each catalog season and manufactures almost 200 million candles. PartyLite debuts around 100 new products each year.

EARLY YEARS

Like many successful companies, the story of PartyLite Worldwide began with a single, dedicated entrepreneur. In this case, it was Mabel Baker, a schoolteacher from Cape Cod, Massachusetts. Around 1905, while teaching her students about local lore and history, Baker had taken note of stories about New England colonists using the local bayberries to produce candles.

Bayberries grew in relative abundance in the region, taking their name from the fact that they thrived in the sandy soil along the nearby shoreline. By this point in history, bayberry candle-making had become largely a thing of the past. It took around 6 to 8 pounds of bayberries to produce one pound of candle wax. The berries had to be repeatedly boiled and strained, with only a thin film of fatty residue retained from each batch for use as wax.

As alternative forms of lighting and candle-making became more widely available, the bayberry process fell by the wayside. Nevertheless, bayberry candles maintained a reputation for a pleasant smell and a reliable, smoothly burning flame and were regarded as something of a regional tradition, particularly around the Christmas holidays.

KITCHEN BUSINESS GROWS

Partly as a hobby, partly as a historical exercise, and partly as a small home business, Baker began producing bayberry candles in her kitchen. At first she simply distributed them to family and friends. The process of making the candles was labor intensive and time consuming.

Pounds and pounds of wild-growing bayberries had to be picked by hand. The cotton wicks were hand braided, and the candles themselves had to be dipped by

---

COMPANY PERSPECTIVES

PartyLite parties are fun! But people buy PartyLite candles because they love the way they look, the way they smell and the way they burn. PartyLite has always offered customers amazing quality—the very best candles you can buy anywhere.

---

hand as many as 35 times apiece to achieve the desired size and shape. After a few years, the response to Baker's products proved overwhelmingly positive. She began receiving requests for candles from people outside her immediate social circles.

BAKER GOES INTO BUSINESS

Baker decided to go into business in 1909. She began by taking custom orders herself, but soon began placing her candles in shops around the region. The new business would be known as Colonial Candle of Cape Cod. During the early part of the 20th century, candles were largely considered utilitarian rather than decorative. People mostly used candles for lighting or ceremonial purposes.

Candles that were pretty to look at or had a nice scent were desirable but not absolutely necessary. The Colonial Candle company, along with a few competitors, helped to change that by focusing on a new emphasis on aroma and appearance in their products. After a decade in business, Colonial Candle's production volume had expanded far beyond the capacity of the Baker home kitchen.

Baker had several employees working in rented commercial space but this proved impractical. In 1921 Baker's husband Walter quit his job to devote himself full time to the candle concern. The couple used the business's profits to build a dedicated candle factory. During the 1920s Colonial Candle of Cape Cod was credited with a number of innovations that helped shape the decorative candle industry.

FIRST SCENTED CANDLES MADE

Walter Baker is credited with developing the process for making solid-colored candles. Colonial Candle is also credited with inventing aromatic candles infused with scented oils. It may also have been the first candle company to offer its own line of candle accessories, such as candleholders, snuffers, and other wares designed specifically for its own candles.

Traditionally, customers purchased these accessories from separate vendors. In the ensuing decades, Colonial Candle of Cape Cod continued to thrive, becoming one of the top decorative candle-makers in the United States. Baker herself remained active in the company until her death in 1965 at the age of 94. By this time, Baker's kitchen table hobby had grown into a $6 million-per-year business.

PARTYLITE TAKES FLIGHT

A few years after the death of its founder, Colonial Candle found itself with a backlog of excess inventory that it was having trouble placing through its regular retail distribution system. Colonial's managers felt the inventory was of high quality and very sellable, but realized that trying to push it into the company's regular distribution stream could glut the market and lead to returns or lowered prices. As something of an experiment, Colonial decided to create a spin-off company, a subsidiary that would distribute the product through a direct sales paradigm.

In direct sales, individual sales agents receive product directly from the manufacturer and sell it in individual transactions, often to friends, acquaintances, and a carefully developed circle of regular customers. Frequently, orders and sales are arranged at organized home parties, a sales method known as the party plan. With their sights set on this potentially lucrative new market, the Colonial Candle team set up PartyLite Gifts, Inc., in 1973.

At first, Colonial Candle's PartyLite division consisted of three employees working together in one small office. Their mission was to design a direct sales program and to begin recruiting individual sales associates. The PartyLite program was ultimately designed with a multilevel marketing structure, typical for direct sales and party plan programs. Under the multilevel marketing paradigm, successful sales associates were encouraged to recruit teams of other salespersons, whom they would then manage and mentor.

NEW SALES STRUCTURE IMPLEMENTED

In return, the original associate receives a portion of his or her team members' sales. When new team members have reached a certain sales threshold, they are able to recruit their own teams. By establishing this sales structure, Colonial Candles was able to essentially wholesale its excess inventory directly to these independent associates who would then be compensated directly with profits from the sales.

KEY DATES

1909: Mabel Baker founds Colonial Candle of Cape Cod.

1973: Colonial Candle creates PartyLite Gifts Inc.

1990: PartyLite is acquired by Blyth, Inc.

1992: PartyLite opens its first international office in Canada.

2013: PartyLite celebrates its 40th anniversary.

The multilevel structure provided an incentive for effective sales associates to continue selling PartyLite products and to expand sales and demand for the product. While the PartyLite company was initially established to handle Colonial Candle products, it became popular and prosperous enough after a few years to justify developing its own product lines under its own brand name.

Colonial's inventory overstock was no longer sufficient to fill the demand for PartyLite products. After less than two decades in business, PartyLite's annual sales were approaching $10 million by the end of the 1980s. The success and reputation of PartyLite, and its parent company Colonial Candles of Cape Cod, had drawn the attention of an industry player with plans that would dramatically affect the fortunes of both companies.

BLYTH BUYS COLONIAL: 1990

In 1990 the owners of Colonial Candle accepted a buyout offer from Blyth, Inc., a candle manufacturer that had built itself into a market force over the previous 15 years, primarily by buying up smaller competitors. Colonial's subsidiary, PartyLite, became part of the acquisition. While the company's headquarters remained in Plymouth, Massachusetts, where it had been for years, the new owners moved its production facilities all the way to a 450,000-square-foot facility in Batavia, Illinois, in 1996.

This was done to take advantage of the production and distribution infrastructure it had already pieced together from previous buyouts. This was not the only change in store for PartyLite. Headed by CEO Robert Blyth Goergen, Blyth continued its aggressive expansion through the 1990s. The company's acquisition tactics appeared to pay off, as Blyth's annual revenues increased from around $200 million at the beginning of the decade to about $1 billion by 2001.

A large part of this success no doubt came from Goergen's respect for the PartyLite business model and Blyth's subsequent focus on expanding the brand. Goergen appreciated the party plan as an appropriate venue for candle sales. "Buying candles is a social event," he told *Forbes.com* in a January 8, 2001, interview, "it brings people together." While Blyth continued selling through traditional retail outlets, it also expanded its focus on direct sales to many of its product lines and subsidiaries during this period.

In fact, Blyth placed so much emphasis on expanding and improving the PartyLite division that it soon outstripped its parent company in terms of profitability and importance. By 2001 nearly half of Blyth's revenues came from the PartyLite division. Ultimately, Blyth would sell the Colonial Candle company, by this time entirely disassociated from PartyLite, in 2011. Meanwhile, PartyLite's market share and revenues continued to grow with each passing year.

INTERNATIONAL EXPANSION

Perhaps the most significant factor in PartyLite's explosive growth during the 1990s was Blyth's decision to take the program international, expanding it across the globe. Beginning with an Ontario-based Canadian office in 1992, Blyth incorporated each foreign branch as a separate subsidiary. PartyLite Canada was followed with an office in Heidelberg, Germany, in 1994 and a U.K. branch in 1996.

In 1997, in anticipation of further European PartyLite companies, Blyth built another production facility in Scansdale-in-Barrow, England. The 101,000-square-foot, custom-built facility added more than 100 full-time workers to the company's payroll. PartyLite continued its European expansion in 1997 with offices in Austria and Switzerland. In 1999 the company brought in Anne M. Butler, a 25-year veteran of the direct sales industry, to head its PartyLite Europe division.

Butler added France and Finland to the company's territories in 1999 before returning to North America with a Mexican branch in 2001. Australia was next in 2002, followed by Sweden in 2003. The same year, Butler became president of PartyLite Worldwide, Inc., the umbrella group that would oversee the entire PartyLite family of companies.

For the next several years, the company focused on Scandinavia, with offices opening in Denmark, Sweden, and Norway between 2003 and 2007. The newly expanding economies of Eastern Europe were next. PartyLite established subsidiaries in Poland, Slovakia, and the Czech Republic during 2009 and 2010. It also added an Italian office during this period. The direct sales model had proven so successful for its original candle business that Blyth had begun experimenting with selling other product lines the same way.

TWO SISTERS LINE INTRODUCED

Most new product lines were established as separate brands or companies under the Blyth umbrella, but one seemed promising enough to fold into the PartyLite company as a brand extension. In 2010 PartyLite sales consultants began selling the Two Sisters Gourmet line of foods and recipes through the same catalog and party structure. The connection between the two lines was made clear with the new brand name, Two Sisters Gourmet By PartyLite.

In addition to its business activities, PartyLite also established a tradition of corporate giving to a number of prominent causes. Beginning in 1997 PartyLite chose the American Cancer Society (ACS) as its primary philanthropic cause, and that focus would continue through the succeeding decades. By 2013 the company had donated more than $14 million to the charity.

EXECUTIVE CHANGES

PartyLite's contributions took the form of direct donations, participation in Relays for Life and other events, and a program in which customers could round up their purchases to the next dollar and donate the change to ACS. In 2012 the company announced that Butler would be stepping down from her position. She was replaced by Robert Goergen Jr., the son of Blyth's CEO.

The following year the junior Goergen became CEO of Blyth, Inc. In addition to his duties as president of PartyLite Worldwide, Inc., Robert Goergen Sr. would remain with Blyth as chairman of its board of directors. Within a year, William C. Looney, the company's vice president for worldwide finance, would be named CFO of PartyLite to take over some of the Goergen Jr.'s former responsibilities as president.

In addition to a new CEO and new CFO, 2013 also saw PartyLite celebrating its 40th anniversary. The company had grown from a kitchen table experiment to a marketing experiment to a company amassing nearly a half-billion dollars in sales annually, with branches in nearly two dozen countries and a loyal sales force of some 60,000 independent operators. An estimated 12 million potential customers attended PartyLite parties annually. PartyLite was the top party-plan candle seller in the world and the 31st-largest direct-selling company in the world overall.

Chris Herzog

PRINCIPAL COMPETITORS

Avon Products Inc.; The Body Shop International plc.; The Yankee Candle Company, Inc.

FURTHER READING

Keogh, James. *Living by Our Wicks. Blyth Industries: The First 20 Years.* New York: Blyth, 1999.

Maiello, Michael. "Blyth: Blyth Spirit." *Forbes.com*, January 8, 2001. Accessed September 29, 2014. http://www.forbes.com/forbes/2001/0108/144.html.

Murphy, Jean. "Candles Centerpiece of PartyLite Business." *Chicago Daily Herald Business Ledger*, February 13, 2012.

Nuyten, Ted. "Rob Goergen New President PartyLite." *Business-ForHome*, January 10, 2012. Accessed September 29, 2014. http://www.businessforhome.org/2012/01/rob-goergen-new-president-party-lite.

Simpson, J. "Sweet Smell of Success for 10-Year-Old PartyLite." *North-West Evening Mail* (UK), December 10, 2007.

Paul Dischamp S.A.S.

Rue des Routiers
Sayat, 63530
France
Telephone: (+33 4) 73 62 81 81
Fax: (+33 4) 73 62 72 72
Web site: http://www.dischamp.com

Private Company
Incorporated: 1989
Employees: 216
Sales: EUR 102 million ($138 million) (2010)
NAICS: 311513 Cheese Manufacturing; 424430 Dairy Product (Except Dried or Canned) Merchant Wholesalers

∎∎∎

Paul Dischamp S.A.S. is one of France's leading cheese producers. The company specializes in the production of cheeses from the Auvergne region, including the region's five protected designation of origin (PDO) cheeses: Saint-Nectaire, Cantal, Salers, Fourme d'Ambert, and Bleu d'Auvergne. Dischamp is the largest producer of Saint-Nectaire cheeses, including the raw-milk PDO variety, and Saint-Nectaire *laitière*, using pasteurized milk. The company produces more than 3,000 metric tons of Saint-Nectaire each year. The company is also a major producer of Cantal cheese, one of France's oldest cheese varieties, with 1,500 metric tons per year. In addition to its PDO cheeses, the company produces a number of other Auvergne-region varieties, including Gaperon, Savaron, Tomme fraîche, Tomme Grise, and Tomme Blanche de Montagne. Altogether, Dischamp produces 7,500 metric tons of cheese per year. The company has a number of production facilities in the region and collects milk from more than 400 Auvergne dairy farmers. Dischamp has also developed a side business in the installation of solar panels on the rooftops of its farmers' barns and hangars. Paul Dischamp remains a family-owned company.

KING'S CHEESE IN 17TH CENTURY

Saint-Nectaire cheese was already considered one of the finest of France's more than 250 cheese varieties at the dawn of the 20th century. Production of the cheese dated back to before the Middle Ages, by peasants in the region of Besse, located in the Auvergne region of the Massif Centrale chain of mountains. The cheese was originally known as *gléo*, or *fromage de siegle*, for the practice of ripening the cheese on a bed of rye straw.

Consumption of the cheese, characterized by a thick, dark rind protecting an unctuous, creamy interior, remained largely reserved to the local market until the Middle Ages, when it became a popular form of payment by peasants to the region's landholders. This cheese, generally made from milk produced during the winter, provided farmers with the ability to produce cheese year-round, alternating the gléo with a hardened cheese called *jouhanal*, one of France's oldest cheeses, which later evolved into the Cantal cheese variety.

By the end of the 16th century, these cheeses played an important role in the livelihood of the region's peasant farmers. During the 17th century, the region's

KEY DATES

1911: Jean Dischamp acquires the A La Renommée des Vrais Saint-Nectaire cheese shop and cellars in Clermont-Ferrand.

1941: Paul Dischamp takes over his father's shop.

1955: Saint-Nectaire is granted protected status as an AOC (*appellation d'origine contrôlée*) cheese.

1969: Company's wholesale business moves to the Rungis wholesale market outside of Paris.

1989: Dischamp acquires La Fromagerie de Grand Mujols.

2007: Dischamp acquires Laiterie de la Montagne and becomes the leading producer of Saint-Nectaire cheese.

2014: Company wins six medals at the Concours General Agricole de Paris.

cheeses fell out of favor with landholders, who developed a preference for cheeses made elsewhere in France, or from other countries altogether. This situation began to change, however, after 1666, when King Louis XIV granted Marechal Henry II de Sennectèrre the barony of Ferté-Saint-Nectaire en Duché-Pairie.

D'AUSSY'S SPECIAL RECOGNITION

Sennectèrre set out to promote the region's cheeses, and the rye cheese in particular, introducing it to the royal court. The cheese, which became known as Sennectèrre's cheese, or Saint-Nectaire, became a favorite at court, and even earned the nickname as "the King's Cheese." Further consecration for the cheese came from Legrand d'Aussy, who published his book, *Voyage à Auvergne*, in 1768.

D'Aussy made special mention of Saint-Nectaire cheese, with the famous phrase, "Si l'on veut vous y régaler, c'est toujours du saint-nectaire que l'on vous annonce." This was translatable as "If one wishes to regale one's guests, one always serves Saint Nectaire." France's declaration of war against Spain, Great Britain, and Holland in 1793 provided the next stage in development for the Saint-Nectaire.

During the war, also known as the War of the First Coalition, soldiers from the Auvergne region arriving in the Netherlands discovered that country's cheeses. Returning from war, they brought back with them new

methods for producing milk and refining cheese, improving the quality of the Saint-Nectaire cheese, while also raising the quantity of cheese produced. The region's cheese makers had also taken to refining the cheese in cellars carved out of the long-dormant volcanoes that formed the region's mountainous terrain.

LEARNING THE CHEESE TRADE

Saint-Nectaire became one of France's most popular cheeses through the 18th and 19th centuries. By the turn of the 20th century, the center of Saint-Nectaire production, although linked to the village of Saint-Nectaire itself, had largely shifted to the city of Clermont-Ferrand, and particularly to the cheese cellars carved from the volcanic tuff in the area around the city's cathedral.

Among these was a small shop and cellar on the Place Hippolyte Renoux, called "A la Renommée des Vrais Saint-Nectaire," or "For the Glory of the True Saint-Nectaire Cheese." The name reflected a growing concern among French and other European producers of regional specialties as they sought to protect both the specificity and the reputation of their products.

This effort, led by the wine industry, sought to codify production of a regional variety, developing strict specifications and guidelines, including limiting production to a defined area. The first official protection efforts were put into place in France, Italy, and Spain at the turn of the century. These would ultimately lead to the adoption of the system of protected geographic status (PGS) by the European Union.

The system created three classes of protected status, starting with the most restrictive, protected designation of origin (PDO), followed by protected geographical indication (PGI), and traditional speciality guaranteed (TSG). In the meantime, the Place Hippolyte Renoux shop changed hands in 1911. The new owner was Jean Dischamp, son of a local farmer. In the sales agreement, the original owner of the shop agreed to provide Dischamp with training in refining Saint-Nectaire cheese.

GROWTH IN THE POSTWAR ERA

Under Jean Dischamp, the shop remained a small, local producer and seller of cheeses. This status was to change only with the arrival of Dischamp's only child, Paul Dischamp, at the shop in 1941. The younger Dischamp had arrived back in Clermont-Ferrand after escaping from a German prison camp. Because Clermont-Ferrand was situated in the so-called Free French Zone, Dischamp was able to take over his father's business for the rest of the war.

Nonetheless, Dischamp's experience in the German camp was to inform his vision of the Europe of the future, which in turned played an important role in the company's postwar growth. Another important part of the company's later growth was Dischamp's marriage to Paulette Bonjean. Her father, Pierre Bonjean, had founded one of the region's largest dairies, the Grande Laiterie d'Argnat in Sayat, in the early 1920s.

The couple had four children, Philippe, Jacques, Pierre, and Jean-Luc. All four would later join the family business and play prominent roles in its expansion. Following the war, Paul Dischamp set in motion his vision for the company's future. With an eye on expanding production, he moved the cheese-making business to the Sayat dairy, which he converted to cheese production. He also built a large-scale refining cellar on the site. Dischamp next purchased a truck, with which he began delivering his cheese beyond the Auvergne region. He also opened a new location in Clermont-Ferrand, on the Place Maréchal Fayolle, as a wholesale center for cheese and other dairy products.

GAINS PROTECTED STATUS: 1955

The company's cheese production in the meantime had received a major boost in 1955, when Saint-Nectaire was granted protected status under France's Appellation d'Origine Contrôlée (AOC) regime. Under the new rules, production of Saint-Nectaire was limited to a small area, primarily in the Puy de Dôme department, as well as in parts of neighboring Cantal.

This area corresponded to the region known as the Monts Dore. Processing of Saint-Nectaire was required to be done only in this area. Milk used for production of the cheese was also required to come from cattle grazing in the Monts Dore region, and it had to be produced at between 750 and 1,200 meters in altitude. The AOC status was further reinforced in 1958, when the members of the young European Community agreed to respect each other's regional product protection regimes.

BUTTER GIANT IN THE SEVENTIES

By the end of the 1960s, however, cheese production had become only a small part of Dischamp's business. During the 1950s Dischamp had expanded his operations into Paris, acquiring Etablissements René Guy, situated at the Halles de Paris wholesale market. That company was renamed as Paul Dischamp Produits Laitiers de France, and it served as the base for the company's expansion throughout France.

In another diversification effort, Dischamp had attempted to develop a business distributing frozen foods, building one of the country's first freezer-equipped warehouses at its Sayat base. This sector was indeed to become a major component of France's retail distribution industry in the future. At the time, however, few households were equipped with home freezers, while the dominance of large-scale supermarkets, and their frozen food sections, would not begin until the late 1960s. The company was soon forced to abandon frozen food distribution.

Dischamp's investment nonetheless provided the company with a new direction, as its refrigerated warehouses offered the perfect environment for stocking butter. Dischamp himself drove his truck to collect butter, especially from a dairy in Normandy. This dairy later grew to become one of France's leading dairy brands, Elle et Vire. Through the 1950s Dischamp focused on collecting and distributing butter in France.

Into the middle of the 1960s after the Treaty of Rome established the basis for the future European Union, Dischamp began expanding his business beyond France. Among the company's most notable markets was Denmark, then emerging as a prominent butter and dairy products center in Europe. Dischamp also attempted a brief foray into retailing, opening a supermarket in Montferrand in 1967. The company was quickly forced to abandon this business, however, after customers of its wholesale dairy products business objected to finding themselves in competition with their supplier.

NEW GENERATION IN 1972

Paul Dischamp died in 1972 at the age of 59. Eldest son Philippe took over as head of the company, alongside his mother. Under Philippe Dischamp's direction, the company grew still more strongly, especially on a European level. The company's refrigerated warehouse grew to span 20,000 square meters. Into the 1980s the company added a second and larger warehouse in Poullaouen, in France's Brittany region. This facility, with a storage space of 40,000 square meters, provided the company with access to another of France's major agricultural markets.

The company later added a third refrigerated warehouse, in Saint Divy, which opened in 1998. Dischamp had become one of France's leading butter distributors. Philippe Dischamp also led the company outside of France, setting up a subsidiary in the Netherlands. Dischamp had been joined by brothers Jacques and, from 1977, Jean-Luc, who took charge of the group's expansion in the Brittany region, while Pierre Dischamp did not join the family company until 1992.

The European butter market was increasingly faced with an oversupply, the result of the surge in milk production following the introduction of industrialized farming methods in the 1950s. As such, Dischamp was careful to maintain a diversified business. In particular, the company set out to expand its production and distribution of cheese. In 1969 the company moved its Paris-based wholesale business to the city's new wholesale market in Rungis, which became one of the largest wholesale markets in Europe.

AOC CHEESE LEADER

The move allowed the company to become an important supplier to the fast-growing, large-scale retail distribution sector. Dischamp also added to its range of cheese varieties. For this, the company remained focused on the Auvergne region. Through the 1980s the region boasted five AOC (and later PDO) cheeses, the most of any other region in France. In addition to Saint-Nectaire, the region's AOC cheeses included Cantal, Salers, Blue d'Auvergne, and Fourme d'Ambert.

In the late 1980s the company supported its growing range of cheeses with the acquisition of a number of other cheese producers in the region. In order to ensure its supply of milk, the company built up its own fleet of milk tankers, collecting both milk and cheese, including Saint-Nectaire and Salers, from a growing network of dairy farmer suppliers.

FOCUSED ON CHEESE FROM 2010

Dischamp added to its list of cheeses into the 1990s, with the purchase of Fromagerie du Grand Murols, the leading producer of Murols, another of the region's most acclaimed cheese varieties. The company also added the production of another regional variety, Gaperon, with the purchase of Le Père Daroit. Dischamp became a major producer of raw milk Cantal cheese as well, buying la Laiterie de Chambernon. Other regional specialties added by the company included Rustou and Savaron.

Dischamp was already one of France's leading dairy companies by the dawn of the 21st century. The company soon emerged as the leader in the Auvergne region, especially of the Saint-Nectaire category. This followed the collapse of one of its main rivals, Groupe Toury, in 2007. Following that company's bankruptcy, Dischamp took over a major part of its operations, the Laiterie de la Montagne, based in Saillant.

This move permitted Dischamp to become the leading producer of Saint-Nectaire cheese. The company also formed a partnership with dairy cooperative Glac to take over Toury's milk collection business. Dischamp took a 30 percent stake in that company, Laitière des Monts d'Auvergne. The retirement of Jacques Dischamp in 2007, and then of Philippe Dischamp in 2009, signaled the start of a new phase in Dischamp's development.

THE TWO DISCHAMPS PART WAYS

Soon after, Jean-Luc and Pierre Dischamp agreed to part ways, with Pierre Dischamp taking over Fromagerie du Grand Murols and Jean-Luc Dischamp remaining leader of Paul Dischamp. Dischamp then began refocusing the company's business around its cheese production. The company sold its Rungis-based wholesale operation in 2009. This was followed by the sale of the group's butter processing and distribution operations in 2010.

This allowed the company to concentrate on developing its three Auvergne-region cheese production facilities, in Sayat, Saint-Nectaire, and Chambernon. Into the decade, the company invested EUR 5 million upgrading its production equipment, as well as its refining cellars for both its Cantal and Saint-Nectaire cheeses. Paul Dischamp had expanded its annual production capacity to 7,500 metric tons, including 3,000 metric tons of Saint-Nectaire cheese.

Despite the increase in quantity, the company nonetheless maintained a strong commitment to quality. This was underscored in 2014, when the company was awarded six medals, including the gold medal for its Saint-Nectaire Fermier AOP, at the Concours General Agricole in Paris. From a single shop in 1911, Paul Dischamp SA had grown into one of France's most-respected cheese producers in the 21st century.

M. L. Cohen

PRINCIPAL SUBSIDIARIES

Collecte Laitière Paul Dischamp; La Coopérative de Chambernon; La Laiterie de la Montagne; Société Laitière Dischamp.

PRINCIPAL DIVISIONS

AOP Cheese; Dairy Products Distribution; International Trading; Dairy Collection.

PRINCIPAL OPERATING UNITS

Saint-Nectaire; Gaperon; Bleu d'Auvergne; Fourme d'Ambert; Cantal; Salers.

PRINCIPAL COMPETITORS

Centrale Coopérative Agricole Bretonne S.C.A.; Coopérative Laitière Ploudaniel S.C.A.; Orlait S.A.S.; Société des Caves et Producteurs Réunis de Roquefort; Soufflet Negoce S.A.S.; Terra Lacta; Terrena S.C.A.; Unibel S.A.; Union Régionale de Coopératives Agricoles.

FURTHER READING

"A 100 Ans, Dischamp se Recentre sur Son Berceau Auvergnat." *Les Marches*, April 21, 2011.

Griffoul, B. "En Auvergne—Dischamp Devient le Leader du Saint-Nectaire." *Reussir*, April 16, 2008.

Therond, Emmanuel. "Jean-Luc Dischamp: Acheter du Fromage, C'est Financer les Biocarburants." *Info Magazine*, June 3, 2013.

Vernet, Arnaud. "Créés en 1911, les Fromages Dischamp Dominent Aujourd'hui le Monde du Saint-Nectaire." *La Montagne*, January 14, 2014.

PCHC-Raketa ZAO

Saint-Petersburg Prospect, 60
Petrodvorets, Saint Petersburg Oblast 198516
Russia
Telephone: (+7 926) 633 73 68
Web site: http://www.raketa.com

Private Company
Founded: 1721
Employees: 110
Sales: $30 million (2014 est.)
NAICS: 334519 Other Measuring and Controlling Device Manufacturing

■ ■ ■

PCHC-Raketa ZAO manufactures watches and related accessories at what is regarded as the oldest factory site in Russia. The company primarily distributes its products in Russia and Europe, though timepiece aficionados in the rest of the world can obtain them on the secondary market relatively easily. Raketa is famous for offering several models that feature a 0 instead of a 12 at the top of the dial. Although the company has produced watches under a number of other labels over the years, Raketa, which means "rocket," remains its flagship brand.

THE FACTORY'S ORIGINS: 1721–1944

The factory site occupied by the Petrodvorets Watch Factory, home of Raketa watches, dates back to October 21, 1721, when Russian monarch Peter the Great ordered the construction of a factory for milling and mounting precious and semiprecious stones in his capital city of Saint Petersburg. The czar had spent his reign modernizing Russia and transforming it into a credible world power. One critical facet of this process was the construction of new palaces, fortresses and civic buildings, all of which demanded a reliable source of decorative stones. The Petrodvorets Lapidary Works, named after its home district, would provide the carvings and ornamental flourishes for Russia's most prominent buildings for the next two centuries, including the elaborate mosaics of St. Isaac's Cathedral and the stately stonework of Lenin's Tomb. Outside Russia, the factory provided stonework for the Louvre and the palaces of Versailles.

After the Russian Revolution, the country's economic decline and decreased emphasis on architectural ostentation and excess led to a new mission and new name for the factory. The year 1930 saw the Lapidary Works transformed into the First State Precision Jewel Cutting Factory. The plant would continue to work with precious stones but would now focus on milling and processing them for industrial, technical, and military uses. In fact, it would be the only such facility in Russia during the prewar period. This unique status may well have contributed to its destruction.

From 1941 until 1944 Saint Petersburg, renamed Leningrad in the wake of the revolution, endured a punishing siege by German forces, resulting in the deaths of more than one million civilians, including one-third of the factory's 600 employees, and the demolition of much of the city's infrastructure. One of

COMPANY PERSPECTIVES

Founded by Peter the Great in 1721, the factory has been producing the watches under the brand name "Raketa" since 1961 after the flight of Yuri Gagarin. This is the oldest manufacturer of Russia and one of the few factories in the world that fully produces its own mechanical movements from A to Z, including hair spring, balance wheel and escapement.

the architectural casualties was the more than 200-year-old stone-cutting factory. Whether the plant was deliberately targeted for destruction or had simply fallen victim to general artillery bombardment is unclear, but when the dust settled, the factory lay in ruins.

RECONSTRUCTION AND A NEW DIRECTION: 1945–60

Almost immediately after the liberation of Leningrad, near the end of the war, came word that the factory would be rebuilt, albeit with an entirely new mission. Concerned that Russia had become overreliant on the importation of consumer goods, Joseph Stalin's regime had embarked on a campaign dedicated to retooling the country's obsolete and redundant industrial facilities for the manufacture of a variety of popular products. Ultimately, it was hoped, this strategy would encourage Russians to boost the country's economy by purchasing domestic goods. Further, the products could bring foreign money into the country if they proved popular as exports.

Under the direction of charismatic manager Leonid Nestorovitch Tkachenko, the former Lapidary Works underwent a four year period of reconstruction, opening in 1949 as the First State Watch Factory and dedicated to producing wristwatches. Stalin himself had chosen the first Russian watch brand name, Pobeda, meaning "victory," to celebrate the end of the war. Pobeda watches had been in production at a number of state factories across Russia for several years when they became the first product line issued by the new plant. Soon, the factory added Zvezda, meaning "star," a brand produced only at the Leningrad site, to its product line.

During the 1950s the factory changed course somewhat, changing its name to Petrodvorets Watch Factory and focusing on the production of men's pocket watches. At the same time the plant converted to an assembly line production process. Previously, watches had

been constructed from start to finish by only one or two employees. The change resulted in a marked increase in the plant's output, which rose to 275,000 watches per year by 1954. Although the assembly line would remain, the pocket watch–centered business model ended just a few years later when a number of developments in Russian technology, national pride, and popular tastes converged to inspire the factory's most popular product line to date.

RAKETA TAKES OFF: 1961–80

In April 1961 Russian cosmonaut Yuri Gagarin became the first human being to enter outer space. The event was a source of great national pride for the Russian population and influenced many aspects of the country's popular and economic culture for years to follow. One of a plethora of products inspired by or named after Gagarin's achievement was the Petrodvorets Watch Factory's new Raketa, or "rocket," model of wristwatch. As a result of its timely release and solid design, the Raketa brand quickly became the factory's most popular product to date. It had become apparent that the era of the pocket watch was quickly coming to an end. Wrist watches were seen as more modern and more convenient and with the success of the new brand, the factory would eventually abandon its pocket watch line.

From its original stand-alone version, the Raketa brand was quickly expanded to include more than two dozen models, all sharing the same basic internal movement design. Variations included watches for the visually impaired and a 24-hour watch, designed for polar explorers. This latter model featured antimagnetic construction and 24 hours on the dial. Other popular Raketa models included the Rossia, the Petrodvorets, and the Rekord. The Rossia was designed with a special shock-resistant mechanism and a separate, central seconds dial. The Petrodvorets, which featured a 0 instead of a 12 at the top of the dial, became one of the company's most famous designs. The Rekord actually used an alternate movement design that enabled it to be enclosed in a much thinner watch casing, at 2.7 millimeters, the thinnest ever produced in Russia. The design won the factory a gold medal at the 1965 Leipzig International Watch Fair.

In 1968 the basic Raketa caliber was overhauled and redesigned by the company's two top technicians, Mikhail Arsentievich Kisilev and Ivan Alekseevich Starkov, who had previously designed the Polar model. The new Raketa mechanism left room for additions the watchmakers had planned for future models. These included a calendar, added in 1969 and a cost-saving screwless balance wheel design introduced in 1972. A self-winding mechanism, added in 1976, was less

KEY DATES

1721:	Factory is founded by Peter the Great for milling precious stones.
1949:	Factory begins producing watches.
1961:	Raketa watch brand is introduced.
2009:	Factory is purchased by a partnership led by Jacques von Polier.
2014:	Company releases updated versions of several classic watch models.

successful. Proving too complex to market at a reasonable price, the design was discontinued by the end of the decade.

During the 1960s and 1970s business at Raketa expanded rapidly. In 1977 the factory closed its last assembly line and moved to a fully automated production system. By the end of the 1970s nearly 8,000 employees produced around 5 million watches each year. Almost a city within a city, the plant supported its own schools and hospital, a stadium for employee events and gatherings, and two orchestras. Employees also enjoyed the use of a Black Sea resort, youth summer camps, and an on-site nuclear fallout shelter capable of hosting the entire work roster. Raketa's economic boom, however, would not last.

THE LONG DECLINE: 1981–2008

Beginning in the early 1980s several factors contributed to a decline in the fortunes of Russia's traditional watch manufacturers, including Raketa. The 1970s had seen the market for traditional mechanical watches overtaken by less expensive and more reliable quartz watches, which were electronically powered. Even though Raketa had begun producing quartz watches, raw materials for watch batteries were difficult to obtain in the Soviet Union during this period. At the same time digital watches grew dramatically in popularity, particularly among younger consumers. Raketa experienced difficulty both in developing a manufacturing infrastructure for digital watches and selling them profitably in competition with inexpensive models sold by Asian manufacturers.

In a final blow to Raketa, the Soviet economy as a whole had begun a period of decline, a state of affairs which contributed greatly to the union's collapse and reorganization in 1991. While a more open and capitalistic economic environment breathed new life into a number of previously state-run industries, Raketa

continued to struggle through the end of the century. Economic deregulation had brought a flood of Chinese-produced watches into the country and allowed a spike in energy prices. During this period the company survived by adding alarm clocks, blood pressure cuffs, and mechanical pressure gauges to its product line. As the factory's fortunes waned, a steady series of layoffs decimated the company's workforce. Ironically, as capitalism spread across Russia and markets became less regulated, the factor that kept Raketa from closing down completely was a handful of grandfathered government contracts.

As the Soviet government had morphed into the new Russian state, many bureaucratic institutions changed slowly or were never altered at all. This included long-standing contracts with Raketa to supply the military and the government with timepieces. With a limited number of Russian suppliers and the low priority assigned to reevaluating such contracts, Raketa continued as the government's primary watch supplier for decades. Ongoing turmoil in the Russian economy, however, reduced the value of even this guaranteed business. By the first years of the new century, the once bustling factory had been reduced to a staff of 100, producing a standardized line of watches mostly for the government. The company continued marketing its wares to the private sector, but with limited resources for research and development, its share of the market had dwindled considerably.

In 2004 the Petrodvorets Watch Factory, owned by a scattered group of investors and former employees, filed for bankruptcy. As a result, the company was split into two divisions, a stripped-down watchmaking operation and a commercial real estate venture, dedicated to leasing the factory's now largely vacant facilities to other businesses. It was the efforts of this division which led to a turnaround in Raketa's fortunes.

THE RAKETA REBIRTH: 2009–14

In 2009 French investment fund manager Jacques Von Polier was attracted by the low rents offered by Raketa's real estate division. Initially interested in starting a new company on the site, Von Polier instead began to mull the possibility of acquiring a going concern with a venerable brand name. Although he knew little about the watch business, Von Polier felt that economic and social tides had turned in Russia and that the Raketa brand, with its decades-old ties to Soviet national pride and achievement could be reinvigorated with a canny marketing effort. "After the fall of the Soviet Union, Russians were rejecting whatever was Russian. ... Russians were almost anti-Russian," he told the *St. Petersburg Times* in 2013, adding, "Now that 20-plus years have passed, you feel that has changed. ... You have the feeling they now begin to appreciate their own country."

When Von Polier and his partner, British banking consultant David Henderson-Stewart, learned that the company was available for a relatively low price, they decided to take the risk. What the pair discovered was initially disheartening. The company was down to fewer than 100 employees, only 30 of whom worked full time. There was no marketing staff and a minimal accounting department. The watchmakers knew their craft but no research and development had been done for 25 years. The factory produced six traditional Raketa models that were shipped regularly to government and private distribution centers. Von Polier did inherit the factory's files containing more than 6,000 ink-and-paper watch designs, a tantalizing glimpse of Raketa's glory days.

One of Von Polier's first steps was to bring in a team of consultants from the Swiss watchmaking industry to evaluate the factory's potential and advise the new owners on the best way to increase the company's production capacity and sales. In addition to technical improvements, the new owners understood the importance of new product and aggressive marketing to revitalizing the brand. In 2010 they signed an agreement with Russian supermodel Natalia Vodianova to produce a new watch model named after her. The design proved popular enough to warrant the addition of additional Vodianova models. Also in 2010, the company reopened the factory's watchmaking school. Raketa hoped to develop its future staff of technicians in house, avoiding the expense of importing talent from outside Russia.

By early 2011 Von Polier had secured a deal with French boutique chain Colette and was courting other European distributors. On the factory floor, Raketa had purchased new equipment from the Swatch Group of Switzerland, boosting its production capacity to around 2,000 watches per month. The following year the company hired Swiss engineer Jean-Claude Quenet, formerly of the Rolex company to oversee production of its new models. These included a new line of self-winding watches, a product the company had originally abandoned in the 1970s. Raketa made the new line, along with the Vodianova models, the focus of its 2012 appearance at the Baselworld watch and jewelry trade show in Switzerland. Although Vodianova was featured heavily in the company's advertising, Von Polier himself became the public face of Raketa during this period, often posing for quirky promotional photos and granting numerous interviews.

In 2013 Raketa expanded its product line further with new marketing tie-ins and returning classics. The company continued its efforts to link the Raketa name with Russian pride and nostalgia by working with members of the royal Romanov family to produce a watch commemorating the Romanov dynasty and by hiring Olympic snowboarding medalists Vic Wild and Alena Zavarzina to help design and promote a line of watches inspired by the Sochi Winter Olympics. In 2014 the company celebrated its own history with updated versions of it Polar 24-hour watch, its waterproof Amphibia model for divers, and even a redesigned Petrodvorets, with its iconic 0 at the top of the dial. In a further nod to history, Raketa obtained the exclusive rights to manufacture Pobeda brand watches, a relaunch of its first product line. In April 2014 Raketa reopened its watch factory museum, which had been closed since the bankruptcy. The factory had seemingly come full circle, beginning again from point zero, much like the hands on its most iconic dial.

Chris Herzog

PRINCIPAL COMPETITORS

Company Volmax; Maktime Watch Factory Ltd.; Vostok Watch Makers Inc.

FURTHER READING

Lakin, Malcolm. "Marvels, Machines and Mechanical Masterpieces." *Europa Star*, July 2012.

Medetsky, Anatoly. "Jacques von Polier Banks on Russian Pride." *St. Petersburg Times*, August 7, 2013.

Muller, Olivier. "The Incredible Story of Raketa Watches." May 2011. Accessed June 23, 2014. http://thewatchlounge.com/the-incredible-story-of-raketa.

Revill, John. "Russians Relaunch Soviet-Era Space Watches." *Emerging Europe* (blog), March 24, 2011. Accessed June 23, 2014. http://blogs.wsj.com/emergingeurope/2011/03/24/russians-resurrect-soviet-era-watch.

Titova, Irina. "Raketa Watch Factory Loved by Brezhnev Looks for Revival." *Moscow Times*, June 17, 2014.

Port of Subs, Inc.

5365 Mae Anne Avenue, Suite A29
Reno, Nevada 89523
U.S.A.
Telephone: (775) 747-0555
Toll Free: (800) 245-0245
Fax: (775) 747-1510
Web site: http://www.portofsubs.com

Private Company
Founded: 1972 as Sub Shop
Sales: $50 million (2013 est.)
NAICS: 722513 Limited-Service Restaurants

■ ■ ■

Port of Subs, Inc., is a privately held company based in Reno, Nevada, that operates the Port of Subs sandwich shop chain of more than 150 units. It includes about 25 company-owned stores, with the remainder franchised operations. Port of Subs locations are mostly found in smaller towns in Nevada, Arizona, California, Idaho, Utah, Washington, and Wyoming. Port of Subs is known for the high-quality, fresh ingredients used to prepare its made-to-order sandwiches. The menu includes typical cold submarine sandwiches as well as hot "grillers," wraps, and salads. For breakfast, Port of Subs offers grillers with egg, bacon, and sausage. Side orders include chips, potato salad, macaroni salad, and dill pickles. Jumbo brownies and chocolate chunk, oatmeal raisin, and chocolate macadamia nut cookies are offered for dessert. Port of Subs stores also offer catering, providing box lunches and sandwich trays, along with wraps and salads, fruit and veggie trays, meat and cheese trays, and dessert trays.

COMPANY FOUNDED: 1972

After graduating from the University of Nevada at Reno, John Larsen began his business career as a public accountant for the gaming industry. He began advising sub shop owners, including Bobby and Andy Spears, a pair of New Jersey–born brothers who in 1972 opened two delicatessens in Sparks, Nevada, under the Sub Shop banner. In need of financial advice, they turned to Larsen. In addition to doing their taxes, Larsen invested in the business.

In 1975 he and his then-wife Patricia, an advertising executive, decided to buy the sandwich shops for $60,000. With two silent partners, they scraped together $10,000 for a down payment, and paid off the balance over the next five years. The Larsens bought out their partners after the first year. One of the first steps taken by the Larsens was to change the sandwich shops' name, which they believed was too generic.

They held a contest for a new name and from the thousands of entries they received, the Larsens selected "Port of Subs." The couple also changed the menu, emphasizing fresh ingredients and made-to-order preparation. They steadily built up a clientele, mostly focusing on the lunch business. "We use a real grass-roots marketing effort to get the word out to the consumer," Patricia Larsen told *Nation's Business* in a July 1990 article. Some of the tools she used included door hangers and direct mail.

COMPANY PERSPECTIVES

Over the years, the Port of Subs brand has become synonymous with quality sandwich making and superior customer service.

With a successful formula in place, Port of Subs began to open new stores between 1976 to 1985, which grew to 10 units, accomplished primarily through the use of cash flow rather than debt and the devotion of the Larsens to the business. "From 1976 to '83, we didn't take a vacation. We didn't take off more than a day a week," John Larsen told the *Arizona Daily Sun* in January 31, 2006.

FRANCHISING BEGINS: 1985

Port of Subs recorded $1.5 million in sales in 1985. By this point, the small chain had caught the notice of people interested in becoming franchisees. After a few years of receiving such requests, the Larsens began developing a franchising model. Finally, in November 1985 they began franchising the Port of Subs concept. To provide start-up capital for the operation, they sold five Port of Subs corporate stores.

The timing for launching a franchised fast-food chain proved poor, however. The stock market soon crashed, the country was embroiled in a savings and loan crisis, and the economy inched toward recession in the late 1980s. Moreover, the Larsens were not prepared for the differences between running a chain of sandwich shops and a franchise organization. During the first two years of franchising, Port of Subs lost more than $400,000.

ADDS KIDS' MEALS: 1988

The Larsens made changes that they hoped would make a difference. In 1988, $1.99 children's meals were introduced. Drive-through lanes were also added. Nevertheless, the company's future was very much in doubt, and in 1990 John Larsen sought help from the Nevada Small Business Development Center. He was unable to answer the first question the counselor asked, "Who is your customer?"

To help Larsen better understand the business that he had been running for the past 15 years, the center assembled a team that included University of Nevada at Reno students to create a customer profile for Port of Subs. Customers were surveyed and individual stores studied to gain a understanding of why some locations succeeded more than others.

With that knowledge in hand, a list of potential sites was created. Larsen also developed a more detailed business plan to help guide the chain into the future and crafted a mission statement to provide employees with a vision for the business. Port of Subs' purpose, simply stated, was to offer a quality product in a clean and appealing atmosphere, coupled with friendly service.

RETURN TO PROFITABILITY: 1991

Aside from gaining a better understanding of their customers and mission, the Larsens took steps to stabilize Port of Subs' finances. All of their available cash was poured into the chain, and they borrowed additional funds to keep the business afloat. At the same time, they found ways to cut expenses without harming the operation. In addition, they improved the way the Port of Subs organization worked by delegating more responsibility to department heads, freeing themselves to focus on big-picture needs.

Steadily, individual stores returned to profitability. After losing $250,000 in 1989, Port of Subs narrowed its loss to $3,000 the following year and recorded a modest profit in 1991, thus setting the stage for a period of accelerated growth. Port of Subs' turnaround was so evident that in 1993 the company won the Nevada small business of the year award. Also in 1993 Port of Subs was recognized by the U.S. Chamber of Commerce and *Nation's Business* magazine.

With a better understanding of site selection, Port of Subs opened several new company-owned stores in Las Vegas and expanded into new markets through franchising. Franchised units at this stage generally relied on funding from the U.S. Small Business Administration. In addition, most of the new stores were opened by existing franchisees and their family and friends, as well as Port of Subs' customers.

Port of Subs mostly targeted smaller population centers, where there was less competition from Subway and other large sandwich shop chains. By 1998 the Port of Subs chain grew to about 90 stores in Nevada, Arizona, California, and Washington. After reaching the 100-unit mark, John Larsen told the press that he planned to make an initial public offering of stock. The offering never took place, however, and Port of Subs remained a private company.

NEW SOURCES OF REVENUE

To add another source of income, Port of Subs began pursuing foodservice contracts in the late 1990s. Clients included high schools, hotel chains, deliberating juries, firefighters for the U.S. Forest Service, and the training academies of the Bureau of Land Management. It was a low-margin business, but it was high volume and also helped to improve recognition of the Port of Subs brand.

Catering also played a growing role in the success of individual stores. For some restaurants, as much as 20 percent of their revenues were generated by catering and foodservice contracts. After recording about $37 million in systemwide sales in 2000, Port of Subs pursued measured growth in the new century. Helping the chain was a growing interest among consumers in eating healthier, a trend that played to the strength of Port of Subs and its reputation for high-quality, fresh ingredients.

The chain expanded to Arizona, and in 2001 Port of Subs entered Idaho, opening its first store in Boise. The following year, three more Port of Subs opened in the area. The chain had not planned to expand into Idaho, but potential franchisees reached out to the Larsens, a reflection of how much the Port of Subs brand was improving its stature in the western United States.

LAUNCHES TV AD CAMPAIGN: 2003

Unlike many of the smaller communities where Port of Subs opened stores, Boise was a market with no shortage of sandwich shops and other fast-food restaurants. Nevertheless, it fared well against the likes of Subway, Quiznos, and Blimpie Subs. Port of Subs took steps to improve brand recognition. In 2003 the chain launched the first television campaign in its history.

By this stage, the chain had grown to 136 units. The three television spots aired in markets in five Western states. A character from the first spot, a fictional employee named Jennifer, was also incorporated in point-of-purchase materials used in the stores. The

Port of Subs chain reached 147 units by the end of 2005.

Many of the stores had been in operation for more than a decade and were beginning to show their age. A Seattle-based design firm was hired and a complete re-branding of the chain was undertaken. A new logo was introduced, featuring a chef character and the slogan "Sliced Fresh Sandwiches!" A store makeover program was also undertaken. Starting with a company-owned unit in Tempe, Arizona, a fresh interior design was unveiled.

New track lighting was installed, and the blue-and-white naval colors that had defined Port of Subs for three decades were replaced with warmer earth tones. Televisions were installed and Wi-Fi became available for customer use. Moreover, the new floor plan helped to speed customers through the food line. The menu was redesigned to help customers decide on their orders more quickly. The chain also installed an online and fax ordering system to allow customers to save time by placing takeout orders in advance.

PRODUCT DEVELOPMENT EMPHASIZED

In 2007 Port of Subs hired its first research and development manager to help develop new products for both the restaurant and catering menus, some of which were limited-time offers. In 2008, for example, Port of Subs offered a barbecue sandwich in honor of the Kentucky Derby, called Kentucky Unbridled. The following year the chain introduced a permanent addition to the menu, the Sliced-Fresh Grillers, as well as the Sliced-Fresh Power-Lunch Box for catered meetings and group events.

The Sliced-Fresh Grillers also filled out the breakfast menu with several new sandwiches. Port of Subs teamed up with larger brands for promotional efforts. In 2010 the chain created a 32-ounce promotional fountain cup program with Coca-Cola and live-events promoter Live Nation.

Each cup came with a peel-and-win label for a variety of concert-related prizes. They ranged from $20 cash cards and music downloads to a VIP Concert Flyaway Trip for two, valued at more than $3,000. In truth, Port of Subs was still very much a regional player with only modest plans for further expansion. In 2010 the chain made a greater commitment to Salt Lake City, Utah, with the opening of the first of several stores in the area.

The chain continued to fill in existing markets as well. In August 2013 Port of Subs opened another store in the Las Vegas area. After more than four decades in business, Port of Subs had carved out a niche in the West. Whether the chain would be able to remain competitive in a crowded field remained an open question.

Ed Dinger

PRINCIPAL DIVISIONS

Finance & Administration; Marketing; Operations; Support.

PRINCIPAL COMPETITORS

Doctor's Associates, Inc.; Kahala Corp.; The Quiznos Master LLC.

FURTHER READING

Ames, Michael D. *Pathways to Success*. San Francisco: Berrett-Koehler Publishers, Inc., 1994.

Gardner, Tom. "Port of Subs Updates by Going Retro." *Arizona Daily Sun*, January 31, 2006.

Liddle, Alan. "Sandwich Shops Spreading Out to Boost Sales." *Nation's Restaurant News*, February 27, 1989, F11.

Martin, Steve. "Nevada-Based Sub Chain Plans to Open Unit in Boise Area." *Idaho Business Review*, June 11, 2001.

Pollock, Dennis. "Port of Subs Will Add 8 Valley Stores." *Fresno Bee*, March 1, 1997, C1.

Whittemore, Meg. "Menus for Growth." *Nation's Business*, July 1990, 56.

Pret A Manger Holdings Ltd.

———————————— ■ ————————————

1 Hudson's Place
London, SW1V 1PZ
United Kingdom
Telephone: (+44 20) 7827 8000
Fax: (+44 20) 7827 8787
Web site: http://www.pret.com

Private Company
Founded: 1983
Employees: 4,000
Sales: £380 million ($626.5 million) (2013 est.)
NAICS: 722513 Limited-Service Restaurants

■ ■ ■

Pret A Manger Holdings Ltd. is the London-based owner and operator of the Pret A Manger chain of quick-serve restaurants. Pret focuses on prepackaged healthful food, including sandwiches, wraps, salads, fruit, and dessert items. Stores also offer breakfast sandwiches and wraps, yogurt pots, hot sandwiches, macaroni and cheese, soups, and oatmeal. In addition to fruit juices, coffee, and hot and cold teas, Pret sells grab-and-go cold pressed bottled juices that blend fruits and vegetables. Products are prepared fresh daily in each store, the leftovers donated to local charities. All Pret stores are corporate owned. Most of the chain's more than 300 stores are located in the United Kingdom, but are also found in the United States in Boston, Chicago, New York City, and Washington, D.C. Pret also has a foothold in France with a dozen locations in Paris, and operates about the same number in Hong Kong. Pret is

owned by an investment group led by Bridgepoint Capital, a pan-European private-equity firm.

ORIGINS: 1983

Pret a Manger grew out of a failed business of the same name. The original Pret was established across from the Hampstead Underground station in London in 1983 by Jeffrey Hyman, who was backed by investors from the advertising and entertainment industries. Credited with naming the shop was Hyman's sister, Valerie Tomalin. She was involved in the fashion industry, where the French term *prêt-à-porter* (ready to wear) was common place. Hence, Pret A Manger signified "ready to eat," an apt name given that the premise behind the new restaurant concept was that the food was prepackaged to speed up service. The French name was also appropriate because it lent an air of sophistication and the original Pret A Manger store mostly offered ready-to-eat French dishes, including filled baguettes and such classics as coq au vin and boeuf bourguignon.

The Hampstead store closed after construction scaffolding was erected on the block. When the work was finally completed, the business was purchased out of liquidation in 1986 by Julian Metcalfe and Sinclair Beecham, who were in their 20s at the time. The two had met while studying at Central London Polytechnic and had grown disenchanted with the sandwiches they bought for lunch while attending classes. They had already attempted to address that problem by opening a wine bar and delicatessen. This business soon closed, losing £80,000. Nevertheless, they were able to borrow £17,000 to acquire Pret. They dropped the emphasis on

French cuisine, replacing it with prepared sandwiches, but retained the prepackaged concept as a way to appeal to time-pressed office workers in search of a quick, healthful lunch.

While Beecham handled business affairs, Metcalfe was the visionary as well as the shop's first cook. He toyed with the Pret concept until he had the right blend of quality and price. The store also dropped the London deli convention of serving meals on plates in favor of the boxed lunch. The revamped Pret found a ready supply of customers, who appreciated the combination of convenience and high-quality food. Before the end of the first year, Pret was serving 7,000 customers a week. After two years, the shop was generating more than £575,000 in annual sales.

Metcalfe and Beecham opened three more Pret shops in London by 1992. To support further growth, they brought in management consultants, who received one-quarter of the company. It proved to be a poor fit for the free-spirited Metcalfe, who balked at the consultants' regimented approach to doing business. It was because of Metcalfe that an anticorporate attitude became part of Pret's brand identity. Eventually, he and Beecham bought out their partners. Despite this unproductive interlude, Pret continued to expand in London, where the brand quickly gained iconic status.

CEO HIRED: 1998

By the fall of 1994 Pret was operating 18 London locations, with a new store opened every six weeks. There was also talk of franchising the Pret concept in hopes of opening 300 to 400 new stores, but that idea never came to fruition. Instead, all Pret stores remained company owned. There were about 60 locations in 1998 when Metcalfe and Beecham began scouting for a seasoned executive to take the quick-serve chain to the next level. Moreover, after a dozen years of working together, their relationship had deteriorated to the point that they barely spoke to one another. In 1998 they brought in Andrew Rolfe to become CEO. Rolfe was a

former PepsiCo executive who had previously run the London KFC operation. He brought more structure to Pret, including new training manuals and improved information technology.

While Metcalfe mostly stepped away from Pret's management, Beecham focused on international expansion, in particular spearheading the entry into New York City. The first U.S. Pret store opened on Broad Street in the Wall Street area of New York in the summer of 2000. By this stage the chain topped the 100-unit mark in the United Kingdom and sales had increased to $121 million. Making the transition to the New York market was not smooth, however. Despite having an American, recent Cornell hotel school graduate Monica Gelinas, to assist Beecham and make some adjustments to the store layout and menu, the New York Pret encountered some growing pains. Unlike Londoners, for example, New Yorkers did not like their sandwiches lathered in mayonnaise, preferring instead a "drier eat." Finding workers with the proper positive Pret attitude was also difficult. To help paper over the churlishness of the local employees, some Pret staff were flown in from London.

More than just establishing a beachhead in the United States, the Broad Street Pret was intended to serve as a showcase for potential investors to help finance the chain's international ambitions. There was some talk in 2001 of making a public offering of stock. Instead, Rolfe found an unlikely partner in McDonald's, which in early 2001 reached an agreement to acquire a one-third interest in Pret for a reported £40 million to £50 million. "Many Pret customers and staff swallowed hard at the potential culture clash," according to a July 1, 2007, *Management Today* article. "Pret preaching how it cares for its customers, staff and ethical living; McDonald's synonymous with globalization, obesity and dead end jobs."

HONG KONG AND JAPAN STORES OPEN: 2002

Although they may not have shared similar brand messages, McDonald's was an ideal partner for a company with international ambitions such as Pret. In July 2001 the chain opened its second New York location in Midtown and announced plans to open 30 more in Manhattan over the next two years. In 2002 Pret stores also opened in Hong Kong and Japan. As was the case in New York, translating the Pret brand to other cultures proved difficult. In Japan, Pret targeted office workers in their mid-20s to mid-30s and hoped to open 30 stores by the end of 2003 and a further 50 locations the following year. The concept, however, never fully took root.

```
╔══════════════════════════════════════════╗
║                                          ║
║              KEY DATES                   ║
║        ──────────────■──────────────      ║
║                                          ║
║  1983:  Original Pret A Manger store opens. ║
║  1986:  Julian Metcalfe and Sinclair Beecham ║
║         relaunch Pret A Manger.          ║
║  2001:  McDonald's acquires a one-third interest. ║
║  2008:  Bridgepoint Capital acquires majority control. ║
║  2012:  First Pret A Manger store opens in Boston. ║
║                                          ║
╚══════════════════════════════════════════╝
```

Pret management soon realized that the chain had attempted to grow too quickly. Pret began losing money, prompting Metcalfe and Beecham in March 2003 to fire Rolfe, as well as Harvey Smyth, Rolfe's deputy chief executive and U.K. managing director. Pret maintained that their departure was by mutual consent, a simple matter of a disagreement over the pace of international expansion. Rolfe told the press that in reality he had been sacked because Metcalfe wanted to regain control of the business and he and Smyth had resisted the move. Indeed, Metcalfe did return to a full-time role, assuming the title of creative director, but other executives were quickly brought in as replacements. A month after the exit of Rolfe and Smyth, Larry Billett was named nonexecutive chairman, and Clive Schlee became CEO.

Although there was some speculation that it was ready to sell its stake in Pret, McDonald's elected to hold its investment for the time being. Pret now entered a period of retrenchment. The chain had hoped to have 40 New York locations by the end of 2004. Instead, six of the 16 stores that it had opened by then were closed. The situation was worse in Japan. After just 18 months in business, Pret closed all of the stores and abandoned the market in 2004. Business in the United Kingdom, on the other hand, remained solid, and slowly Pret began to return to health and resume expansion.

KIOSK FORMAT INTRODUCED: 2006

Always ambitious, Metcalfe in late 2003 began touting a new Pret Café format that he claimed the British people were crying out for. He estimated the country could support 200 to 300 locations. The Pret Café never materialized. Instead, the company adopted an opposite approach. In late 2006 it unveiled a kiosk format. Measuring just three meters by four meters, the outlets allowed Pret to sell prepackaged foods in railway stations, airports, and retail parks.

In late 2006 Pret signed a new lease in New York for the first time in years. The shop would be located across the street from Grand Central Terminal. Having spent the previous year focused on improved sourcing and employee training, Pret believed it was better prepared to expand across Manhattan as well as to other major U.S. cities. Pret also focused on improving same-store sales in the United Kingdom.

With the chain on the rebound, there was talk once more in 2007 of a possible public offering of stock, due in no small measure to some unguarded comments Metcalfe made while attending a book launch. Any plans that may have been in the offing were scrapped, however, when several private-equity firms made unsolicited offers for the company. In March 2008 an agreement was reached to sell a majority interest in Pret for £350 million to a group of investors led by European private-equity firm Bridgepoint Capital and including the American investment bank Goldman Sachs. After the sale of Pret, Beecham remained a non-executive director but had no active role in the company. Instead, he devoted his time to a new hotel venture, while Metcalfe left to start the Itsu sushi restaurant chain.

U.S. EXPANSION

With the deep pockets of its new owners behind it, Pret increased the pace of expansion. In addition to scores of new shops in New York, Pret opened its first store in Washington, D.C., in 2009. A year later, it entered the Chicago market. The first Boston store opened in 2012.

In the meantime Pret entered the French market in 2011 with a pair of stores in Paris. While a French name may have provided a hint of sophistication in other markets, it did not have the same impact on the French. As *Marketing Week*'s Mark Ritson noted in his July 7, 2011, column, "Imagine a new London restaurant called Ready to Eat Foods and you'll get the idea." In any event, the two Paris shops performed well enough that nine others follow in the next three years. Pret was likely to expand further in the United States and perhaps enter new countries. How long its private-equity owners elected to hold onto the investment before deciding to cash in was far less certain.

Ed Dinger

PRINCIPAL SUBSIDIARIES

Pret A Manger (Europe) Ltd.; Pret A Manger (USA) Ltd.

PRINCIPAL COMPETITORS

Eat. The Real Food Co. Ltd.; Marks & Spencer Group P.L.C.; Starbucks Corporation.

FURTHER READING

"Accelerator: From Little Acorns." *Management Today*, July 1, 2007.

Craig, Malcolm. "Sandwich Course." *Leisure & Hospitality Business*, February 22, 2001.

Frumkin, Paul. "McD-Backed Pret A Manger Eyes Larger Bite of Bit Apple." *Nation's Restaurant News*, April 15, 2002.

Kramer, Louis. "Pret A Manger Ready to Take Another Crack at NYC Market." *Nation's Restaurant News*, December 4, 2006.

Maurer, Sherry A. "British Invasion." *Chain Leader*, September 2000.

"Pret A Manger: Bread Winners." *Marketing Week*, August 2, 2007.

Ritson, Mark. "Pret's Brand Promise Lost in Translation." *Marketing Week*, July 7, 2011.

Proto Labs Inc.

———— ■ ————

5540 Pioneer Creek Drive
Maple Plain, Minnesota 55359
U.S.A.
Toll Free: (877) 479-3680
Fax: (763) 479-2679
Web site: http://www.protolabs.com

Public Company
Incorporated: 1999 as Protomold Company Inc.
Employees: 750
Sales: $162.4 million (2013)
Stock Exchanges: New York
Ticker Symbol: PRLB
NAICS: 326199 All Other Plastics Product Manufacturing; 332999 All Other Miscellaneous Fabricated Metal Product Manufacturing

■ ■ ■

Proto Labs Inc. specializes in the rapid manufacture of low-volume runs of parts for a variety of applications, including appliances, medical devices, automotive technology, and electronics. The parts are produced through the company's streamlined injection molding processes, as well as computer-controlled machining tools and three-dimensional (3-D) printing technology.

THE BEGINNING: 1999–2001

In the late 1990s company founder Larry Lukis was already a successful business owner and computer industry innovator. Lukis had helped create LaserMaster, a Minnesota-based designer and manufacturer of computer printers and other desktop publishing hardware, in 1985. After little more than a decade in business, LaserMaster, eventually renamed ColorSpan, had grown into a $100 million business and was entertaining a number of buyout offers. Lukis sensed the time was right to move on and explore other opportunities.

As often happens with innovators, Lukis's next inspiration arose from repeated difficulties and frustrations he had experienced during his time designing new printing technology for his former company. Before any new technology can be mass produced, it must first go through a prototype stage during which a limited number of devices must be produced and tested in order to determine practical and commercial viability. Because most manufacturers that produced parts for electronics based their scheduling and pricing on high-volume business, designers who needed a small number of parts produced, such as Lukis, frequently dealt with prohibitive price quotes and long wait times as they were prioritized behind customers with larger jobs. Certain that the technology sector would expand steadily in the new century, Lukis saw a nascent market for manufacturers who could produce short runs of parts for electronics with a quick turnaround time and competitive pricing.

In 1999 Lukis founded Protomold Company Inc., in the Minneapolis suburb of Maple Plain, and installed himself as chief technological officer. The company would focus on the injection molding of plastic parts for various electronics applications, using customers' existing designs. From the beginning the company focused

COMPANY PERSPECTIVES

As the world's fastest provider of machined and molded parts, we take pride in providing customers real parts really fast.

its marketing efforts on the booming tech start-up sector, a market filled with fresh companies and young inventors who needed to test new products without wasting time or money. While the company used the latest available software and injection molding technology, its business model was fairly simple. Customers would design their own parts and forward the designs to Protomold through the company's website. Protomold would then produce and ship the parts as rapidly as possible.

The model seemed to work. Just over a year later, Protomold had earned around $1 million in revenues. Though Lukis had deliberately limited the operation to an efficient nine employee workforce, the company's success had served to highlight a number of problems with disorganization and administrative inefficiency. Lukis's talents were as a visionary and designer, not a manager. Recognizing that the company's problems would increase with its production volume, he began searching for an experienced administrator to take the reins.

THE NEW CEO: 2001–05

Brad Cleveland had also built a successful career in the Minnesota tech industry. After a decade with MTS Systems Corporation, a venerable Eden Prairie, Minnesota, manufacturer of testing systems and electronic sensors, Cleveland had cofounded a software development company that soon became an MTS subsidiary. In 2001 after four years as the company's vice president, Cleveland spotted an ad in the *Minneapolis Star Tribune* that would change his life. The ad was actually a family-friendly variant of a notice the irascible Lukis had placed on Protomold's website seeking a "No B***S**t CEO" for his company. Cleveland liked Lukis's attitude and business plan and soon found himself Protomold's 10th employee.

Under Cleveland's guidance, Protomold began expanding both its business model and floor space. In 2002 the company began offering a more efficient online pricing service, along with a "manufacturability analysis," which provided customers with projections of the likely pricing and processing time of full production

runs. The following year as business increased the company purchased a new combined design and manufacturing facility that would become known as Plant 1.

By this point Protomold's operations had become even more customer friendly. Using the company website, customers uploaded their own designs in one of several computer-aided-design (CAD) formats. The customer would then receive a price quote, usually within minutes, and shipping could begin as early as the next day. Protomold owed its speed and efficiency to proprietary software which actually went through the process of programming the necessary equipment with the customer's design and estimating the cost. Thus, once the customer completed the approval process online, production could begin instantly. Virtually all of Protomold's manufacturing equipment was and is completely computer controlled.

The next few years saw steady growth at Protomold. By 2004 the company's annual revenues were approaching the $5 million mark. During this period, the company won a number of prestigious honors, including the top spot in the *Minneapolis–St. Paul Business Journal's* list of fastest-growing private companies, number two on the Deloitte Technology Fast 50 list of fastest-growing tech companies in Minnesota, and the Minnesota Tekne award for Best Emerging Company in Advanced Manufacturing. The industry accolades, along with the company's impressive record, inevitably drew the attention of outside investors. In 2005 Private Capital Management, a Minnesota private investment firm, purchased a minority share in the company for $2.5 million. As part of the investment, Brian Smith, president of Private Capital Management, took a seat on the Protomold board of directors. The funding would enable Protomold to expand its operations even further.

GOING GLOBAL: 2005–09

Lukis and Cleveland had long been aware of the existing markets for Protomold's services overseas. While the company was able to accept and produce orders from anywhere in the world, the fast shipping time that distinguished Protomold from many of its competitors would require physical production facilities in the same geographical region as its customers. In 2005 the company created Protomold Ltd., based in a 25,000-square-foot production plant in Telford, England, which would ultimately serve all of the company's European customers. At the same time, Protomold was expanding its domestic production capacity by 50 percent, with the addition of a new 20,000-square-foot facility in Maple Plain. The company's workforce, which had started in the single digits, now included some 200 employees.

KEY DATES

1999: Company is founded as Protomold Company, Inc.
2005: Company opens branch in England.
2009: Protomold is renamed ProtoLabs Inc.
2012: Stock is offered publicly.
2014: Company acquires FineLine Prototyping.

Protolabs continued its expansion in Maple Plain in 2006 with the purchase of the building that would become its new headquarters. In addition to more office space, the building also featured plenty of room for new production lines. By this point, company engineers had perfected and streamlined the injection mold process to the point that they would soon begin offering one day turnaround time on many orders. It was also at this point that the company began looking beyond injection molding and decided that they could apply the company's business model to other forms of production.

In 2007 Protomold added a new product division, Firstcut CNC Machined Parts, to its line of services. Firstcut parts would be actually cut by machine from plastic or metal, rather than molded from plastic. The cutting machines, like most of Protomold's equipment, were completely controlled by computers, a condition known as computer numerical control (CNC). The Firstcut line allowed very small runs of one to ten parts to be produced more economically. Realizing that they might wish to add other service lines in the future, dictated by market demands and technological advancement, the Protomold executive team decided to recast and rename the company to better reflect a variety of possible service offerings. Although the Protomold and Firstcut service brands would remain, they would operate under the umbrella of newly renamed Proto Labs Inc.

In mid-2008 as the Proto Labs reorganization was being finalized, the company received another infusion of investment capital. Boston-based private-equity group North Bridge Growth Equity purchased a large minority share of Proto Labs in exchange for $52 million. By now, Proto Labs was bringing in around $50 million per year and employed almost 300 people at its various production and sales sites. North Bridge had been attracted both by Proto Labs' current revenues and the potential for future revenues from its ongoing global expansion. The company had recently announced plans to open Proto Labs K.K., a full sales and production facility near Tokyo, Japan. The plant would be operational by mid-2009.

GOING PUBLIC: 2010–14

The promise North Bridge had seen in Proto Labs seemed to be justified as the company's revenues continued to climb over the next few years. The year 2010 saw $64.9 million in sales. The following year the figure rose to $98.9 million. Along with rising sales figures, the company also enjoyed a more prominent public profile. In 2010 Proto Labs created the Cool Idea! Award which granted up to $250,000 annually in production services to inventors and innovators who needed help developing product prototypes.

A significant portion of Proto Labs' growth had come from the company's European operation. The company had been forced to find a larger English facility to service its U.K. customers, as well as a bustling trade in Spain, Germany, France, and Italy. The Japanese division also showed steady growth, suggesting the company's best days were yet to come. By February 2012 the Proto Labs board of directors had decided to go public, making a $70 million initial public offering.

Initially priced at $16 per share, Proto Labs stock jumped to $25 after one day of trading on the New York Stock Exchange. While the jump in value seemed to indicate a high level of public confidence in the company, Proto Labs management would learn a lesson about managing a public company just a few months later. In May 2012 along with a report of higher than expected first-quarter earnings, Proto Labs also announced that it would be building a new production facility in Rosemount, Minnesota, and making a considerable investment in technology upgrades at its Maple Plain plant. Wall Street responded unfavorably to the expenditures, dropping the stock's value by 36 percent, an effective loss of $300 million in market value. With market analysts still rating the company favorably and even praising it for putting long-range growth potential before short-term stock losses, the share price would eventually recover. Proto Labs finished 2012 with $126 million in sales.

In October 2013 with Proto Labs firmly established as an industry leader and a Wall Street success story, Cleveland decided it was time to retire, after 12 years as CEO. Lukis, at 65, was also easing toward retirement. He had left his position as chief technological officer, naming as his successor Robert Bodor, Proto Labs' former director of business development. Lukis would remain as the company's chairman.

Cleveland would remain in his position until February 2014, when he turned the office over to his successor, Vicki Holt, a former executive with PPG Industries and Monsanto Corporation. By this point, Proto Labs stock was trading at $80.50 per share and the company had closed out the previous year with $163 million in sales. Holt did not allow the company's solid finances to create an atmosphere of complacency. Within a few months of taking office, she had presided over the opening of a new $19 million, 166,000-square-foot production facility in Plymouth, Minnesota, and facilitated the company's first major acquisition, FineLine Prototyping, a Raleigh, North Carolina, 3-D printing firm. The $38 million purchase would allow Proto Labs to immediately add the rapidly growing 3-D printing market sector to its list of services.

By mid-2014 Proto Labs had a workforce of more than 500 operating at its Minnesota facilities, with another 200 at it international offices. More would soon be added when the new Plymouth facility became fully operational. Although the company's revenues had jumped about 25 percent each year, Holt publicly announced her determination to take Proto Labs' yearly sales to the $1 billion level. One strategy for achieving this goal would be a shift from web-based marketing to actively cultivating business from the research and development divisions of larger corporations. "Do I believe that we can be a $1 billion company? Yes I do," Holt asserted in an interview with the *Minneapolis Star*

Tribune (July 12, 2014), adding, "This is a very strong company. It's just a beautiful financial model."

Chris Herzog

PRINCIPAL SUBSIDIARIES

Proto Labs K.K. (Japan); Proto Labs Ltd. (UK).

PRINCIPAL COMPETITORS

Harbor Plastics Inc.; REO Plastics Inc.; Stratasys Ltd.

FURTHER READING

Black, Sam. "New Proto Labs CEO Vicki Holt Has a Big To-Do List." *Minneapolis–St. Paul Business Journal,* June 13, 2014.

"Brad Cleveland: Proto Labs." *EEWeb Pulse,* August 28, 2012.

DePass, Dee. "New CEO Wants to Turn Proto Labs into a $1 Billion Company." *Minneapolis Star Tribune,* July 12, 2014.

Flaherty, Joseph. "Affordable Injection Molding Transforms Tinkerers into Tycoons." *Wired,* January 30, 2013.

Frisch, Suzy. "Larry Lukis and Brad Cleveland." *Twin Cities Business,* August 2012.

St. Anthony, Neal. "Proto Labs' Chief 'Organizer' Will Search for a Second Act." *Minneapolis Star Tribune,* November 3, 2013.

Red Gold, Inc.

———————————■———————————

1500 Tomato Country Way
Elwood, Indiana 46036-3437
U.S.A.
Telephone: (765) 557-5500
Fax: (765) 557-5501
Web site: http://www.redgold.com

Private Company
Founded: 1942 as Orestes Canning Company
Employees: 1,250
Sales: $375 million (2013 est.)
NAICS: 311421 Fruit and Vegetable Canning

■ ■ ■

Red Gold, Inc., is a leading producer of premium canned and bottled tomato products. The company's offerings include ketchup, tomato juice, crushed and diced tomatoes, pasta sauces, and salsa. Red Gold markets products under its own family of brands, including Red Gold, Redpack, Tuttorosso, and Sacramento, and also makes private-label products for a variety of food retailers. Its products are marketed to consumers via supermarket and club channels, as well as to clients within the foodservice industry.

ORIGINS

Red Gold traces its roots to 1942, when the United States was involved in World War II. To help supply canned products after the bombing of Pearl Harbor, a retired canner named Grover Hutcherson acquired a fire-damaged facility in Orestes, Indiana, formerly operated by the Orestes Packing Company. In partnership with his daughter, Frances (known as Fran), Hutcherson established Orestes Canning Company and relied on local farmers to participate in the venture by growing tomatoes. Early products included both tomato puree and whole peeled tomatoes.

By 1948 the company's products included tomato juice and were marketed under the brand names Indiana's Finest and Indiana Chief. That year management of the company fell to Fran Hutcherson Reichart and her husband, Ernie. In 1952 the company benefited when it gained grocery distributor Shurfine as its first private-label customer. Three years later another plant was acquired in Galveston, Indiana.

Orestes Canning's active involvement in its industry was reflected by Ernie Reichart being named president of the Indiana Canners Association in 1962. The following year the company purchased its very first forklift. Modernization continued in 1964 when gas lines were installed at the Orestes plant, allowing the company to replace coal-powered boilers. The company brought itself in line with other industry players in 1967 by producing products in 14.5-ounce cans.

ACQUISITION OF RED GOLD BRAND

A major development took place in 1970 when Orestes Canning acquired the Red Gold brand from a Trafalgar, Indiana–based cannery. Following the acquisition, the Reicharts changed the company's name to Red Gold,

Inc. Production expanded to include Red Gold–branded ketchup and tomato juice.

It also was during the 1970s that the Reicharts' children became involved in company operations, with Brian Reichart becoming plant manager in 1972. The following year Red Gold's plant in Galveston, Indiana, was repurposed as a warehouse facility. Another significant development occurred during the middle of the decade when Red Gold began using coreless tomatoes.

Red Gold began the 1980s with a leadership change when Brian Reichart was named CEO. Also in 1980, the company acquired a manufacturing plant in Elwood, Indiana, meaning its operations once again included two tomato processing facilities. In addition, Red Gold began serving the contract packaging and foodservice markets. Fettig Transport was acquired in 1981, bolstering the company's distribution capabilities. Red Gold also discontinued the use of its warehouse facility in Galveston. By mid-decade Red Gold was still a small operation, with a workforce of 17 employees. Outside Indiana, few people knew about the company. This soon changed, however. In 1985 Red Gold demolished its Orestes plant and replaced it with a new manufacturing facility. The following year Red Gold transitioned from a seasonal to an annual business, producing products from both concentrated and fresh tomatoes. This allowed the company to offer regular employment opportunities for its workforce, which tripled in size. The color and texture of Red Gold's tomato products was improved in 1988 when the company installed a new evaporator, enabling tomato purees to be concentrated at a lower temperature.

LEADERSHIP CHANGE

Red Gold ushered in the 1990s in growth mode, completing a two-story expansion of its corporate offices and adding an additional 200,000 square feet of warehouse space at its Orestes facility. Ernie and Fran Reichart retired from day-to-day operations, and management of the company was assumed by their children, Brian, Tina, and Gary. Ernie remained involved with the company as chairman.

In 1991 Red Gold's Fettig Transport business was renamed RG Transport. The following year, the company redesigned the look of its Red Gold label. Growth continued in 1993 through the acquisition of a production facility in Paulding, Ohio, along with the Stokely tomato brand. In 1992 Red Gold began producing and marketing diced tomatoes with garlic, basil, and olive oil. After distributing institutional-sized salsa for many years, the company introduced the product to grocery stores in 1993.

By this time Red Gold had partnered with the Indianapolis-based advertising agency Young & Laramore to revitalize its product packaging. The company's products included not only crushed, stewed, and whole tomatoes but also seafood cocktail sauce; chili sauce; ketchup; tomato and vegetable juices; and tomato, spaghetti, marinara, and pizza sauces. These food products were produced using tomatoes grown within a 150-mile radius of its facilities. In addition to the company's own brands, Red Gold produced products for some 200 different private labels, on the strength of approximately 250 employees.

Red Gold continued on a path of expansion in early 1995, acquiring a tomato processing plant in Geneva, Indiana. Two years later the company invested in the facility, adding $1.2 million of machinery and packaging equipment. It also was in 1995 that Red Gold opened a new 575,000-square-foot distribution center in Orestes.

MARKETING INNOVATION

On the marketing front, Red Gold was using a variety of tactics to promote its brand during the mid-1990s. In 1996 the company partnered with Pay Less Supermarket, an independent grocer based in Madison County, Indiana, in a four-week campaign that used store signage, displays, and circulars emphasizing the local ownership of both Red Gold and Pay Less. The company sold 9,000 cases of products in four weeks, with sales that were nine times above normal levels during the campaign's first week.

One particularly innovative marketing idea came from Red Gold's agency, Young & Laramore, in 1997. This involved painting old grain silos throughout the Midwest to resemble cans of the company's tomatoes. Two years later the agency created vibrant red billboards, complete with green tomato stems on top, to promote the brand throughout the Chicago area, where Red Gold had doubled its retail shelf space. The outdoor campaign, which ran during the dreary winter months, featured the tagline "It's Always July."

KEY DATES

1942: Grover Hutcherson and his daughter, Frances, establish Orestes Canning Company.

1970: Orestes Canning acquires the Red Gold brand and renames itself Red Gold, Inc.

2001: Red Gold acquires the tomato products labels of Tri Valley Growers, gaining the Redpack, Tuttorosso, and Sacramento brands.

2012: Headquarters move into a converted elementary school building in Elwood, Indiana.

By the new millennium Red Gold was marketing its own branded products in 10 states throughout the Midwest. The company's product packaging was modified in 2000 to include warm yellow sunrays to emphasize the sun-ripened element of its tomatoes. In addition, Red Gold by this time was also manufacturing products for more than 450 different private labels, both domestically and internationally. The company worked in partnership with approximately 60 different farmers in Ohio, Michigan, and Indiana, who grew its premium tomato seedlings.

GROWING VIA ACQUISITION

Major expansion occurred in early 2001 when Red Gold acquired the tomato products labels of Tri Valley Growers, a cooperative based in San Ramon, California, that had filed for bankruptcy the previous year. Tri Valley's brands (Redpack, Tuttorosso, and Sacramento) were marketed mainly on the East Coast but processed in California. Moving forward, Red Gold began using midwestern tomatoes to make the products. Canning operations were relocated to the company's three plants in Indiana, and roughly 100 additional employees were added to Red Gold's workforce, which already had grown to include 876 people.

Red Gold continued expanding in 2003, acquiring the private-label ketchup operations of Fredonia, New York–based Carriage House. That year, the company also entered into a sponsorship deal with the National Football League's Indianapolis Colts for both the 2003 and 2004 seasons. The deal made Red Gold the official ketchup provider at the RCA Dome and included a variety of marketing opportunities, including branded condiment stations, in-stadium TV advertising, postgame show sponsorship, and advertising and coupon placement in game programs.

By mid-2003 Red Gold was one of only five tomato processors in the Midwest, compared to more than 100 canneries during the 1950s. The company's annual workforce included 1,100 people, with an additional 500 seasonal workers assisting from August to October. Around this time a 15,000-square-foot expansion occurred at Red Gold's Elwood facility, where a high-speed, plastic-bottle ketchup line was added. Brian Reichart remained in charge of the company, with Red Gold management also including his brother, Gary; his sister, Tina Anderson; and his wife, Selita.

CONTINUED GROWTH INITIATIVES

In late 2005 Red Gold announced that it would strengthen its ties with the Hispanic market via the introduction of bilingual packaging for its Redpack product line. Midway through the following year, the company announced growth initiatives at three of its facilities. These included a $5 million, 22,000-square-foot expansion of the Elwood plant; the installation of a new $8 million batching system and cook room at the Geneva plant; and a $7 million, 339,000-square-foot warehouse and rail distribution center at the Orestes facility.

By 2006 Red Gold ranked as the second-leading ketchup manufacturer in the country. Including private labels, products made by the company were sold in 16 countries and throughout the entire United States. In all, Red Gold manufactured 40 different products, up from only three products in 1986. The company consumed 80 percent of all tomatoes grown in the Midwest and 95 percent of the crop harvested in Indiana. With estimated revenues of $230 million, Red Gold's operations included 140 trucks, 15 warehouses, and 3 million square feet of production space in Indiana.

Toward the end of the decade Red Gold introduced a number of new products and packaging options. In 2009 these included a 40-ounce refrigerator-door-fitting ketchup bottle, all-natural ketchup (made with pure cane sugar as opposed to high-fructose corn syrup), and both low-sodium and spicy vegetable juices.

PRIVATE-LABEL SUCCESS

By 2011 challenging economic conditions had made private-label products more appealing to consumers throughout the country. Conditions such as these had helped Red Gold become the largest family-owned private-brand tomato products manufacturer in the nation. Also in 2011, the company spiced up its private-label line by introducing both green and red allergen-free enchilada sauces. Red Gold the following year moved its headquarters into a converted elementary school building located in Elwood, Indiana.

In addition to private-label products, during the economic recession budget-conscious consumers were also opting for canned tomatoes, as opposed to fresh tomatoes, which cost 75 percent more. According to data from the market research firm SymphonyIRI Group, reported in the June 18, 2012, issue of the *Indianapolis Business Journal*, this led to an 18 percent increase in sales of processed tomato products between 2007 and 2011, with sales totaling $1.1 billion by the latter year.

In late 2013 Red Gold received an award from *Progressive Grocer* magazine in recognition of its ability to understand the goals of retailers and help them achieve those goals. In addition to strong connections with retailers, the company also had equally good relationships with its tomato growers. Each year, Red Gold held a growers banquet in Indianapolis that included employees, as well as growers and their families. In 2014, with the fourth generation of the Reichart family involved in the business, Red Gold remained committed to its mission: "To pro-

duce the freshest, best tasting tomato products in the world."

Paul R. Greenland

PRINCIPAL SUBSIDIARIES

RGT Logistics, LLC.

PRINCIPAL COMPETITORS

ConAgra Foods, Inc.; Del Monte Pacific Limited; H.J. Heinz Company.

LP;&-4QFURTHER READING

Doyle, Abbey. "Red Gold Invests $3.5 Million in Elwood: Headquarters to Move into Former School." *Anderson Herald Bulletin*, June 22, 2011.

Human, Dan. "Growth Is in the Can: Tomato Heavyweight Benefiting from Consumers' Thrifty Ways." *Indianapolis Business Journal*, June 18, 2012.

Radice, Carol. "Private-Label Laureates: The *Grocery Headquarters* Private Label Trailblazer Awards Recognize Outstanding Private Label Manufacturers for Their Innovative Excellence and Leadership in the Grocery Industry." *Grocery Headquarters*, February 2011.

Schoettle, Anthony. "Juicy Prospects: While Its Competitors Open Plants on the West Coast, Indiana's Red Gold Becomes a Tomato-Industry Big Boy." *Indianapolis Business Journal*, August 28, 2006.

Restaurant Technologies, Inc.

———■———

2250 Pilot Knob Road, Suite 100
Mendota Heights, Minnesota 55120
U.S.A.
Telephone: (651) 796-1600
Toll Free: (888) 796-4997
Fax: (651) 379-4082
Web site: http://www.rti-inc.com

Private Company
Incorporated: 1998
Employees: 750
Sales: $450 million (2013 est.)
NAICS: 311225 Fats and Oils Refining and Blending

■ ■ ■

Mendota Heights, Minnesota–based Restaurant Technologies, Inc. (RTI), is a leading player in the food-services industry. Specifically, the company provides "oil management" services, which entail the delivery, storage, handling, and disposal of fryer oil, or "yellow grease." RTI serves a customer base that includes approximately 20,000 specialty, quick-serve, and fast-casual restaurants, as well as a wide range of institutions, via a network of 41 oil depots located throughout the United States. The company counts the likes of McDonald's, Burger King, White Castle, KFC, Jack in the Box, Chili's, and Applebee's among its clients.

EARLY HISTORY

RTI traces its origins back to 1998, when the company was established by Paul Plooster, an executive with West

Burnsville, Minnesota–based Minnesota Valley Engineering (MVE). At MVE, the company's engineers had developed an innovative "closed loop" system to equip soda fountains in restaurants with carbon dioxide. Realizing that the same system could be used to manage cooking oil, and discovering that restaurants' cooking oil volume was five times greater than carbon dioxide and soft drink syrup, Plooster identified a new business opportunity.

RTI's system made it easy for restaurants to receive new cooking oil and avoid the unpleasant and sometimes dangerous task of used-oil disposal. The company's system involved the installation of 200-gallon tanks inside restaurants. When new oil was needed, an RTI tanker truck simply connected a hose to fill the tank, while employing a reverse process to remove used oil. Early on, RTI adopted a business model whereby the company, and not its customers, was responsible for the ownership, installation, and servicing of the equipment used in the oil management process.

As a cooking oil supplier, RTI purchased oil in bulk from companies such as Archer Daniels Midland Co. and Cargill Inc. In turn, customers were asked to commit to long-term purchasing contracts, spanning approximately 10 years. With support from a network of roughly 200 individual investors, RTI was spun off from MVE in 1999. That year, the company generated sales of $3.9 million.

A NEW MILLENNIUM

RTI experienced strong growth during the early years of the new millennium. Sales reached $28.5 million in

2002 on the strength of a service network that had grown to include 10,000 restaurants in 30 different cities. Approximately half of those locations were McDonald's restaurants. Sales continued to skyrocket in 2003 and 2004, reaching $52.9 million and $81.0 million, respectively. The company benefited from continued equity investments. These included $20 million from Boston-based Gemini Investors and Boston-based Parthenon Capital LLC in 2001, followed by an additional $10 million in late 2002.

In early 2004 Baltimore-based ABS Capital Partners invested an additional $25 million in the company. In late 2004 the company leased space in Hazelwood, Missouri, which served as a distribution center for its patented cooking-oil systems. In 2005 RTI's sales reached $100 million. That year, Plooster relinquished his role as CEO to Jeffrey Kiesel, a former GE Capital Corp. executive. Plooster remained with the organization for a while as president. Additionally, Ken Larson served as the company's chairman.

By the middle of the decade RTI's majority owners included ABS Capital Partners and Parthenon Capital. The company served its customers with a network of 30 oil depots and a fleet of 90 tanker trucks. RTI managed the supply and disposal of its customers' cooking oil via the use of wireless technology, which provided updates on the volume of oil contained in a given location's storage tank. The same technology allowed the company to provide clients with oil utilization reports. At this time, equipping a restaurant with RTI's system cost about $5,000.

RTI's strong growth was recognized by *Inc.* magazine in 2005, when the company ranked 276th on the publication's Inc. 500 list of the nation's 500 fastest-growing private companies. The organization rounded out the year by bolstering its senior leadership team. Several key executives came on board, including vice president of sales and marketing Lori Ruggiano and vice president of human resources Rick Copeland. Additionally, supply chain director Shane Grutsch was elevated to the role of vice president of supply chain and information technology.

EXPANDS OIL DEPOT NETWORK

After bringing new oil depots online in the communities of Clifton, New Jersey, and St. Louis, Missouri, at the end of 2005, RTI continued expanding its geographic footprint the following year. In 2006 the company added depots in locations such as Hayward, California, to serve San Francisco, and Olathe, Kansas, to serve Kansas City. Other depots included Nashville, Tennessee; Columbia, South Carolina; and Sacramento, California. By the middle of the year RTI's network included 33 depots throughout the country, and its customer base had grown to 12,000 locations.

In early 2006 RTI positioned itself for continued expansion by securing a $50 million credit facility and raising $10 million in new equity from Parthenon Capital and ABC Capital Partners. Later that year the company began providing its customers with zero-transfat, low-linolenic soybean oil. The new product, marketed under the name RTI Max-life ZERO T LL, offered benefits such as longer shelf life and stability, while rivaling the taste of partially hydrogenated oils. The product initially was introduced in the markets of Greensboro, North Carolina, and Newark, New Jersey, as well as Detroit, New York, and Philadelphia.

RTI ended 2006 by receiving an Emerging Growth Award from the Minnesota chapter of the Association for Corporate Growth. The award recognized the company for its commitment to environmental sustainability and social issues within the foodservices industry, as well as strong financial performance. Growth continued early the following year, when the company established its 36th depot with a location in Richmond, Virginia.

CHANGES IN LEADERSHIP

RTI's senior leadership team expanded in mid-2007 when the company named Jon Getzinger as executive vice president of sales and marketing. In October of that year Robert E. Weil was named chief financial officer. By this time the company's customer base had grown to include 15,000 restaurants. RTI was marketing its closed-loop oil management system under the name, MaxLife Total Oil Management Solution. That year, the system was honored with a Tekne Award for outstanding technology achievement and leadership by the Minnesota High Tech Association.

Growth continued as RTI's customer network reached the 16,000 mark by the middle part of 2008. Of these, 13,000 locations were McDonald's restaurants. Revenues continued to climb, reaching $200 million, quadrupling sales figures from five years earlier. In order to remain in growth mode, the company began laying

```
┌─────────────────────────────────────────┐
│                                         │
│              KEY DATES                   │
│              ───────■───────             │
│                                         │
│  1998:  Restaurant Technologies Inc. (RTI) is   │
│         established by Paul Plooster, an executive with │
│         West Burnsville, Minnesota–based Minnesota │
│         Valley Engineering (MVE).       │
│  1999:  RTI is spun off from MVE.       │
│  2010:  Company settles a class-action lawsuit with its │
│         founders and some 260 individual minority │
│         shareholders; headquarters relocate from │
│         Eagan to Mendota Heights, Minnesota. │
│  2011:  Parthenon Capital Partners and ABS Capital │
│         Partners sell the company to Swedish private- │
│         equity firm EQT Partners AB and its $1.74 │
│         billion EQT Infrastructure Fund. │
│  2013:  Oil depots include 41 locations and revenues │
│         reach $450 million.             │
│                                         │
└─────────────────────────────────────────┘
```

the groundwork for expansion into international markets such as Canada and Puerto Rico. Nevertheless, RTI still had plenty of opportunities for domestic growth, considering that its customers represented a mere 10 percent of restaurants offering fried foods.

BIODIESEL OPPORTUNITIES

In addition to selling used yellow grease from restaurants for livestock feed, another new market emerged as demand increased for biodiesel fuels, which could be produced from used cooking oil. At this time RTI was able to receive $.38 per pound for used yellow grease. By this time social media was exploding in popularity, and many companies had adopted policies to restrict employee access at work. At RTI, however, CEO Kiesel allowed his geographically distributed workforce to access social media sites on company laptops.

A recapitalization that occurred in 2009 led to a class-action lawsuit being filed by the company's founders and some 260 individual minority shareholders, who alleged that RTI's owners and senior executives, including CEO Kiesel and CFO Weil, had conspired to devalue their holdings by approximately $39 million.

FACING LEGAL CHALLENGES

Although the company attempted to have the suit dismissed, the request was denied by a U.S. district court judge. Working with a mediator, in late 2010 RTI reached a settlement with the shareholders. Worth at

least $5.5 million, the settlement figure had the potential to become larger in the event RTI was sold for more than $170 million before June 1, 2013. A major development unfolded in November of 2010, when Kiesel revealed that RTI was for sale.

In a November 22, 2010, *Minneapolis Star Tribune* article, Kiesel indicated that new ownership was needed to achieve a higher level of growth and prepare the company for a potential public offering. Majority owner Parthenon Capital was interested in selling its stake in RTI, and Kiesel indicated that ABS Capital also had expressed an interest in selling at least a portion of its stake. To find a potential buyer, the company's equity firm owners retained Chicago-based investment banker William Blair & Co.

In the midst of these changes, RTI relocated its headquarters from Eagan, Minnesota, to a larger, 60,000-square-foot facility in the Minnesota community of Mendota Heights. By this time the company employed approximately 600 people who collectively served 17,000 restaurants. Each year, RTI collected some 150 million pounds of yellow grease. In 2010 an arrangement was made to sell the majority of this grease to the Iowa-based biodiesel fuel refiner, Renewable Energy Group, allowing the company to generate about $30 million annually.

ACQUIRED BY EQT PARTNERS

RTI ultimately found a new owner for its business in early 2011 when Parthenon Capital Partners and ABS Capital Partners sold the company to the Swedish private-equity firm EQT Partners AB and its $1.74 billion EQT Infrastructure Fund. Following the acquisition, Kiesel remained RTI's CEO, while EQT industrial adviser Geoff Roberts was named chairman. One of the things that made RTI attractive to its new owner was the difficult barriers to entry within its particular industry.

EQT also had some experience dealing with edible oils, having acquired Rotterdam-based cooking oil, fats, and biofuels transportation and storage company Koole in 2010. By this time RTI's geographic footprint had expanded to include approximately 75 percent of the major metropolitan markets throughout the United States, which the company served via its network of 36 oil depots.

RTI provided customers with extensive data that helped them to run their businesses more efficiently. This was accomplished via the RTI Total Operations Management online portal, which allowed restaurant managers to monitor oil filtration, quality, and utilization metrics for individual or multiple locations. Toward the end of the year the company received a trademark for a stylized treatment of the RTI name.

EXPANSION CONTINUES

Growth continued as RTI added new restaurants to its customer base. Some of the company's clients were individual restaurants, while others were owners with anywhere from a few locations to hundreds of sites. Examples included the Wild Wing Café in South Carolina, an owner with 18 Jack in the Box restaurants in Texas, and a franchisee with 163 KFC locations throughout the country. RTI's embrace of technology was not limited to its own oil management system. For example, in late 2012 the company began using service life-cycle management and billing software from Astea International Inc.

With tools focused on functions such as scheduling, the software allowed the company to improve the productivity of its field technicians, reduce service costs, and improve customer satisfaction. This was accomplished through the ability to schedule more service calls every day, access customer equipment repair records, and check the availability of parts and inventory. Progress continued in 2013 when RTI brought new oil depots online in Memphis, Tennessee, and Des Moines, Iowa, expanding its total network of depots to 41 locations.

By this time RTI employed 750 people and sales had reached $450 million. Toward the end of the year a survey revealed that 37 percent of the company's employees were completely engaged, compared to a national average of 10 percent. In addition, 85 percent of RTI's workers held their manager and the organization in high regard. With its customer base growing to include some 20,000 locations by 2014, it appeared that RTI was well-prepared to achieve continued growth in the years to come.

Paul R. Greenland

PRINCIPAL COMPETITORS

Don Edward & Company; PFG Holdings, Inc.; SYSCO Corporation.

FURTHER READING

"EQT Infrastructure Signs Definitive Agreement to Acquire RTI." *Entertainment Close-Up*, April 25, 2011.

"Restaurant Technologies Launches Oil Filtration Monitoring Technology; Restaurant Technologies Inc.'s New Filtration Monitoring Technology Records Oil Filtration Process. ..." *Fast Casual*, September 10, 2012.

"Restaurant Technologies: Settles Shareholder Class Action Suit." *Class Action Reporter*, November 16, 2010.

St. Anthony, Neal. "Candor Goes a Long Way at RTI." *Minneapolis Star Tribune*, November 3, 2013.

———. "Finding Gold in Grease; Fast-Growing Restaurant Technologies, Which Provides Cooking Oil Management Services, Is Looking for New Owners and Perhaps a Chance to Go Public." *Minneapolis Star Tribune*, November 22, 2010.

Rocket Fuel Inc.

———■———

1900 Seaport Boulevard
Redwood City, California 94063
U.S.A.
Telephone: (650) 595-1300
Fax: (650) 264-4000
Web site: http://www.rocketfuel.com

Public Company
Incorporated: 2008
Employees: 619
Sales: $240.6 million (2013)
Stock Exchanges: NASDAQ
Ticker Symbol: FUEL
NAICS: 541810 Advertising Agencies

■ ■ ■

Rocket Fuel Inc. is a Redwood City, California–based company that offers a programmatic marketing platform. Using artificial intelligence technology and a real-time optimization engine, Rocket Fuel uses so-called Big Data to help marketers automatically place online, mobile, and digital video advertisements. Not only does Rocket Fuel determine which ad to show to a certain individual at a particular moment, it tracks the effectiveness of advertising and branding campaigns. Rocket Fuel serves such industries as automotive, business-to-business, consumer tech, dining, entertainment, finance, pharmaceutical, politics and advocacy, retail, telecommunications, travel, and publishing.

In addition to its California world headquarters, the company maintains about 20 offices around the world,

such as in New York, London, Paris, and Hamburg. Rocket Fuel's more than 1,200 active customers include 70 of the Advertising Age 100 Leading National Advertisers and more than half of the *Fortune* 100 companies. No single customer accounts for more than 10 percent of its business. Rocket Fuel is a public company, its shares listed on the NASDAQ.

COMPANY FOUNDED: 2008

Rocket Fuel was founded in 2008 by a trio of Yahoo! veterans. The group was led by CEO George H. John, a graduate of Stanford University, where he earned a doctorate in computer science in 1997 while working as a senior data-mining analyst for IBM. He then went to work for E.piphany, Inc. a customer relationship management software company. After a stint with salesforce.com, Inc., he joined Yahoo! Inc. in 2005, serving as senior director for targeting and personalization. The idea behind Rocket Fuel was to use a variety of targeting data to automatically select appropriate Internet ads. The data were secured from social, behavioral, geographical, search, and contextual sources.

Another Rocket Fuel cofounder, Richard Frankel, had served as senior director of product marketing at Yahoo! before leaving to start the company. He also had previous experience with Internet advertising company DoubleClick Inc., serving as general manager. The third cofounder, Abhinav Gupta, was born in India and earned his undergraduate degree in computer science from the Indian Institutes of Technology before coming to the United States to complete his master's degree in computer science at the University of Wisconsin. At

Yahoo! he served as an engineering director and led the development of the company's next-generation behavior-targeting platform.

Rocket Fuel was initially backed by individual angel investors and a Series A round of venture capital funding from Mohr Davidow Ventures and Labrador Ventures that raised $6.8 million in 2008. Rocket Fuel soon began testing its new hybrid ad network, which combined a variety of targeting data with an algorithm to determine the best ads to display to online users. Typical online ad targeting had previously involved a great deal of guesswork. Ad agencies were simply provided with a range of targeting options and had to decide how to make use of the information. Rocket Fuel, on the other hand, automated the process. At the very least, advertisers were able to obtain quicker feedback on the effectiveness of the ads and then refine their targeting process.

NETWORK DEBUT: 2009

Rocket Fuel tested its ad placement network with such major brands as American Express, Dell, Microsoft, and Nike. In August 2009 the network made its public debut. Later in the year, Rocket Fuel raised $3 million in additional funds, the round led by Mohr Davidow. The money was earmarked for the addition of new talent, including Paul Wenz, who was named vice president of business development in October 2009 and brought 13 years of experience in interactive advertising. The New York office, which was instrumental in establishing and maintaining relationships with major advertising agencies, was also expanded. Another one of the new employees, hired in April 2010, was Mark Torrance, who became chief technology officer. He had studied artificial intelligence at both the Massachusetts Institute of Technology and Stanford University before founding a Web company, StockMaster.com, which became the Internet's most popular stock quote site. It was also one of the first users of DoubleClick's ad network. At Rocket Fuel, Torrance joined Gupta to form the company's engineering leadership team.

Rocket Fuel generated $16.5 million in sales in 2010, the first full year the ad network was operational. The company was still in the start-up phase, however,

and in need of additional cash to build the business. In September 2010 Rocket Fuel completed a Series B round of fund-raising, securing $10 million. It was led by Nokia Growth Partners. Mohr Davidow and Labrador Ventures also participated, along with Northgate Capital. Because of Nokia's investment, one of the venture capital firm's directors, Marc Theeuwes, was given a seat on Rocket Fuel's board of directors.

NEW PRODUCTS

Rocket Fuel launched its Brand Booster product in 2010. It included a Real-Time Brand Optimization solution that analyzed the characteristics of a company's audience to improve brand messaging. At the start of 2011 Rocket Fuel introduced another new product, Video Booster. The video targeting solution selected 15- or 30-second "pre-roll" ads to play before a video stream. Once again, it was a matter of presenting the right ad to the right audience in the right medium. In March 2011 Rocket Fuel opened a new office in Detroit to serve the automotive industry. A week later, the company opened its European headquarters in London and made its services available in the United Kingdom. Also in April 2011, Rocket Fuel raised $6.6 million in a Series C round of fund-raising. It was led by Northgate Capital with further backing by investors Mohr Davidow, Labrador Ventures, Nokia Growth Partners, and Wilson Sonsini Goodrich & Rosati.

In November 2011 Rocket Fuel introduced another new product, Social Booster for Facebook. The technology allowed marketers to automatically create, launch, and test thousands of Facebook ads. Campaigns could then be optimized every 10 minutes to help improve performance. The new product helped Rocket Fuel to increase revenues nearly threefold in 2011 to $44.6 million.

Rocket Fuel added a Canadian office in Toronto, Ontario, in 2012. The company also launched a new product, CPG Booster, which focused on the advertising needs of consumer packaged goods companies. Unlike companies in other sectors, most of the sales of CPG companies came from retail stores, although many customers conducted research online. Rocket Fuel made use of loyalty card data and other information to meet the unique needs of this group of clients.

NEW OFFICES OPEN

In order to support international growth and expand staff, Rocket Fuel conducted another round of financing in June 2012. Existing investor Northgate Capital led the $50 million round. Again Mohr Davidow and

Nokia Growth Capital participated, as did new investors Summit Partners and Cross Creek Capital. Rocket Fuel continued to add clients at a rapid pace in 2012. The number of new advertisers increased 93 percent over the previous year. Six new offices opened, including in Amsterdam, Atlanta, Hamburg, Raleigh-Durham, Toronto, and Washington, D.C., which brought the total number of worldwide locations to 15. At the end of 2012, the company reported $106.6 million in revenues.

The number of Rocket Fuel employees grew from 128 at the end of 2011 to 289 at the close of the following year. The ranks swelled further in 2013, despite the automated nature of the company's business. "We plan to increase the number of engineers and customer-facing positions," John told *Silicon Valley Business Journal*, in a January 17, 2013, article. He added: "It's amazing how many times we need somebody to call a customer personally to remind them they need to pay their bill," he explained.

TAKEN PUBLIC: 2013

Because the staff continued to grow, Rocket Fuel's need for space increased as well. In August 2013 the company signed a lease for 145,000 square feet of space in Redwood City, California, at the 10-building campus of Pacific Shores Centers, about four-and-a-half times the space Rocket Fuel currently occupied. While the company was scouting for larger accommodations it was also preparing to make an initial public offering of stock. The offering was completed on September 20, 2013. Rocket Fuel sold 4 million shares at $29 each, netting $116 million for corporate purposes.

Rocket Fuel shares began trading on the NASDAQ. On the first day, the price soared to $56.10, a 94 percent increase. It was not, however, a sustainable level. Although the price per share spiked above $60 several times, it fell steadily. One year after its debut, Rocket Fuel was trading around $15 per share. Rocket Fuel was not alone. Other companies in the ad tech sector were experiencing similar erosions in their stock prices. In an interview with the *Wall Street Journal*'s *CMO Today* blog

on June 26, 2014, John maintained that investors were not afraid of ad tech, nor did they fail to understand the business. "If you're a public company you have to be ready that fashions sort of come and go. ... Being ready for some degree of price movement that is out of your control is something you have to be at terms with before going public," John said.

While the price of the stock fluctuated, John's management team focused on what it was able to control, adding capabilities and doing more business. The company recorded $240.6 million in revenues in 2013 and continued to grow. In February 2014 Rocket Fuel introduced its Mobile Advertising Suite that provided customers with mobile targeting capabilities. Mobile advertising was an especially attractive segment. Mobile ad spending was on pace to double in 2014 to $9.6 billion. In 2017 that amount was projected to grow to $35.6 billion.

NEW HEADQUARTERS OPENS: 2014

With more than 600 employees, Rocket Fuel was more than ready to move into its new corporate headquarters in Redwood City in April 2014. Earlier in the year, the London office moved into a larger space as well, and plans were being made to expand offices in Chicago, Los Angeles, and New York. Rocket Fuel also continued to expand its capabilities. In July 2014 the company unveiled Rocket Fuel Dynamic Personalized Ads, its most sophisticated approach yet to automatically delivering the most effective ad to a consumer.

Rocket Fuel looked to add to its capabilities through external means as well. In September 2014 it completed the acquisition of [x+1], a leading provider of programmatic marketing and data management solutions. The business was folded into Rocket Fuel, and the [x+1] brand was discontinued. As a result of the acquisition, Rocket Fuel combined its artificial intelligence and Big Data optimization technology with [x+1]'s market and data management platform to create a software-as-a-service programmatic marketing platform. Rocket Fuel was now more than just an ad network company. It was able to centrally manage a client's data and use the data to deliver advertising messages across an array of paid and owned channels. It was the beginning of a new stage in the development of Rocket Fuel. Programmatic marketing was still a relatively new field, but clients were becoming more knowledgeable and comfortable with the technology. A so-called second wave of users was likely to emerge and lift Rocket Fuel to profitability in the near future.

Ed Dinger

PRINCIPAL SUBSIDIARIES

Rocket Fuel Ltd.; Rocket Fuel GmbH; Rocket Science Media Inc.

PRINCIPAL COMPETITORS

Facebook, Inc.; Google Inc.; Yahoo! Inc.

FURTHER READING

Donato-Weinstein, Nathan. "Rocket Fuel Quadruples Space in Redwood City." *Silicon Valley Business Journal*, September 18, 2013.

Peak, Krystal. "Rocket Fuel Predicts Shoppers' Habits in Milliseconds." *San Francisco Business Times*, May 11, 2012.

Schonfeld, Erick. "Yahoo Veterans Launch Rocket Fuel, a 'Hybrid' Ad Network." *Tech Crunch*, August 16, 2009.

Schubarth, Cromwell. "Ad Startup Rocket Fuel Hits Gas, Plans to Hire 300." *Silicon Valley Business Journal*, January 17, 2013.

Tadena, Nathalie. "Rocket Fuel CEO George John: Investors Aren't Afraid of Ad Tech." *CMO Today*, June 26, 2014.

The Russ Reid Company Inc.

2 North Lake Avenue, Suite 600
Pasadena, California 91101
U.S.A.
Telephone: (626) 449-6100
Web site: http://www.russreid.com

Wholly Owned Subsidiary of Omnicom Group
Incorporated: 1964
Employees: 250
Sales: $170 million (2011)
NAICS: 541810 Advertising Agencies

■ ■ ■

The Russ Reid Company Inc. is a Pasadena, California–based firm that offers fund-raising and public relations services to nonprofit corporations. Using analytics, Russ Reid designs and executes direct response and digital fund-raising campaigns, producing television specials and designing Web sites, landing pages, time and targeted e-mails, banner ads, and mobile ads. In addition, the firm continues to make use of direct mail, which remains the primary sources of funds raised by charitable and cultural organizations. Russ Reid clients have included the American Red Cross, Billy Graham Crusade, Feed the Children, Girls and Boys Town, Goodwill Industries, Mothers against Drunk Driving, National Audubon Society, and the Salvation Army. In addition, the firm offers government relations and lobbying, as well as database management and analysis. Russ Reid is a unit of advertising giant Omnicom Group.

FOUNDER, CANADA BORN

The man who gave The Russ Reid Company its name was born Russell Charles Reid in Vancouver, Canada, in 1931. He was raised in a fundamentalist church and initially believed he was called to a missionary life. Instead, he went to work in Christian radio and became a program manager in Seattle. He moved to Waco, Texas, in the late 1950s to take a job with Word Publishing, which marketed Christian books and records.

At Word, Reid learned the fundamentals of direct response marketing through the operations of Word's book-of-the-month clubs. In 1964 he struck out on his own, starting The Russ Reid Company to provide marketing services to faith organizations. His first client was Word Publishing. Soon, he began working with small ministries, helping them to tell their stores and raise the funds they needed to operate.

Reid then moved his business to Park Ridge, Illinois. A pivotal moment in the history of the company occurred in 1966 when it landed its first major client, World Vision International, a Christian humanitarian aid organization. At the time, World Vision was operating on an annual budget of about $5 million each year.

Not only did Reid play a key role in World Vision's ability to increase its annual revenue to almost $2 billion, he helped to revolutionize charitable fund-raising techniques. Noticing a personalized direct-mail piece produced by an auto dealership, Reid in 1968 began using computers to insert the recipient's name in solicitation letters for World Vision and other clients.

MOVE TO CALIFORNIA: 1972

As his work with World Vision increased, Reid decided in 1972 to more his headquarters again, this time to Arcadia, California, close to where World Vision was based in Monrovia, California. Until this time, World Vision primarily recruited sponsors by visiting churches. As part of the appeal, the company showed a film depicting problems in the developing world.

After seeing an evangelist on paid-time television, Reid became convinced there was a more effective way for World Vision to add sponsors. In 1972 he suggested that the charity film the plight of children in the third world. The material could then be packaged and shown on television, rather than individual churches, to bring the World Vision story to a much wider audience. When asked what they would do if his idea failed, Reid supposedly joked, "We'll have the most expensive church film in history."

Raising money on television for good causes was hardly novel. In the early 1950s the Muscular Dystrophy Association held the first telethon, which established the template for fund-raising on live television. Other causes followed suit, including the March of Dimes, United Cerebral Palsy, and the Leukemia Society. Because they were live and ran for extended periods, telethons were loose, rambling affairs.

CHILDREN OF ZERO PREMIERES

Russ Reid wanted to change the mold with World Vision by developing a prerecorded, tightly scripted program. He had a star for his production already in mind, television host Art Linkletter, and persuaded him to travel to Hong Kong, Korea, and Vietnam for the first World Vision television special, *Children of Zero*.

It would not be the world's most expensive church film. Instead, it created a blueprint for a new type of televised fund-raising appeal. Unlike the narrow time window of the telethon, the prepackaged special could air on any television station at any time.

Moreover, it packed a more powerful punch than the traditional telethon, which had more time to fill and

tended to become unfocused. The success of *Children of Zero* led to other World Vision specials and other celebrity hosts, including Alex Trebek, the star of popular television game show *Jeopardy*, and Julie Andrews, the acclaimed singer-actress.

GAINS ST. JUDE HOSPITAL: 1982

The World Vision programs also inspired other charitable organizations to hire Reid to produce multi-hour packaged syndicated telethon specials. In 1977 World Vision Canada hired his company and with Reid's help became the largest child sponsorship organization in Canada. In 1982 The Russ Reid Company added St. Jude Children's Research Hospital as a client.

Founded by television star Danny Thomas, St. Jude's was having difficulty raising money through its telethons. Told by a cameraman that the phones always rang for a Russ Reid program, Thomas contacted Reid, who began producing St. Jude's television fund-raising appeals and established a long-term relationship. Another new client in 1982 was Habitat for Humanity. Founded in 1976 by Millard Fuller as a Christian housing ministry to provide low-cost homes for needy families, Habitat was having difficulty in finding support, attracting just 4,000 sponsors.

The Russ Reid Company was quick to exploit the presence of former U.S. President Jimmy Carter on Habitat's board of directors. A series of fund-raising letters in Carter's name were mailed and the response was strong. Over the next five years, Habitat added more than 600,000 new sponsors and became established as an international humanitarian brand.

MADD BECOMES CLIENT: 1981

Reid did not simply rely on clients reaching out to him. In 1981 he and his wife Cathie learned through *People* magazine about the efforts of Candy Lightner to prevent drunk driving after her daughter was killed by a drunk driver. Lightner started an organization called Mothers against Drunk Driving (MADD). Reid contacted her and learned that she was finding it so difficult to find financial backing for MADD that she was on the verge of giving up and returning to her job selling real estate.

Reid persuaded Lightner to let his company develop a direct-mail fund-raising program. She agreed, and quickly MADD's financial picture improved. The relationship was not without conflict, however. In late 1984 the company refused to provide a list of contributors to MADD, which sued in both California and Texas. At issue was the renewal of a contract for direct-mail solicitations that was about to expire. The two parties eventually reached an agreement on a new contract,

```
┌─────────────────────────────────────────┐
│                                         │
│            KEY DATES                    │
│                ■                        │
├─────────────────────────────────────────┤
│  1964:  Russ Reid founds company.       │
│  1966:  World Vision becomes client.    │
│  1998:  Company is sold to Omnicom.     │
│  2001:  Russ Reid retires.              │
│  2013:  Russ Reid Company merges with SCA│
│         Direct.                         │
│                                         │
└─────────────────────────────────────────┘
```

and after five years of working together MADD added more than 450,000 donors.

Another major Russ Reid success story in the 1980s was the Los Angeles Mission. It operated a small homeless shelter in the city's Skid Row district with an annual budget of $125,000. Not only was that amount inadequate to meet the organization's day-to-day needs, the building in which the shelter was located was in desperate need of improvement. The Russ Reid Company took on the mission as a client.

SUCCESS WITH THE MISSION

The initial plan was to run a fund-raising ad in the *Los Angeles Times* with the hope that enough people would donate to at least cover the $1,000 cost of the ad. Receiving $3,000, the mission decided to invest the money in further ads, parlaying $3,000 in ads into $10,000 in donations.

While response to the ads continued to grow, the mission launched a direct-mail program and a public relations campaign conducted by Russ Reid Company that helped to elevate the mission to the top ranks of Los Angeles–area charities. The client's success also resulted in the Russ Reid Company working with other rescue missions across the United States and Canada. The Russ Reid Company continued to grow in the 1990s, serving many long-term clients and picking up new ones.

Not every idea of Russ Reid was successful, however. One notable disappointment was his idea for a National Caring Network in which the company would purchase all of a cable channel's airtime and resell it to nonprofits, essentially creating a 24-hour fund-raising vehicle. It never went beyond the concept stage, however.

OMNICOM ACQUIRES COMPANY: 1998

In 1998 Russ Reid decided to sell his company to Omnicom. He remained in charge for another three years before retiring in 2001 at the age of 70. The company carried on as part of Omnicom's Diversified Agency Services division, owned by a holding company called the Nonprofit Fundraising and Communications Group. Sister companies included Grizzard Communication Group and Steve Cram & Associates.

A fourth company was added in 2002 with the acquisition of Changing Our World, Inc. The three-year-old company was a specialist in capital campaigns, corporate and personal philanthropy, donor research, and e-philanthropy. As a result, Diversified Agency Services was able to offer an unmatched range of services to philanthropic clients.

Succeeding Reid as chief executive officer was Tom Harrison, who had joined the company in 1985 and was well familiar with the operation after serving in various senior management roles. Although Russ Reid was no longer involved with the company he founded, the value of his name as a brand remained undiminished.

GAINS OPERATION SMILE

In the new century the company continued to win clients and take advantage of new tools to help craft further success stories. A case in point was Operation Smile, an organization devoted to providing corrective surgery for children with cleft lips and palates in developing countries. The Russ Reid company developed an innovative "Hometown Heroes" campaign for the organization that targeted a single community for a one-month period.

During that time, the market was saturated with local television and radio coverage, as well as billboards and other outside ads, direct-mail pieces, and e-mail. A local media personality served as an anchor for the multichannel approach. Later iterations of the Operation Smile campaign would also include Facebook and Twitter elements.

NEW CEO IN 2013

In 2013 Harrison stepped down as CEO, turning over day-to-day control to Alan B. Hall while remaining chairman. Hall was another company veteran. He was first hired by Russ Reid in 1990 but left in 1997 to work elsewhere before returning in 2002. He had served as head of business development and director of client services. He later became executive vice president and was promoted to president in 2012, a position he held for one year as he prepared to succeed Harrison.

In the same month that Hall was named CEO, Russ Reid Company was combined with sister company

SCA Direct, the former Steve Cram & Associates. The revamped enterprise retained the Russ Reid name but enjoyed greater scale geographically as well as the types of services it could offer. The end of an era was also marked late in 2013 when Russ Reid died at the age of 82. The company he founded would likely keep his name alive well into the future.

Ed Dinger

PRINCIPAL DIVISIONS

Finance & Administration; Marketing; Operations; Sales; Support.

PRINCIPAL COMPETITORS

The Advocacy Group, Inc.; Ogilvy Public Relations Worldwide, Inc.; Rock, Paper, Scissors, L.L.C.

FURTHER READING

Chawkins, Steve. "Russ Reid Dies at 82." *Los Angeles Times,* December 14, 2013.

"Fundraising Agency SCA Direct Merged into Russ Reid." *NonProfit Times,* August 22, 2013.

"MADD Sues over Contributors List." *Dallas Morning News,* November 16, 1984.

Olcott, William. "The Roots of Fund Raising." *Fund Raising Management,* April 1989.

Tode, Chantal. "Charity Begins with Integration." *DM News,* March 1, 2010.

S. Fischer Verlag GmbH

Hedderichstrasse 114
Frankfurt am Main, 60596
Germany
Telephone: (+49 69) 6062 0
Fax: (+49 69) 6062 319
Web site: http://www.fischerverlage.de

Wholly Owned Subsidiary of Verlagsgruppe Georg von Holtzbrinck GmbH
Founded: 1886
Employees: 158
Sales: EUR 61 million
NAICS: 511130 Book Publishers

■ ■ ■

S. Fischer Verlag GmbH is one of Germany's oldest and most respected publishing houses. Based in Frankfurt am Main, Fischer publishes works of both fiction and nonfiction. Its roster of authors in fiction includes Thomas Mann, Franz Kafka, Gerhardt Hauptmann, and Arthur Schnitzler, as well as contemporary popular fiction. Its nonfiction list encompasses works on history, current events, biography, politics, and natural and social science. Particularly notable in the house's nonfiction line is its *Schwarze Reihe*, a series of books on the National Socialist period. Most of Fischer's book list is now also available in e-book format. In addition to books, Fischer publishes the literary/political journal *Neue Rundschau*. The publisher has a special department that handles publishing and performing rights to radio plays, screenplays, and works for the stage, the S. Fischer

Theater- und Medien Verlag. S. Fischer Verlag is a subsidiary of the Verlagsgruppe Georg von Holtzbrinck.

BOOKSELLER AT AGE 14

The founder of the S. Fischer Verlag GmbH, Samuel Fischer, was born to a German-speaking Jewish family in Hungary in 1859. With just the clothes on his back, Fischer moved to Vienna in 1874, where he went to work as an apprentice in a bookstore and at the same time took business courses in night school. Ten years later he moved to Berlin and went to work for Hugo Steinitz, the owner of a vanity publishing firm. Within a year Fischer had become Steinitz's partner, and two years later, in August 1886, he broke out on his own and founded his own publishing house: S. Fischer Verlag.

Fischer's publishing interests were much different than his former employer's. From the beginning his publications were primarily literary with a strong emphasis on the theater. He was also interested in the work of new writers, so it was not surprising that the first book he published was *Rosmersholm*, a play by the Norwegian playwright Henrik Ibsen, who had caused a stir in Scandinavia but was as yet completely unknown in Germany. Not long after that, however, Ibsen's *A Pillar of Society* was a controversial success in Germany, and Ibsen's work was in demand. The company's first major project was a collected edition of all of Ibsen's work in German translation. Such editions of major authors' collected works remained a hallmark of the Fischer Verlag into the 21st century. Ibsen's work was followed by other representatives of the Scandinavian

COMPANY PERSPECTIVES

The S. Fischer Verlag in Frankfurt am Main is one of Germany's largest quality publishers. The history and tradition continues in today's S. Fischer publishing program.

Naturalist school, as well other foreign work in translation, most notably the works of Leo Tolstoy.

PUBLICATION OF FIRST GERMAN AUTHORS

Fischer expanded beyond books when he established the *Freie Bühne*, a journal of writings for the theater in 1890. In 1905 the journal's name was changed to *Neue Rundschau* (*New Review*), and it was expanded to become a general literary magazine. It eventually began featuring articles on politics and society and quickly assumed its place as the most influential literary journal in Germany until the Nazi takeover in 1933. The magazine featured the firm's first important German author, the playwright Gerhardt Hauptmann. Fischer's important German-language literary discoveries included the writers of the Austrian Wiener Moderne, represented most significantly by Arthur Schnitzler, and Hugo von Hofmannsthal. Their work, unlike that of the Naturalist writers and influenced by the findings of Sigmund Freud, featured dreams, impressions, and the stream of consciousness.

As the dawn of the 20th century approached, the business grew. S. Fischer took on new editors and other staff. Samuel Fischer focused primarily on the firm's business side. At the same time business and organizational structures were put in place to ensure efficient operations. The first telephones and typewriters at S. Fischer, novelties at the time, were installed. Later in the 1890s the company published its first catalog for the book trade and moved into large new premises where it would remain for the next 40 years.

At the beginning of 1897 *Neue Rundschau* published a short story by a promising young author named Thomas Mann. Mann sent other stories, and Fischer collected them in Mann's first book. Finally, the publisher invited Mann to write something longer, such as a novel. Mann responded by submitting the manuscript for *Buddenbrooks*, which would have made a book more than 1,000 pages long. Fischer was greatly impressed by the writing, but he did not believe it economically feasible to publish such a long work. He asked Mann to shorten it by half, and Mann refused. After some soul searching, Fischer accepted the book rather than lose Mann as a house author. A two-volume edition published in 1901 cost 12 marks and did not sell well. Two years later, however, a single-volume edition for 5 marks became a best seller in Germany and secured Fischer Verlag's financial position. That book's popularity never faded. In the second decade of the 21st century, *Buddenbrooks* remained the firm's most successful book ever.

LOWER PRICES ATTRACT NEW READERS

In the 19th century publishers had brought out reduced-price editions of German classics that had passed into the public domain. Fischer introduced a new twist on the idea in 1908 when he launched the Fischer Library of Contemporary Novels, a series of low-priced editions of works by current Fischer authors. Booksellers reacted against the idea, thinking that cheaper versions would cut into the sales of their higher priced, regular editions. Samuel Fischer believed, in contrast, that the less expensive books would attract *new* readers who might not otherwise purchase a book at all. The series proved to be extremely popular and had a minimal effect on other Fischer sales. The firm released a new book in the series every month for the next 16 years. It was such a success that other publishers soon started imitating it.

By the start of World War I Fischer's operations were pushing their physical limits. The firm published 50 new books in 1913, an amount that would not be reached again until after World War II. Fischer's 25th anniversary catalog was 400 pages long with more than 50 pages of backlist and new titles. The war changed everything. Abruptly Fischer and Germany were isolated from the cultural life of the rest of the world. Connections to foreign markets and writers were cut off. Paper supplies were strictly rationed. Specialized staff such as typesetters, printers, and bookbinders were hard to find, many having been called into military service. The situation was so bad that Samuel Fischer proposed to Kurt Wolff, the owner of another important literary publisher, that they merge their two houses. Wolff declined, not wanting to assume co-responsibility for Fischer's numerous financial commitments.

POSTWAR HARDSHIP

The end of the war did not bring an immediate end to hardship. The social and political chaos that followed the defeat, the demands of the victorious Allies, and the abdication of the kaiser, plus growing inflation (it would

KEY DATES

1886: S. Fischer Verlag is founded in Berlin.
1887: Henrik Ibsen's *Rosmersholm* is published.
1890: *Freie Bühne* is founded.
1928: Gottfried Bermann takes over management.
1934: Samuel Fischer dies.
1935: Bermann-Fischer leaves Berlin and establishes Bermann-Fischer Verlag in Vienna.
1940: L.B. Fischer Publishing Corporation is established in New York City.
1947: Bermann-Fischer and Peter Suhrkamp establish a branch in Frankfurt am Main.
1963: Company is acquired by Georg von Holtzbrinck.
2000: Company is reorganized.
2013: Fischer Kinder- und Jugendbuch Verlag is founded.

peak in the hyperinflation of 1923), made the book trade a difficult one. Moreover, with Fischer's advancing age, the question of the future of the firm took on importance. His only son, Gerhardt, had died suddenly at the age of 19, and Fischer rejected the idea of his daughter running the business.

The most important task though in 1919 was to publish the swollen backlog of titles that had piled up during the war years. In all, 73 new titles had been put on hold. However, rising costs and inflation, coupled with declining consumer demand, made the task of publishing them a difficult one. Fischer raised some funds by converting the firm into a stock company in 1921, still retaining 99 percent of the stock himself. Although money was tight, Fischer continued to pursue plans for new collected works editions. At the same time he realized that the economic climate made it unlikely that consumers would be able to afford complete sets, and so decided instead to publish individual volumes separately in uniform editions. Buyers would have the option of purchasing individual works or they could assemble sets over time as new volumes were released. The plan also reduced the financial commitment the company needed to make at the start of a collected works project. A Thomas Mann edition was launched in 1921, followed by Hermann Hesse in 1925.

A SUCCESSOR IS FOUND

The firm finally found a successor in 1928 when Samuel Fischer's son-in-law Gottfried Bermann took over as

business manager. The deal was made complete by Bermann's agreement to change his name to Bermann-Fischer as a sign of continuity in the company. Although he gave up the day-to-day running of the firm, Samuel Fischer continued to retain certain prerogatives in the business. He had the final say over the size of print runs and which authors the house would sign on. His judgment was not always better than Bermann-Fischer's. Ignoring Bermann-Fischer's recommendation, Fischer rejected Erich Maria Remarque's *All Quiet on the Western Front*, a book that went on to become a big success. Although Fischer was opposed, Bermann-Fischer was able to persuade him to publish Alfred Döblin's *Berlin Alexanderplatz*, a novel that went on to sell 20,000 copies in its first two months in bookstores.

Fischer continued to grow even after the onset of the Great Depression, producing a total of 50 new titles in 1930. The coming to power of the Nazi Party in 1933 put an abrupt end to any ambitions of further growth. An essential element of the Nazi ideology was the complete exclusion of Jews from the daily life of Germany, which included the takeover of Jewish-owned businesses. Both Samuel Fischer and Gottfried Bermann-Fischer were from Jewish families and many of the publisher's authors were also Jewish, which made the company a prime candidate for seizure. Unfortunately for Bermann-Fischer, Samuel Fischer had the final say over any move to a location outside Germany, and he seemed oblivious to the danger the Nazis posed to the company and to its people. He was determined to keep book and journal publishing running for as long as possible in Berlin.

Fischer died in 1934, and his wife inherited ownership of the business. Danger of a government takeover loomed larger with every passing day, evidenced by the forced sale to non-Jews of Ullstein, one of Germany's largest publishers. Bermann-Fischer was able to save what he could by making a deal with the Nazi Propaganda Ministry whereby he would leave Germany and give up rights to the name Fischer Verlag in exchange for the rights to any unsold copies of books by authors the Nazis considered undesirable. He moved to Vienna in 1935 and soon had a new house, the Bermann-Fischer Verlag, in operation serving the Austrian and Swiss markets. The German annexation of Austria in March 1938, however, forced the Bermann-Fischers to flee again, this time with little more than the clothes on their backs, first to Amsterdam, then to Stockholm, and finally to the United States.

On Thomas Mann's advice, Bermann-Fischer set up shop in New York City. It was not possible to do business selling books in German in the United States, so, with another publisher-in-exile, Fritz H. Landsdorff, he established an English-language publishing firm. American publishers already held licenses to publish Fischer authors in English, so the new L.B. Fischer firm had to build up a new list from scratch. It was comprised primarily of nonfiction titles, including many books on history. The American firm's greatest success came in 1945 shortly before the end of the war when it received an order from the U.S. government to publish hundreds of thousands of titles for German prisoners of war being interned in the United States.

RETURN TO EUROPE

In February 1946, six months after World War II ended, Bermann-Fischer sold his American publishing house and returned to Germany. The Fischer publishing company in Germany had been taken over by an editor there, Peter Suhrkamp, who had somehow managed to bring it through the war without turning it into a Nazi mouthpiece. The government had ordered it renamed, and when Bermann-Fischer returned it was known as the Suhrkamp Verlag. The firm's offices, archives, and book warehouse were completely destroyed in the last months of the war. Unable to resume publishing without a difficult-to-obtain license, Bermann-Fischer reestablished his company in Vienna in 1947 and in the Netherlands in May 1948. He published books for the markets in the Netherlands, Switzerland, and to a lesser extent, the United States; Germany was still by and large closed to imports.

Peter Suhrkamp, however, was one of the first publishers in Germany to receive a publishing license. Hence Bermann-Fischer had to work with Suhrkamp at first. With Berlin in ruins and located deep inside the Soviet zone of occupation, they opened a branch in West Germany in Frankfurt am Main in 1947. Before long, differences in the visions of Bermann-Fischer and Suhrkamp for the house became apparent. The final straw came when Bermann-Fischer insisted that the Suhrkamp Verlag be returned to him and put under the central management of Bermann-Fischer's publishing house in Amsterdam. Suhrkamp balked, refusing to make a German literary publisher subservient to a foreign company. A lawsuit in German reparations court was avoided at the last minute. According to their final agreement in 1950, Suhrkamp forfeited any claim on Fischer publishing operations in Berlin or Frankfurt, while Bermann-Fischer allowed authors Suhrkamp had published during the war choose to remain with his new house. Some 30 out of 44, including Hesse, stayed with Suhrkamp.

REESTABLISHING S. FISCHER

In the 1950s Bermann-Fischer set out to restore the S. Fischer Verlag to its former position of eminence in German publishing. He reestablished the *Neue Rundschau*. He took out large loans to republish the works of his longtime authors that had long been out of print, including Mann, Schnitzler, and von Hofmannsthal. He brought out other works, long classics elsewhere, in Germany for the first time, including works by Virginia Woolf and Walt Whitman. He obtained licenses for the writing of Franz Kafka.

Fischer played an important role in the paperback revolution in Germany of the 1950s and 1960s. In 1952 he inaugurated the Fischer Bücherei, a line of paperback fiction and nonfiction which soon became a staple of the firm. The inexpensive editions were particularly important to the masses of Germans who were living in poverty after the war. It was met with skepticism from the book trade—just as Samuel Fischer's inexpensive editions had been. It proved once and for all that even paperback nonfiction could be a profitable venture with the publication of a German edition of Lincoln Barnett's *The Universe and Dr. Einstein*, a book that sold more than 100,000 copies in its first months of publication. Other milestones included *Der Nationalsozialismus, Dokumente 1933–45* (*Documents on National Socialism, 1933–45*), one of the first works in Germany that dealt systematically with the Nazi era, and *Fischer Weltgeschichte*, a multivolume series on the history of the world, launched in 1965. A paperback subsidiary, the Fischer Taschenbuch Verlag, was established in 1966.

ACQUISITION BY HOLTZBRINCK

Bermann-Fischer and his wife retired from the operations of the publishing house in 1963. Like his father-in-law, Bermann-Fischer had had concerns about who would takeover the publishing house after his death. The couple had three daughters and no sons. Once it was clear no one in the family would take the company over, plans were made to sell the house, then valued at nearly DEM 7 million (approximately $1.7 million). Among the interested buyers were the DuMont Schauberg Verlag and Kiepenheuer Verlag, both Cologne-based, and Berlin's Verlagshaus Axel Springer. In the end, however, it was the owner of the Deutscher Bücherbund, Georg von Holtzbrinck, who purchased S. Fischer, a takeover that was completed in 1966. It was one of his firm's first acquisitions on the road to its becoming one of the world's largest media conglomerates. Fischer's publishing program remained unchanged under Holtzbrinck. In 1974 Holtzbrinck's daughter Monika Schoeller became Fischer's publisher.

Throughout the 1960s and 1970s, the house showed its commitment time and again to publishing authors of international rank, including Joseph Heller, Thornton Wilder, Doris Lessing, Samuel Beckett, Nadine Gordimer, and André Malraux. Beginning in the 1970s Fischer published a number of young writers from the German Democratic Republic as well, authors whose books could not appear in their home country. With the founding of *Schwarze Reihe* (the Black Series) in 1977, the publisher continued its intensive exploration of the country's Nazi past. The series would eventually come to include more than 250 titles on all aspects of National Socialism. A year later Fischer introduced the Collection S. Fischer, a series dedicated to publishing the first works of promising new writers.

COMPANY IS REORGANIZED

The Fischer Verlag slipped into a serious slump in the latter half of the 1990s. Between 1998 and 2000, the firm had losses of DEM 15 million, a serious number for a modest-sized serious publisher. A reorganization was undertaken with the assistance of consultants from McKinsey & Company. The roots of the problem were identified as bloated corporate bureaucracy, editorial complacency, and simple bad management. In response, strict departmental divisions were done away with and duplication of efforts (imprints that were pursuing essentially the same publishing programs) were combined or eliminated. Publishing operations in general were reorganized into broad new sections responsible for particular types of books, for example, German literature, foreign literature, general nonfiction, how-to books, and popular nonfiction. The marketing and distribution departments were significantly reorganized as well. Part of the plan involved layoffs, and 45 Fischer employees lost their jobs.

As the 21st century got started, a new generation of editors and managers gradually started to take over the reins at Fischer. In October 2002 its publisher of nearly 30 years, Monika Schoeller, retired from day-to-day operations of the house and the younger staff began having more influence on publishing decisions. Another, perhaps less positive, change was that the publisher, which was once in the vanguard of German publishing, began slashing the number of new serious fiction titles published every year. Instead it seemed to be relying on the glories of its own past. In 2002, for example, it announced a major new critical edition of the collected works of Mann. Although it was promised that the new edition would be of interest to general as well as specialist readers, it did not reflect a corporate strategy that

strove to essentially renew the publisher after the doldrums of the late 1990s.

NEW DIVISIONS ESTABLISHED

In the early 21st century other projects from Fischer's long history were taken up. In 2008 the publisher regained the rights to publish the works of Döblin, whose work had not been published by Fischer for some 50 years. In 2010 digitalization of Fischer's 120-year-old literary journal *Neue Rundschau* was completed. The firm made a serious commitment to books for young people around the same time. In 2009 it launched Fischer FJB, an imprint of books for teens. This was followed up in 2013 with the establishment of a new subsidiary, Fischer Kinder- und Jugendbuch Verlag, a new publisher of books for children and the young adult market. This segment of the book market had been growing in Germany as much as in the rest of the world, and the new Fischer publisher was a clear sign that the publisher planned to pursue sales in that market aggressively in the coming years. Whether or not it could return to its place in the upper echelons of German publishing, however, following such a strategy, remained to be seen.

Gerald E. Brennan

PRINCIPAL SUBSIDIARIES

FISCHER Kinder- und Jugendbuch Verlag; Fischer Taschenbuch Verlag GmbH.

PRINCIPAL COMPETITORS

Carl Hanser Verlag GmbH & Co. KG; Philipp Reclam jun. GmbH & Co. KG, Stuttgart; Piper Verlag GmbH; Rowohlt Verlag GmbH; Suhrkamp Verlag GmbH.& Co., Kommanditgesellschaft; Verlagsgruppe Random House GmbH.

FURTHER READING

Mauthner, Martin. *German Writers in French Exile, 1933–1940.* London: Vallentine Mitchell, 2007.

"Nach Hause sind wir nie zurückgekehrt." *Der Spiegel,* no. 1, 1987.

"S. Fischer entlässt 45 Mitarbeiter." *Hamburger Abendblatt,* May 26, 2000.

Schmitter, Elke. "Das Riesenspielzeug." *taz, die tageszeitung,* May 31, 2000.

Stach, Reiner. *100 jahre S. Fischer Verlag, 1886–1986.* Frankfurt am Main: S.Fischer Verlag, 2003.

"Zu verkaufen?" *Der Spiegel,* no. 32, 1962.

Saras SpA

———— ■ ————

S.S. Sulcitana 195 Km 19
Sarroch, 09018
Italy
Telephone: (+39 070) 90911
Fax: (+39 070) 900209
Web site: http://www.saras.it

Public Company
Incorporated: 2006 as Saras SpA
Employees: 2,226
Sales: EUR 11.23 billion ($15.1 billion) (2013)
Stock Exchanges: Milan
Ticker Symbol: SRS
NAICS: 324110 Petroleum Refineries

■ ■ ■

Saras SpA is Italy's leading independent oil refiner. The company operates the largest oil refinery on the Mediterranean, in Saroch, Sardinia, with a total production capacity of 300,000 barrels per day (15 million tons per year). This is equivalent to approximately 15 percent of the total refining capacity in Italy. The company distributes its products, including diesel, gasoline, heating oil, liquefied petroleum gas, naphtha, kerosene, and jet fuel, through its marketing arms Arcola Petrolifera and Deposito di Arcola. Saras is also active in the Spanish petroleum products market, operating a wholesale storage depot in Catagena and a chain of 112 service stations situated primarily on the Spanish

Mediterranean coast. Saras has branched out into power generation, operating its own 575 megawatts (MW) integrated gasification and power generation plant utilizing the heavy residues left over from its refining processes as feedstock. The company has also invested in wind power generation, with a 96-MW wind farm in Ulassai, and operates a water desalination plant. Saras SpA is a public company listed on the Milan Stock Exchange but controlled by the founding Moratti family.

OIL MAGNATE IN THE FORTIES

Born in Somma Lombardo, in Italy's Varese region, in 1909, Angelo Moratti was originally destined to take over his father's pharmacy business. The death of Moratti's mother when he was just eight years ultimately set him on a different path. His father remarried and moved to Milan to operate a new pharmacy on that city's Piazza Fontana. The younger Moratti was unable to get along with his stepmother, however, and after completing elementary school, he left to take a job in a factory producing brass handles.

Moratti later began taking night classes and by the age of 16 had earned his high school diploma. In the meantime, Moratti had already come into contact with what was to become his future career. When he was 14, Moratti had made an attempt to immigrate to the United States, making it as far as the port of Marseille, France. Moratti never shipped out. Instead, his experience in Marseille introduced him to the opportunities presented by the petroleum industry.

MORATTI FOUNDS FIRST BUSINESS

Moratti's interest initially turned toward the distribution of oil products, and specifically toward markets not well-covered by AGIP (Azienda Generale Italiana Petroli), the major Italian oil company. Moratti's chance came when he was assigned to Civitavecchia in order to complete his military service in 1927. While completing his service, Moratti founded his first business distributing lamp oil to local fishermen. During this time, Moratti formed a strong network of relationships in Tuscany and especially in Sardinia, which were to become crucial to his later success.

After leaving the military, Moratti went to work for Società Anonima Permanente Olio (Permolio), Italy's first oil refiner, founded by Count Miani. Moratti became responsible for setting up a distribution network for Permolio, starting from a base in Civitavecchia. This era coincided with the first growth phase of Italy's oil refining industry, centered particularly on the region around Genoa. Several other Italian refineries appeared during this period, while Permolio expanded to include three refineries in Genoa, Milan, and Rome.

Having helped establish Permolio's operations in the south, Moratti once again set out to develop his own business. For this, he moved to Rome, setting up a new distribution company selling oil products to niche markets. In 1935 Moratti moved again, this time to Genoa in order to be closer to the Italian oil industry. While there, Moratti came into contact with Cerutti, who became Moratti's most prominent financial backer.

FIRST REFINERY IN 1950

The growing shortage of petroleum products, and the Fascist government's search for alternative fuels, led Moratti back to Milan in 1937. It was there he became a founding shareholder of the lignite mining concern Società mineraria del Trasimeno (Somintra), which operated a mine in the province of Perugia. Moratti soon acquired full control of the mine, which became an important source of fuel for the duration of the war. Following the war, Moratti managed to maintain control of the mine, in part by promising to invest in other industrial activities, including a brick factory and a glass workshop.

In 1948 the company also made its first venture into electric power generation. At its height, Somintra produced approximately 2 percent of the two Italian lignite supply. Moratti nonetheless recognized that Somintra could not compete with less expensive foreign coal as imports picked up again into the 1950s. At the same time, the discovery and exploitation of the vast oil fields in the Middle East brought about a new shift in fuel policies toward petroleum.

Moratti also correctly guessed that Italy's position on the Mediterranean provided it with a central location between the Middle East oil producers and their European and American customers. In 1948 Moratti joined in on the creation of a new business venture, an oil refinery in Sicily to be built by a new company called RASIOM. This project faced a number of obstacles, most notably Moratti's own lack of experience in the design, engineering, and construction of an oil refinery.

ACQUIRES TEXAS REFINERY

The company quickly hit upon a novel solution to this limitation, however. Instead of building its own refinery, the company acquired an existing refinery, located in Texas, which it dismantled, shipped to Italy, and rebuilt in Augusta, Sicily, in 1949. After a number of setbacks, including losing the blueprints to the refinery, the RASIOM refinery took its first shipment of Middle Eastern oil in 1950.

The following year, after his business partner died, Moratti took full control of the company. By the middle of the decade the refinery had expanded its annual production to five million metric tons. The company achieved still-stronger growth in the second half of the decade, in large part because of its decision to begin refining oil for third parties. The company's largest customer at the time was Esso Standard Italiana, which alone accounted for 80 percent of RASIOM's production.

INDEPENDENT REFINERY IN THE SIXTIES

In 1960 RASIOM and Esso negotiated an agreement not only to extend their contract but also to carry out a major expansion of RASIOM's capacity. As part of that agreement, Esso took a 60 percent stake in RASIOM,

KEY DATES

1927: Angelo Moratti sets up his first business selling lamp oil to fishermen in Civitavecchia.
1948: Moratti founds RASIOM to build an oil refinery in Sicily.
1962: Moratti founds Società Raffinerie Sarde (Saras) to build an oil refinery in Sardinia.
1981: Angelo Moratti dies and the company is taken over by sons Gian Carlo and Massimo.
2001: Company's Sarlux subsidiary begins power generation operations.
2006: Saras goes public on the Milan Stock Exchange.
2013: Saras and Rosneft form a joint venture partnership.

with an option to acquire full control. Moratti agreed to the buyout the following year. Moratti famously placed some of the proceeds of the sale into the purchase of Milan football (soccer) club Inter, sparking a golden period for the club in which it won two European Cups and two other World Cup titles through the next decade.

Moratti, however, had not abandoned the petroleum industry. In 1962 he began making plans to build a new refinery, this time in the southern island province of Sardinia. Moratti chose the tiny village of Sarroch, in Cagliari, as the location for the new refinery, founding Società Raffinerie Sarde SpA (Saras). The choice of location placed the refinery on the route between the Italian-controlled oil fields in Tunisia and the Italian mainland. The Sarroch refinery became operational in 1965.

By then, Moratti had brought son Gian Carlo, born in 1936, into the business. A second son, Massimo, born in 1945, joined the company not long after. From the start, Saras established itself as an independent refinery, providing it with greater flexibility in the increasingly volatile crude oil market. Into the 1970s the company developed a secondary specialty of providing refining services to third-party petroleum product companies. To this end, the company expanded its refinery, adding a topping unit and hydrocracking facility in 1968 and an alkylation plant in 1970.

ACQUIRES SPI: 1972

In parallel with the growth of its third-party services business, Saras invested in other areas of the petroleum

business. In 1972 the Moratti family acquired Società Petrolifera Italiana (SPI), based in Fornovo Taro, in Parma. SPI held one of Italy's oldest oil exploration licenses and had also built up its own refinery and industrial storage complex in Arcola. Saras later sold on the exploration unit, maintaining the Arcola location's industrial operations. Angelo Moratti died in 1981, leaving control of the company to his sons.

Gian Carlo Moratti took over the leadership of the company during this time, later taking the position of chairman, with brother Massimo serving as the company's CEO. Through the 1980s Saras focused on further expansions to its main Sarroch refinery. In 1983 the company added a visbreaking unit and vacuum plant, followed by the addition of a continuous catalytic-reforming unit the following year. By the end of the decade the company had also carried out the expansion of its hydrocracking unit, reaching a capacity of 94,000 barrels per day.

SPANISH ENTRY IN THE NINETIES

Into the 1990s Saras was already the leading independent oil refiner in Italy. The company maintained its edge against its far-larger competitors in Italy and elsewhere by continuously investing in the modernization of its operations. New investments for the company through the turn of the century included the addition of a first mild hydrocracking unit in 1992, a second in 2001, and an etherification plant also in 2001. Saras had been developing its downstream business as well.

The company developed a wholesale business, based at its Arcola facility during the 1990s. The move into wholesale encouraged Saras to expand into another Mediterranean market at the same time, leading the company into Spain. The group's subsidiary there, Saras Energia, set up its own storage facility in Cartagena. Back in Italy, the company explored new expansions to its core operations. The company entered the energy generation business, setting up its own integrated gasification and combined cycle power plant, under subsidiary Sarlux, creating in 1999 a partnership with U.S.-based Enron.

Enron controlled 45 percent of the EUR 1 billion ($1.3 billion) project. The facility, with a generating capacity of 575 MW, was capable of supplying 30 percent of Sardinia's power requirement. Importantly, the power plant made use of the heavy residues left over from the group's refinery operations as its chief feedstock. The Sarlux power plant became operational in 2001.

The association with Enron had by then already come to haunt the company, amid Enron's spectacular collapse at the beginning of the decade. Enron, and its creditors, continued to hold 45 percent of Sarlux. The Morattis made a first effort to take full control of Sarlux in 2002, exercising an option to acquire the Enron stake at a book value of EUR 60 million. Enron's creditors balked, however, seeking as much as EUR 320 million for the stake. In the end, the International Chamber of Commerce sided with Saras, enabling the company to take full control of Sarlux.

PUBLIC OFFERING IN 2006

This decision helped set the stage for the Moratti family's decision to take Saras public, listing the company on the Milan Stock Exchange in April 2006. The initial public offering was a success, raising EUR 2.23 billion in new capital for the company. Saras promptly put its treasury to work, investing strongly in new desulfuring technology in order to meet European objectives for a zero-sulfur gasoline by 2009. The company made strong progress on this effort, already reducing its gasoline levels to just 30 parts per million by 2006, making it the most advanced refinery in Italy.

The company continued investing in desulfuring technology, adding a tail gas treatment and sulfur recovery unit, and a gasoline desulfuring unit in 2008. This permitted the company to achieve sulfur content levels of just 10 parts per million by 2009. The company had invested in modernizing its other technologies, notably for diesel, enabling it to make important advances in its production capacity. Saras soon put this added capacity to work.

In 2009 the company took its first step into the retail market, acquiring a chain of 71 service stations in Spain, located primarily along the country's southern Mediterranean coast. The company invested in expanding the chain, extending its operations to 112 locations by 2014. In 2013 the company also announced its interest in acquiring the 870 Italian service station operations of Shell, after the Anglo-Dutch oil giant announced its interest in selling the division.

Even though petroleum remained the group's primary focus, Saras had also begun investing in the renewable energy sector as well. The company's first investment in this area came in 2005, with the construction of a wind energy farm in Ulassai, with an initial power generating capacity of 72 MW. The company upgraded the site to 96 MW in 2011.

ROSNEFT PARTNERSHIP IN 2013

Saras's power generation operations helped stabilize the company's operations amid the increasingly volatile refining industry in Europe into the decade. Faced with dropping demand in finished oil products, the company went in search of new partners. This led the company to form a joint venture partnership with Russian oil and gas giant Rosneft in 2014. The partnership gave Saras access to Rosneft's upstream activities, while providing the Russian company with an entry into the European downstream market.

As part of the partnership, Massimo and Gian Carlo Moratti transferred nearly 14 percent of Saras's shares to Rosneft. Rosneft president Igor Sechin then took a seat on Saras's board of directors. The Moratti brothers also began to prepare their own succession. Until 2013 the brothers' shares were held in a single vehicle, Angelo Moratti SpA, which maintained majority control of Saras.

In October 2013 the brothers agreed to a demerger of their shares into two separate shareholding companies. These remained linked by a shareholder agreement for at least the next three years, however. Saras continued to suffer from the deteriorating European economic situation into 2014, as it posted losses of EUR 84.1 million ($115.3 million) in 2013.

The company's revenues fell 6 percent that year to EUR 11.23 billion. More bad news came for the company later in 2014. The economic sanctions imposed against Russia, following the country's annexation of Crimea, in Ukraine, forced the companies to place their joint venture on hold. Despite these setbacks, Saras remained hopeful that its partnership with the Russian oil giant would help consolidate its position as Italy's largest oil refiner in the early 21st century.

M. L. Cohen

PRINCIPAL SUBSIDIARIES

Arcola Petrolifera Srl; Deposito di Arcola Srl; Ensar Srl; Parchi Eolici Ulassai Srl; Reasar SA (Spain); Saras Energia Bio SL (Spain); Saras Energia SA (Spain); Sargas Srl; Sarint SA (Spain); Sarlux Srl; Sartec SpA.

PRINCIPAL DIVISIONS

Refining; Power Generation; Marketing; Wind; Other.

PRINCIPAL OPERATING UNITS

Sarroch Refinery; Arcola Petrolifera; Saras Energia.

PRINCIPAL COMPETITORS

Anonima Petroli Italiana; Eni SpA; ExxonMobil; Oliinvest BV; Total SA.

FURTHER READING

"Italian Saras SpA Says Will Continue Iran Oil Imports." *Iranian Government*, March 1, 2012.

"Italy's Saras to Invest EUR1.23 Billion (USD191bn) in 2008–2011 Period." *TendersInfo*, June 26, 2008.

Michaels, Adrian. "Morattis Plan Saras Offering." *Financial Times*, April 24, 2006.

Pozzi, Daniele. "Moratti, Angelo." In *Dizionario Biografico degli Italiani*, vol. 76, 2012.

"Rosneft and Saras Sign Agreement on Cooperation for the Purpose of Establishing a JV." *Web News Wire*, August 6, 2013.

"Sanctions Prevents 'Rosneft' to Create Joint Venture with Saras." *RUPaper.com*, August 12, 2014.

"Saras Adjusted Net Loss Widens to EUR 84.1m in 2013." *SeeNews Italy*, February 21, 2014.

"Saras Interested in Shell's Italian Fuel Stations." *SeeNews Netherlands*, May 7, 2013.

"Saras Ready to Go." *Euroweek*, April 21, 2006.

"Sechin to Take Seat on Board of Italian Saras after Rosneft Buys Stake." *Russia & CIS Business and Financial Newswire*, April 24, 2013.

Schutt Sports, Inc.

710 Industrial Drive
Litchfield, Illinois 62056
U.S.A.
Telephone: (217) 324-3978
Toll Free: (800) 426-9784
Web site: http://www.schuttsports.com

Private Company
Founded: 1918 as W.A. Schutt Manufacturing Company
Employees: 400
Sales: $150 million (2010 est.)
NAICS: 339920 Sporting and Athletic Goods Manufacturing

■ ■ ■

Schutt Sports, Inc., is a Litchfield, Illinois–based sports equipment manufacturer. Football products include helmets, face guards, chin straps, shoulder pads, protective padding, protective and field apparel, training gear, and accessories. Schutt has been supplying major league baseball with bases since the 1930s and also offers helmets, catching gear, umpire gear, training aids, and equipment bags. Schutt is the leading provider of equipment for women's softball, including helmets and catching gear. In addition, Schutt reconditions football helmets and shoulder pads. It also sells a wide variety of football and baseball collectible products, such as miniature team helmets and miniature and full-size home plates, bases, and pitching rubbers. In addition to its Litchfield operation, the company maintains facilities in Easton, Pennsylvania, and Salem, Illinois. Schutt is owned by private-equity firm Platinum Equity LLC.

FOUNDER, A HARDWARE STORE OWNER

Schutt Sports was founded by William A. Schutt, who according to census information was born around 1881. Although trained as a metal worker, Schutt opened a hardware store, Schutt Hardware Co., in Litchfield, Illinois, in 1908. In addition to the retail operation, Schutt used his trade skills to do cornice, skylight, and sheet metal work.

He later formed W.A. Schutt Manufacturing Company to begin manufacturing products of his own design, including a baler for empty cement and plaster sacks. In 1918 Schutt used his welding abilities to invent the eyelets on basketball rims to which a net could be attached. He began manufacturing basketball goals and offered dry line markers for playing fields, laying the foundation for Schutt Sports.

Schutt also began manufacturing javelin hangers and softball catcher's masks. He continued to run the hardware store as well, but finally sold it in 1930. His involvement in football began in 1935 with the manufacture of face guards. At the time, players wore open helmets, and the only facial protection that was available was leather nose guards.

FACE GUARD HISTORY

Schutt's rudimentary face guard was designed by Delby C. Humphrey, who had played center on the Indiana

COMPANY PERSPECTIVES

We build gear for players. Those five words mean everything to us at Schutt Sports. From the manufacturing line to the sales reps on the road to senior management keeping the machine running, all of us are focused on players. The dedicated leaders who devote themselves to the game; every game, every practice and every moment.

State University football team in the late 1920s. The face guard would not be fully embraced by football players for many years, however. According to lore, the modern face guard was first worn by Cleveland Browns quarterback Otto Graham in 1953 after suffering a blow to his teeth.

It was supposedly a makeshift affair but led helmet manufacturer Riddell to develop a helmet with an attached plastic face mask. In truth, Schutt was selling a metal face guard well before Graham and began mass-producing them in the 1950s as players gradually accepted the protective option.

HUMPHREY BUYS COMPANY: 1962

In the meantime, Schutt became involved in baseball by manufacturing bases. In 1939 the company became the exclusive provider of bases to Major League Baseball (MLB). Nevertheless, face guards became Schutt's signature product. Humphrey bought Schutt Manufacturing in 1962 and immediately began lobbying the National Collegiate Athletic Association (NCAA) to finally make football face guards mandatory equipment.

In 1964 Humphrey received a patent on a new loop-strap face guard attachment system. Later in the decade, Humphrey turned over Schutt to his son Bob. Under his leadership the company expanded its face mask business, aided by the device becoming mandatory in football by 1970. Schutt even brought a sense of style to the product. In 1973 the company introduced eight colors, which replaced the traditional white or gray. Schutt also remained involved in the basketball sector.

In 1973 it introduced powder-coated basketball rims. In 1986 Bob Humphrey's daughter Julie Nimmons and her husband Ken bought Schutt Manufacturing along with associate company Schutt Athletic Sales Co., which performed marketing, sales, customer service, and other functions. She had joined the

company four years earlier at the behest of her father and grandfather.

ACQUIRES ATHLETIC HELMET: 1987

While her husband took charge of Schutt Manufacturing, Nimmons became president of Schutt Athletic. In 1987 she took the company into the football helmet business by acquiring Knoxville, Tennessee–based Athletic Helmet Inc., a unit of Bike Athletic Company that also made helmets for baseball, skateboarding, kayaking, windsurfing, mountain climbing, and pro water skiing.

In 1987 Schutt introduced a new football helmet under the AIR brand, becoming the only company that manufactured and distributed both helmets and face guards. Riddell was the only other company that continued to manufacture football helmets in the United States, and the competition between the two companies was fierce. In the face guard market, however, Schutt was a dominant force, controlling 95 percent of the collegiate and professional market, and 75 percent of the much-larger high school market.

NEW NAME: 1992

In 1992 Schutt Athletic Sales Co. was renamed Schutt Sports Group as part of an effort to consolidate the Schutt businesses and lay the foundation for new product development and possible acquisitions. Julie Nimmons acted as chief executive officer of the revamped company, while her husband became executive vice president in charge of product development. A short time later, Schutt acquired Marshall, Michigan–based Ronan and Kunzl, a manufacturer of basketball backboards, the addition of which increased Schutt's annual sales to $20 million.

In 1994 the product development efforts of Athletic Helmet resulted in the introduction of football shoulder pads, marketed under the AIR Blaster name. Later in the year Athletic Helmet moved from Knoxville to Salem, Illinois, occupying a former shoe manufacturing facility. In 1997 Schutt began developing protective softball equipment for women's fast-pitch softball, designed with major input from players. The company introduced equipment that was adapted to the needs of female softball players, such as catcher's equipment shaped for women's bodies and helmets with a ponytail port.

As a result, Schutt became the leading company in women's softball protective gear. Schutt did not neglect its football face guard franchise, however. In 1999 it

<table>
<tr><td colspan="2" align="center">

KEY DATES

</td></tr>
<tr><td>1918:</td><td>William Schutt begins manufacturing eyelets for basketball rims.</td></tr>
<tr><td>1935:</td><td>Schutt manufactures first football face guard.</td></tr>
<tr><td>1962:</td><td>Delby C. Humphrey acquires company.</td></tr>
<tr><td>2010:</td><td>Company declares Chapter 11 bankruptcy protection.</td></tr>
<tr><td>2014:</td><td>Company introduces the SchuttVision football helmet.</td></tr>
</table>

introduced the first face guard using titanium, which proved significantly more enduring than models using other metals. The company also built a collectibles business, offering replica and miniature football helmets from dozens of universities across the United States.

PRODUCT INNOVATIONS

Innovations continued for Schutt in the new century. During the MLB World Series in 2000, the company introduced bases with logos. The following year Schutt added the AIR Advantage helmet, and in 2003 unveiled the DNA Pro football helmet that used thermoplastic urethane (TPU) cushioning, a major improvement over the padding used in helmets for the previous three decades. Another advance in sports equipment Schutt engineered was the 2005 introduction of the Typhoon football shoulder pad, which incorporated climate control technology to better manage a player's body temperature regardless of the weather.

In 2005 Julie and Ken Nimmons decided to bring in equity partners to help expand the business. New Canaan, Connecticut–based private-equity firm Gridiron Capital LLC acquired a majority stake in the company. Later in 2005 some of the cash provided by Gridiron was used to purchase Circle System Group, a company that reconditioned sports equipment, an area in which Schutt was already involved through dealers.

The reconditioning business had outgrown its facility, and the Circle System acquisition allowed Schutt to maintain growth in the sector. Unfortunately, Circle System would soon be embroiled in a financial fraud and bribery scandal. Eventually its longtime president pleaded guilty to a single count of conspiracy to commit mail fraud as part of an effort to overcharge New Jersey schools to recondition athletic equipment.

INTRODUCES AIR XP HELMET

Product innovation at Schutt continued. In 2007 the company introduced the AIR XP football helmet, which was the first in the industry to fit a traditional shell with TPU cushioning, and also unveiled the AIR Flex Shoulder Pads, Schutt's first professional line of football shoulder pads. In 2008 the company revealed its next-generation helmet, the ION4D, featuring a larger shell with additional TPU cushioning as well as the Energy Wedge Faceguard.

Designed to serve as a shock absorber for the helmet, the new face guard represented the first major advancement in face guard design in many years. In 2009 the Flex Line Shoulder Pads line was introduced, building upon the advances made with the AIR Flex Shoulder Pads. Schutt also began working with Atlanta's Hothead Technologies to develop a heat-sensing football helmet to enhance player safety. In addition, Schutt licensed its name to Krypton Sports to produce football gloves, Schutt's first branded shorts, T-shirts, headgear, other apparel, and accessories.

The rivalry with Riddell only intensified in 2008, when Riddell sued Schutt over three patent infringements related to football helmets and face guards. At issue were the earflaps on Schutt's DNA and Ion football helmets that Riddell claimed infringed on the patents it held on its jaw flap. Although Schutt maintained that it could easily modify the shape of its earflap and that it had absolutely no bearing on the effectiveness of the helmet, a jury ruled against Schutt in 2010, awarding Riddell $29 million in damages.

For a small company like Schutt, the amount might prove devastating, especially after the Circle System scandal and the ongoing impact of a recession that resulted in school budget cuts. Schutt appealed the award, countersued Riddell, but also filed for bankruptcy protection in September 2010 as the company was put up for sale.

PLATINUM ACQUIRES SCHUTT: 2010

Ultimately, Schutt settled the matter with Riddell, agreeing to pay $1 million. By then, the company was under new ownership. In December 2010 California-based private-equity firm Platinum Equity LLC won an auction for the company, its $33.1 million winning bid beating out Rawlings Sporting Goods Company, Inc., despite the latter offering $36 million. As part of its bid, Platinum pledged not to close a Pennsylvania plant for at least three months, nor close the Litchfield and Salem plants for one year.

The bankruptcy court judge accepted Platinum's offer, maintaining that it was in the best interest of the company and debtors. Under new ownership, Schutt Sports quickly rebounded. In September 2011 the company reported that sales of football helmets and face guards through the first several months of the year had increased 15 percent over the comparable period the previous year. The company also resumed new product introductions.

In 2013 Schutt introduced a new line of AIR baseball batters' helmets that featured patented impact absorption technology. The warning label in football helmets was also replaced by a new interactive label that could be scanned by a mobile device to provide players, coaches, and parents with the latest information about concussions.

RELEASE OF NEW COLLECTIBLES

In 2014 Schutt unveiled an extensive new line of collectible college football helmets, including the alternate helmets that had become popular at many schools. Also in 2014 Schutt introduced the SchuttVision helmet that incorporated a small video camera above the face mask, developed in conjunction with Louisiana-based Sports Video Innovations. Although the helmet was intended as a coaching and recruiting tool, Schutt was developing wireless capabilities that might change the nature of football coverage on television.

Other new products were also in development, as were new markets. Schutt became the corporate sponsor of a new eight-team American football league in India. Whether the cricket-obsessed country would ever embrace the new sport and create a new market for

Schutt's football equipment remained to be seen. The company, on the other hand, was likely to remain a leader in football, baseball, and softball protective equipment in the United States well into the future.

Ed Dinger

PRINCIPAL DIVISIONS

Baseball; Collectibles; Football; Reconditioning; Softball.

PRINCIPAL COMPETITORS

BRG Sports, Inc.; Rawlings Sporting Goods Company, Inc.; Worth Sports, Inc.

FURTHER READING

Brown, Lisa. "Private Firm Wins Court Approval to Buy Schutt Sports." *St. Louis Post-Dispatch*, December 16, 2010.

———. "Schutt's Football Helmet Gives New Views of the Game." *St. Louis Post-Dispatch*, July 20, 2014.

Dettro, Chris. "Schutt Athletic Changes Name, Plans to Consolidate Business." *Springfield (IL) State Journal-Register*, August 21, 1992.

Engle, Todd. "Saving Face." *Decatur (IL) Herald & Review*, March 20, 2005.

Moore, Rob. "Nimmons Butts Heads with Rival in Football Helmet Biz." *St. Louis Business Journal*, March 29, 1993.

Pierce, Mark. "Firm Has a Head for Sports Gear Business." *Alton Telegraph*, October 3, 1992.

Ryan, Thomas J. "Lean and Mean: Schutt Positions Itself for Growth." *Sporting Goods Business*, June 2007.

Sconza Candy Company

One Sconza Candy Lane
Oakdale, California 95361-7899
U.S.A.
Telephone: (209) 845-3700
Toll Free: (888) SCONZA-1
Fax: (209) 845-3737
Web site: http://www.sconzacandy.com

Private Company
Founded: 1939
Employees: 125 (est.)
Sales: $37 million (2011 est.)
NAICS: 311340 Nonchocolate Confectionery Manufacturing; 311352 Confectionery Manufacturing from Purchased Chocolate

■ ■ ■

Sconza Candy Company is a candy manufacturing company that sells products under its own name and is also one of the industry's largest private-label and contract manufacturers. The company offers both packaged candies and bulk confections and is an organic-certified and kosher-certified confectioner. Sconza is best known for its jawbreakers and such sugar-shell panning candies as Jordan almonds, Boston baked beans, and French burnt peanuts. Other products include chocolate and yogurt panning candies, toffee nuts, tablet candy, yogurt and chocolate-covered pretzels, sour worms, and gummy bears. In addition, Sconza offers seasonal Easter, Halloween, and Christmas candies. Sconza is based in Oakdale, California, where it maintains a 500,000-square-foot manufacturing, packaging, and distribution facility. The company is owned and managed by the third generation of the Sconza family.

FOUNDER, AN ITALIAN IMMIGRANT

Sconza Candy's founder, Vincent Sconza, was born in southern Italy and immigrated to the United States in 1922 at the age of 17. To earn extra money, Sconza and his wife Maria began making peanut brittle in the kitchen of their Oakland, California, home and sold it directly to customers. The candy proved so popular that in 1939, they rented a small storefront in the area and started Sconza Candy Company.

They began adding new candies and soon outgrew the space. In 1948 Sconza Candy moved to a larger location in Berkeley, California. In that same year the company began panning candy and producing hard candies. In 1950 Jawbreakers were introduced. The second generation of the Sconza family became more involved in the business during the post–World War II era, including the Sconzas' eldest son John, who was born in 1932.

His younger brother by five years, James, worked for his father during summer vacations from school. After completing college, James joined Sconza Candy full time in 1960 and gained experience in all aspects of the company. It was he who would eventually inherit the business.

ACQUIRES HROMADA: 1967

Sconza Candy employed only a handful of workers when James Sconza joined his father and brother. The company began to enjoy steady growth in 1967, when it acquired Hromada Candy Company. Hromada was a well-established confectioner and dealer in nuts and confectioner's supplies, located in downtown San Francisco. Subsequently, the Sconza family returned home to Oakland, where it combined the Berkeley and San Francisco operations and would operate for the next four decades.

In addition to the manufacturing plant, the company acquired a nearby 25,000-square-foot warehouse. To better serve the eastern part of the United States, the company later opened a distribution center in Chicago. In addition to serving all 50 states, Sconza Candy products were also distributed to Canada, Mexico, Australia, and the United Kingdom. During the final 20 years of the 20th century, the third generation of the Sconza family joined the company. James Sconza's three children worked their way up in the business in the same manner as their father.

They learned the basics during summer jobs at the plant and later became permanent employees. His son Ron would become plant manager, while daughter Janet Angers became customer service manager. Another daughter, Julie, did not join the company, but in the late 1990s her husband, Greg Cater, became sales manager and played an important role in the growth of Sconza Candy. Although officially retired, Vincent Sconza continued to visit the plant each week until his death at the age of 96 in 2001.

Although Sconza Candy eventually operated out of a 70,000-square-foot production facility in Oakland, the site became cramped by the end of the century. In 1999 James Sconza considered the possibility of moving to a new facility in the Yuba County Industrial Park, but in the end the company remained in Oakland. Despite the limitations of the site, the company expanded on two major fronts at the turn of the century.

ADJUSTING TO NEW TASTES

Sconza Candy had periodically performed contract manufacturing and private-label work but made it a point of emphasis at this time. The company was quick to respond to consumers' changing tastes and was able to take a product idea to the marketplace in just a few months. By 2005 contract manufacturing and private-label candies accounted for about one-fifth of total revenues. Key to the growth of the business was an investment in new packing equipment that allowed Sconza Candy to offer a variety of package types, from 10 grams to five pounds in size.

Sconza Candy's ability to adapt to the times also led to a shift in the branded candy business. Peanut brittle, despite the family's sentimental attachment to the product, was dropped because of diminished popularity. Hard candies, which became a mainstay for the company, were also discontinued as they fell out of favor with younger consumers. Around the turn of the new century, jawbreakers became an area of focus.

Although they were hardly a new product, there was a renewed interest in jawbreakers because of their nostalgic value. The company was just one of two companies in the United States that still produced the candy and the only one that offered large-size varieties. In 2001 Sconza Candy introduced the MegaBruiser, a 16-ounce, 3.875-inch diameter jawbreaker. The novelty item sold particularly well at New York's premier toy retailer FAO Schwarz.

CHOCOLATE PRODUCTS ADDED

More important to the balance sheet was the decision of Sconza Candy to become involved in chocolate confections, a move made to accommodate customer requests. "Going into chocolate was just a natural line extension of what we were already doing," Cater told *Candy Industry* in a January 2005 article. "Our customers wanted us to offer a broader range of candies, so we made the move. It's been good for us and enabled us to expand our core business of panning."

In truth, the company did not expect to enjoy much success with chocolate but demand grew quickly, prompting the investment in new melting and coating machines as well improved air conditioning. Sconza Candy made a greater commitment to the chocolate category in 2005, unveiling a line of gourmet chocolates under its own name, including chocolate-covered berries, fruits, and nuts. Yogurt-covered products were offered as well.

Sconza Candy also kept up with customer interest in healthier products, including reduced sugar and

KEY DATES

1939: Sconza Candy is founded.
1948: Company moves to Berkeley, California.
1967: Hromada Candy Company is acquired.
2008: Sconza Candy moves to Oakdale, California.
2014: Sconza Candy celebrates its 75th anniversary.

sugar-free items. Early in the first decade of the 21st century the company became organic certified, after having become kosher certified a decade earlier. New products in the organic category included Organic Toffee Cashews and Peanuts and Organic Chocolate Raisins, introduced in the summer of 2006.

LIMITED SPACE CAUSES DIFFICULTIES

Sconza Candy was able to expand its business despite the space limitations of its plant. Production, warehousing, and administrative offices were divided among three locations in Oakland. Four employees in the production facility had the sole function of relocating candy and pallets to allow other workers to operate. Moreover, the inability to increase production because of limited space caused the company to miss out on several business opportunities.

The need for a new space had been evident for years, and in the new century Sconza Candy became more active in its search for a new location. When it became apparent that there was no property large enough in Oakland to accommodate the company's needs, management considered moving to other sites on the West Coast.

No existing building met the company's requirements, however. An engineering firm was hired to design a suitable plant while the company scouted for a location. The company secured options on land in British Columbia, Canada, but James Sconza refused to move the business out of the United States. Management then settled on a site in Medford, Oregon, and was close to reaching an agreement when once again, James Sconza halted the deal.

MOVE TO OAKDALE: 2007

Through a newspaper article, Sconza learned in March 2007 that Hershey was moving production to Mexico, and its plant in Oakdale, California, about 85 miles east of Oakland, was up for sale. When James and Ron

Sconza visited the 615,000-square-foot plant situated on 70 acres of land, it became immediately apparent that the site was an ideal fit for Sconza Candy. Although the plant had opened in 1965, it was a top-quality facility that had been well maintained by Hershey.

The 300,000-square-foot-facility design for Sconza Candy, already completed by the engineering firm, could simply be dropped into the existing structure and offer ample space for future growth. In addition, Sconza Candy would be eligible for tax breaks because the factory was included in the enterprise zone of Stanislaus County. Oakdale's city council had just approved a construction project that would create a second entrance to the plant and help Hershey find a buyer.

Another advantage to Oakdale not to be overlooked was its proximity to sources of important ingredients for Sconza Candy, including a variety of nuts, raisins, and other dried fruit. In just two days, Sconza Candy had the Oakdale plant under contract. There were three other suitors for the property, but Sconza Candy found favor with Hershey, which considered it appropriate that the building be occupied by a candy company.

While Hershey had become the object of significant criticism for moving the operation and 575 jobs to Mexico, it had long been considered a good corporate citizen in the community. It had built its visitors' center in the heart of Oakdale. In May of each year it played an important role in the Oakdale Chocolate Festival, which brought thousands of visitors to the town. Although organized by the chamber of commerce, the festival was generally regarded as a Hershey-backed event.

EMPLOYEES MULL MOVE

Hershey continued to operate the Oakdale plant until the end of January 2008, when the company began moving out equipment. Sconza Candy also began its conversion process, planning to transfer production from Oakland to Oakdale in September 2008. The Oakland employees were given the opportunity to move with the company and keep their jobs, but few expressed interest. Buses were chartered and employees were brought to Oakdale to visit, and many changed their minds.

In the end, about half of the company's 100 employees elected not to move their families from Oakland to Oakdale, and many former Hershey employees assumed their places. The company also hired seven former Hershey managers who were well familiar with the Oakdale facility, including 29-year Hershey veteran Eric McDonald, who became director of facilities and maintenance. Completing the move took longer than expected.

Production finally began in Oakdale in mid-November 2008. The company's production capacity increased fivefold, a fact not lost on the candy industry. Sconza Candy received regular calls from potential new customers. In addition to contract manufacturing and private-label opportunities, the new facility helped to spur new product development. The previous research and development unit had been shoehorned into a 400-square-foot space. The new unit enjoyed four times the space.

Although contract manufacturing and private-label work was expanding at a steady pace, it was a sector known for its volatility. Hence, Sconza Candy devoted greater resources to building its branded business. At the start of the second decade of the new century, the company introduced a jawbreaker-on-a-stick product, Lemoncello Almonds, and Carmelized Cashews.

In 2011 the company's premium candies became available for sale online. Sconza Candy introduced the Confection Perfection line of five-ounce pouched candies in 2014. Now 75 years old, the company occupied 500,000 square feet of the former Hershey plant and was making plans to offer viewing tours. The company was fully settled into its new home and poised to enjoy steady growth as it continued this new chapter in its history.

Ed Dinger

PRINCIPAL DIVISIONS

Contract Manufacturing.

PRINCIPAL COMPETITORS

Primrose Candy Co.; SweetWorks, Inc.; Wolfgang Candy Company.

FURTHER READING

Brown, Steven E. F. "Sconza: Responding as America Goes Soft." *San Francisco Business Times*, February 12, 2006.

Fuhrman, Elizabeth. "Panning Traditions." *Candy Industry*, January 2005.

Goll, David. "Sweet Tradition for Jim Sconza." *San Francisco Business Times*, December 29, 2005.

Hightower, Eve. "A Sweet Start." *Modesto Bee*, November 16, 2008.

Pacyniak, Bernard. "Steppin' Up." *Candy Industry*, February 2009.

Salerno, Christina. "Sweet Plans for Hershey Site." *Modesto Bee*, March 22, 2008.

"Sweet Deal." *Modesto Bee*, April 6, 2008.

Shikoku Electric Power Company, Inc.

———■———

2-5, Marunouchi
Takamatsu, Kagawa 760-8573
Japan
Telephone: (+81 87) 821-5061
Fax: (+81 87) 826-1250
Web site: http://www.yonden.co.jp

Public Company
Incorporated: 1951
Employees: 8,506
Sales: ¥636.33 billion ($6.18 billion) (2014)
Stock Exchanges: Tokyo
Ticker Symbol: 95070
NAICS: 221111 Hydroelectric Power Generation; 221112 Fossil Fuel Electric Power Generation; 221113 Nuclear Electric Power Generation; 221114 Solar Electric Power Generation; 221115 Wind Electric Power Generation; 221122 Electric Power Distribution

■ ■ ■

Shikoku Electric Power Company, Inc. (SEPCO) is one of the 10 major regional power companies that generate, transmit, and distribute electricity throughout Japan. The company, referred to in Japan as the Yonden Group, supplies electricity to all four of Shikoku's prefectures including Tokushima, Kochi, Ehime, and Kagawa and serves over four million customers. As of March 2014, its generating capacity was 8,456 megawatts (MW), stemming from nuclear power, oil, coal, liquefied natural gas (LNG), and hydropower

generating operations. The Great East Japan Earthquake and tsunami in March 2011 led to radioactive leaks at the Fukushima Daiichi Nuclear Power Station. As a result, Japan began to overhaul its nuclear program and ordered a shutdown of all nuclear reactors. By 2013 the country was operating without nuclear power. As of September 2014 Japan's Nuclear Regulation Authority had yet to allow SEPCO's Ikata Nuclear Power Plant to resume operations.

FIFTIES FORMATION

SEPCO was formed as a company on May 1, 1951, when the General Headquarters (GHQ) of the Allied powers under General Douglas MacArthur approved a plan submitted by the Japanese government to reorganize and rationalize the electrical power industry. Under the scheme, which was developed in 1948, the nation was divided into nine blocks, each with its own privately owned electric power company (EPC). In 1972 the Okinawa EPC was added as a 10th company.

At the time of inauguration, the nine companies served 16 million customers with a combined capacity of 8,500 MW. Of this, SEPCO's portion was a relatively small 290 MW, or just over 3 percent. Shikoku was the smallest and least developed of Japan's four main islands but since ancient times maintained close ties with the old capital cities in Honshu such as nearby Kyoto, Nara, and more recently Tokyo. It has played an important role as a transit island in shipping between Japan and its trading partners through ports such as Kochi on the south Pacific Coast.

The Yonden Group is committed to the continuous provision of high-quality services, centered on energy, that interconnect with the lives that people lead. In this way, the Yonden Group contributes both to comfortable, safe, and reliable living and to the Shikoku region's development.

Although the chief industries in the region have traditionally been low-technology, such as forestry and handicrafts, there was a boom in the Ehime and Kagawa prefectures in the high-technology sector in the 1980s, prompted in part by the government's "Technopolis" scheme to promote high-technology industry in Shikoku. There was also an increase in tourism on the island, peaking in 1989. Thus the history of electric power on a large scale in Shikoku started in the latter half of the 20th century.

EARLY HISTORY OF JAPAN'S ELECTRIC POWER

The history of electric power in Japan as a whole, however, goes back to 1878 when Professor W. E. Aryton of the Institute of Technology in Tokyo unveiled an arc lamp to celebrate the opening of the Central Telegraph Office. Japan's first electric utility company was established in 1886, seven years after Thomas Edison invented the incandescent lamp in the United States. The company was Tokyo Electric Lighting Company, and its first electric power plant, which was also the first in Japan, was completed in 1887 as a 25-kilowatt (kW) facility in Nihonbashi, Tokyo.

Throughout its history, Japan had been able to assimilate and improve upon outside technology and ideas, and electric power was no exception. After the opening of the Tokyo Electric Lighting plant, many electric utilities started up in main cities. Although demand had increased rapidly, especially since electricity was a great improvement over the troublesome oil lamps then in use, service was generally limited to government and commercial offices and factories. Most of the first plants in Japan were thermal, powered by coal, but in 1891 the first hydroelectric power station was completed in Kyoto. A large part of the demand for electricity came from the electric railways that were springing up all over the country.

Spurred on by these developments, electricity in the form of electric lighting was first introduced to Shikoku

in 1896 by the Tokushima Electric Lighting Company in Tokushima City. The next seven years saw the spread of electric lighting into Shikoku's four prefectures by Takamatsu Lighting, Tosa Lighting, and Iyo Hydroelectric Power, which pioneered hydroelectricity in Shikoku by building the first plant in Ehime prefecture in 1903.

The years 1896 to 1912 saw the rapid development of these four power companies. The turnover of Tokushima Electric, for example, increased 1,000-fold between 1900 and 1912. The most common initial usage of electricity was in the lighting of streets and public areas, but increasingly the upper-class town dwellers had electric lights installed in their homes.

ELECTRIC UTILITY INDUSTRY LAW: 1911

In 1911 the government enacted the Electric Utility Industry Law. The law necessitated government permission for the production and distribution of electric power. By 1920 there were 3,000 power companies in Japan, riding on Japan's economic boom, and the number operating in the towns of Shikoku numbered about 50. The depression of the 1920s in Japan, following its defeat in World War I, was exacerbated by the Great Kanto Earthquake in 1923 and the worldwide market crash in 1929. While the Great Depression did not have an excessive effect on the economy of Shikoku, it did prevent growth during this period.

The period between 1926 and 1937 can be characterized as the era of the "Big Five" in the history of electric power in Japan. It was dominated by Tokyo Electric Lighting and Daido Power in particular. The government regulated the industry by passing four laws in 1938 that ensured state control over prices, plant development, transmission, and all other aspects of the industry. In effect, it had formed one of the largest electric companies in the world with the establishment of JEGTCO (Japan Electric Generation and Transmission Company).

The Allied bombing of Japan from 1943 to 1945 seriously damaged 44 percent of Japan's power stations and devastated Japanese industry. Shikoku, however, not being a strategic target, was largely untouched. The GHQ, which was effectively in charge of Japan from 1945 to 1952, made sweeping changes in Japan's electric power industry.

POSTWAR CHANGES

The Council for Reorganization of Electric Utility Industry was formed in 1949 and chaired by Yasuza-

KEY DATES

1911: Japan enacts the Electric Utility Industry Law.

1948: General Headquarters of the Allied powers creates nine regionally based electricity generation and distribution companies.

1951: SEPCO is incorporated to provide power to the island of Shikoku.

1978: Ikata Nuclear Power Plant goes online.

1995: Japan partially liberalizes its electricity market.

2000: Deregulation begins in the retail sector of Japan's electric power industry.

2008: SEPCO acquires a 5 percent stake in the Ras Laffan C power and desalination project in Qatar.

2011: Great East Japan Earthquake and tsunami leads to a radiation leak at the Fukushima Daiichi Nuclear Power Station.

2012: Ikata Nuclear Power Plant is forced to close as Japan begins to examine its nuclear power program.

emon Matsunaga, former president of Toho Electric Power Company. After much negotiation, a plan was produced that divided the country into nine areas, each with its own privately owned EPC. Thus the Shikoku Electric Power Company was formed, with initial capitalization of ¥400 million ($1.1 million).

The first chairman was Yoichi Takeoka, who was formally in charge of Takamatsu Electric Light Company. Takeoka began a consolidation of SEPCO's facilities and the company embarked on an immediate expansion program. Just two months after the company's establishment, work began on a hydroelectric facility on the Kuro River. Like the rest of Japan, much of the center of Shikoku is mountainous and thus a good source of hydroelectric power, on which most of Shikoku's power facilities at this time operated. The company began to promote the use of electric power in the more rural areas that had previously been uneconomical markets for the smaller utilities in Shikoku.

The central headquarters were rationalized and divisions between the regional offices abolished. Pensions, health care, and insurance were offered on an equal basis to all company employees. Some of the less modern generating facilities were closed and replaced with more efficient plants, with more thermal facilities being built. A listing on the Osaka Stock Exchange in October 1952

was followed by a Tokyo listing in May 1953. By the end of 1953 customer service branches were established in all the major towns of Shikoku, and the capitalization of the company had trebled to ¥1.19 billion.

Also in this year, a pioneering automatic combustion control system was installed on all of SEPCO's transmission and generating equipment to regulate the amount of fuel burned and hence save energy. This was followed in the 1950s and early 1960s with a series of technological upgrades. Emphasis was also placed on the training of staff and customers in the safe use of electrical equipment. As a result, Shikoku had the lowest electricity-related accident rate in the country.

NUCLEAR BEGINNINGS: 1956

In 1956 company president Chikuma Miyagawa initiated research into the use of nuclear power by the company. SEPCO was at this time the most advanced of Japan's nine regional electric utility companies with regards to nuclear power. By 1985 nuclear energy had become the dominant source of power in Shikoku, accounting for 39 percent of the total, and was expected to rise to 50 percent by 2000.

Realizing that the potential of hydroelectric power in the region was ultimately limited, a section was created within the company in 1956 devoted to the development of coal, gas, and oil-fired power. In order to keep abreast of the latest technology in electric power generation, SEPCO sent its chief engineers and planning officers to Europe and the United States on conferences, training courses, and exchange programs. This was typical of Japanese industry at the time, which was desperate for the technological knowledge that it saw as the key to success.

During this period, the company began in earnest the process of closing down redundant transformer substations and replacing them with a smaller number of higher voltage, more efficient units. Also in 1956 by boosting the existing capacity of Hirayama Power Station by 470 kW to 2,900 kW, SEPCO came to own the largest hydroelectric facility in the country and in 1959 began operating the country's first reverse wheel hydroelectric plant, the 11,800-kW facility on Omori River.

The year 1958 saw changes in the organization of the company, with increasing centralization of planning, engineering, and sales operations. In 1960 Miyazawa took over as chairman of the company, which by this time was the largest company in Shikoku with a capitalization of $19 million. For the next decade, like the other EPCs in Japan, SEPCO concentrated on the building of oil-fired generating stations such as the

125-MW plant completed in Tokushima in 1963. Cheap and plentiful Middle Eastern oil and lax environmental controls at the time made this form of generation the most economically attractive.

IKATA NUCLEAR POWER PLANT GOES ONLINE IN 1978

The oil shocks of 1973 and 1978 and increasing emission control quotas changed all this, however, and SEPCO's main priority following these events was the development and construction of a nuclear power station. With technological help from and cooperation with France's nuclear power program, as well as the other domestic companies, Ikata Nuclear Power Plant was completed in 1978 with two initial pressurized water reactors and a combined output of almost 1,200 MW, with an additional 890 MW planned for 1995. Japan's nuclear program was a sensitive public issue and therefore extremely stringent safety controls were laid down. Japan's nuclear energy safety record was one of the world's best at the time, and SEPCO had the additional distinction of operating the world's most efficient reactor.

During the 1970s SEPCO's sales trebled, and although the company's work force remained fairly steady at about 5,000, its revenues and profits increased dramatically. These profits were spent almost entirely on capital investment and research. In the early 1980s, plans for the largest bridge in the world, to link Shikoku with the main island of Honshu, were drawn up. The impressive Seto bridge was completed in 1988 at a cost of about ¥1.13 trillion and had the important effect of creating a tourist boom and urban renewal in the area. For the company, not only did the Seto bridge bring in more business, it could also be used to carry a major trunkline connecting the company with Kansai Electric Power's grid.

The late 1980s saw a slowdown in growth as SEPCO's market matured. To some extent, the company diversified into new areas such as telecommunications with the formation of Shikoku Information & Telecommunication Network and the production of electric power equipment with Techno-Success Company. At the time, it was unlikely that these ventures would contribute significantly to profits and the firm's main emphasis remained on the continued development of the electric power market. Some examples of the company's efforts in this area were the all-electric house, increased customer service, and the application of the hourly rate fluctuation system.

On the international scene, the company continued to exchange information with similar companies worldwide and was a founding member of the World Association of Nuclear Operators formed in 1989. As most of the company's crucial raw materials came from abroad, a tight check was kept on commodity prices, and long-term purchase agreements such as those for uranium from France and Australia were entered into. Financially, the company was in an excellent position, holding a Triple A rating with regard to raising money on the domestic bond market. Overseas, the company conducted two bond issues in Europe in 1989.

To mark the 40th year of business as SEPCO, the company in 1991 launched a new corporate profile based on the environmentally safe and efficient generation of power along with increased provision for the development of customer services related to the core business of power generation.

DEREGULATION BEGINS: 1990–99

In the years leading up to the new century, Shikoku Electric faced a host of challenges brought on by liberalization in Japan's energy sectors. By the mid-1990s, the electricity industry in Japan was undergoing major changes. In 1995 adjustments to the Electricity Utilities Industry Law allowed competition to enter into the electricity generation and supply market. Then, in 1996, a wholesale electric power bidding system enabled nonelectric power companies to sell electricity to electric power companies. Finally, in March 2000, the retail sale of electricity was partially deregulated, allowing large-lot customers, or those demanding large amounts of electricity, to choose their power supplier.

The intent of deregulation was to foster competition, which in turn would lower the electricity costs in the country. The deregulation was slow to change the Japanese industry, however, and during 2001 SEPCO and the nine other regional companies still controlled 99 percent of the market. In fact, only six Japanese-based companies other than the original 10 supplied power to large customers such as retail stores and office buildings. This accounted for a .2 percent share of the overall market.

Nevertheless, SEPCO and its domestic peers were forced to deal with the changes brought on by deregulation. The electric companies were also pushed to seek out and develop environmentally friendly power sources. According to a March 2000 *Business Week* article, nuclear power accounted for nearly 35 percent of Japan's electricity. For much of the 1990s Japan's industry had aggressively focused on shifting from expensive and polluting coal-fired plants to nuclear power. Due to rising concerns over the safety of these nuclear facilities, Japan's government was forced to rethink its expansion efforts, cut back on its nuclear development plans, and find alternative sources of power.

As such, SEPCO worked not only to diversify its holdings in response to the changing business environment but also looked for new alternative methods for generating power. Believing that competition could eventually wreak havoc on its bottom line, the company moved into new business areas, including Internet access, cable television, real estate, engineering, aviation, and energy equipment manufacturing. Cable Media Shikoku Company Inc., a cable television broadcasting and telecommunications subsidiary, was established in 1995. The following year, Netwave Shikoku Company Inc. was created to oversee Internet provider services. The firm also set up subsidiaries related to video production, nursing facilities, and forestation.

MOVING INTO THE NEW MILLENNIUM

While SEPCO set new strategies in place, it faced yet another challenge. During the early years of the new century, Japan's economy was faltering. Demand from steel and manufacturing sectors fell, and in fiscal 2002 electricity sales were lackluster at best. The company's operating revenue fell in 2002 and again in 2003. In order to shore up profits, SEPCO focused on several key initiatives including providing enhanced customer service and consulting services, continual diversification in the energy and telecommunication fields, streamlining costs, and restructuring its businesses into a divisional system.

Over the next several years, SEPCO continued to restructure operations while focusing on new growth areas. Challenges continued as Japan's population was aging, its economy slowing, and its consumers seeking out energy-efficient technologies. With demand in its domestic market weakening, the company looked for growth opportunities abroad.

As part of its international strategy, SEPCO entered the Middle East and Southeast Asia through several independent power producer projects. The company acquired a 5 percent stake in the Ras Laffan C power and desalination project in Qatar in 2008, marking its first investment in an overseas power project. Ras Laffan C went online in 2011. The Barka 3 Project and the Sohar 2 Project began commercial natural gas operations in Oman in April 2013.

OVERCOMING CHALLENGES: 2011–14

While the company worked to diversify its energy portfolio, it remained highly dependent upon its nuclear operations. This dependency proved challenging in the coming years. The Great East Japan Earthquake and tsunami in March 2011 led to radioactive leaks at the Fukushima Daiichi Nuclear Power Station, which was operated by Tokyo Electric Power Co. Inc. As a result of the disaster, Japan began to overhaul its nuclear program and ordered a shutdown of all nuclear reactors. By 2013 Japan was operating without nuclear power.

Before 2011 Japanese reactors provided approximately one-third of the nation's electricity. Without nuclear power, utility firms in Japan were scrambling to provide adequate supply, turning to natural gas and other sources of power. SEPCO saw its profits tumble and quickly set out to streamline operations while applying for a rate increase in February 2013. "With all of our reactors offline, we have made various efforts to cut costs, but the increasing fuel outlays (for nonnuclear thermal power generation) have not been at a level that can be absorbed by such efforts," explained SEPCO president Akira Chiba in a February 2013 *Japan Energy Scan* article.

As of September 2014 Japan's Nuclear Regulation Authority had yet to allow SEPCO's Ikata Nuclear Power Plant to resume operations. By this time, SEPCO had spent nearly $840 million to ensure Ikata met with new safety standards. Company management hoped nuclear activity would resume in the near future.

Meanwhile, Japan's plans for deregulation of its retail electric power sector continued. Deregulation efforts continued to focus on integration of the country's power grid and the establishment of a national transmission oversight entity. Plans to open the market in order to allow consumers to choose their providers were in the works and eventually, Japan's utility firms would be forced to separate power generation and transmission operations. This process was expected to be finalized between 2018 and 2020.

Although the early years of the new millennium proved to be the most challenging period in SEPCO's history, the company was confident in its ability to move forward. As one of Japan's original regional electric utilities, the company stood well positioned to face future obstacles head on.

Dylan Tanner
Updated, Christina M. Stansell

PRINCIPAL SUBSIDIARIES

Shikoku Research Institute Inc.; Yondenko Corporation; Yonden Engineering Company, Inc.; Yonden Consultants Company, Inc.; Shihen Technical Corporation; Shikoku Instrumentation Co., Ltd.; Techno-Success Company, Inc.; Eco-Tech Company, Inc.; Stnet, Inc.;

Cable Media Shikoku Company, Inc.; Cable Television Tokushima, Inc.; Shikoku Air Service Co., Ltd.; Yonden Energy Services Company, Inc.; Ikata Service Company, Inc.; Tachibana Thermal Power Port Service Company, Limited; Sakaide LNG Company, Inc.; Tosa Power, Inc.; Misaki Wind Power Co., Ltd.; Okawara Windfarm Corporation; Ei Wind Power Company, Inc.; Yonden Business Company, Inc.; Yonden Media Works Company, Inc.; Yonden Life Care Company, Inc.; Utazu Kyushoku Service Co., Ltd.; Tokushimaichiko PFI Service Co., Ltd.; SEP International Netherlands B.V.

PRINCIPAL COMPETITORS

The Kansai Electric Power Company Inc.; Nippon Telegraph and Telephone Corporation; The Tokyo Electric Power Company Inc.

FURTHER READING

"Another Japanese Utility Applies for Electricity Rate Hike." *Japan Energy Scan*, February 25, 2013.

Bremner, Brian. "Tokyo's Nuclear Dilemma." *Business Week*, March 15, 2000.

"Ehime Residents Lose Lawsuit over Nuke-Plant Red Tape." *Japan Economic Newswire*, February 9, 2001.

Goto, Yasuhiro. "No Single Recipe for Deregulation of Utilities." *Nikkei Weekly*, March 5, 2001.

History of the Electric Power Industry in Japan. Tokyo: Japan Electric Power Information Center, 1989.

Humber, Yuriy. "Nuclear Power-Less Japan Must Pay for Fuel Imports in Weak Yen." *Business Week*, September 18, 2014.

"Japan Power Firms Pressed for Decision on Aging N-Reactors." *Jiji Press English News Service*, September 9, 2014.

"Nuclear Industry Seeks to Regain Public Trust." *Yomiuri Shimbun/Daily Yomiuri*, November 1, 2003.

"Shikoku Electric Power President Akira Chiba: The Merits of Small." *Electric Daily News*, July 3, 2009.

"Shikoku Electric Sets Up Tree-Planting Firm in Australia." *Jiji Press Ticker Service*, April 7, 2000.

Shoghakn CJSC

Torozyan Street
Nor Hajn Village, 0519
Armenia
Telephone: (374) 010 28 25 92
Fax: (374) 010 28 17 69
Web site: http://www.shoghakn.am

Private Company
Incorporated: 1992
Employees: 1,000
NAICS: 339910 Jewelry and Silverware Manufacturing

■ ■ ■

Shoghakn CJSC is one of the leaders of Armenia's diamond-cutting industry. Founded in the early 1970s, Shoghakn employs 1,200 workers, approximately 90 percent of whom are highly skilled and specialized craftspeople. The company processes up to 30,000 carats of cut diamonds per year, with a diamond yield rate of 40 percent. The company has the capability of cutting diamonds up to five carats in size. Shoghakn focuses entirely on the processing of natural rough diamonds, imported from Russia and elsewhere. The company produces two main categories of diamonds, round diamonds, consisting of a total of 57 facets, and fantasy diamonds, including such cuts as princess, oval, marquise, heart, pear, and baguette shapes. Shoghakn has invested in modern and sophisticated diamond-cutting equipment, incorporating computerized magnification and laser-cutting systems. Much of this equipment was put into place by the company's former

owner, LLD Diamonds Ltd., led by Israeli diamond magnate Lev Leviev.

PRECIOUS STONES INDUSTRY

Armenia held a particular place in the Soviet Union's industrialization efforts. Annexed, along with its Caucasus neighbors, by the Soviet Union in the 1920s, Armenia had already become a major center for industrial investment by the 1930s. The Armenian population itself earned a reputation as hardworking and particularly capable of performing tasks requiring a high degree of precision.

This reputation played a role in the decision by the Soviet government to establish one of the Soviet Union's main centers of precious stone production in Armenia in the 1950s. The construction of Armenia's first large-scale hydroelectric power plant project, known as the Sevan-Hrazdan Cascade, played its own part in the development of this industry.

BUILDING OF POWER PLANT

Construction of the project, consisting of seven hydroelectric power plants situated downstream from Lake Sevan along the Hrazdan River, began in 1936. By the middle of the 1950s the project had reached the area known as Nor Hakn (also transliterated as Hajin or Hakin), with the construction of the Arzni hydroelectric station. The project also included the construction of the Arzni-Shamiram canal.

The commissioning of the power plant in 1956 was accompanied by the creation of a new village, named

COMPANY PERSPECTIVES

The leader of the diamond industry of Armenia, Shoghakn CJSC, is known as a first-rate enterprise in the diamond industry of Armenia.

Nor Hakn, or New Hakn, in commemoration of the village of Hakn, located in the Cilicia region, which had been the site of a battle between Armenians and Turkish forces in 1909. That village had been one of the few in the region to resist the Turkish massacres of the Armenian population during this period.

The existence of the hydroelectric power plant had opened up the potential for new industrial investments. The creation of Nor Hakn came as part of government plans to establish the area as one of the centers of the Soviet precious stones industry. This effort began in 1958, when Ashot Harutyunyan, then a young engineer, began construction of the town's first factory.

The new facility became known as Sapfir Production Company. Initially it specialized in processing sapphires and other gemstones. The Sapfir factory, which later employed some 5,000 people, played a prominent role in the growth of Nor Hakn itself, as the town grew to a population of more than 10,000 residents.

DIAMONDS IN 1971

Harutyunyan's success in building Sapfir caught the attention of Soviet authorities. Into the beginning of the 1970s the Communist Party's Central Committee, led in Armenia by Anton Kochinyan, decided to expand the factory's range of capabilities into the still-more lucrative diamond sector. The first shipments of Russian rough diamonds arrived at the factory soon after. By March 1971 Sapfir had already begun shipping the first Armenian-cut diamonds back to Russia.

By the middle of the decade Sapfir, and Nor Hakn in general, had already succeeded in becoming a main center for diamond processing in the Soviet Union. This position was further underscored with the construction of a new dedicated diamond factory, originally known as the Crystal diamond factory, in 1976. The factory began operating by 1981, and it later became known as Shoghakn.

The success of this facility led to the creation of a number of other diamond-processing plants in the town. At its height, the Nor Hakn diamond industry counted as many as 200 diamond-cutting workshops.

Shoghakn remained by far the largest, employing more than 1,800 workers and producing as much as 100,000 carats of diamonds each year. All of the factory's production was then shipped back to Russia.

RUN BY SOVIET GUIDELINES

Like many Soviet businesses, the factory's operations were less than efficient. The factory was guaranteed a market for its production, regardless of the cost of production. Soviet policies reinforced these operating inefficiencies. Employment was considered one of the basic rights of any Soviet citizen. Industries were also encouraged to place production levels above profits.

As a result, the Shoghakn factory's payroll swelled. By the collapse of the Soviet Union at the end of the 1980s, Shoghakn employed many more people than was necessary. The factory's accounting department, for example, employed more than 50 accountants.

Altogether, the factory employed more than 500 managers and other administrative staff. In this, the company represented another less-appealing side of Soviet life, in that many of these managers were in fact representatives of the Communist Party and members of its secret police.

INDEPENDENT IN 1992

The inefficiencies of the Shoghakn factory, and of parent company Sapfir Production Company, were to come to haunt the company into the 1990s. Armenia itself faced a dramatic reversal of fortunes, starting from the late 1980s. The country was devastated by a major earthquake, measuring 6.9 on the Richter scale, in 1988. The resulting destruction left 25,000 people dead and more than 500,000 homeless. Fears of a Chernobyl-like disaster soon forced the shutdown of Armenia's only nuclear power plant, in Metsamor, the following year.

Armenia suddenly went from a power exporter to becoming heavily reliant on the Hrazdan Thermal Power Plant, the country's only large-scale fossil fuel–based plant. The Hrazdan facility, however, was itself wholly dependent on fuel imports, primarily through neighbor Azerbaijan, for its operations. With the crumbling of the Soviet Empire, however, long-simmering tensions between Armenia and Azerbaijan, primarily centered on the Nagorno-Karabakh region of the latter country, came into the open.

By 1992 the two countries were at war. As a result, Azerbaijan, supported by Turkey, imposed a blockade on imports of oil and gas to Armenia. The country was forced to shut down the Hrazdan Thermal Power Plant. With only the Sevan-Hrazdan Cascade hydroelectric

KEY DATES

1958: Sapfir Production Company is founded in Nor Hakn, Armenia.
1971: Sapfir begins diamond-cutting operations.
1992: Shoghakn becomes an independent company.
2000: LLD Diamonds Ltd., owned by Lev Leviev, acquires Shoghakn.
2010: Another Leviev company forms a joint venture sourcing diamonds from Shoghakn.
2014: Company is acquired by a group of investors through Arister Solutions.

power plants in operation, Armenia experienced severe and widespread power shortages. At its lowest point, the population received power for only an hour or two each day. Like the rest of Armenia's industries, Sapfir and its Shoghakn factory struggled to remain in operation.

In the meantime, the newly elected democratic government began carrying out a series of reforms in preparation for the country's transition to a market-oriented economy. As part of this effort, the government began a restructuring of its industrial operations ahead of their later privatization. Among them, the Shoghakn factory was separated from Sapfir and reincorporated as an independent company, Shoghakn CJSC, in 1992.

STRUGGLING IN THE NINETIES

Shoghakn remained entirely focused on diamond processing. The new company made an attempt to expand these operations. Shoghakn had long specialized in the production of round cut diamonds, a specific type of diamond featuring a total of 57 facets, with 32 facets on the diamonds upper part, and 24 on the lower part. In 1992 the company extended its capacity to include a second category of diamonds known as fantasy diamonds.

These included a larger variety of diamond cuts, including many of the most well-known types of diamonds, such as the marquise, princess, oval, and pear-shaped diamonds. Shoghakn also took steps to address the inefficiencies of its Soviet past. A new director, Gagik Abrahamian, was appointed director general of the company. An electrical engineer, Abrahamian had no prior experience in the diamond trade.

Nonetheless, he took steps toward restructuring the company. Among the first steps of the restructuring was the dismissal of more than 500 of the company's employees, including much of its managerial staff. The company's accounting department, for example, was trimmed down to just two accountants, who were then equipped with computing technology. Armenia's independence, however, nearly spelled the end of Shoghakn as it struggled to make a fresh start.

VARTKESS KNADJIAN SAVES COMPANY

With the separation from the Soviet Union and with the blockade imposed on the country's most prominent trade route to Russia, Shoghakn found itself cut off from its primary source of rough diamonds. Russia cut off its diamond shipments to Armenia completely in 1993. Shoghakn might have folded altogether were it not for the assistance of Vartkess Knadjian.

A diamond dealer based in Antwerp, Belgium, itself one of the world's diamond-trading centers, Knadjian was part of the large Armenian diaspora, which numbered as many as eight million people, compared to fewer than three million citizens in Armenia itself. Knadjian began working with Abrahamian, sharing his strong background in the diamond trade. Knadjian also set himself up as an important ambassador for Shoghakn and the Nor Hakn diamond industry in general.

Although Nor Hakn had been one of the most important suppliers of cut diamonds to the Soviet Union, the town remained more or less unknown outside of the union. Knadjian helped place Abrahamian in contact with South African diamond giant De Beers. Abrahamian traveled to De Beers's office in London for the first time in 1993 and succeeded in persuading De Beers to send a team of technicians to inspect the Shoghakn plant.

DE BEERS CONTRACT IN 1995

By 1995 Shoghakn had succeeded in winning De Beers's confidence. The South African diamond leader began shipping its first rough diamonds to Armenia that year. Within three years, the factory had already succeeded in processing $40 million worth of De Beers's diamonds, which were then shipped to Western Europe for sale. Shoghakn also expanded during this time, adding a second workshop in Stepanakert, the capital of the Nagorno-Karabakh region.

This workshop also allowed the company to skirt the Azeri-Turk blockade of Armenia, which remained in place through the next decades. The contract with De Beers coincided with the restarting of the Metsamor nuclear power plant in 1995. This enabled Armenia not only to pull itself out of its years of economic turmoil but also to emerge as one of the most dynamic of the former Soviet satellite economies at the dawn of the 21st century. In the meantime, Shoghakn's success had inspired a growing number of competitors in Nor Hakn.

Like Shoghakn, this new generation of diamond cutters found partners in the West. Among them, were such companies as Lori Ltd., founded as the first privately owned diamond factory in Armenia, as a subsidiary of Belgium's Arslanian Cutting Work. While this company also benefited from contacts within the Armenian diaspora, others reflected the growing interest of the international market in investing in the country's future.

DIAMOND COMPANY BECOMES RIVAL

In 1998, for example, Shoghakn found itself with a new rival, Diamond Company of Armenia, founded by U.K.-based Ferfano Corporation. The appearance of Diamond Company of Armenia proved a double blow for the company, as Abrahamian left Shoghakn to take over as head of its new rival. Another Belgian company, Rosy Blue, entered Nor Hakn at this time, setting up the Diamond Tech company. Rosy Blue promised to raise its payroll to 1,500 by 2003.

Nor Hakn also attracted interest from another of the world's leading diamond centers, Israel. The first Israeli company to arrive in town was the Tasche Company, which took over the Arevakn diamond processing plant. Although Armenia's economic situation slowly improved through the second half of the decade, Shoghakn's once again faced uncertain times.

The company was affected on the one hand by the continued difficulties of ensuring its raw diamond supply. On the other, the company struggled to compete against its fast-growing rivals. As a result, Shoghakn nearly collapsed once again, shrinking back to just 200 employees at the end of the decade.

NEW OWNER IN 2000

The company's fortunes rose once again, however, with the arrival of a new Israeli investor. In 2000 LLD Diamonds Ltd. paid $370,000 to acquire Shoghakn. LLD was owned by Lev Leviev (also transliterated as Levaev), born in Tashkent, Uzbekistan, in 1956. Leviev's father had been a prominent member of the region's Hasidic Jewish community, while also working as a diamond trader.

In 1971 the family managed to escape from the Soviet Union after Leviev's father was accused of il-

legally smuggling antiques and other goods. Leviev, then 15, took up an apprenticeship at the Zotar diamond-cutting workshop in Kiryat-Malachi. After completing his military service, Leviev married and began his own diamond trading business. In this he was helped by his father-in-law, a successful diamond trader in his own right.

By the middle of the 1980s Leviev had already become one of Israel's diamond industry leaders. Leviev then began his ascension into the world diamond rankings, notably by becoming De Beers's main representative for the Russian, Israeli, Belgian, and Irish markets, starting in 1986. In 1989 Leviev was tapped to become the joint venture partner for the first private diamond business in the Soviet Union as well. Into the 1990s Leviev took sole control of that company.

DE BEERS RELATIONSHIP ENDS: 1995

Leviev broke off his relationship with De Beers in 1995. Instead, in partnership with Bank Leumi, he carried out a major coup, taking control of the holding company Africa-Israel in 1997. That company then began acquiring stakes in a number of major diamond mining businesses in Angola, Namibia, and elsewhere. Leviev also focused on building up an integrated diamond business, adding a string of diamond cutting and polishing companies in India, China, Angola, Russia, and Ukraine.

This latter activity brought Leviev to Nor Hakn, which by then had already acquired a strong reputation for the high quality of its diamond workers. Following its purchase of Shoghakn, LLD invested heavily in modernizing and expanding the factory, with a goal of raising its total production to as high as 30,000 carats per month.

By 2002 the company had already succeeded in raising its capacity to 12,000 carats per month. By the middle of the decade the company not only reached its target but nearly doubled its goal, reaching 50,000 carats per month. The company payroll grew as well, once again reaching more than 1,800 employees by 2007.

SURVIVING A NEW CRISIS

Shoghakn had once again asserted itself as Armenia's leading diamond processor, accounting for 35 percent of the country's total output. The company's success proved short-lived, however. Into the second half of the decade the company, as well as the rest of the Armenian diamond industry, found itself sinking amid the growing volatility of both the diamond and currency markets.

As a result, the Armenian industry found itself unable to compete against lower-priced foreign competitors in Asia and elsewhere. Shoghakn was forced to cut its production to fewer than 4,000 carats per month, laying off all but 300 of its employees. The company's troubles were compounded the following year. In September 2007 the Armenian government had reached a supply agreement with Alrosa, the leading Russian diamond miner, which controlled roughly 27 percent of the world diamond supply.

As part of that agreement, the Armenian government offered significant tax incentives, including a reduction in import duties. This deal placed Alrosa in trouble with the Russian customs service. As a result, Alrosa suspended its shipments of raw diamonds to Armenia in the spring of 2008. The sudden loss of this crucial rough diamond supply came at the worst possible time for the Nor Hakn diamond industry, as the world entered the deepest economic crisis since the Great Depression.

SUCCESSFUL JOINT VENTURE: 2010

The Shoghakn factory was forced to shut down the remainder of its operations, as Leviev shifted his global diamond empire elsewhere. New hope for the factory came in 2010, however. In October of that year another Leviev company, LGC Holdings, formed a marketing and distribution joint venture with M. Fabrikant & Sons for the production of round, brilliant-cut diamonds. Shoghakn's state-of-the-art facility became a supplier to the joint venture, called Brilliant Trading.

With the new deal, Shoghakn once again rebuilt its business, soon reaching production volumes of 25,000–30,000 carats per month. The revived company soon rebuilt its workforce as well to 1,200 employees. With its operations once again growing, Shoghakn also came under new ownership. This occurred in 2014, when a group of investors formed a buyout company, called Arister Solutions, to take over the company. Shoghakn CJSC hoped for a sparkling future as it rebuilt its position as Armenia's diamond-cutting leader in the 21st century.

M. L. Cohen

PRINCIPAL DIVISIONS

Round Diamonds; Fantasy Diamonds.

PRINCIPAL COMPETITORS

Arevakn LLC; Arslanian Cutting Works; Dimotech CJSC; Lori CJSC.

FURTHER READING

Armanakyan, Nazik, and Gayane Abrahamyan. "Armenia Hopes to Become Glittering Gateway for Russian Diamonds." *Eurasia.net*, September 19, 2014.

"Armenia to Increase Polished Production to $400 Million within Three Years." *Israel Diamonds*, February 2004.

"Armenian Shoghakn Diamond Company Reduces Its Monthly Output from 25thnd Carats to 3 or 4 Thousand." *Arka*, November 8, 2007.

Danielyan, Emil. "Yerevan Vows to Shore Up Ailing Diamond Industry." *Arka*, December 2, 2009.

Hakobyan, Tatul. "A Visit to New Hajin." *Arka*, April 18, 2009.

"M. Fabrikant & Sons and Lev Leviev Form Joint Venture." *JewelCAD Design*, October 11, 2012.

Soprema S.A.S.

———————————■———————————

BP 121, 14 rue de Saint Nazaire
Strasbourg, 67100 Cedex 1
France
Telephone: (+33 3) 88 79 84 00
Fax: (+33 3) 88 79 84 01
Web site: http://www.soprema.fr

Private Company
Incorporated: 1941 as Société des Produits et Revête-
    ments d'Etanchéité Mammouth (Soprema)
Employees: 5,200
Sales: EUR 1.81 billion ($2.34 billion) (2013)
NAICS: 324122 Asphalt Shingle and Coating Materials
    Manufacturing; 325520 Adhesive and Sealant
    Manufacturing; 238160 Roofing Contractors

■ ■ ■

Soprema S.A.S. is one of the world's largest and most
innovative developers, producers, and installers of roofing, waterproofing, and insulation systems. The
company operates on an international basis, with 60
subsidiaries in 51 countries providing services to more
than 90 countries. In order to be close to its markets,
Soprema has built a network of 34 factories, including
17 waterproofing plants and 6 insulation factories, as
well as specialized factories producing smoke extraction
systems, steel frames, and geotextiles. Soprema's service
network includes 31 civil engineering and installation
offices, 7 research and development facilities, and 18
training centers. The company has been providing
waterproofing and roofing systems for several major

projects worldwide, including the Eiffel Tower, the
European Parliament in Strasbourg, and the Pentagon in
the United States. Soprema is a privately owned
company, led by its majority shareholder and president
Pierre-Etienne Bindschedler, great-grandson of the
company's founder. Soprema employs more than 5,200
people and generated sales of EUR 1.8 billion ($2.34
billion) in 2013.

MAMMOUTH IDEA IN 1909

Although Charles Geisen started his professional life as a
Latin teacher in Alsace (the hotly disputed, coal-rich
region on the border between France and Germany), he
possessed a broad range of interests. Among them was
science and, in particular, the new chemicals and related
technologies emerging in the early years of the 20th
century. He was interested in securing patents in this
field, and his focus turned to the market for natural
asphalt and coal tar–based bitumen. Long used as roofing and waterproofing materials for terraces and the like,
these materials had become the focus of several new
developments at the turn of the century.

In 1908 Geisen teamed up with a local chemist to
found his own bitumen company, called Usines Alsaciennes d'Emulsions, in Strasbourg. The company set out
to develop and patent its own bitumen-based
waterproofing processes. The company started by
concocting its own range of waterproofing emulsions
and mastic pastes. The application of these waterproofing materials was a messy process, as well as both
extremely time-consuming and labor-intensive. Applying
these coatings to the steeply sloped rooftops in the

snowy Alsace region was especially difficult, and often led to less than reliable results.

Geisen set out to improve the waterproofing process. His moment of inspiration came in 1909, when he recognized the potential for impregnating cloth or another type of material with bitumen, thereby creating a flexible, easy-to-apply waterproofing layer. Geisen soon hit on the use of burlap, made from jute. The highly porous fabric easily absorbed the heated bitumen solution, while the fabric's coarseness reinforced the bitumen's adherence. Burlap also provided superior strength while remaining lightweight. Once cured, the bitumen-jute membrane remained both highly flexible and waterproof, and could easily be rolled out onto rooftops, terraces, and other surfaces.

The discovery of the well-preserved remains of a woolly mammoth in Berezovka, Siberia, provided the name for the new product. Geisen called the new material Mammouth, the French word for "mammoth," to underscore the products superior resistance to the elements. Mammouth became an immediate success, not only in Alsace, but throughout much of the region and beyond. The company also developed a strong expertise in applying the material, allowing it to tackle a number of prominent projects. Among these was the waterproofing of the Viaduc de Langwiese, an important bridge along the Coire-Arose railroad line in Switzerland in 1912. This project later served to underscore the superior resistance of the Mammouth membrane: the covering easily passed inspection nearly 100 years later, requiring no significant intervention.

NEW GENERATION IN 1933

Geisen's company experienced the first of several upheavals. With the outbreak of World War I, the Alsace region, then under German administration, became hostile territory for its French population. In order to preserve his business, Geisen moved to Zurich, Switzerland, founding a new company, Asphalt Emulsion Zurich in 1914. Germany's defeat in 1918 returned the Alsace region to French control. Geisen returned to

Strasbourg that same year, restarting the Usines Alsaciennes d'Emulsions.

Geisen was joined in the business by his son, Pierre Geisen, who had graduated with an engineering degree from the École Centrale des Arts et Manufactures. Geisen took over from his father in 1933, and soon put his engineering background to work on improving the design of its core Mammouth product. The company soon achieved a new breakthrough, with the application of a thin layer of aluminum foil to the Mammouth membrane. The foil layer helped overcome some of the limitations of the original membrane, providing superior resistance to variations in temperature, as well as to weather conditions. The metal layer also provided protection against damaging ultraviolet rays. As a result, the new Mammouth Alu offered still longer-term waterproofing and protection.

The outbreak of World War II, Germany's annexation of Alsace, and its occupation of France forced the Geisen family to move once again. In 1941 Pierre Geisen shifted the company's base to the so-called Unoccupied Zone, also known as Vichy France, named for the administrative capital of the French regime led by Philippe Pétain. Geisen set up shop in Avignon, and opened a new factory under the name of Société des Produits et Revêtements d'Étanchiété Mammouth (SOPREMA).

While the Soprema name proved long lasting, the Avignon factory did not. By the end of the war Allied bombing raids had reduced the site to ruins. Geisen found himself obliged to rebuild the company from scratch. Starting with just two employees, Geisen returned to Strasbourg, laying the foundation for the present-day Soprema.

INNOVATIONS IN THE SEVENTIES

Soprema grew strongly in the postwar era, with its business driven by France's reconstruction effort. The company further benefited from France's robust building sector as the country experience a sustained economic boom through the 1960s. The strong demand for waterproofing products brought the company to the Paris region in the early 1960s. For this, Soprema recognized the advantages of moving closer to the market, opening the first of its extended network of production plants in Louviers, near Paris, in 1962. This also gave the company greater access to the Normandy refinery sector, helping to trim transport costs. The company later added two more factories in France.

Through the 1960s Soprema also took the lead in seeking new waterproofing materials. The company established its own research and development laboratory,

KEY DATES

1908: Charles Geisen founds Usines Alsaciennes d'Emulsions in Strasbourg.

1909: Geisen invents the Mammouth waterproofing membrane.

1933: Pierre Geisen takes over the enterprise from his father.

1941: Geisen establishes Société des Produits et Revêtements d'Étanchiété Mammouth (Soprema).

1962: Company begins building a production network, adding a factory in Louviers, near Paris.

1975: Company introduces its new generation waterproofing membrane, Soprolene.

1992: Pierre-Etienne Bindschedler, grandson of Pierre Geisen, takes over the company.

2006: Soprema acquires Germany's Klewa.

2013: Bindschedler is named Ernst & Young's Entrepreneur of the Year.

and began exploring the use of synthetic textiles, including fiberglass-based textiles. The development of SBS Modified Bitumen by Shell Chemical in the late 1960s provided another important breakthrough for the waterproofing industry. The new bitumen included an added polymer, styrene butadiene styrene (SBS), which provided superior binding of the oil present in bitumen. The resulting emulsion developed a structure more similar to rubber, and shared many similar properties, such as greater flexibility at low temperatures, greater resistance to high temperatures, and improved elasticity and recovery. SBS bitumen also provided greater resistance to aging.

Soprema set to work developing a method for adapting SBS bitumen to its own membrane production. As part of this effort, the company also began experimenting with new compositions for its reinforcing mats. This effort paid off in 1975, when the company released the industry's first SBS bitumen-based waterproofing membrane, called Soprolene. The new membrane incorporated a reinforcing mat composed of a blend of nonwoven polyester and fiberglass.

INTERNATIONAL GROWTH IN THE EIGHTIES

Sopralene's success enabled Soprema to expand beyond France, as the company built up strong exports to other

European markets and to North America. Demand proved especially strong from French-speaking Canada, and in 1978 the company set up its first international subsidiary, in Quebec. Initially established as a sales office, the Canadian subsidiary quickly expanded its role. The company began working with Canada's National Research Council to develop a new air/vapor barrier seal, extending Soprema's technology from the rooftop to the building envelope.

The new product debuted as Sopraseal 180 in 1981. The following year, Soprema's Canadian operation also introduced a line of waterproofing products for such applications as parking deck and building foundations. By 1984 Soprema raised its Canadian presence to the next level, opening a factory in Drummondville, Quebec, that year. By then too the global success of Sopralene enabled the company to expand into a number of new markets, including Switzerland, the United Kingdom, the Benelux markets, and Spain. The company also began expanding its sales into the United States during the decade.

Despite its success, Soprema began to run out of steam toward the end of the decade. In particular, the company had been outpaced in its main French market, ranking only third in the country. The company was especially hard hit by the collapse of the building market, which followed on the stock market crash of 1987, and led the world into a major recession into the beginning of the 1990s. In 1989 Pierre Geisen, who remained at the head of the company, called in his then 29-year-old grandson, Pierre-Etienne Bindschedler, to help revitalize the company's growth.

THE BINDSCHEDLER ERA IN 1992

Bindschedler had grown up in Switzerland, and after earning a degree in business at the University of Lausanne had gone to work in the financial sector, where he specialized in mergers and acquisitions and business auditing. Bindschedler initially intended to remain for only two years with Soprema, and came only to help the company reorganize its flagging business. Instead, Bindschedler found himself at the center of a family conflict, pitting Pierre Geisen, then 83 years old, against other members of the family, who held minority shares in the company.

Bindschedler saw the potential for extending Soprema's technologies beyond its traditional waterproofing market. In 1989, for example, he led the company to develop a new generation of green terrace roofing systems, called Sopranature. For this, the company paired a waterproofing layer with a specially created growing medium. Covering rooftops with vegetation and gardens provided superior thermal and acoustic insulation to buildings, while also providing distinct environmental advantages.

Into the early 1990s Bindschedler became determined to take Soprema into new directions, and especially in developing new and more environmentally friendly waterproofing systems. Bindschedler also sought to extend the company's range of operations into new areas, including civil engineering and the design and installation of roofing systems, as well as related areas, such as insulation.

In 1992 Bindschedler made a bid to take over the company. Bindschedler managed to buy out the minority shareholders in the family by paying an inflated price for their shares. After a bitter battle with Pierre Geisen, Bindschedler managed to gain full control of the company. For this, Bindschedler had been forced to borrow from banks to buy out the rest of the family. It was to take him nearly 20 years to pay off this debt.

GLOBAL LEADER INTO THE TURN OF THE CENTURY

By then, Bindschedler had succeeded in transforming Soprema into one of the world's leading roofing systems and insulation companies. Soprema moved to build on its growing success in the United States, opening its first factory there in Wadsworth, Ohio, in 1993. The company also extended its reach across Canada, adding a second factory in Chilliwack, near Vancouver, in 2000.

Through the decade, the company continued to invest in developing new innovative products and systems. These included the Alsan range of liquid, polyurethane resin-based waterproofing systems, introduced in 1997. That range expanded in 1999 with Alsan Flashing, which could be applied without primer using a brush or roller. These products helped the company's sales increase from EUR 220 million in 1993 to more than EUR 400 million at the beginning of the next decade.

Acquisitions formed a major part of Soprema's growth strategy into the turn of the century. This phase started with the purchase of Antwerp, Belgium–based Bital, another waterproofing membrane specialist, in 2001. In that year also Soprema acquired 50 percent of Canadian roofing and insulation group Convoy. The company moved into Germany in 2006, buying that country's waterproofing membranes leader Klewa, based in Burbach. The following year, Soprema added another market, and another major brand, buying Italy's Flag, and its operations in Chignolo d'Isola and Villa S. Stefano. Also in 2007 the company acquired Netherlands-based Troelstra & Vries.

In 2006 Soprema reached a bitumen supply agreement with the Egyptian government, leading the company to build its first factory in the North African/ Middle East region, in Borg El Arab. The political turbulence in that country ultimately caught up to the company, however. Following the ouster of the Mubarak government, the newly elected Egyptian government discarded Soprema's original supply agreement, significantly raising the price of bitumen while also demanding the company cede ownership of 50 percent of the factory. In response, Soprema shut down the factory in 2011.

By then, however, Soprema's production network had already completed a major expansion, adding a factory in Gulfport, Mississippi, in 2008, and new factories in Poland and France, including a factory producing cellulose wadding in Cestas, near Bordeaux, in 2009. The later factory became part of Soprema's extension into the building insulation sector. This activity received a major new boost in 2010, with the acquisition of Efisol. Although not founded until 1987, Efisol had grown quickly to become the leading French producer of polyurethane-based insulation foams and wadding. The acquisition also gave Soprema three new production facilities in France.

ENTREPRENEUR OF THE YEAR IN 2013

Acquisitions formed only part of Soprema's growth story into the next decade. The company continued to develop itself as a leading roofing systems innovator as well. Soprema's commitment to developing environmentally sustainable roofing and insulating materials had led it to invest in photovoltaic technology. In 2007 the company introduced its Soprasolar system, featuring a waterproofing membrane with integrated photovoltaic cells, allowing rooftops to generate electricity using solar power.

The following year, as Soprema celebrated its 100th anniversary, it also returned to its roots somewhat. In 2008 the company introduced a new and environmentally friendly roofing underlay and rain barrier using natural flax fiber. Other innovations made by the company was its Soprelium waterproofing membrane, which offered a weight reduction as high as 35 percent. The company also developed a highly reflective white-colored waterproofing membrane, helping to keep buildings cooler and thereby offering significant cost savings.

By the end of 2010 Soprema's sales had grown to nearly EUR 1.2 billion. The company continued its string of acquisitions into the decade, most notably of the remaining half of Convoy in Canada. Completed in 2012, this purchase added another $500 million (EUR 300 million) in sales to the group's total. By then Soprema had not only claimed a leading position in the North American market, but had become one of the top three waterproofing and roofing systems groups in the world. At the end of 2013 the company's total revenues topped EUR 1.8 billion ($2.34 billion).

Soprema also set out to expand its horizons beyond its core European and North American market. To this end, the company opened two new sales offices in 2011, in Singapore, and in São Paulo, Brazil. In 2013 Soprema reinforced its presence in southern Europe as well, acquiring Texsa, in Spain. In that year, too, Pierre-Etienne Bindschedler received international recognition, earning the title of Entrepreneur of the Year 2013 from Ernst & Young.

Soprema showed no signs of resting on its laurels. The company announced plans to invest $35 million in expanding its North American presence, with plans to build a new factory in the northeastern United States. The company also expected to add its first production facilities in South America as well. Soprema counted on its long history as an innovator to help it maintain its position as one of the world's leading waterproofing, insulation, and roofing systems specialists in the early 21st century.

M. L. Cohen

PRINCIPAL SUBSIDIARIES

Chignolo d'Isola Flag SpA (Italy); Facadier; Hexadomes S.A.; Soprema AG (Switzerland); Soprema Belgium NV; Soprema Deutschland GmbH; Soprema Inc. (Canada); Soprema Inc. (USA); Soprema Netherlands BV; Soprema Polska Sp.oo; Soprema Spain S.A.; Soprema Svenska AB; Soprema U.K. Ltd.; Technopan S.A.

PRINCIPAL DIVISIONS

Waterproofing; Roofing; Insulation; Civil Engineering.

PRINCIPAL OPERATING UNITS

Mammouth; Soprema; Efisol; Flag; Alsan; Sopralene; Solardis.

PRINCIPAL COMPETITORS

Atlas Roofing; Boral Montoro Proprietary Ltd.; Centimark Corp.; Icopal a/s; Tecta America Corp.

FURTHER READING

Creutz, C. "Pierre-Etienne Bindschedler Entrepreneur de l'Année 2013." *L'Express*, October 21, 2013.

————. "Soprema: Une Histoire de Mammouth." *L'Express*, October 1, 2013.

"Englert and Soprema Announce Alliance," *Roofing Contractor*, March 2008.

"Entrepreneurs de Père en Fils, Les Bindschedler, Seigneurs du Mammouth." *Le Nouvel Observateur*, June 27, 2012.

Freeman, Robert. "Soprema Expansion a 'Vote of Confidence.'" *Chilliwack Progress*, November 8, 2011.

"French Soprema to Close Egyptian Plant." *ADP News France*, May 18, 2011.

Lienhardt, Christian. "Pierre-Etienne Bindschedler Impose Sa Marque." *Les Echos*, October 22, 2013.

————. "Soprema Rachète Convoy et Installe une Nouvelle Usine Outre-Atlantique." *Les Echos*, October 30, 2012.

"Pierre-Etienne Bindschedler: le Pari de l'Innovation." *Success Stories.fr*, December 1, 2013.

Salenty, Patricia. "Soprema: Cap sur l'Amérique du Nord," *L'Express*, October 1, 2013.

"Soprema." *Canadian Business Journal*, September 2014.

"Soprema." *Roofing Contractor*, January 2008.

"Soprema: l'un des Leaders Mondiaux de l'Etanchéité, Ancré en Alsace, Tourné vers l'International." *France 3*, January 6, 2014.

"Soprema Partners with Pfister." *Roofing Contractor*, April 2007.

SoulCycle Holdings LLC

126 Leroy Street
New York, New York 10014
U.S.A.
Telephone: (212) 787-7685
Web site: http://www.soul-cycle.com

Private Company
Incorporated: 2006
Employees: 750
Sales: $100 million (2013 est.)
NAICS: 713940 Fitness and Recreational Sports Centers

■ ■ ■

SoulCycle Holdings LLC owns and operates a chain of fitness studios that offer high-energy training sessions with stationary bicycles. Although a SoulCycle session is more expensive than a typical fitness club workout, the studios have become popular and trendy in major urban centers such as Manhattan, Southern California, Washington, D.C., and the Boston area. In addition to cycling workouts, SoulCycle also offers its customers a variety of branded retail goods, including clothing, accessories, and its own stationary bicycle model.

A SPINNING START-UP IN 2005

When Julie Rice moved to Manhattan from Los Angeles in 2005, she was already addicted to stationary bicycle exercise sessions, also known as "spin classes." The former Hollywood talent agent hoped to start a new life in New York, and one of her first challenges was finding

a bicycle studio that provided the atmosphere and workout style she had enjoyed in California. After several false starts, she discovered a class at Reebok Sports Club taught by Ruth Zukerman.

Zukerman's teaching style emphasized individual pacing rather than competition and incorporated elements of other disciplines, such as yoga-inspired breathing techniques. Rice responded favorably to the instructor's methods, and the two became friends. After a few idle conversations about what it would take to open an independent fitness studio, Zukerman introduced Rice to another student, Elizabeth Cutler, with whom she had had similar discussions. Rice agreed to have lunch with Cutler, and the meeting would change both their lives.

Like Rice, Cutler had also moved to New York fairly recently. A former Colorado real estate broker, Cutler was in the process of recouping a sizable return on an investment in a friend's start-up soda company. She was interested in parlaying the capital into her own start-up, but in the field of fitness rather than soda pop. Rice's creative vision and marketing ability seemed to fit well with Cutler's financial acumen and Zukerman's practical experience as a trainer. In short order, the three were in business together.

2006: THE FIRST STUDIO

Finding a location for the new club proved relatively easy. In the spring of 2006, just a few months after Rice and Cutler's first meeting, the first SoulCycle studio opened for business in a sublet space on West 72nd Street that the partners had found on Craigslist. The building had served as a funeral parlor and more recently as a dance studio, which left it with plenty of open spaces and fixtures appropriate to a fitness club. While the location itself had not been difficult to find, physically converting it into a successful cycling studio brought a number of special challenges.

The first hurdle was letting the public know SoulCycle existed. After signing the lease, the partners discovered that they would not be allowed to attach any signage to the building's historic façade. After scouring the Internet for a bicycle-themed novelty, they purchased a rickshaw on eBay for around $250, painted it in bright colors and chained it to a parking meter out front with the studio's sign prominently attached. When the conspicuous vehicle began accumulating parking tickets, Cutler simply incorporated them into the company's advertising budget.

Adding their own savings to Cutler's soda money, the partners purchased and assembled a front desk from Ikea, around 35 Schwinn stationary bikes, a $20,000 sound system, and 50 pairs of clip-on cycling shoes for patrons to rent. The sound system would become an essential element of the SoulCycle business model. Most cycling studios played pounding, energetic music during sessions to motivate cyclists, and the company would eventually have to invest in heavy soundproofing for each location.

Business did not take off immediately. The partners had estimated the club would need around 100 customers per day to be successful. Yet, some sessions had only one or two clients. Cutler and Rice walked the neighborhood handing out flyers and spent the last $2,500 of their opening budget on promotional T-shirts they handed out to friends. They also provided free classes to various nonprofit groups to get the word out.

During this period SoulCycle developed many of the touches that would ultimately distinguish it from other fitness clubs. One amenity was the use of candlelight during training sessions to provide a more intimate, meditative atmosphere. Instructors would begin each session with meditation, in fact, before beginning slowly and then slowly increasing the pace of the music and pedaling until it reached a crescendo. The pace would then slowly taper off and patrons would spend the last few minutes of the session cooling down and reflecting.

Eventually, SoulCycle's unique approach, a direct contrast to the bright lighting, frenetic music, and competitive atmosphere found at most health clubs, combined with its easy-to-miss signage to give it an underground cachet that made it something of a boutique destination. A few New York–based celebrities, such as actors Kyra Sedgwick and Jake Gyllenhaal had begun to attend classes. Less than a year after opening, the studio hosted an Exercise Your Vote event attended by Bill and Hillary Clinton as part of the latter's presidential campaign. Sessions, though pricy at $32 for 45 minutes were constantly booked solid with a waiting list, and SoulCycle was clearly operating at full capacity. The studio offered as many as 10 classes per day, 7 days a week, serving around 8,000 customers per month with more trying to sign up. Sensing it was time to expand, the partners began scouting new studio locations.

GROWING PAINS

Surprisingly, the successful, young company encountered some difficulty finding landlords willing to offer them a lease. With large, corporate fitness chains scattered throughout the city, a small business, no matter how trendy, was seen as too much of a risk for valuable Manhattan commercial real estate. Ironically, the financial recession of 2008, which brought hardship to businesses across the spectrum, actually provided some relief to SoulCycle. After witnessing mass closings of corporate business locations in the wake of the recession, landlords began to see small, self-contained and financed businesses such as SoulCycle as more likely to stick with their leases for the long term. As the real estate logjam eased and the SoulCycle brand gained popularity, the company would open several new studios in the city, including an Upper East Side studio, a Tribeca facility, and a club near Union Square, as well as two more in the suburbs of Scarsdale and Bridgehampton, by the end of 2011.

As SoulCycle's number of physical locations expanded, so did their revenue stream. In 2009 the company partnered with a food company to market SoulCooler, a line of fresh squeezed juices. The company also began selling its own brand of workout clothing and accessories at studio locations and online, creating a revenue source that would become increasingly important to the company. By 2012 SoulCycle would be marketing its own model of exercise bike.

Meanwhile, the original SoulCycle partnership was going through changes of its own. In 2009 Zukerman

```
┌─────────────────────────────────────────────┐
│                                               │
│              KEY DATES                        │
│                 ──●──                         │
│  2006:  The SoulCycle partners open their first│
│         studio.                               │
│  2007:  SoulCycle launches its retail line.   │
│  2011:  Company is partially acquired by Equinox│
│         Fitness.                              │
│  2012:  Company introduces the SoulCycle Exercise│
│         Bike.                                 │
│  2014:  Company opens its 30th location.      │
│                                               │
└─────────────────────────────────────────────┘
```

left the company under circumstances the three partners chose to keep private. Within a year, however, she had opened Flywheel Sports, a competing cycling studio that also began to expand across the city. To fill Zukerman's position as master trainer, Cutler and Rice eventually brought in Janet Fitzgerald, Rice's former trainer from Los Angeles.

As SoulCycle's popularity grew, the company maintained its boutique price point. The basic rate of $32 per session stayed the same, though customers could buy discounted packages of 10, 20, or 30 sessions. Clients could also sign up for a premium package that offered 50 sessions, with such perks as early sign-up and bikes in the front row, for a fee of $3,000. Even with the new locations, demand for sessions remained high. When online class registration opened each Monday, many sessions sold out within an hour or less.

NEW PARTNERS AND NEW FRONTIERS

In 2011 Cutler and Rice sought to fund even more expansion by selling a portion of their company to Equinox Fitness, a holding company that operated a large number of spas and health clubs in the United States, Canada, and the United Kingdom. Logistical support from Equinox, combined with approximately $20 million in revenue from the sale, would enable the company to open new locations at an accelerated pace. Although the exact terms of the deal were kept confidential, Cutler and Rice reportedly retained a substantial ownership stake in SoulCycle and the company continued to operate as a separate entity.

SoulCycle's next frontier was Rice's former home court of Southern California. Taking advantage of the company's established popularity with the acting and celebrity community, SoulCycle opened six locations in the area over the next few years. Soon the company expanded to the northern end of the state with three San Francisco–area studios. In 2012 music superstar Lady Gaga chose to throw her 26th birthday party at SoulCycle's new West Hollywood location, generating significant publicity. Lady Gaga would also take two custom made SoulCycle bikes on tour with her.

Meanwhile, on the East Coast, SoulCycle had continued to expand through the New York metropolitan area. Locations were added in Greenwich, Connecticut, and Short Hills, New Jersey. Later the suburbs of Bronxville and Rye Brook, New York, were added to the list. On Long Island, the Bridgehampton studio was soon joined by locations in East Hampton, Roslyn Heights, and Water Mill.

LOOKING TO THE FUTURE

In 2013 Cutler and Rice finally decided to abandon the tiny offices they had been working from at SoulCycle's Tribeca location and create a new corporate headquarters in a former jewelry factory near a new studio location in New York's West Village. The 20,000-square-foot office space included training facilities for instructors and office employees, dubbed the SoulUniversity, as well as a photography studio for the company's merchandise catalogs and an employee commissary. The building also hosted the offices of the SoulSocial software programmers who designed the company's class sign-up system and Internet presence. "It is definitely a far cry from the $169 Ikea table we used to sit around," Cutler told the *New York Times* in a July 3, 2013, article.

The SoulSocial team added a critical element to SoulCycle's appeal as the company came to rely more and more on social media to maintain its brand. By 2013 the company had some 30,000 Facebook fans and 25,000 Twitter followers. SoulCycle developed a policy of interacting enthusiastically and personally with its fans on social media and used its website to post success stories and workout advice. The company also used the music service Spotify to create and distribute music playlists designed to maximize workout energy.

Despite the company's growth, SoulCycle did face at least one major challenge, beginning in 2013. In May of that year former employee Nick Oram filed a class-action lawsuit alleging that the company violated New York and California employment law by paying instructors only for the time spent teaching sessions. Like other teachers, fitness instructors also spent a great deal of time training and preparing for their work. Oram's suit alleged that the law required the employees be compensated for this time as well. The suit also criticized the company for its policy of charging customers for missed sessions. In its initial response to the suit, SoulCycle asserted that its wage policies were in accordance with the law.

The year 2014 saw two new additions to the East Coast SoulCycle cluster. In March the company's first Boston-area studio opened in the suburb of Chestnut Hill, Massachusetts. In early August a long-awaited Washington, D.C., location opened on that city's M Street. A second D.C.-area location in Bethesda, Maryland, was also announced. By now the company was operating some 30 stores with plans to add another 15 to 20 over the next two years. With help from Equinox, the company also hoped to add international locations, beginning with London.

In late 2013 Cutler told *Fast Company* magazine that SoulCycle hoped to add about 15 locations a year "until we die." The company's financial outlook seemed to support her optimism. In early 2014 *Forbes* estimated that the company was making $240,000 per day just from cycling sessions. This figure did not include revenue from retail sales, shoe rentals, and various other services. *Forbes* estimated that SoulCycle served some

8,000 riders per day, a figure that would likely increase if the company's plans for expansion came to fruition.

Chris Herzog

PRINCIPAL COMPETITORS

CrossFit Inc.; Flywheel Sports Inc.

FURTHER READING

Brodesser-Akner, Taffy. "SoulCycle's New Spin." *Fast Company*, December 2013/January 2014.

Grigoriadis, Vanessa. "Riding High." *Vanity Fair*, September 2012.

Griswold, Alison. "Here's How SoulCycle Keeps Customers Paying $34 for a Cycling Class." *Business Insider*, December 3, 2013.

McKinney, Sarah. "SoulCycle's Intense Brand Loyalty Is Driving 85% Growth in Profitability." *Forbes*, February 5, 2014.

Morris, Alex. "The Carefully Cultivated Soul of SoulCycle." *New York Magazine*, January 14, 2013.

Satow, Julie. "Even Boutique Gyms Need Back Offices as They Grow." *New York Times*, July 3, 2013.

Springleaf Holdings Inc.

—■—

601 Northwest Second Street
Evansville, Indiana 47708
U.S.A.
Telephone: (812) 424-8031
Web site: http://www.springleaf.com

Public Company
Incorporated: 1920 as Interstate Finance Corporation
Employees: 4,000
Sales: $314.4 million (2013)
Stock Exchanges: New York
Ticker Symbol: LEAF
NAICS: 522291 Consumer Lending

■ ■ ■

Springleaf Holdings LLC, popularly known as Springleaf Financial, provides financial services in 26 states, as well as Puerto and the Virgin Islands. Known as American General Finance until a 2011 name change, the company provides a variety of loan types to consumers with a focus on the subprime market. Subprime borrowers tend to have lower credit scores or other characteristics that add greater risk to their loans and often result in higher fees and interest rates. Springleaf also brokers a variety of insurance products. Springleaf Holdings has been publicly traded since 2013.

THE INTERSTATE YEARS: 1920–67

Springleaf Holdings traces its history to 1920, when a small company known as Interstate Finance Corp. was established in the southwestern Indiana city of Evansville for the purpose of underwriting sales for the Inland Motor Truck Company, also based in Evansville. Interstate began issuing consumer loans in 1928, and, by the following year, the rapidly growing company was writing credit-related insurance policies.

By 1942 Interstate Finance had established three branch offices and, according to one advertisement, offered "friendly financing" in the form of personal loans ranging from $10 to $300, business loans, and a wide range of insurance coverage. The following year, Interstate purchased a local loan company known as the Evansville Morris Plan Co., representing the first in a series of acquisitions that would continue into the 1980s and would prove integral to the company's growth strategy. During this time, Evansville's economy and population were booming, bolstered by the emergence of several local shipyards during World War II, and the insurance and lending businesses in the area also enjoyed steady growth.

By the mid-1950s Interstate had established five branch offices in Evansville, as well as executive offices downtown. During the postwar period of heightened consumerism, Interstate advertisements began emphasizing the financing they made available for automobiles, appliances, televisions, radios, and furniture. The company also strengthened its insurance division, purchasing the Merit Life Insurance Company in 1957. In 1967, Interstate Finance was incorporated as CrediThrift Financial, and, over the next ten years, the company steadily increased its presence, purchasing the assets of Morían Pacific and establishing branch offices throughout the country.

CREDITHRIFT THRIVES: 1968–88

By the early 1980s CrediThrift oversaw operations at 537 branch offices, and its growth and success had attracted the attention of industry leaders, including Houston-based American General Corp., one of the largest providers of retirement annuities, life-insurance products, and loans in the United States. In 1982 American General acquired CrediThrift for $150 million, as part of its plan to embark on one of the most aggressive acquisitions programs in the insurance industry. Unlike many of American General's acquisitions, CrediThrift was accorded considerable autonomy and was allowed to retain many of its top executives, including CEO and Chairperson Wendell L. Dixon, who had been with the company since 1973 and had helped define the terms of the company's sale.

With greater financial resources, CrediThrift began diversifying its offerings. In 1984 the company launched a Visa/MasterCard program through which it offered a credit card called the More Card. Acquisitions also continued under the parentage of American General. In 1983 CrediThrift purchased the assets of General Finance, and, five years later, it acquired CommoLoCo Operations, a loan company based in Puerto Rico, as well as Manufacturers Hanover Consumer Credit Division (Manny Hanny), for which it paid $750 million.

In 1988 CrediThrift reported profits of $85 million on sales of $930 million. The Manny Hanny purchase had effectively doubled the size of CrediThrift's operations. As the company was becoming an increasingly important subsidiary of American General, it proved slow to incorporate and consolidate the operations of its recent acquisitions, which resulted in lower earnings figures for its parent and prompted criticism from Wall Street analysts.

Furthermore, CEO and Chairperson Dixon, then aged 65, retired from CrediThrift in 1988. American General Corp. assumed a greater interest in its subsidiary's day-to-day operations, and dramatic changes in CrediThrift's corporate culture began to take place. First, a management development program, Model-

Netics, was installed at CrediThrift, and, in a process referred to as "enculturation," the company gradually adopted its parent's management techniques and policies. Then American General executives were gradually placed in leadership positions within the Evansville company.

To oversee operations during this transition period, American General sent two of its Houston executives to Evansville: CFO Edwin G. Pickett and Michael G. Atnip, a personal assistant of American General CEO Harold S. Hook. Primary among their concerns for the future of CrediThrift was the standardization of operations among its finance holdings. Toward that end, the company's chief consumer finance companies—CrediThrift, General Finance, and Manufacturers Hanover—were consolidated and the company was renamed American General Finance Corp (AGF).

AMERICAN GENERAL FINANCE: 1988–2000

In 1989, after one year at AGF, Pickett left the company. Also that year, Atnip was named senior vice president of administration, and John J. Bolger, who had assumed leadership upon Dixon's retirement, was replaced by American General executive Roy W. Haley. Several other AGF officials resigned from the company during this time, and two of the company's board members were replaced by American General Corp. executives.

Despite the high turnover rate among its top officials, AGF reported record profits in 1990. Under Haley, AGF became the sixth-largest consumer finance company in the United States in 1990. Relying heavily on feedback from customers, AGF found that its services were generally regarded as superior to those of banks, which were cited as impersonal and, often, uncooperative. In addition to emphasizing personal service, AGF worked to decrease the amount of time involved in processing loan applications.

Employing the services of the telemarketing agency Telenational Marketing, AGF established a one-hour loan service in such test locations as Fresno, California; Orlando, Florida; and Shreveport, Louisiana. Under the program, customers called a toll-free phone number and provided Telenational operators with background information and authorization for the transmittal of credit reports. Telenational operators received the credit reports by facsimile machine and then faxed the completed application to AGF, where loan officers evaluated the information and returned the customers call within an hour, either granting or declining the loan. Another program initiated during this time involved a

```
┌─────────────────────────────────────────────┐
│                                               │
│               KEY DATES                       │
│                  ■                            │
│  ─────────────────────────────────────────   │
│  1920:  Company is founded as Interstate Finance │
│         Corporation.                          │
│  1966:  Name is changed to CrediThrift Financial │
│         Incorporated.                         │
│  1982:  American General Corporation purchases the │
│         company.                              │
│  1988:  Company acquires Manufacturers Hanover │
│         Consumer Services.                    │
│  1990:  Name is changed to American General   │
│         Finance Inc.                          │
│  2001:  Company is acquired by American       │
│         International Group.                   │
│  2010:  Fortress Investment Group acquires the │
│         company.                              │
│  2011:  Name is changed to Springleaf Holdings. │
│  2013:  Company begins trading on the New York │
│         Stock Exchange.                       │
│  2014:  Mortgage division is eliminated.      │
│                                               │
└─────────────────────────────────────────────┘
```

new line of credit cards, referred to as private-label cards, which AGF serviced for retailers across the country. Successful in its own right, the private-label credit card program also afforded AGF access to a wider clientele to which it could market insurance and other financing services.

In April 1990 American General Corp. became the subject of a takeover bid by the Torchmark Corporation, an insurance company based in Birmingham, Alabama, which offered $6.4 billion to acquire the company. When the bid was refused, Torchmark undertook a proxy battle to win seats on the American General board and announced that, if successful, it would sell AGF. Although American General won its battle with Torchmark, CEO Hook announced in May 1990 that American General would be put up for sale. Hook's decision to sell American General was reportedly prompted by his desire to retain the assets of AGF, reflecting the importance and economic potential of AGF as part of the American General package. Moreover, as a subsidiary, AGF was prepared to be sold separately if a buyer was ultimately not found.

Hook took American General off the auction block later that year, and, while several other subsidiaries were then divested, AGF remained under the auspices of American General. Over the next year, operations at AGF were successfully consolidated. By 1992 AGF had extended loans to 2.3 million U.S. families. Acquisitions

that year included Provident Financial Corp. of South Carolina and Credit Centers Inc. of Mississippi.

Under the leadership of Haley's successor, president and CEO Daniel Leitch III, AGF experienced record setting highs in several areas, including earnings, lending volume, and insurance sales. Furthermore, the company's credit card division experienced profit increases of 30 percent, due to continued sales of the More Card as well as rapidly increasing sales of its private-label credit cards. Card servicing growth prompted AGF to open a new 25,000-square-foot facility in Evansville in 1994.

SPRINGLEAF IN THE NEW CENTURY

By the turn of the new century American General Corporation's successes had drawn a new round of interest from potential buyers. In 2001 the conglomerate was acquired by American International Group (AIG), a multinational insurance and financial services giant. Day-to-day operations would proceed normally at AGF for the time being. Steady revenues over the next several years led to the announcement of another major expansion in 2006.

By this point, the company was operating 1,500 branches in 45 states, serving around 2 million customers. AGF claimed some $26 billion in assets and $760 million in pretax revenue for the previous year. In July 2006 AGF chairman and CEO Rick Geissinger announced that the company would build a $35 million, 135,000-square-foot addition to its headquarters building in downtown Evansville. The building would take nearly two years to complete, and before it was fully occupied outside economic forces would present AGF with some of its biggest challenges to date.

As work on the new headquarters proceeded, AGF continued to expand economically. In 2007 the company acquired British finance company Ocean Finance and Mortgages Ltd. The following year it purchased the accounts of 126,000 customers of real estate broker Equity One Inc. By the end of 2008, however, the global economy had entered one of the largest recessions on record, and AGF's parent company AIG sat firmly at the center of the crisis. Much of the crisis centered on the overextended subprime lending market, and companies such as AGF quickly found themselves in trouble as unemployment rose and the housing market, around which so much of its business was structured, struck new lows. During 2009 and 2010 the tightened credit market led AGF to close nearly 200 branches and lay off 1,400 employees.

On the verge of collapse, AIG had been saved by a $182 billion taxpayer bailout. Desperate to balance its books, the company then sold a number of problematic assets, including AGF. Ultimately, AGF was purchased by Fortress Investment Group, a New York–based investment management group, in 2010. Fortress paid just $130 million for an 80 percent stake in the company, while AIG retained the remaining 20 percent. At the time of the sale, AGF carried $20 billion in assets against $18 billion in debts. It had posted losses of $723 million in 2008 and $868 million the following year.

Although the future of AGF seemed less than promising, executives at Fortress undertook a careful rebuilding, rebranding, and restructuring process that began paying off after just a few years. A key strategy was the phasing out of real estate–based lending and refocusing on other types of lending and insurance brokerage. The company stopped issuing new mortgage loans in 2012, while continuing to service existing loans. Other cost-cutting measures included another round of layoffs, more than 800 employees this time, and the closure of another 231 branches. The most visible change during this period was a new name. American General Finance became Springleaf Holdings, doing business as Springleaf Financial, in 2011.

By 2013 Springleaf's restructuring had begun to pay off, with the company showing $45 million in net profits for the first half of the year. The biggest news of the year, however, was the company's initial public offering. Springleaf began trading on the New York Stock Exchange on October 15, 2013, selling 21 million shares at $17 apiece. By the next day the price had jumped to $19.26 per share. By mid-2014 stock prices had risen more than 60 percent.

In the summer of 2014 Springleaf announced that it was closing its real estate division completely, selling some $7 billion in loans and assets. The divestiture also involved the closure of its mortgage servicing center and the elimination of 170 jobs. As recently as 2013 some 50 percent of the company's interest income had derived from mortgage loans, but the loans had become difficult to manage and less lucrative in the wake of the

previous decade's housing crisis. The *Evansville Courier and Press* described Springleaf president and CEO Jay Levine as pleased with the company's new influx of cash and disconnection from the uncertainties of the real estate market. He remarked: "We certainly are in an enviable liquidity position, which gives the company a lot more optionality than it's had in quite some time."

Tina Grant
Updated, Chris Herzog

PRINCIPAL COMPETITORS

Regional Management Corp Inc.; Security Finance Corporation; World Acceptance Corporation.

FURTHER READING

Dugan, Ianthe Jeanne, and Telis Demos. "New Lenders Spring Up to Cater to Subprime Sector." *Wall Street Journal*, March 5, 2014.

Kosman, Josh, and Mark DeCambre. "Fire Sale at AIG-Unit Fetches $130M." *New York Post*, August 12, 2010.

Orr, Susan. "Evansville's Springleaf to Sell Off $7.2 Billion in Remaining Real Estate Assets." *Evansville Courier and Press*, August 9, 2014.

———. "Springleaf Financial Corp. Seeing Some Gain from Last Year's Pain." *Evansville Courier and Press*, May 14, 2013.

Raithel, Tom. "Executive Exchange: Rick Geissinger." *Evansville Business Journal*, April 3, 2007.

Ruquet, Mark E. "AIG Set to Sell Majority Interest in SPRINGLEAF Subsidiary." *National Underwriter Property & Casualty Insurance*, August 16, 2010.

Schawel, David. "Springleaf Holdings and the Re-emergence of Sub-prime Consumer Lending." *Inside Investing* (blog), November 4, 2013. Accessed October 26, 2014. http://blogs.cfainstitute.org/insideinvesting/2013/11/04/springleaf.

Shaw, Dan. "American General Finance Cutting 500 Jobs." *Evansville Courier and Press*, May 5, 2009.

Son, Hugh. "AIG Sells Lender American General to Fortress at a Loss." *Bloomberg*, August 11, 2010.

Spektor, Mike. "Springleaf Talks with Banks about IPO." *Wall Street Journal*, June 10, 2013.

Sudler & Hennessey LLC

---

230 Park Avenue South
New York, New York 10003-1566
U.S.A.
Telephone: (212) 614-4100
Fax: (212) 598-6907
Web site: http://www.sudler.com

Wholly Owned Subsidiary of WPP plc
Founded: 1941
Employees: 930
NAICS: 541819 Advertising Agencies

■■■

Sudler & Hennessey LLC (S&H) is a health care marketing communications subsidiary of WPP plc, a global communications services company. S&H offers a wide range of services to pharmaceutical companies and others in the health care industry, including advertising, direct marketing, and sales promotion programs for prescription drugs and over-the-counter medications. S&H divisions also specialize in market research, strategic planning, medical education, sales training, eHealth solutions, branding, publication strategies, and digital solutions. S&H maintains its headquarters in New York City and a network of 63 offices in 34 countries, including in North America, Europe, and the Pacific Rim. Although little known to the general public because of its narrow focus, S&H is a company with a rich history. It played a major role in the development of contemporary modern advertising and the graphic arts in general.

FOUNDER, BORN 1905

Sudler & Hennessey was founded by Arthur Emory Sudler. He was born in Maryland in 1905 and attended the Baltimore City College and the Maryland Institute of Fine and Applied Art. He then found work in 1930 in the art department of a New York pharmaceutical company, E.R. Squibb & Sons. He became art director and then in 1936 opened his own studio in the Squibb Building, with E.R. Squibb serving as his first client. He also took on work outside of the drug industry. While at Squibb, Sudler had met Matthew Hennessey, who was nine years younger and had started his career in Squibb's advertising department. He soon went to work for Sudler and in 1941 became his partner, resulting in the creation of the Sudler & Hennessey agency.

Hennessey left to serve in the U.S. Army during World War II. When he returned, S&H entered into a golden era. Sudler and Hennessey were both talented artists. Sudler was also an accomplished copywriter; one of his more memorable taglines was "Kiss Hemorrhoids Goodbye!" Moreover, Sudler and Hennessey eagerly recruited equally talented graphic artists, a large number of whom were trained at the School of Art—Cooper Union in New York City. S&H became an incubator for talent in the graphic arts, due in large measure to the creative freedom Sudler and Hennessey afforded their people. Also playing a key role was the creative director of S&H, Herbert Lubalin, another Cooper Union graduate.

COMPANY PERSPECTIVES

We explore the boundary between science and art. Our campaigns combine life-changing healthcare products with creative ideas that fire the imagination.

DISTINGUISHED ALUMNI

S&H's deep roster of design, typographic, and photographic talent literally revolutionized the look of advertising, magazine illustrations, logos, and other visual designs. As the agency's reputation grew, the best talent in the country sought employment with the company, knowing that their portfolios would improve as would their chances of career advancement. Many S&H alumni became art directors at major advertising agencies, and some started their own ad agencies. Notable S&H offspring included George Lois, an artist and designer well known for his covers of *Esquire* magazine, and Helmut Krone, considered by many the pioneer of modern advertising. Another S&H staff member, Andy Warhol, helped to redefine modern art.

In the late 1940s and early 1950s the S&H studio handled a wide range of projects, including consumer advertising, corporate identity, magazine illustrations, record covers, and even store window displays. The NBC television network's peacock logo was an S&H creation. During this period, medical advertising was not a major part of the business, because pharmaceutical companies relied solely on their sales forces rather than mass media. Following the war, however, there was an explosion in prescription drug advertising. In 1953 Sudler and Hennessey decided to focus on the pharmaceutical industry and become a full-fledged advertising agency devoted to the sector. They remained involved in consumer advertising as well through another entity, Sudler Hennessey & Lubalin (SH&L). Although the latter won numerous awards for its work, it was not as profitable as S&H. In 1964 Herb Lubalin left to start his own agency.

Now devoted to pharmaceutical clients, S&H won such early accounts as CIBA and Merrell. The firm had also taken advantage of opportunities internationally, establishing Arranz & Sudler in 1950 to act as an export pharmaceutical advertising agency. Despite a narrower client base, S&H, along with SH&L, continued to develop a style that combined strong visual elements with provocative headlines that would have an impact on consumer advertising that is felt to this day.

RETIREMENT OF SUDLER: 1966

In the early 1960s Sudler began to experience health problems, forcing him to retire from the agency in 1966. He died two years later. When Sudler left the agency, it was generating in excess of $10 million in annual billings. Hennessey now took charge of the agency. Under his leadership, S&H increased billings to more than $30 million by 1972, allowing the agency to lay claim to being the largest medical advertising agency in the United States. It was a distinction S&H would hold for the next 20 years.

In 1973 Hennessey decided to sell S&H to a larger advertising firm, Young & Rubicam. "I had been approached by a number of agencies," Hennessey told *Medical Marketing & Media* in a June 2001 article. He elaborated: "They all wanted to get into our business. But Ed Ney (then chairman of Young & Rubicam) had a marvelous philosophy—one that I really could relate to. He was looking for the very best in each discipline." Thus, S&H was permitted to continue operating as an independent company with Hennessey as its president. Under new ownership, the growth of S&H accelerated. Annual billings increased to $85 million by 1980. The following year S&H appointed 14 vice presidents, including five executive vice presidents. The primary reason for many of the promotions was to relieve Hennessey, now 64 years old, of some of his day-to-day responsibilities.

RETIREMENT OF HENNESSEY: 1984

Hennessey retired in February 1984. He was succeeded as chairman and chief executive officer by 45-year-old William B. Gibson, who had been with S&H since 1970. For the previous two years he had been preparing for his new role by serving as president and chief operating officer. The ties to the founding partners may have been severed, but S&H continued to expand as a part of Young & Rubicam.

The aging of the population helped to spur further growth for S&H and other ad agencies that specialized in the health care sector. For many years pharmaceutical companies had been content to stake out territories based on diseases. Through a gentleman's agreement they generally refrained from encroaching on one another's established territory. With the so-called graying, or aging, of the United States, as members of the baby boom generation entered their senior years, however, there was simply too much potential profit in providing drugs to the elderly to remain on the sidelines as a courtesy.

Pharmaceutical companies now focused on the development of treatments for the chronic diseases of the aged. With multiple products addressing the same disease, however, drug manufacturers had to invest more in advertising to physicians in order to set their products apart. The result was an increased amount of billings for medical ad agencies, especially those such as S&H that had established a consumer advertising division. Sudler & Hennessey Consumer was launched in 1981. Some of the prescription products S&H touted in the late 1980s included the Benylin cough treatment, Caladryl for allergies and skin irritation, Mylanta antacids, Tucks hemorrhoid treatment, and Promega fish oil. By 1988 S&H was reporting annual billings of $185 million, of which $50 million came from the consumer advertising division.

Gibson headed S&H until his retirement in January 1997. During his final year at the helm, the agency posted worldwide billings of about $420 million. His successor as chairman and CEO was Jed Beitler. Unlike Gibson, Beitler did not come up through the S&H ranks. Rather, the 44-year-old was the former president and COO at New York's Harrison & Star LLC, a major health care marketing agency. Growth continued under the new head. In 1997 worldwide billings topped the $500 million mark.

Another significant change took place in 2000 when British advertising company WPP Group acquired Young & Rubicam for $4.7 billion in stock to create the world's largest advertising company. Although the ownership of S&H changed hands, the name remained the same. At the turn of the new century, S&H held the distinction of being the longest continuously operating brand in health care advertising.

NEW CENTURY CHANGES

Although S&H enjoyed a storied past, the firm did change with the times. In 2000 it formed a new division, Avenue-e Health. The health care e-marketing unit offered Internet and interactive media capabilities to provide clients with new ways to reach both physicians and consumers. S&H added to its capabilities on other fronts as well early in the first decade of the 21st century. It acquired HealthAnswers Education in 2003. The Pennsylvania-based company developed sales training and med-ed programs for the pharmaceutical industry. The following year, however, it was spun off from S&H, along with two other units, Emeritus Educations Sciences and Imprint Science.

S&H also placed greater emphasis on expanding its global footprint. Offices were opened throughout Europe, and a Mexico branch was established in 2007 to provide entry into Latin America. To provide greater control over the growing operation, S&H was restructured in 2007 to include eight managing partners. The New York office by itself was now led by three managing partners, each with specific responsibilities.

The steep downturn in the economy at the end of 2008 had an adverse impact on S&H. Nevertheless, it was able to enjoy a good year in 2009. It also acquired a controlling stake in MDS, a China-based health care advertising agency with operations in Shanghai and Beijing. Renamed Sudler MDS, the unit would serve as a regional hub. S&H also grew organically, opening affiliate offices in Moscow and Johannesburg.

In April 2011 Hennessey died of cancer at the age of 95. His passing served as a reminder of how far S&H had come since its founding and of the many contributions the agency had made to the advertising industry and graphic arts. The agency could not, however, rest on its legacy. The business climate remained poor, resulting in only minor growth in 2011. To meet the needs of the day, the agency eliminated its digital unit and instead provided digital training so that all of the creative personnel was versed in digital essentials. S&H opened an office in Brazil through a partnership with Grupo Triunfo and enjoyed some success in Asia and Eastern Europe. The business in Western Europe, on the other hand, did not fare as well. S&H had to contend with another soft year in 2012, but business began to pick up in 2013.

The agency's global approach was also beginning to pay dividends, as was offering its services to a wider market. S&H began working with packaged goods companies about their health claims, such as the Mott's for Tots juice line. The agency also cultivated clients in the health tech arena and formed a unit, Quality Matters, to help health care providers deal with the incentives structure and improved care requirements of the Affordable Care Act. With the deep pockets of its corporate parent for support, and a rich heritage as part of its brand, S&H was well positioned for continued growth in the future.

Ed Dinger

PRINCIPAL OPERATING UNITS

The Americas; Asia Pacific; Europe and Africa.

PRINCIPAL COMPETITORS

CDM World Agency; Inventiv Health, Inc.; Publicis Healthcare Communications.

FURTHER READING

Arnold, Matthew. "Sudler & Hennessey: Using a Broad Base of Knowledge to Go beyond Talking Global to Doing It." *Medical Marketing & Media*, July 2013.

"Arthur E. Sudler, Ad Man, Dies at 63." *New York Times*, April 7, 1968.

Dougherty, Philip H. "An Ad Boom in the Ills of the Elderly." *New York Times*, June 14, 1988.

———. "Sudler & Hennessey Names 14 Vice Presidents." *New York Times*, March 27, 1981.

Parry, Vince. "S&H Celebrates Life at 60." *Medical Marketing & Media*, June 2001.

"Sudler & Hennessey: A Global Slowdown Doesn't Keep This Firm from an International Expansion." *Medical Marketing & Media*, July 2012, 168.

Taboola Inc.

———————— ■ ————————

44 West 18th Street
New York, New York 10010
U.S.A.
Telephone: (212) 206-7663
Web site: http://www.taboola.com

Private Company
Founded: 2007
Employees: 150
Sales: $100 million (2013 est.)
NAICS: 519130 Internet Publishing and Broadcasting
and Web Search Portals

■ ■ ■

Taboola Inc. designs and operates software engines that recommend video content to Internet users, based on content they have previously viewed. The company derives most of its income from paid placement of advertisements and links to commercial Web sites. Taboola's ubiquitous bottom-of-the-page strip of video links, often labeled "Content You May Like," is a familiar sight to users of such popular Web sites as The Huffington Post, TMZ.com, and The Weather Channel. Founded in Israel, the company maintains its headquarters in New York City.

ORIGINS IN ISRAEL

Adam Singolda honed many of the technical skills he would use to shape the Taboola business model during his stint in the Israeli Defense Forces (IDF). Born in Tel Aviv to parents of Moroccan and European ancestry, the mathematically inclined young man found himself assigned to the Algorithm Development Unit of the IDF Intelligence Corps. Specifically, Singolda worked on developing new forms of encryption to protect Israel's data infrastructure. By the time he left the service after nearly seven years, Singolda had been promoted from a lower-status engineer to a full officer.

Singolda's post-military aspirations were modest at first. He hoped to become a teacher and to live a quiet life. The inspiration for what would become a multimillion-dollar company arose when he upgraded his cable package. "There was a moment when I switched my home TV from few channels to 100+ channels, and instead of feeling like I had access to so much content, I felt as if there was nothing to watch," he explained in an interview with Forbes.com, "People don't really wake up in the morning, knowing what they want to learn today."

Pondering the ways in which consumers find content, Singolda identified three primary methods of content discovery as Sharing, Searching, and Opportunistic Happenstance. At this point, before the ascendance of social media giants Facebook and Twitter, sharing links and content had not become as popular, or as easy, as it later would. Rather, the search paradigm stood out as the most dominant method of discovery.

Internet users typed keywords into search engines such as Google or Yahoo to find the content they were after. This presupposed, however, that they knew what they wanted to find. Singolda reflected that some of his most intriguing discoveries had come about through sheer happenstance, while surfing the Internet.

FOCUS ON VIDEO CONTENT

Singolda decided to investigate the possibilities of this third paradigm, helping users to discover content they did not know they were looking for. Singolda decided to focus his efforts on video content. Less quantifiable than text, video offered a steep challenge to anyone attempting to define or classify it with mathematical precision. Nevertheless, with broadband Internet on the rise, the young entrepreneur sensed that video content would become increasingly popular for Internet users across the board.

If he were able to find a way to quantify video and funnel it to consumers who wanted to see it, the rewards would be substantial. He considered it a high-risk, high-reward scenario. Singolda began approaching investors in Israel with his idea, even as he was mulling the possibility of moving to the United States to pursue an MBA.

One of his contacts was so impressed with the scope of Singolda's vision that he offered an investment in the low six figures if Singolda would postpone his MBA plans for a year while working on the business plan. The offer was accepted. Singolda called three friends from his old intelligence unit to offer them jobs with the new company. By July 2007 Taboola Inc. was operating out of the initial investor's office.

EARLY BUZZ

It did not take long for the start-up, named after the Latin words, *tabula rasa*, or "clean slate," to begin attracting further investors. By the end of 2007 the company had attracted $1.5 million in venture capital financing, primarily from the Israel-based Evergreen Venture Partners group. Taboola had obtained the funding based on the launch of its ViDiscovery tool, a basic add-on for commercial Web sites that recommended further videos that customers might enjoy based on their previous video selections.

Evergreen was impressed enough to follow its initial investment with an additional $4.5 million a year later.

Encouraged by the support of the venture capital market, Singolda moved himself and the company's headquarters to New York in May 2009. Around the same time, he hired Lior Golan, former vice president of research and development at Internet security firm Cyota and a fellow IDF veteran, to oversee Taboola's Tel Aviv office and act as the company's chief technology officer.

Singolda would later give Golan credit for much of the company's success. At the time of Golan's hire, however, Taboola was still struggling to settle on a business model that would generate reliable revenues. Initially, many of Taboola's hosting clients had been interested in subscribing to the company's services for a flat monthly fee. Taboola quickly discarded this idea when its projected revenues seemed too low.

The company also toyed with the idea of charging host clients for increased traffic generated by the software. This scheme proved too complicated to implement. Finally, Taboola settled on an ad-supported model, in which hosting Web sites were not charged for the service. Instead, Taboola would derive revenue from ads mixed in with the videos and targeted to users by the company's DiscoverAd and Taboola Analytics software engines.

FACING CHALLENGES

Although the advertising-based approach seemed the most promising model the company had developed to date, Taboola still had a number of problems. First, the paid advertisements the company was attracting simply were not generating sufficient revenue. Also, many prospective clients were wary of attaching too many advertisements to their sites. Finally, the video content ViDiscovery that was recommending seemed limited and sometimes repetitive.

Taboola had contracts with several video content providers, and the engine could only recommend what those providers had to offer. One of the company's earliest content providers was the Israeli service 5min Media, which offered only a few thousand videos. By 2011 Singolda and Golan had hit upon a new business model. Instead of relying on video library services, Taboola would agree to feature virtually any third-party video made available to them, with a few format and content restrictions.

THIRD-PARTY MODEL

A host Web site would feature a bar of Taboola video links with the heading "Content You May Like," "Other Stories of Interest," or something similar. The links were

KEY DATES

2007: Company is incorporated in Israel.
2009: Taboola opens New York headquarters.
2011: Client list expands by 1,400 percent.
2013: Company introduces "Taboola Choice" function.
2014: Taboola enters the Japanese market.

selected for each user by the company's new Engage-Rank algorithm engine, which employed tracking cookies to identify other links the user had chosen and select similar video content.

If the user actually clicked on a Taboola link, Taboola and the host Web site would each receive a few cents from the third-party video provider. The providers generally used the videos to draw traffic to their Web sites. The third-party paradigm finally brought the stream of steady, reliable revenue the company had been searching for.

The smooth and unobtrusive interface, not to mention the money it generated, made the service popular with a number of prominent Web sites, including the *New York Times*, the *Washington Post*, and the *Wall Street Journal*. During 2011 Taboola's publisher client list grew by 1,400 percent. In August of that year the company attracted another round of venture capital investment, netting $9 million from Evergreen and a new investor, New York–based firm Marker LLC.

GLOBAL EXPANSION

By mid-2012 EngageRank was recommending some 800 million videos per day. Taboola's workforce had grown to 65 employees, most of them still operating in Tel Aviv, developing new recommendation algorithms under Golan's direction. The remainder worked in New York with Singolda or in a new office set up in London. In June of that year the company raised another $10 million in venture capital from Evergreen, Marker, and the WGI Group.

At this point, the company's roster of publisher clients, the Web sites that hosted Taboola's video links and split the revenue, had grown to more than 300. More than 130 million Internet users each month clicked on Taboola links. The company had also begun plans for an international expansion. The new London office was run by former Groupon U.K. executive Nadav Rosenberg, who spearheaded a new European business initiative.

Taboola had already put together agreements with several key British, French, and German publisher clients and was developing business relationships in Brazil, Mexico, and Poland. Rosenberg's charge was to expand the company's reach even further. The year 2013 began with one more round of venture funding. Taboola picked up $15 million in funding from a coalition of its previous investors and the Israeli Pitango Venture Capital group.

The same year the company introduced a notable addition to its recommendation engine. Taboola Choice would add an "X" to each video, enabling users to remove it from their feed. A followup interface allowed the user to specify why the video was unwanted. Users might indicate that the video was uninteresting or even offensive.

DEAL WITH NBC SPORTS

Taboola Choice was intended to help the service fine-tune its recommendation algorithm for each user, taking note of previous vetoes and adjusting the feed accordingly. It also gave users a way to flag videos that Taboola might wish to remove from the service entirely. In June of 2013 Taboola inked a lucrative deal with NBC Sports Digital to provide video recommendations for 16 of the company's Web sites. Near the end of the year, the company reached another milestone in its efforts at global expansion.

Singolda recruited former IBM executive Ran Buck to head a new company office in Bangkok, Thailand, to serve the Asian-Pacific market. The move coincided with new publisher client agreements with Hindustantimes.com, Bollywoodlife.com, and several other prominent regional Web sites. Taboola was running on all cylinders. With the expanded publisher client roster, the firm's revenues had grown by a factor of 15 in a little over a year and hovered around the $100 million mark.

In early 2014 the company made the transition to mobile devices, appearing in the apps of several key media services, including the *New York Times* and several British publications. Within months, mobile devices accounted for 20 percent of Taboola's video views. In May 2014 the company continued its international expansion with the announcement of an agreement with New Delhi Television Ltd. to provide content for the Indian media giant's various Web sites and phone apps, which attracted 40 million users each month.

ABER BECOMES CFO

In June, Taboola finalized partnership with Yahoo! Japan. The two companies collaborated to offer Yahoo!

Discovery, a content recommendation platform for Japanese Internet users that drew content from the considerable resources of the Yahoo! News network. Although Singolda had always tried to keep his employee roster and executive staff to a bare minimum, Taboola's dramatic growth compelled him to recruit a new CFO.

David Aber had worked in that position for RRsat Global Communications, DSP Communications, and Powermat Technologies. He joined the Taboola team in June 2014. In addition to the new executive hire, Taboola's increased activity in Europe and Asia had resulted in an accompanying increase in general hiring, more than doubling the company's workforce to around 150.

Although the company had experienced explosive success with its third-party content delivery model, Singolda continued to express broader aspirations for the company. "We want to help every content owner in the world, whether they are using Taboola on their own site as Editors, or as a distribution platform around the web, to have the tools they really need to scale their content business, promote their most valuable assets, and have deep analytics as to what are they getting," he explained to Forbes.com. He continued, "While our space is exciting and growing, I think there is an immense amount of technology to be innovated to allow our space to really grow; we're not there yet."

Chris Herzog

PRINCIPAL COMPETITORS

Google Inc.; Outbrain Inc; Zemanta Inc.

FURTHER READING

Farhi, Paul. "You'll Never Believe How Recommended Stories Are Generated on Otherwise Serious News Sites." *Washington Post*, January 9, 2014.

Gilad, Assaf. "Israeli Outbrain and Taboola in Market War." *Al-Monitor*, October 4, 2013. Accessed October 24, 2014. http://www.al-monitor.com/pulse/business/2013/10/taboola-outbrain-monetized-content-recommendations.html.

Orpaz, Inbal. "Start-Up of the Week/Taboola, Changing the Way We Watch Video." *Haaretz*, October 14, 2012.

Singolda, Adam. "5 Steps to a Manageable Video Strategy." *iMedia Connection*, November 10, 2009. Accessed October 24, 2014. http://www.imediaconnection.com/content/24990.asp.

Taub, Alexander. "How Two Israeli Companies Are Leading the Pack in the AdSense for Content Space." March 28, 2013. Accessed October 24, 2014. http://www.forbes.com/sites/alextaub/2013/03/28/how-two-israeli-companies-are-leading-the-pack-in-the-adsense-for-content-space.

Tarte Cosmetics Inc.

1375 Broadway, Suite 800
New York, New York 10018
U.S.A.
Telephone: (212) 677-3385
Fax: (212) 967-0960
Web site: http://www.tartecosmetics.com

Wholly Owned Subsidiary of Kose Corporation
Founded: 1999
Employees: 60
Sales: $52.4 million (2012)
NAICS: 325620 Toilet Preparation Manufacturing

■ ■ ■

Tarte Cosmetics Inc. manufactures and sells a variety of cosmetic and skin-care products in traditional retail outlets and through its online store. The company emphasizes both personal health and environmental awareness in its ingredients and packaging and makes this emphasis a key component of its marketing appeal. Tarte also pledges that its products will never be tested on animals.

TARTE BEGINS: LATE NINETIES

Maureen Kelly's original life plan did not include founding one of the world's fastest-growing cosmetics company. The daughter of a New York State Supreme Court justice, Kelly had earned a master's degree in psychology from Columbia University and was well on her way to earning her doctorate in the same discipline when she began to realize that her chosen career path was not as fulfilling or interesting to her as she had hoped it would be. In 1998 she married Mark Ludvigsen, a Wall Street bond salesman. Her new husband encouraged her to change careers and explore her lifelong interest in cosmetics.

Since the age of six, when she had concocted a mixture of cough syrup and shaving cream to use as blush on her sister's Holly Hobbie doll, Kelly had experimented with creating her own custom makeup. As a teenager, she had packaged her own lip gloss to give as Christmas gifts and since then had continually dabbled in the hobby. With Ludvigsen's support, Kelly finally quit her PhD program in 1999 and began putting together a business plan. Her first step was to call an old friend.

Troy Surratt, Tarte's first official employee, had done Kelly's makeup for her wedding and the two shared both a rapport and an enthusiasm for cosmetological experimentation. Kelly wanted to create products that were easy to use, attractively packaged, and affordable. Their first product was a gel-based cheek stain, designed to add color to one's features with a minimum of fuss. This was followed by a push-up style blush stick, which enabled the product to be applied with one hand. Working from her one-bedroom apartment, Kelly created the first Tarte line with these and seven other products. Her next challenge was to turn prototypes into actual inventory.

From our award-winning blushes and lip tints to breakthrough Amazonian clay and maracuja complexion products, we're committed to delivering real results for real women. I hope you enjoy your tarte purchase and remember: be green, be smart, be tarte!

HITTING THE SHELVES: 1999–2001

Kelly's initial investment in her new company consisted of $20,000 charged to her credit cards and drawn from savings. That figure would grow to around $100,000 over the next year. To keep overhead low, Tarte continued to operate from Kelly's East Village apartment for the next few years, with friends and family occasionally volunteering to help package and ship product. After a few months, Kelly did add a second official employee to the payroll. Later, the roster doubled to four, the number of seats at Kelly's kitchen table.

Kelly had her first order of 5,000 makeup items manufactured and shipped to her unpackaged to save costs. She had designed her own containers and packaging and ordered them from a Chinese company which also offered to load the unpackaged cosmetics into the containers and complete the packaging for around 45 cents apiece. Having already spent some $18,000 on the order, Kelly decided to save the $2,250 assembly costs by having everything separately shipped to her apartment, where her cohort of volunteers assembled them in exchange for pizza. With a healthy supply of product on hand, Kelly now began reaching out to retailers.

Kelly set her sights high from the beginning, attempting to place Tarte product with such high-end retailers as Henri Bendel and Bergdorf Goodman. It was, in fact, the rivalry between these boutique department stores that first placed Tarte product on store shelves. After multiple unreturned phone calls to Bendel's buyers, Kelly finally reached someone and "suggested" that she had already received orders from Bergdorf Goodman. The Henri Bendel staff believed her and placed an order for $15,700 worth of product. Tarte was in business.

Along with Henri Bendel's order in September 2000 came an invitation to attend a breakfast for the store's new suppliers the following week. With the fashion press in attendance, Kelly worked the room, talking up Tarte and generating coverage that resulted in even more sales. The experience would influence Kelly's subsequent approach to marketing her products. Tarte's earliest marketing efforts would focus on cultivating press coverage and celebrity recommendations. This strategy paid off handsomely in early 2001, when Oprah Winfrey publicly endorsed Tarte lip gloss.

Even as Tarte's reputation grew, Kelly continued to tightly control costs. She relied on media buzz rather than advertising and generated celebrity endorsements by sending out free product. Kelly saved on labor and shipping costs by dropping off orders at store loading docks herself, disguised with a baseball cap. Even as Tarte began developing a reputation as a hot, new industry player, its founder continued to operate out of her small apartment with the help of her parents and siblings whenever they were available.

After a year on the market, Tarte product had begun to move swiftly. The company was not yet profitable, but Kelly had every reason to be optimistic. During this time, however, terrorists attacked the World Trade Center on the morning of September 11, 2001. Kelly's husband, who worked at the center, called her immediately after the attacks to let her know that he was all right and would call her back in a few minutes. She never heard from him again.

CAUTIOUS GROWTH: 2002–05

Devastated by the loss of her husband, Kelly began to regard the new business he had inspired both as a tribute to his spirit and a form of personal therapy. She redoubled her efforts to create new product lines, craft a brand identity, and find new distribution outlets for Tarte. Despite her eagerness to generate sales, Kelly approached the marketplace cautiously. When offers from the large Sephora retail chain and the QVC cable channel came in 2002 and 2003, respectively, she turned both down, afraid that she would not be able meet the order demand. "I didn't want to overpromise and under deliver," she told *Time* magazine in a 2010 interview, adding, "Once you burn a bridge you don't get a second chance."

Sales continued to grow steadily. Tarte brought in more than $2 million in 2003 and continued to attract a celebrity following, which generated even more publicity and sales. Singer Britney Spears and actress Jennifer Garner, among others, sang the praises of Tarte in interviews and magazine profiles. The company had by now begun to develop a brand identity that included both a flair for innovative packaging and accessories, such as powder brushes that incorporated feathers and push-up stick applicators, and a commitment to charitable and environmental causes.

Tarte announced a policy of donating 5 percent of its net profits to a variety of charities. Eventually, the company would adopt homebuilding nonprofit Habitat for Humanity and Dress for Success, a charity devoted to assisting disadvantaged women in the workplace, as its two signature causes. Kelly herself could often be found hammering nails or giving wardrobe and career advice at events held by the two organizations.

By the end of 2003 Tarte's inventory reserves were strong enough for Kelly to go back to Sephora and negotiate a deal. Around the same time, the company's dedicated sales website went online. Previously, Tarte had paid to sell its products on the Beauty.Com retail site. In 2004 the company introduced its first fragrance. The same year, with sales approaching the $3 million mark, Kelly finally decided to move the business out of her apartment and into a ninth-floor suite on Manhattan's West 36th Street. By early 2005 Kelly was ready to go back to QVC.

By all accounts, Tarte's relationship with QVC proved integral to the company's success. Beginning in February 2005 Kelly began appearing personally in segments on the channel to discuss and sell Tarte products. The segments generated enough sales that Kelly was soon making several appearances per month. Kelly also took her hands-on approach to the company's website, making blog posts and chatting with customers in the site's discussion forums.

SUCCESS ATTRACTS A BUYER: 2006–10

Tarte's revenues grew steadily for the next few years. After approaching $10 million in 2006, sales went on to pass $15 million the following year. Also in 2007 Tarte was listed at number 994 on *Inc.* magazine's list of the 5,000 fastest-growing private companies. While undoubtedly pleased with her company's performance, Kelly had even more to celebrate on the personal front

during this period. She had remarried and discovered she was pregnant. She would give birth to a son in early 2008.

Kelly's family life would directly inspire her product line when she made an important discovery during a vacation with her new husband in Brazil. The young entrepreneur had taken note of the soft, unwrinkled skin of the women in a particular village and asked them for beauty tips. They responded by filling a jar with wet clay from the river bank and instructing her to use it as a moisturizer. Kelly took the jar home for analysis, and Tarte's line of Amazonian clay–based cosmetics was soon in development. The line would become a cornerstone of the company's catalog.

Another product line sprang from a partnership with Kelly's friend Scott Borba, who was marketing a line of beverage mixes made from natural ingredients selected to promote skin health. Tarte began by incorporating Borba ingredients into a selection of lip glosses. Marketed under the brand name Inside Out, the glosses were advertised as promoting external beauty and internal health. When the glosses proved popular, Tarte expanded the brand to include lipstick as well.

After passing $20 million in 2009, Tarte's sales would approach $25 million as 2010 drew to a close. The company, once run by pizza-fueled volunteers at a kitchen table, now had 51 employees, a strong industry presence, and celebrity cachet. Inevitably, the company's success attracted a number of prospective buyers, and in 2010 Kelly decided to accept a bid from Encore Consumer Capital, a San Francisco–based private-equity firm. Although the exact amount of the bid was kept private, it was announced that Kelly would retain partial ownership of Tarte and continue to run the company.

NEW OFFICES AND A NEW OWNER: 2011–14

It was business as usual at Tarte after the Encore buyout. The company had continued branding its products as both healthful and environmentally sound. During this period it focused much of its marketing on its "skinvigorating" ingredients which supported skin health while making the customer look good. These ingredients included Amazonian clay, as well as another Amazon-derived substance, maracuja oil, processed from a rainforest fruit. Tarte also touted the use of acai berries, rice bran wax, and other natural substances in its products.

Encore's investment seemed justified when Tarte achieved $39.4 million in sales in 2011 and $52.4 million the following year. By the next year the company had outgrown its 36th Street offices and procured a 15,000-square-foot space on the ninth floor of 1375

Broadway. As the move was underway, Encore Consumer Capital announced that it had agreed to sell its ownership stake in Tarte to the Japanese cosmetics firm KOSE. Kelly also agreed to sell more of her remaining shares to KOSE, which ultimately acquired a 93.5 percent stake in Tarte for about $135 million in a deal closed in April 2014. The acquisition would allow the new owner, which had previously focused on the Asian cosmetics market, to make its first foray into the United States.

KOSE's acquisition of Tarte generated plenty of industry buzz and questions from devoted customers. Initial press releases appeared to settle the issue of Kelly's role under the new ownership. She and her management team would remain in place, running Tarte from its New York headquarters as they had done in the past. Kelly would retain a small ownership stake in the company. Customers also questioned whether Tarte's boycott of animal testing and commitment to environmentally sound business practices would continue under the new ownership. Kelly herself posted assurances on various social media platforms that the company's policies in both these areas would not change. As Tarte began its new life as a KOSE subsidiary, Kelly remained the public face of the company and, for now, the guiding hand.

Chris Herzog

PRINCIPAL COMPETITORS

The Estée Lauder Cos. Ltd.; L'Oréal Group; Mary Kay Inc.; Revlon Inc.

FURTHER READING

Adler, Carlye. "Tarte Cosmetics: A PhD Drop-Out Shakes Up the Beauty Biz." *Time*, September 15, 2010.

Buchanan, Leigh. "How to Start a Beauty Company." *Inc.*, July/August 2009.

Monosoff, Tamara. "Maureen Kelly of Tarte Cosmetics." *Mominventors.com*, March 12, 2009.

Monroe, Valerie. "Success Story: How She Did It—Maureen Kelly." *O: The Oprah Magazine*, April 2008.

Newman, Karen. "Sweet Tarte: Taking Inside-Out Beauty to Heart." *GCI*, October 2007.

Wilson, Sara. "Women on the Rise." *Entrepreneur*, January 2007.

Terra Lacta

BP 29
Surgeres, 17700
France
Telephone: (+33 5) 46 30 30 30
Fax: (+33 5) 46 07 33 58
Web site: http://www.monterralacta.fr

■ ■ ■

Cooperative
Incorporated: 2012
Employees: 950
Sales: EUR 650 million ($850 million) (2013)
NAICS: 424430 Dairy Product (Except Dried or Canned) Merchant Wholesalers

■ ■ ■

Terra Lacta is one of France's leading dairy cooperatives, and the country's largest collector of goat milk. Terra Lacta represents the interests of more than 3,000 dairy farmers, primarily located in the cooperative's Poitou-Charentes base, but also in neighboring areas. Altogether Terra Lacta serves an area comprising eight regions and 22 departments. Milk collection is Terra Lacta's primary activity. The company collects more than 850 million of cow's milk and more than 130 million liters of goat's milk each year. Until 2013 Terra Lacta was also directly active in the production of dairy products, notably ultrahigh-temperature (UHT) milk, butter, and goat cheese, including the production of Protected Designation of Origin cheese under the Charentes-Poitou label. In that year Terra Lacta formed a production partnership with Bongrain SA, one of France's leading dairy products companies, in which Terra Lacta transferred its cheese production to a new company, Fromageries Lescure. As part of this partnership, Terra Lacta acquired 49 percent of Bongrain as well. Terra Lacta also operates a milk collection partnership, Société Laitière des Monts d'Auvergne SAS, with cheese producer Paul Dischamp SA. Terra Lacta generated sales of EUR 650 million ($850 million) in 2013.

FRENCH DAIRY COOPERATIVE ORIGINS IN THE 19TH CENTURY

The cooperative movement came relatively late to France's agricultural sector. Dairy cooperatives had been in existence in the United States since the middle of the 19th century, and the first European dairy cooperatives appeared in England and Italy in the 1870s. In France, however, the first dairy cooperative did not appear until 1887. The cooperative movement nonetheless grew quickly, in large part in order to free France's dairy farmers from their dependence on the country's private dairies and dairy merchants.

A number of other factors stimulated the growth of the dairy cooperative movement. Improvements in agricultural methods had enabled farmers to achieve significant increases both in the quantity and quality of the milk they produced. This increase, however, had the negative effect of reducing the price of milk, placing farmers under growing pressure. This pressure was further increased by the phylloxera plague, which destroyed much of France's wine crop in the Bordeaux and surrounding regions. As a result, many vineyard operators converted their properties to other crops, including dairy farms.

KEY DATES

1893: The Association Centrale des Laiteries Coopératives (ACLC) is created to provide services to dairy cooperatives.

1936: ACLC spins off its commercial operations into Groupement des Laiteries de Coopératives Charentes Poitou (GLAC).

1981: Capribeur becomes part of the GLAC.

1985: Charentes Lait joins the GLAC.

1987: USVAL joins the GLAC.

1995: Lescure-Bougon joins the GLAC.

2007: The GLAC forms a milk-collection joint venture with Paul Dischamp in Auvergne.

2012: The four members of the GLAC merge to form Terra Lacta.

2013: Terra Lacta agrees to transfer its industrial production to Bongrain.

2014: Terra Lacta drivers go on strike protesting new work conditions imposed by Bongrain.

Although dairy farmers found themselves faced with growing competition and sinking milk prices, the period also offered new perspectives with the appearance of the first industrial production methods, permitting the large-scale production of butter and cheese. Investing in these production methods, however, remained out of the reach of individual farmers. Farms in France were largely small scale and family owned and operated, a feature that would continue to characterize the French agricultural sector through much of the 20th century. As a result, the early dairies were largely privately owned businesses, established by wealthy landholders. Among the earliest of these was a dairy set up in Claix, in the Charente region, by Léon de Lescure de Combemary in 1884. Lescure was also the owner of the chateau de Claix.

This region also became the site of the true start of France's dairy cooperative sector, with the founding of butter cooperative in Chaillé, near Surgères, by Eugène Bireau in 1888. Bireau had served in the military in the Jura region in the early 1870s, and had spent time across the border in Switzerland as well. There Bireau had spent time studying the cooperatives then being developed by the Jura region's fruit growers. Returning to his own farm, Bireau set out to adapt the fruit growers' cooperative model to the dairy market. By 1888 he had persuaded 12 other farmers to join him in the creation of a cooperative based in Chaillé. Within just a few months, the cooperative had already attracted more than 40 members.

Under this early model, each farmer took a turn processing the milk of the cooperatives members in order to produce butter. Each farmer then recovered his own portion of skimmed milk, while the cooperative arranged for the butter to be transported for sale in Paris and elsewhere. Word quickly spread of the higher price paid by the cooperative for its members' milk, and in less than a year the cooperative expanded to more than 160 members.

GLAC IN 1936

The success of this early cooperative quickly inspired the creation of many other cooperative dairies in the region. As a result, the Poitou-Charentes region emerged not only as one of France's dairy products centers, but also as the center of the country's cooperative movement. Into the turn of the century, the region's dairy cooperatives also expanded beyond butter production to add cheese production as well. The presence of large numbers of goat farmers in the region also led to the creation of a growing number of dairies producing goat-milk cheeses. Many of these dairies focused on producing round Camembert-style cheeses.

The early growth of the cooperative movement soon led to the creation of the Association Centrale des Laiteries Coopératives (ACLC) in 1893. This body provided a range of services, including coordinating the activities and sales of its cooperative members. The ACLC started out with 20 member cooperatives, with headquarters in Niort, in Deux Sèvres, and offices in Surgères. The ACLC quickly grew to nearly 140 member cooperatives in the early 1930s. In 1936 the ACLC separated its commercial operations, as well as the collection of milk and the transport of dairy products, into a new group, called the Groupement des Laiteries de Coopératives Charentes Poitou (GLAC). This cooperative company became the major component for the future Terra Lacta.

At the same time, the foundation of much of the cooperative's industrial operations had also been put into place. The turn of the century saw a true boom in the creation of both privately held and cooperative dairies in the Poitou-Charentes region. Among these was a large-scale dairy built in Saint Loup-Lamairé by local goat farmers in 1898. The Saint Loup dairy began producing cheese, and later grew into one of the most well-known goat cheese brands. The Saint Loup dairy also became one of the forerunners in the development of another important dairy product category, the production of casein, derived from the whey left over from the cheese-making process. The Saint Loup dairy began this production in 1910. Another important dairy founded during this time was the Bougon cheese cooperative, founded in 1903 in order to produce Camembert-style goat cheese.

The growing clout of the dairy cooperative movement at the dawn of the 20th century helped transform the region's dairy market in other ways. In 1905, for example, a local cooperative in Lezay, also in Deux Sèvres, took over the village's dairy, which had originally been founded as a private company in 1888. Similarly, the Lescure dairy was transferred to a local cooperative, which grew through the next decades to become one of the regions largest dairy cooperatives. Many other cooperative dairies started out by renting facilities from private landowners.

INDEPENDENT IN 1972

The GLAC grew into one of the motors of the Poitou-Charentes' dairy industry. The cooperative invested in developing its own industrial operations, building refrigerated facilities and also providing refrigerated transport for the group's dairy products. The GLAC name itself emerged as one of the leader butter brands in France, and helped raise the reputation of Poitou-Charentes butter as being among France's finest. By the early 1950s GLAC had grown to nearly 150 members of its own.

The ACLC and GLAC had been part of an early movement to consolidate France's highly fragmented dairy industry. In addition to its many dairy cooperatives, Poitou-Charentes alone counted more than 250 dairies, many of which operated on an extremely small scale. France's changing agricultural market in the 1950s and 1960s, and the emergence of new dairy regions, particularly the Brittany region, set the stage for a new wave of consolidation. As a result, a new generation on large-scale, industrial dairy groups began to emerge in France.

In response to the changing market, the GLAC formally separated from the ACLC in 1972. This established the GLAC as an independent cooperative company, with its own industrial operations. In addition to providing collection, storage, and transport services, the GLAC developed its own network of butter and cheese dairies. The GLAC was accorded the legal status as a UCA (Union de Coopératives Agricoles, or farmers' cooperative union).

The French dairy industry was confronted by new challenges through the 1970s and into the 1980s. The adoption of industrial agricultural techniques since the 1950s had resulted in dramatic increases in the quantity of milk produced in France and elsewhere in Europe. By the 1970s the European market was faced with a vast

oversupply, not only of milk but also of butter. Although the development of a number of other dairy products, notably powdered milk, since the 1950s provided new outlets for the dairy industry, the oversupply situation, and resulting collapse in dairy prices, created an increasingly volatile climate. In order to address the situation, the European Community stepped in, instituted a strict quota system among its member nations.

FORMING CAPRIBEUR IN 1981

One result of the quota system was to encourage the growth of a smaller number of major dairy products companies, such as Bongrain, Besnier, and the future Danone and Lactalis groups. These private-sector companies grew to capture significant shares of the French dairy products markets. Faced with these large-scale rivals, France's cooperative movement continued its consolidation through the end of the 20th century.

During this period, the GLAC became the rallying point for a significant part of the Poitou-Charentes region's dairy cooperatives. In this capacity, the GLAC played a major role in helping farmers and their cooperatives survive the financial and economic turbulence of the end of the 1970s. In 1977 the GLAC absorbed the Coopérative Laitière de Gatine et du Centre Ouest (Colagaco), created in 1970. Colagaco was founded to group together several dairies, including the largest, in Mazières en Gatine, founded in 1895; in St. Christophe Sur Roc, founded in 1894; as well as in Ste. Ouenne, Menigoute, and Uzelet, near Ardin. Colagaco ran into trouble during the 1970s and was forced to close several of its dairies before being rescued by the GLAC.

Two years later the GLAC took over another struggling cooperative group, Laiterie Coopérative Saint Loup. This cooperative stemmed from the Saint Loup co-op founded in 1894, which merged with a cooperative in St. Varent in 1960 to form Coop Loup. In 1967 Coop Loup itself became part of the Coopérative Agricole Régionale du Centre Ouest (CARCO), which continued to add new cooperatives and dairies, including a dairy in Cléré, through the 1970s. This expansion was unable to prevent CARCO from going bankrupt, in 1979. The GLAC picked up the remnants of CARCO, including the St. Loup, St. Valent, and Cléré dairies. These were then merged with the Colagaco dairies to form Capribeur in 1981.

NEW MEMBERS IN THE EIGHTIES

Through the 1980s the GLAC added two other major members to its union. The first of these was Charentes Lait, which was created in order to group together four dairy cooperatives in the Charente-Maritime region. These cooperatives had themselves been founded in 1965, as part of an effort to consolidate the region's dairy cooperatives, and included the Union des Coopératives Laitières d'Aunis, the Coopérative Charente Seuldre, the Centrale Laitière des Agriculteurs Charentais, and the Union des Laiterie Coopérative du Bocage Saintongeais. Each of these companies produced approximately 50 million liters of milk per year, giving Charente Lait a total production of 190 million liters when it joined the GLAC in 1985.

The GLAC extended its reach into another of the Poitou-Charente region's departments, the Vienne, in 1987, with the addition of USVAL. This cooperative had been established in 1965 as Union des Laiteries de Sud Vendée Agricole, and grouped around the St. Michel-en-l'Herm dairy, one of the oldest in the reached, founded in 1892. USVAL grew to include such major regional dairies as the Fromagerie de Nailliers, inaugurated in 1894, and the Mareuil-sur-Lay dairy cooperative, founded in 1895, and the Le Langon dairy cooperative, founded in 1899. Through the 1970s USVAL added several more cooperatives and dairies, including Sopraval in 1976. Sopraval brought several new dairies to USVAL including in Allonnes, Chinon, and Champigny.

By the early 1990s the Poitou-Charentes region had become the clear center of France's goat-milk production, representing nearly 80 percent of the country's total production of goat-milk cheese. By then, the GLAC had raised itself to the top of the sector, vying only with rival Lescure-Bougon for the lead. Lescure-Bougon itself had been created only in 1991, uniting two of the region's leading dairy brands, including Lescure butter and Bougon goat cheese.

Spared from the quota system affecting the cow's milk dairy industry, the goat-milk sector nonetheless experienced pressures of its own. In response to the imposition of quotas, a growing number of dairy farmers had begun converting part of their own production to goat's milk. As a result, the market experienced a surge in goat-milk volumes through the end of the 1980s and into the 1990s, resulting in significant price drops. In the meantime, France's dairy industry began bracing itself for the creation of the European Union in 1992. The ending of trade barriers among the member nations promised a new and still more competitive dairy market into the turn of the century.

EXPANDING AT THE TURN OF THE CENTURY

This situation led Lescure-Bougon to join up with the three other dairy unions under the GLAC to form

France's uncontested goat-milk leader, and one of its largest dairy cooperatives altogether. The expanded GLAC now represented annuals sales of FRF 2.5 billion (approximately $400 million), and accounted for 40 percent of France's goat-milk production. The GLAC had now gained sufficient scale to confront the increasingly competitive French dairy market, as well as the growing internationalization of the European dairy industry.

The expanded cooperative started off strongly, carrying out significant investments in expanding and modernizing its production capacity. This included spending 100 million francs to upgrade Lescure-Bougon's Fromagerie de Saint-Saviol dairy, France's leading producer of packaged goat cheese. In 2000 the GLAC invested another 107 million francs to expand its dairy in Mareuil-sur-Lay-Dissais with the capacity to produce 30 million liters per year of UHT milk, under the Le Petit Vendéen brand name. The investment also permitted the GLAC to begin packaging its UHT milk in plastic bottles, as these began to grow in popularity against the segment's traditional carton-based packaging.

Into the second half of the decade the GLAC spotted an opportunity to extend its reach into new territories. Following the collapse of the Toury group, a leading dairy group in the Auvergne and surrounding regions, the GLAC teamed up with that region's Paul Dischamp cheese group to acquire Toury's milk collection business. For this, the partners created a joint venture, La Société Laitière des Monts d'Auvergne SAS in 2007.

BECOMING TERRA LACTA IN 2012

The GLAC was not immune to the growing difficulties of France's dairy sector into the end of the decade. The industry was once again facing a new turbulent period, in the run-up to the abolition of the quota system, slated for 2015. This promised to introduce still more competition in the industry, especially given the expansion of the European Union to 25 member states by then. The GLAC began preparations for this event, carrying out a restructuring of its organization, including bringing in a new president, Alain Lebret, in 2010.

The GLAC also set out to join in the new consolidation of the French dairy industry. In June 2010 the company announced plans to merge its operations with Eurial, the dairy cooperative leader in the Loire-Atlantique region. Eurial had also been extending its reach into the Poitou-Charentes region, notably through its acquisition of the Soignon goat cheese brand. The merger was slated to create a new challenger to French dairy cooperative group Sodiaal, which had claimed the country's number one spot after its merger with Entremont.

Discussions between the GLAC and Eurial continued through the next year. In the end, however, the two groups were unable to work out an agreement, and by November 2011 the companies, both of which were rumored to be facing growing financial problems, called off the merger. Instead, the GLAC attempted to take on the increasingly competitive market alone. In January 2012 the four cooperative member groups of the GLAC agreed to merge into a single, unified organization. The new group took on a new name, Terra Lacta, and took its place as the eighth-largest dairy group in France.

The move, however, proved too little too late. Amid the morose European dairy market, Terra Lacta's financial problems continued to build through the year. At last, in 2012, the company was forced to seek the shelter of a new partner, Bongrain, then one of France's leading private-sector cheese producers. In July 2013 Terra Lacta and Bongrain worked out a partnership agreement, in which Terra Lacta agreed to transfer its industrial cheese production to Bongrain, in exchange for a 49 percent in a new joint-venture partnership, Fromageries Lescure. Terra Lacta also transferred its butter production, as well as its production of cream, milk powder, and casein to Bongrain's Compagnie Laitière Européenne, taking a stake in that company as well.

Much of this transfer was carried out by the end of 2013. Into 2014 the Terra Lacta refocused around its core business of collecting and transporting milk for its 3,000 dairy farmers. This business was further extended by the group's continued stake in the Société Laitière des Monts d'Auvergne SAS partnership. The streamlined group remained under pressure, however. In May 2014 the company was confronted by a strike among its drivers, who objected to new work conditions imposed by Bongrain. Although this strike lasted only two days, it signaled the difficulties of reconciling Terra Lacta's cooperative past with its future as a partner to one of France's largest private-sector dairy companies.

M. L. Cohen

PRINCIPAL SUBSIDIARIES

Fromageries Lescure (49%); Compagnie Laitière Européenne; GLAC; Société Laitière des Monts d'Auvergne SAS.

PRINCIPAL DIVISIONS

Milk Collection; Cheese; Butter.

PRINCIPAL OPERATING UNITS

Bougon Lescure; GLAC.

PRINCIPAL COMPETITORS

Eurial; Lactalis International SNC; Société des Produits Laitière SNC; Sodiaal International SA; Terrena S.C.A.; Unibel S.A.

FURTHER READING

Aubril, Sylvain. "Bongrain Devrait Mettre la Main sur les Marques de Beurre et de Fromage de Terra Lacta." *LSA*, October 18, 2012.

Best, Dean. "Annual Sales Up at Dairy Group Bongrain." *just-food.com*, February 18, 2014.

———. "End of Dairy Quotes Makes EU Mergers Inevitable." *just-food.com*, June 16, 2010.

Bonnardel, Xavier. "Terra Lacta Officialise Son Union avec Bongrain." *Ouest France*, June 26, 2013.

Bremaud, Nicole. "Grève des Chauffeurs de la Collecte de Lait de Terra Lacta." *France 3*, May 28, 2014.

Dartigues, Daniel. "Le Glac Veut Grandir et Devient Terra Lacta." *Sud Ouest*, January 20, 2012.

"La Fusion Entre Eurial et le Glac au Point Mort." *Sud Ouest*, November 12, 2011.

Lemaire, Pierre-Maire. "Le Nouveau Visage de Terra Lacta." *Sud Ouest*, October 28, 2013.

Riffard, Xavier. "Ex Toury—Le Glac et la Fromagerie Dischamp Ont Confiance en l'Avenir." *L'Auvergne Agricole*, October 10, 2007.

"Terra Lacta: Les Chauffeurs Mettent Fin à Leur Grève." *Ouest-France*, May 28, 2014.

Toho Co., Ltd.

■

1-2-1, Yuraku-cho
Chiyoda-ku
Tokyo, 100-8415
Japan
Telephone: (+81 3) 3591 1221
Fax: (+81 3) 3580 8900
Web site: http://www.toho.co.jp

Public Company
Founded: 1932
Employees: 3,040 (2013)
Sales: ¥202.27 billion ($1.96 billion) (2012)
Stock Exchanges: Tokyo
Ticker Symbol: 9602
NAICS: 512110 Motion Picture and Video Production;
512120 Motion Picture and Video Distribution;
512131 Motion Picture Theaters (Except Drive-Ins)

■ ■ ■

Toho Co., Ltd., is one of the top Japanese filmmakers
and one of the oldest in that country. Known worldwide
for unleashing Godzilla in 1954, Toho has grown
steadily to become a nearly $1 billion international
entertainment company. In addition to film production
and distribution, the company operates a large network
of theaters in Japan.

COMPANY FOUNDED: 1932

Toho was founded in 1932. From the start, it faced serious competition in the entertainment industry, notably

Shochiku Company Ltd. Shochiku was Japan's oldest
cinema company, founded in 1895 to promote Kabuki
theater. Undeterred, Toho wasted little time before
producing some of Japan's top films. In 1954 Akira Kurosawa directed the smash hit *Seven Samurai* for Toho,
starring Toshiro Mifune.

Kurosawa would go on to direct such movies as *The
Hidden Fortress* (1958), *Yojimbo* (1961), and *Sanjuro*
(1962). Other important directors, including Masaki
Kobayashi (*Harakiri*, 1962; *Rebellion*, 1967) and Kiha-
chi Okamoto (*Samurai Assassin*, 1965; *Sword of Doom*,
1966; *Kill*, 1968), worked for Toho as well. Actors who
first signed with Toho and later went on to stardom
included Kumi Mizuno (*Frankenstein Conquers the
World*, 1965; and several Godzilla movies, 1965–99)
and Haruo Nakajima, whose face was never seen until
the 1970s, playing Gojira, or Godzilla.

In 1959 Toho released its 100th film, the three-and-
a-half-hour epic *Nippon Tanjou* (*The Birth of Japan*).
Known as the Japanese version of *The Ten Command-
ments*, the movie, directed by Hiroshi Inagaki, featured
every major actor under contract to the studio, including Mifune, Mizuno, Ganjiro Nakamura, Hajime Izu,
Akira Takarada, Akira Kubo, Eijiro Tono, Jun Tazaki,
Yoshio Kosugi, Kyoko Kagawa, Akihito Hirata, and
Takashi Shimura.

CALLING ALL MONSTERS: 1954

Toho made another huge mark on the world when a giant, prehistoric, underwater lizard made his first appearance terrorizing Tokyo in 1954 in a Japanese movie
called *Gojira*. Two years later, *Godzilla, King of the*

Monsters! appeared in the United States with new footage. It featured Raymond Burr, who went on to fame on television as detective Perry Mason. It was one of the first post–World War II Japanese films to commercially break through the U.S. market. Burr would reappear in *Godzilla 1985* (1985), commemorating the 30th anniversary of the lizard's debut.

In 1955 *Godzilla Raids Again* hit the world. Godzilla would not resurface for nearly eight years, when he began coming face-to-face with other famous monsters of filmland. Veteran monster King Kong put in an appearance in *King Kong tai Godzilla* (1963). Giant flying moth Mothra debuted in *Mosura* (1962) and costarred with Godzilla in *Mosura tai Godzilla* (1964). Rodan, a prehistoric pterodactyl, appeared in *Sora no Daikaiju Radon* (1956) first, then costarred with Godzilla later in *Kaiju Daisenso* (1968).

Ghidra, a three-headed monster from outer space, joined the lizard in *Ghidorah Sandai Kaiju Chikyu Saldai no Kessan* (1964). Ebirah, an enormous lobster, appeared in *Nankai no Kai Ketto* (1966). Godzilla's son debuted in *Gojira no Musuko* (1966). Other monster costars appeared throughout Godzilla's career, including a huge blob of sludge named Hedora (*Gojira tai Hedora*, 1971), Gigan (*Godzilla tai Gigan*, 1972), Megalon (*Gojira tai Me garo*, 1973), Mechagodzilla (*Gojira tai MekaGojira*, 1974), and Biollante (*Gojira tai Bioliante*, 1989). Just about every monster showed up in *Destroy All Monsters* (1968).

AUDIENCES GET SMALLER

Toho continued attracting talent into the 1980s. Director Juzo Itami debuted in 1984 with *The Funeral* and filmed nine other movies. Almost all of these films starred his wife, Nobuko Miyamoto, including *Tampopo* (1985), *A Taxing Woman* (1987), and *The Gentle Art of Japanese Extortion* (1992). The number of movie screens in Japan dwindled over the period from 1960 to 1990.

By 1991 there were only about 2,000 screens in the entire country, some 600 of which were reserved exclusively for Japanese films. Most of these were produced and/or distributed by Japan's Big Three studios of Toho, Shochiku, and Toei Co. Ltd., which had allied itself with Shochiku for greater distribution.

The choke hold on the limited number of screens, and the split caused by the "cinema warfare" of Toho versus Shochiku/Toei, made it very difficult for foreign filmmakers to show their movies at all, and never at both Toho *and* Shochiku/Toei theaters. U.S. blockbuster *Back to the Future II* opened in only eight theaters in Tokyo and 160 throughout Japan.

Even giant Japanese corporations Sony, which owns Columbia Pictures, and Matsushita, which owned MCA, bowed to the iron grip of Toho and Shochiku. Matsushita began working with Shochiku to open video theaters in which to show its films. Sony, on the other hand, made a saber-rattling gesture of fighting back, opening its own independent theaters starting in 1984, but the 100-seat theaters were created to show mostly Japanese films and not intended for major international distribution.

ALLIANCE FORMED: 1991

In the spring of 1991, Time Warner Inc. allied with Osaka-based Nichii Co. The company renamed Mycal Corporation, one of Japan's largest retail companies, to construct 30 multiplex theaters in Japanese suburbs, each featuring six to 12 screens. With $12.50 ticket prices, and with U.S. movie rentals bringing $236 million from Japan, it was hoped the new theaters would capture more of the huge Japanese market. Even Time Warner, however, located its theaters in areas where they would not directly compete with Toho- or Shochiku-owned theaters.

By the end of 1991 Toho had turned total sales revenues of $1.2 billion, while closest competitor Shochiku topped $400 million. Toei allied with Saban Entertainment to produce the hit television series *Mighty Morphin's Power Rangers* and the subsequent movie. They also diversified into real estate. In 1992 Toho, which then owned 158 theaters, sold the rights for a Godzilla movie to U.S. filmmaker TriStar.

Toei expanded slightly, building 10 new theaters, and creating Sun Stripe Pictures for coproduction of movies with U.S. companies. Nikkatsu went under in 1993. Toho flexed its huge legal tail in 1994, when it swatted Kia Motor Co. with a lawsuit for using a giant lizard monster resembling Godzilla. The monster clawed its way through power lines in its ads, along with the slogan, "There's only one thing more frightening to

KEY DATES

1932: Company is founded.
1954: *Godzilla* and *The Seven Samurai* are released in Japan.
1956: *Godzilla, King of the Monsters!* is released in the United States.
1959: Company releases its 100th film.
1963: Toho begins producing live theater in Japan.
1977: Isao Matsuoka becomes president of Toho.
1984: Toho revives the dormant *Godzilla* franchise.
1998: American version of *Godzilla* is released.
2003: Toho purchases Virgin Cinemas Ltd.'s Japanese theaters.
2014: Second American version of *Godzilla* is released.

Japan. Aaaaaaaaaaaaaaagh! A well-made car for under $9,000." Kia also supplied dealers with 25-foot-tall inflatable reptiles during the advertising campaign.

Toei and Saban allied that year with Italian broadcaster RTL Television to coproduce *V.R. Troopers* and *Cybertron*, companion shows to *Power Rangers*. Toei Animation allied with DIC Productions for domestic syndication and merchandising rights to the half-hour animated strip *Sailor Moon*, a $1.5 billion Japanese entertainment phenomenon featuring a 14-year-old female action hero.

GODZILLA'S DEATH AND REBIRTH

In 1995 Toho made one last domestic Godzilla film, *Godzilla vs. Destroyer*, killing off the monster. Speculation abounded about whether this was truly the end of the great lizard, a media fascination surpassed only by the death of Superman in the same decade. Toho capped 1996 with $953.8 million in total revenue and $5.4 million net income.

In 1997 television networks and book publishers moved visibly into movie production. *Mononoke Hime* (*Princess Mononoke*) was produced by Studio Ghibli Co., one of two film production companies affiliated with Tokuma Shoten (Publishing) Co., the other being Daiei Co. Directed by one of Japan's best-loved animated filmmakers, Hayao Miyazaki (*My Neighbor Totoro*, 1993), the Toho-distributed *Mononoke* made over $108 million in its first seven weeks.

Two previous Ghibli releases, *Pom Poko* (1994) and *Whispers of the Heart* (1995), brought in $22.8 million

and $16 million, respectively, making them huge successes. Disney consequently picked up Ghibli's list for worldwide distribution. Toei distributed Kadokawa Shoten (Publishing) Co.'s science fiction feature *Evangelion* in 1997, which made nearly $13.8 million in four months. Steven Spielberg's *The Lost World: Jurassic Park* opened on more than 300 screens in Japan, along with a huge merchandising deal with Mycal.

Toho posted total revenue of $905.4 million and net income of $6.7 million. By the end of 1998 over 153 million movie tickets were sold in Japan, topping the 150 million mark for the first time since 1986. Domestic box-office revenues for the year reached an all-time record high of ¥193.4 billion, compared to the U.S. market in 1996, where 1.3 billion movie tickets were sold, bringing in $26 billion in revenue.

THEME PARK OPENS: 1995

Things were looking up for the Japanese film industry as a whole. This was not the case, however, for veteran film house Shochiku. In an attempt to diversify its holdings, and as a centenary celebration of its founding, Shochiku dismantled part of its Ofuna Studio and opened the theme park Kamakura Cinema World in 1995. The ¥15 billion park was a dismal failure, closing just three years later in December 1998. Father-and-son management team Toru and Kazuyoshi Okuyama were fired. The company began moving away from production of "artsy" films, focusing more on commercially oriented movies.

Shochiku lost over 5 percent of its workforce that year, and 6.3 percent of total revenue from 1997, falling to $463.4 million, and posting a net loss of $120.2 million. In an effort to revitalize itself, Shochiku began an extensive restructuring effort, which included selling its headquarters building in Tokyo in February 1999 and naming executive vice president Nobuyoshi Ohtani, a grandson of the company's founder, to the top post.

The following month, the company announced cutbacks in its film production schedule, slashing the number of films to be produced in 1999 and 2000 to about five or six per year, with Shochiku veteran Yoji Yamada of the Tora-san series directing most of them. Shochiku, in a bold move, also announced that it would abolish its block booking policy, allowing affiliated movie houses to show foreign movies as well as its own.

Toei was also struggling in 1998, cutting over 7 percent of its workforce and posting total revenues of $600.9 million, a 14.5 percent loss from the previous year. Net income climbed just over 5 percent to $6.1 million. Toho, however, had a fabulous year, with hit movies for 1998 including *Odoru Daisosasen* (*Bayside Shakedown*), produced in affiliation with Fuji TV. It was based on the latter's hit television police series.

GODZILLA RETURNS

The company reduced its own in-house production schedule and began buying movies from other distributors. It also began refurbishing its affiliated movie houses. Their big hit came that year when TriStar Pictures brought the 54-year-old lizard and veteran of 22 Japanese films back to the big screen in the United States with *Godzilla*. It was written by Dean Devlin and directed by Roland Emmerich, the duo behind blockbuster film *Independence Day*, and starred Matthew Broderick.

Godzilla's own Web site appeared (www.godzilla.com) and the licensing frenzy began. Toys, lunch boxes, action figures, all of which Toho had been producing for years, hit the U.S. market with a vengeance, along with video games. Toho closed 1998 with total revenue of ¥83.84 billion ($927 million), up 2.4 percent from 1997. Net income jumped 33 percent to $4.5 million. The company also added dramatically to its workforce, topping out at near 1,500 employees, a 178 percent increase. Godzilla would return to the silver screen in December 1999 in *Godzilla: Millennium*, propelling the lizard into another century of fame.

NEW VENTURES

By 2003 Toho was ready to shore up its steady film production revenues with a reinvigoration of its already successful theater business. That year, the company negotiated the purchase of Virgin Cinema's 81-screen network of Japanese theaters for ¥10 billion ($83 million). The acquisition brought Toho's total screens in the country to 365, surpassing Warner Mycal's 337 and making it the largest Japanese film exhibitor.

Over the next several years, Toho concentrated on expanding and overhauling its theater business. One strategy was a focus on building and acquiring large cinema multiplexes, which quickly added to Toho's total operating screens. By 2006 the company had more than 500 individual screens in operation. That year, Toho's theaters set a new record, selling 35.5 million tickets and earning ¥45 billion ($387 million.) The company's executives, however, were canny enough to avoid sacrificing issues of quality to sheer quantity.

An article in the August 23, 2007, issue of *Variety* quoted Chikara Murikami, president of Toho's cinema division, as saying, "These days, people can watch DVDs at home on a large, clear screen. So it is vital for us to increase the different types of attractions that we offer." Toho's response to the quality issue included a proactive and early adaptive approach to the new digital projection technologies emerging at the time, as well as concessions to the physical comfort of theater audiences.

In 2005 Toho introduced 4K DCI Pure Cinema projection to its theaters. This system, well ahead of the curve of digital projection technology, was the first of its kind in Japan and anticipated the industry-wide changeover to digital projection that would take place over the next few years. In addition to pleasing the eyes of its audiences, Toho sought to increase its bottom line by pleasing the rest of their bodies as well.

JAPANESE THEATERS UPDATED

Japanese theaters, particularly in crowded multiplexes, had a sometimes deserved reputation for being small and cramped. Toho addressed this problem by redesigning many theaters to add more elbow room and by launching a prototype "Premiere" theater in the upscale Roppongi Hills shopping complex. The nine-screen complex featured spacious, comfortable seating, a full dining menu, and the largest movie screen in the country.

As Toho's theatrical exhibition division sought to solidify its dominance in Japan, its film production division continued to make waves globally. Toho had released several successful anime films over the past several years. In particular, *Spirited Away* (2001) and *Howl's Moving Castle* (2004) had proven highly successful in Japan, the United States, and across the world.

FRANCHISE GROWS

The Godzilla franchise had continued to prove profitable as the company released a third series of films in the first years of the new millennium, even garnering a star for the big lizard on Hollywood's Walk of Fame as the series came to a close with *Godzilla: Final Wars* in 2004. After a decade of dormancy, Toho set out to revive its flagship character once again with the release of a new American version of *Godzilla* in 2014. Toho's part of the deal primarily involved licensing the intellectual property rights and retaining Japanese distribution rights to the film. The film would actually be coproduced by Warner Brothers and Legendary Pictures, who would distribute it worldwide.

The deal guaranteed profitability for Toho, who assumed no financial risk and would be paid regardless of the film's box-office performance. Further, if the film proved successful, Toho would earn further revenue and benefit in the long term from further films and increased interest in the franchise. With a successful theater chain, respectable revenues from its annual slate of films and the rights to one of the most popular franchises in entertainment history, Toho continued rampaging along in the wake of its iconic creature.

Daryl F. Mallett
Updated, Chris Herzog

PRINCIPAL SUBSIDIARIES

Toho Costume Company Limited; Toho E.B. Company Limited; Toho International Ltd.; Toho Music Corporation; Toho Pictures Incorporated.

PRINCIPAL COMPETITORS

Shochiku Co. Ltd.; Toei Co. Ltd.; Tokyo Theaters Co. Ltd.

FURTHER READING

Bull, Brett. "Digital Key to Plex Pleasures: Theater Upgrades, Building Spree Feed Sector's Growing Bottom Line." *Variety*, August 27, 2007, B4.

Galbreith, Stuart. *The Toho Studios Story: A History and Complete Filmography.* Lanham, MD: Scarecrow Press, 2008.

Kalat, David. *A Critical History and Filmography of Toho's Godzilla Series.* 2nd ed. Jefferson, NC: McFarland, 2010.

Mermelstein, David. "Film Catalog Yields Artistic Gems with Global Impact." *Variety*, August 27, 2007, B1.

Miyao, Daisuke. *The Oxford Handbook of Japanese Cinema.* New York: Oxford University Press USA, 2014.

Richie, Donald. *A Hundred Years of Japanese Film.* New York: Kodansha USA, 2002.

Schilling, Mark. "Hitting the Box Office Strike Zone: With a String of No. 1 Pics at the B.O., Toho's Mastery of the 'Production Committee' System Is the Secret behind Its Dominance." *Variety*, August 27, 2007, B2.

———. "Toho Chief Says U.S. Key to Asian Aud Increases." *Daily Variety*, March 12, 2007, A3.

Sharp, Jasper. *Historical Dictionary of Japanese Cinema.* Lanham, MD: Scarecrow Press, 2011.

Standish, Isolde. *A New History of Japanese Cinema: A Century of Narrative Film.* New York: Bloomsbury Academic, 2006.

Tezuka, Yoshiharu. *Japanese Cinema Goes Global: Filmworkers' Journeys.* Hong Kong: Hong Kong University Press, 2011.

Tokyo Joe's Inc.

7332 South Alton Way, Suite K
Centennial, Colorado 80112
U.S.A.
Telephone: (303) 825-0321
Fax: (303) 721-6194
Web site: http://www.tokyojoes.com

Private Company
Incorporated: 1993
Employees: 450
Sales: $31 million (2014)
NAICS: 722511 Full-Service Restaurants

∎ ∎ ∎

Tokyo Joe's Inc. operates a growing chain of fast-casual restaurants that serve Japanese-inspired, health-conscious cuisine. The chain's menu features a variety of noodle bowls, which can be customized by patrons, as well as a selection of salads, soups, and sushi. The restaurants are popular for their modern Asian décor, casual atmosphere, and affordable prices. In addition to food, Tokyo Joe's also serves several proprietary brands of tea.

THE ENTREPRENEUR: EARLY NINETIES

As the prospective owner of a Japanese restaurant, Larry Leith cut a rather unlikely figure. By his early 30s, Leith had spent his adult life following his passions, first as a professional skier and later as the manager of a ski shop on a mountain near Vail, Colorado. The late 1980s

brought an interest in classic cars that drew him away from the Colorado snows to the arid desert of Scottsdale, Arizona, where he used his savings to open a garage that specialized in restoring vintage automobiles. After six years, however, Leith's interest in the business had waned and he began contemplating a return to his home state.

Leith had developed an obsession with opening a restaurant, despite the notoriously high failure rate of start-up food enterprises. Around this same time, several fast-casual restaurant chains had begun to spring up around Colorado. A new dining concept combining the counter-service model used by fast-food stores with higher-quality food with a more traditional dining atmosphere, the fast-casual market appealed to diners interested in a quality meal at affordable prices. New fast-casual players included the Qdoba Mexican Grill and Chipotle chains. The success of these companies, with their Mexican-inspired names and menus, suggested to Leith that ethnic cuisine might attract more attention, and diners, than traditional burgers and fries.

Leith's first step was to sell his Arizona car business and head back to Colorado in 1993, settling in the Denver area. Living off the proceeds from the sale, the young entrepreneur began putting together a business plan and educating himself about Japanese cuisine. After considering his options, Leith had settled on a Japanese restaurant for several reasons. First, he enjoyed the cuisine himself. Second, the market was already crowded with Mexican, Chinese, and Italian eateries, and Japanese restaurants were still something of a novelty at the time. Finally, after conducting a little culinary research, Leith decided that Japanese cooking tended to be one of the most healthful ethnic cuisines, with its emphasis on lean meat and fish, vegetables, and steaming rather than frying. Athletic and health-conscious, Leith wanted to offer a nutritious, low-calorie alternative in a field filled with fatty, high-calorie menu items.

A SLOW START-UP: 1993–95

Although Leith actually incorporated his business shortly after arriving in Colorado, he took an unusually long time to get the first store up and running. A 10-month start-up schedule stretched out to more than two years, as the project encountered some snags, including reluctance by commercial landlords to rent to an inexperienced restaurateur. The delay did allow Leith time to more fully research and develop his business plan, however. One of the earliest decisions had been the restaurant's name. Leith felt that the combination of "Tokyo" with the quintessentially American name "Joe" would subtly reassure patrons and make them more comfortable with the still-unfamiliar Japanese recipes.

Tokyo Joe's two year start-up phase also allowed its founder time for a crash course in his new field. Although he intended to eventually hire a chef, Leith developed the menu himself, spending months poring over Japanese cookbooks and figuring out which dishes would be most palatable to American tastes and could be prepared quickly and affordably. He ultimately developed the concept of Tokyo Joe's signature Noodle Bowls, which began with a common noodle or rice base and could then be customized according to a number of house recipes or the patron's own specifications. At the same time he was soaking in knowledge from cookbooks, Leith was receiving a more practical education from an unpaid internship at a Japanese restaurant. Although his new restaurant needed a menu, it also needed an owner who knew the restaurant business.

By the time Leith finally found a viable location for his restaurant, his cash reserves were running low. Funds from the car shop sale had dwindled and he had been forced to sell his own classic car, a 1973 BMW, to make ends meet. Help came in the form of an old friend. Todger Anderson, who had helped Leith fund the car shop, agreed to become a silent partner in Tokyo Joe's with a $220,000 investment. Leith and his wife Betsy had already put around $130,000, essentially their life

savings, into the project. The money and effort landed them an unassuming space in a strip mall in the Denver-area suburb of Englewood. By early 1996 Tokyo Joe's was ready to open.

OPEN FOR BUSINESS: 1996

By the morning of March 13, 1996, Tokyo Joe's opening day, Leith's savings had dwindled to the point that he was forced to charge his $1,000 mortgage payment on his credit card. What he lacked in cash resources, however, the young entrepreneur made up with determination and business savvy. He had prepared for his restaurant's grand opening by issuing direct-mail coupons, hanging up a large open-for-business sign, and little more. The first day's customers were unaware of his final promotional tactic until they entered the store: all orders that day were on the house. Leith simply gave away his food as a show of appreciation for the patrons who were willing to take a chance on a new restaurant. Even though the offer lasted only one day, word spread quickly. By the time Leith ran out of food and locked the doors that night, he had given away 800 free meals.

The unique promotion and the stampede of diners that resulted generated a great deal of much-needed attention in local media and dining circles. The fledgling restaurant in its out-of-the-way strip mall location needed all the attention it could get, if it was to stay alive in the crowded restaurant market. The combination of popular buzz and the novelty of fast Japanese food brought a steady stream of customers in the days and weeks that followed. After two months, the business had turned a profit, an impressive feat for a new restaurant with an inexperienced owner.

Much of Tokyo Joe's success could likely be attributed to Larry Leith's tireless attention during this early phase. Hovering in the store from early morning until long after closing, Leith made a point to introduce himself to every customer and remember their names, or at least their usual orders. He did eventually hire a general manager, but paid the more experienced employee a higher salary than he himself was drawing. As revenues grew and the small location became increasingly crowded, it became apparent that another Tokyo Joe's location was in order. Eight months after his grand opening, Leith cut the ribbon on his second store. From that point on, Tokyo Joe's would add one or two more stores every year. The chain was off and running.

TOKYO JOE'S EVOLVES: 1997–2009

The restaurant remained decidedly budget-conscious during its early years. Food was served with disposable

```
┌─────────────────────────────────────────────┐
│                                               │
│              KEY DATES                        │
│          ─────────────◆─────────────          │
│                                               │
│   1993:  Company is founded.                  │
│   1996:  First Tokyo Joe's location opens.    │
│   2009:  Tokyo Joe's opens 20th location.     │
│   2013:  Gridiron Capital LLC acquires        │
│          majority stake in company.           │
│   2014:  Company opens its first store        │
│          outside Colorado.                    │
│                                               │
└─────────────────────────────────────────────┘
```

plates, cups, and utensils. To save labor costs, there was no traditional table service. Customers simply picked their own food up from the counter. This enabled Leith to keep prices low from the beginning, with the typical Tokyo Joe's entrée selling for $5 to $6.

Despite the affordable price point, Leith made every effort to keep his food quality high and to point this factor out to customers at every opportunity. Ingredients were purchased fresh, with little of the prepackaged and processed foods served at most other restaurants. Tokyo Joe's dishes avoided such additives as monosodium glutamate and used organic produce and meats; the restaurant did not offer fried menu items.

As the chain became more successful, Leith began to rethink its no-frills dining room sensibilities. Tokyo Joe's now had the funding to add distinctive décor and architecture, conceived by Leith and executed by Jeff Sheppard, a local architect. Generally inspired by Asian design concepts, the Tokyo Joe's look featured an open kitchen; sculpted steel fixtures; and a black, red, and yellow color scheme. The disposable plates and bowls were replace by colorful ceramics. Wait staff now delivered orders to customers at their tables.

By 2004 Tokyo Joe's had 11 Denver-area locations bringing in a little over $1 million annually apiece. The typical store remained fairly small, with 90 seats and an average of 2,000 square feet of space. The chain's menu had been expanded and improved under the auspices of Paris-trained corporate chef Ray Berman, who fine-tuned the chain's noodle bowl line and changed the sushi preparation process so that rolls could be custom-prepared for each order, rather than premade at the beginning of the shift. Berman also helped to establish a children's menu.

Beyond his emphasis on his customers' health and satisfaction, Leith also fostered a teamlike corporate culture in which employees at all levels were to be treated with equal respect. The restaurant developed a reputation for tolerating tattoos and piercings on their

serving staff and using the slogan "The Few. The Proud. The Pierced." in hiring ads and employee handbooks. The Bathroom Rule was another symbol of equality within the Tokyo Joe's workforce. At closing time, a location's restrooms were to be cleaned by the most senior employee on the premises, even if that employee was Leith himself. One perk that did apply to managers only was a vacation house in Maui the company purchased in 2006, which senior staff members could use for one week a year each.

NEW OWNERS AND NEW FRONTIERS: 2009–14

The 20th Tokyo Joe's location opened for business in 2009. The stores were still bringing in an average of $1.3 million apiece annually. Leith had up to this time kept his company local, adding locations in metropolitan Denver and a few outlying suburbs. One reason he had kept his stores in such a relatively tight cluster was that they were all within easy driving distance of one another, and he could visit multiple locations per day. With some 350 employees and annual revenues of about $22 million a year, however, Leith decided to risk expanding the chain beyond his driving range.

By 2013 the chain had grown to 25 stores and even the energetic Leith had begun to struggle to keep up with the operation in the hands-on style he preferred. At the same time, the steady growth and reliable revenue stream of the Tokyo Joe's chain had drawn the attention of a potential investor. While Leith remained the company's chief executive, partner Anderson and Leith's former wife also held ownership shares and early that year, New Haven, Connecticut–based investment firm Gridiron Capital made the trio an offer to acquire Tokyo Joe's. After some deliberation, they accepted. The exact terms of the deal, which closed April 16, 2013, were kept confidential, but it was reported that Gridiron acquired majority interest in the company for roughly $75 million.

Although Leith would not be leaving the company he had founded and fostered, there would be changes under the new ownership. Leith would be replaced as CEO by Greg MacDonald, former chief executive at the nationally successful Quiznos subs chain. Gridiron apparently intended to expand Tokyo Joe's beyond its Denver territory and felt it needed an executive with MacDonald's experience to do so. Leith would become the chain's chief innovation officer, developing ideas for menu items and promotional themes as he had done so successfully in the past.

Gridiron's plans for large-scale expansion became clearer in May 2014, when the company opened its first store outside Colorado, in Mesa, Arizona, and announced plans for 29 more Arizona locations over the next five years. As it began laying out its plans for this new territory, Tokyo Joe's also began developing a franchise program. Previously, all locations had been 100 percent company owned. Now the company announced it would license the Tokyo Joe's concept to independent restaurateurs, focusing on those who could operate multiple locations, and hoped to have as many as 24 franchised locations open within three years.

By mid-2014, Tokyo Joe's was operating 29 locations in Colorado and Arizona, and had serious plans to double that number in the near future. Beyond Arizona, the company was investigating the possibility of opening company stores in Texas and California and franchise locations in Nebraska and the Kansas City, Missouri, area. The sharp expansion represented a departure from the controlled growth of the company's previous 18 years, but Leith expressed cautious optimism in an interview with the *Denver Business Journal*. "We've probably grown too slow by many people's standards," he admitted, adding, "It's never going to be about hitting a number. It's going to be about doing the right things."

Chris Herzog

PRINCIPAL COMPETITORS

Chipotle Mexican Grill Inc.; Noodles & Company; Panda Restaurant Group Inc.

FURTHER READING

Berta, Dina. "Fast Casual Players: Tokyo Joe's." *Nation's Restaurant News*, January 31, 2005.

Brandau, Mark. "Franchisees Wanted." *Nation's Restaurant News*, May 26, 2014.

Del Rey, Jason. "How to Start a Restaurant." *Inc.*, July/August, 2009.

Kneiszel, Judy. "One to Watch: Tokyo Joe's." *QSR*, June 2014.

Sealover, Ed. "Serious Growth Ahead for Tokyo Joe's." *Denver Business Journal*, April 4, 2014.

———. "Tokyo Joe's Gearing Up for Biggest Expansion in Its History." *Denver Business Journal*, April 1, 2014.

Tokyu Land Corporation

■

1-21-2, Dogenzaka
Shin Nanpeidai Tokyu Building
Shibuya-ku
Tokyo, 150-0043
Japan
Telephone: (+81 3) 3545-80633
Web site: http://www.tokyu-land.co.jp

■■■

Wholly Owned Subsidiary of Tokyu Fudosan Holdings Corporation
Incorporated: 1953 as Tokyu Real Estate Co., Ltd.
Employees: 17,106
Sales: ¥595.86 billion ($6.34 billion) (2013)
NAICS: 236115 New Single-Family Housing Construction (Except For-Sale Builders); 236220 Commercial and Institutional Building Construction; 531110 Lessors of Residential Buildings and Dwellings; 531190 Lessors of Other Real Estate Property

■ ■ ■

Tokyu Land Corporation is a leading property developer in Japan. The company is involved in the development, construction, and sale of condominiums, detached housing, housing sites, country houses, and custom-built housing. It also has operations in real estate leasing and property management, and operates leisure and sports facilities including resort hotels, golf courses, ski resorts, and senior housing. Tokyu Land became a wholly owned subsidiary of Tokyu Fudosan Holdings Corporation in 2013.

EARLY HISTORY

Since its inception, Tokyu Land was associated closely with the Tokyu Corporation, a diversified Japanese company with roots in the electric railway industry. In 2013 Tokyu Corporation still owned approximately 16 percent of Tokyu Land Corporation. Tokyu Real Estate Co., Ltd., was set up in December 1953 as a subsidiary of the Tokyo Electric Express Railway Company, which became known as the Tokyu Corporation. Tokyu Real Estate was to run the urban development, gravel transportation, and recreational property businesses of its parent.

The business of managing recreation grounds was handed back to Tokyo Electric Express Railway later in 1953, and Tokyu Real Estate quickly expanded into other areas. In 1954 the company acquired two other Tokyo Electric Express Railway operations, the Japanese Enterprise Company and Tokyu Construction Industry, operating an insurance agency, warehousing, and construction businesses. Within two years the warehousing operations and the gravel business were spun off to affiliated companies, the Yokohama Cooperative Wharf Company and the Tokyu Gravel Company, respectively.

ENTERS REAL ESTATE LEASING

In 1955 the company entered the real estate leasing market. In 1959 the Tokyu Construction Company took over the construction business. Tokyu Real Estate focused on the sale and development of real estate. By 1961 the company traded on the first section of the Tokyo Stock Exchange. The islands of Japan had limited real estate resources, so the price of land was typically very high.

Real estate prices remained high, with exceptions being in the 1970s and during the economic crisis that followed the burst of Japan's economic bubble in the early 1990s. Land in the city of Tokyo was particularly expensive in the 1980s. Fear of earthquakes kept the height of office and residential buildings in the Japanese capital at fewer than 30 stories. In the most fashionable district of the city, a single square meter cost $450,000 in 1988. Tokyu Land operated in a market where demand was perennially higher than supply.

In 1970 Tokyu Real Estate entered into a joint venture with Levitt & Sons, the largest U.S. homebuilder. The newly formed company was 40 percent owned by Tokyu Real Estate and was slated to produce 30,000 modular housing units in Japan within a few years. The company's push into prefabricated housing was supported by the Tokyu Corporation's development of new railway connections between Tokyo and the surrounding areas.

OVERCOMING CHALLENGES

In the early 1970s Tokyu Real Estate Co., Ltd., changed its name to Tokyu Land Corporation. Also during the early 1970s Prime Minister Kakuei Tanaka's plan to redistribute Japan's industrial development away from the traditional centers of Tokyo and Osaka encouraged a wave of land speculation that raised real estate prices all over Japan. The flames were further fueled by the easy availability of credit.

In addition to land speculation, the popularity of suburban housing led many to believe that residential building would represent a major growth industry in the near future. The recession of 1974 quickly put the skids on this flurry of speculation. The effect of the recession on real estate prices was devastating. Tokyo land prices went into decline for the first time since 1936. Many investors had come to view Japanese real estate as an invincible investment and were shocked when the bottom fell out of the market.

Hundreds of Japanese companies, including several large ones, went bankrupt due to their real estate investments. The crash of the real estate market took a heavy toll on Tokyu Land Corporation. The company lost money on its own holdings, and it suffered from Japanese consumers' fear of buying property. Tokyu Land was the last of Japanese real estate's Big Three to recover from the crunch. Profits were down through fiscal 1976.

The residential market was the first to rebound. Demand for houses showed an upturn in the spring of 1976. Luxury apartments in the big cities were in great demand, a trend that continued into the 1980s. In 1977 and 1978 land prices rose steadily, and in 1979 increases reached double digits, 10 percent nationally and 18.5 percent in Tokyo.

NEW GROWTH AREAS

Tokyu Land followed a policy of expanding its overseas business to 10 percent of its total assets during the 1980s. Its parent company, Tokyu Corporation, had started a major resort development in Hawaii in 1970, starting with a golf course and hotel. By 1987 Tokyu Land was offering Hawaiian condominiums for sale. In 1980 Tokyu Land established a subsidiary in Singapore and began several major commercial and residential development projects there.

In the early 1980s the market for new housing in Japan slowed. An oversupply of houses and a widening gap between housing prices and purchasing power were the main causes. The government under Prime Minister Yasuhiro Nakasone instituted an urban-renewal program to stimulate new construction and to replace old urban dwellings with new. Local governments were encouraged to relax restrictions. This cooperation was not immediate, and the plan got off to a slow start.

Although the housing market was slow, the Japanese real estate industry was reaping profits from other areas. Commercial property values in Tokyo were rising, nearly doubling in 1984. In 1985 Tokyu Land instituted a five-year plan to expand its rental property holdings. Construction on four large buildings intended to provide a steady source of rental income began in 1987. By March 1990 rental property made up about 15 percent of Tokyu Land's total income.

Between 1983 and 1987 Tokyo's commercial property increased in value by 160 percent. The city's importance as a commercial center insured that office vacancies were almost nonexistent. Fear that prices would get out of control as they had in the mid-1970s prompted the government to take action. Starting in August 1987 all property transactions involving more than 500 square meters in Tokyo required governmental approval.

KEY DATES

1953: Tokyu Real Estate Co., Ltd., is established.

1955: Company enters real estate leasing.

1961: Company trades on the first section of the Tokyo Stock Exchange.

1990: Japan's bubble economy bursts.

2001: Tokyu Land and Tokyu Corporation establish Tokyu Real Estate Investment Management, Inc.

2005: Tokyu Land has posted ¥350 billion in losses.

2007: Tokyu Land Capital Management Inc. is created as a real estate investment fund management firm.

2011: Forms condominium development partnership with PT Jakarta Setiabudi Internasional Tbk.

2012: Activia Properties Inc. lists on the Tokyo Stock Exchange.

2013: Tokyu Fudosan Holdings Corporation is created as a holding company; Tokyu Land becomes a wholly owned subsidiary.

EYEING OVERSEAS REAL ESTATE

Tax breaks for speculative land deals were abolished in 1988. The Ministry of Finance also warned banks against making too many property loans. In the late 1980s Japanese investors began to grow more interested in real estate investments overseas. Real estate in the United States could be a far more profitable investment property than in Japan. The annual yield on investment for an office building in Tokyo in 1987 was about 2 percent, compared to 5 to 8 percent in the United States.

The advantages were clear, and Japanese investment in U.S. properties became newsworthy. Tokyu Land played upon a growing Japanese penchant for American-style architecture in a unique way in 1989. The company hired a U.S. architectural firm to design Beverly Hills–style luxury houses in Tokyo's suburbs. The houses, built on half-acre lots, 10 times the usual size, offered large yards with tennis courts, swimming pools, and spacious interiors.

BUBBLE BURSTS IN THE NINETIES

In the early 1990s Tokyu Land Corporation had continued to add to its rental properties, viewing them as a stable source of income. Because Tokyo appeared likely to remain the unrivaled commercial center of Japan, Tokyu Land expected property in the Tokyo area to remain extremely valuable and expanded its sales force there. Also, massive land reclamation projects in Tokyo Bay promised new opportunities in commercial real estate.

Problems rose once again, however, as Japan's bubble economy burst in the early 1990s. From 1985 through 1990 real estate prices had soared as both commercial and individual investors had easy access to credit. At the same time, interest rates on loans were low. Japan's stock market crashed in 1990 and by December, the market had lost over $2 trillion in value.

At this time there was a sharp decline in real estate prices and the number of underperforming, or bad loans, skyrocketed. Japan's economy entered a recessionary period that would last over a decade. Harsh market conditions forced Tokyu Land to revamp operations as it saw its land investments lose nearly 50 percent of their value. The company began to look for new growth opportunities to bolster its bottom line as demand for offices and condominiums in Tokyo's market slowly recovered.

MOVING FORWARD

At the start of the 21st century, Tokyu Land entered the real estate investment trusts (REITs) market. These were investment trusts set up to invest in office buildings, apartments, and various forms of real estate. A July 2001 *Reuters News* article explained how they worked. "Under the REITs system, fund managers collect money from investors to buy buildings and assets, and pay dividends to the investors based on rental income and proceeds from assets sales."

REITs, which were popular in the United States, slowly began to gain popularity in the Japanese market and were seen as necessary to aid in the recovery of the real estate market. As such, Tokyu Land and Tokyu Corporation established Tokyu Real Estate Investment Management, Inc., as a real estate investment consulting firm in 2001. This company went public in 2003.

Japan's real estate market showed signs of recovery during the early years of the new millennium and Tokyo Land's financial performance slowly rebounded. From 1990 through 2005 the company posted approximately ¥350 billion in losses related to impaired property assets, appraisal losses, and capital losses from the sale of land. By focusing on growth opportunities, including increasing its revenues from property rentals, Tokyo Land was able to secure profit growth.

TOTSUKA TOKYU PLAZA OPENS

Tokyu Land Capital Management Inc. was created in 2007 as a real estate investment fund management firm. Two years later Tokyu Land SC Management Inc. was established as a commercial facility management firm. In 2010 Totsuka Tokyu Plaza opened. The Futako Tamagawa Rise Shopping Center opened the following year along with Abeno Market Park Q's Mall, one of the largest shopping malls in Osaka.

During 2011 the company expanded its Indonesian operations when it formed a condominium development partnership with Indonesian developer PT Jakarta Setiabudi Internasional Tbk. Activia Properties Inc. was listed on the Tokyo Stock Exchange in 2012 and was created to oversee the company's commercial and office REIT. Comforia Residential REIT, Inc., a residential REIT was listed the following year.

CREATING A HOLDING COMPANY

During 2013 the company joined with Tokyu Livable Inc. and Tokyu Community Corp. to create Tokyu Fudosan Holdings Corporation. The creation of a new holding company helped to consolidate operations and would better position Tokyu Land for future growth. The company was delisted from the Tokyo Stock Exchange later that year and moved forward as a wholly owned subsidiary of the Tokyu Fudosan Holdings.

Looking to the future, Tokyu Land focused on positioning itself as a leading property developer. During 2014 the company created its Tower Condominium Project Team to develop tower condominium projects in Kansai. It also looked for international growth opportunities and planned for additional expansion in the United States and China.

Thomas M. Tu
Updated, Christina M. Stansell

PRINCIPAL COMPETITORS

Mitsubishi Estate Co., Ltd.; Mitsui Fudosan Co., Ltd.; Sumitomo Realty & Development Co., Ltd.

FURTHER READING

Kaneko, Natsuki. "Shrinking Debt Spurs Tokyu Land to Expand." *Nikkei Weekly*, August 22, 2005.

Obayashi, Yuka. "Tokyu Land Eyes Signs of Property Mkt Recovery." *Reuters News*, July 23, 2001.

"Realtors, Builders See Higher Profits on Property Mkt Recovery." *Nikkei Report*, November 11, 2004.

"3 Tokyu Land Group Firms to Merge under Holding Company." *Nikkei Report*, May 11, 2013.

"Tokyu Land Looking to Expand on Foreign Soil." *Nikkei Weekly*, September 12, 2011.

"Tokyu Land Seeks Stable Haven in Rent Income." *Nikkei Report*, July 17, 2007.

"Tokyu Land Sets Up Tower-Condo Team in Kansai." *Fudousan Keizai Weekly*, August 19, 2014.

Virbac Corporation

3200 Meacham Boulevard
Fort Worth, Texas 76137
U.S.A.
Telephone: (817) 831-5030
Toll Free: (800) 338-3659
Fax: (817) 831-8327
Web site: http://www.virbaccorp.com

Wholly Owned Subsidiary of Virbac S.A.
Incorporated: 1987 as Virbac Inc.
Employees: 269
Sales: $70.7 million (2014)
NAICS: 325412 Pharmaceutical Preparation
Manufacturing

■ ■ ■

Virbac Corporation is a Fort Worth, Texas–based manufacturer of health and pet-care products, primarily for cats and dogs, in categories such as antiparasitics, antibiotics, behavioral health, dental health, dermatology, endocrinology, euthanasia, nutrition, and urology. Virbac also makes pesticides and agricultural chemicals, engages in contract manufacturing, and provides a range of services aimed at helping veterinarians to expand and manage their practices. Virbac is a wholly owned subsidiary of France-based Virbac S.A.

EARLY YEARS

Virbac considers its founder to be Roger Brandt, a Texas businessman involved in the pharmaceutical industry. In 1981 he spotted an opening in the pet-care field to produce skin care products developed specifically for dogs. At the time, veterinarians had nothing to prescribe for dogs other than human dermatological products, but these were not suited to the task. Brandt formed a company called Allerderm in 1982 to address this need, initially producing anti-itch shampoos. Over the next five years the business established itself in the pet-care field and attracted the attention of Virbac SA, a global veterinary pharmaceutical manufacturer.

The French company acquired Allerderm in 1987 and changed its name to Virbac Inc. Part of the company was then sold in a public stock offering held in 1994. Virbac performed well in the 1990s, as did the entire pet industry, which was worth about $25 billion by the later years of that decade, and enjoyed annual growth in the 15 percent range.

By 1999 Virbac was doing about $15 million a year in sales. To form a larger and more competitive business, at that time the company was merged with a larger pet-care company. Named Agri-Nutrition Group, the St. Louis–area manufacturer of dental hygiene, nutritional, and grooming products for cats and dogs was doing about $35 million in business each year.

AGRI-NUTRITION GAINS INDEPENDENCE

Agri-Nutrition grew out of the Health Industries Business of Purina Mills Inc. In 1993 an investor group acquired the unit through a subsidiary called PM Resources, Inc. (PM standing for Purina Mills), which then became part of a Delaware corporation, PM Agri-

Nutrition Group, formed three months later. In July 1994 the company was taken public, netting $12.1 million that was used to fuel expansion.

The company assumed the Agri-Nutrition Group Ltd. name in March 1995, and by the end of the month paid $3.3 million for Zema Corporation, a North Carolina maker of health care and pet grooming products. In August of that year Agri-Nutrition spent another $5.5 million for St. JON Laboratories, a Los Angeles–based company that manufactured oral hygiene, dermatological, and gastrointestinal products for cats and dogs and also maintained a London-based subsidiary, St. JON VRx Products.

Next, in September 1997 Agri-Nutrition paid nearly $2.5 million in cash and stock to acquire Mardel Laboratories, a Glendale Heights, Illinois, company that manufactured and marketed pet-care products for cats, dogs, birds, small animals, and freshwater and marine fish. It also offered pond accessories. Agri-Nutrition split its business into two units, the Pet Health Care Division, focusing on pet owners, and PM Resources, which took care of the company's private-label and contract manufacturing operations.

MERGER COMPLETED: 1999

Although Agri-Nutrition was more than twice as large as Virbac Inc., the later was considered the acquirer because its parent company, Virbac SA, received 60 percent of the voting stock of the combined business. The merger was completed in March 1999, with Pascal Boissy, president of Virbac SA, assuming the chairmanship, and Virbac's CEO Dr. Brian A. Crook staying on as chief executive. Agri-Nutrition's CEO, Bruce G. Baker, became an executive vice president of the enlarged company, which settled on the large Fort Worth facility as its headquarters.

Crook's tenure, however, would be brief. Within a matter of weeks he resigned and was replaced by Thomas L. Bell. The son of a truck driver, the 40-year-old Bell had devoted his adult working life to the animal and livestock health care industry. After earning a chemistry degree, with a minor in business administra-

tion, from Mount Union College in Ohio, he took a job as a sales representative in the animal health division of Diamond Shamrock. Several years later he joined the Fort Dodge Animal Health subsidiary of American Cyanamid, where he spent 13 years, eventually rising to the rank of vice president for the International Animal Health and Nutrition Division.

STREAMLINES OPERATIONS

Virbac devoted the rest of 1999 to consolidating and streamlining its business. Agri-Nutrition's Chicago and Los Angeles distribution facilities were shut down and their operations transferred to Fort Worth. All of the Chicago manufacturing was also moved to Texas, along with most of the Los Angeles manufacturing operations, leaving only a limited amount of production and marketing business to be conducted in California.

In time, that also was eliminated, leaving just the manufacturing units in Fort Worth and the St. Louis area. With its house in order, Virbac anticipated that within a few years it would increase revenues, which totaled less than $44 million in fiscal 1999, to $100 million by the end of 2004, as well as $20 million in earnings. Management was banking on its relationship with Virbac SA to spur growth.

The company also was riding the wave of the pet industry, which then was one of the strongest-growing sectors of the U.S. economy. It signed agreements to have Virbac SA distribute its products internationally, as well as to distribute Virbac SA's products in the United States and Canada. Virbac also had two drugs in development to treat horse parasites, and pharmaceutical giant Pfizer was set to market and distribute them under a 15-year agreement, pending approval from the Food and Drug Administration (FDA).

SUCCESS AFTER MERGER

Virbac achieved a solid start in its first full year since the merger, recording sales of $53.7 million in 2000, a 10 percent improvement over the combined sales from the previous year. As a result of increased sales and cost savings from the consolidation of the two operations, the company realized net income of more than $3.6 million. Virbac benefited from the increased sale of oral hygiene and dermatological products and a bump in its contract manufacturing business.

The company's consumer brands division also acquired the rights to Pet-Tabs, a cat and dog nutritional supplement. Business was also boosted in 2001 with the introduction of Iverhart Plus, a dog heartworm prevention product. In addition, the

---

KEY DATES

1982: Allerderm is founded.

1987: Virbac SA acquires Allerderm, which is renamed Virbac Inc.

1993: Agri-Nutrition is founded.

1994: Agri-Nutrition is taken public.

1999: Virbac and Agri-Nutrition merge.

2004: Accounting errors lead to the resignation of Virbac's CEO and CFO.

2006: Virbac reaches a settlement with the Securities and Exchange Commission in connection with its alleged violation of federal securities laws; Virbac S.A. acquires full ownership of Virbac Corp.

2008: Company sells its consumer brands division to Sergeant's Pet Care Products Inc.

2014: Paul Hays is named president and CEO, North America.

---

company gained FDA approval for the two Pfizer products and began manufacturing Worm-X, a dog wormer, and Virbamec, a wormer for cattle. To accommodate expanded production, a 1,500-square-foot manufacturing suite was added to its plant in Bridgeton, Missouri.

COMPETITION INTENSIFIES

At the end of 2001 management reported revenues of $60.6 million and net income of $1.3 million, far short of being on pace with the company's aforementioned goals. Eventually, these numbers came under scrutiny. In the meantime, the task of reaching the $100 million level grew even more difficult as Virbac began experiencing increased competition in the pet store sales channel, as well as from products sold by mass merchants, affecting sales in all product categories.

To offset this deteriorating situation, the company began seeking ways to sell their products through mass-market outlets such as supermarkets, drugstore chains, and discounters. Revenues also were hurt by the decision to cut back on low-margin contract manufacturing in order to devote resources to Virbac's branded products. For 2002 management reported sales of $63.8 million and net income of $3.4 million.

In 2003 Virbac sought to improve its product mix by increasing its presence in the animal pharmaceutical business through acquisitions. In August it added Del-

marva Laboratories, a small Virginia-based veterinary pharmaceuticals company that manufactured two antibiotics and two euthanasia drugs. A month later Virbac paid $15.1 million for the veterinary medicine business of King Pharmaceuticals, a Tennessee pharmaceutical company that primarily manufactured drugs for human consumption and was looking to divest noncore products.

As a result, Virbac added several products in the small-animal endocrinology market, as well as products to treat gland-related conditions. The most important of these was Soloxine, used in dogs as a thyroid hormone replacement. Other King products included Pancrezyme, Tumil-K, Uroeze, and Ammonil.

SCANDAL EMERGES

Wall Street was pleased with the acquisitions, as reflected by the rising price of company shares, which reached a high of $8.73 at the end of October. Just two weeks later, however, Virbac became mired in scandal. An outside auditor, PricewaterhouseCoopers, raised serious questions about the company's accounting practices and refused to sign off on its third-quarter numbers.

The price of Virbac shares plunged, slipping 22 percent before the NASDAQ halted the trading of the stock until the company was able to provide some clarification. In mid-December 2003 Virbac admitted that it had been improperly counting revenue since 2001. At the same time it announced that Bell was taking a voluntary leave of absence with pay until an investigation was completed by the company's audit committee. David Eller, a Houston drug industry executive, was hired to step in as interim CEO.

According to the *Fort Worth Star-Telegram*, Virbac booked revenues for products that were either returned later or destroyed after the lapse of their expiration date. Moreover, the company "shipped products from its veterinary division to wholesalers during the final days of several quarters to boost revenues in those quarters but held off on final delivery until the subsequent quarters had begun."

Virbac also "booked revenue from some products in its manufacturing and livestock division at the time of shipment. Those orders should have been treated as consignments, with no revenue counted until Virbac had been paid, the company said." As a result, Virbac's net income had been inflated by $900,000 in 2001 and $1.3 million in 2002. Reported sales fell from $60.6 million to $56.3 million in 2001, and $62 million from $63.8 million in 2002.

DELISTING AND LEGAL ENTANGLEMENTS

Law firms representing shareholders wasted little time in filing lawsuits against Virbac, alleging it had misrepresented its financial condition. Then, in January 2004 the NASDAQ delisted the company. Bell, along with CFO Joseph Rougraff, resigned. The Securities and Exchange Commission (SEC) soon launched a probe, the scope and nature of which was uncertain until January 2005, when the company received a "Wells notice," a formal warning the SEC issues to companies, indicating that the commission might pursue civil action.

Not only did the company face the prospect of SEC penalties and have to contend with shareholder suits, it also had to deal with lenders. Virbac's mounting legal and accounting fees left insufficient cash to repay borrowing. As a result, in May 2005 the company announced that if lenders failed to renegotiate the terms of several loans it might seek bankruptcy protection. At this time, the company's stock continued to trade over the counter.

Following Bell's resignation the company named Dr. Erik R. Martinez as its new president and CEO. In an effort to improve customer service, the company also placed the leadership of sales and marketing activities for its consumer brands and veterinary divisions under a single leader. By September Virbac had renegotiated and extended its credit facility with lenders, including majority shareholder Virbac S.A.

ACQUIRED BY VIRBAC S.A.

In December 2005 Virbac S.A. offered to acquire full ownership of Virbac Corp. in a $37 million cash deal, for $4.15 per share. This involved the acquisition of the 39.7 percent of the company's outstanding common stock that Virbac S.A. did not already own. Virbac Corp. formed a special committee to evaluate the offer, which was initially rejected. A positive development took place in May 2006, when Virbac Corp.'s stock began trading on the NASDAQ Capital Market.

In July 2006 Virbac achieved another important milestone when the company reached a settlement with the SEC in connection with its alleged violation of federal securities laws. Although it did not admit or deny any wrongdoing, and did not have to pay a fine, the company agreed to consent to an injunction requiring compliance with federal securities laws, and to provide compliance, accounting, and regulatory training to select personnel. At the same time Virbac S.A. increased its offer to acquire Virbac to $43.8 million, or $4.85 per share.

Virbac S.A. increased its offer to acquire full ownership of Virbac Corp. twice more, increasing it to $5.25 per share and ultimately $5.75 per share in October 2006. The offer was completed in November, when Virbac S.A.'s indirect, wholly owned subsidiary, Labogroup Holding Inc., secured 100 percent of Virbac Corp.'s shares. Public trading of Virbac Corp.'s shares ceased, and the company became an indirect, wholly owned Virbac S.A. subsidiary.

SELLS CONSUMER BRANDS DIVISION

Virbac rounded out the decade by selling its consumer brands division to Omaha, Nebraska–based Sergeant's Pet Care Products Inc. in 2008. The division included Virbac's aquatic products, dental solutions products, and external and internal health care products, sold under brand names such as WormX, WormXPlus, Mardel, LiveMeter, Petrodex, and Zema. Early the following decade parent Virbac S.A. continued to expand its broader animal health business.

For example, the company offered a global vaccine platform for large animals, which it had grown via acquisitions of laboratories in Australia, Colombia, and New Zealand. By 2013 Virbac had established a collaboration and licensing agreement with NovaBay Pharmaceuticals Inc., acquiring worldwide rights to the compound auriclosene, which was used in conjunction with urinary catheters.

Progress continued in late 2013 when Virbac received the Veterinary Oral Health Council's Seal of Acceptance for its VeggieDent Tartar Control Chews, which reduced halitosis, plaque, and calculus in dogs. In early 2014 the company announced that it had appointed Paul Hays as president and CEO, North America. Heading into 2015 the future appeared to be bright for Virbac. The company had recovered from significant difficulties, and as part of Virbac S.A., appeared to be positioned for continued growth and success.

Ed Dinger
Updated, Paul R. Greenland

PRINCIPAL SUBSIDIARIES

PM Resources, Inc.; St. JON Laboratories, Inc.; Virbac AH, Inc.; Virbac Canada, Inc.

PRINCIPAL COMPETITORS

Bayer HealthCare Animal Health Division; Farnam Companies, Inc.; Merial, Inc.

FURTHER READING

"Colombia: Virbac Grows Sales of Veterinary Medicines." *South American Business Information*, September 20, 2012.

"NovaBay Signs License Agreement with Virbac for Animal Health." *Midnight Trader Live Briefs*, May 28, 2013.

Perotin, Maria M. "Texas-Based Animal Health Products Maker Admits to Inflating Revenue." *Fort Worth Star-Telegram*, December 19, 2003.

Shlachter, Barry. "Trading of Stock Halted for Fort Worth, Texas, Animal Health Products Maker." *Fort Worth Star-Telegram*, November 14, 2003.

Wahlstrom Group LLC

800 Connecticut Avenue
Norwalk, Connecticut 06854
U.S.A.
Toll Free: (800) 348-6347
Web site: http://www.wahlstrom.com

Wholly Owned Subsidiary of The Interpublic Group of Companies Inc.
Founded: 1954 as Wahlstrom & Company
Employees: 210
Sales: $200 million (2013 est.)
NAICS: 541810 Advertising Agencies

■ ■ ■

Wahlstrom Group LLC is a Norwalk, Connecticut–based directory marketing company. The company offers clients in the United States, Canada, and the Caribbean such services as Yellow Pages advertising, for both printed book and online directories; White Pages listings; interactive services, including search engine marketing and online display ad placement; business listing management, ensuring that online brick-and-mortar business information is accurate; social media monitoring to help shape a client's brand; and mobile media advertising advice. In addition to its Connecticut home, Wahlstrom maintains offices in Chicago, Minneapolis, and Philadelphia. Wahlstrom is a wholly owned subsidiary of The Interpublic Group of Companies Inc. (IPG) and part of the Orion Holdings division of IPG Mediabrands, created by IPG to manage its global media-related assets.

A MOMENT OF INSPIRATION

The Wahlstrom Group was founded by Frederick D. Wahlstrom. After graduating from Purdue University, he went to work in the magazine advertising field in Chicago in the mid-1930s, selling ad space for such magazines as *Coronet*, *Esquire*, and *This Week*. It was during the 1930s that he noticed an advertisement for an Arrow shirt and decided to purchase one. Finding a store that actually sold that particular shirt, however, proved difficult. The experience gave Wahlstrom a business idea: connecting national advertisements to local providers.

After eight years in the magazine business, Wahlstrom went to work as a field representative for the Association of National Advertisers, Inc. (ANA), an advertising industry trade association. Under the auspices of the ANA-sponsored Distribution Council, a nonprofit entity for which he served as president, Wahlstrom was able to flesh out his idea for a localized national advertising plan. Dubbed "Operator 25," it was unveiled at the Waldorf-Astoria Hotel in New York City following an ANA board meeting in July 1948. Under the plan, subscribing companies informed consumers in their national advertising that if they wanted to find a local dealer, they could call their local Western Union office and ask for Operator 25. In each Western Union office, a specially trained operator was made available to provide assistance.

Operator 25 enjoyed some success for a few years, but Wahlstrom found another way to connect national companies and local dealers: the Yellow Pages. The combination of telephone listings and advertising was

COMPANY PERSPECTIVES

Our mission is to deliver data-driven marketing solutions with a local point of view. Your top priorities are ours—developing the optimal local media mix for the best return on your investment.

almost as old as the instrument itself. Just two years after the introduction of the telephone, the New Haven District Telephone Company created the first directory in 1878. Although just a single page, it laid the foundation for the millions of "phone books" that would be printed in the years ahead. In the 1880's, according to lore, a telephone directory printer ran out of white paper and began using yellow instead. Soon the "yellow pages" became standard. It was also during this period that the Chicago printing firm RR Donnelley began to sell classified telephone directory ads, giving birth to the Yellow Pages industry as telephone companies across the country tapped into this new source of revenue.

Initially, directory advertising was simply seen as a way to offset printing costs. In time, however, it became a significant profit center, especially after World War II. When the war came to an end in 1945, some 14 million telephones were in service in the United States. Five years later the amount doubled. Moreover, the Yellow Pages had become accepted by both merchants and consumers, the former willing to advertise in the directories because a large percentage of the people who used the Yellow Pages were ready and motivated buyers. The widespread distribution and increasing popularity of the Yellow Pages also presented Wahlstrom with a new for-profit opportunity to bring together national companies, local merchants, and customers.

WAHLSTROM & COMPANY FORMED: 1954

In 1954 Wahlstrom established Wahlstrom & Company in Stamford, Connecticut. National companies hired Wahlstrom to place their ads in local telephone directories across the country with tie-ins to local dealers, the so-called closed national trademark plan. It was a novel concept, and Wahlstrom & Company was the first company to be recognized in the telephone industry as a special Yellow Pages agency. One of Wahlstrom's earliest clients was insurer Aetna, Inc., a relationship that would carry on to the present day.

To help grow the business, Wahlstrom hired Francis J. Barton. A New York City native, Barton earned his

college degree from City College of New York. He then served a tour of duty in Vietnam as a Marine captain before joining St. Regis Paper Company and becoming involved in Yellow Pages advertising. A St. Regis division was one of Wahlstrom & Company's clients, and Wahlstrom persuaded Barton to join him in 1970. The agency was still privately held, but that came to an end in 1973 when major advertising firm Foote, Cone & Belding acquired the business.

WAHLSTROM DIES: 1978

After Wahlstrom died in 1978, Barton was named president of Wahlstrom & Company. He took over a company that was preeminent in its field. A year later Wahlstrom became the first authorized selling representative recognized by the American Association of Advertising Agencies. It remained on the cutting edge of the Yellow Pages industry by being the first agency to use computers to administer Yellow Pages programs for its national clients. Wahlstrom was also prepared for the revolution that was about to take place after AT&T, in response to an antitrust lawsuit, was forced to dismantle the Bell System that had provided local telephone service for more than century. On January 1, 1984, the system was broken into seven regional concerns, the so-called Baby Bells, and in the process the Yellow Pages industry exploded.

Immediately after the breakup of the Bell System, many new telephone directories with Yellow Pages were introduced, each vying for advertising dollars. Soon the number of directories in the United States doubled to more than 6,000, some of which were directed at niche markets, such as the Silver Pages, a directory aimed at older Americans. Many of the directories, whether independent or subsidiaries of the regional Bells, also began to invade one another's territories. Barton summed up the situation in a *New York Times* article from December 22, 1987: "We had a century-old business that had been operating in a monopolistic cocoon. Now there is a choice of media."

FRESH CHALLENGES

Specialty Yellow Pages ad agencies such as Wahlstrom faced a host of new challenges. The days of simply placing an ad for a client in the only directory in a market were over. Before the Bell breakup, a company could achieve national Yellow Pages coverage for an outlay of less than $100,000. With the proliferation of books, however, several million dollars would have to be spent to achieve total coverage. Wahlstrom now had to become even more of a full-service agency. It advised clients about which directories offered the best return

KEY DATES

1954: Frederick Wahlstrom forms a Yellow Pages' advertising agency.
1973: Company is sold to Foote, Cone & Belding.
1978: Founder Wahlstrom dies.
2002: Company merges with Bozell Yellow Pages to create Wahlstrom Group LLC.
2010: Kathleen DeCaire-Aden is named CEO.

for their ads and then tracked the results. In addition, Wahlstrom offered design services, creating ads and then tailoring them for specific markets. The agency became the perennial winner of the creative media award in its category from influential trade publication *Marketing and Media Decisions.*

Abiding by the guidelines established by the Yellow Pages Publishers Association, Wahlstrom served only clients that generated 30 percent of their sales revenue from outside their home state. They also had to advertise in 20 telephone directories in three states. Most Wahlstrom clients spent more than $100,000 on ads, appearing in 1,000 to 2,000 books.

Foote, Cone & Belding was not alone in seeing the value of a specialty firm like Wahlstrom. Other large advertising agencies acquired Yellow Pages specialists to provide clients with yet another service. Wahlstrom also became involved in the sector's consolidation. In 1988 it acquired Philadelphia-based McCrea Associates, which had been in the Yellow Pages business for 27 years.

More dramatic changes were in store for Wahlstrom and the Yellow Pages industry in the final decade of the century. Wahlstrom was part of an effort called Brand Sell to use Yellow Pages ads to support a company's brand-building efforts rather than tout a specific product. New media was also revolutionizing the industry. Experiments were conducted with Talking Yellow Pages, making use of the telephone, and AT&T marketed a videophone that could be made available in public spaces as a type of consumer directory. Both would pale in comparison to the Internet, which began to become a commercial force with the introduction of the first Web browser in 1994.

The Electronic Yellow Pages (EYP) quickly revolutionized the Yellow Pages industry. By 1997 there were more than 265 EYP directories on the Internet. To serve its clients, Wahlstrom began working with both traditional Yellow Pages publishers and the new online providers. The company would also branch into search

engine marketing to better serve clients. Despite the new online option, traditional Yellow Pages remained a lucrative business at the turn of the century.

MERGER: 2002

In 2002 Wahlstrom was merged with Bozell Yellow Pages to create Wahlstrom Group LLC, a unit of IPG-owned Initiative Media. The enlarged Wahlstrom kept its Connecticut headquarters and maintained full-service offices in Chicago; Dallas; Irvine, California; Los Angeles; Louisville, Kentucky; Minneapolis; Morris Plains, New Jersey; Philadelphia; and Toronto, Canada. In addition to the United States and Canada, the agency did business in the Caribbean. Late in 2002 Wahlstrom also received a new CEO, Peter Broadbent. He had been with the company since 1983 and served as president since 1998. He took the reins of a company that ranked as the second-largest certified marketing representative in the industry with annual billings of about $175 million.

Wahlstrom continued to adapt to the times in the first decade of the 21st century. In addition to the Internet, the Yellow Pages industry took advantage of mobile telephones that soon evolve into smartphones, making AT&T's videophone of the previous generation somewhat prescience. In addition, Wahlstrom offered services to help clients take full advantage of the opportunities afforded by social media.

Broadbent left Wahlstrom in 2009. Taking charge of the company as president was Geoff Kehoe, previously the director of e-commerce marketing for Motorola. A year later, he was replaced by Kathleen DeCaire-Aden, who assumed the title of CEO. She had also worked at Motorola, serving as global director of e-commerce marketing. She made it clear that she would pursue cross-platform expansion, using all available tools to help national companies reach customers at the local level.

That which Frederick Wahlstrom once considered "local" had changed. Local was more than physical; it was now digital and virtual. Wahlstrom became one of the leading media agencies that offered what were called geo-targeted leads. No longer did advertisers rely on customers to pick up a telephone directory and leaf through the Yellow Pages to find them. They could now send notices to potential consumers on their mobile phones as they approached a merchant using location targeting. It was still a blunt instrument, however, one that did not take context into account.

Wahlstrom would also evolve as an organization. In December 2010 IPG moved it and two other media specialty units into Orion Holdings. As part of the restructuring, Debbie Lance assumed leadership as executive vice president/managing director. Regardless of who was in charge or where it fell in an organizational chart, Wahlstrom continued to face the perpetual challenge of adapting to the way consumers responded to new technologies in order to serve the commercial needs of its clients.

Ed Dinger

PRINCIPAL COMPETITORS

CoBrand Media; Millard Rosenberg National Yellow Pages, Inc.; VendAsta Technologies Inc.

FURTHER READING

Borowski, Neill. "War of the Yellow Pages." *Philadelphia Inquirer*, July 7, 1985.

Dougherty, Philip H. "Competition Grows in the Yellow Pages." *New York Times*, December 22, 1987.

Eder, Peter F. "Big Changes: Ahead for Telephone Directories." *Futurist*, April 1999.

Mangan, Dan. "Clients Look to Wahlstrom for Green Light before Advertising in the Yellow Pages." *Fairfield County Business Journal*, August 24, 1992.

"New Plan Started for National Ads." *New York Times*, July 16, 1948.

Turmelle, Luther. "No Yellowing of These Pages." *New Haven Register*, September 19, 1999.

Wanzl GmbH & Co. Holding KG

Bubesheimer Strasse 4
Leipheim, 89340
Germany
Telephone: (+49 8221) 729-0
Web site: http://www.wanzl.com

Private Company
Founded: 1947 as Werkstatt für Waagenbau und Reparaturdienste
Employees: 4,400 (2013)
Sales: EUR 530 million ($684 million) (2012)
NAICS: 333924 Industrial Truck, Tractor, Trailer, and Stacker Machinery Manufacturing; 332618 Other Fabricated Wire Product Manufacturing; 326199 All Other Plastics Product Manufacturing

■ ■ ■

Wanzl GmbH & Co. Holding KG is the holding company of the Wanzl group, the world's leading manufacturer of shopping carts. Headquartered in Leipheim in Bavaria, Wanzl produces roughly 2.5 million shopping carts per year in its production plants in Germany, France, the United Kingdom, the Czech Republic, and China. In North America the company owns the Canadian Cari-All Group, a leading shopping cart supplier of the Cari-All, Technibilt, and Rondi brands manufactured by Technibilt in the United States and Industries Rondi in Canada.

Wanzl is also an internationally leading producer of luggage carts, which are in use in more than 300 airports around the world. Other Wanzl divisions supply hotels and warehouses with multifunctional carts and storage systems and offer the complete interior design of retail stores.

POSTWAR PRODUCTION BEGINS

Before Rudolf Wanzl Sr. settled in Leipheim, Bavaria, the mechanic ran his own agricultural machinery workshop in Nazi-occupied Olmütz, Czechoslovakia. After World War II, the German-speaking population, including Rudolf Wanzl Sr. and his family, was expelled from the country. While his father set up a scale manufacturing and mechanical repair workshop in Leipheim, Rudolf Wanzl Jr. became a trainee at the Augsburg subsidiary of U.S.-based National Cash Register Company (NCR).

The company asked Wanzl to manufacture a dozen wire shopping baskets for the self-service shop exhibition at its showroom in Augsburg. Wanzl Jr., along with his father, made them at their workshop. Wanzl Jr. went to the United States on an exploratory trip. It was there he saw the first shopping cart, a movable metal frame with wheels and two wire baskets attached to it. Fascinated with the idea of self-service shopping, which was still unknown in Germany at the time, 23-year-old Wanzl Jr. decided to start his own business.

Back in Germany he and his father, with a few helpers, worked day and night to fill the first incoming orders for shopping baskets from retail store owners who had visited NCR's showroom. In 1948 Wanzl Sr. and Wanzl Jr. decided to join forces with the Siegel brothers, two experienced businessmen from their home region. Together, they established the partnership Wanzl & Sie-

COMPANY PERSPECTIVES

Wanzl solutions are always synonymous with exceptional quality, attractive aesthetics and distinctive design combined with optimum ergonomics. As a high-performance and value-oriented family company, as well as a quality leader, our name is our guarantee that we will contribute to the success of our customers with ideas, creativity and service—both now and in the future.

gel OHG in 1948. When a consumer co-op in Hamburg opened its first self-service store in 1949, Wanzl & Siegel delivered 100 baskets and built the first 40 shopping carts. In 1950 Wanzl Jr. patented his stackable shopping basket with a hinged handle in Germany, which became a best seller.

SIEGEL BROTHERS LEAVE

One year later he received a patent on the first shopping cart with four flexible wheels and a fixed basked. Marketed under the name Concentra, the simple construction, with its modern but timeless design, set a benchmark for the coming decades. When the Siegel brothers left the company at the end of 1954 and established their own shopping cart factory, Wanzl Sr. and Wanzl Jr. renamed the business Wanzl & Sohn Drähte und Metallwarenfabrik.

Realizing the enormous market potential of his invention, Wanzl Jr. learned everything he could about the self-service shopping culture in the United States. He held lectures on the subject, where he also presented his first shopping cart models to potential customers. Wanzl quickly established personal contacts to several managers of retail store chains in big German cities such as Cologne, Düsseldorf, and Berlin. As the German economic miracle grew in the 1950s, the number of self-service retail stores grew rapidly, from about 200 in 1954 to roughly 1,400 in 1956. By then Wanzl employed a staff of 74, and sales reached DEM 1 million.

GERMAN SELF-SERVICE BOOM

The continued rapid spread of self-service supermarkets in West Germany was the main driving force behind Wanzl's dynamic growth in the 1960s. In addition to technical insight and entrepreneurial vision, Wanzl Jr.

had a talent for building rapport with his customers, who were the heads of purchasing at big German retail companies. As the latter set up an extensive network of self-service outlets across the country, Wanzl produced the shopping carts for the new stores they opened.

As the number and size of orders increased, the company transitioned to the industrial mass production of shopping carts. By 1966 about 400 people worked for Wanzl, generating DEM 16 million in annual sales. At the beginning of the 1970s the construction of new retail outlets in Germany moved from the inner cities to the suburbs, and all of them were equipped with shopping carts.

The company's new shopping cart models were equipped with a foldable children's seat. In addition, a foldable back allowed several shopping carts to be stacked into each other in a row, which saved retailers valuable sales floor space. When German retailers complained about losing money through shopping cart theft, Wanzl developed a patented, coin-operated locking mechanism attached to the handlebars, cutting their losses roughly in half.

The 1970s in Germany saw the rise of new discount and drugstore retail chains, followed by the mushrooming of home improvement and garden superstores in the 1980s, which contributed largely to Wanzl's continued growth. During the same period Wanzl ventured into Western Europe. The company established subsidiaries in France, Belgium, and the Netherlands, and later in Switzerland, Austria, and the United Kingdom. In 1982 a production facility was built in Sélestat, France. This step established Wanzl firmly in the French market, where the Carrefour group, one of Europe's biggest retail companies, become a Wanzl customer.

VENTURING INTO EASTERN EUROPE

In the late 1980s Wanzl was operating at the upper limit of the company's production capacity. Consequently, a large property in Leipheim was acquired, where a new production facility was soon to be built. The surprising opening of the Berlin Wall in November 1989 resulted in an unexpected boom in the West German retail industry. As soon as the new factory in Leipheim was finished in 1990, Wanzl received large orders from the big retail chains setting up new outlets all over eastern Germany.

Within one year the company's sales climbed by 50 percent, or DEM 100 million, while its workforce grew by more than 600 employees. When the large German retail chains Wanzl had served for more than three

KEY DATES

1947: Rudolf Wanzl Sr. establishes a scale manufacturing and mechanical repair workshop in Leipheim.

1951: The Concentra shopping cart with flexible wheels and a fixed basket is patented.

1982: Wanzl sets up its first production facility abroad in France.

1995: A production facility in the Czech Republic starts operations.

2000: Production of shopping carts begins in Shanghai.

2003: The new Tango line of plastic shopping carts is launched.

2012: North American shopping cart manufacturer Cari-All Group is taken over.

decades ventured further into Eastern Europe in the early 1990s, the company followed suit. After the foundation of the Czech Republic in 1991 Wanzl Jr. returned to his home region, where a new factory was built in Olmütz in 1995. The new plant supplied mostly semifinished products to Wanzl's factories in Germany.

Between 1991 and 1994 the company also set up sales subsidiaries in Hungary and Poland. By the mid-1990s the Wanzl group reported annual sales of more than DEM 300 million. In 1991 Wanzl established its new Shop Solutions business division. It started building shelf systems for its retail customers and helped them with the interior design of new outlets. Ten years after its foundation Wanzl's shop solutions division had built the interior of approximately 3,000 retail outlets and equipped them with shelf systems, according to *Lebensmittel Zeitung*, on March 1, 2002.

GOING GLOBAL

In 1998 Wanzl Jr. handed the day-to-day management of the company over to his son, Gottfried Wanzl, so he could have more time to dream up new Wanzl products. At the dawn of the 21st century the Wanzls decided to continue their international expansion strategy. In 1998 the company opened a sales subsidiary in Spain.

Having established a strong market position in Western and Eastern Europe, they followed in the footsteps of large German retailers such as Metro AG to conquer new markets elsewhere in the world. After a new subsidiary had been founded in China in 1998, the company leased a factory in Shanghai and started the production of shopping carts for the Asian market in 2000. In the following year Wanzl opened sales offices in South Korea, Russia, Slovakia, and Italy.

In 2002 a subsidiary was founded in Melbourne, Australia. According to *Lebensmittel Zeitung*, on October 2, 2003, Wanzl had established subsidiaries in 12 counties and employed about 2,500 staff worldwide. In the second half of the decade the company opened additional sales offices in Ukraine, the United Arab Emirates, and India. In 2007 Wanzl moved its production in China to a newly built factory in Shanghai. By the end of the decade about two-thirds of the company's total sales were generated outside on Germany.

DIVERSIFICATION AND INNOVATION

At the beginning of the 21st century Wanzl offered more than 200 versions of shopping carts. However, the rapid expansion of large retail companies in Eastern Europe had long passed its peak. Wanzl customers in Western Europe ordered new carts, but mainly to maintain their existing inventory. To continue on its growth path, the company applied its know-how to similar products in other industries. As Wanzl had helped millions of shoppers to conveniently haul their groceries and other goods to the supermarket checkout counter, they then set out to help millions of travelers move their luggage around and conveniently do their shopping at airports and train stations.

In 2001 Wanzl's newly established Airport and Security division started providing some of the world's largest airports, such as in Paris, Tokyo, Dubai, and Shanghai, with special luggage carts featuring a grip brake. One year later Wanzl launched its new Logistics and Industry division, which targeted potential industrial clients as a supplier of multifunctional carts and storage systems for warehouses and logistics centers.

TRIM TROLLEY INTRODUCED: 2004

In 2006 the company's Hotel Service division was established to market products such as multipurpose carts and flexible storage products. The year 2003 had seen the launch of a new generation of Wanzl shopping carts. The new Tango line featured a shopping basket made of lightweight plastic, instead of steel wire, which was available in bright colors. One year later Wanzl introduced the new Trim Trolley in the United Kingdom.

Equipped with a sensor to calculate the calories burned during a shopping trip, the Trim Trolley also featured an additional wheel, the resistance of which could be raised to make pushing the cart through the store more of a workout. By 2007, when the company celebrated its 50th anniversary, Wanzl had sold over 25 million shopping carts worldwide. With shopping carts still accounting for almost half of its total sales, the company was busier than ever before.

ACQUISITIONS FOR FUTURE GROWTH

In 2007 Wanzl took over the German production of its bankrupt partner-turned-competitor, Draht- und Metallwarenfabrik BrüderSiegel GmbH & Co. KG in Jettingen-Scheppach. That company was by then the country's second-largest shopping cart manufacturer, according to *Lebensmittel Zeitung* on August 24, 2007. However, rising prices for steel and fuel, as well as the growing number of competitors from abroad with products made in Asia, increased the pressure on prices later in the decade. In 2010 Wanzl's Shop Solutions division acquired Unseld Innenausbau und Ladenbau GmbH, a shop interior outfitter in Ulm with 30 employees, and subsidiaries in Austria and Switzerland.

After 40 years of working relentlessly on building the family business, Wanzl Jr. died at age 86 on February 8, 2011. About one year later the Wanzl group acquired the Canadian Cari-All Group, a leading shopping cart supplier of the Cari-All, Technibilt, and Rondi brands serving more than 850 retail customers in North America. The deal included Industries Rondi Inc. in Montreal, Canada, and Technibilt in Newton, North Carolina, as well as distribution centers in North Las Vegas, Nevada, and Montreal, Canada.

GLOBAL LEADER

As reported by *Südwest Presse* on November 17, 2012, Wanzl received orders in that year alone to produce 6,000 luggage carts for Incheon International Airport near Seoul in South Korea, and 5,200 carts for Hong Kong International Airport. By then Wanzl was a globally leading company in that market segment, having provided luggage carts to over 300 airports around the world. By 2013 Wanzl produced roughly 2.5 million shopping carts per year, which were used by millions of people in supermarkets and warehouses.

The company's luggage carts were in use in over 300 airports around the world. With retail markets stagnating in Western Europe, Wanzl saw potential for future growth in Asia and South America as well as in new products for hotels and warehouses. At the company's newly built Creative Center that opened in 2009, engineers and designers were working on Wanzl's "intelligent" shopping cart of the future.

It might feature an electric motor for a smoother shopping trip. Its onboard computer would entertain kids with the latest computer games, guide shoppers to their desired destination in the store, automatically scan the goods placed into the cart, and use radio frequency identification (RFID) technology to transmit the sum total to the automated checkout counter.

Evelyn Hauser

PRINCIPAL SUBSIDIARIES

Wanzl Metallwarenfabrik GmbH; Mouldtec Kunststoff GmbH; Wanzl Commercial Equipment (Shanghai) Co. Ltd. (China); Wanzl SAS (France); Storetec Ltd. (UK); Cari-All Products Inc. (Canada); Technibilt, Ltd. (USA); Industries Rondi Inc. (Canada); Wanzl spol. s r.o. (Czech Republic).

PRINCIPAL DIVISIONS

Retail Solutions; Shop Solutions; Logistics + Industry; Airport + Security Solutions; Hotel Service.

PRINCIPAL COMPETITORS

Caddie Strasbourg S.A.S; Changshu Yirunda Business Equipment Factory; Creaciones Marsanz S.A.; La Fortezza S.p.A.; Mago Group; Tegometall International Sales GmbH; Unarco Industries LLC.

FURTHER READING

Dobelmann, Cathrin. "Wer steckt hinter dem Einkaufswagen?" *Stern*, April 26, 2007.

Evans, Doris. "Wanzl agiert flexibel und weltweit." *Lebensmittel Zeitung*, March 1, 2002.

"Grossauftrag für Wanzl aus Südkorea." *Südwest Presse*, November 17, 2012.

"Harris Williams Helps Cari-All Group in Sale to Wanzl." *Entertainment Close-Up*, January 23, 2012.

Hörmann, Friedrich. *Rudolf Wanzl: Auf Draht*. Glött, Germany: Friedrich Hörmann Biografien, 2005.

Konrad, Jörg. "Wanzl übernimmt Siegel." *Lebensmittel Zeitung*, August 24, 2007.

Lauer, Marco. "Revolution auf Rollen." *brand eins Wirtschaftsmagazin*, February 25, 2011.

Mertens, Bernd. "Meister des Alltags." *Wirtschaftswoche*, June 24, 2013.

"Shop till You Drop Pounds." *Progressive Grocer*, July 10, 2004.

Vonhoff, Peter. "Die Metallverarbeitung lebt von Ideen." *Lebensmittel Zeitung*, October 2, 2003.

Wenzel, Horst. "Schwer auf Draht." *Lebensmittel Zeitung*, November 28, 2008.

Warburtons Ltd.

Hereford House
Hereford Street
Bolton, Lancashire BL1 8JB
United Kingdom
Telephone: (+44 1204) 531004
Fax: (+44 1204) 523361
Web site: http://www.warburtons.co.uk

Private Company
Incorporated: 1921
Employees: 4,500
Sales: £562.1 million ($926.8 million) (2013 est.)
NAICS: 311812 Commercial Bakeries

■ ■ ■

Warburtons Ltd. is the United Kingdom's largest independent baked goods company. Based in Bolton, the company's headquarters are just across the road from the original grocery store opened by the Warburton family in 1870. The company operates 12 bakeries across the United Kingdom, backed by a network of 13 depots and its own fleet of heated delivery vehicles. Warburtons doubled in size during the first decade of the 21st century, and the company produces more than two million fresh baked breads and other bakery products each day. According to the company, more than a quarter of all bakery product consumed in the United Kingdom are produced by Warburtons. The company remains a privately held, family-owned company.

FROM GROCER TO BAKER

Warburtons originated as a small grocers shop in the town of Bolton, England, opened by Thomas Warburton with the financial backing of his brother George in the 1870s. Much of the credit for the family's future direction and success goes to Thomas's wife Ellen Warburton. When sales at the grocery hit a dip in the mid-1870s, Ellen Warburton turned to baking bread at the back of the store. Within an hour of marketing, she had sold every loaf.

The Blackstone Road shop quickly became known for Ellen Warburton's breads and cakes, and within two weeks the family decided to convert the grocery into a full-fledged bakery. In that year, 1876, the shop raised a new sign, "Warburtons' The Bakers." The bakery provided the Warburtons with a comfortable living. The growing business also provided employment for George Warburton's son Henry, who in 1890 joined his aunt and uncle as an apprentice at the age of 16.

From the start, Henry Warburton became highly involved in the business, and by the age of 25 after becoming a master baker, took over the bakery. The younger Warburton played a major role in transforming the bakery from a small artisan's shop into an industrial bakery. By 1897 the business had outgrown its original premises, and in that year opened a dedicated bakery, the Diamond Jubilee Bakery, nearby. This facility supplied the original shop, which continued to do a brisk business.

Warburtons was developing from a local to a regional favorite. As its market increased, the company continued to expand its production, and by the

COMPANY PERSPECTIVES

In our business, we see ambition as being absolutely fundamental to our future success. Continual innovation underpins our business model, whether it's continuing to bring new variants of our products to our consumers, delivering wheat- and gluten-free products for those who have intolerances or branching out into the snacks market. In fact, our ambition is to be one of the world's best family food businesses.

outbreak of World War I had moved three more times. Until then, the company had been housed in existing buildings, which were outfitted to accommodate its growing range of baking equipment and machinery. In 1915, however, Warburtons moved into its first purpose-built bakery facility, which was called the Model Bakery, and later became known as the Back o'th'Bank House.

INVESTING FOR SUCCESS

Henry Warburton remained at the head of the company, which was formally incorporated in 1921, until his death in 1936. Throughout this period, Warburtons continued to invest in its production equipment. In 1921, for example, the company added a specialized packaging machine, enabling it to supply its packaged breads to the Bolton area and then to the Lancashire region's grocery trade. This allowed the company to grow still more strongly, and by 1937 the company's factory had once again become too small.

By then the company had also been hard hit by the difficult financial environment of the time. The company, led by Henry's three sons, decided to invest in new-generation machinery. The new equipment included a Simplex Continuous Oven, vastly increasing productivity. At the same time, Warburtons added a traveling oven, further increasing capacity. In this way, Warburtons evolved into one of the Lancashire region's most technologically advanced bakery groups by the outbreak of World War II.

The third generation of the Warburton family, led by Derrick Warburton, took over the company's operations during World War II. With the end of the war and the end of rationing, Warburtons resumed its commitment to investment and expansion. In the early 1950s the company made the important decision to expand its operations by acquiring a number of small bakeries in the northern region of England.

EXPANSION AND DIVERSIFICATION

Over the next decade the company expanded its industrial plant, and by the mid-1960s operated five full-scale baked goods factories. The rise of the supermarket sector in the United Kingdom during this time provided a ready market for Warburtons' packaged breads. Under Derrick Warburton the company carefully developed the Warburton brand, establishing a reputation for the company's commitment to quality.

In order to achieve this, the company also began working closely not only with its flour suppliers, but also with wheat farmers themselves. Canada especially emerged as a major source for the company's wheat. Warburtons' early quality commitment placed it in a strong position to conquer space on the supermarket shelves, and in customers' pantries. The company continued to expand the reach of its operations, and in order to maintain proximity with its new markets, began building new bakeries.

At the end of the 1960s, for example, Warburtons had added a sixth bakery, in Burnley. The company continued to expand into the 1970s, aided by the rapidly growing supermarket sector. The transformation of the retail market, however, meant that Warburtons could no longer rely on the small grocer to guide consumers' bread purchases.

Warburtons therefore began to develop a formal marketing program for the first time during the 1970s. As part of this effort, the company also developed and launched a range of new products. This effort had begun in the 1960s and included the successful Milk Roll, launched in 1965. This bread remained one of the company's best sellers into the next century.

EXTENDING ITS REACH

Warburtons began a drive to solidify its position in its northern regional base in the 1980s. The company added a presence in the Yorkshire region in 1984, supported by the addition of a new bakery in Wakefield that year. By the end of the decade, the company had also opened a bakery in Newcastle, allowing it to add the northeast region to its operations.

Then, in 1990 Warburtons expanded its operations again through the acquisition of Sayers, a Liverpool-based bakery group that operated more than 120 shops in the United Kingdom. By the 1990s Warburtons had succeeded in becoming one of northern England's leading bread companies. The steady growth of the Warburtons' bakery business had enabled the family to pursue numerous investments over the previous decades.

```
┌─────────────────────────────────────────┐
│                                         │
│              KEY DATES                  │
│                 ■                       │
│  ┌───────────────────────────────────┐  │
│                                         │
│  1876: Ellen Warburton begins baking    │
│        bread at a grocery store         │
│        operated by husband Thomas       │
│        Warburton in Bolton, England.    │
│  1921: Warburtons formally incorporates.│
│  1959: Company acquires Soreen malt     │
│        cakes brand.                     │
│  1965: Company launches best-selling    │
│        Milk Roll product.               │
│  1984: Warburtons enters Yorkshire      │
│        region with bakery in Wakefield. │
│  1992: Company sells U.S. subsidiary to │
│        Au Bon Pain as part of           │
│        streamlining of operations.      │
│  2003: Warburtons completes             │
│        streamlining with sale of Soreen │
│        to Inter Link Foods.             │
│  2007: Warburtons launches new          │
│        advertising campaign to          │
│        underscore transformation into   │
│        nationally operating company.    │
│  2009: Company opens a bakery in        │
│        Bristol.                         │
│  2013: Giles Food Ltd. is acquired.     │
│                                         │
└─────────────────────────────────────────┘
```

By the early 1990s Warburtons had become, in fact, a somewhat diversified company operating in a variety of areas beyond its core baked breads business. Among these was the production of malt cakes, which came through the purchase of the Soreen brand in 1959. Warburtons subsequently built Soreen into the United Kingdom's third-largest producer of malt cakes and similar snacks. The company also developed a business producing pot pies and other savory products under the Peter Hunt name.

ACQUIRES SAYERS: 1990

That business was expanded in 1990, when Warburtons acquired Sayers and transferred its savory products operations to Peter Hunt. Further afield, Warburtons entered the United States in the early 1980s, setting up a subsidiary that developed a chain of more than 100 bakery cafés under the Warburtons Bakery Café brand.

The arrival of a new generation of Warburtons in 1991 ultimately led to a shift in direction for the company. Under the leadership of comanaging directors Ross and Brett Warburton, and aided by another cousin, Jonathan Warburton, the company launched a restructuring in order to refocus its operations around its core baked breads business.

Part of this strategy was an exit from its U.S. operations, completed with the sale of the Warburtons Bakery

Café chain to Au Bon Pain Inc. in 1992. Over the next decade Warburtons continued to streamline its operations, completing the process with the sale of the Soreen brand in 2003 to Inter Link Foods for £9.1 million.

BAKING TOWARD NATIONAL SCALE

Part of the motivation behind Warburtons' streamlining effort came from its new goal of redeveloping itself as a truly national brand. In support of this strategy, the company launched an ambitious bakery-building program starting in the mid-1990s. In 1995, for example, the company added the East Midlands region to its range of operations, with construction of a bakery in Eastwood, Nottingham.

That factory also represented the first "greenfield" construction made by the company since the construction of the Model Bakery back in 1912. Warburtons next targeted Scotland, entering that market in 1998 with the launch of a bakery in Bellshill. This bakery was soon followed by commissioning of a bakery in Wednesbury, which extended the Warburtons brand into the West Midlands region.

Warburtons quickly gained a strong share in each new market. In Scotland, for example, Warburtons' rapid growth led to the expansion of its Bellshill facility in 2004. Encouraged, the company set its ambitions still higher. The company targeted the all-important London market in 2003, adding a site in Enfield. This was followed by the construction of a new "super bakery" for the Yorkshire region, which was opened in Tuscany Park in 2005.

ENTRY INTO WALES

For its entry into Wales, Warburtons purchased a bakery in Newport that year. In the meantime, growing demand for Warburtons' breads led it to buy a new facility in Stockton, in order to supply the north England region. By 2006 Warburtons claimed to reach some 80 percent of the U.K. population, with only the region south of the Thames posing a gap on the company map.

In that year, however, Warburtons announced its intention to double the capacity of its Enfield factory by the beginning of 2007. The extension of the Enfield site, which included the addition of a production line making crumpets, cost the company more than £45 million to complete. At the same time, Warburtons expanded its Newport factory, a move that allowed the company to deepen its penetration into the southwest region.

By mid-2007 Warburtons laid claim to being the United Kingdom's leading independent national baked goods brand, with a coverage of more than 95 percent of the population and sales of more than £405 million ($800 million) at that time. Also that year, the company launched its first nationwide advertising campaign, with the tagline "Bakers Born & Bred."

GROWTH CONTINUES

Growth continued over the next several years as Warburtons focused on maintaining its leadership position in the U.K. market. As part of its strategy, the company continued to expand and upgrade its bakery operations. During 2009 it opened a bakery in Bristol, which could produce more than 1.5 million products a week to serve customers in southwest England.

By 2012 Warburtons had invested over £370 million to build new bakeries, revamp existing locations, and to upgrade its distribution networks. During 2012 the company opened a new facility in Bolton, claiming it was the most technically advanced bakery in Europe. In addition to bolstering production operations, Warburtons moved into new markets and expanded its product offerings. In 2010 the company added new sandwich wraps and thins to its produce lineup.

During 2011 the company began selling its products in Tesco stores in Eastern Europe. It also became the first baker in the United Kingdom to enter the baked snacks market with the launch of its Baked Pitta Chips. It also opened a gluten-free facility in Newburn in response to growing demand for gluten-free products. Warburtons also updated the look of its brand that year, adopting a new logo for its products. In 2013 the company launched a line of cakes including chocolate brownies, Bakewell squares, lemon cakes, and millionaire's shortbread.

The company also grew via acquisition as this time. Warburtons acquired Giles Food Ltd. in 2013. Giles Food produced garlic breads, dough balls, French and Italian breads, Danish pastries, tarts, and buns that were sold to retailers, restaurants, pub chains, and catering companies. By this point, Warburtons was the largest bakery brand in London, overtaking competitors Hovis Ltd. and the Kingsmill brand, which was owned by Allied Bakeries.

CHANGING STRATEGIES

Although Warburtons experienced success during this time, not all ventures proved profitable. The company scaled back its international ambitions and shuttered operations in France and central Europe in 2013 due to high distribution costs and its inability to secure a partnership with a suitable manufacturing firm. It had also ended its foray into Eastern Europe at the end of 2012 for similar reasons.

The company pulled its bagged pita snacks from store shelves in 2014 due to lackluster sales. During 2014 the company set plans in motion to build a new factory on its site in Burnley to manufacture its sandwich wraps and thins. It also expanded into the Channel Islands that year, selling its bread in over 50 stores in Jersey and Guernsey.

Sales and profits were on the rise and Warburtons could claim to be the second-largest grocery brand in the United Kingdom after Coca-Cola based on sales. With a history dating back more than 135 years, the Warburtons name would no doubt remain one of the United Kingdom's most prominent and well-loved food brands for years to come.

M. L. Cohen
Updated, Christina M. Stansell

PRINCIPAL COMPETITORS

Associated British Foods plc; Memory Lane Cakes Ltd.; Premier Foods plc.

FURTHER READING

"Alternative Lines Boost Warburtons' Profits." *British Baker*, July 11, 2014.

Best, Dean. "UK: Warburtons Eyes New Plant." *Just-Food*, January 2, 2014.

"Bread for South." *Grocer*, October 18, 2003.

Carmichael, Mary. "Warburtons Wants to Roll Out Bread UK-Wide." *Grocer*, July 1, 2006.

"A Focus on Appealing and Sophisticated Premium Lines in Stand-Out Packaging Has Turned Bakery into a £2bn Market, with Warburtons Doing Particularly Well." *Grocer*, December 11, 2004.

Hunt, Julian. "Quality and Tradition: A Tasty Recipe for Growth." *Grocer*, September 3, 2005.

"Major TV Ads to Build on Heritage." *Grocer*, December 16, 2006.

Montague-Jones, Guy. "Warburtons Bread Makes Debut in Channel Islands." *Grocer*, April 12, 2014.

———. "Warburtons Launches Its First Cakes." *Grocer*, November 30, 2013.

"Warburtons Expands Scottish Operation with £14 Million Bakery Extension." *Food Trade Review*, March 2004.

Watkins Manufacturing Corporation

1280 Park Center Drive
Vista, California 92081
U.S.A.
Telephone: (760) 440-5488
Web site: http://www.hotspring.com

Wholly Owned Subsidiary of Masco Corporation
Incorporated: 1977
Employees: 1,100
Sales: $125 million (2013 est.)
NAICS: 326191 Plastics Plumbing Fixture
   Manufacturing

■■■

Vista, California–based Watkins Manufacturing Corporation is one of the world's leading manufacturers of portable outdoor spas, also known as hot tubs. The company offers products in all price points, ranging in size from two-person to eight-person models. The company's flagship brand is Hot Spring, which the company claims is the world's top-selling portable spa brand. Other premium brands include Limelight and Highlife and cost as much as $15,000. Mid-price spas are sold under the Caldera Spas brand, while at the lower end is the Freeflow brand, offering spas for less than $2,000. Watkins also sells replacement spa covers, cover lifters, spa steps, water care and spa maintenance products, and entertainment systems that include wireless television and sound systems. Production is conducted at a 300,000-square-foot-plant in Vista and 160,000 square feet of manufacturing space in two

plants in Mexico. Through a dealer network, the company is able to sell to all 50 states and more than 60 countries. Watkins is a subsidiary of *Fortune* 500 company Masco Corporation, best known as the manufacturer of Delta Faucets.

HOT TUB INDUSTRY TAKES SHAPE

Watkins Manufacturing was founded by brothers Jon and Jeff Watkins, who grew up around the pool business in Southern California. Their father operated one of the first pool chemical service companies. The older of the two brothers, Jon, started his own pool maintenance company in Escondido, California, in 1970 as a franchisee of Pool Chlor. Around 1975 he began to notice fewer people using their pools if they also owned a hot tub. Home hot tubs were hardly new in California. The first ones likely began appearing in the late 1950s, made from discarded wine barrels and redwood vats. The following decade of hippies and free love brought hot tubs to the consciousness of Americans, albeit with overtones of sex and drugs. Wooden hot tubs were not especially trustworthy, given to leaks and providing an ideal breeding ground for bacteria, mold, and slime. The introduction of the fiberglass shell at the end of the 1960s, followed by more reliable heaters, pumps, and filters began to make hot tubs a true consumer product.

Eager to tap into the growing home spa market, Jon Watkins decided to build portable spas as an adjunct to his pool maintenance business. He enlisted the help of his brother Jeff, a civil engineer, and together they began developing a self-contained spa in an Escondido garage. Building a workable fiberglass spa was not especially challenging for the pair, which often tinkered together on backyard inventions while growing up. In that same Escondido garage, they had also once tried to build a fiberglass boat. It would take about two years to develop a reliable hot tub product that could be operated at a reasonable price. Finally in 1977, after spending about $100,000 in developmental costs, they launched Watkins Manufacturing Corporation and began sell their spa.

THIRD PARTNER ADDED

Watkins sold about 100 spas in the first 18 months through the pool maintenance company and a small store, but the company was running short on money and decided to take on a partner, O. Thomas Neal, who was a member of a barbershop quartet with Jeff Watkins. A year earlier Neal had been shown the spa, and he had told the brothers that he was ready to become involved if they needed an investor. Neal became a one-third partner in Watkins Manufacturing, but he was far from a silent partner. As a national account executive for a store fixture company, he brought a great deal of sales experience to the table.

Neal attempted to sell spas from the company store, but there was little traffic. After visiting a trade show, he became convinced that the company needed to establish a dealer network. To build one, he purchased a mobile home, attached a trailer with a hot tub, and took to the road with his wife. In the ensuing weeks, they would travel 35,000 miles through 25 states, paying cold-call visits to pool companies they found in the phonebook. Persuading the pool companies to become dealers proved difficult, largely because Neal had been preceded by other California hot tub companies that had proven to be less than reliable. Neal also reached out directly to consumers through advertising and generated a great deal of interest through a toll-free telephone number. Business began to pick up, and during the final months of 1978 through 1979, Watkins sold about 800 spas.

While better marketing was important, an even more important factor in the success of the company was the decision to drop fiberglass in favor of a new material. Everyone in the spa industry relied on fiberglass, but it had two major drawbacks. The material lost its effectiveness after prolonged exposure to sun and water, and molding was problematic, making it difficult to mass produce hot tub shells in a cost-effective manner. The Watkins brothers learned about a thermoplastic called Rovel that Uniroyal Co. unveiled in the pages of *Popular Science* in August 1980. Not only was the material affordable, it was waterproof and able to withstand continuous exposure to the sun. Many uses were found for Rovel, including pickup truck rooftop covers and football helmets, but the Watkins thought it to be an ideal material for hot tubs because it was not affected by sunlight, hot water, or chemicals. Moreover, Rovel could be molded and mass produced. The company performed the molding at a 30,000-square-foot plant in San Marcos, California, and the new spas were then assembled in an 87,000-square-foot plant in Carlsbad, California.

To make the switch to the new material, Watkins borrowed $30,000, a move that appeared extremely risky at the time, requiring that the three partners pledge their homes as security. Also important was gaining a certification of safety from Underwriters Laboratory (UL) for the spa, despite the dangerous combination of water, electricity, and humans. Watkins Manufacturing offered the first home spa product to receive UL's blessing, which became an important selling point.

MASCO ACQUIRES WATKINS MANUFACTURING: 1986

In 1985 the company began selling spas through Sears and Price Clubs stores, which helped in fiscal 1986 to boost revenues to $25.2 million. In 1986 the company was on its way to increasing sales to about $30 million, representing an 8 percent market share, when it caught the attention of Masco Corporation, a fast-growing company that was on an acquisition spree. Masco made a bid for Watkins Manufacturing, which the Watkins brothers and Neal decided to accept. Although they had established a 350-dealer national dealer network and had opened a distribution center in Tennessee to serve the eastern United States, the partners believed that as a part of Masco the company would enjoy greater clout in the marketplace. Moreover, all three men were allowed to continue running the company as an independent subsidiary. Jon Watkins stayed until 1989. Neal also left to start a new venture, Neal Energy Management, but Jeff Watkins remained president until his retirement in 1997.

Under Masco's ownership, Watkins enjoyed steady growth. In 1990 the company moved into a new

KEY DATES

1977: Jon and Jeff Watkins begin manufacturing hot tubs.
1986: Masco Corporation acquires Watkins Manufacturing.
1990: New plant opens in Vista, California.
1999: Caldera Spas is acquired.
2011: Freeflow Spas brand is acquired.

250,000-square-foot plant on a 20-acre site in Vista, California, that was designed by Jeff Watkins. By now annual sales topped $60 million, due in large measure to a television advertising budget the company could now afford as a part of Masco. In addition to its flagship Hot Spring brand, the company sold spas under the Tiger River spas and Hot Spot names. Sales continued to climb in the 1990s, reaching about $90 million in 1995. Further growth was hindered as a roaring economy led to a labor shortage in Southern California. To increase production, Watkins in 1996 expanded to Mexico, where the company would operate a pair of plants in Tijuana, one owned and the second leased. To support international sales, Watkins also opened a manufacturing operation in Auckland, New Zealand.

JEFF WATKINS RETIRES: 1997

After Jeff Watkins retired in 1997, he was succeeded as president by longtime employee Steven M. Hammock. He had joined Watkins Manufacturing in 1982 as promotions manager. Five years later Hammock was promoted to general manager. Under his leadership, the company now made plans for a major plant expansion, adding 102,000 square feet of space to the Vista facility. The extra room was needed to keep up with growing demand from aging baby boomers who appreciated the therapeutic effects of spas. While Watkins was building onto its Vista plant, it was also looking for acquisition opportunities. In 1999 the company acquired El Cajon, California–based Caldera Spas & Baths, which manufactured spas as well as whirlpools, baths, and gazebos. Established in 1976, the Caldera Spas brand was retained to help fill out Watkins' product lines with a mid-priced option. The 75,000-square-foot plant in El Cajon was also kept until production could eventually be moved to Vista.

The sale of home spas was adversely affected in 2001 by the energy crisis that resulted in rolling blackouts in California, a key market for the industry.

In truth, modern spas used far less electricity than older versions, but energy efficiency figures did little to persuade skittish customers. Numerous orders were canceled and fewer people were visiting showrooms. For many dealers, it was the worst selling environment they had experienced in more than 20 years. Once the crisis was averted, however, spa sales began to pick up again in California.

In 2003 Watkins manufactured its 600,000th spa. With the pace of sales increasing, the company would manufacture the one millionth unit just five years later. To commemorate the occasion, the spa was auctioned off online. The proceeds were matched by Watkins and donated to the National Fallen Firefighters Foundation.

FREEFLOW BRAND ACQUIRED: 2011

Industry-wide, spa sales tapered off in 2009 and 2010. As a subsidiary of Masco, Watkins was better able to weather the storm and actually take advantage of poor business conditions. In December 2011 Watkins expanded its new product lines by acquiring the assets of Ontario, California–based American Hydrotherapy System and its FreeFlow Spas brand. FreeFlow was a low-priced brand that complimented Watkins' premium and mid-priced lines. FreeFlow hot tub shells were produced using a rotational molding technique that eliminated the internal support frame of the more expensive models. In 2012 Watkins also acquired another low-price brand, Aquaterra Spas, which were sold exclusively through Costco.

Spa sales began to rebound in 2012. With products at all price points, Watkins was well positioned for future growth, which might well come from international sales. The company was now exporting to about 70 countries, with Western Europe its largest market outside of the United States. Foreign customers now accounted for 25 percent of the 50,000 to 60,000 spas Watkins manufactured each year. Because the American market was more mature, international sales were likely to increase further in the years ahead and serve as the company's primary engine for ongoing growth.

Ed Dinger

PRINCIPAL SUBSIDIARIES

Hot Spring Spa Australia Pty. Ltd.; Hot Spring Spas New Zealand Ltd.; Tapicerias Pacifico, S.A. de C.V. (Mexico).

PRINCIPAL COMPETITORS

Aquatic Co.; Jacuzzi Brands, Inc.; Kohler Co., Inc.

FURTHER READING

Finch, Erika Ayn. "Spa-Maker to the World." *North County (CA) Times*, September 3, 2003.

Maio, Pat. "Watkins Poised to Make a Bigger Splash in Hot Tub Market." *North County (CA) Times*, February 13, 2012.

Riggs, Rod. "Garage Project Becomes Big Business." *San Diego Union*, November 13, 1988.

————. "Masco Buys Carlsbad Watkins Manufacturing." *San Diego Union*, December 19, 1996.

————. "Watkins Will Double Output at New Spa Plant." *San Diego Union*, June 3, 1990.

Spaulding, Richard. "Plunge into Hot Tubs Pays Off for Brothers." *San Diego Evening Tribune*, January 29, 1996.

W.B. Doner & Co.

25900 Northwestern Highway
Southfield, Michigan 48075
U.S.A.
Telephone: (248) 354-9700
Fax: (248) 827-8440
Web site: http://www.doner.com

Private Company
Incorporated: 1937
Employees: 544
Sales: $88.3 million (2013 est.)
NAICS: 541810 Advertising Agencies

■■■

W.B. Doner & Co. is one of the largest independently owned advertising agencies in North America. The firm offers a full range of services that include creation of advertising campaigns, media buying, account planning, sales promotion, and social media. Doner works with many well-known clients including ADT, Minute Maid, Owens Corning, DuPont, JCPenney, Marie Callender's, Chrysler, and Chiquita. Beyond its Detroit-area headquarters the agency has offices in Atlanta, Los Angeles, Cleveland, and London. Its capabilities include the Doner Social Currency Index, which monitors brand visibility, as well as a digital technology hub named the Digital Underground.

EARLY YEARS

The roots of W.B. Doner & Co. date to 1937, when Wilfred Broderick "Brod" Doner founded an advertising agency in Detroit. Doner, who was just 23, gradually built up the firm's client base during the late 1930s and 1940s. By the early 1950s, when the company had begun doing television commercials, its accounts included Speedway 79 Gasoline and E-Z Pop popcorn.

In 1954 Doner won the account of National Brewing Company, based in Baltimore, and when that firm offered a building for Doner to use, the agency added an office there. It opened in January 1955 and was headed by a new recruit, 26-year-old Herbert Fried. Fried had studied business and marketing, and he had worked for several agencies in Chicago before joining Doner. Although National Brewing was the only account in Baltimore for the first two years, the office later began to win work for other clients such as First National Bank.

During the 1960s Doner continued to grow, creating memorable ad campaigns for the likes of Colt 45 Malt Liquor and Hygrade Ball Park Franks. For the latter, the firm came up with the classic, "They plump when you cook 'em," slogan, which debuted in 1966. Another notable Doner campaign, for Tootsie Roll, asked the question, "How many licks does it take to get to the center of a Tootsie Pop?" The tagline was introduced in 1968 and used for many years afterward.

NEW LEADERSHIP

In 1973 Herb Fried was named chairman and CEO of the company, having already served as president since 1968. Fried remained in the Baltimore area, and the firm designated its Detroit and Baltimore offices as co-

---

COMPANY PERSPECTIVES

We seek out unique intersections of culture, commerce and consumer life and turn them into Ideas That Move People.

---

headquarters. To keep up with the activities of both branches, Fried took frequent trips to Detroit.

During the 1970s Doner's work included the "Scrubbing Bubbles" campaign for Dow and the creation of the Vlasic Stork character for Vlasic Pickles. The decade also saw the firm add a number of important new accounts, including United Brands' Chiquita Banana division, May Department Stores Co., Lionel Trains, and Dutch Boy, Inc. Doner had acquired a reputation for creating advertisements that produced sales on the retail level, and many clients sought it out for this specialization.

Although the firm's clients typically paid the agency the industry standard 15 percent of billings, meaning the total advertising budget, this began to change in the late 1970s. Doner began to work with its clients to find less rigid ways of charging them for their advertising services. In some cases the agency accepted fees based on the sales results of its advertising.

In 1981 several key members of Doner's Baltimore staff left to form a rival agency, Smith, Burke and Azzam. They took an estimated 30 percent of the office's clients with them, including restaurant chain Roy Rogers and hotel franchiser Quality International. Doner subsequently filed suit against the parties involved, including Roger Gray, Barry L. Smith, and Eugene Azzam. Ultimately, the claim was settled for a reported $300,000.

CREATIVITY CAMPAIGNS CONTINUE

During the 1980s the company continued to come up with creative and successful campaigns for a variety of clients. The "Zoo Stars" ad for the Detroit Zoo, which featured talking animals, won a number of awards and was later adopted as the official commercial of the National Zoo Association. Ads for Canadian Tire and Klondike bars were well-received during the early 1980s as well, with the "What would you do for a Klondike bar" line being used for years afterward. The company also was hired to work for the Michigan State Lottery.

In 1984 an office was opened in Toronto, which joined an existing location in Montreal to give Doner

offices in Canada. The year 1985 saw the company begin working for Little Caesars. At the time the Detroit-based pizza restaurant chain had 700 locations. Over the next three years Doner's ads helped the chain double this amount of outlets and triple the number of markets it served.

In 1986 Doner bought the Chicago-based ad agency, Lou Beres and Associates, which handled billings of some $17 million and accounts that included Turtle Wax and Florsheim. Owner Beres was retained to serve as managing director of the office, which would employ approximately 25 and take on the name of its new parent. The move was made in part to serve the new G. Heileman Brewing Company account, which was worth $4 million in billings. In 1987 Doner also added a Hispanic unit to handle specialized advertising.

INTERNATIONAL GROWTH

In early 1988 Doner scored a major coup, when it was assigned the British Petroleum (BP) worldwide retail gasoline account. The work had grown out of a small job done for Standard Oil in 1984 to promote six auto repair shops in Toledo, Ohio. This later led to contracts with sister companies Gulf, Sohio, and Boron, and after BP took control of Standard the new parent company selected Doner to boost its profile around the world, an assignment that was expected to involve some $30 million in annual billings.

Doner would create the ads, with media-buying handled by BP's agencies in its various international markets. To service the account Doner opened an office in London, which soon helped bring in other foreign assignments. Over the next four years Doner's overseas work jumped from 5 percent to 30 percent of its total billings. The late 1980s saw other major clients such as Arby's, La-Z-Boy, Iams, and B.F. Goodrich added to the firm's roster.

Memorable work of the era included a series of television spots for Red Roof Inns featuring comedian Martin Mull. By 1989 Doner was planning campaigns worth more than $300 million in billings and taking in $52.1 million in revenues. At this time the firm employed a staff of 550, including 325 employees in the Detroit suburb of Southfield, where the company had moved into new offices in October 1988.

Some 140 other staffers were in Baltimore, with the rest in satellite offices in Boston, Chicago, Cleveland, St. Petersburg, Florida, London, Toronto, and Montreal. Doner had no presence in the advertising mecca of New York, but despite its "outsider" status, in March 1989 the firm was named runner-up as Agency of the Year by the influential trade publication *Advertising Age*, which ranked Doner as the nation's 26th-largest agency.

KEY DATES

1937: Wilfred Broderick Doner founds an ad agency in Detroit, Michigan.

1955: Firm opens a second office in Baltimore, Maryland, run by Herb Fried.

1986: Chicago office opened with purchase of Lou Beres and Associates.

1988: Doner wins $30 million British Petroleum retail account; London office opens.

1995: Company purchases GGK London.

1997: $240 million Mazda account is won.

1998: Firm wins $160 million Blockbuster account.

2003: Baltimore is office closed and its operations moved to Southfield.

2008: Doner's Serta Counting Sheep are given a place on the Advertising Walk of Fame on New York's Madison Avenue.

2012: Agency holding group, MDC Partners, purchases a substantial minority stake in Doner.

DEATH OF FOUNDER

In January 1990 founder and patriarch Brod Doner passed away at the age of 75. More than 40 years after starting the company he had remained a vital presence there, at the end serving as president of its executive committee. As Fried told *Crain's Detroit Business*, his guiding philosophy had been, "creativity comes first, and everything else is secondary." Doner was praised for his ethics and family-oriented values, and his professional way of conducting business.

Because of Doner's personal convictions, the company had never taken assignments from cigarette makers or the National Rifle Association. After Doner's death, the firm expanded its executive committee from two to six members and gave Fried the position of chairman. Other changes that took place at this time included the sale of the Chicago office and the opening of a new one in Dallas to serve an account with Ford dealership associations in that area.

A joint venture also was formed with Grey Advertising, Inc., of New York to do work for the BP account, with Grey handling media buying and other services through its network of European offices. In 1991 Doner bought into Luscombe & Partners, the fourth-largest independent advertising agency in Australia. In early 1992 Doner laid off 24 employees because of declining revenues caused by the stagnant U.S. economy.

A number of the firm's clients, including the Ford dealerships and the Michigan-based appliance store chain Highland Superstores, were seeing drastic sales declines, which left them with fewer dollars to spend on advertising. The company also was hurt by the decision of the Michigan State Lottery to find a new agency, as well as the bankruptcy of longtime client Eckerd Drug Stores.

DALE BECOMES CEO: 1992

Some new accounts were landed during the year, however, including Rose's Stores, a 217-outlet chain of discount department stores located in the southeastern United States. In June 1992 Doner president Jim Dale was promoted to the jobs of CEO and chairman, while Fried kept his role as chairman of the executive committee. A 25-year company veteran, Alan Kalter, who was based in Detroit, was given the job of president. At the same time Steve LaGattuta, vice chairman of international business development, resigned.

LaGattuta had been credited with boosting the company's international profile, but was reportedly upset at having been passed over for the president's job. Since Brod Doner's death about a dozen key executives had left the company, which was still trying to redefine itself in his absence.

In 1993 Doner lost the Vlasic Pickle account, which it had held for 27 years. Vlasic had been purchased by Campbell Soup Company, which was consolidating its advertising with several other agencies. Doner also had recently lost Hygrade Food Products Corporation, which had been acquired by Sara Lee.

NEW OPPORTUNITIES

The company's fortunes began improving at the start of 1994. At that time the company signed six major new accounts worth $40 million in billings. These included Frank's Nursery & Crafts, Musicland Stores Corporation, National Car Rental System, Inc., and National Tire Warehouse, which was owned by Sears.

In the spring of 1994 Doner formed a public relations division at its Baltimore co-headquarters. Additional accounts added during the year and into early 1995 included supermarket chain Kroger, for its Michigan stores. Other accounts were Prudential Senior-Care and G. Heileman Brewing, which the firm had lost four years earlier. Coca-Cola also tapped the agency for a Christmas season promotion and other tasks. The year was strong for Doner, with billings increasing nearly 20 percent, to $450 million.

In April 1995 chairman and CEO Dale announced he was leaving the company to pursue a writing career.

The CEO role was taken by Kalter, while Fried became chairman. After his elevation to the top post, Kalter announced that Doner would establish a series of "centers of excellence" at the firm's 11 offices worldwide. These would consist of specializations in different areas, such as direct marketing, which was already in place in Baltimore. Other specializations included automobile and retail advertising, which had been established in Southfield, and media, promotions, and research, which would be added later.

Although Doner's Southfield office was twice as large, Baltimore typically had been the home of the firm's top officer. At times the two co-headquarters competed against each other for business. In some instances, such as the recently won Coke assignment, both agencies claimed they would be performing the work, although it was later determined that it actually would be done in Southfield.

ACQUIRES GGK LONDON

In October 1995 Doner bought GGK London, an offshoot of GGK International, whose clients included Equifax and Marie Curie Cancer Care. GGK London was merged into Doner's existing London office, which then took the name Doner Cardwell Hawkins, after two former GGK executives who helped run the operation. Doner recently had won a number of important new accounts, including Lowe's Home Improvement Warehouse, lawn equipment maker Cub Cadet, and ABC Warehouse, a Michigan-based appliance chain.

The year 1996 started off on a solid note, when G. Heileman Brewing expanded Doner's assignment to cover its entire advertising program. Other new work included U.S. Cellular's $25 million account, and Color Tile, worth $20 million. Other companies were Hill Stores Co. of Massachusetts, with billings of $10 million, and Nordic Track, which billed for $5 million. In April Doner restructured its media planning operations, consolidating the work in Southfield.

The firm then spun off its rapidly growing Doner Direct unit, which handled direct marketing. Doner Direct employed 30 and had accounts worth $48 million in billings. It remained headquartered in the firm's Baltimore office.

FIRE DAMAGES HEADQUARTERS: 1996

On August 4, 1996, Doner suffered a catastrophe when the company's Southfield headquarters building was ravaged by fire. The blaze, which started after-hours in an empty office, extensively damaged the second floor of the structure, where much of the firm's creative work was done. Fortunately, most of the crucial computer data files were salvaged. Temporary quarters were hastily secured, and some employees worked from home in the fire's immediate aftermath. The disaster did not scare away clients.

New accounts brought in during the latter half of the year included Loyola University Medical Center and the $15 million to $20 million ad work of the Bennigan's and Steak & Ale restaurant chains, owned by S&A Restaurant Corporation. Early 1997 saw the addition of Bush Brothers & Co., the leading maker of baked beans in the United States, an account that was worth $5 million in billings.

ESTABLISHES DONER PUBLIC AFFAIRS

In the spring of 1997 the company formed Doner Public Affairs in its Florida office to provide consulting services for political candidates. Its first client was New York mayor Rudolph Giuliani, then seeking reelection. Doner hired noted political advertising expert Adam Goodman to run the agency. He had worked with a number of Republican candidates including Senator Trent Lott and Wisconsin governor Tommy Thompson.

During the year Doner also added the work of Stroh Brewery Co., which had acquired G. Heileman in August 1996, and Florists' Transworld Delivery (FTD). In October 1997 Doner won its biggest assignment to date, triumphing over a number of larger agencies to secure the North American advertising for Mazda Motor of Japan, whose sales had been in decline. The $240 million account was a feather in Doner's cap, as the firm had never been the agency of record for an automaker, even though it had worked for a number of regional Ford dealership groups over the previous 17 years.

To avoid a possible conflict of interest, Doner gave up this work, which was worth $100 million. Moving forward, Doner opened an office near Mazda's U.S. headquarters in Irvine, California. In December the firm's Canadian unit, Doner Schur Peppler, was renamed Doner Canada, and plans were laid for expansion there, due largely to the new Mazda assignment. Doner's annual revenues stood at $62.6 million.

CONSOLIDATES HEADQUARTERS

In January 1998 Fried sold his majority ownership stake in the firm, ceding the chairmanship to Kalter, although he stayed involved as a consultant. At that time Doner named Southfield as its sole headquarters, letting 24 of the 195 Baltimore employees go a few weeks later.

Major accounts for Arby's and Bush Brothers were shifted to Southfield as well.

Work that stayed in Baltimore included Ikon Office Solutions and the newly won Teligent, which billed for an estimated $5 million to $10 million. In June 1998 Doner moved back into its Southfield headquarters, 22 months after the building had been gutted by fire. A third floor was added in the reconstruction process, increasing the usable space to 106,000 square feet.

In the months after the fire, the firm had added 90 employees at the location, for a total of 405. Doner was experiencing a growth spurt, and when the $160 million Blockbuster video store account was won in the fall, it put the firm above $1 billion in annual billings for the first time. The company was working on upgrading its own image and asked media outlets to refer to it as "Doner," rather than "W.B. Doner and Co." The company's official name was not changed, although it filed an "also doing business as" notice with the state of Michigan.

During 1999 the firm won the $60 million Progressive Corporation insurance account and other work from AutoTrader.com and ADT Security Services, Inc., although it lost $15 million in billings from long-term client Iams. For 1999 Doner's revenues topped out at nearly $100 million, with the company employing 832. *Adweek* magazine named the firm one of its agencies of the year, ranking it fourth in the country in terms of management, growth, and creative effort.

A NEW MILLENNIUM

The year 2000 was another strong one for Doner, which saw billings top $1.5 billion, helped in part by the acquisition of such major new accounts as Owens Corning and Serta. New ads for Mazda, with their "Zoom-Zoom" tagline, helped further boost the carmaker's sales, which had been on an upswing since Doner had begun working for the company. In 2001 Doner won assignments to work for cable giant Cox Communications, as well as Sherwin-Williams; Mail Boxes, Etc.; and PNC Bank, among others.

The firm's revenues for the year hit $114.2 million, although billings dropped to $1.2 billion as the U.S. economy faltered. In 2002 Doner was chosen to create ads for Helzberg Diamonds, Heinz Pet Products, and DuPont's Corian and Zodiaq product lines. In March legal proceedings began in a lawsuit filed in 2000 against Doner and Mazda by rock musician Rob Zombie, who claimed unauthorized use of one of his songs in a Doner-created spot. The company settled with Zombie for an undisclosed amount.

BALTIMORE OFFICE CLOSES: 2003

By fall the busy firm was looking for additional office space in Southfield, having already outgrown the addition to its headquarters there. Doner was handling work worth $1.6 billion in billings at this time. In June 2003 Doner announced it would close its Baltimore office, moving all operations there to Southfield.

The move came amid rapid consolidation in the advertising industry, which left Doner as the largest independently owned agency in the United States. The decision to combine the firm's two main offices was a response to the new climate, according to Fried, as well as due to the relative difficulty of recruiting top talent to Baltimore and the dwindling opportunities there for local advertising work.

Detroit had by this point evolved into one of the major U.S. advertising centers, although still ranked behind New York, Chicago, and Los Angeles. During the second half of 2003 Doner secured Six Flags Inc., the largest regional theme park company in the world, as a client. The firm became Six Flags' agency of record for both domestic and international advertising, gaining an account worth $90 million.

Other new accounts that year included Home & Garden TV, Outback Steakhouse, and Carpet One. Progress continued in mid-2004 when Doner was chosen to handle the $150 million advertising account for Circuit City, which then operated a chain of more than 600 consumer electronics stores in the United States, as well as more than 1,000 locations in Canada.

LOSES KEY ACCOUNTS

It also was in 2004 that Doner's longtime client, Arby's, announced that it would put its $15 million advertising account up for review. Although Doner was invited to participate, the agency declined, acknowledging that the sandwich shop was in search of a new agency relationship. By 2006 the agency was handling accounts with combined billings of about $2 billion. That year, the nation's leading indoor water park operator, Great Wolf Resorts, Inc., named Doner as its agency of record.

In addition, the agency was chosen to assist the Greater Cleveland Marketing Alliance with a branding effort for northeast Ohio, helping the region compete for travel and tourism dollars and business expansion projects. Creative campaigns continued during the latter part of the decade. Midway through 2008 Doner developed new brand icons for the multiservice broadband communications and entertainment company Cox Communications.

Specifically, Doner created characters called Digis to position Cox as a leading provider of broadband Internet, high-definition television, and DVR services. A major development took place later that year when Doner's Serta Counting Sheep officially gained iconic status and were given a place on the Advertising Walk of Fame on New York's Madison Avenue, which also featured the likes of the AFLAC duck and the M&M characters.

PROMOTES CHOICE HOTELS

During the latter part of 2009 Doner became the creative promotion agency for Choice Hotels International, Inc., which operated more than 5,800 hotels under a variety of names, including Comfort Suites, Comfort Inn, Econo Lodge, and Quality Inn. The agency rounded out the year by extending an existing relationship with MediaBank, a leading provider of analytics software for advertising agencies.

Specifically, Doner used MediaBank's software for the management of its media procurement activities. Doner withstood a major blow in 2010 when the agency lost Mazda, which spent approximately $150 million per year on advertising, as an account. Neither the automaker nor Doner gave specific reasons for the change.

By this time Doner was owned by Tim Blett, David DeMuth, and Rob Strasberg. DeMuth and Strasberg provided the agency with leadership as co-CEOs and co–chief creative officers. Despite losing the Mazda account, Doner proceeded to gain new accounts, including retail advertising assignments for Chrysler Group LLC, as well as advertising for AutoZone and Perkins restaurants.

MDC PARTNERS ACQUIRES STAKE

Another major change took place in early 2012 when the agency holding group MDC Partners purchased a substantial minority stake in Doner. The deal, which was estimated to be in the $15 million to $20 million range, included an option for MDC to acquire a major-

ity stake in Doner in the future. At that time MDC held either partial or full ownership of some 50 different advertising agencies.

Moving forward as a member of the MDC Partners network, Doner proceeded to do work for clients such as JCPenney and Coca-Cola. The agency also developed the Doner Social Currency Index, a tool for monitoring brand visibility, as well as a digital technology hub named the Digital Underground. In 2014 Doner worked in partnership with Bellefaire JCB to develop an integrated campaign focused on generating awareness about youth homelessness throughout northeast Ohio.

That year, the agency also teamed up with Eyeview to create a digital campaign for the PGA Tour. Doner also developed a new national advertising campaign for its longtime client Serta. With about $1.5 billion in billings, a proven track record, and a history of many memorable campaigns, Doner appeared to be positioned for continued success in 2015 and beyond.

Frank Uhle
Updated, Paul R. Greenland

PRINCIPAL COMPETITORS

BBDO Worldwide Inc.; Campbell Ewald Company; Team One.

FURTHER READING

Byland, Kathleen. "Creative Still Drives Doner." *Crain's Detroit Business*, July 30, 1990.

Elliott, Stuart. "After Time of Tumult, Doner Sells a Stake to MDC." *New York Times*, April 4, 2012.

"Eyeview and Doner Media Partner on PGA Tour Advertising Campaign." *Professional Services Close-Up*, May 14, 2014.

Roberts, Graeme. "US: Mazda Changes Ad Agency." *just-auto global news*, June 22, 2010.

"Serta Debuts New National Advertising Campaign 'Always Comfortable'; Campaign Launches across Television and Online Introducing the New iComfort Sleep System by Serta." *Marketwired*, May 21, 2014.

WeberHaus GmbH & Co. KG

———————•———————

Am Erlenpark 1
Rheinau-Linx, 77866
Germany
Telephone: (+49 7853) 83-0
Fax: (+49 7853) 83-341
Web site: http://www.weberhaus.de

Private Company
Founded: 1960
Employees: 1,000
Sales: EUR 184 million ($237 million) (2012)
NAICS: 236115 New Single-Family Housing Construction (Except For-Sale Builders); 236116 New Multifamily Housing Construction (Except For-Sale Builders); 236220 Commercial and Institutional Building Construction; 523930 Investment Advice

■ ■ ■

WeberHaus GmbH & Co. KG is one of Germany's leading manufacturers of prefabricated homes. Headquartered in Rheinau-Linx in southwestern Germany, the company operates two production plants for prefabricated home components. Using wood mainly from suppliers in the region as raw material, the company builds wooden frame-type structures, mainly single-family homes, but also town houses, apartment buildings, and commercial buildings. In addition to its core market in southern Germany, where the company generates roughly one-third of total sales, WeberHaus is also active in other Western European countries, including Austria, France, Luxembourg, Switzerland, Great Britain, and Ireland. The company's financing arm, WeberHaus Finanzierungsservice GmbH, offers individual financing plans to the company's customers.

WOODWORKING TO HOME BUILDING

When master carpenter Hans Weber took over the woodworking shop of Jacob Gerold in Linx, a small town in the upper Rhine region close to the French border near Strasbourg, he was only 23 years old. Born in the Dutch East Indies, where he spent his early childhood, Weber was the son of a German construction project manager who died during World War II. He lived in Japan with his mother and two siblings during the war. In October 1947 Weber came to Germany, to him a foreign country.

After finishing school, the teenager followed in the footsteps of his father and grandfather and learned carpentry at a local woodworking shop. For four years he worked for several construction companies before he received his master craftsman certificate in 1959. Back in Linx, his parents' hometown nestled between hilly vineyards and the foothills of the Black Forest with 850 inhabitants, he started his own business in January 1960.

With Gerold as an experienced adviser and one apprentice as a helper, Weber took on his first projects, mainly the building of roof structures. However, due to adverse weather conditions during the winter months, most projects were running behind schedule. Weber had to purchase wood and other materials and pay his helpers wages while payment for his work was delayed.

CHANGING TRADITIONAL GERMAN STYLE

Four months after he had started his business, the young entrepreneur ran out of money. Luckily, he received a loan from a local bank that was looking for new clients. Fascinated by the wooden-frame houses built in Scandinavia and the United States, Weber decided to build new homes that could be erected within a short time using prefabricated components. He acquired a license for the construction technology and rented an old gym for building the wooden frames and wall components.

His first customer was his sister Gretel. Brick construction was the norm in Germany, and even skeptical observers who were unsure about the durability of wooden homes were surprised by how quickly the project was completed. To make the house look like a "normal" German-style brick building, Weber plastered the outer walls of the wooden structure.

SUCCESS WITH PREFABRICATED HOMES

Riding on the wave of the postwar construction boom in Germany in the early 1960s, Weber's enterprise grew quickly. His first project attracted a steady stream of curious visitors to his sister's home and new customers into his office. By the end of 1961 Weber had built two more homes using the new technology. The elements for the wooden frames were precut and the wall panels assembled in advance, a novelty at the time.

Several helpers erected the structure in only one day. Completing the home took about two months. Subcontractors provided plumbing fixtures, heating systems, and electrical installations. In 1962 Weber bought an additional site in Linx, and a production hall was built. An architect in Linx became an important business partner who educated prospective homeowners about Weber's prefabricated houses.

In 1963 Hans Weber's wife Christel, an accountant, joined the business and took care of administrative and financial matters. In the same year Weber secured two contracts for his first larger projects, including four row houses and a hotel in Altglashütten in the Black Forest. The company was moved to a bigger site, where the Webers moved into their own newly built home, located at the center of their family enterprise.

An assembly hall for stairs was built at the new location in 1964. By the mid-1960s Weber employed 15 workers. In 1965 they built 17 homes. In the same year the company founder traveled to the United States where he learned firsthand about the latest advances in wood construction technology. Weber purchased a truck-mounted hydraulic crane with a telescopic arm for lifting heavy equipment and bulky components. Building material and machinery, as well as the prefabricated modules, were transported to the construction sites on a special trailer, pulled by an old passenger car. In 1969 WeberHaus completed 70 homes and generated DEM 2.3 million in sales.

RAPID GROWTH DURING RECESSION

In 1970 Hans Weber decided to focus solely on building new homes using prefabricated components. In the same year the company built 40 new homes. While the oil price shock of 1973 caused a severe recession in Germany that resulted in a significant downturn in the construction industry, WeberHaus experienced a decade of rapid growth. Two years later Weber invested in a new 30,000-square-meter production hall and increased the company's workforce to 100 to keep up with the rapidly increasing demand.

In 1973 an additional production hall was built and equipped with state-of-the-art machinery. In these modern production facilities the company was able to manufacture two homes per day. The industrial construction of residential buildings called for standardized designs. By the mid 1970s WeberHaus had developed 28 different types of modular homes in various sizes. Exhibits of model homes became an important marketing tool for the company.

In cooperation with a nationally distributed magazine for aspiring homeowners, WeberHaus built model homes for exhibition purposes in two German cities. Showcase homes were also exhibited at the company's production locations in Linx and Wenden-Hünsborn. By the end of the decade there were 14 steady exhibitions with 50 Weber homes on display.

KEY DATES

1960: Carpenter Hans Weber takes over a woodworking shop in Linx.

1961: Company starts building prefabricated wooden-frame houses.

1978: A second production plant is set up in Wenden-Hünsborn.

1991: Low-energy consumption technology is introduced as a standard.

2000: Company's "World of Living" theme park opens in Linx.

2007: Financing subsidiary WeberHaus Finanzierungsservice is established.

2010: The surplus energy-generating home "generation5.0" is introduced.

Soon the company invested two-digit sums in marketing programs, in addition to strengthening its sales organization.

DIVERSIFICATION AND EXPANSION

WeberHaus also developed new technologies that improved the production processes as well as product quality. The installation of prefabricated stairs in the framing made it easier for construction workers to move between floors. WeberHaus also developed large prefabricated roof panel modules, a novelty at the time. The combination of wooden beams with concrete plates and insulation materials in ceiling components decreased the noise from footsteps overhead.

To further increase its capacity and to extend its geographic reach to northwestern Germany, the company set up a second production facility in Wenden-Hünsborn near Siegen, west of Cologne, in 1978. In the same year annual revenues passed the DEM 100 million mark. In 1979 WeberHaus employed a workforce of 760 and built 860 new homes. However, as the German economy got back into gear in the late 1970s, the company had a hard time keeping up with the rising demand. Altogether WeberHaus set up 3,142 new buildings from 1970 to 1979.

IMPROVING PRODUCTION AND RANGE

As the idea of environmentally friendly technologies took root in Germany, wooden homes were seen by many as an environmentally friendly alternative to conventional brick or concrete structures. Moreover, roughly every seventh homebuyer chose a prefabricated home. In 1980 for the first time, WeberHaus built more than 1,000 houses in one year. One of them was the new home of Hans Weber, who moved with his family to a new site farther away from the factory buildings at company headquarters in Linx.

With an additional 1,300 new homes in the company's order books, Weber again significantly expanded production capacity to manufacture about 24 houses per week. In 1982 the company won a contract to build a new multipurpose community center in Linx. However, in a stagnating economic environment and a saturated residential construction market, the number of orders WeberHaus received declined in the following years.

To defend its market position against fierce competition the company took a number of measures, such as reducing its workforce to 960 at the end of 1982. On the other hand WeberHaus opened four new exhibition centers and further automated production. Outer wall elements became about one-third thicker, which increased the thermal insulation by 75 percent. WeberHaus also doubled its warranty on primary structures to 10 years.

INCREASES CUSTOMIZATION

As customers asked for more individual designs, WeberHaus introduced a new generation of homes with more customizable elements, such as curved bay windows, roofed terraces, walls in different angles, and round arches on pillars. In 1985 and 1987 the company opened large builders' centers in Linx and Wenden-Hünsborn, where interior designers advised prospective customers on what type of home might best meet their needs.

With the introduction of a model for a luxury villa built with prefabricated components, WeberHaus demonstrated that ready-to-set-up homes might also be an option for more affluent customers. At the end of the 1980s the company was leading the German market in its field and, for the first time in six years, sold more than 1,000 homes in one year, grossing DEM 220 million in 1989.

NEW MARKETS, NEW DESIGNS

The reunification of West and East Germany in 1990 opened up a new market for WeberHaus. Many East Germans realized their chance for a dream home, and many of them were able to pay for it in cash out of their savings. The first Weber house in eastern Germany was built in June 1990. In order to be able to meet the expected increase in order volume, WeberHaus set up a third factory in Mainburg, Bavaria, which started operations in May 1992.

New staff from eastern Germany was hired and trained on the job. In February 1993 the first branch in eastern Germany was set up in Erfurt. In 1993 orders from eastern Germany accounted for one-fifth of the total annual order volume. WeberHaus built about 300 homes annually in the new eastern German states. Sales peaked in 1994 at DEM 410 million. Additional branches were established there in the following years, with staff increasing to 110 by 1996.

Besides eastern Germany, WeberHaus also ventured into Austria in the 1990s, where the company built a town-house complex near Vienna worth DEM 7.2 million in 1994. Because Linx was located at the French border, WeberHaus also employed about 50 workers from France who commuted daily to Germany. However, the company's attempt to establish a stronger foothold in the French market was not successful.

Looking for ways to solidify its position as a leading player in Germany, energy efficiency became a major focus of WeberHaus. As early as in 1991 the company introduced low energy-consumption technology as a standard in all models. A result of publicly subsidized research, in cooperation with the Fraunhofer Institute as well as with heating equipment and electronics manufacturers, the company developed innovative designs for low-energy-consumption houses.

ÖVOLUTION MODEL LAUNCHED: 1997

First launched in 1997, the "Övolution" model home featured a solar-energy-based heating system and won numerous design and environmental awards. To revive the business in its core market WeberHaus also introduced a number of house models in the mid-1990s. For the upper price segment the company offered homes in country-typical designs, including the Italian-style "Toscana" model with a pillar-lined entrance and balcony, and the North American–style "ParkLane" model, a large-area, one-story bungalow with white wood panels on the outside and an extended roof.

For the lower-priced end of the market, WeberHaus launched a series of standardized basic prefabricated models with the option of the home buyer doing part of the interior finish himself. WeberHaus's order volumes plummeted in the late 1990s as new competitors from Eastern European countries entered the market, who offered significantly lower prices for their prefab homes

and construction services. In 2002 the new factory in Mainburg was closed.

CONSOLIDATION AND INNOVATION

Despite difficult market conditions at the turn of the new millennium, company founder Hans Weber realized a personal dream in 2000. After acquiring an 75,000-square-meter site in Linx, he invested approximately EUR 20 million in an infotainment-style theme park. Opened in October 2000 the World of Living was a journey through different historical living environments, from ancient Egypt to a spaceship. It also featured a WeberHaus exhibition center with dozens of model homes.

One of them was the prototype of a "passive house" with a futuristic design and an solar-powered energy management system that reduced its heating energy consumption by 90 percent. A long-term investment in raising the company's visibility, the World of Living attracted some 60,000 visitors per year. In 2005 WeberHaus, in cooperation with London-based project developer William Verry Ltd., won a contract in the "Design for Manufacture" competition, financed by the British government.

As reported by *dpa* on December 8, 2005, the project included several apartment buildings as well as single-family homes and town houses on two sites in southern England. In the following years WeberHaus continued to market to prospects in Great Britain. As *Immobilien Zeitung Aktuell* reported on March 10, 2006, exports accounted for roughly 13 percent of the company's total revenues. In 2007 WeberHaus built its first houses in Ireland.

SURVIVING CONSTRUCTION RECESSION

The company also intensified its marketing efforts in Switzerland, Scotland, and Spain. The expiration of government subsidies for German home buyers in 2005 caused a severe recession in the residential construction sector. According to *dpa* on October 17, 2007, the number of issued building licenses dropped by 47 percent in the first half of that year.

In September 2007 the company established its new financing arm, WeberHaus Finanzierungsservice, offering tailored financing plans for home buyers. However, the global financial crisis of 2008 exacerbated the difficult economic situation and WeberHaus slipped into the red, as reported by *Handelsblatt*, on November 23, 2009. To cut costs the company reduced its workforce by roughly 9 percent and outsourced its logistics unit.

MEETING FUTURE CHALLENGES

In 2010 the company's 50th anniversary year, Weber-Haus built its 30,000th house. In the same year the company founder's son-in-law Ralph Mühleck, a business consultant who had become the new CEO in 1999, resigned. According to *Immobilien Zeitung* on January 28, 2010, he and the Weber family had different opinions on the company's strategic positioning. Thereafter, Hans Weber and his 46-year-old daughter Heidi Weber-Mühleck jointly managed the company.

Looking ahead, the Webers envisioned an innovative family enterprise that was deeply rooted in its home region, with modest business activities in neighboring countries. In addition to residential construction, the company was planning to tackle the market for commercial and institutional buildings. Another emerging market of the near future was the renovation and modernization of existing structures, implementing energy-saving and environmentally sound technologies.

Following the low-energy concept in its own building design, the roofs of the company's production halls were equipped with solar panels on an area of 7,000 square meters in 2011, generating 25 percent of the power needed for running the facility. In an economic climate with historically low interest rates on one hand, but shortening product cycles and consumers' increasing demands on individual design and functionality on the other, the Webers saw themselves well-positioned to remain a leading player in the market.

ÖVONATURTHERM
INTRODUCED: 2011

In the same year WeberHaus introduced its innovative wall component "ÖvoNaturTherm." Due to its increased thickness, the outer wall component greatly improved the thermodynamic and insulating qualities of the buildings. It was a major element in the company's award-winning "generation5.0" single family home, which produced more energy than it consumed. The remainder could be used, for example, to recharge the battery of an electric vehicle in the garage.

By 2014 WeberHaus was offering other innovative solutions that addressed many of the challenges of the early 21st century, from flexible, low-budget "micro homes" for young adults to barrier-free houses for the elderly. Environmental options included eco-friendly materials and insulated walls against electromagnetic radiation for the health conscious, as well as energy-self-sufficient homes for the cost-conscious to extravagant designs for the demanding upscale customer. In May 2014 the company presented its latest innovation, a prefabricated wooden-frame-type, five-story apartment building.

Gerald Brennan

PRINCIPAL SUBSIDIARIES

WeberHaus Finanzierungsservice GmbH.

PRINCIPAL COMPETITORS

FingerHaus GmbH; Huf Haus GmbH & Co. KG; OKAL Haus GmbH; SchwörerHaus KG; Streif Haus GmbH.

FURTHER READING

Granzow, Axel. "Sparprogramm bringt Weberhaus nach vorn." *Handelsblatt*, November 23, 2009.

Simon, Frank, and Hermann Strasser. *Hans Weber: LebensTräume*. Bühl, Germany: ikotes e.K., 2012.

"WeberHaus gewinnt Wettbewerb in Grossbritannien." *dpa*, December 8, 2005.

"WeberHaus GmbH; Musterhauscenter der etwas anderen Art." *Immobilien Zeitung*, November 2, 2000.

"WeberHaus gut positioniert." *dpa*, October 17, 2007.

"WeberHaus will nach Umsatzrückgang nun wieder mehr Häuser bauen." *Immobilien Zeitung Aktuell*, March 10, 2006.

Westat, Inc.

—■—

1600 Research Boulevard
Rockville, Maryland 20850
U.S.A.
Telephone: (301) 251-1500
Web site: http://www.westat.com

Employee-Owned Company
Founded: 1961
Employees: 2,044
Sales: $582.5 million (2013)
NAICS: 541910 Marketing Research and Public Opinion Polling

■ ■ ■

Westat, Inc., is an employee-owned market research and statistical survey services provider. The Rockville, Maryland–based company designs surveys and clinical trials, collects and manages data, and analyzes the information. Westat also offers communications and social marketing services, helping clients to leverage data accumulated through social media sources. Westat serves both the public and private sectors, including the military, in such areas as health, social policy, education, information systems, and transportation. In addition to its 27-acre Maryland campus, Westat maintains regional offices in the United States in Atlanta, Georgia; Cambridge, Massachusetts; Raleigh/Durham, North Carolina; Philadelphia, Pennsylvania; and Houston, Texas. International locations include Beijing, China; Liberia, Costa Rica; Addis Ababa, Ethiopia; New Delhi, India; Johannesburg, South Africa; and Bangkok, Thailand.

COMPANY ORIGINS

Westat was founded by Edward C. Bryant, a University of Wyoming professor of statistics, and two of his students, James Daley and Donald W. King. Bryant was born in Wyoming in 1915, the son of homesteaders. Although he grew up under modest circumstances, he managed to attend the University of Wyoming in Laramie. After earning a master's degree in business in 1940, he joined the Interstate Commerce Commission in Washington, D.C., as a junior statistician.

World War II soon intervened, and he went to work for the War Production Board before joining the army in 1943. After completing officer training, he was assigned to the Pentagon the following year, serving as a statistician. In 1947 Bryant returned to the University of Wyoming to teach statistics.

After earning his PhD in statistics from Iowa State University, he became a full professor at the University of Wyoming, where he established the department of statistics, as well the statistics laboratory, and the computing center. Laramie's high altitude did not agree with a heart condition that had troubled Bryant throughout his life. Taking the advice of his doctor, Bryant decided in 1961 to move and began looking for a new teaching post.

ESTABLISHING WESTAT

In the meantime, Daley and King, who had just earned their master's degrees in statistics under Bryant, were looking for work. Daley suggested that the three of them start a statistical consultancy to serve the needs of both government and commercial clients. They agreed and formed a partnership that was initially based in Colorado. They called the business Westat, which stood for "western statistics."

The early years of Westat were difficult, as the company was able to land only a variety of small contracts. The first job was a customer survey for a bank in Golden, Colorado, that served only 80 individuals. Other early contracts included serving as an expert witness in a lawsuit to determine the worth of a uranium mine, helping a construction company with the problem of quality control in its crushed rock, and working with the Humane Society to help determine the necessity of using live animals in research. The company generated revenues of only $2,000 in its first year. To keep the business afloat, Bryant sold his house.

MAJOR BREAK: 1962

Despite the founders' lack of business experience, Westat held on until it received its first significant break in 1962. The company was hired to provide statistical and experimental design services to the U.S. Patent Office for a five-year project. As part of the job, Westat received office space and secretarial support, prerequisites that strengthened the young company's thin balance sheet. Moreover, work with the Patent Office opened the door to other government business.

Westat was incorporated in 1963. Because the company began winning more government contracts, the headquarters was moved from Colorado to Washington, D.C., in 1966. A year earlier, Bryant had open-heart surgery, which greatly improved his health and allowed him to make the move to the East. Westat was soon joined by another University of Wyoming graduate, Morris Hansen, who accepted a position at Westat after retiring from the U.S. Census Bureau.

HANSEN'S EARLY YEARS

Born in 1910 Hansen had earned an accounting degree from the University of Wyoming in 1934 and then went to work for the Census Bureau. In Washington, he also furthered his education in statistics, an area of personal interest, and he earned a degree in the subject from American University. During his time at the Census Bureau, Hansen pioneered a number of statistical concepts, including sampling techniques and the total survey error perspective in the design of surveys.

Hansen joined Westat as a senior vice president and continued to influence the science of statistical surveys. At Westat he would lead such major government projects as the consumer price index and the National Assessment of Educational Progress. Not only did Hansen bring a wealth of government contacts that helped Westat to secure more business, his arrival at Westat led to a string of former Census Bureau statisticians joining the company for second careers. The bureau's influence on the company was so pronounced that in government circles Westat was often called "Census West."

AMERICAN CAN ACQUIRES WESTAT

In the later 1960s Westat expanded beyond pure statistical services, adding research capabilities to win a wider range of contracts. By 1970 the company reached the $1 million mark in annual revenues. In order to maintain growth, more funding was necessary. Hence, in 1970 Westat agreed to sell a 60 percent controlling interest to American Can Company (ACC) for $750,000.

The deal also brought an ACC employee, Joseph A. Hunt, who became the chief financial officer. Over the next few years, ACC increased its holdings to 78 percent. With the backing of its new corporate parent, Westat grew rapidly, increasing revenues to $5 million in 1975.

A key contract during this period was the company's first longitudinal study, conducted on behalf of the Public Employment Program. In 1974 Westat began a three-year contract, its first national household study, for the National Survey of Family Growth (NSFG).

EMPLOYEES ACQUIRE WESTAT: 1977

Westat was generating about $10 million in annual sales in 1977 when the NSFG contract ended and ACC announced that Westat was up for sale. Westat's executives were determined to buy back the company rather than deal with new ownership and searched for a way to finance the purchase. Finally, they established the Westat Employee Stock Ownership Plan, and in 1978 this entity acquired ACC's 78 percent interest.

Although the price of the transaction was not made public, it was understood that it would be mostly financed by a $1.2 million loan. Independent once again, Westat continued to grow as Hunt took over as president while Bryant remained as chairman. In 1980 the company reached the $20 million mark in revenues. By this point, Westat had outgrown its office. In 1981 the company moved to its new headquarters in Rockville, Maryland.

It was in Rockville that Westat soon won a number of significant contracts, including the Employment Opportunity Pilot Projects for the U.S. Department of Labor. In addition, Westat received three long-term projects that would extend into the next century, the National Assessment of Educational Progress, National Health and Nutrition Examination Survey, and National Medical Expenditure Survey.

Westat also became involved in large medical survey projects, such as the Vietnam Veterans' Birth Defects Study and the Reye's Syndrome Study. Significant new clients in the 1980s included the Centers for Disease Control and Prevention, U.S. Department of Agriculture, Environmental Protection Agency, U.S. Department of Education, National Institutes of Health, National Cancer Institute, and National Center for Health Statistics.

ACQUIRES CROSSLEY SURVEYS

Westat grew through external means as well. In 1983 it acquired Crossley Surveys, which operated as an independent subsidiary. Another giant in statistics, Archibald M. Crossley, had founded it. Along with George Gallup and Elmo Roper, Crossley was considered one of the founders of modern public-opinion polling. He had started Crossley Inc. in New York in 1926 as a market-research firm and devised the first radio audience measurement system before becoming better known for public opinion polling.

In 1954 Crossley joined forces with Stewart, Dougall & Associates to create Crossley Surveys. In 1985 Bryant retired and became chairman emeritus, but he stayed on as a consultant for the next 20 years. He passed away at the age of 92 in 2008. Morris succeeded Bryant as chairman and remained actively involved in the Westat's work up until his death at the age of 79 in 1990. Westat veteran Joseph Wakesberg became the new chairman.

CROSSLEY SURVEY SOLD: 1994

With Hunt still serving as president and CEO, Westat's steady growth continued in the 1990s, this despite shedding Crossley Surveys. Westat sold the business to Roper Starch Worldwide Inc. in 1994. Even without Crossley's contribution to the balance sheet, Westat increased revenues from about $75 million in 1991 to $119 million in 1994. By this stage, the company was operating interview centers in Gaithersburg and Frederick, Maryland, and Oceanside, California.

The opening of a new behavioral research facility in Rockville helped Westat to maintain its momentum in the second half of the decade. The 1990s was also a period of transition, as surveys went from paper-based to electronic-based. Revenues topped the $250 million level in 2000. They grew to more than $285 million in 2001. The full-time staff also swelled to 1,500. Aiding the sales increase was the 2001 acquisition of Applied Logic Associates.

The Houston-based company provided clinical trial services to pharmaceutical and biotechnology companies, adding to Westat's clinical trial capabilities. By this point, the company had expanded the number of telephone research centers to nine across the United States. In the new century, Westat focused on international expansion. By the end of the first decade of the 21st century the company established operations in six international locations.

HUNT STEPS DOWN: 2011

At the start of the 2010s, Westat employed about 2,000 on a full-time basis and posted annual revenues in excess of $500 million. Instrumental to the company's growth for the previous 30 years had been its president and CEO, Hunt. He finally stepped down in 2011, but remained vice chairman. Taking the reins from him was 62-year-old James E. Smith, who had been with Westat since 1985 and rose through the ranks.

Hunt left Smith with a company that was well-established and fiscally healthy. Smith soon expanded

Westat further. In 2012 Westat acquired GeoStats LP. The Atlanta-based firm provided transportation consulting services, collecting, and analyzing transportation data for both government and commercial clients. Although the office was retained, GeoStats was folded into existing Westat operations.

The budget sequestration in 2013, which caused automatic spending cuts in the federal government, had an adverse impact on Westat, as it did on many other companies that depended on government contracts. Nevertheless, Westat was able to increase revenues 17 percent to $582.5 million in 2013. Of that amount, just $18.8 million, or 3.2 percent, came from outside the country. Whether Westat would be able to expand its international business in the years ahead, or remain dependent on its government business, remained a question yet to be answered.

Ed Dinger

PRINCIPAL DIVISIONS

Engineering & Research; IT & IS; Operations.

PRINCIPAL COMPETITORS

IMS Health Holdings, Inc.; The Kantar Group; Nielsen NV.

FURTHER READING

"American Can Plans Westat Share Deal." *New York Times*, June 7, 1978.

"Obituary: Edward C. Bryant." *Amstat News*, March 2008.

Rothman, Robert. "Working behind the Scenes on Reports, Md. Company Finds Its Strength in Numbers." *Education Week*, October 21, 1992.

"Top 25 Global Marketing/Ad/Opinion Research Firms Profiles." *Marketing News*, August 18, 1997.

"Top 50 Y.S. Marketing/Ad/Opinion Research Firms Profiles." *Marketing News*, June 8, 1992.

"Westat Inc." *Marketing News*, June 10, 2002.

Winn Inc.

—■—

15648 Computer Lane
Huntington Beach, California 92649
U.S.A.
Telephone: (714) 373-6271
Toll Free: (877) 854-7601
Fax: (714) 379-5463
Web site: http://www.winngrips.com

Private Company
Incorporated: 1977
Employees: 15
Sales: $30 million (2013 est.)
NAICS: 339920 Sporting and Athletic Goods
Manufacturing

■ ■ ■

Winn Inc. is a privately held sports equipment manufacturer based in Huntington Beach, California. Winn specializes in sports' grips through the use of advanced polymers. The company's primary business is golf, offering premium products that are categorized as comfort grips, responsive grips, and putters grips. Winn also offers golf grips specifically designed for women and juniors. Additionally, Winn manufactures grips for fishing rods, including fly rod grips, split grips, and full-rear grips. Winn products are sold through a network of distributors. The company is owned and managed by its founder, Dr. A. Ben Huang.

FOUNDER, TAIWAN BORN

Born in Taipei, Taiwan, in 1935, Ben Huang earned a bachelor's degree in mechanical engineering from the National Taiwan University. He received a scholarship from the University of Illinois to pursue his doctorate but first had to complete a two-year commitment to the air force. In 1959 he immigrated to the United States to continue his postgraduate education. His PhD thesis caught the attention of a National Aeronautics and Space Administration (NASA) recruiter, leading to a job offer shortly before Huang completed his degree in 1963. As a result, Huang became involved in the race to the moon, working on Dr. Wernher von Braun's team in the development of the space craft for the Apollo flights. In particular, Huang's group created a shock-absorbing material that provided protection for the spacecraft as it reentered the earth's atmosphere. Huang also accepted a position at Georgia Institute of Technology (Georgia Tech) in 1964, establishing the school's Graduate Aerospace Engineering PhD program.

Huang continued to work at NASA and teach at Georgia Tech until 1973, when he decided to switch gears and return home to Taiwan to try his hand at business. An ardent tennis player, Huang hoped to take advantage of a surge in interest in the sport that had caused a global tennis ball shortage. With help from a contact in the Taiwan rubber industry, he was able to secure an alliance with Japan's Showa Rubber Company to start a tennis ball factory in Taiwan. Further, he negotiated an agreement with sporting goods companies Spaulding and Wilson to purchase all of the tennis balls he could produce. What Huang did not take into account was the slim margin in tennis balls. It was a high-volume business, and he found it difficult to compete against his much larger competitor, General Tire, which made tennis balls under the Penn and Wilson brands.

COMPANY PERSPECTIVES

The pioneer of polymer golf grips, Winn strives to innovate the highest performing, most technologically advanced premium golf grips to facilitate the learning and enjoyment of golf at every level.

Huang diversified, offering synthetic tennis racket strings, as opposed to traditional gut, that he began producing in a factory he opened in northern Taipei in 1975. A year later, the plant began producing the Gutex and Gutite brands of synthetic strings, supplying such major tennis brands as Dunlop, Head, Penn, and Wilson. The tennis string business was also highly competitive, and he lacked an edge in the market. His synthetic strings did not hold much advantage over gut. While the former lasted longer, the latter played better.

FORMATION OF WINN INCORPORATED: 1977

Huang returned to the United States with his family in 1977, settling in California. He established Winn Incorporated and set up a sales and marketing arm for his Taiwan tennis products factories. Winn Inc. would also serve as Huang's sporting goods brand. To expand his line of tennis products, Huang took advantage of the work he did with NASA to create a synthetic shock-absorbing material for use in tennis racket grips that would weigh less and perform better than leather. Introduced in 1980, Winn's synthetic tennis grips, marketed under the Absorb-Mor, Anti-Shok, and SuperTech labels, revolutionized the sport.

Winn's shift in focus from tennis to golf began in 1993 when Huang decided to take up golf. His home near the company's headquarters in Huntington Beach, California, overlooked the 10th hole of the SeaCliff Country Club. He took golf lessons and quickly realized that it was a difficult game to play. It was also hard on the hands because he often mishit. In addition, he grew frustrated with the rubber grips that became so slippery he had to hold the club tighter, resulting in extra tension in his arms and shoulders that made it more difficult to produce a smooth swing.

INTRODUCTION OF FIRST GOLF GRIP: 1995

A trained engineer, Huang began to analyze golf grips and realized that traditional rubber grips were simply too heavy and distorted a golf club's idea weight distribution. He then used his experience developing a shock absorption material for NASA and tennis racket grips to tackle the problem of golf grips. He began experimenting with a high-tech polymer, Elastom ETM, for which he would receive several patents in the United States, Europe, and Japan. He used the material to develop his first golf grip, The Classic, which he unveiled at the 1995 Professional Golfers' Association (PGA) International Golf Show in Las Vegas. The grips became generally available for sale the following year.

Winn golf grips offered more than just superior performance. Huang designed them so that they could be easily and quickly replaced by the golfer at home or even on the course. Traditional rubber grips had to be taken to a pro shop to have them cut off and a new set glued on. Winn grips, on the other hand, simply wrapped around the club and were anchored by finishing tape.

Golf grips quickly supplanted tennis grips as Winn's focus. Not only were there more golf players to serve than tennis players, golfers carried a dozen or more clubs in their bags that required grips, far more than the typical tennis player owned rackets. Initially, Winn grips were mostly sold in regripping kits at pro shops and sporting goods stores, but soon club manufacturers, such as Goodwin Golf, began using Elastom grips for their club lines. Bullet Golf also became a customer, and Winn began talking to the likes of Calloway, Cobra, and Wilson Sports about using the grips.

OPENING OF CHINESE PLANT

After recording just $7,000 in sales in 1995, Winn golf grips generated about $800,000 in 1996 and $5 million the following year. To keep up with demand for the golf grips, Winn opened a plant in Guangzhou, China, in the late 1990s. In addition to making regular trips to oversee construction, Huang continued to serve as the head of Winn's research and development efforts, making further improvements to the company's golf grip technology. In 1999 the company introduced the Excel golf grip, using the patented ETX15 material.

As the new century dawned, Winn continued to expand its golf grip business, due in large measure to a growing number of top professional golfers switching to Winn grips. Helping to promote the product line was Butch Harmon, best known as the swing teacher for professional golfers Tiger Woods and Phil Mickelson. Harmon became Winn's spokesperson in 2000. The company also introduced a new grip, this one designed specifically for putters. Because of the unique requirements of the putter, which differed greatly from woods

KEY DATES

1977:	Huang starts Winn Inc. as U.S. marketing arm for Taiwan tennis ball business.
1980:	Winn introduces synthetic tennis grips.
1995:	Winn introduces golf grips.
2009:	Winn introduces fishing rod grips.
2013:	DuraTech grips are introduced.

and irons, the polymer used to make the new grip promoted feel, an important element in effective putting.

A testament to the effectiveness of Winn's golf grips was the emergence of similar products in the marketplace, some of which the company believed were using Huang's patented technology. In 2000 Winn filed patent-infringement lawsuits in U.S. District Court in Santa Ana, California, against two grip manufacturers: Kingwood, Texas–based Kelmac Grips and Taiwan's Karakal Grips. Although the case against Kelmac would soon be settled and voluntarily dismissed, Karakal would eventually accuse Winn of violating its Chinese patents. In 2002 Winn would also file a patent infringement lawsuit against the Eaton Corporation and its Golf Pride Grip division. The matter was settled in October of the following year. In 2006 Winn sued Compgrip USA Corp. over patent infringement charges. Winn won a summary judgment on the matter in April 2007.

Despite the legal distractions, Winn maintained the growth of its golf business early in the first decade of the 21st century. A growing number of professional golfers used the grips and helped to drive sales, as did more aggressive marketing. In 2002 Winn putter grips were used by the winner on 23 PGA Tour events. Even more important, three of the four major men's tournaments that year used Winn putter grips.

INTRODUCTION OF V17AVS MATERIAL: 2003

To increase production, the company opened its third factory in 2001. It included a state-of-the-art material production operation and quality-control department, as well as a research and development unit where Huang further refined the polymers he used to make golf grips. In 2003 Winn introduced another new material, V17 AVS, a proprietary polymer with a tacky quality that was well suited for putters because it offered the same feel and grip no matter the weather conditions. Aside from new high-tech materials, Winn also attempted to increase grip sales through styling. In 2003 the company launched the Collegiate Series of grips that featured school colors as well as the name and logo that spiraled through the entire grip.

Grips using the V17 material with Advanced Vertical Seam technology were introduced in 2004 and expanded upon the following year. In 2007 the company introduced the Dura-Soft V17 material as well as PCi Polymer Cord Integration. The latter combined polymers and cord material at the molecular level to combine the firmness that came with polymer grips and the control afforded by cord. The technology was refined further for the benefit of professional players, resulting in the 2009 introduction of the PCi Triple Line. In November 2009 Huang announced his latest breakthrough, Winnlite Grip Technology. Using an advanced injection molding process, he was able to reduce weight to about half of a conventional grip. The result was improved swing speed that led to greater distances and higher trajectories that improved accuracy.

INTRODUCTION OF FISHING ROD GRIPS: 2009

Winn also took advantage of its golf grip technology in 2009 to enter new markets. The company developed grips for fishing rods, hand tools and bicycle handles. The fishing tackle business proved especially attractive and became a key secondary market for Winn. At the start of the 2010s, the company developed new technologies and products for both golf and fishing applications. In 2012 the WinnDry polymer was introduced for the golf market. This new tacky material was ideally suited for excellent performance in all weather conditions. WinnDry was also incorporated into new fishing rod grips.

In 2013 Winn combined the WinnDry polymer with the Elastrom ETX rubber compound to create the first polymer/rubber hybrid grip, offering slip-resistant, all-weather performance in a highly durable material. The new grip, fashioned for both golf clubs and fishing rods, was christened DuraTech. Other innovative materials were likely to follow as Winn maintained its position as a leading company in the development of new grip styles and materials.

Ed Dinger

PRINCIPAL OPERATING DIVISIONS

Fishing; Golf.

PRINCIPAL COMPETITORS

Karakal Far East Ltd.; Lamkin Grips; Tacki-mac.

FURTHER READING

Donohue, Steve. "Winn Grips Goes Collegiate." *Golf World*, July 25, 2003.

"Fast Talk." *Orange County Register*, October 20, 1997.

Johnson, E. Michael. "Winn Launches New Grips." *Golf World Business*, June 2000.

Morita, Tad. "One for the Gripper." *Transpacific*, May 1997.

Reger, John. "Grip on the Game." *Orange County Register*, November 14, 1996.

Wright & McGill
Company

4245 East 46th Avenue
Denver, Colorado 80216
U.S.A.
Telephone: (720) 941-8700
Fax: (303) 321-4750
Web site: http://www.wright-mcgill.com

Private Company
Founded: 1925
Employees: 275
Sales: $126 million (2010 est.)
NAICS: 339920 Sporting and Athletic Goods
Manufacturing

■ ■ ■

Wright & McGill Company is a Denver, Colorado–based sporting goods company devoted to the development and manufacture of fishing equipment. The company is best known for its Eagle Claw brand of fish hooks. Wright & McGill also offers a wide variety of rods and reels, flies, tools and accessories, waders, bibs, tackle bags, and tackle packs. Products are sold through a network of dealers as well as through online retailers. The company's professional staff includes top anglers Brent Chapman, Rick Clunn, Skeet Reese, and Blair Wiggins. Wright & McGill also sponsors about 20 other men and women professionals. Wright & McGill is a privately held company, owned by Lee McGill, grandson of one of the company's cofounders.

COMPANY FOUNDED: 1925

Wright & McGill's founders were cousins Andrew Douglas McGill and Stanley Malcolm Wright, both avid fly fishermen. In the early 1920s McGill worked as a salesman for Denver's Whitney Sporting Goods. Frustrated one day by his hand-tied trout fishing flies, which too quickly became water-logged and sank, he developed a way to waterproof his flies. He then hired the fly tiers at Whitney to make the new flies, which he dubbed "Wiltless Wing" dry flies. He then sold them through Denver's two largest sporting goods stores, Gart Brothers and Dave Cook Sporting Goods. McGill's employer was not pleased with the side venture, however, and fired him. Believing his trout flies could become a profitable business, McGill then asked Wright to be his business partner.

Born in 1892, the son of a tanner, Wright studied at the Denver School of Commerce and the American Institute of Banking to prepare for a career in banking. In 1910 he became a bank clerk and after 10 years rose to the rank of teller. Nevertheless, he agreed to go into business with McGill, forming Wright & McGill in 1921 or 1925, depending on the source. What is not in doubt is that the business prospered through the sale of trout flies. In 1927, the company published its first mail-order catalog.

INSPIRATION FOR THE EAGLE
FISKHOOK

It was another afternoon of poor fishing that provided McGill with the inspiration for what would become the signature product of Wright & McGill. Around 1930, he was fishing and finding it difficult to hook and hold his catches. According to company lore, McGill noticed a pair of eagles flying overhead. He watched one of them land on a tree limb across the stream and observed the firm grip and penetration the bird achieved with its talons. McGill then took a close look at one of his fishing hooks. Dragged across his fishing creel it failed to penetrate the leather. An adjustment with his fishing pliers that bent the point of hook inward allowed it to catch the leather. McGill tried fishing with the modified hook and was pleased with the results.

McGill returned to the Wright & McGill offices, where his partner Wright, a bird-watcher, kept some reference books. McGill found a detailed picture of an eagle's claw, and it served as a template for his new hook and the first major advancement in hook design in many years. Once the design was completed, Wright & McGill had to contend with the problem of mass production, in particular tempering the hooks without breaking them. The thin tip had to be tempered just as much as the body, which was hundreds of times thicker than the point. New machinery had to be devised for tempering as well as grinding the points, but eventually the production obstacles were overcome and Wright & McGill began to market the hook under the Eagle Claw name. It quickly became a best seller for the company.

A major reason for the popularity of the Eagle Claw hook was that by then the country had been plunged into the Great Depression that aside for some temporary upticks spanned the entire decade of the 1930s. Although many people continued to fish for sport, a sizable number were simply trying to feed their families, and Eagle Claw hooks were an investment that paid off. For Wright & McGill, the sale of Eagle Claw hooks played an important role in the company staying afloat during these lean times. The company also continued to sell Wiltless Wing Trout Flies, as well as other patterns, including Ginger Quill, the Gunnison, and Royal Coachman.

The Depression finally came to an end in the early 1940s when the economy roared back to life as a result of spending on the military during World War II. The war caused a shortage in the silk gut imported from Spain that Wright & McGill used for the leaders that attached to their flies. Instead, the company now used

nylon, recently invented by DuPont, as a substitute. The work between Wright & McGill and DuPont would ultimately result in the development of new types of fishing lines. Like most companies, Wright & McGill found a way to make money during the war as a military supplier. Unlike many firms, however, Wright & McGill did not manufacture products that were unusual to their operation. Rather, they furnished fishhooks that were packaged in survival kits found on ships and planes.

FISHING RODS ADDED: 1946

Following the war, Wright & McGill expanded its range of fishing products. In 1946 a subsidiary was formed to produce and sell fishing rods. The new company leased the factory of Denver's Goodwin Granger & Co., a well-respected maker of bamboo cane rods. Wright & McGill also briefly retained the services of Goodwin Granger's master rodmaker, Swedish-born William Phillipson, who soon left to start his own company. After five years, Wright & McGill acquired the Goodwin Granger company from the widow of Goodwin Granger, who had died in 1931. During this time, the United States was involved in the Korean War, which resulted in a shortage of the Topkin bamboo cane used in making fishing rods. The fiberglass rod had been developed in the 1940s, and Wright & McGill began producing their own fiberglass rods in 1951. The new style grew increasingly more popular over the years, eventually supplanting bamboo as the predominant material for fishing rods.

To keep up with demand for its fishing products, Wright & McGill expanded its operations in the early 1950s. A new plant was built in Greeley, Colorado. It opened in 1953 and began producing fishhooks that were sold around the world. A second plant opened in Greeley a year later to manufacture fiberglass fishing rods.

FOUNDERS PASS AWAY

Wright died in Los Angeles in April 1956, and McGill bought out his partner's interest in Wright & McGill. As the decade came to a close, McGill's health began to fail, too. In February 1960 following a lengthy illness, he died in his home at the age of 71. His wife Madeline now became president of Wright & Gill, and their son Leland also played a major role in the management of the company. In that same year, the company opened a fishhook factory in the Pine Ridge Sioux Indian Reservation in South Dakota, providing much needed jobs. Residents learned how to tie flies and leaders and other skills. Even before Pine Ridge, Wright & McGill

KEY DATES

1925: Stanley Wright & Andrew McGill found company.
1946: Subsidiary is formed to make and sell fishing rods.
1956: Wright dies; McGill becomes sole owner.
1971: Company moves into new Denver home.
2012: Donn Schaible succeeds John Jilling as president.

had forged a reputation as a progressive company, hiring women, minorities, and disabled employees years before the concept of equal opportunity came into vogue. Madeline McGill continued the tradition. In 1971 she implemented "The New Life" policy. In the belief that a company devoted to making leisure time products should be an advocate of more leisure time for workers, the policy established a four-day workweek for Wright & McGill employees. Further, they received numerous four-day weekends and 40 hours of pay for 37 hours of work each week. It was also in 1971 that the company moved into its present-day home in Denver.

Wright & McGill grew organically as well as externally in the 1960s and 1970s. In addition to flies, hooks, and rods, the company began selling a free-line spinning reel. The company made a major breakthrough in fishhook technology in 1985 with the introduction of the Lazer Sharp fishhook, which used a chemical process to sharpen the tip, allowing the hooks to be extremely sharp as well as smooth and strong. Also during this period, the company expanded its range of fishhooks through the acquisition of the Kahle Horizontal Hook Co.

Wright & McGill grew its business internationally in the 1990s. In order to serve the needs of anglers and differing conditions around the globe, the company modified the sizes and styles of its fishhooks. Also important to the effort was the addition of distributors who understood the international markets. As a result, Wright & McGill began to carve out a sizeable market share in Canada and Mexico, as well as Europe and the Pacific Rim. In the latter half of the 1990s, the company began to focus on South America.

NEW CENTURY, CONTINUED GROWTH

Growth continued for Wright & McGill in the new century, led by new president John Jilling, who had

been with the company for more than 20 years. To better serve customers, it began marketing the products of Terminal Tackle Co. in 2002. The 1,500 tackle items included fishing lines, nets, tools, and accessories. In that same year, Wright & McGill completed another acquisition, Camdenton, Missouri–based Laker by Jadico, an importer of rods, reels, and other fishing products that were made available for private-label programs to major American retailers. The business was renamed Laker Fishing Tackle Company.

Wright & McGill enjoyed less success with the 2003 acquisition of Red Bluff, California–based Lightning Bait. The company offered the Crave and Nitro lines of bait and scent items. Although it helped to fill out Wright & McGill's product line, the bait line did not perform especially well. In 2011 Wright & McGill dropped it.

Wright & McGill also grew organically in the first decade of the 21st century. The company enjoyed success with the 2004 launch of rods endorsed by top professional anglers. The Skeet Reese signature S-Curve rods performed especially well. Other top professionals soon signed up with Wright & McGill to develop their own signature rods, including Rick Clunn, Tony Roach, and Trevor Storlie. The company did not neglect its flagship fishhook business, remaining on the leading edge of technology. Making use of medical tool technology, the company introduced the Lazer TroKar fishhook in 2009, representing the industry's first "surgically sharpened" fishhook.

In 2012 Jilling retired after 13 years as president and 35 years with the company. He was succeeded by Donn Schaible, who had been the company's chief financial officer. He took the helm of a business that was already well established in the freshwater fishing market. With the new Lazer TroKar hooks, Wright & McGill now began a concerted effort to become a major player in the saltwater sector. New equipment was installed to produce the bigger hooks that would be required, and samples were given out to top saltwater fishing captains. The effectiveness of the Lazer TroKar hooks quickly won converts. The saltwater market was likely to become an important avenue of growth for Wright & McGill in the years ahead.

Ed Dinger

PRINCIPAL SUBSIDIARIES

Laker Fishing Tackle Company.

PRINCIPAL COMPETITORS

Gamakatsu USA, Inc.; O. Mustad & Son AS; Rapala VMC OYJ.

FURTHER READING

"Andrew D. McGill Dies in Denver." *Greeley Daily Tribune*, February 9, 1960.

Bates, Joseph D., Jr. "The Bird That Built a Tackle Business." *San Antonio Light*, June 25, 1967.

Geiger, Robert E. "Making Hooks Is Bigger Task Than Hooking Fish." *Paris (TX) News*, May 18, 1941.

"New Working Policy Initiated at Wright and McGill Plants." *Greeley Tribune*, February 27, 1971.

Spencer, John. "Wright and McGill's Fine Products Are the Standard of Fishing Tackle." *Redding Record Searchlight*, December 4, 2010.

Wright, Sharon. "Eagle Claws Has Been Reeling in Customers since 1925." *Denver Business Journal*, October 14, 2011.

Zieralski, Ed. "Eagle Claw Hopes to Hook Southern California Anglers on New TroKars." *San Diego Union-Tribune*, March 8, 2013.

ZTE Corporation

ZTE Plaza, Keji Road South
Hi-Tech Industrial Park
Nanshan District
Shenzhen, 518057
China
Telephone: (+86 755) 2677 0282
Fax: (+86 755) 2677 0286
Web site: http://www.zte.com.cn

Public Company
Founded: 1985
Employees: 69,093
Sales: RMB 75.23 billion ($12.42 billion) (2013)
Stock Exchanges: Hong Kong; Shenzhen
Ticker Symbol: 00763
NAICS: 334220 Radio and Television Broadcasting and Wireless Communications Equipment Manufacturing

■ ■ ■

ZTE Corporation is one of the world's leading manufacturers of telecommunications equipment. The company has positioned its product line as one of the world's most comprehensive and vertically integrated, spanning nearly every segment of both the fixed-line and mobile/wireless telecommunications sectors. The company's products include base stations, broadband networking equipment and systems, and switching equipment and systems, as well as software and support services. ZTE has also been making a push to become one of the world's largest manufacturers of mobile handsets, which it markets under its own global ZTE brand. The company has announced plans to raise its handset sales to as many as 100 million smartphones by 2015, up from just 15 million in 2011 and 50 million in 2012.

ZTE has also ventured into the production of tablet computers, which it sells under the Optik name in partnership with Sprint Nextel in the United States. ZTE operates on a global basis, with sales and operations spanning 160 countries, including 17 research and development centers in China, France, and India. With a research team of more than 30,000, ZTE has also taken the global lead in telecommunications patents. Ninety percent of the company's more than 2,000 patents were developed in-house. China, where ZTE supplies most of the country's major telecommunication services providers, represented nearly 47.5 percent of ZTE's total revenues, while Europe, the Americas, and Oceania contributed nearly 26.4 percent. The rest of Asia added 18.4 percent, while Africa contributed 7.8 percent. ZTE is listed on the Hong Kong and Shenzhen Stock Exchanges. The company is led by founder and chairman Hou Weigui and president Shi Lirong. In 2013 ZTE reported sales of RMB 75.23 billion ($12.42 billion).

SEMICONDUCTOR ORIGINS IN 1985

Born in 1942, Hou Weigui became the deputy chief engineer of a research laboratory in Xian, Shaanzi Province, which operated under the auspices of the People's Republic of China's former Ministry of

COMPANY PERSPECTIVES

ZTE has the most complete telecommunications product line in the world, covering every vertical sector of wireless networks, core networks, access & bearer networks, services and terminals markets. With its independent and creative R&D capability and customer-oriented and market-driven strategy, ZTE is capable of developing and producing market-leading, first-class technologies in wireless, switching, access, optical transmission, data, handsets and telecommunications software. ZTE uses this expertise to provide end-to-end solutions tailored to the specific needs of customers around the world.

Aeronautics. In the early 1980s Hou recognized the new opportunities presented by the Communist Party's economic reform policies, which had been initiated in the late 1970s.

In 1984 Hou left Xian for Shenzhen, the first of the free-trade zones established as part of the government's economic reforms. Companies located in the zone benefited from a greater access to foreign investment capital and technologies, as well as a proximity to the Hong Kong market. Hou was joined by six other engineers, and in 1985 created Zhongxing Semiconductor Co. Ltd. This company initially operated under the auspices of the aeronautics industry, and was initially founded to develop semiconductors and other electronic components.

Starting from a single, cramped office, Zhongxin Semiconductor grew slowly through the decade, developing a range of small electronic parts and components, while it built up its technological capacity. By the beginning of the 1990s Hou had already turned the company toward the production of components for the telecommunications industry, starting with switches. The company quickly became a major supplier of components to the Chinese telecommunications sector, which at the time was only just beginning to develop after decades of neglect under communist rule.

Hou recognized the importance of research and development in building the company. This investment enabled Zhongxing to implement a multiproduct research and development strategy. In this way, Zhongxing developed a broad range of research interests, spanning the fixed-line and mobile and wireless sectors. Through the first half of the decade, the company's

products extended across such applications as transmission, wireless switching, videoconferencing, and power supply systems.

GOING PUBLIC IN 1993

In 1993 Hou, serving as chairman, restructured the company as Zhongxing New Telecom Corporation. The new company featured a range of state-owned corporations as its shareholders, became the first in China to adopt a form of collective operations. Hou himself became a major shareholder of the company, which quickly changed its name to Shenzhen Zhongxingxin Telecommunications Equipment Company Ltd. Other shareholders included China Precision Machinery Import & Export Shenzhen Company, Lishan Microelectronics Corporation, Shenzhen Zhaoke Investment Development Company Ltd., Hunan Nantian (Group) Company Ltd., Jilin Posts and Telecommunications Equipment Company, and Hebei Posts and Telecommunications Equipment Company and incorporated in People's Republic of China.

The company's breakthrough came in 1996, when it became the first in China to develop a digital SPC exchange based on its own technology. This success paved the way for the company to go public, marking another first for the Chinese telecommunications sector, with a listing on the Shenzhen Stock Exchange. The company once again changed its name, becoming ZTE Corporation. Hou's shares in the company were worth more than RMB 150 million (approximately $25 million) at the time.

Hou quietly set to work transforming ZTE into one of China's leading telecommunications equipment suppliers. ZTE also became the first Chinese telecom company to begin exploring sales outside of China. In 1998, for example, the company won its bid for the construction of a turnkey telecommunications network in Pakistan, in a deal worth $95 million. The company opened its first foreign office soon after, in Islamabad. The following year the company completed its first shipment to Africa, of a videoconferencing system to Kenya.

TECHNOLOGY LEADER INTO 2000

ZTE soon established itself as a technology leader in China. The company became the first to introduce a dual-band handset in 1999, once again based on its own technology. The company also began winning orders to implement telecommunications networks for China's fast-growing telecom giants, including a contract for China Telecom in 1999.

1985: Hou Weigui founds Zhongxing Semiconductor Co. Ltd. in Shenzhen, China.

1993: Company becomes Zhongxing New Telecom Corporation and specializes in telecommunications equipment with Hou as chairman.

1997: Company goes public as ZTE Corporation on the Shenzhen Stock Exchange.

2004: ZTE lists its shares on the Hong Kong Stock Exchange.

2010: Company enters the market for smartphone handsets.

2014: ZTE announces plans to open a global network operations center in India.

The company in the meantime had been investing in developing its code division multiple access (CDMA) technology, as the new protocol appeared set to become the mobile telecommunications standard into the new century. CDMA was a channel access method used by various radio communication technologies in which several transmitters could send information simultaneously over a single communication channel. By 2000 ZTE had completed its first CDMA-based network. The company also became the first in the world to produce a CDMA-based handset with a removable SIM card. These investments paid off as the group secured contracts with two of China's top telecommunications groups, China Netcom and China Unicom. For the latter, the company implemented China's first full-scale CDMA network, with the capacity to handle 1.1 million phone lines.

Although ZTE invested heavily in developing its own technologies, the company also developed a range of partnerships with many of the world's leading technology and telecommunications equipment companies. The company teamed up with Intel's Chinese arm in 2002, for example, in order to develop new third-generation (3G) mobile technologies and equipment. Through the middle of the decade, ZTE entered a long series of partnerships, with companies including Alcatel, Ericsson, Qualcomm, Cisco, France Telecom, Telecom Egypt, Telefonicon, and Hutchison.

These partnerships also helped raised the group's international profile. In 2003 the company teamed up with BSNL in India, building that country's largest CDMA-based mobile network. The group also entered a partnership with Greece's OTE, building a broadband network for the 2004 Olympic Games in Athens. In that year too the company's technology backed the implementation of the first 3G network in Africa, in Tunisia.

HONG KONG LISTING IN 2004

ZTE confirmed its status as a growing contender for the global telecommunications equipment market in 2004, when it became the first Chinese company with a listing on the Shenzhen Stock Exchange to add its listing to the Hong Kong Stock Exchange as well. This listing, which made the company's shares available to the international investment community, also played a crucial role in ZTE's efforts to challenge its main rival, Huawei Technologies, at that time the largest and most well-known Chinese telecommunications equipment supplier.

By 2005 ZTE had already claimed the lead in China's wireless equipment market, having installed a total capacity of more than 100 million phone lines worldwide. The company also became one of the world's top three producers of DSLAM equipment. Also in 2005 the company made a major push into the European markets. This enabled the company to form a long-term strategic partnership with France Telecom, by then one of the world's leading telecommunications services providers. As part of that partnership, ZTE became the global supplier of ADSL equipment for the French company. The partnership later expanded to include a range of equipment, including fixed-line network access and terminal equipment.

ZTE next set its sights on cracking the North American market. The company made some headway in this effort in 2006, when it won a contract to supply 3G terminals to Canada's Telus. The company continued to build up its range of partnerships as well, with such companies as building terminals and handsets for such companies as Portugal Telecom, Vodafone, Hutchison, and Telefonica.

By the end of 2007 ZTE internationalization strategy had successfully raised the percentage of foreign sales to 60 percent of its total. After winning a contract to supply 51 percent of China Mobile's CDMA equipment supply, the company consolidated its position as the world leader in CDMA equipment. By then ZTE had also become one of the world's top four suppliers of GSM equipment. The company also made its entry into the U.S. market, reaching an agreement to supply WiMAX equipment to Sprint Nextel.

SMARTPHONE FOCUS FROM 2010

ZTE continued to win respect from the global telecommunications market. By 2008 the company's client list counted more than 500 operators in 140 countries, including more than half of the top 100 services providers. The group also won international recognition for the quality of equipment, including being named by Frost & Sullivan as the World Best CDMA Equipment Manufacturer for 2009.

One of ZTE's fastest-growing operations was its production of mobile handsets. By the beginning of 2009 ZTE had already become the world's sixth-largest producer of handsets, generally produced for third parties. In the United States, for example, the company scored a major success with its line of low-priced handsets developed for MetroPCS. Into the next decade, however, ZTE shifted its attention to the booming smartphone market, while also setting its sights on building the ZTE brand as an international leader as well.

ZTE's massive research and development component, which by then counted more than 30,000 research professionals, enabled the company to leapfrog the competition. In 2010 the company shipped some 3.75 million smartphones. Just one year later, the company's smartphone sales had already risen to 15 million. By the beginning of 2013 the company had already cracked the top four, and ranked as the fastest-growing smartphone maker, trailing only Apple.

ZTE BRAND IN 2012

ZTE established itself as a low-priced alternative to competitors including Apple and Samsung. The company nonetheless incorporated its share of innovative designs and features. In 2011, for example, the company introduced the first of a line of simplified handsets designed for children, which became a best seller in Japan. By the beginning of 2013 the company had already sold two million of the handsets. In that year, the company announced that it was on track to top sales of 50 million smartphones by the end of the year, up from 35 million in 2012. The company also announced it expected its smartphone sales to reach 100 million by 2015.

Part of this growth was expected to come from increasing acceptance of the ZTE brand. In 2012, for example, the company introduced a new low-priced, but full-featured smartphone, called the Slate, which it began marketing in Germany under its brand name. The rollout was a strong success, leading the company to expand its sales to other European markets. ZTE released a number of models for the European market, most notably the ZTE Open, the first smartphone to feature the new Firefox OS open-source operating system, introduced in 2014.

ZTE's record had begun making its rivals nervous. As one Samsung official told *Trusted Reviews* in 2011: "We simply cannot make handsets as cheaply as [ZTE] can," adding, "and we cannot buy ZTE to make this problem go away because it is partly owned by the Chinese government. You do not push your luck with the Chinese government unless you want to lose access to a market of over a billion people."

ZTE, however, had its own government worries. In 2012 the company found itself under scrutiny from U.S. lawmakers, which alleged that ZTE and Huawei represented a security risk for the United States in that they could not be trusted to be free of influence from the Chinese governments. Both companies rejected these claims. Nonetheless, ZTE continued to struggle to expand its presence in the U.S. market. The group made new inroads, when it reached a new partnership with Sprint Nextel to introduce a line of tablets under the Optik name, starting from 2012.

ZTE made better progress in other markets, such as India. In 2014 the company expanded its presence in that market by setting up a new global network operations center, making that country its base of operations for its expansion into Southeast Asian markets such as Indonesia and Malaysia, and African markets, including Kenya and Nigeria.

The company had also continued to expand its presence in other directions. In 2014 the company was recognized as the leading provider of videoconferencing equipment to the Asian Pacific region. By then ZTE's R&D efforts were also recognized, when the company claiming one of the top rankings in the World Intellectual Property Organization's annual patent applicants table. With more than 2,300 patent filings, ZTE had claimed the top position in 2011 and 2012, although slipping back to the second spot behind Panasonic in 2014. Hou Weigui, who remained the company's chairman, had successfully steered ZTE from a small Shenzhen office to become one of the world's leading telecommunications equipment companies in the early 21st century.

M. L. Cohen

PRINCIPAL SUBSIDIARIES

PT ZTE Indonesia; Shenzhen Zhonxing Telecom Technology and Service Company Ltd.; Shenzhen ZTE Mobile Telecom Company Ltd.; Zhongxing Software; ZTE (Hangzhou) Company Ltd.; ZTE (Malaysia) Corporation Sdn. Bhd.; ZTE (Thailand) Co., Ltd.; ZTE Do Brasil Ltda; ZTE HK; ZTE ICT Company Ltd.; ZTE Telecom India Private Ltd.; ZTESoft Technology Company Ltd.

PRINCIPAL DIVISIONS

Manufacturing; Information Technology; Telecommunication Services.

PRINCIPAL COMPETITORS

Apple Corporation; HTC Corporation; Huawei Technologies Ltd.; Motorola Mobility Holdings Inc.; Nokia Telecommunications Ltd.; Phillips Electronics North America Corp.; Samsung Corporation; Siemens AG.

FURTHER READING

Chiang, Benjamin. "Racing the West Head to Head." *Commonwealth Magazine*, June 7, 2012.

Dickie, Mure, and Alexandra Harney. "ZTE Focuses on the World's Rich Pickings." *Financial Times*, February 20, 2004.

Gale, Sophie. "Upwardly Mobile." *Trade Finance*, December 2002.

Hille, Kathrin. "Range of Problems behind ZTE Profit Plunge." *Financial Times*, August 23, 2012.

Kelly, Gordon. "Who Is ZTE & Why Are Rivals Running Scared?" *Trusted Reviews*, July 15, 2011.

Rahul, Kumar. "Getting Smart." *India Business Journal*, August 1, 2014.

Woyke, Elizabeth, "ZTE's Smart Phone Ambitions," *Forbes*, March 16, 2009.

"ZTE Awarded Contract for Nationwide LTE Network Deployment in Slovakia by SWAN." *Worldwide Computer Products News*, August 28, 2014.

"ZTE Delivers Milestone Handset; Celebrating 15th Anniversary of Terminals Division." *Wireless News*, April 29, 2013.

"ZTE Is Number 2 in World Intellectual Property Organization Patent Table." *Telecom Tiger*, March 21, 2014.

"ZTE Raises European Profile." *Telecommunications*, June 2005.

"ZTE Retains No. 1 Position in Asia Pacific Video-Conferencing Market." *Communications Today*, June 11, 2014.

"ZTE Successfully Takes over Network Operations for E-Plus Group in Germany." *Telecom Tiger*, February 27, 2014.

Cumulative Index to Companies

Listings in this index are arranged in alphabetical order under the company name. Company names beginning with a letter or proper name such as Eli Lilly & Co. will be found under the first letter of the company name. Definite articles (The, Le, La) are ignored for alphabetical purposes as are forms of incorporation that precede the company name (AB, NV). This index is cumulative with volume numbers printed in bold type. Updates to entries that appeared in earlier volumes are signified by the notation (upd.).

Numbers

Guitar Center, Inc., **29** 221–23; **68** 192–95 (upd.)

Guittard Chocolate Company, **55** 183–85

Gulf + Western Inc., **I** 451–53 *see also* Paramount Communications; Viacom Inc.

Gulf Agency Company Ltd., **78** 133–36

Gulf Air Company, **56** 146–48

Gulf Island Fabrication, Inc., **44** 201–03

Gulf States Toyota, Inc., **115** 233–36

Gulf States Utilities Company, **6** 495–97 *see also* Entergy Corp.

GulfMark Offshore, Inc., **49** 180–82; **126** 182–86 (upd.)

Gulfport Energy Corporation, **119** 217–20

Gulfstream Aerospace Corporation, **7** 205–06; **28** 169–72 (upd.)

Gund, Inc., **96** 159–62

Gunite Corporation, **51** 152–55

The Gunlocke Company, **23** 243–45

Gunnebo AB, **53** 156–58

Gunvor S.A., **162** 226–30

GUS plc, **47** 165–70 (upd.)

Guthrie Theater, **136** 222–225

Guthy-Renker Corporation, **32** 237–40; **119** 221–26 (upd.)

Guttenplan's Frozen Dough Inc., **88** 151–54

Guy Degrenne SA, **44** 204–07

Guyana Telephone and Telegraph Company Limited, **157** 219–23

Guyenne et Gascogne S.A., **23** 246–48; **107** 173–76 (upd.)

GVT S.A., **127** 165–68

Gwathmey Siegel & Associates Architects LLC, **26** 186–88

GWR Group plc, **39** 198–200

GXS Inc., **150** 225–31

Gymboree Corporation, **15** 204–06; **69** 198–201 (upd.)

H

H&E Equipment Services, **128** 254–58

H&M Hennes & Mauritz AB, **98** 181–84 (upd.)

H&R Block, Inc., **9** 268–70; **29** 224–28 (upd.); **82** 162–69 (upd.)

H-P *see* Hewlett-Packard Co.

H.B. Fuller Company, **8** 237–40; **32** 254–58 (upd.); **75** 179–84 (upd.); **158** 271–77 (upd.)

H. Betti Industries Inc., **88** 155–58

H.D. Vest, Inc., **46** 217–19

H. E. Butt Grocery Company, **13** 251–53; **32** 259–62 (upd.); **85** 164–70 (upd.)

H.F. Ahmanson & Company, **II** 181–82; **10** 342–44 (upd.) *see also* Washington Mutual, Inc.

H.H. Brown Shoe Co., Inc., **159** 135–38

H. J. Heinz Company, **II** 507–09; **11** 171–73 (upd.); **36** 253–57 (upd.); **99** 198–205 (upd.)

H.J. Russell & Company, **66** 162–65

H. Lundbeck A/S, **44** 208–11; **147** 147–51 (upd.)

H.M. Payson & Co., **69** 202–04

H.O. Penn Machinery Company, Inc., **96** 163–66

H.P. Hood L.L.C., **117** 130–33

The H.T. Hackney Company, **144** 206–09

The H.W. Wilson Company, **66** 166–68

Ha-Lo Industries, Inc., **27** 193–95 *see also* Halo Branded Solutions, Inc.

The Haartz Corporation, **94** 223–26

Haas Automation, Inc., **154** 219–22

Haas Outdoors, Inc., **147** 152–54

Habanos, S.A., **157** 224–28

Habasit AG, **121** 230–33

Habersham Bancorp, **25** 185–87

The Habitat Company LLC, **106** 213–17

Habitat for Humanity International, Inc., **36** 258–61; **106** 218–22 (upd.)

Hach Co., **18** 218–21

Hachette Filipacchi Medias S.A., **21** 265–67

Hachette Livre SA, **IV** 617–19; **163** 203–07 (upd.)

Hachijuni Bank Ltd., **144** 210–14

Haci Omer Sabanci Holdings A.S., **55** 186–89; **138** 132–36 (upd.)

Hackman Oyj Adp, **44** 212–15

Hackney *see* The H.T. Hackney Company.

Hadco Corporation, **24** 201–03

Häfele GmbH & Co Kommanditgesellschaft, **127** 169–73

Haeger Industries Inc., **88** 159–62

Haemonetics Corporation, **20** 277–79; **122** 192–96 (upd.)

Haftpflichtverband der Deutschen Industrie Versicherung auf Gegenseitigkeit V.a.G. *see* HDI (Haftpflichtverband der Deutschen Industrie Versicherung auf Gegenseitigkeit V.a.G.).

Hagemeyer N.V., **39** 201–04

Haggar Corporation, **19** 194–96; **78** 137–41 (upd.)

Haggen Inc., **38** 221–23

Hagoromo Foods Corporation, **84** 175–178

Hahn Automotive Warehouse, Inc., **24** 204–06

Haier Group Corporation, **65** 167–70

Haights Cross Communications, Inc., **84** 179–182

The Hain Celestial Group, Inc., **27** 196–98; **43** 217–20 (upd.); **120** 152–56 (upd.)

Hainan Airlines Co., Ltd., **162** 231–34

Hair Club For Men Ltd., **90** 222–25

Hajoca Corporation, **131** 137–40

Hakuhodo DY Holdings Inc., **6** 29–31; **42** 172–75 (upd.); **144** 215–20 (upd.)

HAL Inc., **9** 271–73 *see also* Hawaiian Airlines, Inc.

Hal Leonard Corporation, **96** 167–71

Haldor Topsøe Holding A/S, **151** 201–04

Hale-Halsell Company, **60** 157–60

Half Price Books, Records, Magazines Inc., **37** 179–82

Halfords Group plc, **110** 200–04

Hall, Kinion & Associates, Inc., **52** 150–52

Halliburton Company, **III** 497–500; **25** 188–92 (upd.); **55** 190–95 (upd.); **127** 174–81 (upd.)

Hallmark Cards, Inc., **IV** 620–21; **16** 255–57 (upd.); **40** 228–32 (upd.); **87** 205–212 (upd.)

Halloren Schokoladenfabrik AG, **142** 231–35

Halma plc, **104** 179–83

Halo Branded Solutions, Inc., **151** 205–09 (upd.)

Halo Burger Inc., **156** 159–62

Halwani Brothers Co., **153** 171–74

Hamilton Beach Brands, Inc., **17** 213–15; **143** 179–83 (upd.)

Hammacher Schlemmer & Company Inc., **21** 268–70; **72** 160–62 (upd.)

Hammerson plc, **IV** 696–98; **40** 233–35 (upd.); **133** 165–69 (upd.)

Hammond Manufacturing Company Limited, **83** 179–182

Hamon & Cie (International) S.A., **97** 190–94

Hamot Health Foundation, **91** 227–32

Hampshire Group Ltd., **82** 170–73

Hampson Industries PLC, **122** 197–200

Hampton Affiliates, Inc., **77** 175–79

Hampton Industries, Inc., **20** 280–82

Hana Financial Group Inc., **150** 232–36

Hancock Fabrics, Inc., **18** 222–24; **129** 150–53 (upd.)

Hancock Holding Company, **15** 207–09

Handleman Company, **15** 210–12; **86** 185–89 (upd.)

Handspring Inc., **49** 183–86

Handy & Harman, **23** 249–52

Hanesbrands Inc., **98** 185–88

Hang Lung Group Ltd., **104** 184–87

Hang Seng Bank Ltd., **60** 161–63

Hanger Orthopedic Group, Inc., **41** 192–95; **129** 154–58 (upd.)

Hangzhou Wahaha Group Co., Ltd., **119** 227–30

Haniel *see* Franz Haniel & Cie. GmbH.

Hanjin Shipping Co., Ltd., **50** 217–21; **150** 237–44 (upd.)

Hankook Tire Company Ltd., **105** 200–03

Hankyu Corporation, **V** 454–56; **23** 253–56 (upd.)

Hankyu Department Stores, Inc., **V** 70–71; **62** 168–71 (upd.)

Hanmi Financial Corporation, **66** 169–71

Hanna Andersson Corp., **49** 187–90

Hanna-Barbera Cartoons Inc., **23** 257–59

Hannaford Bros. Co., **12** 220–22; **103** 211–17 (upd.)

Hanover Compressor Company, **59** 215–17

Hanover Direct, Inc., **36** 262–65

Hanover Foods Corporation, **35** 211–14; **154** 223–27 (upd.)

Hansen Natural Corporation, **31** 242–45; **76** 171–74 (upd.) *see also* Monster Beverage Corporation.

Hansgrohe AG, **56** 149–52

Hanson Building Materials America Inc., **60** 164–66

Macmillan, Inc., **7** 284–86

The MacNeal-Schwendler Corporation, **25** 303–05

MacNeil Automotive Products Limited, **162** 293–96

MacNeil/Lehrer Productions, **87** 296–299

Macquarie Group Ltd., **69** 246–49; **148** 365–70 (upd.)

Macromedia, Inc., **50** 328–31

Macrovision Solutions Corporation, **101** 314–17

Macy's, Inc., **94** 284–93 (upd.); **156** 264–73 (upd.)

Mad Catz Interactive, Inc., **154** 287–90

MADD *see* Mothers Against Drunk Driving.

Madden's on Gull Lake, **52** 231–34

Madeco S.A., **71** 210–12

Madeira Wine Company, S.A., **49** 255–57; **156** 274–78 (upd.)

Madelaine Chocolate Novelties, Inc., **104** 280–83

Madge Networks N.V., **26** 275–77

Madhvani Group of Companies, **143** 303–06

Madison Dearborn Partners, LLC, **97** 258–61

Madison Gas and Electric Company, **39** 259–62

Madison-Kipp Corporation, **58** 213–16

Madison Square Garden, LP, **109** 385–89

Madrange SA, **58** 217–19

Mag Instrument, Inc., **67** 240–42; **156** 279–82 (upd.)

Magazine Luiza S.A., **101** 318–21

Magellan Aerospace Corporation, **48** 274–76; **136** 333–337 (upd.)

MaggieMoo's International, **89** 312–16

Magic Seasoning Blends Inc., **109** 390–93

magicJack VocalTec Ltd., **154** 291–94

Magma Copper Company, **7** 287–90 *see also* BHP Billiton.

Magma Design Automation Inc., **78** 203–27

Magma Power Company, **11** 270–72

Magna International Inc., **102** 248–52

Magna Steyr AG and Company KG, **113** 232–36

Magnetek, Inc., **15** 287–89; **41** 241–44 (upd.); **158** 363–67 (upd.)

Magneti Marelli Holding SpA, **90** 286–89

Magnotta Winery Corporation, **114** 280–83

Magnum Hunter Resources Corporation, **151** 267–70

Magyar Telekom Rt, **78** 208–11

Magyar Villamos Muvek Zrt, **113** 237–41

Mahindra & Mahindra Ltd., **120** 225–29

Mahle GmbH, **156** 283–88

Mahou S.A., **142** 287–91

MAI Systems Corporation, **11** 273–76

Maid-Rite Corporation, **62** 235–38

Maidenform Brands, Inc., **20** 352–55; **59** 265–69 (upd.); **157** 261–66 (upd.)

Mail Boxes Etc., **18** 315–17; **41** 245–48 (upd.) *see also* U.S. Office Products Co.

Mail-Well, Inc., **28** 250–52 *see also* Cenveo Inc.

Mail.Ru Group Limited, **133** 275–78

MAIN *see* Makhteshim-Agan Industries Ltd.

Main Line Health, **126** 226–29

Maine & Maritimes Corporation, **56** 210–13

Maine Central Railroad Company, **16** 348–50

Maines Paper & Food Service Inc., **71** 213–15

Mainfreight Limited, **119** 311–15

Maïsadour S.C.A., **107** 252–55

Maison Louis Jadot, **24** 307–09

Majesco Entertainment Company, **85** 225–29

Majestic Star Casino, LLC, **153** 257–60

Majestic Wine plc, **153** 261–64

The Major Automotive Companies, Inc., **45** 260–62

Major League Baseball, **163** 272–75

Major League Baseball Players Association, **154** 295–98

Make-A-Wish Foundation of America, **97** 262–65

Makedonski Telekom AD Skopje, **113** 242–46

MakerBot Industries, LLC, **151** 271–75

Makhteshim-Agan Industries Ltd., **85** 230–34

Makino Milling Machine Co., Ltd., **159** 225–28

Makita Corporation, **22** 333–35; **59** 270–73 (upd.); **152** 300–04 (upd.)

MAKO Surgical Corporation, **140** 284–87

Makro Cash and Carry UK Holding Ltd., **146** 258–61

Malaco Records Inc., **145** 233–36

Malayan Banking Berhad, **72** 215–18

Malayan Banking Berhad, **149** 226–30 (upd.)

Malaysia Dairy Industries Private Ltd., **156** 289–92

Malaysian Airline System Berhad, **6** 100–02; **29** 300–03 (upd.); **97** 266–71 (upd.)

The Malcolm Group Ltd., **130** 319–22

Malcolm Pirnie, Inc., **42** 242–44

Malden Mills Industries, Inc., **16** 351–53 *see also* Polartec LLC.

Malév Plc, **24** 310–12

Mallinckrodt Group Inc., **19** 251–53

Malt-O-Meal Company, **22** 336–38; **63** 249–53 (upd.)

Mammoet Transport B.V., **26** 278–80

Mammoth Mountain Ski Area, **101** 322–25

Man Aktiengesellschaft, **III** 561–63

Man Group PLC, **106** 290–94

MAN Roland Druckmaschinen AG, **94** 294–98

Management and Training Corporation, **28** 253–56

Management Action Programs, Inc., **123** 247–50

Manatron, Inc., **86** 260–63

Manchester United Football Club plc, **30** 296–98

Mandalay Resort Group, **32** 322–26 (upd.)

Mandom Corporation, **82** 205–08; **162** 297–301 (upd.)

Mane USA Inc., **131** 234–37

Manhattan Associates, Inc., **67** 243–45

Manhattan Beer Distributors LLC, **114** 284–87

Manhattan Construction Company *see* Rooney Holdings Inc.

Manhattan Group, LLC, **80** 228–31

The Manhattan Mortgage Co., Inc., **125** 229–32

Manheim, **88** 244–48

Manila Electric Company, **56** 214–16; **148** 371–75 (upd.)

Manischewitz Company *see* B. Manischewitz Co.

Manitex International, Inc., **144** 301–04

Manitoba Telecom Services, Inc., **61** 184–87

Manitou BF S.A., **27** 294–96

The Manitowoc Company, Inc., **18** 318–21; **59** 274–79 (upd.); **118** 269–76 (upd.)

Mann+Hummel Holding GmbH, **159** 229–32

Manna Inc., **164** 242–45

Manna Pro Products, LLC, **107** 256–59

Mannatech Inc., **33** 282–85

Mannesmann AG, **III** 564–67; **14** 326–29 (upd.); **38** 296–301 (upd.) *see also* Vodafone Group PLC.

Mannheim Steamroller *see* American Gramophone LLC.

Manning Selvage & Lee (MS&L), **76** 252–54

MannKind Corporation, **87** 300–303

Manor Care, Inc., **6** 187–90; **25** 306–10 (upd.) *see also* HCR ManorCare, Inc.

ManpowerGroup Inc., **9** 326–27; **30** 299–302 (upd.); **73** 215–18 (upd.); **152** 305–10 (upd.)

Mansfield Oil Company, **117** 247–50

ManTech International Corporation, **97** 272–75

Manufacture Prelle & Cie, **118** 277–80

Manufactured Home Communities, Inc., **22** 339–41

Manufacturers Hanover Corporation, **II** 312–14 *see also* Chemical Bank.

Manulife Financial Corporation, **85** 235–38

Manutan International S.A., **72** 219–21

Manville Corporation, **III** 706–09; **7** 291–95 (upd.) *see also* Johns Manville Corp.

MAPCO Inc., **IV** 458–59

Mapfre S.A., **109** 394–98

MAPICS, Inc., **55** 256–58

Maple Grove Farms of Vermont, **88** 249–52

Maple Leaf Foods Inc., **41** 249–53; **108** 327–33 (upd.)

Maple Leaf Sports & Entertainment Ltd., **61** 188–90; **125** 233–37 (upd.)

Maples Industries, Inc., **83** 260–263

Maranello Rosso Collezione, **146** 262–65

Media Wales Limited, **159** 237–40

Mediacom Communications Corporation, **69** 250–52

MediaNews Group, Inc., **70** 177–80

Mediaset SpA, **50** 332–34; **132** 264–67 (upd.)

MediaTek, Inc., **139** 291–96

Medical Action Industries Inc., **101** 338–41

Medical Information Technology Inc., **64** 266–69; **157** 276–81 (upd.)

Medical Management International, Inc., **65** 227–29

Medical Mutual of Ohio, **128** 329–33

Medical Staffing Network Holdings, Inc., **89** 320–23

Medicine Shoppe International, Inc., **102** 253–57

Medicis Pharmaceutical Corporation, **59** 284–86

Medidata Solutions, Inc., **124** 229–32

Medifast, Inc., **97** 281–85

MedImmune LLC, **35** 286–89; **153** 285–88 (upd.)

Mediobanca SpA, **149** 247–51

Mediolanum S.p.A., **65** 230–32; **134** 204–07 (upd.)

Medipal Holdings Corporation, **120** 239–43

Medis Technologies Ltd., **77** 257–60

MediSys Health Network, **161** 275–78

Meditrust, **11** 281–83

Medley Indústria Farmacêutica Ltda., **155** 367–69

Medline Industries, Inc., **61** 204–06

Medochemie Ltd., **152** 322–25

MedQuist Inc., **124** 233–36

Medtox Scientific, Inc., **139** 297–301

Medtronic, Inc., **8** 351–54; **30** 313–17 (upd.); **67** 250–55 (upd.); **144** 323–30 (upd.)

Medusa Corporation, **24** 331–33

Meetic S.A., **129** 236–39

Meezan Bank Limited, **161** 279–83

MEGA Brands, Inc., **61** 207–09; **151** 285–89 (upd.)

MegaChips Corporation, **117** 259–62

Megafoods Stores Inc., **13** 335–37

Megastudy Company Ltd., **127** 253–56

Meggitt PLC, **34** 273–76

Meguiar's, Inc., **99** 282–285

Meidensha Corporation, **92** 242–46

Meier & Frank Co., **23** 345–47 *see also* Macy's, Inc.

Meijer, Inc., **7** 329–31; **27** 312–15 (upd.); **101** 342–46 (upd.)

Meiji Dairies Corporation, **II** 538–39; **82** 231–34 (upd.)

Meiji Holdings Co., Ltd., **139** 302–05

Meiji Mutual Life Insurance Company, **III** 288–89

Meiji Seika Kaisha Ltd., **II** 540–41; **64** 270–72 (upd.)

Meissen Porcelain *see* Staatliche Porzellan-Manufaktur Meissen GmbH.

Mel Bay Publications, Inc., **142** 292–95

Mel Farr Automotive Group, **20** 368–70

Melaleuca, Inc., **31** 326–28; **151** 290–94 (upd.)

Melamine Chemicals, Inc., **27** 316–18 *see also* Mississippi Chemical Corp.

Melco Crown Entertainment Limited, **103** 262–65

Melissa & Doug, LLC, **123** 270–73

Melitta Unternehmensgruppe Bentz KG, **53** 218–21

Mellanox Technologies, Ltd., **141** 334–37

Mello Smello *see* The Miner Group International.

Mellon Financial Corporation, **II** 315–17; **44** 278–82 (upd.) *see also* Bank of New York Mellon Corporation.

Mellon-Stuart Co., **I** 584–85 *see also* Michael Baker Corp.

The Melting Pot Restaurants, Inc., **74** 186–88

Melville Corporation, **V** 136–38 *see also* CVS Corp.

Melvin Simon and Associates, Inc., **8** 355–57 *see also* Simon Property Group, Inc.

MEMC Electronic Materials, Inc., **81** 249–52

Memorial Sloan-Kettering Cancer Center, **57** 239–41

Memry Corporation, **72** 225–27

Menard, Inc., **104** 310–14 (upd.)

Menasha Corporation, **8** 358–61; **59** 287–92 (upd.); **118** 286–93 (upd.)

Menchie's Group, Inc., **148** 376–79

Mendocino Brewing Company, Inc., **60** 205–07

Mengniu Dairy *see* China Mengniu Dairy Company Limited

The Men's Wearhouse, Inc., **17** 312–15; **48** 283–87 (upd.)

The Mentholatum Company Inc., **32** 331–33

Mentor Corporation, **26** 286–88; **123** 274–78 (upd.)

Mentor Graphics Corporation, **11** 284–86; **125** 244–49 (upd.)

MEPC plc, **IV** 710–12

Meralco *see* Manila Electric Company

MercadoLibre, Inc., **128** 334–38

Mercantile Bankshares Corp., **11** 287–88

Mercantile Stores Company, Inc., **V** 139; **19** 270–73 (upd.) *see also* Dillard's Inc.

Mercer International Inc., **64** 273–75

The Merchants Company, **102** 258–61

Mercian Corporation, **77** 261–64

Merck & Co., Inc., **I** 650–52; **11** 289–91 (upd.); **34** 280–85 (upd.); **95** 268–78 (upd.)

Merck KGaA, **111** 304–10

Mercury Air Group, Inc., **20** 371–73

Mercury Communications, Ltd., **7** 332–34 *see also* Cable and Wireless plc.

Mercury Computer Systems Inc., **145** 247–50

Mercury Drug Corporation, **70** 181–83

Mercury General Corporation, **25** 323–25

Mercury Interactive Corporation, **59** 293–95

Mercury Marine Group, **68** 247–51

Mercury Radio Arts, Inc., **132** 268–72

Meredith Corporation, **11** 292–94; **29** 316–19 (upd.); **74** 189–93 (upd.)

Merge Healthcare, **85** 264–68

Merial Ltd., **102** 262–66

Meridian Audio Ltd., **130** 327–31

Meridian Bancorp, Inc., **11** 295–97

Meridian Bioscience, Inc., **115** 315–18

Meridian Gold, Incorporated, **47** 238–40

Meridian Industries Inc., **107** 265–68

Merillat Industries, LLC, **13** 338–39; **69** 253–55 (upd.)

Merisant Worldwide, Inc., **70** 184–86

Merisel, Inc., **12** 334–36

Merit Energy Company, **114** 302–05

Merit Medical Systems, Inc., **29** 320–22; **135** 249–53 (upd.)

Meritage Homes Corporation, **26** 289–92; **157** 282–87 (upd.)

MeritCare Health System, **88** 257–61

Meritor, Inc., **159** 241–47 (upd.)

Merix Corporation, **36** 329–31; **75** 257–60 (upd.)

Merkle Inc., **114** 306–09

Merkur - trgovina in storitve, d.d., **130** 332–35

Merlin Entertainments Group Ltd., **105** 300–03

Mermaid Marine Australia Limited, **115** 319–23

Merriam-Webster Inc., **70** 187–91

Merrill Corporation, **18** 331–34; **47** 241–44 (upd.)

Merrill Lynch & Co., Inc., **II** 424–26; **13** 340–43 (upd.); **40** 310–15 (upd.); **138** 227–33 (upd.)

Merry-Go-Round Enterprises, Inc., **8** 362–64

The Mersey Docks and Harbour Company, **30** 318–20

Mervyn's California, **10** 409–10; **39** 269–71 (upd.) *see also* Target Corp.

Merz Group, **81** 253–56

Mesa Air Group, **11** 298–300; **32** 334–37 (upd.); **77** 265–70 (upd.)

Mesaba Holdings, Inc., **28** 265–67

Messaggerie Italiane SpA, **134** 208–11

Messerschmitt-Bölkow-Blohm GmbH., **I** 73–75 *see also* European Aeronautic Defence and Space Company EADS N.V.

Mestek, Inc., **10** 411–13

Mestemacher GmbH, **127** 257–61

Met-Pro Corporation, **128** 339–43

Metabolix, Inc., **154** 315–18

Metal Box plc, **I** 604–06 *see also* Novar plc.

Metal Management, Inc., **92** 247–50

Metaleurop S.A., **21** 368–71

Metalico Inc., **97** 286–89

Metallgesellschaft AG, **IV** 139–42; **16** 361–66 (upd.)

Metalurgica Mexicana Penoles, S.A. *see* Industrias Penoles, S.A. de C.V.

Metatec International, Inc., **47** 245–48

Metavante Corporation, **100** 288–92

Metcash Limited, **58** 226–28; **129** 240–44 (upd.)

Mullen Advertising Inc., **51** 259–61; **153** 298–302 (upd.)

Mullen Group Ltd., **141** 361–64

Multi-Color Corporation, **53** 234–36; **126** 251–55 (upd.)

Multiband Corporation, **131** 271–74

Multimedia, Inc., **11** 330–32

Multimedia Games, Inc., **41** 272–76

Mumias Sugar Company Limited, **124** 257–61

Münchener Rückversicherungs-Gesellschaft, **III** 299–301; **46** 303–07 (upd.); **144** 340–46

Munir Sukhtian Group, **104** 340–44

Munro & Company, Inc., **149** 285–88

Muralo Company Inc., **117** 270–73

Murata Manufacturing Company Ltd., **134** 216–20

Murdock Holding Company, **127** 280–83

Murdock Madaus Schwabe, **26** 315–19

Murphy Family Farms Inc., **22** 366–68 *see also* Smithfield Foods, Inc.

Murphy Oil Corporation, **7** 362–64; **32** 338–41 (upd.); **95** 283–89 (upd.)

Murphy's Pizza *see* Papa Murphy's International, Inc.

Murugappa Group, **142** 305–09

The Musco Family Olive Co., **91** 334–37

Musco Lighting, **83** 276–279

Muscular Dystrophy Association, **133** 291–94

Museum of Modern Art, **106** 308–12

Musgrave Group Plc, **57** 254–57

Music Choice, **143** 337–40

Music Corporation of America *see* MCA Inc.

Music Sales Group Limited, **151** 308–11

Musician's Friend, Inc., **159** 262–65

Musicland Stores Corporation, **9** 360–62; **38** 313–17 (upd.)

Musson Ltd., **156** 312–16

Mutual Benefit Life Insurance Company, **III** 302–04

Mutual Life Insurance Company of New York, **III** 305–07

The Mutual of Omaha Companies, **98** 248–52

Mutuelle Assurance des Commerçants et Industriels de France (Macif), **107** 283–86

Muzak Holdings LLC, **18** 353–56; **136** 356–360 (upd.)

MWA *see* Modern Woodmen of America.

MWH Preservation Limited Partnership, **65** 245–48

MWI Veterinary Supply, Inc., **80** 265–68

MXL Industries, Inc., **120** 259–62

Mycogen Corporation, **21** 385–87 *see also* Dow Chemical Co.

Myers Industries, Inc., **19** 277–79; **96** 293–97 (upd.)

Mylan Inc., **I** 656–57; **20** 380–82 (upd.); **59** 304–08 (upd.); **122** 288–93 (upd.)

Myllykoski Oyj, **117** 274–78

MYOB Ltd., **86** 286–90

Myriad Genetics, Inc., **95** 290–95

Myriad Restaurant Group, Inc., **87** 328–331

MySpace.com *see* Intermix Media, Inc.

N

N. Kohl Grocer Company, **160** 256–59

N.F. Smith & Associates LP, **70** 199–202

N.K. Shacolas (Holdings) Ltd., **152** 342–45

N M Rothschild & Sons Limited, **39** 293–95

N.V. *see under first word of company name*

NAACP *see* National Association for the Advancement of Colored People.

Naamloze Vennootschap tot Exploitatie van het Café Krasnapolsky *see* Grand Hotel Krasnapolsky N.V.

Nabisco Brands, Inc., **II** 542–44 *see also* RJR Nabisco.

Nabisco Foods Group, **7** 365–68 (upd.) *see also* Kraft Foods Inc.

Nabors Industries Ltd., **9** 363–65; **91** 338–44 (upd.)

NACCO Industries, Inc., **7** 369–71; **78** 232–36 (upd.); **162** 302–06 (upd.)

NACHA–The Electronic Payments Association, **151** 312–16

Nadro S.A. de C.V., **86** 291–94

Naf Naf SAS, **44** 296–98; **143** 341–45 (upd.)

NAFA *see* North American Fur Auctions.

Nagasakiya Co., Ltd., **V** 149–51; **69** 259–62 (upd.)

Nagase & Co., Ltd., **8** 376–78; **61** 226–30 (upd.)

Nagoya Railroad Company Ltd., **153** 303–07

NAI *see* Natural Alternatives International, Inc.; Network Associates, Inc.

Najafi Companies, LLC, **135** 268–72

Naked Juice Company, **107** 287–90

Naked Pizza North American Franchising LLC, **137** 309–13

Naked Wines Ltd., **148** 393–96

Nalco Holding Company, **I** 373–75; **12** 346–48 (upd.); **89** 324–30 (upd.)

Nam Tai Electronics, Inc., **61** 231–34; **129** 249–53 (upd.)

Namco Bandai Holdings Inc., **106** 313–19 (upd.)

Namibia Breweries Ltd., **138** 259–62

Nammo A.S., **153** 308–12

Nan Ya Plastics Corporation, **150** 317–21

Nantucket Allserve, Inc., **22** 369–71

Napster, Inc., **69** 263–66

Narodowy Bank Polski, **100** 297–300

NAS *see* National Audubon Society.

NASCAR *see* National Association for Stock Car Auto Racing.

NASD, **54** 242–46 (upd.)

The NASDAQ Stock Market, Inc., **92** 256–60

Nash Finch Company, **8** 379–81; **23** 356–58 (upd.); **65** 249–53 (upd.); **141** 365–70 (upd.)

Nashua Corporation, **8** 382–84; **151** 317–21 (upd.)

Naspers Ltd., **66** 230–32; **144** 347–51 (upd.)

Nastech Pharmaceutical Company Inc., **79** 259–62

Nasty Gal Inc., **162** 307–10

Nathan's Famous, Inc., **29** 342–44; **134** 221–25 (upd.)

Nation Media Group, **116** 357–61

National American University Holdings, Inc., **140** 312–15

National Amusements Inc., **28** 295–97; **136** 361–366 (upd.)

National Aquarium in Baltimore, Inc., **74** 198–200

National Association for Stock Car Auto Racing, Inc., **32** 342–44; **125** 268–73 (upd.)

National Association for the Advancement of Colored People, **109** 404–07

National Association of Securities Dealers, Inc., **10** 416–18 *see also* NASD.

National Audubon Society, **26** 320–23; **134** 226–31 (upd.)

National Australia Bank Ltd., **111** 315–19

National Auto Credit, Inc., **16** 379–81

National Bank of Canada, **85** 291–94

National Bank of Greece S.A., **41** 277–79; **133** 295–99 (upd.)

National Bank of Kuwait SAK, **145** 260–64

The National Bank of South Carolina, **76** 278–80

National Bank of Ukraine, **102** 287–90

National Beverage Corporation, **26** 324–26; **88** 267–71 (upd.)

National Broadcasting Company, Inc., **II** 151–53; **6** 164–66 (upd.); **28** 298–301 (upd.) *see also* General Electric Co.

National Can Corp., **I** 607–08

The National Capital Bank of Washington, **154** 323–26

National Car Rental System, Inc., **10** 419–20 *see also* Republic Industries, Inc.

National Cattlemen's Beef Association, **124** 262–66

Nationa CineMedia, Inc., **103** 266–70

National City Corporation, **15** 313–16; **97** 294–302 (upd.)

National Collegiate Athletic Association, **96** 298–302

National Convenience Stores Incorporated, **7** 372–75

National Council of La Raza, **106** 320–23

National Discount Brokers Group, Inc., **28** 302–04 *see also* Deutsche Bank A.G.

National Distillers and Chemical Corporation, **I** 376–78 *see also* Quantum Chemical Corp.

National Educational Music Co. Ltd., **47** 256–58

National Enquirer see American Media, Inc.

National Envelope Corporation, **32** 345–47 *see also* NE Opco, Inc.

National Equipment Services, Inc., **57** 258–60

National Express Group PLC, **50** 340–42

National Film Board of Canada, **154** 327–30

National Financial Partners Corp., **65** 254–56

National Football League, **29** 345–47; **115** 344–49 (upd.)

National Frozen Foods Corporation, **94** 319–22

National Fuel Gas Company, **6** 526–28; **95** 296–300 (upd.)

National Geographic Society, **9** 366–68; **30** 332–35 (upd.); **79** 263–69 (upd.)

National Grape Co-operative Association, Inc., **20** 383–85

National Grid plc, **135** 273–76

National Grid USA, **51** 262–66 (upd.); **155** 375–80 (upd.)

National Gypsum Company, **10** 421–24 *see also* \New NGC Inc.

National Health Laboratories Incorporated, **11** 333–35 *see also* Laboratory Corporation of America Holdings.

National HealthCare Corporation, **139** 315–19

National Heritage Academies, Inc., **60** 211–13

National Hockey League, **35** 300–03; **146** 284–89 (upd.)

National Home Centers, Inc., **44** 299–301

National Instruments Corporation, **22** 372–74; **161** 302–06 (upd.)

National Intergroup, Inc., **V** 152–53 *see also* FoxMeyer Health Corp.

National Iranian Oil Company, **IV** 466–68; **61** 235–38 (upd.)

National Jewish Health, **101** 356–61

National Journal Group Inc., **67** 256–58

National Kidney Foundation, **137** 314–18

National Media Corporation, **27** 336–40

National Medical Enterprises, Inc., **III** 87–88 *see also* Tenet Healthcare Corp.

National Medical Health Card Systems, Inc., **79** 270–73

National Oil Corporation, **66** 233–37 (upd.)

National Oilwell Varco, Inc., **54** 247–50; **139** 320–25 (upd.)

National Organization for Women, Inc., **55** 274–76

National Patent Development Corporation, **13** 365–68 *see also* GP Strategies Corp.

National Penn Bancshares, Inc., **103** 271–75

National Picture & Frame Company, **24** 345–47

National Power PLC, **12** 349–51 *see also* International Power PLC.

National Presto Industries, Inc., **16** 382–85; **43** 286–90 (upd.); **130** 344–51 (upd.)

National Public Radio, Inc., **19** 280–82; **47** 259–62 (upd.); **132** 308–13 (upd.)

National R.V. Holdings, Inc., **32** 348–51

National Railroad Passenger Corporation (Amtrak), **22** 375–78; **66** 238–42 (upd.)

National Record Mart, Inc., **29** 348–50

National Research Corporation, **87** 332–335

National Retail Systems, Inc., **158** 372–75

The National Rifle Association of America, **37** 265–68; **112** 285–90 (upd.)

National Sanitary Supply Co., **16** 386–87

National Sea Products Ltd., **14** 339–41 *see also* High Liner Foods Inc.

National Semiconductor Corporation, **II** 63–65; **6** 261–63; **26** 327–30 (upd.); **69** 267–71 (upd.); **158** 376–81 (upd.)

National Service Industries, Inc., **11** 336–38; **54** 251–55 (upd.)

National Standard Co., **13** 369–71

National Starch and Chemical Company, **49** 268–70

National Steel Corporation, **12** 352–54 *see also* FoxMeyer Health Corp.

National Technical Systems, Inc., **111** 320–23

National TechTeam, Inc., **41** 280–83 *see also* Stefanini TechTeam Inc..

National Thoroughbred Racing Association, Inc., **58** 244–47; **127** 284–89 (upd.)

National Transcommunications Ltd. *see* NTL Inc.

The National Trust, **110** 333–37

National Weather Service, **91** 345–49

National Westminster Bank PLC, **II** 333–35

National Wildlife Federation, **103** 276–80

National Wine & Spirits, Inc., **49** 271–74; **156** 317–21 (upd.)

Nationale-Nederlanden N.V., **III** 308–11

Nationale Portefeuille Maatschappij (NPM) *see* Compagnie Nationale à Portefeuille.

NationsBank Corporation, **10** 425–27 *see also* Bank of America Corporation

Nationwide Children's Hospital, **138** 263–67

Nationwide Mutual Insurance Company, **108** 358–62

Native New Yorker Inc., **110** 338–41

NativeX LLC, **154** 331–34 (upd.)

Natori Company, Inc., **108** 363–66

Natra S.A., **158** 382–86

Natrol, Inc., **49** 275–78

Natura Cosméticos S.A., **75** 268–71; **152** 346–50 (upd.)

Natural Alternatives International, Inc., **49** 279–82

Natural Beauty Bio-Technology Ltd., **127** 290–93

Natural Gas Clearinghouse *see* NGC Corp.

Natural Gas Services Group, Inc., **157** 295–98

Natural Grocers by Vitamin Cottage, Inc., **111** 324–27

Natural Ovens Bakery, Inc., **72** 234–36

Natural Selection Foods, **54** 256–58

Natural Wonders Inc., **14** 342–44

Naturally Fresh, Inc., **88** 272–75

The Nature Conservancy, **28** 305–07; **138** 268–72 (upd.)

Nature's Path Foods, Inc., **87** 336–340

Nature's Sunshine Products, Inc., **15** 317–19; **102** 291–96 (upd.)

Natus Medical Incorporated, **119** 322–26

Natuzzi Group *see* Industrie Natuzzi S.p.A.

NatWest Bank *see* National Westminster Bank PLC.

Naumes, Inc., **81** 257–60

Nautica Enterprises, Inc., **18** 357–60; **44** 302–06 (upd.)

Navarre Corporation, **24** 348–51

Navarro Discount Pharmacies, **119** 327–32

Navigant International, Inc., **47** 263–66; **93** 324–27 (upd.)

The Navigators Group, Inc., **92** 261–64

Navios Maritime Holdings Inc., **150** 322–25

NaviSite, Inc., **128** 344–48

Navistar International Corporation, **I** 180–82; **10** 428–30 (upd.); **114** 310–19 (upd.)

NAVTEQ Corporation, **69** 272–75

Navy Exchange Service Command, **31** 342–45

Navy Federal Credit Union, **33** 315–17

NBBJ, **111** 328–31

NBC *see* National Broadcasting Company, Inc.

NBD Bancorp, Inc., **11** 339–41 *see also* Bank One Corp.

NBGS International, Inc., **73** 231–33

NBSC Corporation *see* National Bank of South Carolina.

NBTY, Inc., **31** 346–48; **132** 314–18 (upd.)

NCAA *see* National Collegiate Athletic Assn.

NCC AB, **121** 313–16

NCH Corporation, **8** 385–87

NCI Building Systems, Inc., **88** 276–79

NCL Corporation Ltd., **79** 274–77; **159** 266–70 (upd.)

NCNB Corporation, **II** 336–37 *see also* Bank of America Corp.

NCO Group, Inc., **42** 258–60; **131** 275–78 (upd.)

NCR Corporation, **III** 150–53; **6** 264–68 (upd.); **30** 336–41 (upd.); **90** 303–12 (upd.)

NCsoft Corporation, **137** 319–22

NDB *see* National Discount Brokers Group, Inc.

NE Opco, Inc., **135** 277–80 (upd.)

The Neat Company Inc., **137** 323–26

Nebraska Book Company, Inc., **65** 257–59

Nebraska Furniture Mart, Inc., **94** 323–26

Nebraska Public Power District, **29** 351–54

NEBS *see* New England Business Services, Inc.

O

Oak Industries Inc., **21** 396–98 *see also* Corning Inc.

Oak Technology, Inc., **22** 389–93 *see also* Zoran Corp.

Oakhurst Dairy, **60** 225–28

The Oakland Raiders, A California Limited Partnership, **129** 284–87

Oakleaf Waste Management, LLC, **97** 312–15

Oakley, Inc., **18** 390–93; **49** 297–302 (upd.); **111** 358–65 (upd.)

Oaktree Capital Management, LP, **71** 254–56; **154** 335–39 (upd.)

Oakwood Homes Corporation, **13** 155; **15** 326–28

OAO AVTOVAZ *see* AVTOVAZ Joint Stock Co.

OAO Gazprom, **42** 261–65; **107** 317–23 (upd.); **157** 198–203 (upd.)

OAO LUKOIL, **40** 343–46; **109** 428–36 (upd.)

OAO NK YUKOS, **47** 282–85

OAO Severstal *see* Severstal Joint Stock Co.

OAO Siberian Oil Company (Sibneft), **49** 303–06

OAO Surgutneftegaz, **48** 375–78; **128** 358–64 (upd.)

OAO Tatneft, **45** 322–26 *see also* Tatneft Joint Stock Co.

Obagi Medical Products, Inc., **95** 310–13

Obayashi Corporation, **78** 266–69 (upd.); **149** 298–302 (upd.)

Oberg Industries, Inc., **151** 327–30

Oberoi Group *see* EIH Ltd.

Oberthur Technologies S.A., **113** 277–81

Oberto Sausage Company, Inc., **92** 288–91

Obie Media Corporation, **56** 260–62

Obrascon Huarte Lain S.A., **76** 291–94

Observer AB, **55** 286–89

OC Oerlikon Corporation AG, **120** 292–96

Ocado Group PLC, **141** 377–80

Occidental Petroleum Corporation, **IV** 480–82; **25** 360–63 (upd.); **71** 257–61 (upd.); **152** 375–81 (upd.)

Océ N.V., **24** 360–63; **91** 359–65 (upd.)

Ocean Beauty Seafoods, Inc., **74** 209–11

Ocean Bio-Chem, Inc., **103** 308–11

Ocean Group plc, **6** 415–17 *see also* Exel plc.

Ocean Spray Cranberries, Inc., **7** 403–05; **25** 364–67 (upd.); **83** 284–290

Oceana Group Ltd., **123** 291–95

Oceaneering International, Inc., **63** 317–19

Ocesa *see* Corporación Interamericana de Entretenimiento, S.A. de C.V.

O'Charley's Inc., **19** 286–88; **60** 229–32 (upd.)

OCI *see* Orascom Construction Industries S.A.E.

OCI Company Ltd., **149** 303–07

Oclaro, Inc., **151** 331–34

OCLC Online Computer Library Center, Inc., **96** 324–28

The O'Connell Companies Inc., **100** 306–09

Octel Messaging, **14** 354–56; **41** 287–90 (upd.)

Ocular Sciences, Inc., **65** 273–75

Odakyu Electric Railway Co., Ltd., **V** 487–89; **68** 278–81 (upd.); **138** 281–85 (upd.)

Oddbins Ltd., **160** 281–85

Odebrecht S.A., **73** 242–44

oDesk Corporation, **157** 320–23

Odetics Inc., **14** 357–59

Odfjell SE, **101** 383–87

ODL, Inc., **55** 290–92

Odlo Sports Group AG, **120** 297–300

The Odom Corporation, **126** 279–82

Odwalla Inc., **31** 349–51; **104** 349–53 (upd.)

Odyssey Marine Exploration, Inc., **91** 366–70

Odyssey Re Holdings Corporation, **139** 345–48

OEC Medical Systems, Inc., **27** 354–56

OENEO S.A., **74** 212–15 (upd.)

Oettinger IMEX AG, **149** 308–13

Office Depot, Inc., **8** 404–05; **23** 363–65 (upd.); **65** 276–80 (upd.); **133** 321–27 (upd.)

OfficeMax Incorporated, **15** 329–31; **43** 291–95 (upd.); **101** 388–94 (upd.)

OfficeTiger, LLC, **75** 294–96

Officine Alfieri Maserati S.p.A., **13** 376–78 *see also* Maserati S.p.A.

Offset Paperback Manufacturers Inc., **145** 290–93

Offshore Logistics, Inc., **37** 287–89

Ogden Corporation, **I** 512–14; **6** 151–53 *see also* Covanta Energy Corp.

OGE Energy Corp., **135** 289–92 (upd.)

OGF S.A., **113** 282–86

Ogilvy Group Inc., **I** 25–27 *see also* WPP Group.

Oglebay Norton Company, **17** 355–58

Oglethorpe Power Corporation, **6** 537–38

Ogletree, Deakins, Nash, Smoak & Stewart, P.C., **152** 382–85

Ohbayashi Corporation, **I** 586–87

Ohio Art Company, **14** 360–62; **59** 317–20 (upd.); **143** 346–51 (upd.)

Ohio Bell Telephone Company, **14** 363–65 *see also* Ameritech Corp.

Ohio Casualty Insurance Company, **11** 369–70; **143** 352–56

Ohio Edison Company, **V** 676–78

Ohio National Financial Services, Inc., **118** 327–30

OhioHealth Corporation, **139** 349–53

Oil and Natural Gas Commission, **IV** 483–84; **90** 313–17 (upd.)

Oil-Dri Corporation of America, **20** 396–99; **89** 331–36 (upd.)

Oil States International, Inc., **77** 314–17

Oil Transporting Joint Stock Company Transneft, **92** 450–54

The Oilgear Company, **74** 216–18

Oji Paper Co., Ltd., **IV** 320–22; **57** 272–75 (upd.); **128** 365–70 (upd.)

OJSC Novolipetsk Steel, **99** 311–315

OJSC Wimm-Bill-Dann Foods, **48** 436–39

OKI Electric Industry Company Ltd., **II** 72–74; **15** 125; **21** 390; **164** 262–66 (upd.)

Oklahoma City Thunder *see* Professional Basketball Club, LLC.

Oklahoma Gas and Electric Company, **6** 539–40 *see also* OGE Energy Corp.

Okuma Holdings Inc., **74** 219–21

Okura & Co., Ltd., **IV** 167–68

Olam International Ltd., **122** 311–14

Olan Mills, Inc., **62** 254–56; **160** 286–90 (upd.)

Olav Thon Gruppen AS, **162** 321–24

Old America Stores, Inc., **17** 359–61

Old Dominion Freight Line, Inc., **57** 276–79; **123** 296–300 (upd.)

Old Dutch Foods, Inc., **118** 331–34

Old Kent Financial Corp., **11** 371–72 *see also* Fifth Third Bancorp.

Old Mutual PLC, **IV** 535; **61** 270–72; **139** 354–58 (upd.)

Old National Bancorp, **15** 332–34; **98** 266–70 (upd.)

Old Navy, Inc., **70** 210–12; **138** 286–90 (upd.)

Old Orchard Brands, LLC, **73** 245–47

Old Republic International Corporation, **11** 373–75; **58** 258–61 (upd.); **144** 366–71 (upd.)

Old Spaghetti Factory International Inc., **24** 364–66

Old Town Canoe Company, **74** 222–24

Old Vic Productions plc, **108** 371–74

Old World Industries, LLC, **146** 300–03

Oldcastle, Inc., **113** 287–90

Oldenburg Group Inc., **113** 291–95

Olga's Kitchen, Inc., **80** 274–76; **160** 291–94 (upd.)

Olhausen Billiards Manufacturing, Inc., **162** 325–28

Olin Corporation, **I** 379–81; **13** 379–81 (upd.); **78** 270–74 (upd.)

Olivetti S.p.A., **34** 316–20 (upd.)

Olsten Corporation, **6** 41–43; **29** 362–65 (upd.) *see also* Adecco S.A.

Olvea Group, **156** 338–42

Olympia & York Developments Ltd., **IV** 720–21; **9** 390–92 (upd.)

Olympia Sports Center, **122** 315–17

Olympic Air Group, **122** 318–21

Olympic Entertainment Group A.S., **117** 291–94

Olympic Steel, Inc., **136** 371–374

Olympus Corporation, **106** 332–36

OM Group, Inc., **17** 362–64; **78** 275–78 (upd.)

OMA *see* Grupo Aeroportuario del Centro Norte, S.A.B. de C.V.

Omaha Steaks International Inc., **62** 257–59

Omax Corporation, **164** 267–70

Omega Protein Corporation, **99** 316–318 *see also* Harbinger Group Inc.

Omega World Travel Company, **141** 381–84

O'Melveny & Myers, **37** 290–93

OTR Express, Inc., **25** 368–70
Otsuka Holdings Co., Ltd., **139** 369–73
Ottakar's plc, **64** 302–04
Ottaway Newspapers, Inc., **15** 335–37
Otter Products, LLC, **144** 372–75
Otter Tail Power Company, **18** 402–05;
   132 336–42 (upd.)
OtterBox *see* Otter Products, LLC.
Otto Bremer Foundation *see* Bremer
   Financial Corp.
Otto Fuchs KG, **100** 310–14
Otto Group, **106** 342–48 (upd.)
Otto Versand GmbH & Co., **V** 159–61;
   15 338–40 (upd.); **34** 324–28 (upd.)
Outback Steakhouse, Inc., **12** 373–75; **34**
   329–32 (upd.) *see also* OSI Restaurant
   Partners, Inc.
Outboard Marine Corporation, **III**
   597–600; **20** 409–12 (upd.) *see also*
   Bombardier Inc.
Outdoor Research, Incorporated, **67**
   288–90
Outdoor Systems, Inc., **25** 371–73 *see also*
   Infinity Broadcasting Corp.
Outlook Group Corporation, **37** 294–96
Outokumpu Öyj, **38** 335–37; **108**
   375–80 (upd.)
Outrigger Enterprises, Inc., **67** 291–93
Outward Bound USA, **111** 376–79
Overhead Door Corporation, **70** 213–16
Overhill Corporation, **51** 279–81
Overland Storage Inc., **100** 315–20
Overnite Corporation, **14** 371–73; **58**
   262–65 (upd.)
Oversea-Chinese Banking Corporation
   Ltd., **153** 340–43
Overseas Shipholding Group, Inc., **11**
   376–77
Overstock.com, Inc., **75** 307–09; **159**
   314–18 (upd.)
Overwaitea Food Group, **121** 325–28
Owens & Minor, Inc., **16** 398–401; **68**
   282–85 (upd.)
Owens Corning, **III** 720–23; **20** 413–17
   (upd.); **98** 285–91 (upd.)
Owens-Illinois, Inc., **I** 609–11; **26**
   350–53 (upd.); **85** 311–18 (upd.); **162**
   336–43 (upd.
Owosso Corporation, **29** 366–68
Oxbow Corporation, **160** 299–02
Oxfam GB, **87** 359–362
Oxford Health Plans, Inc., **16** 402–04
Oxford Industries, Inc., **8** 406–08; **84**
   290–296 (upd.)
OXXO *see* FEMSA Comercio, S.A. de
   C.V.
Oxylane Group, **142** 319–22
Oy Karl Fazer Ab, **127** 309–12
OYO Geospace Corporation, **139** 374–78
OZ Minerals Limited, **139** 379–82
Ozburn-Hessey Logistics, LLC, **149**
   320–23

P

P&C Foods Inc., **8** 409–11
P & F Industries, Inc., **45** 327–29
P&G *see* Procter & Gamble Co.
P&H *see* Palmer and Harvey Group PLC.

P.A.M. Transportation Services, Inc., **131**
   292–95
P.C. Richard & Son LLC, **23** 372–74;
   118 335–38 (upd.)
P.F. Chang's China Bistro, Inc., **37**
   297–99; **86** 317–21 (upd.)
P.H. Glatfelter Company, **8** 412–14; **30**
   349–52 (upd.); **83** 291–297 (upd.)
P.W. Minor and Son, Inc., **100** 321–24
PACCAR Inc., **I** 185–86; **26** 354–56
   (upd.); **111** 380–84 (upd.)
Pacer International, Inc., **54** 274–76
Pacer Technology, **40** 347–49
Pacers Basketball, LLC, **149** 324–28
Pacific Aerospace & Electronics, Inc., **120**
   301–04
Pacific Basin Shipping Ltd., **86** 322–26
Pacific Clay Products Inc., **88** 292–95
Pacific Coast Building Products, Inc., **94**
   338–41
Pacific Coast Feather Company, **67**
   294–96
Pacific Coast Restaurants, Inc., **90** 318–21
Pacific Continental Corporation, **114**
   320–23
Pacific Dunlop Limited, **10** 444–46 *see
   also* Ansell Ltd.
Pacific Enterprises, **V** 682–84 *see also*
   Sempra Energy.
Pacific Ethanol, Inc., **81** 269–72
Pacific Gas and Electric Company, **V**
   685–87 *see also* PG&E Corp.
Pacific Internet Limited, **87** 363–366
Pacific Islands Trade and Invest, **146**
   308–11
Pacific Mutual Holding Company, **98**
   292–96
Pacific Sunwear of California, Inc., **28**
   343–45; **104** 363–67 (upd.)
Pacific Telecom, Inc., **6** 325–28
Pacific Telesis Group, **V** 318–20 *see also*
   SBC Communications.
PacifiCare Health Systems, Inc., **11**
   378–80
PacifiCorp, Inc., **V** 688–90; **26** 357–60
   (upd.)
Packaging Corporation of America, **12**
   376–78; **51** 282–85 (upd.)
Packard Bell Electronics, Inc., **13** 387–89
Packeteer, Inc., **81** 273–76
PacketVideo Corporation, **112** 303–06
Paddock Publications, Inc., **53** 263–65
Paddy Power plc, **98** 297–300
PAETEC Holding Corporation, **128**
   380–83
PagesJaunes Groupe SA, **79** 306–09
Paging Network Inc., **11** 381–83
Pagnossin S.p.A., **73** 248–50
PaineWebber Group Inc., **II** 444–46; **22**
   404–07 (upd.) *see also* UBS AG.
Paiste AG, **115** 379–82
Pakistan International Airlines
   Corporation, **46** 323–26; **149** 329–33
   (upd.)
Pakistan State Oil Company Ltd., **81**
   277–80
PAL Holdings, Inc., **122** 327–33 (upd.)

Palace Sports & Entertainment, Inc., **97**
   320–25
Palfinger AG, **100** 325–28
PALIC *see* Pan-American Life Insurance
   Co.
Pall Corporation, **9** 396–98; **72** 263–66
   (upd.)
Palm Beach Tan, Inc., **163** 307–10
Palm Breweries NV, **113** 296–99
Palm Harbor Homes, Inc., **39** 316–18
Palm, Inc., **36** 355–57; **75** 310–14 (upd.)
Palm Management Corporation, **71**
   265–68
Palmer & Cay, Inc., **69** 285–87
Palmer and Harvey Group PLC, **114**
   324–28
Palmer Candy Company, **80** 277–81
Palmer Co. *see* R. M. Palmer Co.
Palo Alto Networks, Inc., **148** 407–10
Palo Alto Research Center Incorporated,
   129 288–92
Paloma Industries Ltd., **71** 269–71
Palomar Medical Technologies, Inc., **22**
   408–10
Pamida Holdings Corporation, **15** 341–43
Pampa Energía S.A., **118** 339–42
The Pampered Chef Ltd., **18** 406–08; **78**
   292–96 (upd.)
Pamplin Corp. *see* R.B. Pamplin Corp.
Pan American Energy LLC, **133** 334–37
Pan-American Life Insurance Company,
   48 311–13
Pan American World Airways, Inc., **I**
   115–16; **12** 379–81 (upd.)
Panalpina World Transport (Holding)
   Ltd., **47** 286–88
Panamerican Beverages, Inc., **47** 289–91;
   54 74
PanAmSat Corporation, **46** 327–29
Panasonic Corporation, **160** 303–07
   (upd.)
Panattoni Development Company, Inc.,
   99 327–330
Panavision Inc., **24** 372–74; **107** 340–44
   (upd.)
Pancho's Mexican Buffet, Inc., **46** 330–32
Panda Power Funds, **160** 308–12
Panda Restaurant Group, **35**
   327–29; **97** 326–30 (upd.)
Pandora A/S, **160** 313–16
Pandora Media Inc., **123** 301–04
Panera Bread Company, **44** 327–29; **119**
   353–57 (upd.)
Panhandle Eastern Corporation, **V** 691–92
   see also CMS Energy Corp.
Panhandle Oil and Gas Inc., **146** 312–15
Panrico S.A., **123** 305–08
Pantone LLC, **53** 266–69; **164** 279–83
   (upd.)
The Pantry, Incorporated, **36** 358–60;
   124 280–83 (upd.)
Panzani, **84** 297–300
Papa Gino's Holdings Corporation, Inc.,
   86 327–30
Papa John's International, Inc., **15**
   344–46; **71** 272–76 (upd.); **162**
   344–49 (upd.)

Puck Lazaroff Inc. *see* The Wolfgang Puck Food Company, Inc.

Pueblo Xtra International, Inc., **47** 311–13

Puerto Rico Electric Power Authority, **47** 314–16

Puget Sound Energy Inc., **6** 565–67; **50** 365–68 (upd.)

Puig Beauty and Fashion Group S.L., **60** 243–46

Pulaski Furniture Corporation, **33** 349–52; **80** 296–99 (upd.)

Pulitzer Inc., **15** 375–77; **58** 280–83 (upd.)

Pulmuone Holdings Company Limited, **140** 353–56

Pulsar Internacional S.A., **21** 413–15

Pulte Homes, Inc., **8** 436–38; **42** 291–94 (upd.); **113** 310–15 (upd.)

PUMA AG Rudolf Dassler Sport, **35** 360–63; **120** 336–41 (upd.)

Pumpkin Masters, Inc., **48** 330–32

Pumpkin Patch Limited, **129** 302–05

Punch International N.V., **66** 258–60

Punch Taverns plc, **70** 240–42; **151** 353–56 (upd.)

Punjab National Bank, **149** 363–67

Puratos S.A./NV, **92** 315–18

Pure Fishing, Inc., **136** 392–395

Pure World, Inc., **72** 285–87

Purina Mills, Inc., **32** 376–79

Puritan-Bennett Corporation, **13** 419–21

Purity Wholesale Grocers, Inc., **144** 385–88

Purolator Products Company, **21** 416–18; **74** 253–56 (upd.)

Pusser's West Indies Ltd., **160** 330–34

Putt-Putt Golf Courses of America, Inc., **23** 396–98

Putzmeister Holding GmbH, **145** 325–29

PVC Container Corporation, **67** 312–14

PW Eagle, Inc., **48** 333–36 *see also* JM Eagle

PWA Group, **IV** 323–25 *see also* Svenska Cellulosa.

Pyramid Breweries Inc., **33** 353–55; **102** 343–47 (upd.)

Pyramid Companies, **54** 303–05

PZ Cussons Plc, **72** 288–90; **150** 361–65 (upd.)

Q

Q.E.P. Co., Inc., **65** 292–94

Qantas Airways Limited, **6** 109–13; **24** 396–401 (upd.); **68** 301–07 (upd.); **137** 336–44 (upd.)

Qatar Airways Company Q.C.S.C., **87** 404–407

Qatar National Bank SAQ, **87** 408–411

Qatar Petroleum, **IV** 524–26; **98** 324–28 (upd.)

Qatar Telecom QSA, **87** 412–415

QBE Insurance Group Limited, **139** 417–22

QCR Holdings, Incorporated, **157** 347–50

Qdoba Restaurant Corporation, **93** 358–62

QIAGEN N.V., **39** 333–35; **121** 351–55 (upd.)

QinetiQ Group PLC, **128** 384–88

QLT Inc., **71** 291–94

QNB Corporation, **134** 290–93

QRS Music Technologies, Inc., **95** 349–53

QSC Audio Products, Inc., **56** 291–93

QSS Group, Inc., **100** 358–61

Quad/Graphics, Inc., **19** 333–36

Quadrangle Group LLC, **150** 366–70

Quaker Chemical Corp., **91** 388–91

Quaker Fabric Corp., **19** 337–39

Quaker Foods North America, **II** 558–60; **12** 409–12 (upd.); **34** 363–67 (upd.); **73** 268–73 (upd.)

Quaker State Corporation, **7** 443–45; **21** 419–22 (upd.) *see also* Pennzoil-Quaker State Co.

Quaker Steak & Lube Franchising Corp., **159** 352–55

QUALCOMM Incorporated, **20** 438–41; **47** 317–21 (upd.); **114** 337–43 (upd.)

Quality Chekd Dairies, Inc., **48** 337–39

Quality Dining, Inc., **18** 437–40

Quality Distribution, Inc., **160** 335–38

Quality Food Centers, Inc., **17** 386–88 *see also* Kroger Co.

Quality Houses PCL, **149** 368–71

Quality King Distributors, Inc., **114** 344–47

Quality Systems, Inc., **81** 328–31

Quanex Corporation, **13** 422–24; **62** 286–89 (upd.)

Quanta Computer Inc., **47** 322–24; **110** 385–89 (upd.)

Quanta Services, Inc., **79** 338–41; **159** 356–60 (upd.)

Quantum Chemical Corporation, **8** 439–41

Quantum Corporation, **10** 458–59; **62** 290–93 (upd.)

Quark, Inc., **36** 375–79

Quarto Group Inc., **131** 312–16

Québec Hydro-Electric Commission *see* Hydro-Quebec.

Quebecor Inc., **12** 412–14; **47** 325–28 (upd.); **133** 367–71 (upd.)

Queensland Treasury Corporation, **124** 317–20

Quelle Group, **V** 165–67 *see also* Karstadt Quelle AG.

Quest Diagnostics Inc., **26** 390–92; **106** 383–87 (upd.)

Questar Corporation, **6** 568–70; **26** 386–89 (upd.); **127** 332–37 (upd.)

Questex Media Group LLC, **134** 294–97

The Quick & Reilly Group, Inc., **20** 442–44

Quick Restaurants S.A., **94** 357–60

Quicken Loans, Inc., **93** 363–67

Quidel Corporation, **80** 300–03

The Quigley Corporation, **62** 294–97

Quiksilver, Inc., **18** 441–43; **79** 342–47 (upd.)

QuikTrip Corporation, **36** 380–83; **130** 400–04 (upd.)

Quill Corporation, **28** 375–77; **115** 403–06 (upd.)

Quilmes Industrial (QUINSA) S.A., **67** 315–17

Quiñenco S.A., **133** 372–75

Quinn Emanuel Urquhart Oliver & Hedges, LLP, **99** 350–353

QuinStreet Incorporated, **124** 321–24

Quintiles Transnational Corporation, **21** 423–25; **68** 308–12 (upd.)

Quixote Corporation, **15** 378–80

Quiznos Corporation, **42** 295–98; **117** 332–37 (upd.)

Quovadx Inc., **70** 243–46

QVC Inc., **9** 428–29; **58** 284–87 (upd.)

Qwest Communications International, Inc., **37** 312–17; **116** 400–05 (upd.)

R

R&B, Inc., **51** 305–07

R&R Partners Inc., **108** 407–10

R.B. Pamplin Corp., **45** 350–52; **134** 298–301 (upd.)

R.C. Bigelow, Inc., **49** 334–36; **138** 338–42 (upd.)

R.C. Willey Home Furnishings, **72** 291–93

R.G. Barry Corp., **17** 389–91; **44** 364–67 (upd.)

R. Griggs Group Ltd., **23** 399–402; **31** 413–14; **149** 372–76 (upd.)

R.H. Kuhn Company, Inc., **117** 338–41

R.H. Macy & Co., Inc., **V** 168–70; **8** 442–45 (upd.); **30** 379–83 (upd.) *see also* Macy's, Inc.

R.H. Reny, Inc., **147** 355–58

R.J. Reynolds Tobacco Holdings, Inc., **30** 384–87 (upd.)

R. L. Polk & Co., **10** 460–62; **123** 328–33 (upd.)

R. M. Palmer Co., **89** 362–64

R.P. Scherer Corporation, **I** 678–80 *see also* Cardinal Health, Inc.

R.R. Bowker LLC, **100** 362–66

R.R. Donnelley & Sons Company, **IV** 660–62; **38** 368–71 (upd.); **113** 316–21 (upd.)

R.T. Vanderbilt Company, Inc., **117** 342–45

Rabobank Group, **26** 419; **33** 356–58; **116** 406–09 (upd.)

RAC *see* Roy Anderson Corp.

Racal-Datacom Inc., **11** 408–10

Racal Electronics PLC, **II** 83–84 *see also* Thales S.A.

RaceTrac Petroleum, Inc., **111** 415–18

Racing Champions Corporation, **37** 318–20 *see also* RC2.

Rack Room Shoes, Inc., **84** 314–317

Rackspace Hosting, Inc., **125** 336–40

RAD Data Communications Ltd., **134** 302–05

Radeberger Gruppe AG, **75** 332–35

Radian Group Inc., **42** 299–301 *see also* Onex Corp.

Radiant Systems Inc., **104** 383–87

Radiation Therapy Services, Inc., **85** 344–47

TI Group plc, **17** 480–83
TIAA-CREF *see* Teachers Insurance and Annuity Association-College Retirement Equities Fund.
Tianjin Flying Pigeon Bicycle Co., Ltd., **95** 421–24
Tibbett & Britten Group plc, **32** 449–52
TIBCO Software Inc., **79** 411–14
TIC Holdings Inc., **92** 376–379
Ticketmaster, **13** 508–10; **37** 381–84 (upd.); **76** 349–53 (upd.)
Tidewater Inc., **11** 522–24; **37** 385–88 (upd.)
Tieto Oyj, **117** 407–11
Tiffany & Co., **14** 500–03; **78** 396–401 (upd.); **159** 416–22 (upd.)
TIG Holdings, Inc., **26** 486–88
Tiger Aspect Productions Ltd., **72** 348–50
Tiger Brands Limited, **112** 420–24
Tigre S.A. Tubos e Conexões, **104** 446–49
Tilcon-Connecticut Inc., **80** 373–76
Tilia Inc., **62** 363–65
Tillamook County Creamery Association, **111** 460–63
Tilley Endurables, Inc., **67** 364–66; **127** 398–402 (upd.)
Tillotson Corp., **15** 488–90
Tilly's, Inc., **160** 415–18
TIM *see* Telecom Italia Mobile S.p.A.
Tim-Bar Corporation, **110** 459–62
Tim Hortons Inc., **109** 543–47 (upd.)
TIM Participações S.A., **126** 394–97
Timber Lodge Steakhouse, Inc., **73** 341–43
The Timberland Company, **13** 511–14; **54** 375–79 (upd.); **111** 464–70 (upd.)
Timberline Software Corporation, **15** 491–93
TimberWest Forest Corp., **114** 449–52
Time Inc., **125** 413–16
Time Out Group Ltd., **68** 371–73
Time Warner Inc., **IV** 673–76; **7** 526–30 (upd.); **109** 548–58 (upd.)
The Times Mirror Company, **IV** 677–78; **17** 484–86 (upd.) *see also* Tribune Co.
TIMET *see* Titanium Metals Corp.
Timex Group B.V., **7** 531–33; **25** 479–82 (upd.); **111** 471–77 (upd.)
The Timken Company, **8** 529–31; **42** 381–85 (upd.); **113** 423–28 (upd.)
TINE SA, **152** 447–50
Tipco Foods PCL, **160** 419–23
Tipiak S.A., **113** 429–33
Tiscali SpA, **48** 396–99
TISCO *see* Tata Iron & Steel Company Ltd.
Tishman Construction Company, **112** 425–28 (upd.)
Tishman Speyer Properties, L.P., **47** 403–06; **112** 429–34
Tissue Technologies, Inc. *see* Palomar Medical Technologies, Inc.
Titan Cement Company S.A., **64** 379–81
The Titan Corporation, **36** 475–78
Titan International, Inc., **89** 445–49
Titan Machinery Inc., **103** 446–49
Titanium Metals Corporation, **21** 489–92

TiVo Inc., **75** 373–75; **154** 422–26 (upd.)
TJ International, Inc., **19** 444–47
The TJX Companies, Inc., **V** 197–98; **19** 448–50 (upd.); **57** 366–69 (upd.); **120** 435–40 (upd.)
TLC Beatrice International Holdings, Inc., **22** 512–15
TMP Worldwide Inc., **30** 458–60 *see also* Monster Worldwide Inc.
TMX Group Inc., **136** 453–456
TNK-BP, **129** 396–400
TNT Express N.V., **146** 422–29 (upd.)
TNT Freightways Corporation, **14** 504–06
TNT Limited, **V** 523–25
TNT Post Group N.V., **27** 471–76 (upd.); **30** 461–63 (upd.) *see also* TPG N.V.
Tnuva Food Industries Ltd., **111** 478–81
Tobu Railway Company Ltd., **6** 430–32; **98** 404–08 (upd.)
Today's Man, Inc., **20** 484–87
TODCO, **87** 439–442
The Todd-AO Corporation, **33** 400–04 *see also* Liberty Livewire Corp.
Todd Shipyards Corporation, **14** 507–09
Todhunter International, Inc., **27** 477–79
Tod's S.p.A., **145** 408–12
Tofutti Brands Inc., **64** 382–84; **142** 420–24 (upd.)
Tohan Corporation, **84** 402–405
Toho Co., Ltd., **28** 461–63; **164** 393–97 (upd.)
Tohoku Electric Power Company Inc., **V** 726–28; **144** 471–76 (upd.)
The Tokai Bank, Limited, **II** 373–74; **15** 494–96 (upd.)
Tokheim Corporation, **21** 493–95
Tokio Marine and Fire Insurance Co., Ltd., **III** 383–86 *see also* Millea Holdings Inc.
Tokyo Dome Corporation, **118** 445–48
Tokyo Electric Power Company, **V** 729–33; **74** 343–48 (upd.)
Tokyo Gas Co., Ltd., **V** 734–36; **55** 372–75 (upd.); **148** 472–78 (upd.)
Tokyo Joe's Inc., **164** 398–401
TOKYOPOP Inc., **79** 415–18
Tokyu Corporation, **V** 526–28; **47** 407–10 (upd.)
Tokyu Department Store Co., Ltd., **V** 199–202; **32** 453–57 (upd.); **107** 434–40 (upd.)
Tokyu Land Corporation, **IV** 728–29; **164** 402–05 (upd.)
Tolko Industries Ltd., **114** 453–56
Toll Brothers Inc., **15** 497–99; **70** 323–26 (upd.); **147** 410–15 (upd.)
Toll Holdings Limited, **143** 432–35
Tollgrade Communications, Inc., **44** 424–27; **129** 401–05 (upd.)
Tom Brown, Inc., **37** 389–91
Tom Doherty Associates Inc., **25** 483–86
Tombstone Pizza Corporation, **13** 515–17 *see also* Kraft Foods Inc.
Tomen Corporation, **IV** 224–25; **24** 488–91 (upd.)

Tomkins plc, **11** 525–27; **44** 428–31 (upd.)
Tommy Bahama Group, Inc., **108** 491–95
Tommy Hilfiger Corporation, **20** 488–90; **53** 330–33 (upd.)
TomoTherapy Incorporated, **121** 409–12
Tomra Systems ASA, **103** 450–54
Tom's Foods Inc., **66** 325–27
Tom's of Maine, Inc., **45** 414–16; **125** 417–20 (upd.)
TOMS Shoes, Inc., **152** 451–55
TomTom N.V., **81** 388–91; **163** 353–57 (upd.)
Tomy Company Ltd., **65** 341–44
Tone Brothers, Inc., **21** 496–98; **74** 349–52 (upd.)
Tonen Corporation, **IV** 554–56; **16** 489–92 (upd.)
TonenGeneral Sekiyu K.K., **54** 380–86 (upd.)
Tong Yang Cement Corporation, **62** 366–68
Tonka Corporation, **25** 487–89
Too, Inc., **61** 371–73
Toolex International N.V., **26** 489–91
Tootsie Roll Industries, Inc., **12** 480–82; **82** 392–96 (upd.)
Top Pot Inc., **132** 424–27
Topa Equities Ltd., **136** 457–460
The Topaz Group, Inc., **62** 369–71
Topco Associates LLC, **60** 302–04; **141** 483–86 (upd.)
Topcon Corporation, **84** 406–409
Toppan Printing Co., Ltd., **IV** 679–81; **58** 340–44 (upd.); **152** 456–61 (upd.)
The Topps Company, Inc., **13** 518–20; **34** 446–49 (upd.); **83** 400–406 (upd.)
Tops Appliance City, Inc., **17** 487–89
Tops Markets, LLC, **60** 305–07; **136** 461–466 (upd.)
Toray Industries, Inc., **V** 383–86; **51** 375–79 (upd.); **152** 462–68 (upd.)
Torchmark Corporation, **9** 506–08; **33** 405–08 (upd.); **115** 458–64 (upd.)
Toresco Enterprises, Inc., **84** 410–413
Toridoll Corporation, **134** 427–30
Torm A/S, **145** 413–17
The Toro Company, **7** 534–36; **26** 492–95 (upd.); **77** 440–45 (upd.)
Toromont Industries, Ltd., **21** 499–501
The Toronto-Dominion Bank, **II** 375–77; **49** 395–99 (upd.); **135** 375–80 (upd.)
Toronto Maple Leafs *see* Maple Leaf Sports & Entertainment Ltd.
Toronto Raptors *see* Maple Leaf Sports & Entertainment Ltd.
Tororo Cement Limited, **135** 381–84
Torraspapel S.A., **142** 425–29
The Torrington Company, **13** 521–24 *see also* Timken Co.
Torstar Corporation, **29** 470–73 *see also* Harlequin Enterprises Ltd.
Tory Burch LLC, **141** 487–91
Tosco Corporation, **7** 537–39 *see also* ConocoPhillips.
Toshiba Corporation, **I** 533–35; **12** 483–86 (upd.); **40** 435–40 (upd.); **99** 453–461 (upd.)

Index to Industries

Accounting

American Institute of Certified Public
  Accountants (AICPA), 44
Andersen, 29 (upd.); 68 (upd.)
Automatic Data Processing, Inc., III; 9
  (upd.); 47 (upd.); 126 (upd.)
BDO Seidman LLP, 96
BKD LLP, 96
CPP International, LLC, 103
CROSSMARK, 79; 159 (upd.)
Deloitte Touche Tohmatsu International,
  9; 29 (upd.)
Ernst & Young Global Limited, 9; 29
  (upd.); 108 (upd.)
FTI Consulting, Inc., 77
Grant Thornton International Ltd., 57;
  135 (upd.)
Huron Consulting Group Inc., 87
JKH Holding Co. LLC, 105
KPMG International, 33 (upd.); 108
  (upd.)
L.S. Starrett Co., 13
LarsonAllen, LLP, 118
McLane Company, Inc., 13
NCO Group, Inc., 42
Paychex Inc., 15; 46 (upd.); 120 (upd.)
PKF International, 78
Plante & Moran, LLP, 71
PRG-Schultz International, Inc., 73
PricewaterhouseCoopers International
  Limited, 9; 29 (upd.); 111 (upd.)
Resources Connection, Inc., 81
Rothstein, Kass & Company, P.C., 131
RSM McGladrey Business Services Inc.,
  98
Saffery Champness, 80
Sanders\Wingo, 99
Schenck Business Solutions, 88

StarTek, Inc., 79
Travelzoo Inc., 79
UHY International Limited, 161
Univision Communications Inc., 24; 83
  (upd.)

Advertising & Business Services

1-800-FLOWERS.COM, Inc., 26; 102
  (upd.)
24/7 Media, 49; 139 (upd.)
4imprint Group PLC, 105
ABM Industries Incorporated, 25 (upd.);
  128 (upd.)
Abt Associates Inc., 95
Acacia Research Corporation, 144
Accenture Ltd., 108 (upd.)
AchieveGlobal Inc., 90
Ackerley Communications, Inc., 9
Ackerman McQueen, Inc., 164
ACNielsen Corporation, 13; 38 (upd.)
Acosta Sales and Marketing Company,
  Inc., 77
Acsys, Inc., 44
Adecco S.A., 36 (upd.); 116 (upd.)
Adelman Travel Group, 105
Adia S.A., 6
Administaff, Inc., 52
The Advertising Council, Inc., 76
The Advisory Board Company, 80
Advo, Inc., 6; 53 (upd.)
Aegis Media Ltd., 6; 154 (upd.)
Affiliated Computer Services, Inc., 61
Affinion Group, Inc., 121
AHL Services, Inc., 27
Airbnb, Inc., 148
AirMedia Group, Inc., 163
AKQA Inc., 148

Alibaba.com, Ltd., 119
Alion Science and Technology
  Corporation, 128
Allegis Group, Inc., 95
AlliedBarton Security Services LLC, 128
  (upd.)
Alloy, Inc., 55
Altavia S.A., 164
Amdocs Ltd., 47
American Building Maintenance
  Industries, Inc., 6
Amey Plc, 47
Analysts International Corporation, 36
APAC Customer Services Inc., 127
aQuantive, Inc., 81
Aquilex Holdings LLC, 139
Arbitron Inc., 38; 149 (upd.)
Armor Holdings, Inc., 27
Asatsu-DK Inc., 82
Ashtead Group plc, 34
Astral Media Inc., 126
Astro-Med, Inc., 135
Auction Systems Auctioneers &
  Appraisers, Inc., 159
Avalon Correctional Services, Inc., 75
Babcock International Group plc, 69; 161
  (upd.)
Bain & Company, 55; 157 (upd.)
Barrett Business Services, Inc., 16; 154
  (upd.)
Barton Protective Services Inc., 53
Bates Worldwide, Inc., 14; 33 (upd.)
Bearings, Inc., 13
Belfor Holdings Inc., 128
Berlitz International, Inc., 13; 39 (upd.)
Bernard Hodes Group Inc., 86
Bernstein-Rein, 92
Big Flower Press Holdings, Inc., 21
Billing Concepts, Inc., 26; 72 (upd.)

Aerospace

Agribusiness & Farming

Airlines

The Yokohama Rubber Company,
    Limited, V; 19 (upd.); 91 (upd.)
Yulon Motor Co., Ltd., 147
ZAP Jonway, 140
ZF Friedrichshafen AG, 48
Ziebart International Corporation, 30; 66
    (upd.)

Beverages

A & W Brands, Inc., 25
A. Smith Bowman Distillery, Inc., 104
Accolade Wines Ltd., 158
Adolph Coors Company, I; 13 (upd.); 36
    (upd.)
A.G. Barr p.l.c., 64; 163 (upd.)
Ajegroup S.A., 92
Alaskan Brewing Company, 162
Ale-8-One Company Bottling Company,
    Inc., 117
Allied Domecq PLC, 29
Allied-Lyons PLC, I
Altia plc, 145
Anadolu Efes Biracilik ve Malt Sanayii
    A.S., 95
Anchor Brewing Company, 47
Andrew Peller Ltd., 101
Angostura Holdings Ltd., 114
Anheuser-Busch InBev, I; 10 (upd.); 34
    (upd.); 100 (upd.)
Apple & Eve L.L.C., 92
Arcus-Gruppen AS, 141
Asahi Breweries, Ltd., I; 20 (upd.); 52
    (upd.); 108 (upd.)
Asia Pacific Breweries Ltd., 59; 150 (upd.)
Aston Manor Brewery Company Limited,
    163
Athenian Brewery S.A., 145
August Schell Brewing Company Inc., 59
Bacardi & Company Ltd., 18; 82 (upd.)
Baltika Brewery Joint Stock Company, 65
Banfi Products Corp., 36; 114 (upd.)
Baron de Ley S.A., 74; 152 (upd.)
Baron Philippe de Rothschild S.A., 39
Barry's Tea, Ltd., 143
Bass PLC, I; 15 (upd.); 38 (upd.)
Bavaria N.V., 121
Bavaria S.A., 90
Bayerische Staatsbrauerei Weihenstephan,
    164
BB&R Limited, 122
BBAG Osterreichische
    Brau-Beteiligungs-AG, 38
Beam Inc., 132 (upd.)
Bell's Brewery, Inc., 117
Belvedere S.A., 93
Ben Hill Griffin, Inc., 110
Berentzen-Gruppe AG, 113
Beringer Blass Wine Estates Ltd., 22; 66
    (upd.)
The Bernick Companies, 75
Birra Peroni Industriale S.p.A., 145
Bitburger Braugruppe GmbH, 110
Blue Bottle Coffee Inc., 161
Blue Ridge Beverage Company Inc., 82
Bodegas Barbadillo S.L., 148
Bodegas Riojanas S.A., 158
Boizel Chanoine Champagne S.A., 94
Bols Distilleries NV, 74

The Boston Beer Company, Inc., 18; 50
    (upd.); 108 (upd.)
Boyd Coffee Company, 164 (upd.)
Brauerei Beck & Co., 9; 33 (upd.)
Brauerei C. & A. Veltins GmbH & Co.
    KG, 120
Breckenridge Holding Company, 160
Brick Brewing Co. Limited, 130
Britannia Soft Drinks Ltd. (Britvic), 71
Bronco Wine Company, 101
The, Brooklyn Brewery, 109
Brouwerijen Alken-Maes N.V., 86
Brown-Forman Corporation, I; 10 (upd.);
    38 (upd.); 114 (upd.)
Budweiser Budvar, National Corporation,
    59
Cadbury Schweppes PLC, 49 (upd.)
Cains Beer Company PLC, 99
California Dairies Inc., 111
Cameron Hughes Wine, 103
Canandaigua Brands, Inc., 13; 34 (upd.)
Cantine Giorgio Lungarotti S.R.L., 67
Caribou Coffee Company, Inc., 28; 97
    (upd.)
Carlsberg A/S, 9; 29 (upd.); 98 (upd.)
Carlton and United Breweries Ltd., I
Carolina Beverage Corporation, 152
Casa Cuervo, S.A. de C.V., 31
Cascade Brewery Company Pty. Ltd., 143
Casella Wines Pty Limited, 132
Castel Frères S.A.S., 156
Cavit s.c., 130
Central European Distribution
    Corporation, 75
Cerveceria Polar, I
The Chalone Wine Group, Ltd., 36
Champagne Bollinger S.A., 114
Champagne Louis Roederer S.A., 160
The Charmer Sunbelt Group, 95
China Mengniu Dairy Company Limited,
    158
City Brewing Company LLC, 73
Clearly Canadian Beverage Corporation,
    48
Clement Pappas & Company, Inc., 92
Click Wine Group, 68
Coca Cola Bottling Co. Consolidated, 10
The Coca-Cola Company, I; 10 (upd.);
    32 (upd.); 67 (upd.); 141 (upd.)
Coca-Cola Hellenic Bottling Company
    S.A., 144
Coffee Holding Co., Inc., 95
Columbia Distributing Co., 128
Companhia de Bebidas das Américas, 57
Compañia Cervecera de Canarias S.A.,
    160
Compania Cervecerias Unidas S.A., 70
Compañía Vinícola del Norte de España
    S.A., 158
Constellation Brands, Inc., 68 (upd.); 158
    (upd.)
Corby Distilleries Limited, 14
Cott Corporation, 52; 149 (upd.)
Craft Brew Alliance, Inc., 140
D. Canale Beverages LLC, 138
D.G. Yuengling and Son, Inc., 38; 137
    (upd.)
Dairylea Cooperative Inc., 111

Dallis Coffee, Inc., 86
Daniel Thwaites Plc, 95
Davide Campari-Milano S.p.A., 57
Dean Foods Company, 21 (upd.)
Delicato Vineyards, Inc., 50
Deschutes Brewery, Inc., 57
Desnoes and Geddes Limited, 79
Diageo plc, 79 (upd.); 155 (upd.)
Direct Wines Ltd., 84
Distell Group Ltd., 126
Distillerie Tuoni Canepa Srl, 149
Distilleries Company of Sri Lanka PLC,
    147
Distillers Company PLC, I
DMK Deutsches Milchkontor GmbH,
    158
The Double Cola Company, 160 (upd.)
Double-Cola Co.-USA, 70
Dr Pepper Snapple Group, Inc., 9; 32
    (upd.); 124 (upd.)
Drie Mollen Holding B.V., 99
Drinks Americas Holdings, LTD., 105
Dynasty Fine Wines Group Ltd., 160
E. & J. Gallo Winery, I; 7 (upd.); 28
    (upd.); 104 (upd.)
East Africa Breweries Limited, 116
East African Breweries Ltd., 138
Eckes-Granini Group, 56; 136 (upd.)
The Edrington Group Ltd., 88
Embotelladora Andina S.A., 71
Embotelladoras Arca, S.A.B. de C.V., 119
Empresas Polar SA, 55 (upd.)
Energy Brands Inc., 88
Everards Brewery Ltd., 123
F. Korbel & Bros. Inc., 68
Faygo Beverages Inc., 55
Federico Paternina S.A., 69
Ferolito, Vultaggio & Sons, 27; 100
    (upd.)
Fiji Water LLC, 74
Florida's Natural Growers, 45; 146 (upd.)
Fomento Económico Mexicano S.A.B. de
    C.V., 128 (upd.)
Foster's Group Limited, 7; 21 (upd.); 50
    (upd.); 111 (upd.)
Francis Ford Coppola Winery, LLC, 162
Freixenet S.A., 71
Frucor Beverages Group Ltd., 96
Fuller Smith & Turner P.L.C., 38; 160
    (upd.)
G. Heileman Brewing Company Inc., I
The Gambrinus Company, 40; 157 (upd.)
Gano Excel Enterprise Sdn. Bhd., 89
Garagiste Inc., 161
The Gatorade Company, 82
Geerlings & Wade, Inc., 45
General Cinema Corporation, I
George A. Dickel & Co., 143
Glazer's Wholesale Drug Company, Inc.,
    82
Gluek Brewing Company, 75
Golden State Vintners, Inc., 33
Gonzalez Byass S.A., 148
Gosling Brothers Ltd., 82
Grand Metropolitan PLC, I
Grands Vins Jean-Claude Boisset S.A., 98
Great Lakes Brewing Company, 156

The South African Breweries Limited, I; 24 (upd.)
South Beach Beverage Company, Inc., 73
Southcorp Limited, 54
Southern Wine and Spirits of America, Inc., 84
Spadel S.A./NV, 113
SPB, LLC (dba Stevens Point Brewery), 156
Starbucks Corporation, 13; 34 (upd.); 77 (upd.)
The Stash Tea Company, 50
Sterling Vineyards, Inc., 130
Stewart's Beverages, 39
Stone Brewing Company, 153
The Stroh Brewery Company, I; 18 (upd.)
Suntory Ltd., 65
Surinaamse Brouwerij N.V., 156
Sutter Home Winery Inc., 16
Taittinger S.A., 43; 125 (upd.)
Taiwan Tobacco & Liquor Corporation, 75
Takara Holdings Inc., 62
Tampico Beverages, Inc., 147
Tanzania Breweries Limited, 124
Tata Tea Ltd., 76
Teavana Holdings, Inc., 137
Teekanne Holding GmbH, 145
Tennent Caledonian Breweries UK Ltd., 147
The Terlato Wine Group, 48
Tetley USA Inc., 88
TINE SA, 152
Todhunter International, Inc., 27
Total Beverage Solution, 151
Triarc Companies, Inc., 34 (upd.)
Trinchero Family Estates, 107 (upd.)
Tropicana Products, Inc., 73 (upd.)
Tsingtao Brewery Company, Limited, 49; 129 (upd.)
Tully's Coffee Corporation, 51
Underberg AG, 92
Unilever, II; 7 (upd.); 32 (upd.); 89 (upd.)
Unión de Cervecerias Peruanas Backus y Johnston S.A.A., 92
United Breweries (Holdings) Limited, 143
V&S Vin & Sprit AB, 91 (upd.)
Van Houtte Inc., 39
Vermont Pure Holdings, Ltd., 51
Veuve Clicquot Ponsardin SCS, 98
Vin & Spirit AB, 31
Viña Concha y Toro S.A., 45; 163 (upd.)
Viña San Pedro Tarapacá S.A., 119
Vincor International Inc., 50
Vinmonopolet A/S, 100
Vranken Pommery Monopole S.A., 114
W.J. Deutsch & Sons, Ltd., 126
Warsteiner Group, 113
Welsh Whisky Company Ltd., 153
Wente Family Estates, 141
Whitbread PLC, I; 20 (upd.); 52 (upd.); 97 (upd.)
Whyte & Mackay Ltd., 144
Widmer Brothers Brewing Company, 76
Willamette Valley Vineyards, Inc., 85
William Grant & Sons Ltd., 60
The Wine Group, Inc., 39; 114 (upd.)

The Wolverhampton & Dudley Breweries, PLC, 57
Wray & Nephew Group Ltd., 98
Wuliangye Group Company Ltd., 144
Yantai Changyu Pioneer Wine Company Ltd., 127
Young & Co.'s Brewery, P.L.C., 38
Young's Market Company, LLC, 32; 118 (upd.)

Bio-Technology

Actelion Ltd., 83
Affymetrix Inc., 106
Agenus Inc., 158
Agria Corporation, 101
Amersham PLC, 50
Amgen, Inc., 10; 30 (upd.)
Amyris, Inc., 152
ArQule, Inc., 68
Becton, Dickinson and Company, I; 11 (upd.); 36 (upd.); 101 (upd.)
BioClinica, Incorporated, 129
Biogen Idec Inc., 14; 36 (upd.); 71 (upd.); 152 (upd.)
bioMérieux S.A., 75
Bio-Rad Laboratories, Inc., 93
Bio-Reference Laboratories, Inc., 122
bluebird bio, Inc., 162
BTG Plc, 87
Caliper Life Sciences, Inc., 70; 143 (upd.)
Cambrex Corporation, 44 (upd.)
Cardiac Science Corporation, 121
Celera Genomics, 74
Celgene Corporation, 67; 137 (upd.)
Centocor Inc., 14
Cepheid, 77; 161 (upd.)
Charles River Laboratories International, Inc., 42; 128 (upd.)
Chiron Corporation, 10; 36 (upd.)
Codexis, Inc., 130
Covance Inc., 30; 98 (upd.)
CryoLife, Inc., 46; 149 (upd.)
Cytyc Corporation, 69
Delta and Pine Land Company, 33
Dionex Corporation, 46
Dyax Corp., 89
Ebro Foods S.A., 118
Embrex, Inc., 72
Emergent BioSolutions Inc., 137
Enzo Biochem, Inc., 41
eResearch Technology, Inc., 115
Eurofins Scientific S.A., 70
Genentech, Inc., 32 (upd.)
Gen-Probe Incorporated, 79
Genzyme Corporation, 38 (upd.); 152 (upd.)
Gilead Sciences, Inc., 54; 125 (upd.)
Grifols, S.A., 152
Harvard Bioscience Inc., 142
Hindustan Lever Limited, 79
Howard Hughes Medical Institute, 39
Huntingdon Life Sciences Group plc, 42
iCAD, Inc., 151
IDEXX Laboratories, Inc., 23; 107 (upd.)
ImClone Systems LLC, 58; 160 (upd.)
Immunex Corporation, 14; 50 (upd.)
IMPATH Inc., 45
Incyte Genomics, Inc., 52

Inverness Medical Innovations, Inc., 63
Invitrogen Corporation, 52
The Judge Group, Inc., 51
Kendle International Inc., 87
Landec Corporation, 95
Life Technologies, Inc., 17
Life Technologies Corporation, 77; 133 (upd.); 156 (upd.)
Lonza Group Ltd., 73
Luminex Corporation, 122
Martek Biosciences Corporation, 65
Medarex, Inc., 85
MedImmune LLC, 35; 153 (upd.)
Medtronic, Inc., 8; 30 (upd.); 67 (upd.)
Meridian Bioscience, Inc., 115
Millipore Corporation, 25; 84 (upd.)
Minntech Corporation, 22
Monogram Biosciences, Inc., 146
Monsanto Company, I; 9 (upd.); 29 (upd.); 152 (upd.)
Mycogen Corporation, 21
Nektar Therapeutics, 91
New Brunswick Scientific Co., Inc., 45
Novozymes A/S, 118
Omrix Biopharmaceuticals, Inc., 95
Pacific Ethanol, Inc., 81
Pharmion Corporation, 91
QIAGEN N.V., 39; 121 (upd.)
Quintiles Transnational Corporation, 21
RTI Biologics, Inc., 96
Seattle Genetics, Inc., 137
Seminis, Inc., 29
Senomyx, Inc., 83
Serologicals Corporation, 63
Sigma-Aldrich Corporation, I; 36 (upd.); 93 (upd.)
Solazyme, Inc., 137
Starkey Laboratories, Inc., 52; 157 (upd.)
STERIS Corporation, 29; 132 (upd.)
Stine Seed Company, 162
Stratagene Corporation, 70
Talecris Biotherapeutics Holdings Corp., 114
Tanox, Inc., 77
TECHNE Corporation, 52; 133 (upd.)
Transgenomic, Inc., 146
Trinity Biotech plc, 121
TriPath Imaging, Inc., 77
Verenium Corporation, 151
Viterra Inc., 105
Waters Corporation, 43; 163 (upd.)
Whatman plc, 46
Wilmar International Ltd., 108
Wisconsin Alumni Research Foundation, 65
Wyeth, Inc., 50 (upd.); 118 (upd.)

Chemicals

A. Schulman, Inc., 8; 49 (upd.); 133 (upd.)
Aceto Corp., 38
Adeka Corporation, 160 (upd.)
Agrium Inc., 155
Air Products and Chemicals, Inc., I; 10 (upd.); 74 (upd.); 148 (upd.)
Airgas, Inc., 54
Akzo Nobel N.V., 13; 41 (upd.); 112 (upd.)

Conglomerates

Construction

Containers

Molins plc, 51
National Can Corporation, I
Owens-Illinois, Inc., I; 26 (upd.); 85
   (upd.); 162 (upd.)
Packaging Corporation of America, 51
   (upd.)
Pochet SA, 55
Primerica Corporation, I
Printpack, Inc., 68
PVC Container Corporation, 67
Rexam PLC, 32 (upd.); 85 (upd.); 162
   (upd.)
Reynolds Metals Company, 19 (upd.)
Royal Packaging Industries Van Leer N.V.,
   30
RPC Group PLC, 81
Sealright Co., Inc., 17
Shurgard Storage Centers, Inc., 52
Silgan Holdings Inc., 128
Smurfit Kappa Group plc, 112 (upd.)
Smurfit-Stone Container Corporation, 26
   (upd.); 83 (upd.)
Sonoco Products Company, 8; 89 (upd.)
Tetra Laval International S.A., 53; 141
   (upd.)
Thermos Company, 16
Tim-Bar Corporation, 110
Toyo Seikan Kaisha, Ltd., I
U.S. Can Corporation, 30
Ultra Pac, Inc., 24
Viatech Continental Can Company, Inc.,
   25 (upd.)
Vidrala S.A., 67; 161 (upd.)
Vitro Corporativo S.A. de C.V., 34
Winpak Ltd., 121

Drugs & Pharmaceuticals

A.L. Pharma Inc., 12
A. Nelson & Co. Ltd., 75
Abbott Laboratories, I; 11 (upd.); 40
   (upd.); 93 (upd.)
Aché Laboratórios Farmacéuticas S.A., 105
Acorda Therapeutics, Inc., 148
Actavis Group hf., 103
Actelion Ltd., 83; 162 (upd.)
Adolor Corporation, 101
Advanced BioHealing Inc., 139
Aelia SAS, 145
Akorn, Inc., 32
Albany Molecular Research, Inc., 77; 161
   (upd.)
Alfresa Holdings Corporation, 108
Allergan, Inc., 77; 148 (upd.)
Alpharma Inc., 35 (upd.)
ALZA Corporation, 10; 36 (upd.)
Amarin Corporation plc, 141
American Home Products, I; 10 (upd.)
American Oriental Bioengineering Inc., 93
American Pharmaceutical Partners, Inc.,
   69
Amersham PLC, 50
Amgen, Inc., 10; 89 (upd.)
Amylin Pharmaceuticals, Inc., 67
Andrx Corporation, 55
Angelini SpA, 100
Angiotech Pharmaceuticals, Inc., 128
Aspen Pharmacare Holdings Limited, 112
Astellas Pharma Inc., 97 (upd.)

AstraZeneca PLC, I; 20 (upd.); 50 (upd.);
   121 (upd.)
AtheroGenics Inc., 101
Avanir Pharmaceuticals, Inc., 162
Axcan Pharma Inc., 85
Barr Pharmaceuticals, Inc., 26; 68 (upd.)
Bayer AG, I; 13 (upd.); 41 (upd.); 118
   (upd.)
Berlex Laboratories, Inc., 66
BioCryst Pharmaceuticals, Inc., 154
Biovail Corporation, 47
Block Drug Company, Inc., 8
Boiron S.A., 73
Bristol-Myers Squibb Company, III; 9
   (upd.); 37 (upd.); 111 (upd.)
BTG Plc, 87
C.H. Boehringer Sohn, 39
Cahill May Roberts Group Ltd., 112
Cangene Corporation, 150
Caraco Pharmaceutical Laboratories Ltd.,
   149
Caremark Rx, Inc., 10; 54 (upd.)
Carter-Wallace, Inc., 8; 38 (upd.)
Catalent Pharma Solutions, Inc., 122
Celgene Corporation, 67; 137 (upd.)
Cephalon Technology, Inc, 45; 115 (upd.)
China Biologic Products, Inc., 125
Chiron Corporation, 10
Chugai Pharmaceutical Co., Ltd., 139
   (upd.)
Chugai Pharmaceutical Co., Ltd., 50
Ciba-Geigy Ltd., I; 8 (upd.)
Clinical Data, Inc., 125
CSL Limited, 112
Cubist Pharmaceuticals, Inc., 123
D&K Wholesale Drug, Inc., 14
Daiichi Sankyo Co., Ltd., 136
Dechra Pharmaceuticals PLC, 126
DepoMed, Inc., 141
Diplomat Specialty Pharmacy, Inc., 139
Discovery Partners International, Inc., 58
Dr. Reddy's Laboratories Ltd., 59
Egis Gyogyszergyar Nyrt, 104
Eisai Co., Ltd., 101
Elan Corporation PLC, 63; 151 (upd.)
Eli Lilly and Company, I; 11 (upd.); 47
   (upd.); 109 (upd.)
Emergent BioSolutions Inc., 137
Endo Pharmaceuticals Holdings Inc., 71
Eon Labs, Inc., 67
Express Scripts Inc., 44 (upd.)
F. Hoffmann-La Roche Ltd., I; 50 (upd.)
Farmacias de Similares S.A. de C.V., 158
Ferring Pharmaceuticals S.A., 119
Fisons plc, 9; 23 (upd.)
Forest Laboratories, Inc., 52 (upd.); 114
   (upd.)
FoxMeyer Health Corporation, 16
Fujisawa Pharmaceutical Company, Ltd.,
   I; 58 (upd.)
G.D. Searle & Co., I; 12 (upd.); 34
   (upd.)
Galenica AG, 84
Gedeon Richter plc, 122
GEHE AG, 27
Genentech, Inc., I; 8 (upd.); 75 (upd.);
   152 (upd.)
Genetics Institute, Inc., 8

Gentium S.p.A., 162
Genzyme Corporation, 13, 77 (upd.); 152
   (upd.)
Glaxo Holdings PLC, I; 9 (upd.)
GlaxoSmithKline plc, 46 (upd.); 119
   (upd.)
Green Cross Corp., 138
Grifols, S.A., 152
Groupe Fournier SA, 44
Groupe Léa Nature, 88
Grupo EMS, 141
H. Lundbeck A/S, 44; 147 (upd.)
Hauser, Inc., 46
Heska Corporation, 39; 151 (upd.)
Hexal AG, 69
Hi-Tech Pharmacal Co., Inc., 137
Hikma Pharmaceuticals Ltd., 102
Hospira, Inc., 71; 148 (upd.)
Huntingdon Life Sciences Group plc, 42
ICN Pharmaceuticals, Inc., 52
ICU Medical, Inc., 106
Idera Pharmaceuticals Inc., 128
Immucor, Inc., 81
Insys Therapeutics, Inc., 155
Integrated BioPharma, Inc., 83
Isis Pharmaceuticals, Inc., 144
IVAX Corporation, 55 (upd.)
Janssen Pharmaceutica N.V., 80
Jazz Pharmaceuticals plc, 149
Johnson & Johnson, III; 8 (upd.)
Jones Medical Industries, Inc., 24
The Judge Group, Inc., 51
Kerr Drug, Inc., 133
King Pharmaceuticals Inc., 54; 132 (upd.)
Kinray Inc., 85
Kos Pharmaceuticals, Inc., 63
Kyowa Hakko Kogyo Co., Ltd., 48 (upd.)
Laboratoires Arkopharma S.A., 75
Laboratoires Pierre Fabre S.A., 100
Lannett Company, Inc., 126
Leiner Health Products Inc., 34
Lek farmacevtska druzba d.d., 130
Ligand Pharmaceuticals Incorporated, 47
London Drugs Limited, 46; 135 (upd.)
MannKind Corporation, 87
Marion Merrell Dow, Inc., I; 9 (upd.)
Matrixx Initiatives, Inc., 74
McKesson Corporation, 12; 47 (upd.)
Medco Health Solutions, Inc., 116
Medicis Pharmaceutical Corporation, 59
Medley Indústria Farmacêutica Ltda., 155
Medochemie Ltd., 152
Meiji Holdings Co., Ltd., 139
Merck & Co., Inc., I; 11 (upd.); 34
   (upd.); 95 (upd.)
Merck KGaA, 111
Merial Ltd., 102
Merz Group, 81
Miles Laboratories, I
Millennium Pharmaceuticals, Inc., 47
Millennium: The Takeda Oncology
   Company, 164 (upd.)
Mitsubishi Tanabe Pharma Corporation,
   139
Moore Medical Corp., 17
Murdock Madaus Schwabe, 26
Mylan Inc., I; 20 (upd.); 59 (upd.); 122
   (upd.)

Myriad Genetics, Inc., 95
Nadro S.A. de C.V., 86
Nastech Pharmaceutical Company Inc., 79
National Patent Development
    Corporation, 13
Natrol, Inc., 49
Natural Alternatives International, Inc., 49
Nektar Therapeutics, 91
Novartis AG, 39 (upd.); 105 (upd.)
Noven Pharmaceuticals, Inc., 55
Novo Nordisk A/S, I; 61 (upd.); 144
    (upd.)
Obagi Medical Products, Inc., 95
Omnicare, Inc., 49
Omrix Biopharmaceuticals, Inc., 95
Ono Pharmaceutical Co., Ltd., 128
Onyx Pharmaceuticals, Inc., 110
Otsuka Holdings Co., Ltd., 139
Par Pharmaceutical Companies, Inc., 65
PDL BioPharma, Inc., 90
Perrigo Company, 12; 59 (upd.); 118
    (upd.)
Pfizer Inc., I; 9 (upd.); 38 (upd.); 79
    (upd.)
Pharmaceutical Product Development,
    Inc., 125
Pharmacia & Upjohn Inc., I; 25 (upd.)
Pharmacyclics, Inc., 148
Pharmion Corporation, 91
PLIVA d.d., 70
PolyMedica Corporation, 77
POZEN Inc., 81
QLT Inc., 71
The Quigley Corporation, 62
Quintiles Transnational Corporation, 21
R.P. Scherer, I
Ranbaxy Laboratories Ltd., 70
ratiopharm Group, 84
Reckitt Benckiser plc, II; 42 (upd.); 91
    (upd.)
Recordati Industria Chimica e
    Farmaceutica S.p.A., 105
Regeneron Pharmaceuticals, Inc., 152
Roberts Pharmaceutical Corporation, 16
Roche Bioscience, 14 (upd.)
Roche Holding AG, 109
Rorer Group, I
Roussel Uclaf, I; 8 (upd.)
Salix Pharmaceuticals, Ltd., 93
Sandoz Ltd., I
Sankyo Company, Ltd., I; 56 (upd.)
Sanofi SA, 139
The Sanofi-Synthélabo Group, I; 49
    (upd.)
Santarus, Inc., 105
Schering AG, I; 50 (upd.)
Schering-Plough Corporation, I; 14
    (upd.); 49 (upd.); 99 (upd.)
Seattle Genetics, Inc., 137
Sepracor Inc., 45; 117 (upd.)
Serono S.A., 47
Shionogi & Co., Ltd., III; 17 (upd.); 98
    (upd.)
Shire PLC, 109
Sigma-Aldrich Corporation, I; 36 (upd.);
    93 (upd.)
Sigma Pharmaceuticals Ltd., 121
SmithKline Beecham plc, I; 32 (upd.)

Solvay S.A., 61 (upd.)
Squibb Corporation, I
Sterling Drug, Inc., I
Stiefel Laboratories, Inc., 90
Sun Pharmaceutical Industries Ltd., 57;
    138 (upd.)
The Sunrider Corporation, 26
SurModics, Inc., 142
Syntex Corporation, I
Takeda Pharmaceutical Company Limited,
    I; 115 (upd.)
Taro Pharmaceutical Industries Ltd., 65
Teva Pharmaceutical Industries Ltd., 22;
    54 (upd.); 112 (upd.)
UCB Pharma SA, 98
United Drug PLC, 121
United Therapeutics Corporation, 144
The Upjohn Company, I; 8 (upd.)
Valeant Pharmaceuticals International,
    Inc., 125 (upd.)
Vertex Pharmaceuticals Incorporated, 83
Vétoquinol S.A., 156
Virbac Corporation, 74; 164 (upd.)
Vitacost.com Inc., 116
Vitalink Pharmacy Services, Inc., 15
Warner Chilcott Limited, 85
Warner-Lambert Co., I; 10 (upd.)
Watson Pharmaceuticals Inc., 16; 56
    (upd.); 122 (upd.)
The Wellcome Foundation Ltd., I
WonderWorks, Inc., 103
Wyeth, Inc., 50 (upd.); 118 (upd.)
XOMA Ltd., 117
Yuhan Corporation, 142
Zentiva N.V./Zentiva, a.s., 99
Zhejiang Medicine Company Ltd., 131
Zila, Inc., 46

Education & Training
ABC Learning Centres Ltd., 93
ACT, Inc., 114
American Management Association, 76
American Public Education, Inc., 108
Anhanguera Educacional Participações
    S.A., 122
Apollo Group, Inc., 24; 119 (upd.)
Archipelago Learning, Inc., 116
Arthur Murray International, Inc., 136
    (upd.)
Avenues World Holdings LLC, 146
Benesse Corporation, 76
Berlitz International, Inc., 13; 39 (upd.)
Bridgepoint Education, Inc., 108
Cambium Learning Group, Inc., 135
Capella Education Company, 109
Career Education Corporation, 45; 128
    (upd.)
ChartHouse International Learning
    Corporation, 49
Childtime Learning Centers, Inc., 34
Computer Learning Centers, Inc., 26
Corinthian Colleges, Inc., 39; 92 (upd.)
Cornell Companies, Inc., 112
Council on International Educational
    Exchange Inc., 81
The Culinary Institute of America, 122
Demos S.A., 145
DeVry Inc., 29; 82 (upd.)

ECC International Corp., 42
EdisonLearning, Inc., 37; 151 (upd.)
Educate Inc., 86 (upd.)
Education Management Corporation, 35;
    120 (upd.)
Educational Testing Service, 12; 62 (upd.)
FlightSafety International, Inc., 9; 20
    (upd.); 143 (upd.)
Franklin Institute, 132
Frasca International, Inc., 147
GP Strategies Corporation, 64 (upd.)
Grand Canyon Education, Inc., 133
Green Dot Public Schools, 99
Grupo Positivo, 105
Harvard University, 125
Huntington Learning Centers, Inc., 55
ITT Educational Services, Inc., 39; 76
    (upd.)
Jones Knowledge Group, Inc., 97
Kaplan, Inc., 42; 90 (upd.)
KinderCare Learning Centers, Inc., 13
Knowledge Learning Corporation, 51; 115
    (upd.)
Knowledge Universe Education LLC, 143
    (upd.)
K12 Inc., 118
Kumon Institute of Education Co., Ltd.,
    72
Le Cordon Bleu International B.V., 67;
    161 (upd.)
LeapFrog Enterprises, Inc., 54; 139 (upd.)
Learning Care Group, Inc., 76 (upd.)
The Learning Company Inc., 24
Learning Tree International Inc., 24
Lincoln Educational Services Corporation,
    111
LPA Holding Corporation, 81
Lynda.com, Inc., 152
Management and Training Corporation,
    28
Measurement Incorporated, 129
Megastudy Company Ltd., 127
Mount Sinai Medical Center, 112
National American University Holdings,
    Inc., 140
National Heritage Academies, Inc., 60
New Horizons Worldwide, Inc., 120
New Oriental Education and Technology
    Group, 150
The New School, 103
Noah Education Holdings Ltd., 97
Nobel Learning Communities, Inc., 37;
    76 (upd.)
Plato Learning, Inc., 44
The Princeton Review, Inc., 42; 124
    (upd.)
Renaissance Learning, Inc., 39; 100 (upd.)
Rocketship Education, 146
Rosetta Stone Inc., 93
Scientific Learning Corporation, 95
Strayer Education, Inc., 53; 124 (upd.)
Sylvan Learning Systems, Inc., 35
The Teaching Company, LLC, 126
Udacity, Inc., 161
United States Air Force Academy, 152
Whitman Education Group, Inc., 41
Youth Services International, Inc., 21

Electrical & Electronics

SCI Systems, Inc., 9
Scientific-Atlanta, Inc., 45 (upd.)
Scitex Corporation Ltd., 24
Seagate Technology, 8; 34 (upd.); 105 (upd.)
Semitool, Inc., 79 (upd.)
Semtech Corporation, 32; 134 (upd.)
Sennheiser Electronic GmbH & Co. KG, 66
Sensormatic Electronics Corp., 11
Sensory Science Corporation, 37
SGI, 29 (upd.)
Sharp Corporation, II; 12 (upd.); 40 (upd.); 114 (upd.)
Sheldahl Inc., 23
Shure Inc., 60
Siemens Aktiengesellschaft, II; 14 (upd.); 57 (upd.); 137 (upd.)
Sierra Nevada Corporation, 108
Sigma Designs, Inc., 150
Silicon Graphics Incorporated, 9
Silicon Image Inc., 145
Silicon Laboratories Inc., 145
Silicon Storage Technology, Inc., 146
Siltronic AG, 90
Skullcandy, Inc., 123
Skyworks Solutions, Inc., 143
SL Industries, Inc., 77
Sling Media, Inc., 112
SMA Solar Technology AG, 118
SMART Modular Technologies, Inc., 86
Smiths Industries PLC, 25
Solectron Corporation, 12; 48 (upd.)
Sonus Networks Inc., 126
Sony Corporation, II; 12 (upd.); 40 (upd.); 108 (upd.)
SoundWorks, Inc., 154 (upd.)
Spansion Inc., 80
Sparton Corporation, 18; 140 (upd.)
Spectrum Control, Inc., 67
Spire Corporation, 129
SPX Corporation, 10; 47 (upd.); 103 (upd.)
Square D, 90
Standex International Corporation, 17; 44 (upd.); 133 (upd.)
Static Control Components, Inc., 145
Sterling Electronics Corp., 18
STMicroelectronics N.V., 52; 138 (upd.)
Strix Ltd., 51
Stuart C. Irby Company, 58
Sumitomo Electric Industries, Ltd., II; 138 (upd.)
Sun Microsystems, Inc., 7; 30 (upd.); 91 (upd.)
Sunbeam-Oster Co., Inc., 9
SunPower Corporation, 91
Suntech Power Holdings Company Ltd., 89
Suntron Corporation, 107
SunWize Technologies, Inc., 114
Synaptics Incorporated, 95
Syneron Medical Ltd., 91
SYNNEX Corporation, 73; 158 (upd.)
Synopsys, Inc., 11; 69 (upd.)
Syntax-Brillian Corporation, 102
Sypris Solutions, Inc., 85
SyQuest Technology, Inc., 18

Taiwan Semiconductor Manufacturing Co., Ltd., 47; 139 (upd.)
Tamura Corporation, 155
Tandy Corporation, II; 12 (upd.)
TASER International, Inc., 62; 140 (upd.)
Tatung Co., 23
TDK Corporation, II; 17 (upd.); 49 (upd.); 114 (upd.)
TEAC Corporation, 78
Tech Data Corporation, 10; 74 (upd.); 162 (upd.)
Technicolor, 154 (upd.)
Technitrol, Inc., 29
Tech-Sym Corporation, 18
Tektronix, Inc., 8
Teledyne Technologies Inc., I; 10 (upd.); 62 (upd.); 143 (upd.)
TeleNav, Inc., 141
Telvent GIT, S.A., 150
Telxon Corporation, 10
Teradyne, Inc., 11; 98 (upd.)
Tesla Motors, Inc., 124
Texas Instruments Incorporated, II; 11 (upd.); 46 (upd.); 118 (upd.)
Thales S.A., 42; 144 (upd.)
Thomas & Betts Corporation, 11; 54 (upd.); 114 (upd.)
THOMSON multimedia S.A., II; 42 (upd.)
THQ, Inc., 92 (upd.)
The Titan Corporation, 36
TiVo Inc., 75; 154 (upd.)
TomTom N.V., 81
Tops Appliance City, Inc., 17
Toromont Industries, Ltd., 21
Tower Semiconductor Ltd., 150
Trans-Lux Corporation, 51
Trimble Navigation Limited, 40
Trio-Tech International, 129
TriQuint Semiconductor, Inc., 63
TT electronics plc, 111
TTM Technologies, Inc., 150
Turtle & Hughes Inc., 137
Tweeter Home Entertainment Group, Inc., 30
Ultimate Electronics, Inc., 69 (upd.)
Ultrak Inc., 24
Ultralife Corporation, 58; 157 (upd.)
Uniden Corporation, 98
Unisys Corporation, 112 (upd.)
United Microelectronics Corporation, 98
Universal Electronics Inc., 39; 120 (upd.)
Universal Lighting Technologies, 157
Universal Security Instruments, Inc., 96
Varian, Inc., 12; 48 (upd.)
Veeco Instruments Inc., 32
VIASYS Healthcare, Inc., 52
Viasystems Group, Inc., 67
Vicon Industries, Inc., 44
Victor Company of Japan, Limited, II; 26 (upd.); 83 (upd.)
Videocon Industries Ltd., 147
Vishay Intertechnology, Inc., 21; 80 (upd.)
Vitesse Semiconductor Corporation, 32
Vitro Corp., 10
Vizio, Inc., 100
VLSI Technology, Inc., 16

Volterra Semiconductor Corporation, 128
Vorwerk & Co. KG, 112 (upd.)
VTech Holdings Ltd., 77
WABCO Holdings Inc., 136
Wells-Gardner Electronics Corporation, 43
WESCO International, Inc., 116
Westinghouse Electric Corporation, II; 12 (upd.)
Winbond Electronics Corporation, 74
Wincor Nixdorf Holding GmbH, 69 (upd.)
Wintek Corporation, 135
Wistron Corporation, 126
WuXi AppTec Company Ltd., 103
Wyle Electronics, 14
Xantrex Technology Inc., 97
Xerox Corporation, III; 6 (upd.); 26 (upd.); 69 (upd.); 147 (upd.)
Yageo Corporation, 16; 98 (upd.)
York Research Corporation, 35
ZAGG Inc., 161
Zenith Data Systems, Inc., 10
Zenith Electronics Corporation, II; 13 (upd.); 34 (upd.); 89 (upd.)
ZF Electronics Systems Pleasant Prairie LLC, 149
Zoom Telephonics, Inc., 18
Zoran Corporation, 77
Zumtobel AG, 50; 157 (upd.)
Zytec Corporation, 19

Engineering & Management Services

AAON, Inc., 22
Aavid Thermal Technologies, Inc., 29
Acciona S.A., 162
Acergy SA, 97
Acorn Energy, Inc., 129
AECOM Technology Corporation, 79; 158 (upd.)
Aker ASA, 128
Alliant Techsystems Inc., 30 (upd.); 77 (upd.); 148 (upd.)
Altran Technologies, 51
AMEC plc, 112
American Science & Engineering, Inc., 81
Amey Plc, 47
Analytic Sciences Corporation, 10
Arcadis NV, 26
Argonne National Laboratory, 137
Arthur D. Little, Inc., 35
Asteelflash Group, 153
Ausenco Limited, 129
The Austin Company, 8; 72 (upd.)
Autostrada Torino-Milano S.p.A., 101
Babcock International Group plc, 69; 161 (upd.)
Balfour Beatty plc, 36 (upd.); 144 (upd.)
BE&K, Inc., 73
Bechtel Corporation, I; 24 (upd.); 99 (upd.)
Bertrandt AG, 126
Bilfinger Berger SE, I; 55 (upd.); 141 (upd.)
Birse Group PLC, 77
Black & Veatch Corporation, 22; 130 (upd.)

UGL Limited, 137
United Dominion Industries Limited, 8; 16 (upd.)
URS Corporation, 45; 80 (upd.)
VA TECH ELIN EBG GmbH, 49
VECO International, Inc., 7
Vinci, 43
Volkert and Associates, Inc., 98
VSE Corporation, 108
Waterman Group PLC, 140
The Weir Group PLC, 85
Willbros Group, Inc., 56
Willdan Group, Inc, 140
Wisconsin Lift Truck Corp., 130
WS Atkins Plc, 45
WSP Group plc, 126

Entertainment & Leisure

4Kids Entertainment Inc., 59
7digital Limited, 125
19 Entertainment Limited, 112
24 Hour Fitness Worldwide, Inc., 71
40 Acres and a Mule Filmworks, Inc., 121
155 East Tropicana, LLC, 124
365 Media Group plc, 89
888 Holdings plc, 124
A&E Television Networks, 32
Aardman Animations Ltd., 61; 136 (upd.)
ABC Family Worldwide, Inc., 52
Academy Music Group, Ltd., 141
Academy of Motion Picture Arts and Sciences, 121
Academy of Television Arts & Sciences, Inc., 55
Acclaim Entertainment Inc., 24
Activision, Inc., 32; 89 (upd.)
Acushnet Company, 64
Adams Golf, Inc., 37; 139 (upd.)
Adelman Travel Group, 105
AEI Music Network Inc., 35
AFC Ajax NV, 132
Affinity Group Holding Inc., 56
Airtours Plc, 27
Alamo Drafthouse Cinemas, LLC, 135
Alaska Railroad Corporation, 60
Alcon Entertainment LLC, 137
Aldila Inc., 46
All American Communications Inc., 20
The All England Lawn Tennis & Croquet Club, 54
Allen Organ Company, 33
Allgemeiner Deutscher Automobil-Club e.V., 100
Alliance Entertainment Corp., 17
Alternative Tentacles Records, 66
Alvin Ailey Dance Foundation, Inc., 52
Amalgamated Holdings Limited, 139
Amaury Sport Organisation, 134
Amblin Entertainment, 21
AMC Entertainment Inc., 12; 35 (upd.); 114 (upd.)
Amer Group plc, 41
American Golf Corporation, 45
American Gramaphone LLC, 52
American Kennel Club, Inc., 74
American Museum of Natural History, 121
American Skiing Company, 28

Ameristar Casinos, Inc., 33; 69 (upd.); 155 (upd.)
AMF Bowling, Inc., 40
Amscan Holdings, Inc., 61; 124 (upd.)
Anaheim Angels Baseball Club, Inc., 53
Anchor Gaming, 24
Annapurna Pictures, 161
Anytime Fitness LLC, 164
AOL Time Warner Inc., 57 (upd.)
Apollo Theater Foundation, Inc., 109
Applause Inc., 24
Apple Corps Ltd., 87
Aprilia SpA, 17
Arena Leisure Plc, 99
Argosy Gaming Company, 21
Aristocrat Leisure Limited, 129 (upd.)
Aristocrat Leisure Limited, 54
Arizona Cardinals Football Club LLC, 129
Arizona Professional Baseball LP, 134
Arsenal Holdings plc, 79; 159 (upd.)
The Art Institute of Chicago, 29
The Arthur C. Clarke Foundation, 92
Arthur Murray International, Inc., 32; 136 (upd.)
Artisan Entertainment Inc., 32 (upd.)
Asahi National Broadcasting Company, Ltd., 9
Aspen Skiing Company, 15; 129 (upd.)
Aston Villa plc, 41
Atari S.A., 9; 23 (upd.); 66 (upd.); 132 (upd.)
Athlete's Performance, Inc., 153
The Athletics Investment Group, 62
Atlanta National League Baseball Club, Inc., 43
The Atlantic Group, 23
Atom Factory, 158
Audible, Inc., 79; 159 (upd.)
Augusta National Inc., 115
Australian Baseball Federation Incorporated, 161
Autotote Corporation, 20
Avedis Zildjian Co., 38
Aztar Corporation, 13
Bad Boy Worldwide Entertainment Group, 58
Bad Robot Productions, 152
Baker & Taylor Corporation, 16; 43 (upd.)
Baldwin Piano & Organ Company, 18
Ballet Theatre Foundation, Inc., 118
Bally Total Fitness Holding Corp., 25
Baltimore Orioles L.P., 66
Barden Companies, Inc., 76
The Baseball Club of Seattle, LP, 50
The Basketball Club of Seattle, LLC, 50
BCD Holdings N.V., 141
Beggars Group, 99; 161 (upd.)
Bell Media, Inc., 126
Bell Sports Corporation, 16; 44 (upd.)
BenQ Corporation, 67
Bertelsmann A.G., IV; 15 (upd.); 43 (upd.); 91 (upd.)
Bertucci's Inc., 16
Bet365 Group Limited, 163
Big 5 Sporting Goods Corporation, 55; 150 (upd.)

Big Apple Circus, 156
Big Fish Games, Inc., 108
Big Idea Entertainment, LLC, 49; 154 (upd.)
BigBen Interactive S.A., 72
The Biltmore Company, 118
BioWare ULC, 81; 163 (upd.)
Black Diamond Equipment, Ltd., 62; 121 (upd.)
Black Rock City LLC, 142
Blair & Associates Ltd. (dba VCI Entertainment), 164
Blockbuster Inc., 9; 31 (upd.); 76 (upd.)
Blue Note Label Group, 115
Bobcats Basketball Holdings, LLC, 140
Boca Resorts, Inc., 37
Bolshoi Ballet, 156
Bonneville International Corporation, 29
Booth Creek Ski Holdings, Inc., 31
Boston Basketball Partners L.L.C., 14; 115 (upd.)
Boston Professional Hockey Association Inc., 39
Boston Sox Baseball Club Limited Partnership, 124
The Boston Symphony Orchestra Inc., 93
The Boy Scouts of America, 34; 164 (upd.)
Boyd Gaming Corporation, 43; 132 (upd.)
Boylesports Holdings Ltd., 129
Boyne USA Resorts, 71
Brass Eagle Inc., 34
Bravo Company, 114
Brillstein-Grey Entertainment, 80
British Broadcasting Corporation Ltd., 7; 21 (upd.); 89 (upd.)
The British Film Institute, 80
The British Museum, 71; 149 (upd.)
British Sky Broadcasting Group plc, 20; 60 (upd.); 139 (upd.)
Broadway Video Entertainment, 112
Brooklyn Academy of Music, 132
Brooklyn Nets Company, 145
Brunswick Corporation, III; 22 (upd.); 77 (upd.); 158 (upd.)
Buccaneers Limited Partnership, 135
Buffalo Bills, Inc., 140
Burgett, Inc., 97
Burton Snowboards Inc., 22
Busch Entertainment Corporation, 73
bwin.party digital entertainment plc, 129
C. Bechstein Pianofortefabrik AG, 96
C.F. Martin & Co., Inc., 42
C3 Presents, LLC, 157
Cablevision Systems Corporation, 7; 30 (upd.); 109 (upd.)
California Sports, Inc., 56
Callaway Golf Company, 15; 45 (upd.); 112 (upd.)
Camelot Group plc, 110
Canadian Broadcasting Corporation, 109 (upd.)
The Canadian Football League, 154
Canlan Ice Sports Corp., 105
Canterbury Park Holding Corporation, 42
Capcom Company Ltd., 83
Capital Cities/ABC Inc., II

Financial Services: Banks

Financial Services: Excluding Banks

Food Products

Mars, Incorporated, 7; 40 (upd.); 114 (upd.)
Mars Petcare US Inc., 96
Martha White Foods Inc., 104
Maruha Nichiro Holdings, Inc., 75 (upd.); 152 (upd.)
Maryland & Virginia Milk Producers Cooperative Association, Inc., 80
The Maschhoffs, 82
Massimo Zanetti Beverage Group S.p.A., 145
Mastellone Hermanos S.A., 101
Masters Gallery Foods, Inc., 160
Mastronardi Produce Limited, 141
Maui Land & Pineapple Company, Inc., 29; 100 (upd.)
Mauna Loa Macadamia Nut Corporation, 64
Maverick Ranch Association, Inc., 88
Maxfield Candy Company, 153
McCadam Cheese Company Inc., 123
McCain Foods Limited, 77
McCormick & Company, Inc., 7; 27 (upd.); 127 (upd.)
McIlhenny Company, 20; 124 (upd.)
McKee Foods Corporation, 7; 27 (upd.); 117 (upd.)
McLeod Russel India Limited, 128
Mead Johnson Nutrition Company, 84; 153 (upd.)
Medifast, Inc., 97
Meiji Dairies Corporation, II; 82 (upd.)
Meiji Holdings Co., Ltd., 139
Meiji Seika Kaisha, Ltd., II; 64 (upd.)
Menchie's Group, Inc., 148
Merisant Worldwide, Inc., 70
Mestemacher GmbH, 127
Meyer Natural Angus L.L.C., 112
Michael Foods, Inc., 25; 127 (upd.)
Michigan Turkey Producers Co-op, Inc., 115
Mid-America Dairymen, Inc., 7
Midwest Grain Products, Inc., 49
Mike-sell's Inc., 15; 131 (upd.)
Milk Specialties Company, 120
Milnot Company, 46
Mitr Phol Sugar Corporation Ltd., 142
Mizkan Group Corporation, 137
Molinos Río de la Plata S.A., 61
Monfort, Inc., 13
Monogram Food Solutions, LLC, 163
Monterey Gourmet Foods, Inc., 135
Morinaga & Co. Ltd., 61; 149 (upd.)
Morinda Holdings, Inc., 82
Morley Candy Makers, Inc., 149
Mountain Man Nut & Fruit Co., 123
Mountaire Corp., 113
Moy Park Ltd., 78
Mrchocolate.com LLC, 105
Mrs. Baird's Bakeries, 29
Mrs. Fields' Original Cookies, Inc., 27; 104 (upd.)
Mt. Olive Pickle Company, Inc., 44; 140 (upd.)
MTR Foods Pvt. Ltd., 55; 145 (upd.)
Murphy Family Farms Inc., 22
The Musco Family Olive Co., 91
Nabisco Foods Group, II; 7 (upd.)

Nantucket Allserve, Inc., 22
Nathan's Famous, Inc., 29
National Presto Industries, Inc., 16; 43 (upd.); 130 (upd.)
National Sea Products Ltd., 14
Natra S.A., 158
Natural Ovens Bakery, Inc., 72
Natural Selection Foods, 54
Naturally Fresh, Inc., 88
Nature's Path Foods, Inc., 87
Nature's Sunshine Products, Inc., 15; 102 (upd.)
Naumes, Inc., 81
Nestlé S.A., II; 7 (upd.); 28 (upd.); 71 (upd.); 148 (upd.)
New Britain Palm Oil Limited, 131
New England Confectionery Co., 15
New World Pasta Company, 53; 156 (upd.)
Newhall Land and Farming Company, 14
Newly Weds Foods, Inc., 74
Newman's Own, Inc., 37; 125 (upd.)
Nichiro Corporation, 86
Niman Ranch, Inc., 67
Nippon Meat Packers, Inc., II; 78 (upd.)
Nippon Suisan Kaisha, Ltd., II; 92 (upd.)
Nishimoto Trading Co. Ltd., 146
Nisshin Seifun Group Inc., II; 66 (upd.)
Nissin Foods Holdings Company Ltd., 75; 142 (upd.)
Norbest, Inc., 145
Nordzucker AG, 121
NORPAC Foods, Inc., 163
Norseland Inc., 120
Northern Foods plc, 10; 61 (upd.); 126 (upd.)
Northland Cranberries, Inc., 38
Nortura S.A., 153
Nurture, Inc., 159
The NutraSweet Company, 8; 107 (upd.)
Nutreco Holding N.V., 56
Nutrexpa S.A., 92
Nutriset S.A., 129
NutriSystem, Inc., 71
Oakhurst Dairy, 60
Oberto Sausage Company, Inc., 92
Ocean Beauty Seafoods, Inc., 74
Ocean Spray Cranberries, Inc., 7; 25 (upd.); 83 (upd.)
Oceana Group Ltd., 123
Odwalla Inc., 31; 104 (upd.)
OJSC Wimm-Bill-Dann Foods, 48
Olam International Ltd., 122
Old Dutch Foods, Inc., 118
Olga's Kitchen, Inc., 80
Olvea Group, 156
Omaha Steaks International Inc., 62
Omega Protein Corporation, 99
Orange Leaf Holdings LLC, 131
Oregon Freeze Dry, Inc., 74
Ore-Ida Foods Inc., 13; 78 (upd.)
Organic To Go Food Corporation, 99
Organic Valley (Coulee Region Organic Produce Pool), 53
Oriental Yeast Company Ltd., 127
Original Honey Baked Ham Company of Georgia, Inc., 153
Orkla ASA, 18; 82 (upd.); 162 (upd.)

Oscar Mayer Foods Corp., 12
OSI Group, 128
Otis Spunkmeyer, Inc., 28
Otsuka Holdings Co., Ltd., 139
Overhill Corporation, 51
Oy Karl Fazer Ab, 127
Palmer Candy Company, 80
Panrico S.A., 123
Panzani, 84
Papetti's Hygrade Egg Products, Inc., 39
Paradise, Inc., 151
Parmalat S.p.A., 50; 135 (upd.)
Patrick Cudahy Inc., 102
Paul Dischamp S.A.S., 164
Pendleton Grain Growers Inc., 64
Penford Corporation, 55
Penzeys Spices, Inc., 79
Pepperidge Farm, Incorporated, 81; 162 (upd.)
PepsiCo, Inc., I; 10 (upd.); 38 (upd.); 93 (upd.)
Perdigao SA, 52
Perdue Incorporated, 7; 23 (upd.); 119 (upd.)
Perfection Bakeries, Inc., 123
Perfetti Van Melle S.p.A., 72
Performance Food Group, 96 (upd.)
Perkins Foods Holdings Ltd., 87
Perry's Ice Cream Company Inc., 90
Pescanova S.A., 81
Pet Incorporated, 7
Petrossian Inc., 54
PEZ Candy, Inc., 38; 145 (upd.)
Philip Morris Companies Inc., 18 (upd.)
Phillips Foods, Inc., 63
Phillips Foods, Inc., 90 (upd.)
PIC International Group PLC, 24 (upd.)
Pierre's Ice Cream Company, 160
Pilgrim's Pride Corporation, 7; 23 (upd.); 90 (upd.)
The Pillsbury Company, II; 13 (upd.); 62 (upd.)
Pinguin SA/NV, 148
Pinnacle Foods Finance LLC, 126
Pioneer Food Group Ltd., 160
Pioneer Hi-Bred International, Inc., 9
Pizza Inn Holdings, Inc., 46; 138 (upd.)
Plum Organics, Inc., 155
Poore Brothers, Inc., 44
Popchips Inc., 138
PowerBar, Inc., 44 (upd.); 134 (upd.)
Precision Foods, Inc., 120
Premium Brands Holdings Corporation, 114; 140 (upd.)
Premium Standard Farms, Inc., 30
Princes Ltd., 76
The Procter & Gamble Company, III; 8 (upd.); 26 (upd.); 67 (upd.)
Prosper De Mulder Limited, 111
Provimi S.A., 80
Punch Taverns plc, 70; 151 (upd.)
Puratos S.A./NV, 92
Purina Mills, Inc., 32
Quaker Foods North America, 73 (upd.)
Quaker Oats Company, II; 12 (upd.); 34 (upd.)
Quality Chekd Dairies, Inc., 48
R.C. Bigelow, Inc., 49; 138 (upd.)

Food Services, Retailers, & Restaurants

Health, Personal & Medical Care Products

NeighborCare, Inc., 67 (upd.)
Neutrogena Corporation, 17
New Dana Perfumes Company, 37
Neways Inc., 78
Nikken Global Inc., 32
Nobel Biocare Holding AG, 119
Novo Nordisk A/S, I; 61 (upd.); 144 (upd.)
Nutraceutical International Corporation, 37; 124 (upd.)
NutriSystem, Inc., 71
Nutrition 21 Inc., 97
Nutrition for Life International Inc., 22
Obagi Medical Products, Inc., 95
Ocular Sciences, Inc., 65
OEC Medical Systems, Inc., 27
OraSure Technologies, Inc., 75
Orion HealthCorp, Inc., 164
Orion Oyj, 72
Orthofix International NV, 72
Orthovita, Inc., 119
Osteotech, Inc., 119
Otsuka Holdings Co., Ltd., 139
Parfums Givenchy S.A., 100
Patterson Dental Co., 19
Pearle Vision, Inc., 13; 115 (upd.)
Perfumania Holdings, Inc., 150
Perrigo Company, 12; 59 (upd.); 118 (upd.)
Personna American Safety Razor Company, 119 (upd.)
PhotoMedex, Inc., 154
Physician Sales & Service, Inc., 14
Physio-Control International Corp., 18
Playtex Products, Inc., 15
PolyMedica Corporation, 77
The Procter & Gamble Company, III; 8 (upd.); 26 (upd.); 67 (upd.)
Proteus Digital Health, Inc., 158
PSS World Medical, Inc., 115 (upd.)
Puritan-Bennett Corporation, 13
PZ Cussons Plc, 72; 150 (upd.)
Quest Diagnostics Inc., 26; 106 (upd.)
Quidel Corporation, 80
Reckitt Benckiser plc, II; 42 (upd.); 91 (upd.)
Redken Laboratories Inc., 84
Reliv International, Inc., 58
Remington Products Company, L.L.C., 42
ResMed, Inc., 125
Retractable Technologies, Inc., 99
Revlon Inc., III; 17 (upd.); 64 (upd.)
Roche Biomedical Laboratories, Inc., 11
Rockwell Medical Technologies, Inc., 88
Rotech Healthcare Inc., 157
S.C. Johnson & Son, Inc., III; 28 (upd.); 89 (upd.)
Safety 1st, Inc., 24
Sage Products Inc., 105
St. Jude Medical, Inc., 11; 43 (upd.); 97 (upd.)
Schering-Plough Corporation, I; 14 (upd.); 49 (upd.); 99 (upd.)
Schiff Nutrition International, Inc., 140
Sephora Holdings S.A., 82
Shaklee Corporation, 39 (upd.)
Shionogi & Co., Ltd., III; 17 (upd.); 98 (upd.)

Shiseido Company, Limited, III; 22 (upd.); 81 (upd.); 162 (upd.)
Slim-Fast Foods Company, 18; 66 (upd.)
Smith & Nephew plc, 17; 133 (upd.)
SmithKline Beecham PLC, III
SoftSheen/Carson Products, 31; 132 (upd.)
Sola International Inc., 71
Sonic Innovations Inc., 56; 142 (upd.)
SonoSite, Inc., 56; 161 (upd.)
Sonova Holding AG, 136
Spacelabs Medical, Inc., 71
Span-America Medical Systems, Inc., 147
Spenco Medical Corporation, 142
STAAR Surgical Company, 57
Starkey Laboratories, Inc., 52; 157 (upd.)
The Stephan Company, 60
STERIS Corporation, 29; 132 (upd.)
Straumann Holding AG, 79
Stryker Corporation, 11; 29 (upd.); 79 (upd.)
Summer Infant, Inc., 150
Sunrise Medical Inc., 11
Sybron International Corp., 14
Synergetics USA, Inc., 124
Syneron Medical Ltd., 91
Synthes, Inc., 93
Sysmex Corporation, 146
Tambrands Inc., 8
Tarte Cosmetics Inc., 164
Teleflex Inc., 122
Terumo Corporation, 48; 137 (upd.)
Thane International, Inc., 84
Theranos, Inc., 162
Thermo Fisher Scientific Inc., 105 (upd.)
Thoratec Corporation, 122
TomoTherapy Incorporated, 121
Tom's of Maine, Inc., 45; 125 (upd.)
Transitions Optical, Inc., 83
The Tranzonic Companies, 37
Turtle Wax, Inc., 15; 93 (upd.)
Tutogen Medical, Inc., 68
Unicharm Corporation, 84
United States Surgical Corporation, 10; 34 (upd.)
Urban Decay Cosmetics LLC, 138
USANA, Inc., 29
Utah Medical Products, Inc., 36
Varian Medical Systems, Inc., 122 (upd.)
Ventana Medical Systems, Inc., 75
VHA Inc., 53
VIASYS Healthcare, Inc., 52
Vion Food Group NV, 85
VISX, Incorporated, 30
Vitacost.com Inc., 116
Vitamin Shoppe, Inc., 60; 147 (upd.)
VNUS Medical Technologies, Inc., 103
Wahl Clipper Corporation, 86
Water Pik Technologies, Inc., 34; 83 (upd.)
Weider Nutrition International, Inc., 29
Weleda AG, 78
Wella AG, III; 48 (upd.)
Werner & Mertz GmbH, 142
West Pharmaceutical Services, Inc., 42
William Demant Holding A/S, 126
Wright & Filippis, Inc., 156
Wright Medical Group, Inc., 61

Wyeth, Inc., 50 (upd.); 118 (upd.)
Young Innovations, Inc., 160 (upd.)
Zila, Inc., 46
Zimmer Holdings, Inc., 45; 120 (upd.)
ZOLL Medical Corporation, 150

Health Care Services

Acadian Ambulance & Air Med Services, Inc., 39
Accretive Health, Inc., 150
Addus HomeCare Corporation, 135
Adventist Health, 53
Advocat Inc., 46
Allied Healthcare Products, Inc., 24
Almost Family, Inc., 93
Alterra Healthcare Corporation, 42
Amedisys, Inc., 53; 106 (upd.)
American Dental Partners Inc., 123
American Diabetes Association, 109
American Healthways, Inc., 65
American Hospital Association, 124
American Medical Alert Corporation, 103
American Medical International, Inc., III
American Medical Response, Inc., 39
AMERIGROUP Corporation, 69; 162 (upd.)
AmeriSource Health Corporation, 37 (upd.)
AmerisourceBergen Corporation, 64 (upd.); 141 (upd.)
Amil Participações S.A., 105
AmSurg Corporation, 48; 122 (upd.)
The Andrews Institute, 99
Applied Bioscience International, Inc., 10
Apria Healthcare Group Inc., 123
Ardent Health Services LLC, 114
Ascension Health, 114
Aspen Dental Management, Inc., 156
Assisted Living Concepts, Inc., 43
ATC Healthcare Inc., 64
Banner Health, 119
Baptist Health Care Corporation, 82
beBetter Networks Inc., 123
Best Doctors, Inc., 159
The Betty Ford Center at Eisenhower, 126
Beverly Enterprises, Inc., III; 16 (upd.)
Bio-Reference Laboratories, Inc., 122
Bon Secours Health System, Inc., 24
Bostwick Laboratories, Inc., 129
Bravo Health Insurance Company, Inc., 107
British United Provident Association Limited, 79; 159 (upd.)
Bronson Healthcare Group, Inc., 125
Bronx-Lebanon Hospital Center, 125
Brookdale Senior Living, 91
C.R. Bard Inc., 9; 65 (upd.)
Cancer Treatment Centers of America, Inc., 85
Capital Senior Living Corporation, 75
Cardinal Health, Inc., 18; 50 (upd.); 115 (upd.)
Caremark Rx, Inc., 10; 54 (upd.)
Catholic Health Initiatives, 91
Catholic Healthcare West, 128
Centene Corporation, 150
CHE Trinity, Inc., 163
Chemed Corporation, 13; 118 (upd.)

Hotels

Sunstone Hotel Investors Inc., 131
Super 8 Motels, Inc., 83
Thistle Hotels PLC, 54
Trusthouse Forte PLC, III
Vail Resorts, Inc., 43 (upd.)
WestCoast Hospitality Corporation, 59
Westin Hotels and Resorts Worldwide, 9;
  29 (upd.)
Whitbread PLC, I; 20 (upd.); 52 (upd.);
  97 (upd.)
Woolworths Limited, 137
Wyndham Worldwide Corporation, 99
  (upd.)
Wynn Resorts, Limited, 128
Xanterra Parks & Resorts, Inc., 133

Information Technology

3M Cogent, Inc., 151
3Com Corporation, 11; 34 (upd.); 106
  (upd.)
The 3DO Company, 43
A.B. Watley Group Inc., 45; 138 (upd.)
AboutTime Technologies, LLC, 146
Accelrys, Inc., 158
AccuWeather, Inc., 73
ActivIdentity Corporation, 135
Acxiom Corporation, 35
Adaptec, Inc., 31
Adobe Systems Inc., 10; 33 (upd.); 106
  (upd.
Advanced Internet Technologies, Inc., 119
Advanced Micro Devices, Inc., 6; 30
  (upd.); 99 (upd.)
Advanced Technology Investment
  Company LLC, 161
Affecto Plc, 151
Agence France-Presse, 34
Agilent Technologies Inc., 38; 93 (upd.)
Akamai Technologies, Inc., 71
Aladdin Knowledge Systems Ltd., 101
Aldus Corporation, 10
Alibaba.com, Ltd., 119
Alion Science and Technology
  Corporation, 128
Allen Systems Group, Inc., 59
Allied Digital Services Ltd., 119
Allscripts-Misys Healthcare Solutions Inc.,
  104
Alorica, Inc., 139
Altair Engineering, Inc., 128
AltaVista Company, 43
Altiris, Inc., 65
Amazon.com, Inc., 113 (upd.)
Amdahl Corporation, III; 14 (upd.); 40
  (upd.)
Amdocs Ltd., 47
America Online, Inc., 10; 26 (upd.)
American Business Information, Inc., 18
American Management Systems, Inc., 11
American Software Inc., 25
American Systems Corporation, 119
AMICAS, Inc., 69
Ampex Corporation, 17
Amstrad PLC, III
Analex Corporation, 74
Analog Devices, Inc., 10; 157 (upd.)
Analytic Sciences Corporation, 10
Analytical Surveys, Inc., 33

Anam Group, 23; 135 (upd.)
Ancestry.com Inc., 116
Anker BV, 53
Ansoft Corporation, 63
ANSYS, Inc., 115
Antenna Software Inc., 156
Anteon Corporation, 57
AOL Time Warner Inc., 57 (upd.)
Apple Computer, Inc., III; 6 (upd.); 77
  (upd.)
aQuantive, Inc., 81
Arbitron Inc., 38; 149 (upd.)
Ariba, Inc., 57; 139 (upd.)
Ariba, Inc., 57
Asanté Technologies, Inc., 20
Ascential Software Corporation, 59
ASI Computer Technologies, Inc., 122
AsiaInfo Holdings, Inc., 43
ASK Group, Inc., 9
Ask Jeeves, Inc., 65
ASML Holding N.V., 50; 144 (upd.)
AST Research Inc., 9
Astro-Med, Inc., 135
At Home Corporation, 43
AT&T Bell Laboratories, Inc., 13
AT&T Corporation, 29 (upd.)
AT&T Istel Ltd., 14
athenahealth, Inc., 128
Atheros Communications Inc., 119
Atos Origin S.A., 69
Attachmate Corporation, 56; 135 (upd.)
AuthenTec, Inc., 124
Autodesk, Inc., 10; 89 (upd.)
Autologic Information International, Inc.,
  20
Automatic Data Processing, Inc., III; 9
  (upd.); 47 (upd.); 126 (upd.)
Automattic Inc., 148
Autotote Corporation, 20
Avantium Technologies BV, 79
AVG Technologies N.V., 148
Avid Technology Inc., 38
Avocent Corporation, 65
Aydin Corp., 19
Baan Company, 25
Baidu.com Inc., 95
Baker & Taylor, Inc., 122 (upd.)
Baltimore Technologies Plc, 42
Bankrate, Inc., 83
Banyan Systems Inc., 25
Battelle Memorial Institute, Inc., 10; 140
  (upd.)
Bazaarvoice, Inc., 140
BBN Corp., 19
BEA Systems, Inc., 36
Bell and Howell Company, 9; 29 (upd.)
Bell Industries, Inc., 47
Billing Concepts, Inc., 26; 72 (upd.)
Blackbaud, Inc., 85
Blackboard Inc., 89
Blizzard Entertainment, 78
Blogmusik SAS, 157
Bloomberg L.P., 21; 126 (upd.)
Blue Martini Software, Inc., 59
BMC Software, Inc., 55; 162 (upd.)
Bolt Technology Corporation, 146
Boole & Babbage, Inc., 25
Booz Allen Hamilton Inc., 10; 101 (upd.)

Borland International, Inc., 9
Bowne & Co., Inc., 23
Brightcove Inc., 151
Brite Voice Systems, Inc., 20
BroadSoft, Inc., 150
Brocade Communications Systems Inc.,
  106
Broderbund Software, 13; 29 (upd.)
Brooks Automation Inc., 145
BTG, Inc., 45
Bull S.A., 43 (upd.)
The Burton Group plc, V
Business Objects S.A., 25
CA Inc., 116
CACI International Inc., 21; 72 (upd.);
  155 (upd.)
Cadence Design Systems, Inc., 11
Caere Corporation, 20
Cahners Business Information, 43
CalComp Inc., 13
Callidus Software Inc., 156
Cambridge Technology Partners, Inc., 36
Candle Corporation, 64
Canon Inc., III; 18 (upd.); 79 (upd.)
Cap Gemini S.A., 37; 145 (upd.)
Captaris, Inc., 89
Carbonite, Inc., 141
CareerBuilder, Inc., 93
CareTech Solutions, 128
Caribiner International, Inc., 24
Cass Information Systems Inc., 100
Catalina Marketing Corporation, 18; 150
  (upd.)
C-Cube Microsystems, Inc., 37
CDC Corporation, 71
CDW Computer Centers, Inc., 16
Cerner Corporation, 16
CGI Group Inc., 137
ChaCha Search, Inc., 152
Check Point Software Technologies Ltd.,
  119
CheckFree Corporation, 81
Chegg Inc., 144
Cheyenne Software, Inc., 12
Chickasaw Nation Industries, Inc., 155
China UnionPay, 161
CHIPS and Technologies, Inc., 9
Ciber, Inc., 18
Cincom Systems Inc., 15
Cirrus Logic, Incorporated, 11
Cisco Systems, Inc., 11; 77 (upd.)
Cisco-Linksys LLC, 86
Citizen Watch Co., Ltd., III; 21 (upd.);
  81 (upd.)
Citrix Systems, Inc., 44; 131 (upd.)
ClickSoftware Technologies Ltd., 158
CMGI, Inc., 76
CNET Networks, Inc., 47
Cogent Communications Group, Inc., 55
Cognizant Technology Solutions
  Corporation, 59; 139 (upd.)
Cognos Inc., 44
Collabera, Inc., 150
Commodore International Ltd., 7
CommVault Systems, Inc., 144
Compagnie des Machines Bull S.A., III
Compaq Computer Corporation, III; 6
  (upd.); 26 (upd.)

Insurance

Andreas Stihl AG & Co. KG, 16; 59
    (upd.)
ANDRITZ AG, 51; 147 (upd.)
Apator S.A., 153
Apogee Enterprises, Inc., 163 (upd.)
Applica Incorporated, 43 (upd.)
Applied Extrusion Technologies Inc., 126
Applied Films Corporation, 48
Applied Materials, Inc., 10; 46 (upd.)
AptarGroup, Inc., 69
Aqua Lung International, 141
Aquatic Company, 121
Arc International, 76; 157 (upd.)
Arçelik A.S., 100
Arctic Cat Inc., 16; 40 (upd.); 96 (upd.)
AREVA NP, 90 (upd.)
Ariens Company, 48
The Aristotle Corporation, 62
Armor All Products Corp., 16
Armstrong Holdings, Inc., III; 22 (upd.);
    81 (upd.)
Armstrong World Industries, Inc., 162
    (upd.)
Art's Way Manufacturing Co., Inc., 101
Asahi Glass Company Ltd., III; 48 (upd.);
    168 (upd.)
Ashley Furniture Industries, Inc., 35; 122
    (upd.)
Assa Abloy AB, 112
Associated Materials, LLC, 130
Asti Corporation, 153
Atlantis Plastics, Inc., 85
Atlas Copco AB, III; 28 (upd.); 85 (upd.)
Atrion Corporation, 163
Atrium Companies, Inc., 121
Atwood Mobil Products, 53
Austin Powder Company, 76
AXT, Inc., 129
AZZ Incorporated, 93
B&W Group Ltd., 126
B.J. Alan Co., Inc., 67
The Babcock & Wilcox Company, 82
Badger Meter, Inc., 22; 130 (upd.)
Baldor Electric Company, 21; 97 (upd.)
Baldwin Technology Company, Inc., 25;
    107 (upd.)
Ball Watch Company SA, 148
Ballantyne Strong, Inc., 27; 146 (upd.)
Bally Manufacturing Corporation, III
Baltimore Aircoil Company, Inc., 66
Bandai Co., Ltd., 55
Barmag AG, 39
Barnes Group Inc., 13; 69 (upd.)
Barry-Wehmiller Companies, Inc., 90
Bassett Furniture Industries, Inc., 18; 95
    (upd.)
Bath Iron Works Corporation, 12; 36
    (upd.); 136 (upd.)
Baxi Group Ltd., 96
BCP Imports, LLC, 120
Beaulieu of America, L.L.C., 121
Beckman Instruments, Inc., 14
Behr Process Corporation, 115
BEI Technologies, Inc., 65
Bekaert S.A./N.V., 90
Bel-Art Products Inc., 117
Belleek Pottery Ltd., 71
Bemis Manufacturing Company, 148

Benjamin Moore & Co., 13; 38 (upd.);
    115 (upd.)
Benninger AG, 107
Berger Bros Company, 62
Bernina Holding AG, 47
Berwick Offray, LLC, 70
Bianchi International (d/b/a Gregory
    Mountain Products), 76
BIC Corporation, 8; 23 (upd.)
The Bing Group, 60
Binks Sames Corporation, 21
Binney & Smith Inc., 25
Bissell Homecare, Inc., 9; 30 (upd.); 147
    (upd.)
The Black & Decker Corporation, III; 20
    (upd.); 67 (upd.)
Blodgett Holdings, Inc., 61 (upd.)
Blount International, Inc., 12; 48 (upd.);
    163 (upd.)
BLRT Grupp A.S., 117
Blyth, Inc., 18; 74 (upd.); 152 (upd.)
Bodum Design Group AG, 47
The Boler Company, 127
Bombril S.A., 111
Borrego Solar Systems, Inc., 111
Borroughs Corporation, 110
Boston Scientific Corporation, 37; 77
    (upd.); 152 (upd.)
Boston Whaler, Inc., 120
Boyd Specialty Sleep, 148
The Boyds Collection, Ltd., 29; 151
    (upd.)
BPB plc, 83
Bradley Corporation, 118
Brady Corporation, 78 (upd.)
Brammer PLC, 77
Breeze-Eastern Corporation, 95
Brenco, Inc., 104
Bridgeport Machines, Inc., 17
Bridgewater Interiors, LLC, 149
Briggs & Stratton Corporation, 8; 27
    (upd.)
BRIO AB, 24; 103 (upd.)
BRITA GmbH, 112
Broan-NuTone LLC, 104
Brother Industries, Ltd., 14
Brown & Sharpe Manufacturing Co., 23
Brown Jordan International Inc., 74
    (upd.)
Broyhill Furniture Industries, Inc., 10
Bruker Corporation, 113
Brunswick Corporation, III; 22 (upd.); 77
    (upd.); 158 (upd.)
BSH Bosch und Siemens Hausgeräte
    GmbH, 67
BTR Siebe plc, 27
BTU International, Inc., 160
Bucher Industries AG, 134
Buck Knives Inc., 48; 147 (upd.)
Buckeye Technologies, Inc., 42
Bulgari S.p.A., 20; 106 (upd.)
Bulova Corporation, 13; 41 (upd.)
Bundy Corporation, 17
Bunn-O-Matic Corporation, 147
Burelle S.A., 23
Bush Industries, Inc., 20; 147 (upd.)
Butler Manufacturing Company, 12; 62
    (upd.)

California Cedar Products Company, 58
Cameron International Corporation, 110
Campbell Scientific, Inc., 51
Canam Group Inc., 114
CandyRific, LLC, 163
Cannondale Corporation, 21
Canon Inc., III; 18 (upd.); 79 (upd.); 158
    (upd.)
Capewell Components Holding Company,
    160
Capstone Turbine Corporation, 75
Caradon plc, 20 (upd.)
The Carbide/Graphite Group, Inc., 40
Carbo PLC, 67 (upd.)
Cardo AB, 53
Carl Geringhoff Vertriebsgesellschaft mbH
    & Co. KG, 144
Carrier Corporation, 7; 69 (upd.)
Cascade Corporation, 65
Catalina Lighting, Inc., 43
CE Franklin Ltd., 138
Cendres+Métaux Holding S.A., 153
Central Sprinkler Corporation, 29
Centuri Corporation, 54
Cepheid, 77; 161 (upd.)
Cerro Wire LLC, 143
Cervélo Cycles Inc., 134
Champion Enterprises, Inc., 17
Chance Rides Manufacturing, Inc., 162
The Character Group plc, 140
Charisma Brands LLC, 74
The Charles Machine Works, Inc., 64
Chart Industries, Inc., 21; 96 (upd.)
Chatham Created Gems, Inc., 123
Chemring Group plc, 113
Chittenden & Eastman Company, 58
Chris-Craft Corporation, 9; 31 (upd.); 80
    (upd.); 162 (upd.)
Christian Dalloz SA, 40
Christofle SA, 40
Chromcraft Revington, Inc., 15
Chugoku Marine Paints Ltd., 145
Cincinnati Lamb Inc., 72
Cincinnati Milacron Inc., 12
Cinemeccanica SpA, 78
Cinram International Income Fund, 43;
    136 (upd.)
Circon Corporation, 21
CIRCOR International, Inc., 115
Citizen Watch Co., Ltd., III; 21 (upd.);
    81 (upd.)
Clarion Technologies, Inc., 146
Clark Associates, Inc., 142
Clark Equipment Company, 8
The Clark Grave Vault Company, 142
Clean Diesel Technologies Inc., 143
Clopay Corporation, 100
ClosetMaid Corporation, 136
Cloverdale Paint Inc., 115
Club Car, LLC, 134
Cognex Corporation, 76
Colfax Corporation, 58
Colt's Manufacturing Company, LLC, 12;
    140 (upd.)
Columbia Manufacturing, Inc., 114
Columbus McKinnon Corporation, 37
Compagnie Financière Richemont S.A.,
    50; 137 (upd.)

Materials

Mining & Metals

Nonprofit & Philanthropic Organizations

Paper & Forestry

Associated Wholesalers Inc., 153
Au Printemps S.A., V
Audio King Corporation, 24
Aurora Wholesalers, LLC, 140
Auto Value Associates, Inc., 25
Autobytel Inc., 47
AutoNation, Inc., 50; 114 (upd.)
AutoTrader.com, L.L.C., 91
AutoZone, Inc., 9; 31 (upd.); 110 (upd.)
AVA AG (Allgemeine Handelsgesellschaft der Verbraucher AG), 33
Aveve S.A./NV, 123
Aviall, Inc., 73; 150 (upd.)
Aviation Sales Company, 41
AWB Ltd., 56
B&D Industrial, Inc., 136
B & H Foto and Electronics Corporation, 126
B&B Equipment and Supply Inc., 163
B. Dalton Bookseller Inc., 25
B2W Companhia Global do Varejo, 117
Babbage's, Inc., 10
Baby Superstore, Inc., 15
Baccarat, 24
Bachman's Inc., 22
Bailey Nurseries, Inc., 57
Baker & Taylor, Inc., 122 (upd.)
Ball Horticultural Company, 78
Balsam Brands LLC, 164
Banana Republic Inc., 25
Barnes & Noble, Inc., 10; 30 (upd.); 75 (upd.)
Barnes & Noble College Booksellers, Inc., 115
Barnett Inc., 28
Barneys New York Inc., 28; 104 (upd.)
Barrett-Jackson Auction Company L.L.C., 88
Barrow Industries, Inc., 123
Basketville, Inc., 117
Bass Pro Shops, Inc., 42; 118 (upd.)
Baumax AG, 75
BB&R Limited, 122
Beacon Roofing Supply, Inc., 75; 163 (upd.)
Beate Uhse AG, 96
bebe stores, inc., 31; 103 (upd.)
Bed Bath & Beyond Inc., 13; 41 (upd.); 109 (upd.)
Belk, Inc., V; 19 (upd.); 72 (upd.); 152 (upd.)
Belnick, Inc., 155
Ben Bridge Jeweler, Inc., 60; 143 (upd.)
Benetton Group S.p.A., 10; 67 (upd.)
Berean Christian Stores, 96
Bergdorf Goodman Inc., 52
Bergen Brunswig Corporation, V; 13 (upd.)
Bernard Chaus, Inc., 27
Best Buy Co., Inc., 9; 23 (upd.); 63 (upd.); 141 (upd.)
Bestseller A/S, 90
Beter Bed Holding N.V., 123
Bhs plc, 17
Big A Drug Stores Inc., 79
Big Dog Holdings, Inc., 45
Big Lots, Inc., 50; 110 (upd.)
Big O Tires, Inc., 20

Bijoux Terner, LLC, 160
Bilia AB, 145
Birks & Mayors Inc., 112
Birthdays Ltd., 70
Blacks Leisure Group plc, 39
Blair Corporation, 25; 31 (upd.)
Blish-Mize Co., 95
Blokker Holding B.V., 84
Bloomingdale's Inc., 12
Blue Nile, Inc., 61; 121 (upd.)
Blue Square Israel Ltd., 41
Bluefly, Inc., 60; 147 (upd.)
BlueLinx Holdings Inc., 97
Bob's Discount Furniture LLC, 104
The Bombay Company, Inc., 10; 71 (upd.)
The Bon Marché, Inc., 23
The Bon-Ton Stores, Inc., 16; 50 (upd.)
Booker Cash & Carry Ltd., 68 (upd.)
Books-A-Million, Inc., 14; 41 (upd.); 96 (upd.)
Bookspan, 86
The Boots Company PLC, V; 24 (upd.)
Borders Group, Inc., 15; 43 (upd.)
Borsheim's Jewelry Company, Inc., 154
Boscov's Department Store, Inc., 31
Bossini International Holdings Ltd., 164
Boston Proper, Inc., 131
Boulanger S.A., 102
Bowlin Travel Centers, Inc., 99
Boyd Specialty Sleep, 148
The Boyds Collection, Ltd., 29; 151 (upd.)
Bradlees Discount Department Store Company, 12
Brake Bros Ltd., 45; 149 (upd.)
Bricorama S.A., 68
Briscoe Group Ltd., 110
Brodart Company, 84
Broder Bros., Co., 38; 136 (upd.)
Brooks Brothers Inc., 22; 115 (upd.)
Brookstone, Inc., 18; 147 (upd.)
The Buckle, Inc., 18; 115 (upd.)
Buffalo Exchange Ltd., 153
Buhrmann NV, 41
Build-A-Bear Workshop, Inc., 62; 129 (upd.)
Bunzl plc, IV; 31 (upd.); 137 (upd.)
Burdines, Inc., 60
Burkhart Dental, Inc., 121
Burlington Coat Factory Warehouse Corporation, 10; 60 (upd.); 130 (upd.)
Buttrey Food & Drug Stores Co., 18
buy.com, Inc., 46
C&A, V; 40 (upd.); 136 (upd.)
C&J Clark International Ltd., 52
C. Kersten en Co. N.V., 157
C.C. Filson Company, 130
CA Immobilien Anlagen AG, 142
Cabela's Incorporated, 26; 68 (upd.); 155 (upd.)
Cablevision Electronic Instruments, Inc., 32
Caché, Inc., 124 (upd.)
Cache Incorporated, 30
Cactus S.A., 90
Caldor Inc., 12
Calendar Holdings, LLC, 149

Calloway's Nursery, Inc., 51
Camaïeu S.A., 72
Camelot Music, Inc., 26
Campeau Corporation, V
Campmor, Inc., 104
Campo Electronics, Appliances & Computers, Inc., 16
Car Toys, Inc., 67
Carol Wright Gifts Inc., 131
The Carphone Warehouse Group PLC, 83
Carrefour SA, 10; 27 (upd.); 64 (upd.); 137 (upd.)
Carson Pirie Scott & Company, 15
Carter Hawley Hale Stores, Inc., V
Carter Lumber Company, 45
Cartier Monde, 29
Casas Bahia Comercial Ltda., 75
Casey's General Stores, Inc., 19; 83 (upd.)
Castorama-Dubois Investissements SCA, 104 (upd.)
Castro Model Ltd., 86
Casual Corner Group, Inc., 43
Casual Male Retail Group, Inc., 52
Catherines Stores Corporation, 15
CDS (Superstores International) Limited, 126
CDW Computer Centers, Inc., 16
Celebrate Express, Inc., 70
Celebrity, Inc., 22
CellStar Corporation, 83
Cencosud S.A., 69; 137 (upd.)
Central European Distribution Corporation, 75
Central Garden & Pet Company, 23
Central Retail Corporation, 110
Century Tokyo Leasing Corporation, 158
Cenveo, Inc., 71 (upd.); 148 (upd.)
Chadwick's of Boston, Ltd., 29
Charlotte Russe Holding, Inc., 35; 90 (upd.)
charming charlie, Inc., 155
Charming Shoppes, Inc., 38
Chas. Levy Company LLC, 60
Chegg Inc., 144
Cherry Brothers LLC, 105
Chesbro Music Co., 142
Chiasso Acquisition LLC, 53; 145 (upd.)
The Children's Place Retail Stores, Inc., 37; 86 (upd.)
China Nepstar Chain Drugstore Ltd., 97
Chongqing Department Store Company Ltd., 105
Christian Dior S.A., 49 (upd.)
Christopher & Banks Corporation, 42
Cifra, S.A. de C.V., 12
Circuit City Stores, Inc., 9; 29 (upd.); 65 (upd.)
Clare Rose Inc., 68
Clinton Cards plc, 39; 130 (upd.)
The Clothestime, Inc., 20
CML Group, Inc., 10
Coach, Inc., 45 (upd.); 99 (upd.)
Coast Distribution System, Inc., 140
Coborn's, Inc., 30
Coflusa S.A., 120
Coinmach Laundry Corporation, 20
Coldwater Creek Inc., 21; 74 (upd.); 152 (upd.)

Furniture Row, LLC, 136
Future Shop Ltd., 62; 151 (upd.)
G&K Holding S.A., 95
G.I. Joe's, Inc., 30
Gadzooks, Inc., 18
Galeries Lafayette S.A., V; 23 (upd.)
Galiform PLC, 103
Gallery Furniture Inc., 149
Galyan's Trading Company, Inc., 47
GameFly, Inc., 137
Gander Mountain, Inc., 20; 90 (upd.)
Gantos, Inc., 17
The Gap, Inc., V; 18 (upd.); 55 (upd.);
    117 (upd.)
Garden Ridge Corporation, 27
Gart Sports Company, 24
Gazelle, Inc., 148
GEHE AG, 27
General Binding Corporation, 10; 73
    (upd.)
General Host Corporation, 12
General Parts, Inc., 122
Genesco Inc., 17; 84 (upd.)
Genovese Drug Stores, Inc., 18
Genuine Parts Company, 45 (upd.)
Gerald Stevens, Inc., 37
Gerhard D. Wempe KG, 88
GIB Group, V; 26 (upd.)
Gibbs and Dandy plc, 74
GiFi S.A., 74
Glentel Inc., 122
Global Custom Commerce, Inc., 163
Global Imaging Systems, Inc., 73
Globex Utilidades S.A., 103
Globus SB-Warenhaus Holding GmbH &
    Co. KG, 120
Gold Standard Enterprises, Inc., 148
Golfsmith International Holdings, Inc.,
    120
GOME Electrical Appliances Holding
    Ltd., 87; 153 (upd.)
The Good Guys, Inc., 10; 30 (upd.)
Goody's Family Clothing, Inc., 20; 64
    (upd.)
Gordmans Stores, Inc., 74; 150 (upd.)
Gottschalks, Inc., 18; 91 (upd.)
Graff Diamonds International Limited,
    144
Grafton Group plc, 104
Grand Piano & Furniture Company, 72
GrandVision S.A., 43
The Great Universal Stores plc, V; 19
    (upd.)
Griffin Land & Nurseries, Inc., 43
Grossman's Inc., 13
Groupe Alain Manoukian, 55
Groupe Castorama-Dubois
    Investissements, 23
Groupe Go Sport S.A., 39
Groupe Lapeyre S.A., 33
Groupe Monnoyeur, 72
Groupe Zannier S.A., 35
Grow Biz International, Inc., 18
Grupo Casa Saba, S.A. de C.V., 39
Grupo Elektra, S.A. de C.V., 39; 144
    (upd.)
Grupo Eroski, 64

Grupo Gigante, S.A.B. de C.V., 34; 140
    (upd.)
Grupo Martins, 104
Grupo Sanborns, S.A. de C.V., 107 (upd.)
Gruppo Coin S.p.A., 41
GS Holdings Corp., 135
GSC Enterprises, Inc., 86
GT Bicycles, 26
GTSI Corp., 57
Guilbert S.A., 42
Guitar Center, Inc., 29; 68 (upd.)
GUS plc, 47 (upd.)
H&M Hennes & Mauritz AB, 29; 98
    (upd.)
Hahn Automotive Warehouse, Inc., 24
Hajoca Corporation, 131
Hale-Halsell Company, 60
Half Price Books, Records, Magazines
    Inc., 37
Halfords Group plc, 110
Hallmark Cards, Inc., IV; 16 (upd.); 40
    (upd.); 87 (upd.)
Hammacher Schlemmer & Company Inc.,
    21; 72 (upd.)
Hancock Fabrics, Inc., 18; 129 (upd.)
Hankyu Department Stores, Inc., V; 62
    (upd.)
Hanover Compressor Company, 59
Hanover Direct, Inc., 36
Happychic S.A., 142
Harbor Freight Tools USA, Inc., 152
Harold's Stores, Inc., 22
Harrods Holdings Ltd., 47; 154 (upd.)
Harry Winston Inc., 45; 104 (upd.)
Harsco Corporation, 8; 105 (upd.)
Haruyama Trading Company Limited,
    150
Harvey Norman Holdings Ltd., 56; 136
    (upd.)
Hästens Sängar AB, 121
Hastings Entertainment, Inc., 29; 104
    (upd.)
Haverty Furniture Companies, Inc., 31;
    136 (upd.)
Hayneedle Incorporated, 116
Headlam Group plc, 95
Hechinger Company, 12
Heilig-Meyers Company, 14; 40 (upd.)
Heinrich Deichmann-Schuhe GmbH &
    Co. KG, 88
Helzberg Diamonds, 40; 156 (upd.)
HEMA B.V., 111
Hengdeli Holdings Ltd., 127
Henry Modell & Company Inc., 32; 135
    (upd.)
Hensley & Company, 64; 146 (upd.)
Hertie Waren- und Kaufhaus GmbH, V
hhgregg Inc., 98
Highsmith Inc., 60
Hills Stores Company, 13
Hines Horticulture, Inc., 49
HMV Group plc, 59
Hobby Lobby Stores Inc., 80; 163 (upd.)
The Hockey Company, 34; 70 (upd.)
Holiday Companies, 120
Holiday RV Superstores, Incorporated, 26
Holland & Barrett Retail Limited, 118

The Home Depot, Inc., V; 18 (upd.); 97
    (upd.)
Home Hardware Stores Ltd., 62
Home Interiors & Gifts, Inc., 55
Home Product Center plc, 104
Home Retail Group plc, 91; 153 (upd.)
Home Shopping Network, Inc., V; 25
    (upd.)
HomeBase, Inc., 33 (upd.)
Hornbach Holding AG, 98
Hot Topic Inc., 33; 86 (upd.); 156 (upd.)
House of Fabrics, Inc., 21
House of Fraser Ltd., 45; 159 (upd.)
Houston Wire & Cable Company, 97
HSN, 64 (upd.)
Hudson's Bay Company, V; 25 (upd.); 83
    (upd.)
The Hut Group Ltd., 149
Huttig Building Products, Inc., 73
Hy-Vee, Inc., 36; 120 (upd.)
Ideal Shopping Direct PLC, 131
Ihr Platz GmbH + Company KG, 77
IKEA International A/S, V; 26 (upd.)
InaCom Corporation, 13
Inchcape PLC, III; 16 (upd.); 50 (upd.);
    133 (upd.)
Indigo Books & Music Inc., 58; 134
    (upd.)
Ingram Micro Inc., 52; 157 (upd.)
Insight Enterprises, Inc., 18
Interbond Corporation of America, 101
Intermix Media, Inc., 83
Intimate Brands, Inc., 24
Intres B.V., 82
Isetan Company Limited, V; 36 (upd.)
Isetan Mitsukoshi Holdings Ltd., 114
    (upd.)
Ito-Yokado Co., Ltd., V; 42 (upd.)
It's Greek to Me, Inc., 159
J&R Electronics Inc., 26
J.A. Riggs Tractor Co., 131
J. Baker, Inc., 31
J. C. Penney Company, Inc., V; 18 (upd.);
    43 (upd.); 91 (upd.)
J. Front Retailing Co., Ltd., 149 (upd.)
The J. Jill Group Inc., 35; 90 (upd.)
J.L. Hammett Company, 72
J. W. Pepper and Son Inc., 86
Jack Schwartz Shoes, Inc., 18
Jacobson Stores Inc., 21
Jalate Inc., 25
James Beattie plc, 43
James Richardson Corporation Proprietary
    Ltd., 138
JAND, Inc., 152
Jay Jacobs, Inc., 15
Jennifer Convertibles, Inc., 31
Jetro Cash & Carry Enterprises Inc., 38
Jewett-Cameron Trading Company, Ltd.,
    89
JG Industries, Inc., 15
JJB Sports plc, 32
JM Smith Corporation, 100
Jo-Ann Stores, Inc., 72 (upd.)
Joe's Sports & Outdoor, 98 (upd.)
John Lewis Partnership plc, V; 42 (upd.);
    99 (upd.)
Jordan-Kitt Music Inc., 86

W.S. Badcock Corporation, 107
W.W. Grainger, Inc., V; 26 (upd.); 68
  (upd.); 133 (upd.)
Waban Inc., 13
Wacoal Corp., 25
Waldenbooks, 17; 86 (upd.)
Walgreen Co., V; 20 (upd.); 65 (upd.);
  133 (upd.)
Wall Drug Store, Inc., 40
Wal-Mart de Mexico, S.A. de C.V., 35
  (upd.)
Wal-Mart Stores, Inc., V; 8 (upd.); 26
  (upd.); 63 (upd.); 141 (upd.)
Walter E. Smithe Furniture, Inc., 105
The Warehouse Group Limited, 125
Warners' Stellian Inc., 67
Waterstone's Booksellers Ltd., 131
Watsco Inc., 134 (upd.)
WAXIE Sanitary Supply, 100
Weiner's Stores, Inc., 33
West Marine, Inc., 17; 90 (upd.)
The Wet Seal, Inc., 18; 70 (upd.); 156
  (upd.)
Weyco Group, Incorporated, 32
WH Smith PLC, V; 42 (upd.); 126 (upd.)
The White House, Inc., 60
Whitehall Jewellers, Inc., 82 (upd.)
Wickes Inc., V; 25 (upd.)
Wilco Farm Stores, 93
Wilkinson Hardware Stores Ltd., 80
William Doyle Galleries, Inc., 134
Williams Scotsman, Inc., 65; 163 (upd.)
Williams-Sonoma, Inc., 17; 44 (upd.);
  103 (upd.)
The Willis Music Company, 156
The Wills Group, Inc., 138
Wilsons The Leather Experts Inc., 21; 58
  (upd.)
Wilton Products, Inc., 97
WinCo Foods Inc., 60; 159 (upd.)
Windstream Corporation, 83
Wine.com, Inc., 126
Winmark Corporation, 74
WinWholesale Inc., 131
Wolohan Lumber Co., 19
Wolverine World Wide, Inc., 59 (upd.)
Woolworth Corporation, V; 20 (upd.)
Woolworths Group plc, 83
Woolworths Limited, 137
Woot, Inc., 118
World Duty Free Americas, Inc., 29
  (upd.)
X5 Retail Group N.V., 162
Yamada Denki Co., Ltd., 85
The Yankee Candle Company, Inc., 37
Yingli Green Energy Holding Company
  Limited, 103
Younkers, 76 (upd.)
Younkers, Inc., 19
Z Gallerie, Inc., 141
Zale Corporation, 16; 40 (upd.); 91
  (upd.)
Zany Brainy, Inc., 31
Zappos.com, Inc., 73; 147 (upd.)
Zara International, Inc., 83
Ziebart International Corporation, 30
Zion's Cooperative Mercantile Institution,
  33

Zipcar, Inc., 92
Zones, Inc., 67
Zulily, Inc., 155
Zumiez, Inc., 77

Rubber & Tires
Aeroquip Corporation, 16
AirBoss of America Corporation, 108
Avon Rubber p.l.c., 108
Bandag, Inc., 19
The BFGoodrich Company, V; 19 (upd.)
Bridgestone Corporation, V; 21 (upd.); 59
  (upd.); 118 (upd.)
Canadian Tire Corporation, Limited, 71
  (upd.); 148 (upd.)
Carlisle Companies Incorporated, 8
Compagnie Générale des Établissements
  Michelin, V; 42 (upd.); 117 (upd.)
Continental AG, V; 56 (upd.); 130 (upd.)
Continental General Tire Corp., 23
Cooper Tire & Rubber Company, 8; 23
  (upd.); 121 (upd.)
Day International, Inc., 84
Elementis plc, 40 (upd.)
General Tire, Inc., 8
The Goodyear Tire & Rubber Company,
  V; 20 (upd.); 75 (upd.); 155 (upd.)
Hankook Tire Company Ltd., 105
The Kelly-Springfield Tire Company, 8
Kumho Tire Company Ltd., 105
Les Schwab Tire Centers, 50; 117 (upd.)
Myers Industries, Inc., 19; 96 (upd.)
Nokian Tyres Plc, 126
Pirelli & C. S.p.A., V; 15 (upd.); 158
  (upd.)
Rent-a-Wheel, Inc., 152
Safeskin Corporation, 18
Sumitomo Rubber Industries, Ltd., V; 107
  (upd.)
Tillotson Corp., 15
Treadco, Inc., 19
Trelleborg AB, 93
Ube Industries, Ltd., III; 38 (upd.)
The Yokohama Rubber Company,
  Limited, V; 19 (upd.); 91 (upd.)

Telecommunications
4Kids Entertainment Inc., 59
A.S. Eesti Mobiltelefon, 117
A.H. Belo Corporation, 30 (upd.)
Abertis Infraestructuras, S.A., 65; 139
  (upd.)
Abril S.A., 95
Acme-Cleveland Corp., 13
ADC Telecommunications, Inc., 10; 89
  (upd.)
Adelphia Communications Corporation,
  17; 52 (upd.)
Adtran, Inc., 22; 147 (upd.)
Advanced Fibre Communications, Inc., 63
AEI Music Network Inc., 35
Aeroflex Holding Corporation, 128
AirTouch Communications, 11
Al Jazeera Media Network, 159 (upd.)
Alaska Communications Systems Group,
  Inc., 89
Albtelecom Sh. a, 111
Alcatel S.A., 36 (upd.)

Alcatel-Lucent, 109 (upd.)
Allbritton Communications Company,
  105
Alliance Atlantis Communications Inc., 39
ALLTEL Corporation, 6; 46 (upd.)
América Móvil, S.A. de C.V., 80; 158
  (upd.)
American Tower Corporation, 33; 144
  (upd.)
Ameritech Corporation, V; 18 (upd.)
Amper S.A., 153
Amstrad plc, 48 (upd.)
Anaren, Inc., 33; 128 (upd.)
AO VimpelCom, 48
AOL Time Warner Inc., 57 (upd.)
Arch Wireless, Inc., 39
ARD, 41
Aricent Group, 154
ARINC Inc., 98
ARRIS Group, Inc., 89
Ascent Media Corporation, 107
Ascom AG, 9
Aspect Telecommunications Corporation,
  22
Astral Media Inc., 126
Asurion Corporation, 83
AT&T Inc., V; 29 (upd.); 68 (upd.); 137
  (upd.)
AT&T Bell Laboratories, Inc., 13
AT&T Wireless Services, Inc., 54 (upd.)
Atlantic Tele-Network, 119
Avaya Inc., 104
Axiata Group Bhd, 164 (upd.)
Basin Electric Power Cooperative, 103
BCE Inc., V; 44 (upd.); 133 (upd.)
Beasley Broadcast Group, Inc., 51
Belgacom, 6
Bell Atlantic Corporation, V; 25 (upd.)
Bell Canada, 6
Bell Media, Inc., 126
BellSouth Corporation, V; 29 (upd.)
Belo Corporation, 98 (upd.)
Bertelsmann A.G., IV; 15 (upd.); 43
  (upd.); 91 (upd.)
BET Holdings, Inc., 18
Bezeq The Israel Telecommunication
  Corporation Ltd., 150
Bharti Airtel Limited, 128
Bharti Tele-Ventures Limited, 75
BHC Communications, Inc., 26
Birch Communications, Inc., 146
Blackfoot Telecommunications Group, 60
Blonder Tongue Laboratories, Inc., 48;
  132 (upd.)
Bogen Communications International,
  Inc., 62; 151 (upd.)
Boingo Wireless, Inc., 139
Bonneville International Corporation, 29;
  151 (upd.)
Bouygues S.A., I; 24 (upd.); 97 (upd.)
Brasil Telecom Participações S.A., 57
Brightpoint Inc., 18; 106 (upd.)
Brite Voice Systems, Inc., 20
British Broadcasting Corporation Ltd., 7;
  21 (upd.); 89 (upd.)
British Columbia Telephone Company, 6
British Telecommunications plc, V; 15
  (upd.)

Textiles & Apparel

Waste Services

Geographic Index

Albania

Algeria

Andorra

Angola

Argentina

Armenia

Australia

Ube Industries, Ltd., III; 38 (upd.); 111 (upd.)
ULVAC, Inc., 80
Unicharm Corporation, 84
Uniden Corporation, 98
Unitika Ltd., V; 53 (upd.)
Uny Group Holdings Co., Ltd., V; 49 (upd.); 144 (upd.)
Ushio Inc., 91
Victor Company of Japan, Limited, II; 26 (upd.); 83 (upd.)
Wacoal Corp., 25
West Japan Railway Co., 138
Yamada Denki Co., Ltd., 85
Yamaha Corporation, III; 16 (upd.); 40 (upd.); 99 (upd.)
Yamaichi Securities Company, Limited, II
Yamato Transport Co. Ltd., V; 49 (upd.)
Yamazaki Baking Co., Ltd., 58; 156 (upd.)
The Yasuda Fire and Marine Insurance Company, Limited, III
The Yasuda Mutual Life Insurance Company, III; 39 (upd.)
The Yasuda Trust and Banking Company, Ltd., II; 17 (upd.)
Yazaki Corporation, 150
The Yokohama Rubber Company, Limited, V; 19 (upd.); 91 (upd.)
Yoshinoya D & C Company Ltd., 88
Zojirushi Corporation, 125

Jordan

Arab Potash Company, 85
Hikma Pharmaceuticals Ltd., 102
Munir Sukhtian Group, 104
Nuqul Group of Companies, 102
Royal Jordanian Airlines Company PLC, 133
KazMunayGas JSC, 156

Kenya

Bamburi Cement Limited, 116
East Africa Breweries Limited, 116
East African Breweries Ltd., 138
Equity Bank Limited, 116
Kenya Airways Limited, 89
Kenya Power and Lighting Company Limited, 124
Mumias Sugar Company Limited, 124
Nation Media Group, 116
Safaricom Limited, 116
Spinners & Spinners Ltd., 155

Kuwait

Agility Public Warehousing Company KSC, 150
Kuwait Airways Corporation K.S.C., 68; 158 (upd.)
Kuwait Flour Mills & Bakeries Company, 84
Kuwait Petroleum Corporation, IV; 55 (upd.); 124 (upd.)
National Bank of Kuwait SAK, 145
Zain, 102
Dao-Heuang Group Ltd., 163

Latvia

A/S Air Baltic Corporation, 71; 163 (upd.)

Lebanon

Blom Bank S.A.L., 102
Middle East Airlines - Air Liban S.A.L. 79

Lesotho

Letšeng Diamonds (Pty) Ltd., 146
Standard Bank Lesotho Limited, 146

Libya

Libya Insurance Company, 124
National Oil Corporation, IV; 66 (upd.)
Sahara Bank, 116

Liechtenstein

Hilti Corporation, 53; 140 (upd.)
Hoval AG, 164
Liechtensteinische Landesbank AG, 121

Lithuania

Orlen Lietuva, 111
TEO LT, AB, 144
UAB Koncernas MG Baltic, 117

Luxembourg

ARBED S.A., IV; 22 (upd.)
ArcelorMittal, 108
Cactus S.A., 90
Cargolux Airlines International S.A., 49
Elcoteq SE, 113
Elite World S.A., 94
Esprito Santo Financial Group S.A., 79 (upd.)
Flint Group, 154 (upd.)
Gemplus International S.A., 64
Intelsat S.A., 129
L'Occitane International S.A., 132
Metro International S.A., 93
Millicom International Cellular S.A., 115
RTL Group S.A., 44; 142 (upd.)
Skype Technologies S.A., 108
Société Luxembourgeoise de Navigation Aérienne S.A., 64
Sword Group SE, 157
Tenaris SA, 63; 144 (upd.)

Macedonia

Makedonski Telekom AD Skopje, 113

Malaysia

AirAsia Berhad, 93
Axiata Group Bhd., 164 (upd.)
Berjaya Group Bhd., 67
Gano Excel Enterprise Sdn. Bhd., 89
Genting Berhad, 65; 140 (upd.)
IOI Corporation Bhd, 107
Kim Loong Resources Bhd, 160
Kumpulan Fima Bhd., 117
Malayan Banking Berhad, 72; 149 (upd.)
Malaysian Airlines System Berhad, 6; 29 (upd.); 97 (upd.)
MISC Bhd., 138
Perusahaan Otomobil Nasional Sdn. Bhd., 62; 151 (upd.)

Petroliam Nasional Bhd (PETRONAS), IV; 56 (upd.); 117 (upd.)
PLUS Malaysia Bhd., 152
PPB Group Berhad, 57; 138 (upd.)
Sime Darby Berhad, 14; 36 (upd.); 136 (upd.)
Telekom Malaysia Bhd, 76
UEM Group Bhd., 130
United Plantations Bhd., 117
Yeo Hiap Seng Malaysia Bhd., 75

Malta

Air Malta p.l.c., 137
Bank of Valletta PLC, 111

Mauritius

Air Mauritius Limited, 63; 140 (upd.)

Mexico

ABC Aerolíneas, S.A. de C.V., 126
Alfa, S.A. de C.V., 19
Altos Hornos de México, S.A. de C.V., 42
América Móvil, S.A.B. de C.V., 80; 158 (upd.)
Apasco S.A. de C.V., 51
Banco Azteca, S.A., Institución de Banca Múltiple, 113
Bolsa Mexicana de Valores, S.A. de C.V., 80; 145 (upd.)
Bufete Industrial, S.A. de C.V., 34
Casa Cuervo, S.A. de C.V., 31
Celanese Mexicana, S.A. de C.V., 54
CEMEX, S.A.B. de C.V., 20; 59 (upd.); 122 (upd.)
Cifra, S.A. de C.V., 12
Cinemas de la República, S.A. de C.V., 83
Comisión Federal de Electricidad, 108
Compañia Industrial de Parras, S.A. de C.V. (CIPSA), 84
Compartamos, S.A.B. de C.V., 152
Consorcio ARA, S.A. de C.V. 79
Consorcio Aviacsa, S.A. de C.V., 85
Consorcio G Grupo Dina, S.A. de C.V., 36
Controladora Comercial Mexicana, S.A. de C.V., 36; 157 (upd.)
Controladora Mabe, S.A. de C.V., 82
Controladora Vuela Compañía de Aviación, S.A.B. de C.V., 155
Coppel, S.A. de C.V., 82
Corporación Geo, S.A. de C.V., 81
Corporación Interamericana de Entretenimiento, S.A. de C.V., 83
Corporación Internacional de Aviación, S.A. de C.V. (Cintra), 20
Desarrolladora Homex, S.A. de C.V., 87
Desc, S.A. de C.V., 23
Diconsa S.A. de C.V., 126
Editorial Televisa, S.A. de C.V., 57
El Puerto de Liverpool, S.A.B. de C.V., 97
Embotelladoras Arca, S.A.B. de C.V., 119
Empresas ICA Sociedad Controladora, S.A. de C.V., 41
Farmacias de Similares S.A. de C.V., 158
FEMSA Comercio, S.A. de C.V., 148
Fomento Económico Mexicano S.A.B. de C.V., 128 (upd.)

Monaco

Mongolia

Nepal

The Netherlands

Netherlands Antilles

New Zealand

Nigeria

North Korea

Norway

Oman

Pakistan

Panama

Papua New Guinea

Paraguay

Peru

Banco de Crédito del Perú, 93
Compañía de Minas Buenaventura S.A.A.,
 93; 142 (upd.)
Corporación José R. Lindley S.A., 92
Grupo Brescia, 99
Petróleos del Perú – Petroperú S.A., 153
Southern Peru Copper Corporation, 40
Telefónica del Perú S.A.A., 119
Unión de Cervecerias Peruanas Backus y
 Johnston S.A.A., 92
Volcan Compañia Minera S.A.A., 92

Philippines

Bank of the Philippine Islands, 58
Benguet Corporation, 58
Jollibee Foods Corporation, 134
Manila Electric Company, 56; 148 (upd.)
Mercury Drug Corporation, 70
PAL Holdings, Inc., 122 (upd.)
Petron Corporation, 58; 147 (upd.)
Philippine Airlines, Inc., 6; 23 (upd.)
Philippine Long Distance Telephone
 Company, 152
San Miguel Corporation, 15; 57 (upd.);
 118 (upd.)

Poland

Agora S.A. Group, 77
Apator S.A., 153
Bank Handlowy w Warszawie S.A., 126
KGHM Polska Miedz S.A., 98
LOT Polish Airlines (Polskie Linie
 Lotnicze S.A.), 33
Narodowy Bank Polski, 100
NG2 S.A., 120
PGE Polska Grupa Energetyczna S.A., 158
Polski Koncern Naftowy ORLEN S.A.,
 77; 157 (upd.)
Telekomunikacja Polska SA, 50
Zakłady Azotowe Puławy S.A., 100

Portugal

Banco Comercial Português, SA, 50
Banco Espírito Santo e Comercial de
 Lisboa S.A., 15
BRISA Auto-estradas de Portugal S.A., 64
Cimentos de Portugal SGPS S.A.
 (Cimpor), 76
Corticeira Amorim, Sociedade Gestora de
 Participaço es Sociais, S.A., 48
EDP - Energias de Portugal, S.A., 111
 (upd.)
Electricidade de Portugal, S.A., 47
Galp Energia SGPS S.A., 98
Grupo Média Capital, SGPS S.A., 143
Grupo Portucel Soporcel, 60
Jerónimo Martins SGPS S.A., 96
José de Mello SGPS S.A., 96
Madeira Wine Company, S.A., 49; 156
 (upd.)
Mota-Engil, SGPS, S.A., 97
Petróleos de Portugal S.A., IV
Portugal Telecom SGPS S.A., 69; 144
 (upd.)
Sonae SGPS, S.A., 97
TAP—Air Portugal Transportes Aéreos
 Portugueses S.A., 46

Transportes Aereos Portugueses, S.A., 6

Puerto Rico

Popular, Inc., 108 (upd.)
Puerto Rico Electric Power Authority, 47

Qatar

Al Jazeera Media Network, 159 (upd.)
Aljazeera Satellite Channel 79
Industries Qatar QSC, 162
Masraf Al Rayan, 153
Qatar Airways Company Q.C.S.C., 87
Qatar General Petroleum Corporation, IV
Qatar National Bank SAQ, 87
Qatar Petroleum, 98
Qatar Telecom QSA, 87

Romania

Dobrogea Grup S.A., 82
InterAgro S.A., 149
TAROM S.A., 64

Russia

A.S. Yakovlev Design Bureau JSC, 15;
 138 (upd.)
Aeroflot - Russian Airlines JSC, 6; 29
 (upd.); 89 (upd.)
Alfa Group, 99
Alrosa Company Ltd., 62
AO VimpelCom, 48
Aviacionny Nauchno-Tehnicheskii
 Komplex im. A.N. Tupoleva, 24
AVTOVAZ Joint Stock Company, 65
Baltika Brewery Joint Stock Company, 65
Bolshoi Ballet, 156
CJSC Transmash Holding, 93
Evraz Group S.A., 97
OAO Gazprom Neft, 42; 107 (upd.); 157
 (upd.)
Golden Telecom, Inc., 59
Interfax News Agency, 86
Interros Holding Company, 158
Irkut Corporation, 68
Mail.Ru Group Limited, 133
Mechel OAO, 99
Mobile TeleSystems OJSC, 59
OJSC MMC Norilsk Nickel, 48; 137
 (upd.)
OAO LUKOIL, 40; 109 (upd.)
OAO NK YUKOS, 47
OAO Siberian Oil Company (Sibneft), 49
OAO Surgutneftegaz, 48; 128 (upd.)
OAO Tatneft, 45
Oil Transporting Joint Stock Company
 Transneft, 93
OJSC Novolipetsk Steel, 99
OJSC Wimm-Bill-Dann Foods, 48
PCHC-Raketa ZAO, 164
RAO Unified Energy System of Russia, 45
Rosneft, 106
Rostelecom Joint Stock Co., 99
Rostvertol plc, 62
RusHydro Group Joint Stock Co., 150
Russian Aircraft Corporation (MiG), 86
Russian Railways Joint Stock Co., 93
S7 Airlines, 127
Sberbank, 62; 138 (upd.)

Seventh Continent Joint Stock Co., 141
Severstal Joint Stock Company, 65; 138
 (upd.)
Sistema JSFC, 73; 151 (upd.)
Stroygazconsulting Group of Companies
 Ltd., 162
Sukhoi Design Bureau Aviation
 Scientific-Industrial Complex, 24
Tatneft Joint Stock Co., 142 (upd.)
TNK-BP, 129
Ural Mining and Metallurgical Company,
 162
Volga-Dnepr Group, 82
X5 Retail Group N.V., 162

San Marino

Gruppo Asset Banca S.p.A., 146
Maranello Rosso Collezione, 146

Saudi Arabia

Al Rajhi Bank, 158
Arab National Bank, 133
Dallah Albaraka Group, 72
Halwani Brothers Co., 153
Kingdom Holding Co., 156
Saudi Arabian Airlines Corporation, 6; 27
 (upd.); 122 (upd.)
Saudi Arabian Oil Company, IV; 17
 (upd.); 50 (upd.)
Saudi Basic Industries Corporation
 (SABIC), 58; 117 (upd.)
Saudi Electricity Co., 155
Saudi Telecom Company, 137
The Savola Group, 142

Scotland

Alexander Dennis Limited, 136
Arnold Clark Automobiles Ltd., 60
CJ Lang and Son Ltd., 138
Distillers Company PLC, I
General Accident PLC, III
The Governor and Company of the Bank
 of Scotland, 10
Linn Products Ltd., 147
Scottish & Newcastle plc, 15; 35 (upd.)
Scottish Hydro-Electric PLC, 13
Scottish Media Group plc, 32
Scottish Midland Co-operative Society
 Limited, 154
ScottishPower plc, 19
Stagecoach Holdings plc, 30
The Standard Life Assurance Company,
 III
Tennent Caledonian Breweries UK Ltd.,
 147

Senegal

Banque Centrale des États de l'Afrique de
 l'Ouest, 151
Groupe Mimran, 155

Singapore

Asia Pacific Breweries Ltd., 59; 150 (upd.)
Avago Technologies Limited, 150
Boustead Singapore Ltd., 127
City Developments Limited, 89
Creative Technology Ltd., 57

CellStar Corporation, 83
The CementBloc Inc., 161
Cendant Corporation, 44 (upd.)
Centel Corporation, 6
Centene Corporation, 150
Centennial Communications Corporation, 39
The Center for Creative Leadership, 155
Centerior Energy Corporation, V
Centerplate, Inc. 79
CenterPoint Energy, Inc., 116
Centex Corporation, 8; 29 (upd.); 106 (upd.)
Centocor Inc., 14
Central and South West Corporation, V
Central European Distribution Corporation, 75
Central Florida Investments, Inc., 93
Central Garden & Pet Company, 23; 58 (upd.)
Central Hudson Gas and Electricity Corporation, 6
Central Maine Power, 6
Central National-Gottesman Inc., 95
Central Newspapers, Inc., 10
Central Park Conservancy, 163
Central Parking System, 18; 104 (upd.)
Central Soya Company, Inc., 7
Central Sprinkler Corporation, 29
Central Vermont Public Service Corporation, 54
Centuri Corporation, 54
Century 21 Inc., 123
Century Aluminum Company, 52
Century Business Services, Inc., 52
Century Casinos, Inc., 53
Century Communications Corp., 10
Century Theatres, Inc., 31
CenturyLink, Inc., 9; 54 (upd.); 141 (upd.)
Cenveo, Inc., 71 (upd.); 148 (upd.)
Cephalon Technology, Inc, 45; 115 (upd.)
Cepheid, 77; 161 (upd.)
Ceradyne, Inc., 65
Cerberus Capital Management, L.P., 123
Cerner Corporation, 16; 94 (upd.)
Cerro Wire LLC, 143
CertainTeed Corporation, 35
Certegy, Inc., 63
Cessna Aircraft Company, 8; 27 (upd.); 147 (upd.)
CF Industries Holdings, Inc., 99
CH Energy Group, Inc., 123 (upd.)
CH2M HILL Companies Ltd., 22; 96 (upd.)
ChaCha Search, Inc., 152
Chadbourne & Parke, 36
Chadwick's of Boston, Ltd., 29
The Chalone Wine Group, Ltd., 36
Chamber of Commerce of the United States of America, 143
Champion Bus, Inc., 156
Champion Enterprises, Inc., 17
Champion Industries, Inc., 28; 151 (upd.)
Champion International Corporation, IV; 20 (upd.)
Championship Auto Racing Teams, Inc., 37

Chance Rides Manufacturing, Inc., 162
Chancellor Beacon Academies, Inc., 53
Chancellor Media Corporation, 24
Chaparral Energy, LLC, 139
Chaparral Steel Co., 13
Chargers Football Company LLC, 153
Charisma Brands LLC, 74
Charles Komar & Sons, Inc., 156
Charles M. Schulz Creative Associates, 114
The Charles Machine Works, Inc., 64
Charles River Laboratories International, Inc., 42; 128 (upd.)
The Charles Schwab Corporation, 8; 26 (upd.); 81 (upd.); 158 (upd.)
The Charles Stark Draper Laboratory, Inc., 35
Charlotte Russe Holding, Inc., 35; 90 (upd.)
The Charmer Sunbelt Group, 95
charming charlie, Inc., 155
Charming Shoppes, Inc., 8; 38
Chart House Enterprises, Inc., 17
Chart Industries, Inc., 21; 96 (upd.)
Charter Communications, Inc., 33; 116 (upd.)
Charter Financial Corporation, 103
Charter Manufacturing Company, Inc., 103
ChartHouse International Learning Corporation, 49
Chas. Levy Company LLC, 60
Chase Corporation, 140
Chase General Corporation, 91
The Chase Manhattan Corporation, II; 13 (upd.)
Chateau Communities, Inc., 37
Chatham Created Gems, Inc., 123
Chattanooga Bakery, Inc., 86
Chattem, Inc., 17; 88 (upd.)
Chautauqua Airlines, Inc., 38
CHE Trinity, Inc., 163
Check Into Cash, Inc., 105
Checker Motors Corp., 89
Checkers Drive-In Restaurants, Inc., 16; 74 (upd.); 152 (upd.)
CheckFree Corporation, 81
Checkpoint Systems, Inc., 39
Cheddar's Casual Café, Inc., 138
The Cheesecake Factory Inc., 17; 100 (upd.)
Chef Solutions, Inc., 89
The Chefs' Warehouse, Inc., 157
Chegg Inc., 144
Chelsea Milling Company, 29
Chelsea Piers Management Inc., 86
Chemcentral Corporation, 8
Chemed Corporation, 13; 118 (upd.)
Chemfab Corporation, 35
Chemical Banking Corporation, II; 14 (upd.)
Chemical Waste Management, Inc., 9
Chemi-Trol Chemical Co., 16
Chemonics International, Inc., 155
ChemTreat, Inc., 129
Chemtura Corporation, 91 (upd.)
Cheniere Energy, Inc., 160
CHEP Pty. Ltd., 80

Cherokee Inc., 18; 161 (upd.)
Cherry Brothers LLC, 105
Cherry Central Cooperative, Inc., 137
Cherry Lane Music Publishing Company, Inc., 62
Chesapeake Corporation, 8; 30 (upd.); 93 (upd.)
Chesapeake Energy Corporation, 132
Chesapeake Utilities Corporation, 56; 130 (upd.)
Chesbro Music Co., 142
Chesebrough-Pond's USA, Inc., 8
Chester, Inc., 149
Chesterman Company, 146
Chevron Corporation, 103 (upd.)
ChevronTexaco Corporation, IV; 19 (upd.); 47 (upd.)
Cheyenne Software, Inc., 12
CHF Industries, Inc., 84
CHHJ Franchising LLC, 105
Chi-Chi's Inc., 13; 51 (upd.)
Chiasso Acquisition LLC, 145 (upd.)
Chiasso Inc., 53
Chiat/Day Inc. Advertising, 11
Chic by H.I.S, Inc., 20
Chicago and North Western Holdings Corporation, 6
Chicago Bears Football Club, Inc., 33
Chicago Blackhawk Hockey Team, Inc., 132
Chicago Board of Trade, 41
Chicago Mercantile Exchange Holdings Inc., 75
Chicago National League Ball Club, Inc., 66
Chicago Professional Sports Limited Partnership, 151
Chicago Review Press Inc., 84
Chicago Symphony Orchestra, 106
Chicago Theatre Group, Inc., 158
Chicago Transit Authority, 108
Chicago White Sox, Ltd., 125
Chickasaw Nation Industries, Inc., 155
Chicken of the Sea International, 24 (upd.); 106 (upd.)
Chick-fil-A Inc., 23; 90 (upd.)
Chico's FAS, Inc., 45
ChildFund International, 106
ChildrenFirst, Inc., 59
Children's Comprehensive Services, Inc., 42
Children's Healthcare of Atlanta Inc., 101
Children's Hospital of Philadelphia, 149
Children's Hospitals and Clinics, Inc., 54
The Children's Place Retail Stores, Inc., 37; 86 (upd.)
Childtime Learning Centers, Inc., 34
Chiles Offshore Corporation, 9
Chindex International, Inc., 101
Chipotle Mexican Grill, Inc., 67; 133 (upd.)
CHIPS and Technologies, Inc., 9
Chiquita Brands International, Inc., 7; 21 (upd.); 83 (upd.)
Chiron Corporation, 10; 36 (upd.)
Chisholm-Mingo Group, Inc., 41
Chittenden & Eastman Company, 58
The Chlorine Institute Inc., 146

Collins Bus Corporation, 151 (upd.)
The Collins Companies Inc., 102
Collins Industries, Inc., 33
Colonial Pipeline Company, 139
Colonial Properties Trust, 65
Colonial Williamsburg Foundation, 53
Colony Capital, LLC, 133
Color Kinetics Incorporated, 85
Color Spot Nurseries, Inc., 123
Colorado Baseball Management, Inc., 72
Colorado Boxed Beef Company, 100
Colorado MEDtech, Inc., 48
Colt Industries Inc., I
Colt's Manufacturing Company, LLC, 12;
  140 (upd.)
Columbia Distributing Co., 128
Columbia Forest Products, 78; 161 (upd.)
The Columbia Gas System, Inc., V; 16
  (upd.)
Columbia House Company, 69
Columbia Manufacturing, Inc., 114
Columbia Sportswear Company, 19; 41
  (upd.); 148 (upd.)
Columbia TriStar Motion Picture Group,
  II; 12 (upd.); 140 (upd.)
Columbia/HCA Healthcare Corporation,
  15
Columbian Home Products, LLC, 121
Columbus McKinnon Corporation, 37
Comair Holdings Inc., 13; 34 (upd.)
Combe Inc., 72; 151 (upd.)
Comcast Corporation, 7; 24 (upd.); 112
  (upd.)
Comdial Corporation, 21
Comdisco, Inc., 9
Comerica Incorporated, 40; 101 (upd.)
COMFORCE Corporation, 40
Comfort Systems USA, Inc., 101
Command Security Corporation, 57; 140
  (upd.)
Commerce Bancshares, Inc., 116
Commerce Clearing House, Inc., 7
Commercial Contracting Group, Inc., 164
Commercial Credit Company, 8
Commercial Federal Corporation, 12; 62
  (upd.)
Commercial Financial Services, Inc., 26
Commercial Metals Company, 15; 42
  (upd.); 125 (upd.)
Commercial Vehicle Group, Inc., 81
Commodore International Ltd., 7
Commonwealth Edison Company, V
Commonwealth Energy System, 14
Commonwealth Telephone Enterprises,
  Inc., 25
CommScope, Inc., 77
Communications Systems, Inc., 139
Community Bank System, Inc., 143
Community Coffee Co. L.L.C., 53
Community Health Systems, Inc., 71; 158
  (upd.)
Community Newspaper Holdings, Inc.,
  91
Community Psychiatric Centers, 15
CommVault Systems, Inc., 144
Compaq Computer Corporation, III; 6
  (upd.); 26 (upd.)
Compass Bancshares, Inc., 73

Compass Diversified Holdings, 108
Compass Minerals International, Inc. 79;
  162 (upd.)
CompDent Corporation, 22
Compellent Technologies, Inc., 119
CompHealth Inc., 25
Complete Business Solutions, Inc., 31
Complete Production Services, Inc., 118
Comprehensive Care Corporation, 15
CompuAdd Computer Corporation, 11
CompuCom Systems, Inc., 10
CompuDyne Corporation, 51
CompUSA, Inc., 10; 35 (upd.)
CompuServe Interactive Services, Inc., 10;
  27 (upd.)
Computer Associates International, Inc.,
  6; 49 (upd.)
Computer Data Systems, Inc., 14
Computer Learning Centers, Inc., 26
Computer Sciences Corporation, 6; 116
  (upd.)
Computer Services, Inc., 122
Computerland Corp., 13
Computervision Corporation, 10
Compuware Corporation, 10; 30 (upd.);
  66 (upd.)
CompX International Inc., 130
Comsat Corporation, 23
comScore, Inc., 119
Comshare Inc., 23
Comstock Resources, Inc., 47; 126 (upd.)
Comtech Telecommunications Corp., 75
Comverge, Inc., 135
Comverse Technology, Inc., 15; 43 (upd.)
ConAgra Foods, Inc., II; 12 (upd.); 42
  (upd.); 85 (upd.)
Conair Corporation, 17; 69 (upd.)
Concentra Inc., 71
Concepts Direct, Inc., 39
Concho Resources, Inc., 139
Concord Camera Corporation, 41
Concord EFS, Inc., 52
Concord Fabrics, Inc., 16
Concord Music Group, Inc., 118
Concur Technologies, Inc., 106
Concurrent Computer Corporation, 75
Condé Nast Publications, Inc., 13; 59
  (upd.); 109 (upd.)
Cone Mills LLC, 8; 67 (upd.)
Conexant Systems Inc., 36; 106 (upd.)
Confluence Holdings Corporation, 76
Congoleum Corporation, 18; 98 (upd.)
CONMED Corporation, 87
Connecticut Light and Power Co., 13
Connecticut Mutual Life Insurance
  Company, III
The Connell Company, 29; 104 (upd.)
Conner Peripherals, Inc., 6
Connetics Corporation, 70
Conn's, Inc., 67
Conn-Selmer, Inc., 55; 154 (upd.)
ConocoPhillips, IV; 16 (upd.); 63 (upd.);
  141 (upd.)
Conrad Industries, Inc., 58
Conseco, Inc., 10; 33 (upd.); 112 (upd.)
Conso International Corporation, 29
CONSOL Energy Inc., 59; 144 (upd.)

Consolidated Delivery & Logistics, Inc.,
  24
Consolidated Edison, Inc., V; 45 (upd.);
  112 (upd.)
Consolidated Freightways Corporation, V;
  21 (upd.); 48 (upd.)
Consolidated Graphics, Inc., 70
Consolidated Natural Gas Company, V;
  19 (upd.)
Consolidated Papers, Inc., 8; 36 (upd.)
Consolidated Products Inc., 14
Consolidated Rail Corporation, V
Constar International Inc., 64
Constellation Brands, Inc., 68 (upd.); 158
  (upd.)
Constellation Energy Group, Inc., 116
  (upd.)
Consumers Power Co., 14
Consumers Union, 26; 118 (upd.)
Consumers Water Company, 14
The Container Store Group Inc., 36; 154
  (upd.)
ContiGroup Companies, Inc., 43 (upd.)
Continental Airlines, Inc., I; 21 (upd.); 52
  (upd.); 110 (upd.)
Continental Bank Corporation, II
Continental Cablevision, Inc., 7
Continental Can Co., Inc., 15
The Continental Corporation, III
Continental General Tire Corp., 23
Continental Grain Company, 10; 13
  (upd.)
Continental Graphics Corporation, 110
Continental Group Company, I
Continental Medical Systems, Inc., 10
Continental Resources, Inc., 89
Continucare Corporation, 101
Continuum Health Partners, Inc., 60
Control Data Corporation, III
Control Data Systems, Inc., 10
Control4 Corporation, 161
ConvaTec Inc., 150
Convergys Corporation, 119
Converse Inc., 9; 31 (upd.)
Con-way Inc., 101
Cook Group Inc., 102
Cooker Restaurant Corporation, 20; 51
  (upd.)
Cooley LLP, 161
CoolSavings, Inc., 77
Cooper Cameron Corporation, 20 (upd.);
  58 (upd.)
The Cooper Companies, Inc., 39; 125
  (upd.)
Cooper Industries plc, II; 44 (upd.); 133
  (upd.)
Cooper Tire & Rubber Company, 8; 23
  (upd.); 121 (upd.)
Cooperative for Assistance and Relief
  Everywhere, Inc., 152
Coopers & Lybrand, 9
Cooper's Hawk Winery & Restaurants,
  LLC, 163
CoorsTek, Incorporated, 151
Copano Energy, L.L.C., 139
Copart Inc., 23
The Copley Press, Inc., 23
The Copps Corporation, 32

McDonald's Corporation, II; 7 (upd.); 26 (upd.); 63 (upd.); 144 (upd.)
McDonnell Douglas Corporation, I; 11 (upd.)
McGrath RentCorp, 91
The McGraw-Hill Companies, Inc., IV; 18 (upd.); 51 (upd.); 115 (upd.)
MCI WorldCom, Inc., V; 27 (upd.)
McIlhenny Company, 20; 124 (upd.)
McJunkin Corporation, 63
McKee Foods Corporation, 7; 27 (upd.); 117 (upd.)
McKesson Corporation, I; 12; 47 (upd.); 108 (upd.)
McKinsey & Company, Inc., 9; 145 (upd.)
McLanahan Corporation, 104
McLane Company, Inc., 13
McLaughlin & Moran, Inc., 134
McLeodUSA Incorporated, 32
McMenamins Pubs and Breweries, 65
McMurry, Inc., 105
MCN Corporation, 6
McNaughton Apparel Group, Inc., 92 (upd.)
MCSi, Inc., 41
McWane Inc., 55; 132 (upd.)
MDU Resources Group, Inc., 7; 42 (upd.); 114 (upd.)
MDVIP, Inc., 118
Mead & Hunt Inc., 113
The Mead Corporation, IV; 19 (upd.)
Mead Data Central, Inc., 10
Mead Johnson Nutrition Company, 84; 153 (upd.)
Meade Instruments Corporation, 41
Meadowcraft, Inc., 29; 100 (upd.)
MeadWestvaco Corp., 76 (upd.); 138 (upd.)
Measurement Incorporated, 129
Measurement Specialties, Inc., 71
Mecklermedia Corporation, 24
Medarex, Inc., 85
Medco Containment Services Inc., 9
Medco Health Solutions, Inc., 116
MedeAnalytics Inc., 153
MEDecision, Inc., 95
Media Arts Group, Inc., 42
Media Cybernetics, Inc., 159
Media General, Inc., 7; 38 (upd.)
Media Sciences International, Inc., 104
Mediacom Communications Corporation, 69
MediaNews Group, Inc., 70
Medical Action Industries Inc., 101
Medical Information Technology Inc., 64; 157 (upd.)
Medical Management International, Inc., 65
Medical Mutual of Ohio, 128
Medical Staffing Network Holdings, Inc., 89
Medicine Shoppe International, Inc., 102
Medicis Pharmaceutical Corporation, 59
Medidata Solutions, Inc., 124
Medifast, Inc., 97
MedImmune LLC, 35; 153 (upd.)
Medis Technologies Ltd., 77

MediSys Health Network, 161
Meditrust, 11
Medline Industries, Inc., 61
MedQuist Inc., 124
Medtox Scientific, Inc., 139
Medtronic, Inc., 8; 30 (upd.); 67 (upd.); 144 (upd.)
Medusa Corporation, 24
Megafoods Stores Inc., 13
Meguiar's, Inc., 99
Meier & Frank Co., 23
Meijer, Inc., 7; 27 (upd.); 101 (upd.)
Mel Bay Publications, Inc., 142
Mel Farr Automotive Group, 20
Melaleuca, Inc., 31; 151 (upd.)
Melamine Chemicals, Inc., 27
Melissa & Doug, LLC, 123
Mellon Bank Corporation, II
Mellon Financial Corporation, 44 (upd.)
Mellon-Stuart Company, I
The Melting Pot Restaurants, Inc., 74
Melville Corporation, V
Melvin Simon and Associates, Inc., 8
MEMC Electronic Materials, Inc., 81
Memorial Sloan-Kettering Cancer Center, 57
Memry Corporation, 72
Menard, Inc., 34; 104 (upd.)
Menasha Corporation, 8; 59 (upd.); 118 (upd.)
Menchie's Group, Inc., 148
Mendocino Brewing Company, Inc., 60
The Men's Wearhouse, Inc., 17; 48 (upd.)
The Mentholatum Company Inc., 32
Mentor Corporation, 26; 123 (upd.)
Mentor Graphics Corporation, 11; 125 (upd.)
Mercantile Bankshares Corp., 11
Mercantile Stores Company, Inc., V; 19 (upd.)
Mercer International Inc., 64
The Merchants Company, 102
Merck & Co., Inc., I; 11 (upd.); 34 (upd.); 95 (upd.)
Mercury Air Group, Inc., 20
Mercury Computer Systems Inc., 145
Mercury General Corporation, 25
Mercury Interactive Corporation, 59
Mercury Marine Group, 68
Mercury Radio Arts, Inc., 132
Meredith Corporation, 11; 29 (upd.); 74 (upd.)
Merge Healthcare, 85
Merial Ltd., 102
Meridian Bancorp, Inc., 11
Meridian Bioscience, Inc., 115
Meridian Gold, Incorporated, 47
Merillat Industries Inc., 13
Merillat Industries, LLC, 69 (upd.)
Merisant Worldwide, Inc., 70
Merisel, Inc., 12
Merit Energy Company, 114
Merit Medical Systems, Inc., 29; 135 (upd.)
Meritage Homes Corporation, 26; 157 (upd.)
MeritCare Health System, 88
Meritor, Inc., 159 (upd.)

Merix Corporation, 36; 75 (upd.)
Merkle Inc., 114
Merrell Dow, Inc., I; 9 (upd.)
Merriam-Webster Inc., 70
Merrill Corporation, 18; 47 (upd.)
Merrill Lynch & Co., Inc., II; 13 (upd.); 40 (upd.); 138 (upd.)
Merry-Go-Round Enterprises, Inc., 8
Mervyn's California, 10; 39 (upd.)
Mesa Air Group, Inc., 11; 32 (upd.); 77 (upd.)
Mesaba Holdings, Inc., 28
Mestek Inc., 10
Met-Pro Corporation, 128
Metabolix, Inc., 154
Metal Management, Inc., 92
Metalico Inc., 97
Metatec International, Inc., 47
Metavante Corporation, 100
Meteor Industries Inc., 33
Method Products, Inc., 132
Methode Electronics, Inc., 13
Methodist Hospital of Houston, 132
MetLife, Inc., 143 (upd.)
MetoKote Corporation, 120
Metris Companies Inc., 56
Metro Information Services, Inc., 36
Metrocall, Inc., 41
Metro-Goldwyn-Mayer Inc., 25 (upd.); 84 (upd.)
Metromedia Company, 7; 14; 61 (upd.)
Metropark United States, Inc., 124
MetroPCS Communications, Inc., 132
Metropolitan Baseball Club Inc., 39
Metropolitan Financial Corporation, 13
Metropolitan Life Insurance Company, III; 52 (upd.)
The Metropolitan Museum of Art, 55; 115 (upd.)
Metropolitan Opera Association, Inc., 40; 115 (upd.)
Metropolitan Transportation Authority, 35; 146 (upd.)
The Metropolitan Water District of Southern California, 161
Mexican Restaurants, Inc., 41
Meyer Natural Angus L.L.C., 112
MFS Communications Company, Inc., 11
MGA Entertainment, Inc., 95
MGIC Investment Corp., 52; 143 (upd.)
MGM MIRAGE, 17; 98 (upd.)
MGM/UA Communications Company, II
Miami Heat Limited Partnership, 125
Miami Herald Media Company, 92
Miami Marlins, 135
Miami Subs Corporation, 108
MiaSolé, 146
Michael & Susan Dell Foundation, 137
Michael Anthony Jewelers, Inc., 24
Michael Baker Corporation, 14; 51 (upd.); 126 (upd.)
Michael C. Fina Co., Inc., 52
Michael Foods, Inc., 25; 127 (upd.)
Michaels Stores, Inc., 17; 71 (upd.)
Michigan Bell Telephone Co., 14
Michigan National Corporation, 11
Michigan Sporting Goods Distributors, Inc., 72

Teknor Apex Company, 97
Tektronix Inc., 8; 78 (upd.)
Telcordia Technologies, Inc., 59; 129
  (upd.)
Tele-Communications, Inc., II
Teledyne Brown Engineering, Inc., 110
Teledyne Technologies Inc., I; 10 (upd.);
  62 (upd.); 143 (upd.)
Teleflex Inc., 122
Teleflora LLC, 123
Telemundo Communications Group, Inc.,
  154
TeleNav, Inc., 141
TelePacific Communications Corporation,
  139
Telephone and Data Systems, Inc., 9; 124
  (upd.)
TeleTech Holdings Inc., 153
The Television Food Network, G.P., 118
Tellabs, Inc., 11; 40 (upd.)
Telsmith Inc., 96
Telular Corporation, 129
Telxon Corporation, 10
Temple-Inland Inc., IV; 31 (upd.); 102
  (upd.)
Tempur-Pedic Inc., 54
Ten Thousand Villages U.S., 108
Tenaska Energy, Inc., 128
Tenet Healthcare Corporation, 55 (upd.);
  112 (upd.)
TenFold Corporation, 35
Tengasco, Inc., 99
Tennant Company, 13; 33 (upd.); 95
  (upd.)
Tenneco Inc., I; 10 (upd.); 113 (upd.)
Tennessee Football, Inc., 129
Tennessee Valley Authority, 50; 143 (upd.)
The Tennis Channel, Inc., 126
TEPPCO Partners, L.P., 73
Teradata Corporation, 150
Teradyne, Inc., 11; 98 (upd.)
Terex Corporation, 7; 40 (upd.); 91
  (upd.)
The Terlato Wine Group, 48
Terra Industries, Inc., 13; 94 (upd.)
TerraCycle Inc., 136
Terremark Worldwide, Inc., 99
Tesla Motors, Inc., 124
Tesoro Corporation, 7; 45 (upd.); 97
  (upd.)
TESSCO Technologies Incorporated, 119
Tessera Technologies, Inc., 119
The Testor Corporation, 51
Tetley USA Inc., 88
Teton Energy Corporation, 97
Tetra Tech, Inc., 29; 134 (upd.)
Texaco Inc., IV; 14 (upd.); 41 (upd.)
Texas Air Corporation, I
Texas Industries, Inc., 8
Texas Instruments Incorporated, II; 11
  (upd.); 46 (upd.); 118 (upd.)
Texas Monthly, Inc., 142
Texas Pacific Group Inc., 36
Texas Rangers Baseball Club, 51; 159
  (upd.)
Texas Roadhouse, Inc., 69; 141 (upd.)
Texas Utilities Company, V; 25 (upd.)
Textron Inc., I; 34 (upd.); 88 (upd.)

Textron Lycoming Turbine Engine, 9
Tha Row Records, 69 (upd.)
Thane International, Inc., 84
Theatre Development Fund, Inc., 109
Theranos, Inc., 162
Thermadyne Holding Corporation, 19
Thermo BioAnalysis Corp., 25
Thermo Electron Corporation, 7
Thermo Fibertek, Inc., 24
Thermo Fisher Scientific Inc., 105 (upd.)
Thermo Instrument Systems Inc., 11
Thermo King Corporation, 13
Thermos Company, 16
Thermotech, 113
Things Remembered, Inc., 84
Thiokol Corporation, 9; 22 (upd.)
Thomas & Betts Corporation, 11; 54
  (upd.); 114 (upd.)
Thomas & Howard Company, Inc., 90
Thomas Cook Travel Inc., 9; 33 (upd.)
Thomas H. Lee Co., 24
Thomas Industries Inc., 29
Thomas J. Lipton Company, 14
The Thomas Kinkade Company, 156
  (upd.)
Thomas Nelson, Inc., 14; 38 (upd.)
Thomas Publishing Company, 26
Thomaston Mills, Inc., 27
Thomasville Furniture Industries, Inc., 12;
  74 (upd.)
Thompson Creek Metals Company Inc.,
  122
Thomsen Greenhouses and Garden
  Center, Incorporated, 65
Thomson Industries Inc., 136
Thor Equities, LLC, 108
Thor Industries Inc., 39; 92 (upd.)
Thoratec Corporation, 122
Thorn Apple Valley, Inc., 7; 22 (upd.)
Thornton Tomasetti, Inc., 126
Thos. Moser Cabinetmakers Inc., 117
ThoughtWorks Inc., 90
Thousand Trails Inc., 33; 113 (upd.)
THQ, Inc., 39; 92 (upd.)
Thrifty PayLess, Inc., 12
Thrillist Media Group, Inc., 147
Thrivent Financial for Lutherans, 111
  (upd.)
Thumann Inc., 104
Thunderbird Resources LP, 161
TIBCO Software Inc., 79
TIC Holdings Inc., 92
Ticketmaster, 76 (upd.)
Ticketmaster Group, Inc., 13; 37 (upd.)
Tidewater Inc., 11; 37 (upd.)
Tiffany & Co., 14; 78 (upd.); 159 (upd.)
TIG Holdings, Inc., 26
Tilcon-Connecticut Inc., 80
Tilia Inc., 62
Tillamook County Creamery Association,
  111
Tillotson Corp., 15
Tilly's, Inc., 160
Tim-Bar Corporation, 110
Timber Lodge Steakhouse, Inc., 73
The Timberland Company, 13; 54 (upd.);
  111 (upd.)
Timberline Software Corporation, 15

Time Inc., 125
Time Warner Inc., IV; 7 (upd.); 109
  (upd.)
The Times Mirror Company, IV; 17
  (upd.)
Timex Group B.V., 7; 25 (upd.); 111
  (upd.)
The Timken Company, 8; 42 (upd.); 113
  (upd.)
Tishman Construction Company, 112
Tishman Speyer Properties, L.P., 47; 112
  (upd.)
The Titan Corporation, 36
Titan International, Inc., 89
Titan Machinery Inc., 103
Titanium Metals Corporation, 21
TiVo Inc., 75; 154 (upd.)
TJ International, Inc., 19
The TJX Companies, Inc., V; 19 (upd.);
  57 (upd.); 120 (upd.)
TLC Beatrice International Holdings, Inc.,
  22
TMP Worldwide Inc., 30
T-Netix, Inc., 46
TNT Freightways Corporation, 14
Today's Man, Inc., 20
TODCO, 87
Todd Shipyards Corporation, 14
The Todd-AO Corporation, 33
Todhunter International, Inc., 27
Tofutti Brands, Inc., 64; 142 (upd.)
Tokheim Corporation, 21
Tokyo Joe's Inc., 164
TOKYOPOP Inc. 79
Toll Brothers Inc., 15; 70 (upd.); 147
  (upd.)
Tollgrade Communications, Inc., 44; 129
  (upd.)
Tom Brown, Inc., 37
Tom Doherty Associates Inc., 25
Tombstone Pizza Corporation, 13
Tommy Bahama Group, Inc., 108
TomoTherapy Incorporated, 121
Tom's Foods Inc., 66
Tom's of Maine, Inc., 45; 125 (upd.)
TOMS Shoes, Inc., 152
Tone Brothers, Inc., 21; 74 (upd.)
Tonka Corporation, 25
Too, Inc., 61
Tootsie Roll Industries, Inc., 12; 82 (upd.)
Top Pot Inc., 132
Topa Equities Ltd., 136
Topco Associates LLC, 60; 141 (upd.)
The Topps Company, Inc., 13; 34 (upd.);
  83 (upd.)
Tops Appliance City, Inc., 17
Tops Markets, LLC, 60; 136 (upd.)
Torchmark Corporation, 9; 33 (upd.); 115
  (upd.)
Toresco Enterprises, Inc., 84
The Toro Company, 7; 26 (upd.); 77
  (upd.)
The Torrington Company, 13
Tory Burch LLC, 141
Tosco Corporation, 7
Total Beverage Solution, 151
Total Entertainment Restaurant
  Corporation, 46